The
Foundations
of Modern
Education

John Amos Comenius, 1592–1670
Father of Modern Education

FOURTH EDITION

The Foundations of Modern Education

Elmer Harrison Wilds

Kenneth V. Lottich
Montana State University

HOLT, RINEHART AND WINSTON, INC.
New York • Chicago • San Francisco • Atlanta
Dallas • Montreal • Toronto • London • Sydney

Again to
Robert Ulich
"For he who can view things
in their connexion is a dialectician. . . ."

Book VII, THE REPUBLIC

Copyright 1936, 1942 by Elmer Harrison Wilds,
© 1961, 1970 by Holt, Rinehart and Winston, Inc.
All rights reserved
Library of Congress Catalog Card Number: 79–114839
SBN: 03-079740-3
Printed in the United States of America
1 2 3 4 5 6 7 8 9 22 0 1 2 3 4

Preface

The decades since the publication of earlier editions of *The Foundations of Modern Education* have been crucial, even as that of today is crucial, and the human crises that have occurred represent significant catalysts of change we must understand to comprehend today's dilemmas. Although it is no easy task to essay either the interpretation and evaluation of what is truly contemporary or to evaluate the past in fresh and new frameworks and terms, the present edition of *Foundations* represents such an effort.

With the passing years—particularly the late 1960s, which witnessed the first successful heart transplant, the near-synthesis of life in the test tube, and the landing of men on the moon—it has become increasingly clear that man exists in a historical and scientific continuum. Nor does this sequence exclude education, its philosophies, and its policies. Indeed, it is primarily in the study of *education* that the social, scientific, and historical processes become most meaningful. For, as Robert Ulich has said, "One cannot comprehend the nature of the educational process without seeing it in its historical context."[1]

In this book the historical matrix is continually consulted; for it is only through the use of a morphology that involves the physical setting, social-political relations, religion, technology, and history that educational analogies and differences become comprehensible. But learning the history or philosophy of education should not be equated with the memorization of a catalog of chronology or the recognition of a galaxy of figures, however great! Rather, the total interrelationship of the parties to our morphology constitutes the source of understanding.

This volume, as did the First Edition, written solely by Dr. Wilds, represents a method of treatment that is held to be distinctively different from that found in other works on the history and philosophy of education. In addition to its morphology, *Foundations* provides a multiple approach to the study of individual movements or philosophies; its purpose is to present the evolution of educational theory from the day of primitive man to the present age; and it attempts not only to relate the

---

[1] *The Education of Nations* (Cambridge, Mass.: Harvard University Press, 1967), p. vii.

history of education with corresponding social movements but also to illuminate the significance of contemporary accomplishments and their adjacent problems.

Through an analysis of the varying conceptions of education in the writings of outstanding educational thinkers and reformers, *Foundations* points out the implications of ancient and current educational opinions. By tracing the influence of changing social, political, economic, and religious views upon the development of educational thought, it seeks to provide a sound basis for the reinterpretation and evaluation of present-day theories and routines.

Nor does this book fail to recognize that in recent years the emphasis in history of education courses has shifted from a detailed description of educational institutions and practices to an analysis of their foundations or underlying theories. The tendency to subordinate matters such as school administration and legislation and to emphasize the philosophies that have influenced educational practice through the centuries in order to study their effects on all phases and conditions of education is heartily approved. The authors, believing this tendency should be encouraged, trust that their work will be of value in producing this effect.

The First Edition of *Foundations* was intended not as another factual textbook in the history of education, but primarily as a history of educational thought, with only scant emphasis on the record of educational practice. The philosophies and concepts of education that have developed in more than four thousand years were presented in as unbiased and objective a manner as possible. In this Fourth Edition the conflict between progressivism and essentialism and the new recourses to idealism and existentialism are recognized and discussed; the student is acquainted with each point of view so that he will be able to evaluate and adopt the philosophy of his choice or inclination. But he may, if he feels it preferable, choose what he deems the best elements from several correlative (or even conflicting) philosophies and fuse them into his own personal eclectic system of educational thought.

Understandably, it will be possible to dwell at length only on those sections of the world's history that pertain to Western civilization, although in the earlier chapters the Near East serves as a focus. Professor Tom B. Jones puts our chosen emphasis as follows:

> If we seek to understand the modern world fully we must appreciate, among other things, the reality that the dominant and most complex civilization of the twentieth century is the one we call "Western" which was, for centuries, the possession of Europe and parts of the New World, but which has now been diffused over the entire globe, and is affecting vitally other civilizations and cultures.[2]

---

[2] Reprinted with permission from Jones, *From Tigris to Tiber* (Homewood, Ill.: The Dorsey Press, 1969), p. 4.

Through Jones' reasoning and the limiting size of our present volume we have omitted the larger portion of Asia's educational history and have had to dispense with mention of Latin America, Africa, and Australia.

However, throughout the later chapters, the contemporary demand for a treatment of comparative education is recognized, and Chapter 21 is devoted to a quick survey of educational ideologies in both the Free World and behind the Iron Curtain. Thus, the current ideological schism is observed, and the relationship of new totalitarian influences to education is examined. Recent recourses to nationalism in both the older and newer areas of the globe are considered in the light of their meaning for educational practice.

By retaining a basically American focus in the last six chapters of *Foundations,* the authors' intent is to emphasize the significance of the remarkable effort of the United States in universal education and, at the same time, to highlight some of the discrepancies that have become more visible in recent years. Thayer and Levit posit this dilemma in practical terms:

> The American's faith in education, then, has both persisted and expanded throughout the years. However, as a result of the uses to which this faith has been put, problems have arisen. Principles and procedures that in a simple and relatively homogeneous community seemed self-evident have become less so—have even become questionable—in today's complex and heterogeneous society.[3]

By utilizing chronological order in presenting varying philosophies the authors have attempted to maintain the historical approach and to avoid swinging too far in the direction of a conventional treatment of educational philosophies, that is, through the "isms." Thus the organization of the book makes it suitable for an orthodox course in history of education as well as for a newer arrangement which combines history and philosophy of education. Further, this text may be used as a supplement in courses such as Introduction to Education, Principles of Teaching, or Foundations of Education.

Material is offered in twenty-one chapters, ordinarily a semester's study at the rate of approximately one chapter per week. Each chapter aims at a thorough explanation of a particular period or movement in the development of educational theory and practice; and each chapter emphasizes the application of this information to contemporary demands. This plan allows the use of *Foundations* through the selection of chapters appropriate for courses which may continue for one term or quarter, and should a year's program be desired, this book will be adequate when supplemented by some of the references for further study placed at the

---

[3] V. T. Thayer and Martin Levit, *The Role of the School in American Society,* 2d ed. (New York: Dodd, Mead & Company, Inc., 1966), p. 14.

conclusion of each chapter. Moreover, this Fourth Edition includes, as a special feature, a copious selection of apposite paperback books at the end of each chapter.

The subject matter of the volume is uniquely organized on the basis of selective continuity. Each chapter treats each of the following phases of education: (1) aims; (2) types; (3) content; (4) agencies; (5) organization; and (6) methods. Consequently the history of the curriculum or the history of school organization, or the history of method—any, or all of these—may be traced readily from their beginnings to modern times.

Specifically, each chapter includes an overview containing a summary of the geographical, social, political, economic, and religious influences (our morphology) underlying the period, motive, or movement under consideration; the relationship of this chapter to the preceding one, and a brief survey of the chapter's subject matter. Second, each chapter provides an exposition, through which the concept or philosophy is studied in its application to the six aspects of education mentioned above. Such an arrangement permits each of these significant foci to be emphasized and its importance to the pattern of education to be heightened.

1. Under *aims* the underlying purposes of education, its philosophy or ideology, its historical determinants, and tribal or national goals are stressed.

2. *Types* considers the various forms in which education appears within a given society or culture; for example, religious or moral instruction, vocational training, physical education, military or civic training, the liberal arts, esthetics.

3. *Content* emphasizes the selection of traditions, experiences, learnings, skills, crafts, or group activities thought to be valuable within a culture, or whatever is the basis for that culture's formal or informal education.

4. By *agencies* is meant the specific influence of the clan, the tribe or nation, the home (including parental instruction), the church or other religious orientation, apprenticeship, the formal school, or the teaching role of the social ethos.

5. *Organization* refers to the several gradations, age levels, or special plateaus (usually of formal education) within the educational system. In contemporary situations organization may refer also to single ladder or multitrack, common or elite systems, academic, vocational, or polytechnical education, or other arrangements.

6. *Method* includes the devices, procedures, or direction of the formal school as well as the more informal influences of the society, culture, or polity. It may, and frequently does, involve participation (actual or vicarious), initiation, emulation, imitation, and various forms of discipline. Method as a term represents an entity that may be either concrete or abstract, depending on its context or usage.

It is the authors' belief that such a six-pronged attack on each of the main topics presents a greater opportunity for the student's summarization and comparison of philosophies and methods, essential features in contemporary educational analysis.

Finally there is, following each chapter, a compilation of complementary or collateral readings. These references contain parallel selections from other authors and special monographs—historical, sociological, or philosophical—selected to enhance the student's interest and appreciation of the men and movements under consideration. The generous listing of available and inexpensive paperbacks is a modern feature with strong educational value.

The authors wish to acknowledge their debts to the late Dean Ellwood P. Cubberley of Stanford University; to the late Dean Henry Wyman Holmes, former Dean Francis Keppel, and Professors Robert Ulich and S. Willis Rudy, all of the Graduate School of Education, Harvard University; and their appreciation to the many friends, colleagues, and students, contact with whom has served to catalyze, clarify, and encourage the authors' thought about educational theory and practice. The junior author wishes to mention especially his debt to Professors Hugh C. Black, University of California at Davis, Donald S. Seckinger, California State College, Everett D. Lantz, University of Wyoming, and Theodore H. E. Chen and William O'Neill of the University of Southern California, all of whom, by their interest and counsel, helped to make *Foundations* a better book.

Special thanks are offered to the librarians and staffs of the Firestone Library, Princeton University; the University of Arizona, Tucson; and the Arizona State University, Tempe. Grateful appreciation is extended also to Deborah Doty and Jeanette Ninas Johnson of Holt, Rinehart and Winston for their editorial help and guidance, and to those writers and publishers who so courteously granted permission to use copyrighted materials.

Scottsdale, Arizona   K. V. L.
May 1970

Contents

CHAPTER 1

Education for Tribal Conformity

Down how many roads among the stars must man propel himself in search of the final secret? The journey is difficult, immense, at times impossible. Yet that will not deter some of us from attempting it.[1]

HOW EDUCATION BEGAN

The road man has traveled from his early beginnings has involved a long hard climb and has taken hundreds of thousands of years. Breasted, the archeologist, asserts that "the fact that man possessed the capacity to make this climb—to rise from savagery to an accumulated culture—and at the time when it had never been done before, constitutes the greatest episode in the history of the universe."[2] Sometimes by chance, more often by conscious effort, man learned first to adapt himself to nature, then to harness nature for his own service. His perhaps unforeseen goal was nothing less than the control of his environment, the mastery of his external circumstances. Generation after generation contested in this struggle. Childe comments:

> Man's social heritage is a tradition which he begins to acquire only after he has emerged from his mother's womb. Changes in culture and tradition can be initiated, controlled, or delayed by the conscious and deliberate choice of their human authors. . . . An invention is not an accidental

---

[1] Loren Eiseley, *The Immense Journey* (New York: Random House, Inc., 1957). Eiseley's work, beautifully written, is found in several editions.

[2] James Henry Breasted's *The Conquest of Civilization* (New York: Harper & Row, Publishers, 1926 and 1938) presents the story of man's upward march from the perspective of a generation ago; Eiseley, in *The Immense Journey*, uses a contemporary approach, yet the inherent drama is the same.

mutation of the germ plasm, but a new synthesis of the accumulated experience.[3]

Through his accumulation of a social heritage man learned little by little to multiply his powers of communication; through his development of institutions such as language, customs, and laws he organized his society; through his discovery or invention of better modes of transportation and travel he broadened his world view. Man gradually learned to dream dreams and to see visions of a better life. The creative development of aspirations and ideals such as those expressed in art, literature, and religion aided his steep ascent. His changing conceptions of how this learning was and is to be achieved and transmitted constitute the history of his educational thought.

The thought processes of men are determined by their environmental relationships. Doubtless the earliest man could concentrate only scarcely and momentarily on anything beyond food and safety. As an anthropologist reports, when he asked his aboriginal baggage-carrier what he was thinking of, the honest man replied, "Nothing, I have plenty to eat." But as man's culture developed, his horizons tended to enlarge. With the achievement of civilization came an advance in ideas about education; with the application of theories came a further advance in civilization.

Thus, man's attainment in social living occurs through an evolutionary process which has passed from aboriginal stages to a contemporary heterogeneous level. Certain phases of this evolution may be termed accidental, involuntary, incidental, and undirected by man; but much of the cultural, or superorganic, development was conscious, voluntary, and directed. Man became intent on changing his existence from the unplanned to the planned. This conscious, or voluntary, control of his present and future constitutes man's educational thinking. As the chapter continues we shall attempt to discover the beginnings of such a heritage among contemporary man's ancestors, the early peoples.

It is difficult to say just when education began. While education is as old as life, some prefer to term its earliest forms *enculturation*.[4] Indeed, education antedates man, for the animals of prehistoric ages must have consciously or unconsciously passed on to their offspring the tricks by which they were able to survive against the dangers of starvation or attack by their enemies. Education, organized or unorganized, has existed as long

---

[3] V. Gordon Childe, *Man Makes Himself* (New York: New American Library of World Literature, Inc., 1951), p. 21. Reprinted with permission of C. A. Watts & Co. Ltd., London, original publishers.

[4] "Enculturation" may be defined as "the processes by which an infant becomes indoctrinated into a cultural tradition." Some anthropologists consider it a more inclusive term than the related concept "socialization." From an unpublished manuscript by Joseph S. Roucek and Kenneth V. Lottich.

as life. But with the advent of culture, education began to play an increasingly important role in the drama of human development.[5]

Education occurred long before anyone thought about it; people thought about education long before anyone wrote about it; and people wrote about education long before there was a problem of education. Primitive education is education reduced to its basic terms.

The making of man continued for eons before man himself was capable of taking a hand in the process. There was a time, perhaps thousands of years, in which education was conducted chiefly on the organic plane. Nature taught through a highly selective process, designated by Wallace and Spencer as "survival of the fittest." The individuals and groups with characteristics and traits favorable to life in the environment in which they found themselves survived and thus were able to reproduce their kind and to perpetuate these favorable traits. Those not so fortunate died and disappeared from the scene. Such is one explanation of the instincts and reflexes, which are still a part of man's psychological equipment.

THE ROLE OF CULTURE

But before we consider primitive education, we must mention the process by which man passed from lower to higher forms of living. This advance was made possible through the development of *culture*, which the British anthropologist Tylor, in his classic interpretation, defines as "that complex whole which includes knowledge, belief, art, morals, law, custom, and any other capabilities acquired by man as a member of society."[6] Another and later definition of culture is indebted to Tylor:

> The essential part of culture is to be found in the social traditions of the group, that is, in knowledge, ideas, beliefs, values, standards, and sentiments. . . . The overt part of culture is to be found in the actual behavior of the group, usually in its usages, customs, and institutions . . . but tradition as the subjective side of culture, is the essential core.[7]

In any discussion of preliterate education the force of tradition must be admitted. The evolution of even a simple culture required millennia.

One of the difficulties in studying primitive man is that his "immense

---

[5] For a most interesting and eloquent presentation of the epic of man's history see Henry Field, *The Track of Man* (New York: Dell Publishing Co., Inc., 1967).

[6] Edward B. Tylor, *Primitive Culture*. A reprint of the first edition. (New York: Brentanos, 1924), p. 1. This original commentary on the meaning of culture has, of course, been greatly expanded. For a critical review of the concepts and definitions of culture see Alfred Louis Kroeber and Clyde Kluckhohn, *Culture* (New York: Random House, Inc., 1963); and Leslie A. White, *The Science of Culture* (New York: Grove Press, Inc., 1949).

[7] Charles A. Ellwood in *The Dictionary of Sociology*. H. F. Fairchild, Ed. (Totowa, N.J.: Littlefield, Adams & Company, 1944.)

journey" took thousands and thousands of years, and is thus difficult to reduce to simplicity. For primitive man passed through many stages in his development, just as the development of modern man has required many stages. Certain phases in his evolution are conventionally distinguished. Yet the essential legacy was man himself. Hawkes says:

> The inheritance which the Prehistoric Age received from the Prehuman Age was immense and powerful. It was the whole body of man and the environment in which he was to live, that basic inheritance which all later ages could take for granted. . . . While civilizations have come and gone we still are born to the identical equipment of body and limbs already shaped a hundred thousand years or more ago—yes, down to our scratching nails and that tendency to long canine teeth. . . . But the fact that the human stock grew from a creature that walked upright and was ancestral to ourselves and the great apes cannot be denied.[8]

Given man as basic, three stages in his primeval development have been suggested:

> The *Eolithic,* in which man's only implements were those of wood, horn, bone, or rock, retrieved from the soil and utilized as they were found, and his only shelter was appropriative: the bushes and caves supplied by nature;
> The *Paleolithic,* in which implements of rough stone, crudely hacked into shape as axes, arrowheads, hammers, and spearheads prevailed, and man's shelter was adaptive: rocks, reeds, and bushes bent into rude bowers or dwelling places;
> The *Neolithic,* in which stone implements were polished and keenly sharpened, thus being made far superior to their earlier prototypes; and shelter was created out of materials converted from their natural state into blocks, beams, or boards.

However, there is a great deal of difference between the Paleolithic way of life of Neanderthal man, poor, fearful, and rude, squatting and trembling in his drafty cave, grimacing and chattering like an ape, and that of Neolithic man as represented by the early American Indian, skilled in shelter making, the domestic arts, hunting, fishing, and agriculture. Yet both are classified here as "primitives," for we cannot in brief space treat adequately the part played by education at each stage. Arbitrarily, we shall have to strike an average and consider aboriginal life in general.

Although when later dealing with historic eras we can extract material from the records and writings of seminal thinkers and philosophers, in discussing the educational concepts of truly primitive people we must

---

[8] Jacquetta Hawkes and Sir Leonard Woolley, *Prehistory and The Beginnings of Civilization.* History of Mankind Series, vol. i. (New York: Harper & Row, Publishers, 1963), p. 46.

depend on other sources. Whatever ideas preliterate peoples had concerning education were perpetuated by word of mouth from generation to generation. In the usual course of events these ideas were part of the lore of shamans and priests, revealed only to their proteges. Yet we can get some knowledge of prehistoric life from archeologists who have studied the relics of extinct communities: potsherds, weapons of war, and charms or ornaments used for personal adornment; from physical anthropologists who, as anthropometrists, have studied comparatively the skeletal remains of long-vanished races for the length of the limbs, the cephalic index, or the capacity of the braincase; or from ethnologists, culturologists, or social anthropologists who have visited and recorded their analyses of those primitive, or aboriginal, tribes still found in isolated or remote areas. Such students of early man and present-day aborigines have provided what knowledge we possess of preliterate, or prehistoric, peoples. But the emphasis in such study has recently shifted:

> What impressed the student of human behavior like Franz Boas was the *diversity* of human cultures. And so Boas and his colleagues stressed the uniqueness of every human society. . . . Commonalities and regularities were obscured, and the insight that every culture is a complex solution to a set of common problems by a sentient animal with a universal sharing of biological and intellectual propensities was temporarily lost. But the pendulum of study and thought reached full swing in the direction of exclusive interest in the uniqueness of culture during the thirties, and now the search for regularities in human culture, preconditioned by the bio-emotional brotherhood of man, is clearly under way.[9]

Benedict, drawing on her own field research and that of others, has produced a popular and comparative review of three widely diverse primitive peoples: the Pueblo of New Mexico, the Dobu of Melanesia, and the Kwakiutl of Northwest North America.[10] Both unique and general features are shown, some of which will be considered later in this chapter. Mead has completed a number of such studies based on her experience in the South Seas and in America. Although the cultural pattern in each of these societies is quite different, common bonds exist in the societies' need for complex systems of rules and regulations and for rudimentary educational routines. And the review of man's precultural activity includes much more. Hawkes believes:

> What it will prove most important to remember is that our species did not only inherit . . . its bodily equipment, dominated by its subtly elaborated brain, but also highly charged emotional centers and all that

---

[9] George D. Spindler, *Education and Culture* (New York: Holt, Rinehart and Winston, Inc., 1963), pp. 18–19.

[10] Ruth Benedict, *Patterns of Culture* (Boston: Houghton Mifflin Company, Sentry Books, 1965).

strange ancient furniture of the unconscious mind. Man emerged bringing
with him hate, fear and anger, together with love and the joy of life in
their simple animal form. He also brought the social heritage of family
affection and group loyalty.[11]

This human heredity of physique, emotion, and a penchant for group
organization was to lead to the development of educational objects and
strategies.

EARLY MAN'S APPROACH TO EDUCATION

Aims

Aboriginal education is almost unconscious of its simple, yet completely compulsive, objectives. Although when judged alongside contemporary life, the aims, goals, and ideals of primitive education appear to be
few in number, every development that could possibly secure early man's
survival was of utmost importance. Again Childe says:

> Natural history traces the emergence of new species each better adapted
> for survival, more fitted to obtain food and shelter, and so to multiply.
> Human history reveals man creating new industries and new economies
> that have furthered the increase of his species and thereby vindicated
> its enhanced fitness.[12]

The aboriginal educational system, if indeed it could be called a
system, did not require complexity to develop in the individual those
qualities and characteristics deemed necessary for his well-being and the
welfare of his group. Very likely early man philosophized little; his concern
was with immediates: how to satisfy his hunger, how to protect himself
against the elements, how to avoid injury or death. Tied to the present, he
neither understood nor anticipated the future. "Sufficient unto the day is
the evil thereof," may well have been his maxim. Apparently, at first, he
gave little thought to where he was going or from whence he had come.
Aboriginal man was but dimly conscious of his entity and his ends. He
concentrated on things to be done, the ways of doing them, the very need
of doing them. Much of his activity must have been on the instinctive level,
and whatever education there was may be considered unconscious imitation.
"Like father, like son" may well have originated here.

The basic aim of primitive education was security; for the fundamental problem of prehistoric man was how to stay alive, to protect himself
and his family from the destructive forces of nature and from both animal
and human enemies. Fear, undoubtedly, was a stimulus for most action:

---

[11] Hawkes and Woolley, p. 47.
[12] Childe, p. 20.

In the beginning there was fear; and fear was in the heart of man; and fear controlled man. At every turn it overwhelmed him, leaving no moment of ease.[13]

Fire, storm, thunder, and death left in the mind of early man feelings of awe and fear, stimulating him to action and urging him to bequeath to his offspring those behaviors which proved most effective. Thus, fear was one of the earliest motives for education. Early man was a slave to his needs and to his dread of the unseen. His educational aim, if he was conscious of one at all, was to prepare his offspring to obtain the necessities of life for self and family, and to propitiate the invisible powers presumed to exist in his natural surroundings.

The aborigine feared inanimate objects because he endowed them with life or considered them manifestations of occult powers, which, he believed, could destroy him if they so willed. Trees, stones, storms, or fire held properties of being, he thought, that could be turned against him. His respect for them gave rise to the earliest religion, animism. Yet it would be a mistake to think that he worshipped a rock as a rock. Hocart, in *The Life-giving Myth*, points out that "there is no such thing as 'nature-worship.' Nobody ever worshipped the sun simply as the sun. It is worshipped as it is deified."[14]

Primitive man believed that a spirit controlled each material existence; perhaps through his dream sequences, he came to conceive of a dual world of body and mind. At first man was conscious of only two kinds of spirits: those that were neutral, demanding no solicitude; and those that were hostile, and to be propitiated, deceived, or driven away. Security from the dreaded invisible powers came when man began to explore the possibility of reconciliation through the ceremonies and rituals of magic.

Security was the original purpose of these magic ceremonies and of the taboos, restraints, and customs placed by the old upon the young to preserve the amnesty apparently granted by the gods to the tribe. The second aim of primitive education was conformity, for conformity is a requisite of social security. Common danger brought early men into families, clans, and tribes and with such togetherness came the oldest problem of social life, that of conformity. Fitting the individual to the group then constituted the major part of his education, for the individual had to conform both for his safety and that of the group. Tribal consciousness rather than individual consciousness was emphasized. Obviously, the welfare of the tribe rather than recognition of any individual right was of paramount concern.

---

[13] Lewis Browne, *This Believing World* (New York: Crowell-Collier and Macmillan, Inc., 1954), p. 27.

[14] A. M. Hocart, *The Life-giving Myth* (New York: Grove Press, Inc., 1953), p. 7.

At first this process of developing conformity was followed without a conscious aim. Man engaged in it without theorizing. When individuals drew together into social units, as was necessary for survival, likenesses among those in the group were essential for the comfort and stability of each. Consequently, without conscious effort, the grouping became an educational force, which stamped out eccentricities and impelled each individual toward uniformity. When an individual achieved group standards his education was complete; and general social approval or disapproval was a sufficient force to compel each member to stay within the cultural limits of his group.

As primitive man began to think in "educational" terms, it seemed no problem to him; he merely continued to do consciously what he had been doing naturally: adjusting each individual to his material and spiritual environment through the already arrived at, prescribed ways of doing things in work and worship considered salutary by the tribe. For primitive life tended to repress, not to encourage, individual variation and to maintain an unvarying level of adherence to tradition and to the customs of the tribe. As Hart observes:

> Each new child was a task to be dealt with as occasion arose; but *the elders of the group knew what to do with him.* They knew what their job was; they were able to break him in—to the uses and ways of life— or they were able to throw him out. They had no alternative, no choice, and no problem. The matter was never questioned.[15]

For millennia, then, education was nothing but enculturation, that is, the imposing of group characteristics upon children. The object of primitive organization was to create what Sir Walter Bagehot has called "the cake of custom." Choice or chance was to determine nothing. The guiding rule was the status quo. The dominant aim was to weed out variations at birth or in early childhood. For a member to deviate from the ancient customs and usage of his tribe was the unpardonable sin.

Types

Preliterate education contained, in rudimentary form, both universal types of education: (1) practical education, which refers to the seen and (2) theoretical education, which refers to the unseen.

The practical education of primitive man included the simpler forms of domestic, vocational, physical, military, and moral training. These types of education, when freed from the aboriginal standard of static adjustment to environment, became the foundations of economics, sociology, politics, and ethics. They educate for all work activities which deal with the material aspects of human life.

---

[15] Joseph Kinnan Hart, *Creative Moments in Education* (New York: Holt, Rinehart and Winston, Inc., 1931), p. 1.

Early man's theoretical education covered religious, literary, musical, artistic, medical, and intellectual learning, which are the prototypes forming the bases of religion, the arts, medicine, science, and philosophy. Originally, these disciplines had basic contact with the so-called worship activities, those concerned with the spiritual or abstract aspects of man's existence.

The separation suggested above is, however, more apparent than real because, while the theoretical forms of primitive education dealt with the spiritual and unseen, they were applied to practical efforts to obtain security from the occult forces. In fact, many worship activities were actually work activities. Worship among the aborigines was largely physical. So in a way all aboriginal education was practical: education was but an adjustment to life and a propitiation of the unseen forces to make life less hazardous. But such goals fell far short of being an introduction to an abundant life.

Content

Fundamentally, the education, or enculturation, of early man rested on three processes: (1) the physical training necessary to satisfy his primal urges for food, shelter, and clothing; (2) the spiritual, or ceremonial and sacramental training considered necessary that he might reconcile the unseen world to himself and family; and (3) the social knowledge of the customs, taboos, and restraints essential for harmonious living with the members of his tribal group. Anthropological studies show how different modes of life, or "destiny ideas," controlled these folkways, customs, and mores.

Benedict was one of the first (c. 1930) to implement the theories of psychoanalysis that keys, or clews, exist which serve to explain human behavior through reference to the taboos and drives of aboriginal peoples. Utilizing the *Gestalt* (configuration) principle (which we discuss in Chapter 16), Benedict saw cultures as material and spiritual entities; she applied to groups the psychological concepts conventionally associated with individuals; looking for ruling motivations, she borrowed the terminology of Oswald Spengler, German author of *Decline of the West*.

Thus Benedict listed several ruling motivations that she deemed characteristic of culture-types. The *Apollonian* appeared to her, as to Spengler, to typify the soul of the classic world—"a cosmos ordered in a group of excellent parts," that is, an ideal or idealized world, with conspicuous absence of conflict and competition; the *Dionysian*, as identified by Friedrich Nietzsche, alluded to a world in frenzy, characterized by a life geared only to the present and rich in terms of excess and prodigality; the *Egyptian* also identified an ancient stage in the human drama, but lacked the joyfulness of the Apollonian, for the Egyptian saw himself "as moving down a narrow and inexorably prescribed life-path, to come, at last, before the judges of the dead"; the *Faustian*, an advanced culture-type, denominated a force "endlessly combatting obstacles, inevitable, the culmination of past choices and experiences."[16] Its essence is conflict, yet personal as opposed to general, and not necessarily entailing strife on any solely materialistic plane. In Goethe's rendition of the Faust legend we find this prototype of an individual seeking such transcendence:

> A longing pure and not to be described
>> Drove me to wander over woods and fields;
> And in a mist of hot, abundant tears
>> I felt a world arise and live for me.[17]

When applied to culture as a pattern, the Faustian is more typical of later stages in man's history, especially those dominated by ideals of bridging the gap between experience and total knowledge. Nor does the Faustian, as a culture-type, appear to apply as generally as, for example, the Apollonian. If the terms *Apollonian* and *Dionysian* are sensed as implying a dualism in man's nature, then the resultant conflict becomes the core of all the West's great literature. Here, however, we are concerned with cultures rather than with man as an individual; and, although Benedict has been criticized for her penchant for applying individual concepts to groups, we shall use her distinctions from time to time.

The mode of life and education found in aboriginal societies visited by contemporary anthropologists undoubtedly typifies that of early man. Boys were taught to hunt, to fish, to fight, and to create and wield instruments for these pursuits. Girls were taught to care for children, to prepare food, to manufacture clothing and the implements and utensils demanded by their tasks. Normally women were expected to construct and maintain the dwelling. All these tasks were relatively simple and could be learned by simple methods.

Acts of appeasement or worship were more involved, and training in the magical rites by which spirits were to be placated was much more complex. Ingenuous animistic explanations of sun, moon, stars, storms, and seasons—all the ordinary processes of nature as well as the extraordinary—were transmitted from the wise men of the tribe to their proteges. These sometimes garish interpretations represented the beginnings of science and philosophy. Primitive man's ability to speak of and explain his unusual experiences and to decorate and embellish such tales in "rites of intensification" was a development in the genesis of history and literature.

The ceremonies and rituals by which the gods were appeased were largely concerned with symbols of two types: the audible and the visible. As spoken symbols increased in number, we find the origin of language

---

[16] Benedict, pp. 52–55, 79, 89–90.
[17] Johann Wolfgang von Goethe, *Faust*, Book I.

and music.[18] In the development of visible symbols in the shape of totems, altars, and statues are found the beginnings of art, architecture, and picture writing. But we should note that for early man, the symbol, instead of merely representing the spirit, contained its essence; the symbol was as much the thing as the thing itself. To destroy the statue of a spirit was to destroy the spirit; to eat the symbol of a spirit in the form of a cake was to partake of the spirit's essence; to pronounce the name of the spirit was to breathe the spirit's very substance. Customarily the name of a spirit was taboo and not to be uttered except by a holy man at a holy moment and then perhaps under very secret circumstances.

Fetishes were commonly used. These were natural or manufactured objects in which the essence of the spirit was deemed to dwell, and the possession of which supposedly gave its holder power to control the spirit. Learning the magic rites connected with animism, fetishism, totemism, and tabooism was quite a complicated procedure for neophytes.

For example, Benedict tells how the sorcerers of Dobu used witchcraft and incantations to influence the sweet potatoes growing in the gardens of the islands. The Dionysian Dobuan culture is characterized by strong personalism and violence so the potatoes are thought of as persons; the islanders believe the potatoes can wander at night from garden to garden. Thus the sorcerers' charms are designed to keep the yams at home.[19] The Kwakiutl likewise used magic in their activities.

Medicine and religion were one for primitive peoples. They thought that disease was caused by evil influences; the important thing was to know how to drive these away. A usual practice was to make the body so uncomfortable that an evil spirit no longer cared to dwell there, but charms and incantations also were used. Evil had to be driven or coaxed out. Generally the exercise of this treatment resided with the shaman, or medicine man, who practiced a crude type of medical science. The acquisition of shamanic lore constituted a rustic type of medical education.

Yet early man did not disregard his physical condition; the history of physical education began here. Thomas Woody's *Life and Education in Early Societies* demonstrates that care of bodily development and physical health represents one of man's earliest and most urgent concerns.[20] Since his primary anxiety was for the protection of himself and family from other people as well as wild beasts, it was essential that he develop a strong, vigorous body. Different tribes undertook physical exercise in various ways. Exercises were devised to develop the constitutions of the young, to give strength to their limbs and adroitness to their actions, to arouse their

---

[18] See Mario Pei, *The Story of Language* (New York: New American Library of World Literature, Inc., 1966), chs. 1 and 2.

[19] Benedict, pp. 131–140.

[20] (New York: Crowell-Collier and Macmillan, Inc., 1949), pp. 10–43.

martial fervor, to incite them to deeds of daring and danger. From infancy they were primed in the arts of dodging and turning, perhaps to be able later to avoid the missiles that might be aimed at them. Youths sometimes buffeted their parents as a training to forestall cowardice; adolescents were often forced to endure their fathers' blows without flinching. So the content of early education was practical; even education in magic had practical aims.

Agencies

Utilitarian education was imparted to primitive youth by the basic social group, the family, usually considerably more extensive than its modern counterpart. In fact, an "extended family" of preliterate days comprised a large number of people of varying degrees of social relationship; and within the family, each young person had his own special position just as adult members had theirs. The security gained allowed for as full a development of personality and prowess as the tribe permitted. The women of the family taught the girls the female duties of household management and child rearing, while the men, of course, instructed the boys, whose male duties included hunting, fishing, fighting, making tools and weapons, and learning how to propitiate the tribal spirits, or gods.

When a boy knew as much as his father or guardian his formal education stopped; when a girl's knowledge equaled that of her mother her training was complete. As Spencer has rightly observed, "The end to be attained in both cases is the same; the exact reproduction of the knowledge or skill of the parent. Variation has no place in this scheme of education, for the children are not supposed to make any advance beyond the attainments of their parents."[21] Primitive man had a crude Apollonian society.

Within the social system, however, a degree of specialization gradually evolved; one or several persons in a group came to be able to do a thing better than anyone else; one man learned, by accident or by simple trial and error, to make a sharper spear, ax, or pruning hook; another a more shapely piece of pottery, a more useful basket, or statue of a god. Sometimes these "specialists" were keen enough to keep their secret to themselves or to pass them on only to their offspring. More often, children of other members of the tribe came to them for instruction. Thus there developed a more definite division of labor, based on knowledge and skill, and a trend toward such imparting of knowledge and specialized technique. Crafts and professions were in the process of being born.

At first, all religious instruction was in the hands of the immediate or extended family. This was a most logical procedure, for those spirits which gave the greatest concern were, of course, those of deceased members of a family. These, it was believed, still occupied a position in the family and

---

[21] F. C. Spencer, *Education of the Pueblo Child* (New York: Columbia University Press, 1899).

were as a rule friendly toward it as long as traditions were followed. Thus, one's ancestors provided a focus for family worship and, in a sense, became gods.

The office of placator of the family gods rested on the family father, he being the oldest, the most experienced, and the closest to the spirits of those who had passed on. He was responsible for training the young to conduct themselves in a manner pleasing to the ancestral spirits. Hence the father taught his offspring the value of work, the necessity for fighting to maintain the group, the advantages of living together harmoniously, the proper relations of the sexes, the taboos and restraints peculiar to the tribe, and all other things indispensable to living a life satisfactory to the canons of the family spirits.

As families united into larger groups and their customs were added to the social inheritance, it became necessary to worship not only as families but also as tribes. This required a tribal chief, who might be chosen for his strength, physique, age, or ability in council. He might be called medicine man, shaman, wizard, witch doctor, or priest. His primary duties were to propitiate the spirits, especially the evil ones, and to instruct others in the dances, ceremonies, incantations, and rituals—all the wild, fanciful, bewildering forms of worship found among primitive peoples. Indeed, certain anthropologists trace the beginnings of religion to the group solidarity and ecstasy aroused by the dance and its ordinances.[22]

With the formation of a priesthood came another differentiation in the education of early man. At first, the chief merely taught where and when the act was to be performed and the exact mode of performance. Next came the question, "Why?" Consequently, the priest had to offer a special type of explanation or knowledge dealing with the reasons for his rites; this knowledge forms our earliest distinct body of intellectualized subject matter.

To better carry from one generation to another these special perceptions or intuitions, classes were set up to train tribal youths who were to become priests or religious leaders; and the priests began to formulate systematically a body of knowledge which remained secret except to their own fraternity. The priests' inquiry into the why and wherefore of things stimulated primitive intellectual development and provided the first intellectual differentiation. Out of such inquiry developed a large body of theoretical knowledge and, with this knowledge, the need to find means of permanent recording. The development of writing, an alphabet, and recorded literature was a logical sequence to priestly inquiry, although in most early civilizations learning was closed to all but the priesthood and a privileged nobility. Nevertheless, this formation of a priestly class advanced

---

[22] See Emile Durkheim, *The Elementary Forms of Religious Life*, trans. from the French (New York: Crowell-Collier and Macmillan, Inc., Collier Books, 1961).

the functions of education in several important ways. It led to (1) the formation of a definite body of subject matter, (2) the rise of a teaching class, and (3) the development of a language and a literature. These attainments marked the constitution of education as a distinct and essential institution.

Methods

The earliest method utilized in education was that of organic education. Jean Baptiste de Lamarck (1774–1829) first offered the theory that all organisms, including man, evolved gradually in response to conditions which affected their growth. Lamarck contended that new structures arose as adjustments or adaptations to environment and either developed through use or disappeared through disuse. For example, if someone learned the efficacy of a scowl or gesture, the action became one of his responses to similar situations; the same occurred when someone learned to clench his fist, or to throw a stone, or to hold and hurl a club. Such mechanisms, once acquired, were satisfying because they brought results. So they became fixed in the individual and were transmitted, according to Lamarck and his followers, *biologically* to his descendants and thus became inherent in the organism. "All that has been acquired or altered in the organization of individuals during their life is preserved by generation and transmitted to the new individuals which proceed from those which have undergone the change," said Lamarck in his promulgation of the now generally rejected theory of evolution through the inheritance of such features.[23]

In 1859 Charles Darwin advanced another interpretation of the origin of traits and characteristics. Darwin believed that new characteristics arose as chance variations in individual organisms. Those traits establishing usefulness in the "struggle for existence" enabled organisms possessing them to survive so they could reproduce their kind, thus passing such positive traits on to future generations. Individuals holding negative, or nonprogressive traits, failed to survive until they could reproduce, thus unfavorable traits disappeared. Hugo De Vries extended Darwin's idea of chance variations by demonstrating the occurrence of mutations, unique pronounced accidental variations, which he maintained accounted for radical changes in organic evolution.

Regarding the variations which played so indispensable a role in his theory, Darwin could only say "we are profoundly ignorant of the cause of each slight variation or individual difference." This ignorance was not

---

[23] A similar explanation, proposed by Tromfim D. Lysenko, a Soviet agronomist, was accepted by the Central Committee in 1948 as the basis for biology teaching in the U.S.S.R. Since Lysenko's theories are in line with Marxist ideology they found favor in the Soviet Union for a number of years, but have now been discredited. See E. W. Caspari and R. E. Marshak, "The Rise and Fall of Lysenko," *Science*, vol. 149 (July 16, 1965), pp. 275–278.

completely dispelled until almost a century later, in 1953, when James D. Watson and Francis Crick at the Cavendish Laboratory in England demmonstrated how the individual's basic characteristics are passed through the genes from generation to generation. These singular properties are found in the molecule DNA (deoxyribonucleic acid), a determiner found within the cell of every living body. The DNA molecule is a long string of smaller molecules, or nucleotides, which are arranged in a manner different in each organism. This sequence determines which proteins will be brought together in the body cells. These proteins control body chemistry and all the traits of the person. A modification of the nucleotides in DNA constitutes a mutation.[24] Mutations thus are changes in the body chemistry of the individual which are transmitted to his descendants; the self-duplication of the gene makes the process possible and, while Darwin did not understand the chemical basis of heredity, the mutation is the inheritable variation which forms the basis of his theory of evolution.

These biological processes, whether one relates them to Darwin, De Vries, or Watson and Crick, comprise what we mean by the term *organic method*, a mode generally considered to be beyond the power of man himself.[25]

We must turn now to the method of unconscious imitation, in which man takes some share in the educative process, but without awareness of his role and without theorizing. Long before man made any conscious attempts to enculturate his children, his children began to educate themselves through their unconscious duplication of the activities of their parents and other members of their family or tribe. Much of such unconscious imitation was performed as play, which is actually a form of education. The child's games and amusements were small replicas of the activities of adult life. His toys were miniatures of the implements used by his elders. For example, American Indian children played with a log in the water, paddling about as though it were a canoe; young boys made tiny bows and arrows and hurled them at marks; girls made small cooking utensils and feigned the preparation of food. Most sports were imitations of the serious life of the tribe: the council, the buffalo hunt, war, and the ritualistic ceremonies to appease the spirit world.

Even as aboriginal father and mother enlisted the child's aid in performing the many tasks involved in group life, they were hardly aware that they were educating. Both imitation through play and imitation through

---

[24] For a lucid explanation of the causes of mutations and the cosmic forces in the evolution of man see Robert Jastrow, *Red Giants and White Dwarfs* (New York: Harper & Row, Publishers, 1967), pp. 120–167. For an informative biographical report of the DNA discovery see James D. Watson, *The Double Helix* (New York: Atheneum Publishers, 1968).

[25] In 1969 the frontiers of genetics were pushed back still further with the isolation of a gene by Jonathan Beckwith, James Shapiro, and Lawrence Eron at Harvard University, making theoretically possible control of heredity on simple cellular levels.

work, effective though they might be, were experienced largely at the unconscious level.

The wholly conscious method represents a third stage in the development of primitive education. Now an awareness of what was being planned and executed obtained; from the learner's standpoint education was still imitation, but from the teacher's viewpoint it was teaching by example. A primitive man watching his neighbor acquire efficiently the necessities of existence, or a youth observing the actions of the elders of the tribe consciously endeavored to duplicate others' efforts for the satisfaction of their own wants. Older members of the tribe, not being able to utilize the methods of instruction developed by historic peoples, consciously attempted to direct the attention of the young to such examples.

Our survey would be incomplete without mention of another preliterate means of training: trial and error. This process, however, could only be used in the few cases in which the action either did not conflict with tribal customs, taboos, rites, and restraints, or might occur as the result of an accident. When a trial proved successful, it could be repeated; when painful results followed, the procedure was abandoned, or so reasoned the early learner. But in primitive days any procedure that resulted in even a little success might be continued indefinitely. Charles Lamb tells a delightful story of the discovery of roast pig through the mishap of a burning pigsty. And it is not unlikely that pottery making arose from the accidental burning of a basket in which fresh clay had been carried; at least it is generally supposed that the manufacture of glass occurred after experience with a campfire on a sandy beach.

When the earliest teaching class, the priests, arose and was entrusted with the education of the young, the method generally used was indoctrination. Instruction dealt, for the most part, with the formal aspects of worship; what to do and how to do it. Even when the reasons for religious conduct were inculcated (usually only in the training of acolytes for the temple), the education was invariably of the type that taught what to think, rather than how to think.

Yet man's capability suggests his uniqueness; and the fact that primitive teachers called for perfection in areas they considered worth teaching should be an incentive to modern education. As Boyd says,

> Achievements in [primitive] art so perfect as those which appear in the best of the animal pictures engraved on horn and ivory or drawn on cave walls could only have been attained by definite teaching. Concerning the Why and the How of this teaching we can never hope to know anything, and can only speculate whether, like the wall-paintings, it may not have had its origin in some [primordial] religious impluse.[26]

[26] William Boyd, *The History of Western Education*, 8th ed., rev. by Edmund J. King (New York: Barnes & Noble, Inc., 1966), p. 1.

Since man is the only organism on this planet with a true language, he alone can store his accumulated knowledge—the *superorganic*, as Alfred Louis Kroeber has called it— and through education pass it on beyond individual memory.[27] This extraordinary ability, plus the fact that man is capable of high acts of heroism and self-denial as well as guilt for depraved acts, stamps him as enormously different from the most cleverly trained animal.

Organization

There was indeed little organization in the contemporary sense in primitive education. There were no grades of instruction or levels of schooling. Most education might better be called training, given in rather random fashion, quite incidental to other survival activities and the regular duties of family and tribe. Custom, once determined, required of the individual strict obedience through imitation of the approved ways.

The exception to a generally diffuse educational organization among primitive peoples was the prevalent and significant ceremony of initiation. Through ritualistic observance the adolescent youth achieved manhood and tribal membership. Almost without exception, boys at the onset of puberty were taken aside by the shaman or a tribal committee and in secret underwent a series of complicated ceremonies, the token of their acceptance into full-fledged fellowship. In some cultures girls as well as boys were included in these puberty rites and had to pass through certain observances attendant on their newly achieved biological maturity.

Ritualistic ordinances likewise offered their opportunities for instruction. As Charles points out:

> The fundamental business of growing up is accomplished everywhere; and although methods and forms of behavior vary tremendously in different primitive cultures, they usually are dramatic. Whether in puberty rites or in their educational equivalents, the overwhelming purpose of this dramatization is to emphasize and impress beyond the shadow of a doubt that childhood and all its parts have been left behind; to make sure that the individual has received communion with the deepest cultural ideals; and to announce and stress that henceforth he is an adult, responsible for his own acts and for his share of group responsibilities.[28]

During initiation ceremonies the youths were taught the ancient secrets of the tribe, shown its holy objects, informed of the proper relation-

---

[27] Alfred Louis Kroeber, "The Superorganic," *American Anthropologist*, vol. 19 (1917), pp. 163–213.

[28] Lucille H. Charles, "Growing up through Drama," *Journal of American Folklore*, vol. 59 (1946), p. 261. As quoted in Frank W. Young, *Initiation Ceremonies, A Cross-Cultural Study of Status Dramatization* (Indianapolis: The Bobbs-Merrill Company, Inc., 1965), p. 9; see also pp. 9–41 for a supplementary interpretation of ritual from the individual or "inside," viewpoint.

ship of the sexes, and all practical and theoretical training deemed essential for their own well-being and the welfare of the group. In dramatic fashion they sometimes were tortured to reveal their strength and their willingness to suffer without complaint and to keep the mysteries of their tribe. It is a mark of educational development that their elders thoroughly grasped the importance of such high and exciting moments of emotional and intellectual awakening to demonstrate and inculcate useful lessons.[29]

Moreover the efficacy of such exercises was shared by those participating in the ceremonials, which were stimulating and uplifting. Spencer and Gillin, writing of the aborigines of central Australia, report that the natives themselves say the rituals have power to strengthen and enlighten those who receive them, and to produce "very good and great" men. From the practical standpoint alone, the ceremonies represent an important way station in male progress into the confidence and councils of the tribe.[30]

Margaret Read, telling of the Ngoni of east-central Africa, summed up their mode of child training as the inculcation of, as Ngoni adults understood it, "respect." By demonstrating respect in language, posture, and action, a child or adult was believed to share in the honor he was thus acknowledging. A person, failing to convey respect, lost face accordingly.[31] Boys were taught their tribal roles through life in the common "boys' dormitory" and in the activities of cattle tending, listening to their elders at the kraal gate, through discussion groups, and, as time permitted, in school. Girls were taught in home surroundings by the women of the tribe, but especially in their "girls' circle," where, through personal relations and the telling and hearing of tales and legends they achieved the essentials of a practical and cultural education. If exceptional, and the parents agreed, they were sent to school along with the boys.[32]

As we see, participation in the ordinances and ceremonies of one's society, together with an incidental apprenticeship to the daily and seasonal activities of the family and tribe constituted the basic educational program found in primitive cultures.[33] It was usually adequate, however, to set the

---

[29] See Benedict, pp. 22–27, for further description of the "rites of passage" and "rites of intensification" in primitive societies.

[30] Baldwin Spencer and F. J. Gillin, *Native Tribes of Central Australia* (London: Macmillan & Co., Ltd., 1938), especially chs. vii, viii, and ix on initiation.

[31] Margaret Read, *Children of Their Fathers, Growing up among the Ngoni of Malawi* (New York: Holt, Rinehart and Winston, Inc., 1968), pp. 15–18.

[32] Read, pp. 48–59.

[33] The educational system of each tribe or nation is unique and it is only by close observation and comparison that its real significance and goals are revealed. More than a century ago Marc-Antoine Jullien de Paris (1775–1848), in a call for a greater comprehensiveness in the study of education, wrote: "Education, as other sciences, is based on facts and observations, which should be ranged in analytical tables, easily compared, in order to deduce principles and definite rules. Education should become a positive science instead of being ruled by narrow and limited opinions, by whims and arbitrary decisions of administrators, to be turned away from the direct line which it should follow, either by the prejudice of a blind routine or by

cake of custom to insure the perpetuation of the tribe. For this reason, *conformity in work and worship* may be advanced as the means whereby group security was attained, and as the chief goal in primitive and preliterate societies. But, we may note in passing for the benefit of those who disclaim the regimented features of tribal society that, while individualism undoubtedly suffered severely, the resultant society was generally an integrated one.

REFERENCES

Barnes, Harry Elmer, *An Intellectual and Cultural History of the Western World*. New York: Random House, Inc., 1937. Pp. 27–61.

Benedict, Ruth, *Patterns of Culture*. Boston: Houghton Mifflin Company, 1934.

Bohannan, Paul, *Africa and the Africans*. Garden City, N.Y.: Natural History Press, 1964.

Boyd, William, *The History of Western Education*, 8th ed., rev. by Edmund J. King. New York: Barnes & Noble, Inc., 1966. Pp. 1–3.

Breasted, James Henry, *The Conquest of Civilization*. New York: Harper & Row, Publishers, 1926 and 1938. Pp. 3–39.

Browne, Lewis, *This Believing World*. New York: Crowell-Collier and Macmillan, Inc., 1954. Pp. 27–65.

Butts, R. Freeman, *A Cultural History of Western Education*. New York: McGraw-Hill, Inc., 1955. Pp. 1–6.

Childe, V. Gordon, *Man Makes Himself*. New York: New American Library of World Literature, Inc., 1951.

Clark, John G. D., and Stuart Piggott, *Prehistoric Societies*. New York: Alfred A. Knopf, 1965.

Cornwall, I. W., *The World of Ancient Man*. New York: New American Library of World Literature, Inc., 1964.

Dawson, Christopher, *The Age of the Gods*. New York: Sheed & Ward, Inc., 1933. Pp. 3–107.

———, *The Dynamics of World History*. New York: Sheed & Ward, Inc., 1957. Pp. 3–110.

Eby, Frederick, and Charles F. Arrowood, *The History and Philosophy of Education, Ancient and Medieval*. Englewood Cliffs, N.J.: Prentice-Hall, Inc., 1940. Pp. 1–35.

Eiseley, Loren, *The Immense Journey*. New York: Random House, Inc., 1957.

---

the spirit of some system and innovation." (*L'Esquisse et vues préliminaires d'un ouvrage sur l'Éducation Comparée*, Paris, 1817. As quoted in Pedro Rosselló, *Marc-Antoine Jullien de Paris*, Geneva, 1943.) Arthur Henry Moehlman suggests a morphology consisting of the philosophy, people, the geography, historical determinants, and technology for use in the study of a system of education in its own culture pattern. (Arthur Henry Moehlman and Joseph S. Roucek Eds., *Comparative Education*, New York: Holt, Rinehart and Winston, Inc., 1952.) We recommend such a comparative approach to the study of the educational records of the past and present and have attempted to utilize it in this work.

Frazer, Sir James G., *The Golden Bough*, one vol. ed. New York: Cro-well-Collier and Macmillan, Inc., 1922.

———, *The New Golden Bough—A New Abridgement of the Classic Work*, edit. and with notes and foreword by Theodor H. Gaster. New York: Criterion Books, Inc., 1959.

Hart, Joseph Kinnan, *Creative Moments in Education*. New York: Holt, Rinehart and Winston, Inc., 1931. Pp. 1–26.

Hawkes, Jacquetta, and Sir Leonard Woolley, *Prehistory and The Beginnings of Civilization*. History of Mankind Series, vol. i. New York: Harper & Row, Publishers, 1963.

Jung, Carl G. (Ed.), *Man and His Symbols*. New York: Doubleday & Company, Inc., 1964. Especially pp. 104–157.

Kroeber, Alfred Louis, *Anthropology*. New York: Harcourt, Brace & World, Inc., 1948.

Malinowski, Bronislaw, *Magic, Science and Religion and Other Essays*. New York: The Free Press, 1948.

Mayer, Frederick, *A History of Educational Thought*. Columbus, Ohio: Charles E. Merrill Books, Inc., 1960.

Messenger, James F., *An Interpretative History of Education*. New York: Thomas Y. Crowell Company, 1931. Pp. 9–16.

Mulhern, James, *A History of Education*, 2d ed. New York: The Ronald Press Company, 1959. Pp. 1–54.

Myers, Edward D., *Education in the Perspective of History*. New York: Harper & Row, Publishers, 1960.

Nakosteen, Mehdi, *The History and Philosophy of Education*. New York: The Ronald Press Company, 1965. Pp. 9–22.

Pei, Mario, *The Story of Language*, rev. ed. Philadelphia: J. B. Lippincott Company, 1965.

Pfeiffer, John E., *The Emergence of Man*. New York: Harper & Row, Publishers, 1969.

Piggott, Stuart (Ed.), *The Dawn of Civilization*. New York: McGraw-Hill, Inc., 1961.

Power, Edward J., *Main Currents in the History of Education*. New York: McGraw-Hill, Inc., 1962. Pp. 1–6.

Shaw, Charles Gray, *Trends of Civilization and Culture*. New York: American Book Company, 1932.

Smith, William A., *Ancient Education*. New York: Philosophical Library, Inc., 1955. Pp. 254–294.

Spencer, Baldwin, and F. J. Gillin, *Native Tribes of Central Australia*. London: Macmillan & Co., Ltd., 1938. Chs. vii, viii, ix.

Spencer, F. C., *Education of the Pueblo Child*. New York: Columbia University Press, 1899.

Starr, Chester G., *A History of the Ancient World*. New York: Oxford University Press, 1965. Pp. 3–26.

Stewart, George R., *Man: An Autobiography*. New York: Random House, Inc., 1946.

Tylor, Edward B., *Primitive Culture*. Reprint of the 1st ed. New York: Brentanos, 1924.

Ulich, Robert, *Education and the Idea of Mankind.* New York: Harcourt, Brace & World, Inc., 1964.
Wendt, Herbert, *It Began in Babel.* Boston: Houghton Mifflin Company, 1962.
Wissler, Clark, *Man and Culture.* New York: Thomas Y. Crowell Company, 1923. Pp. 1–20, 47–72.
Woody, Thomas, *Life and Education in Early Societies.* New York: Crowell-Collier and Macmillan, Inc., 1949. Pp. 10–43.

SELECTED PAPERBACKS

Beck, Robert Holmes, *A Social History of Education.* Englewood Cliffs, N.J.: Prentice-Hall, Inc., 1965.
Benedict, Ruth, *Patterns of Culture.* Boston: Houghton Mifflin Company, Sentry Books, 1965; New York: New American Library of World Literature, Inc., 1946.
Boas, Franz, *The Mind of Primitive Man.* New York: The Free Press, 1965.
———, *Race, Language and Culture.* New York: The Free Press, 1966.
Breasted, James Henry, *Ancient Times,* 2d ed., vol. i, *The Ancient Near East.* Boston: Ginn & Company, 1966.
Brown, Ina Corrine, *Understanding Other Cultures.* Englewood Cliffs, N.J.: Prentice-Hall, Inc., 1963.
Carrington, Richard, *A Million Years of Man.* New York: New American Library of World Literature, Inc., 1963.
Castle, Edgar Bradshaw, *Ancient Education and Today.* Baltimore: Penguin Books, Inc., Pelican Books, 1961.
Cheney, L. J., *A History of the Western World from the Stone Age to the Twentieth Century.* New York: New American Library of World Literature, Inc., 1959.
Childe, V. Gordon, *The Dawn of European Civilization.* New York: Random House, Inc., Vintage Books, 1965.
———, *Man Makes Himself.* New York: New American Library of World Literature, Inc., 1951.
———, *Prehistory of European Society.* Baltimore: Penguin Books, Inc., 1958.
———, *What Happened in History.* Baltimore: Penguin Books, Inc., 1961.
Darwin, Charles, *Voyage of the Beagle.* New York: Doubleday & Company, Inc., Anchor Books, 1962.
Durkheim, Emile, *The Elementary Forms of Religious Life,* trans. from the French. New York: Crowell-Collier and Macmillan, Inc., Collier Books, 1961.
Eiseley, Loren, *The Immense Journey.* New York: Random House, Inc., Vintage Books, 1965.
Fallers, Lloyd A., *Bantu Bureaucracy.* Chicago: University of Chicago Press, 1965.

Field, Henry, *The Track of Man*. New York: Dell Publishing Co., Inc., Laurel Books, 1967.

Frankfort, Henri, *The Birth of Civilization in the Near East*. Garden City, N.Y.: Doubleday & Company, Inc., Anchor Books, 1956.

Frazer, Sir James. *The New Golden Bough*, abr. and edit. with notes and foreword by Theodor H. Gaster. New York: New American Library of World Literature, Inc., 1964.

Gay, John, and Michael Cole, *The New Mathematics and an Old Culture, A Study of Learning among the Kpelle of Liberia*. New York: Holt, Rinehart and Winston, Inc., 1967.

Hawkes, Jacquetta, *History of Mankind, Cultural and Scientific Development*, vol. i, pt. i, *Prehistory*. New York: New American Library of World Literature, Inc., 1965.

Henry, Jules, *Jungle People*. New York: Alfred A. Knopf, 1961.

Hocart, A. M., *The Life-giving Myth*. New York: Grove Press, Inc., 1953.

Hollister, C. Warren, *Roots of the Western Tradition*. New York: John Wiley & Sons, Inc., 1966. Pp. 1–8.

Jones, Tom B., *From the Tigris to the Tiber*. Homewood, Ill.: The Dorsey Press, 1969.

Jung, Carl G., *Psyche and Symbol*. New York: Doubleday & Company, Inc., 1958.

Kluckhohn, Clyde, *Mirror for Man*. New York: Fawcett Publications, Inc., 1949.

Kroeber, Alfred Louis, and Clyde Kluckhohn, *Culture*. New York: Random House, Inc., 1963.

Leakley, L. S. B., *Adam's Ancestors, The Evolution of Man and His Culture*. New York: Harper & Row, Publishers, 1960.

Linton, Ralph, *The Tree of Culture*. New York: Random House, Inc., Vintage Books, 1960.

Mead, Margaret. *Coming of Age in Samoa*. New York: New American Library of World Literature, Inc., 1949.

Montagu, F. Ashley, *Man: His First Million Years*. New York: New American Library of World Literature, Inc., 1959.

Morris, Desmond, *The Naked Ape*. New York: Dell Publishing Co., 1967.

Pei, Mario, *The Story of Language*. New York: New American Library of World Literature, Inc., 1966.

Read, Margaret, *Children of Their Fathers, Growing up among the Ngoni of Malawi*. New York: Holt, Rinehart and Winston, Inc., 1968.

Ross, Ralph, *Symbols & Civilization*. New York: Harcourt, Brace & World, Inc., 1962.

Shapiro, Harry L. (Ed.), *Man, Culture and Society*. New York: Oxford University Press, 1960.

Simpson, George Gaylord, *The Meaning of Evolution*. New York: New American Library of World Literature, Inc., 1951.

Spindler, George D., *Education and Culture*. New York: Holt, Rinehart and Winston, Inc., 1963.

Sumner, William Graham, *Folkways*. New York: New American Library of World Literature, Inc., 1960.

White, Leslie A., *The Science of Culture*. New York: Grove Press, Inc., 1949.

Woolley, Sir Leonard, *Digging Up the Past,* Baltimore: Penguin Books, Inc., 1960.

————, *History of Mankind, Cultural and Scientific Development,* vol. i, pt. ii, *The Beginnings of Civilization*. New York, New American Library of World Literature, Inc., 1965.

Young, Frank W., *Initiation Ceremonies, A Cross-Cultural Study of Status Dramatization*. Indianapolis: The Bobbs-Merrill Company, Inc., 1965.

CHAPTER 2

The Preservation of Social Stability

*You who wander about the public square; would you achieve success?
Then seek out the first generations. Go to school, it will be of benefit
to you. My son, seek out the first generations, inquire of them!*[1]

EARLY CIVILIZATIONS

Several thousand years ago tribesmen began to emerge from their
primordial stages into the earliest known civilizations. What distinguishes
this transition from the prehistoric? Some anthropologists claim that early
civilizations began when men forced nature to their will by applying water,
wind, and fire to their needs; when they established themselves as temporary masters of their environment by forging iron implements and keener
weapons, by using sails for their manually propelled canoes and boats, or
by irrigating their lands for tillage. Others maintain that man developed
more sophisticated means to transfer himself from simple primitive societies
to the more complex stages of social living called civilization.

Almost half a score of "determiners" have been suggested,[2] among
them (1) discovery of symbolization and writing,[3] (2) development of
"logical presuppositions," (3) artificial control of the sex drive, (4) urbanization, (5) "challenge and response," (6) invention of mechanical, steam,

---

[1] Samuel Noah Kramer (Trans.), *History Begins at Sumer* (New York: Doubleday
& Company, Inc., Anchor Books, 1959).

[2] See Kenneth V. Lottich, "Some Distinctions between Culture and Civilization,"
Social Forces, vol. 28, no. 3 (March, 1950), pp. 240–250. V. Gordon Childe in
Man Makes Himself (New York: New American Library of World Literature, Inc.,
1951), lists nineteen major contributions by which early men achieved mastery of
their environment.

[3] Mario Pei, *The Story of Language* (New York: New American Library of World
Literature, Inc., 1966), pp. 12–14, contrasts the human ability to symbolize with
that of other species.

and petroleum engines, and (7) "a newly developed individuality." The British Lord Cromer adds, "Civilization began with the lash."

Still other writers allege that civilization arose when social classes and castes developed, when the blood ties that held primitive tribes and clans together became weaker, and persons holding common occupations and duties were brought into closer relationships and socioeconomic organization.[4] Certainly, as conditions changed, differentiation occurred between the roles and employment of the sexes, families, individuals, and clans or totems. These differentiations doubtless precipitated the origins of classes and castes.

As clearly illustrated by Sumer and Egypt, the oldest caste, the priesthood, grew out of the performance of shamans and other intermediaries or propitiators, whose existence was noted in most primitive tribes; thus, the priestly class became a group set aside from the common people, who valued and considered their services indispensable. The attainment of superior methods for the production of weapons and other implements by certain individuals, or families, paved the way for development of the artisan class. The vigor, prowess, and dedication of warriors set them apart as a protective and ruling class.

Social relations became more complex with the advent of such distinctions among people; eventually the three broad social classes or, even, castes that have played their part in world history appeared: (1) priests, performing the rites that shielded man from supernatural fears and invisible enemies; (2) soldiers or military rulers, defending men from their visible foes and preserving law and order; and (3) the common folk, working to produce food, tools, clothing, and shelter, the general necessities of life. These divisions were not, of course, equal; the upper classes, sometimes through warriors, sometimes by priests, most frequently ruled. The worker or producer usually had a subservient role, although the security of the group was greatly dependent on his industry and effort.

Although man's inventiveness is well shown in his creation of tools, weapons, and machines, nonmaterial developments continued to play a large part in the growing complexity of his newly structured social life. Primitive man, through the discovery of fire making had advanced his skill in the useful and esthetic arts; the invention of writing speeded his entrance into civilization.[5] In fact most ancient cultures are evaluated in terms of

[4] F. Ashley Montagu, in *Race, Science and Humanity* (Princeton, N.J.: D. Van Nostrand Company, Inc., 1963), argues that distinctions based on the so-called primitive level of life are as inadmissible as those based on race or color. Here, however, we are speaking only of cultures in terms of "simplicity" or complexity as the terminology "primitive cultures" and "ancient civilizations" suggest (regardless of the fact that there is perhaps no such thing as a really "simple" culture).

[5] Jacquetta Hawkes and Sir Leonard Woolley, *Prehistory and The Beginnings of Civilization*. History of Mankind Series, vol. i. (New York: Harper & Row, Publishers, 1963), pp. 166–167.

their peoples' ability with the strange but civilizing characters first chosen to record history and the spoken word. At the earliest, writing was wholly pictorial (alphabets of symbols developing only through a long and fascinating evolution[6]). This new mode of communication made possible the compilation and retention of the sacred tradition and laws hitherto handed down solely by word of mouth. These holy scripts became the prevailing curriculum and constituted the first textbooks. Further, in order to provide a specific systematic instruction in the use and veneration of the sacred word, the institution which came to be known as the *school* was established.

For many centuries it was held that the human species arose in western Asia, but it is now considered more likely that Africa was the birthplace of man.[7] And it is fairly safe to say that civilization was born either in middle-eastern Asia or eastern Africa, along the great water courses. For our purpose, we have selected Sumer as representative of the early origins in Asia and Egypt as representative of civilization in northeast Africa.[8]

These ancient civilizations, conventionally called Oriental, may be classified for our purposes on the basis of their languages as Indo-European (including Aryan Persian and Hindu); Turanian (Chinese and Mongolian); Semitic (Assyrian, Babylonian, Hittite, Phoenician, and Hebrew); and Hamitic (including Coptic, Ethiopian, Egyptian, and Minoan).

Throughout the Eastern Hemisphere the first civilizations appear to have developed in fluvial valleys.[9] Four sites of the earliest development were along the Tigris-Euphrates, the Indus, the Hwang Ho, and the Nile. Other strong groups originated in the plateau regions adjacent to the great rivers and the sea, on nearby islands, and in the Fertile Crescent, that upland area extending from the Mediterranean to the Persian Gulf. Indeed, a little later, important clusters of mankind learned to adapt to the semiarid lands of central and western Asia, Africa, and even the desert itself.

Distinguishing features of the transition from primitive cultures to the early civilizations were the use of copper (later mixed with tin to produce

---

[6] Oscar Ogg, *The 26 Letters* (New York: Thomas Y. Crowell Company, 1961).

[7] Hawkes and Woolley, pp. 48–49.

[8] This is not to say that there were not other influential civilizations in Africa. See Basil Davidson, *The Lost Cities of Africa* or *Old Africa Discovered* (Boston: Little, Brown & Company, 1900); *Africa, History of a Continent* (New York: Crowell-Collier and Macmillan, Inc., 1966); *The African Past* (Boston: Little, Brown & Company, 1964); or Chancellor Williams, *The Rebirth of African Civilization* (Washington, D.C.: Public Affairs Press, 1961); J. C. De Graft-Johnson, *African Glory, The Story of a Vanished Negro Civilization* (New York: Walker and Company, 1967).

[9] Conversely, the leading civilizations in the Western Hemisphere arose in plateau regions. As a significant departure the student might investigate early American cultures, the Inca, Maya, Aztec, Chichba, and others. A comprehensive single source, Jacquetta Hawkes, *The World of the Past*, 2 vols. (New York: Alfred A. Knopf, Inc., 1963) is both authoritative and interesting.

bronze) and the development of urban life. Actually, the transition to the *Chalcolithic* from the Neolithic was accomplished in many Far East, Middle East, and Near East settings as early as the fifth or fourth millennium B.C. The growth of the city was made possible by the development of a surplus of goods and services resulting in the creation of a trading economy that permitted larger concentrations of people and a concomitant diversification of activity. Authorities differ as to the prime reason for urbanization, but the cities of the copper age were seats of political power, trade, and religion. The existence of the city with its manifold activities is, of course, a hallmark of those cultures sometimes termed *civilizations*.

In order to learn the origins and status of education in the Eastern world, it will suffice to consider developments in Sumer, China, India, and Egypt as typical. And it should be noted that the term "Oriental" as used here has nothing to do with color or race; the Greek heritage, so largely accepted in the Western world, defines the *Orient*, or lands of the rising sun, as those countries and people east of the Aegean Sea. Today, the designations *Near East, Middle East*, and *Far East* are more frequently used, although Durant in his monumental *Story of Civilization* calls the first volume *Our Oriental Heritage*.[10] It is with this great tradition that we are now concerned.

THE ORIENTAL CONCEPTION OF EDUCATION

What was the position of education among these early Eastern peoples? What was the authority of the state? What rights to education and individuality did the populations have? What was the position of religion and its interpreters? What was religion's attitude toward, and its relationship to, education? All of these questions and many more are the province of educational history and its philosophy.

Oriental education, as represented by the philosophies and processes of the fluvial civilizations, exhibits a distinctive role when compared with that of primitive peoples, but lacks the freedom of later cultures such as that of the Athenian Greeks, the Italian Renaissance city-states and at least the stated goals of contemporary Western education. The aims and operation of Oriental education were closely controlled and dominated by the external authority of the state, the ruler, or unvarying custom. Individuality was suppressed; one person, unless he were the king, counted for nothing. Oriental education dictated what the person should do, feel, and think. In practice, it recapitulated and summed up the past for the individual in order that he might not depart from it or advance beyond it. Thus, an omnipotent authority of tradition, varying among different nations but

---

[10] New York: Simon and Schuster, Inc., 1935.

essentially the same, determined the character of man's education and directed his destiny.

In China the antecedent of ancestral beliefs, customs, and opinions ruled; in India the authority of the traditions of caste; in Sumer the authority of the national deities, as interpreted by their priests and votaries. In Egypt religion, as reflected through its deification of the Pharaoh and its learned priesthood, together with a great concern for life after death, became the leading motif. Somewhat differently, Persian education aimed at crystallizing rather than refining culture. The predominant aims of its teaching were practical rather than literary or scholastic.

The Persians wished to produce no great body of science or literature; instead they strove to produce a nation of warriors, physically fit and valiant, with all the virtues of a good soldier. Although their religious prophet Zoroaster taught a highly ethical religion, Persian life did not become otherworldly. In its fundamental purposes, Persian education was military rather than priestly. It aimed at fixing and disseminating national ideals. In order to develop a strong national life Zoroastrian virtues were to be inculcated—virtues much like those stressed two thousand years later, in early modern times, by Catholic Jesuits and Puritan Protestants.[11]

To sum up, the general purpose of early Oriental education was not to produce ideal men and women, but to prepare them as raw material to adjust to their place in the established order, as the tradition or necessity of their culture directed. As in primitive cultures, youth were taught to know their place and to play their part, the chief difference being only that the arena, being a state or national setting, was much more extensive. And as in primitive times, duties and obligations were emphasized rather than individual rights and privileges.

In the Oriental programs of education discussed here and in Chapter 3, we find as a common characteristic that training was concerned with fixing existing standards and perpetuating national standards, not with individual development. Instruction was geared toward building and maintaining an accepted national life.[12] And the system chosen was exceedingly successful in attaining its objective. For example, the Hindus and the Chinese, although overrun or harassed by conquerors many times, have preserved their national cultures for more than four thousand years. To

---

[11] Although Persian culture and education are not treated further in this volume, the student is referred to Richard N. Frye, *The Heritage of Persia* (Cleveland: The World Publishing Company, 1963). An excellent account of one of the world's great civilizations, ancient Persia (before the Islamic movement), Frye may profitably be read with other pre-Hellenic narratives, especially that of Durant in *The Story of Civilization.*

[12] See Sir Leonard Woolley, *History of Mankind, Cultural and Scientific Development,* vol. i, pt. ii, *The Beginnings of Civilization* (New York: New American Library of World Literature, Inc., 1965), pp. 393–399, for graphic discussion and interpretation of school methods in several of the early Eastern civilizations.

secure social stability, to ensure the stability of society, the perpetuity of family and empire, and the conservation of the past were their aims. The static, even negative, characteristic of such goals is an explanation of their success, for as an amateur marksman might observe, "A stationary target is more readily hit than a moving one."

This pattern of self-satisfaction with their educational arrangements, which prevailed among the early Eastern peoples, may be considered one of the first educational "philosophies." The tendency to be content with the status quo and to follow blindly and slavishly the traditions of the past raises a real barrier to political and social advancement. Yet such conservatism has been a dominant influence over many centuries of educational organization and when irrationally maintained is still one of the chief obstacles to an instructional program that can serve as an auxiliary to social improvement and individual development. But, since modes and expressions of education varied considerably among ancient civilizations, let us consider two prominent examples separately beginning with Sumer.

History Begins at Sumer

At the eastern end of the Fertile Crescent lies the once fruitful Plain of Shinar, adjacent to and containing the lower basin of the Tigris and Euphrates rivers, which flow into the Persian Gulf. Here under a variety of names flourished one of the most amazing of the Asian fluvial civilizations, as ancient perhaps as those of Africa. An Indo-European group, now known as the Sumerians, came into the alluvial plain from the upland region of interior Asia and sometime before 4000 B.C. began the reclamation of the swamps around the mouths of the great rivers.

The Sumerians settled first at the lower end of the rivers, not very distant from the gulf, which in about 6500 B.C. was 100 miles above its present location. They irrigated their fields and raised domestic animals: sheep, cattle, goats, and asses. Soon their original mud huts developed into towns, in which they built *ziggurats*, step-towers to their gods, especially Enlil, deity of the air. When a high priest of the city of Erech levied tribute on peoples from the Persian Gulf to the Mediterranean Sea, Sumeria formed the earliest known empire. Remains of their trade-empire have been found as far east as India. Their temples and priest-kings represent firsts for all civilization.[13]

City planning and arrangement appear to have developed from the planting of the tower-temple in what became the heart of the city. This step-tower was actually an artificial mountain, reminiscent perhaps of the

---

[13] See Kramer's *History*, pp. 1–125, for twenty-seven firsts attributed historically to the Sumerians. See also Edward Chiera, *They Wrote on Clay* (Chicago: University of Chicago Press, 1938). Page 167 shows the remains of an ancient schoolroom; p. 170 an early "copy-book" with the teacher's model inscription. Chiera writes of later civilizations of Mesopotamia as well as Sumer.

hills the Sumerians left behind when they descended into the twin valleys. About the ziggurat were placed business offices and storehouses and dwelling places for the priests, who also had charge of the lands surrounding the temple manor. With their corps of scribes, they carried on huge business in the name of the god, who the people believed owned the land and all those within it. The chief priest (*patesi*) may also be called king, and his duties were temporal as well as spiritual. Around the whole temple establishment ran a formidable wall—somewhat like that of the Kremlin in the U.S.S.R. today—which served not only to protect the sacradotal class and holy mound but also to separate the common people from their rulers.

Breasted describes the activities at this sanctuary:

> Under the shadow of the tower-temple the peasant brought in his offering, a goat and a jar of water containing a few green palm branches intended to symbolize the vegetable life of the land, which the god maintained by the annual rise of the river. (The jar with the green palm branches in it later became "the tree of life," a symbol often depicted on the monuments of the land.) [The peasant was not only] praying that there might be plentiful waters and generous harvests, but praying also for deliverance from the destroying flood which the god had once sent to overwhelm the land.[14]

In the work of record keeping and the affairs of the temple the Sumerians made use of their most significant contribution to world civilization, the cuneiform system of writing. Small wedge-shaped characters were scratched or pressed into clay, which if considered worth keeping, was baked in the sun, creating a permanent record, of the highest value to later researchers. Thus, the first written documents in the world were discovered about three-quarters of a century ago at Erech, the ancient Sumerian capital.

Kramer reports the discovery of a clay tablet composed, it is thought, by a "school father" about 2000 B.C. In this tale the "school son" is unsuccessful at school and dreads being tardy "lest his teacher cane him." Finally, after he has been beaten and told that his copy of the lesson is not satisfactory, he invites the *ummia* (expert, professor) home to dinner. When the ummia is received by the family, he is wined and dined, presented with a new robe and a ring, and as a result realizes that his charge is a sincere seeker of knowledge! The professor then makes this little speech:

---

[14] James Henry Breasted, *The Conquest of Civilization* (New York: Harper & Row, Publishers, 1926 and 1938), pp. 129–130. See also Leonard Cottrell, *The Quest for Sumer* (New York: G. P. Putnam's Sons, 1965). The same work, identical except for pictures, published in England with the title, *The Land of Shinar* (London: Souvenir Press, 1965).

Young man, because you did not neglect my word, did not forsake it, may you reach the pinnacle of the scribal art, may you achieve it completely. . . . Of your brothers may you be their leader, of your friends may you be their chief, may you rank the highest of the schoolboys. . . . You have carried out well the school's activities, you have (now) become a man of learning.[15]

Of course, Sumerian education was not universal and was the prerogative of only the wealthy classes. For one reason, the poor could not afford the time required. The "tablet-place" prepared its students for writing and counting; its graduates found in commerce or in government positions of far greater importance than comparable roles today. Childe demonstrates the superiority of Sumerian mathematics over that of Egypt,[16] and cuneiform characters were known all over the Middle East.

Sumerian Attitudes toward Education

Aims

Sumerian education had as its goal the training of scribes and bookkeepers for ecclesiastical, commercial, and political duties in the temple, countinghouse, and palace. Frequently these three institutions behaved as one, the earliest rulers being priests who controlled the lands and business of the god as well as conducted his sacraments at the holy tower. Later stages saw the establishment of royalty as such and the beginnings of a commercial merchant-trader class. In the preceding illustration our school son was undoubtedly the offspring of a rich trader or caravansary operator. Yet, as we shall note in reference to Egypt, the temple drew its share of middle-class scribes and other linguistically oriented personnel.

According to Kramer, there were junior and superior scribes, temple scribes, and the king's men, highly specialized writers for special administrative activities of all kinds, and those scribes who became, like Joseph in Egypt, perhaps the highest servants or functionaries of king or emperor.[17] Moreover, the existence of schools entailed the existence of a group of teachers trained or educated in the business of instructing others. That such a group existed in Sumer is easily revealed by a survey of the literature created and the fact that Sumerian civilization was able to maintain itself for several millennia.

A further aim of Sumerian education is revealed by the concluding phrases of the tablet quoted at the beginning of this chapter. Here a father

---

[15] Kramer, *History*, p. 9.

[16] Childe, pp. 156–174. See also Robert M. Adams, Jr., in *Level and Trend in Early Sumerian Civilization* (Photolithed doctoral dissertation, University of Chicago, 1956), pp. 85ff. Expands the picture of the temple manor and commercial institutions of early Sumer. See also W. F. Leemans, *The Old-Babylonian Merchant, His Business and His Social Position* (Leiden: E. J. Brill, 1950), pp. 1–5.

[17] Kramer, *History*, pp. 12–15.

is admonishing his son to follow a wise path and, indeed, to learn the meaning of *namlulu* (humanity):

> May you find favor before your god,
> May your humanity exalt you, neck and breast,
> May you be the head of your city's sages,
> May your city utter your name in favored places,
> May your god call you by a good name.[18]

Types

Clearly, we may assume that the "writing school" constituted the main type of Sumerian education. Having devised the method, these Fertile Crescent people for reasons of pride and utility sought to perpetuate it. But teaching writing involved not merely the making of signs and scribbles; vocabulary became a large part of the instruction. And with a slight bow to Aristotle (who 2000 years later arrived on the scene) categories were established, lists of like and unlike, names of fish, birds, animals, stones, trees, and gods. With only a little exaggeration one can easily imagine Sumerian children busily playing "animal, mineral, or vegetable?"

Mathematics assumed an important role (in some respects the system based on 60s had definite advantages in the years 3000 and 2000 B.C.), while certain professors took it upon themselves to construct a dictionary of Sumerian words and phrases. All in all, it is clear that Sumerian education was utilitarian, but also dedicated to the enhancement and preservation of unique cultural legends and inventions.

No doubt there was vocational (apprentice) education too. The clay tablets do not, for obvious reasons, show this; but the existence of a linguistic, mathematical, and recording sector of the population indicates the need for others who were underlings, relegated to hewing wood and drawing water, or slaves, who came at beck and call.

Content

The most important items in the curriculum were, of course, reading and writing, since the Sumerians had developed the remarkable cuneiform system as an aid to priestly activity and commerce. Their language became a foundation stone for all Near Eastern literature, sacred and heroic, and has a beauty hardly reconcilable with the immediate concerns of such a utilitarian and ancient people. Numbers too played their part, but it is doubtful if the very young did more than count. Nevertheless, Western school children in their games have for many centuries recited the "Eeny, meeny, miny, mo," attributed to the ancient East.

Astronomy was highly utilized by the priesthood in their prediction

---

[18] Kramer, *History*, p. 16.

of the seasons, and as an unfortunate by-product astrology, later to be highly emphasized by the Chaldeans, developed. Medicine, including surgery, flourished; and some Sumerian skulls show evidence of a most efficient trepanning; surgical instruments crop up regularly in Sumerian archeological finds. But it was in architecture and hydraulics that these Tigris-Euphrates people shone; their canal systems were marvelous and can be traced across the delta even today. With irrigation, naturally we must mention their agriculture, the chief source of their wealth. Thus, the work of the servants of the temple manor was highly organized and prescribed, with apprenticeship a condition for efficient labor.

Wonderful imagination and taste is shown in Sumerian jewelry designed in copper, gold, and silver; the bakers, brewers, carpenters, wheelwrights, ship-builders, smiths, and seal-cutters likewise demanded emulation. Law, art, poetry, and music flourished. The harp reconstructed from remains in the death-pit at Ur indicates an attachment to music, even to its provision in the "second life," probably another element in the content of Sumerian teaching and knowledge.[19]

Agencies

Much more is assumed than known about the schools, yet even though in 1894 in the old Sumerian city of Shuruppak the remains of what has been described as the oldest school building were uncovered. Clay tablets bearing the exercises of children of 2000 B.C. lay on the floor and the six rooms that surrounded a court perhaps open to the sun resemble a modern schoolroom arrangement. The enclosure marks a building about 55 feet square, the walls being, still today, about 8 or 9 feet in height.

The temple schools no doubt were more elaborate than the school discovered. One can picture sections of great halls or curtained alcoves dedicated to the training of young priests and even scribes for government or commerce. There must have been a hierarchy of students, the more proficient or advanced for the temple receiving at least some sacred or even occult knowledge, perhaps astronomy and mathematics for the prediction of seasons for planting and reaping and for the announcement of propitious times for undertakings such as trading missions or sea voyages. The existence of a learned class, steeped in what was already known as natural phenomena, was a distinct advantage to Sumerian civilization.

That there were highly skilled trades or professions entails a strong system of apprenticeship or perhaps apprentice schools. The beautiful work

---

[19] See the remarkable description of ancient Sumerian life and custom in Sir Leonard C. Woolley and others, *The Ur Excavations*, vol. ii, *The Royal Cemetery, Predynastic and Sargonid Graves Excavated between 1926 and 1931.* (London and Philadelphia: The Trustees of the two museums [British and University of Pennsylvania], 1934.) Hawkes and Woolley show a remarkable diagram of an early Sumerian school, p. 661.

done in gold, silver, and copper could hardly have been the product of untrained hands; the making of bread and beer indicates a body of knowledge or experience valuable to those who practiced these arts. Hydraulics too must have had centers for study; the remains of aqueducts and irrigation channels indicate a highly developed science of water control.

Mallowan observes that inside these Sumerian cities:

> . . . the people not only developed the skills and trades of the architect, the sculptor, the metal-worker, the jeweller and all the other attendant craftsmen of an active corporation, but through a learned and astute priesthood and clerisy made decisive steps in social organization and speculative thought, involving the great and cardinal invention of writing.[20]

Organization

Since the Sumerians invented writing (by the cuneiform system) it is logical to assume that they built some of the first schools. Kramer has maintained that they spread writing, as a means of acquiring knowledge, throughout the known world.[21] And as we have noted, in the last century a building and materials indicating the existence of formally organized classes and schools were unearthed. As early as 3000 B.C. there were Sumerian scribes or teachers whose business was to carry on the light of learning. The texts or word-study lists on tablets of sun- or oven-baked clay covered grammatical items, lists of plants, animals, or gods, tables of common objects, and records of administrative and commercial items.

The tablet-house (*edubba*) must have been for a favored few engaged in administration, commerce, or the work of the temple. But because of the far-flung operations of the temple, which was in some ways similar to the activities of a modern international banking and trust organization, and the proliferation of Sumer's economic activities, geographically situated halfway between the Mediterranean world and India, a large number of trainees was necessary.

Nor was the cultural urge absent. Sumerians highly esteemed literature, including poetry and music. For those of wealth and position, who could afford the leisure, these were keys to advanced learning. Farmers and skilled workers were perhaps trained on the job or through apprenticeship. This interest in things Sumerian was again reflected by the successors to the Sumerian state. After the change in rule Sumerian schools vanished, but Sumerian as a language and Sumerian literature continued to be utilized, much as Latin was during the Middle Ages. Babylonian scholars hoped

[20] M. E. L. Mallowan, *Early Mesopotamia and Iran* (New York: McGraw-Hill, Inc., 1965), p. 8. See also ch. iii, "The Invention of Writing," pp. 59–71. This book, printed in England, is beautifully illustrated in black and white and color.

[21] Samuel Noah Kramer, *The Sumerians, Their History, Culture, and Character* (Chicago: University of Chicago Press, 1963), see especially pp. 229–248, ch. 6, "The Sumerian School."

by the use of the Sumerian hymns and incantations to perfect their higher
education and perhaps to gain supernatural reward.[22]

Methods

As indicated, the school head in Sumeria was a school-father, or
ummia, and the student a school-son. This terminology establishes a large
part of the relationships in the school and indicates something of its method.
The headmaster appears to have been a demanding personage who flogged
his pupils unmercifully when they transgressed his rules or did not prepare
their tablets properly. There were assistant teachers known as "big
brothers"; specialized personnel such as "the man in charge of Sumerian";
"the man in charge of drawing"; and, of course, the gatekeeper, proctors,
and monitors.

Actually the method used was simple. As in all primitive education
it was imitation. The student either copied and reproduced the characters
or figures of the masters, or copied and memorized long lists of items.
On the part of the professors one also finds the preparation of dictionaries and grammars, of mathematical tables and questions, and editions
of Sumerian classics, legends, and other literary productions, of which
hundreds including poetry, epic prose, proverbs, essays, and fables have
survived.

Of the day's work Kramer reports the setting of the pattern by the
"big brother," the making of a fresh clay tablet, the execution of the assignment, and the resulting praise or penalty. The reverence with which some
men regarded their schoolboy training comes through clearly in the following retort to an unworthy opponent:

> I was raised on Sumerian, I am the son of a scribe. But you are a
> bungler, a windbag. When you try to shape a tablet you can't even
> smooth the clay. When you try to write a line, your hand can't manage
> the tablet. . . . You "sophomore," cover your ears! Cover your ears!
> Yet you claim to know Sumerian like me![23]

India: The Aryan Heritage

The vast peninsula of India, which forms virtually a subcontinent,
was like Sumer settled about 4000 years ago by Indo-Europeans, a proto-
Nordic people of the stock from which modern Europeans arose. According
to Huntington the geographical influences of a monsoon land greatly
affected the life of its people:[24] the climate was then, as now, sticky and

---

[22] Childe, p. 175.

[23] Kramer, *The Sumerians*, p. 242. The Sumerians, as a nation, disappeared from
history about 2000 B.C., but much of their culture, including language and writing,
was continued by the Amorites, Assyrians, Kassites, and Chaldeans.

[24] See Ellsworth Huntington, *The Mainsprings of Civilization* (New York: John
Wiley & Sons, Inc., 1965) for a vigorous interpretation of geographical conditioning,
warmly disputed by some others.

enervating; physical activity must take this into consideration. Fortunately, the rich, fertile valleys and the productive uplands made it possible to extract a living without undue labor; and several crops could be grown throughout a year. The worth of the land itself, a rich tropical savanna, attracted other peoples and India became a battleground. A powerful soldier class became necessary for the defense of the country, but the military was not dominant, being under the authority of a priestly class.

As the population increased, so did the prevalence of disease, poverty, and famine. It is alleged that these burdens and contemplation of the vicissitudes of life tended to develop a religion of mysticism and fatalism, although the doctrine of *karma*, or retribution, rests on personal activity rather than on divine will. Thus karma teaches the reward of good and the punishment of evil, even to future reincarnations.

The prevailing religion of India, Brahmanism, holds that the world is an illusion; Brahma, the world spirit, the all-pervading spiritual presence, is the only ultimate reality; and the termination of life is the loss of individual personality and absorption into Brahma. Since God was conceived as abiding everywhere, in everything, the multitude, but not the educated classes, came to practice a form of polytheism, in which various objects of nature were worshipped as particles emitted by Brahma. Among the upper orders religion was a mystical philosophy, among the common folk it hardly rose above superstition.

But the Hindu religious mentality was not slothful. It attempted to solve the riddle of existence and man's purpose in the universe, even as contemporary philosophers and savants seek answers. As Max Muller has written:

> If I were asked under what sky the human mind . . . has most deeply pondered over the greatest problems of life, and has found solutions of some of them which well deserve the attention even of those who have studied Plato and Kant—I should point to India. And if I were to ask myself from what literature we . . . who have been nurtured almost exclusively on the thoughts of Greeks and Romans, and of one Semitic race, the Jewish, may draw the corrective which is most wanted in order to make our inner life more perfect, more comprehensive, more universal, in fact more truly human a life, not for this life only, but a transfigured and eternal life—again I should point to India.[25]

Dependent on their historical origins and religious beliefs, the Indians built a system of government and education based on castes, higher and lower orders of society each with prescribed duties and roles. No other civilization has developed so rigid a caste arrangement as that of ancient

---

[25] As quoted in Huston Smith, *The Religions of Mankind* (New York: Harper & Row, Publishers, 1958), pp. 13–14.

India. The complicated scheme of social differentiation prohibited members of one group from eating, sleeping, or marrying with those outside their group. By disobeying one of the numerous and complex regulations relating to caste, a Hindu might lose his position within society. While one could not rise above one's order, one could easily sink to a lower level or become an outcaste.

This arrangement into castes, since the class positions were fixed, came early in India's history. Four castes were developed—each of which was divided in the course of time into a host of minor, but significant, subdivisions.[26] At the top of the social ladder were the *Brahmans*, priests and teachers, the intellectual rulers; next were the *Kashatriyas*, the military caste, soldiers and warlords; below were the *Vaisayas*, the artisans, shopkeepers, and money-handlers; at the bottom, the *Sudras*, menial workers and serfs. And, in addition to these principal groups, there existed a huge mass of submerged and helpless outcastes, or untouchables, *Pariahs*.[27] The accident of birth determined caste; thus, one's life and educational opportunities were closely circumscribed.

Early Hindu Attitudes toward Education

Aims

Ancient Hindu education was dominated by unique religious beliefs and by the caste system. Its chief aims were (1) to strive for individual excellence through knowledge and contemplation of philosophic truth, to prepare for the life to come rather than for the activities of this existence, to hasten by seeking perfection the final absorption into the infinite and universal spirit; and (2) through the use of precedent, history, and strict observance of custom to preserve the caste system—a valid objective for an Apollonian society, but one in which, unfortunately, not all classes could share equally.

The Hindu educational system, therefore, was concerned with the development of spiritual and emotional attitudes rather than with the acquisition of new knowledge, the ultimate goal being the attainment of a state of perfection through worthiness as exemplified in self-control. Intellectual education was the prerogative of the priestly and teaching class; they needed command of the ancient literature, so that they could recite the national religious hymns. Priests needed to develop skill in intoning the

---

[26] See Mark Naidis, *India, A Short Introductory History* (New York: Crowell-Collier and Macmillan, Inc., 1966) for a concise interpretation of early Indian history. Also Michael Edwardes, *A History of India* (New York: Farrar, Straus & Giroux, 1961), pp. 27ff. Edwardes writes of pre-Aryan civilization of Harappa and Mohenjo-Daro in the Indus valley, pp. 21–23; Hawkes and Woolley discuss the Indusian cultural remains on pp. 748–752.

[27] We are, of course, speaking of ancient India. The most severe feature of this system—untouchability—is now outlawed by the Republic of India (1947).

sacred prayers, in performing the established sacraments. Brahmans, as official representatives of Hindu culture, had evolved an elaborate system of rites and ceremonies, in which each neophyte had to be trained. Other castes, believing in the effectiveness of the sacraments, felt utterly dependent upon priestly ministration for deliverance from sin, for only by such intervention could they hope for happiness in this world or a serene existence in the hereafter.

The Brahmans, as the caste with the most at stake and the greatest prestige, were the sustaining influence in the system. Through their teaching and priestly prerogatives they allowed each member of the lower castes education in the religious observances suitable for his caste and, through his own efforts or that of his family group, the vocational training necessary for him to play his role: the farmer in his field, the artisan at his craft, and the merchant or money-lender at his business.

Types

Hindu education was predominantly religious, for the culture itself was dedicated to the things of the spirit. Motwani says, "There was harmony within and without, and inward realization of the Eternal became a dominant aspiration of people's lives. There was an attitude of identification, not conflict, a search of the One, not of the many."[28] Education imparted the customs and traditional modes of conduct that were to fit its sharers for their "proper" places in life. It was moral, ethical, and ascetic in its emphasis upon self-discipline, for the Vedas say, "The Truth is one; sages [merely] call it by different names."

Intellectual education was confined to the highest caste and was purely theoretical, limited to the knowledge of ancient tradition and lacking in practical applications to alleviate poor living conditions or aid an overcrowded population. Nor did women receive an intellectual education; their role was only to minister to men and to bear children.

As in other eastern countries, little provision was made for physical education or hygiene, although much of the student's day was spent outdoors. Bathing, however, appears to have played an important part in Hindu life. Vocational training, domestic training, and even military training were all acquired by the primitive methods of imitation and drill.

Content

The Brahman curriculum was literary. Its chief emphasis was on the Hindu and pre-Hindu sacred writings in Sanskrit, the language of learning. But in the training college, or *parishads*, the course of study also included consideration of such acquired lore as astronomy, mathematics, history,

---

[28] Kewal Motwani, *India: A Synthesis of Cultures* (Bombay: Thacker & Company, Ltd., 1947), pp. 47–73, "Religion and Philosophy."

grammar, law, and medicine. Candidates for the priesthood studied linguistics, philosophy, and theology.

In literature Brahman study centered on the Vedas, collections of ancient religious wisdom, the *Rig Veda*, the *Sama Veda*, the *Yajur Veda*, and the *Atharva Veda*; on the Angas, volumes of Hindu "scientific" and philosophical knowledge; and on the *Code of Manu*, a compilation of ethics, customs, and tradition. Perhaps because of their pantheistic viewpoint, the Hindus gave attention likewise to speculative and mathematical science. Contemporary Western arithmetical notation, including the symbol "0," originated in India, As early as 500 B.C., the Hindus developed an algebra said to be superior to that of Greece and later disseminated throughout the West by the Arabs. The Hindus possessed an elementary knowledge of medicine and developed an organized approach to grammar and rhetoric.

Although physical education as such was not a part of the curriculum, much attention was given to sports such as archery and wrestling. Dancing, associated with religion, was from time to time considered a subject, but eventually became the heritage of the lower classes. Military training involved the use of the horse (which had been brought to India by the Aryans) and chariot, as well as the utilization in war of elephants. Yoga, which involves many highly stylized exercises in posture and breathing, was practiced. Eighty-four postures were considered best; thirty-two were "useful in this world."

Agencies and Organization

As in most well-developed primitive societies, education in early India was received for the most part through the family in the home or place of work. The few first-level schools were quite simple and merely furthered the mother's teaching, which the child received until about the age five. If schooling were possible (considering the family's wealth and social status), the boy was then placed under a professional teacher, a Brahman, who was paid for his services by voluntary gifts, since it was deemed a disgrace to accept a salary for teaching. Teachers were highly respected, and often received more reverence than parents. The *guru*, or teacher, frequently taught outdoors, in the open air under a large tree. Classes, of not more than fifteen pupils, were small and lasted several hours, after which various group and individual responsibilities were discharged; there was no time for sloth.

> . . . students were subject to a rigorous discipline, within the framework of which they received religious or scientific instruction. They slept on a litter of rushes, arose before dawn, and had as their first duty that of greeting their guru reverently by touching his feet. They were required to show total and prompt obedience to him standing upright with their hands pressed together whenever they addressed him. [But] the guru

was not a tyrant and made every effort to teach his pupils the rules without ever misrepresenting the truth.[29]

Intellectual training centered on religious and philosophical study and, as higher education, was conducted at the parishads, where the Brahman class was educated. The complete course usually required twelve years. In time, the restrictions were relaxed to admit children of the *Kashatriya* and *Vaisayas* castes. Monasteries, when established, also became important foci of learning; it is obvious that the Hindu considered high education of vast importance. Education was a badge of rank as well as a chief hope for religious salvation. Naidis says candidly, "By deliberately restricting the spread of sacred knowledge, the priests had a powerful weapon to use to their own advantage."[30]

Methods

Imitation and memorization were the basic methods of learning. The Vedas, written in rhythmic metrical form lent themselves to this mode of study. Progress was slow. The pupils shouted lines until they could repeat them without error. The teacher, who was required to cover the whole curriculum before beginning to teach, wrote models for class reproduction. Writing was learned through imitating the master's copy, the pupils utilizing first sand and then palm leaves. Although the school was a loud one, procedures were carried on in a dignified fashion befitting the position and training of its teacher. Sonnenschein describes the ancient method of oral teaching:

> At the beginning of each lesson the pupils embrace the feet of their teacher and say "Read, Sir." The teacher then proceeds to pronounce words which the pupils repeat after him until the words are learned. In this manner they go on until they have finished a *prasna* (three verses of about forty syllables). After the prasna is finished, they have all to repeat it once more, and then go on learning it by heart, pronouncing every syllable with high accent.[31]

Unsophisticated though such a venerable method may appear, the practical result of this mnemonic teaching is the carefully preserved purity and integrity of the original language, Sanskrit. The Veda texts have been handed down with such accuracy that there is hardly a variant reading or an uncertain accent.

Indian discipline was mild. "Good instruction," repeated the *Code*

---

[29] Jeannine Auboyer, *Daily Life in Ancient India* (New York: Crowell-Collier and Macmillan, Inc., 1965), p. 170. See also pp. 3–113, chs. i–iv, "Family Life and Organization."

[30] Naidis, p. 11.

[31] Sonnenschein, "Schools of Antiquity," in *Cyclopedia of Education* (London: Gale & Polden, Ltd., 1926–28), p. 382.

of Manu, "must be imparted to the pupil in an agreeable manner, and a teacher must use sweet, gentle words."

And lest Western students imagine that the schools described were ineffectual in their preparation for life, it must be said that their essential concern was the values of Hindu culture rather than vocational or professional training. Hindu life was a reflection of these educational values; if the Hindu personality and the European-American personality appear to differ, this does not suggest that the more mechanistic culture of the West can sit in judgment on that of the East.[32] Indeed, when judged by the standards of both ancient and modern Hindu culture, Western life is both materialistic and self-seeking, which the East, with its long history of transcendental philosophy, cannot easily condone. Hence, the methodology of ancient Hindustan was not really "quaint." Geared to a class (caste) society, this educational system for thousands of years protected its bona fide culture and insured social stability within a whole subcontinent.

REFERENCES

Auboyer, Jeannine, *Daily Life in Ancient India.* New York: Crowell-Collier and Macmillan, Inc., 1965. Pp. 3–113, 117–214.

Barnes, Harry Elmer, *An Intellectual and Cultural History of the Western World.* New York: Random House, Inc., 1937. Pp. 63–112.

Breasted, James Henry, *The Conquest of Civilization.* New York: Harper & Row, Publishers, 1926 and 1938. Pp. 43–110, 187–211.

Browne, Lewis, *This Believing World.* New York: Crowell-Collier and Macmillan, Inc., 1964. Pp. 75–89, 119–165, 169–196, 199–219.

Butts, R. Freeman, *A Cultural History of Western Education,* 2d ed. New York: McGraw-Hill, Inc., 1955. Pp. 6–18.

Cottrell, Leonard, *The Quest for Sumer.* New York: G. P. Putnam's Sons, 1965.

Davidson, Basil, *Africa, History of a Continent.* New York: Crowell-Collier and Macmillan, Inc., 1966.

————, *The African Past.* Boston: Little, Brown & Company, 1964.

Dawson, Christopher, *The Age of the Gods.* New York: Sheed & Ward, Inc., 1933. Pp. 141–165, 287–308.

————, *The Dynamics of World History.* New York: Sheed & Ward, Inc., 1957. Pp. 111–147.

Durant, Will, *The Story of Civilization,* pt. i, *Our Oriental Heritage.* New York: Simon and Schuster, Inc., 1935. Pp. 112–823.

---

[32] For a cogent and provocative analysis of these poles of dissent see F. S. C. Northrop, *The Meeting of East and West* (New York: Crowell-Collier and Macmillan, Inc., 1946). Northrop implies that interworld differences arise because of fundamental contrasting modes of thought, East and West; the Western mode, says Northrop, rests on "concepts derived through postulation," the Eastern on "concepts derived by intuition." Yet he does not see these obvious divergences as inherently fateful; Northrop believes in eventual rapprochement through a slightly different orientation on the part of each.

Eby, Frederick, and Charles F. Arrowood, *The History and Philosophy of Education, Ancient and Medieval.* Englewood Cliffs, N.J.: Prentice-Hall, Inc., 1940. Pp. 36–107.

Fairservis, Walter A., *India.* Cleveland: The World Publishing Company, 1900.

Frye, Richard N., *The Heritage of Persia.* Cleveland: The World Publishing Company, 1963.

Good, Harry G., *A History of Western Education,* 2d ed. New York: Crowell-Collier and Macmillan, Inc., 1960. Pp. 6–17.

Hawkes, Jacquetta, and Sir Leonard Woolley, *Prehistory and The Beginnings of Civilization.* History of Mankind Series, vol. i. New York: Harper & Row, Publishers, 1963.

Huntington, Ellsworth, *Mainsprings of Civilization.* New York: John Wiley & Sons, Inc., 1965.

Jung, Carl G. (Ed.), *Man and His Symbols.* London: Aldus Books, 1900.

Knight, Edgar W., *Twenty Centuries of Education.* Boston: Ginn & Company, 1940. Pp. 33–40.

Kramer, Samuel Noah, *History Begins at Sumer.* Indian Hills, Colo.: Falcon Wing's Press, 1956.

———, *The Sumerians, Their History, Culture, and Character.* Chicago: University of Chicago Press, 1963.

———, and Editors of Time-Life Books, *Cradle of Civilization.* New York: Time, Inc., 1967.

Latourette, Kenneth Scott, *A Short History of the Far East,* 3rd ed. New York: Crowell-Collier and Macmillan, Inc., 1957. Pp. 37–77, 78–189.

Lin Yutang, *The Wisdom of India and China.* New York: Random House, Inc., 1942.

Majumdar, R. C. (Ed.), *The History and Culture of the Indian People: Ancient India,* rev. ed., vol. i. London: Verry, 1964.

Mayer, Frederick, *A History of Educational Thought.* Columbus, Ohio: Charles E. Merrill Books, Inc., 1960. Pp. 28–73.

Messenger, James F., *An Interpretative History of Education.* New York: Thomas Y. Crowell Company, 1931. Pp. 17–28.

Montagu, F. Ashley, *Race, Science, and Humanity.* Princeton, N.J.: D. Van Nostrand Company, Inc., 1963.

Motwani, Kewal, *India: A Synthesis of Cultures.* Bombay: W. Thacker and Co., Ltd., 1947.

Mulhern, James, *A History of Education,* 2d ed. New York: The Ronald Press Company, 1959. Pp. 55–128.

Myers, Edward D., *Education in the Perspective of History.* New York: Harper & Row, Publishers, 1960. Pp. 49–70, 307–312.

Naidis, Mark, *India, A Short Introductory History.* New York: Crowell-Collier and Macmillan, Inc., 1966.

Nakosteen, Mehdi, *The History and Philosophy of Education.* New York: The Ronald Press Company, 1965. Pp. 23–59.

Northrop, F. S. C., *The Meeting of East and West.* New York: Crowell-Collier and Macmillan, Inc., 1946.

Ogg, Oscar. *The 26 Letters.* New York: Thomas Y. Crowell Company, 1961.

Oppenheim, A. Leo, *Letters from Mesopotamia.* Chicago: University of Chicago Press, 1967.

Panikkar, K. M., *India, Past and Present.* Englewood Cliffs, N.J.: Prentice-Hall, Inc., 1964.

Power, Edward J., *Main Currents in the History of Education.* New York: McGraw-Hill, Inc., 1962. Pp. 6–20, 27–29.

Reischauer, E. D., and John K. Fairbank, *East Asia, The Great Tradition.* Boston: Houghton Mifflin Company, 1958.

Roux, Georges, *Ancient Iraq.* Cleveland: The World Publishing Company, 1964.

Smith, William A., *Ancient Education.* New York: Philosophical Library, Inc., 1955. Pp. 3–49, 50–68, 69–87.

Starr, Chester G., *A History of the Ancient World.* New York: Oxford University Press, 1965. Pp. 27–142, 164–181.

Toynbee, Arnold J., *A Study of History,* one vol. ed., abr. by D. C. Somervell. New York: Oxford Unversity Press, 1946. Pp. 12–47.

Ulich, Robert, *Three Thousand Years of Educational Wisdom.* Cambridge, Mass.: Harvard University Press, 1954. Pp. 3–13, 14–28.

Wolpert, Stanley A., *India.* Englewood Cliffs, N.J.: Prentice-Hall, Inc., 1965.

Woody, Thomas, *Life and Education in Early Societies.* New York: Crowell-Collier and Macmillan, Inc., 1949. Pp. 47–194.

Woolley, Sir Leonard C., *The Sumerians.* New York: Oxford University Press, 1928.

SELECTED PAPERBACKS

Allchin, Bridget and Raymond, *Birth of Indian Civilization.* Baltimore: Penguin Books, Inc., 1968.

Ardrey, Robert, *African Genesis.* New York: Dell Publishing Co., 1967.

Breasted, James Henry, *Ancient Times,* 2d ed., vol. i, *The Ancient Near East.* Boston: Ginn & Company, 1966.

Chakravorty, P. M., *Caste System in India.* Banaras: Missirpokhra, 1960.

Fairservis, Walter A., Jr., *The Origins of Oriental Civilization.* New York: New American Library of World Literature, Inc., 1959.

Frye, Richard N., *The Heritage of Persia.* New York: New American Library of World Literature, Inc., 1966.

Gurney, O. R., *The Hittites.* Baltimore: Penguin Books, Inc., 1954.

Hawkes, Jacquetta. *History of Mankind, Cultural and Scientific Development,* vol. i. pt. i, *Prehistory.* New York: New American Library of World Literature, Inc., 1965.

Hollister, C. Warren, *Roots of the Western Tradition.* New York: John Wiley & Sons, Inc., 1966.

Huntington, Ellsworth, *The Mainsprings of Civilization.* New York: New American Library of World Literature, Inc., 1944.

Jones, Tom B., *From the Tigris to the Tiber*. Homewood, Ill.: The Dorsey Press, 1969. Pp. 19–39, 48–51.

Leakey, L. S. B., *Adam's Ancestors*. New York: Harper & Row, Publishers, 1960.

Leemans, W. F., *The Old-Babylonian Merchant, His Business and His Social Position*. Leiden: E. J. Brill, 1950.

McEvedy, Colin, *The Penguin Atlas of Ancient History*. Baltimore: Penguin Books, Inc., 1968.

Maxwell, Gavin, *People of the Reeds*. New York: Pyramid, 1966.

Mellaart, James. *Earliest Civilizations in the Near East*. New York: McGraw-Hill, Inc., 1965.

Moscati, Sabatino, *Face of the Ancient Orient*. New York: Doubleday & Company, Inc., 1962.

Nikhilananda, Swami (Ed.), *The Upanishads*. New York: Harper & Row, Publishers, 1964.

Oliver, Roland, and J. D. Fage, *A Short History of Africa*. Baltimore: Penguin Books, Inc., 1962.

Pei, Mario, *The Story of Language*. New York: New American Library of World Literature, Inc., 1966.

Ross, Ralph, *Symbols & Civilization*. New York: Harcourt, Brace & World, Inc., 1962.

Roux, Georges, *Ancient Iraq*. New York: New American Library of World Literature, Inc., 1965.

Saggs, H. W. I., *The Greatness that was Babylon*. New York: New American Library of World Literature, Inc., 1962.

Sandars, N. K., *The Epic of Gilgamish*. Baltimore: Penguin Books, Inc., 1960.

Smith, Huston, *The Religions of Mankind*. New York: New American Library of World Literature Inc., 1961.

Woolley, Sir Leonard C., *Digging Up the Past*, 2d ed. Baltimore: Penguin Books, Inc., 1954.

———, *History of Mankind, Cultural and Scientific Development*, vol. i, pt. ii, *The Beginnings of Civilization*. New York: New American Library of World Literature, Inc., 1965.

CHAPTER **3**

Social
Stability
and Cultural
Achievement

Nowhere is civilization so perfectly mirrored as in speech. If our knowledge of speech, or the speech itself, is not yet perfect, neither is civilization.[1]

OTHER CRADLES OF CIVILIZATION

The cultures of Sumer and early India revolved around two of man's greatest achievements: the invention of a sophisticated system of writing and the creation of one of the world's preeminent languages. Cuneiform, later to be used by Akkadians, Assyrians, Babylonians, and Persians, conserved the record of civilization's origins and also served the practical purposes of school instruction and commerce. In India, Sanskrit, the closest cousin of later Western (Indo-European) languages, likewise became an agency for the preservation of a civilized past with a sacred literature and, at the same time, offered an example of purity and permanence exhibited by few other tongues.

In China and Egypt we find other cradles of civilization eminently worthy of consideration for their contribution to history and the history of instruction. China (*Chung-kuo*, the Middle Kingdom) offers the remarkable example of a social organization, with an accompanying literature, language, and educational system, founded on family and nation—the two elements that have guaranteed China a continuous chronicle of more than 4000 years. The Egyptian emphasis was on the afterlife, another notable

---

[1] Mario Pei, *The Story of Language* (Philadelphia: J. B. Lippincott Company, 1965).

45

contribution, which although not entirely unique, is unparalleled in man's immense journey from cave to cathedral.

China and Its People

The early history of China, like that of other countries of fluvial Asia, is masked by obscurity. Claims of a Chinese civilization extending as far back as five thousand years, perhaps to 4000 or 3000 B.C. have been made; and recent discoveries appear to place the prehistoric period of China even earlier. The first dynastic era has been dated as 1994 B.C., although another authority claims 2205 B.C. as the date of first historic event. Goodrich reports that the people of this early epoch, the *Hsia*, knew agriculture and sericulture, used bronze weapons and chariots, and had developed a system of writing.[2] Their use of the wheel suggests the existence of a culture perhaps equivalent to that of Mesopotamia of about 2100 B.C. and perhaps little inferior to that of the Indus or of the Sea-Kings of Crete.

Dynasty followed dynasty but the life of the people remained crystalized in fixed forms; and ideas and beliefs continued very much the same from generation to generation. Thus, Chinese development was, well into the twentieth century, basically different from that of the Western world. Although Taoism and Buddhism became popular, the dominating Chinese motives were those summarized by Confucius (551–478 B.C.). His writings, representing the accumulated wisdom of many hundred years, became a guide to generations of Chinese. It is largely from the literary works attributed to Confucius, his followers, and other Chinese philosophers that we have received most of our knowledge of Chinese educational thought. Indeed, many of these early Sinic educational practices actually survived until the end of World War II, in 1945.[3]

The Early Chinese Approach to Education

Aims

The traditional ambition of the Chinese people was to remain as they were, firm in their belief that they had achieved the summit of civilization, and to seek to preserve their past. Deviation from ancestral custom was viewed with extreme disfavor; every effort was made to mold the present and future upon the pattern of their golden ages. Formal education was confined to a painstaking study of ancient Sinic classics.

The teachings of Confucius focus on the idea of noble living. They make human relationships, order, duty, morality, matters of prime importance. They stress the value of his five fundamental relationships: (1) be-

---

[2] L. Carrington Goodrich, *A Short History of the Chinese People* (New York: Harper & Row, Publishers, 1943), pp. 6–8.

[3] For a résumé of Chinese history from *Hsia* to *Ch'ing* see Kenneth Scott Latourette, *China* (Englewood Cliffs, N.J.: Prentice-Hall, Inc., 1964), ch. ii, pp. 44–100.

tween sovereign and subject, (2) between father and child, (3) between husband and wife, (4) between brother and brother, and (5) between friend and friend. These affinities are based, in turn, upon a doctrine of submission; the subject submits to his ruler, the child to his father, the wife to her husband, the brother to his brother, and the friend to his friend. Then there are the five cardinal virtues, idealizing the life and government of the Middle Kingdom: (1) benevolence, or universal charity; (2) justice; (3) order, or conformity to established usage; (4) prudence, or rectitude of the heart and mind; and (5) fidelity, or pure sincerity. Confucius believed that peace would result from following these prescriptions. As a social philosopher, endeavoring to establish the cornerstone of his doctrine, *Tien Jen Hsiang-yu* (heaven and man in partnership), "he dreamed of a realm which would embrace all Chinese—indeed all civilized men, for so he regarded the Chinese. His intent was [the production of] an ideal human society."[4]

Confucius' frequently aphoristic precepts represented for his followers statements of purpose and genuine pearls of universal wisdom. For example:

At fifteen I was bent on learning;
At thirty I stood fast;
At forty I had no doubts;
At fifty I knew the will of God;
At sixty my ear was open to the truth;
At seventy I could follow my desires without transgressing the square (i.e. the bounds of right).
A man's character is formed by the Odes, developed by the Rites, and perfected by Music.
The princely man thinks of virtue; the mean man of gain.
Do not unto others what you do not like done unto yourself.
Rotten wood cannot be carved, and a dung wall ought not to be whitewashed.
The princely man is catholic, not narrow; the small-minded man is narrow, not catholic.
Observe a man's actions; scrutinise his motives; take note of the things that give him pleasure. How then can he hide from you what he really is?
When you see a good man, think of emulating him; when you see a bad man, examine your own heart.
Virtue cannot live in solitude; neighbours are sure to grow up around it.
We ought to have wholesome respect for our juniors. Who knows but that by-and-by they may prove themselves equal to the men of today?
It is only when the cold season comes that we know the pine and cypress to be evergreens.
He who requires much from himself and little from others will be secure from hatred.

4 Latourette, p. 55.

It is the man that is able to develop his virtue, not virtue that develops
the man.

The real fault is to have faults and not try to amend them.

Where there is education, there is no distinction of class.

Men who differ in their principles cannot help each other in their plans.

Men's natures are alike; it is their habits that carry them far apart.

Only two classes of men never change: the wisest of the wise and the
dullest of the dull.[5]

There are nine traditional volumes with which the name of Confucius
is usually associated. Five of these are called Classics: (1) the *Shu King*,
or *Book of History*, an outline of history before the time of Confucius;
(2) the *Shi King*, or *Book of Odes*, an outline of poetry; (3) the *Yi King*,
or *Book of Changes*, an outline of prophecy and augury; (4) the *Li Ki
King*, or *Book of Rights*, an outline of social etiquette; and (5) the *Hsiao
King*, or *Book of Filial Piety*. Some of the material in these classics was
undoubtedly written by Confucius himself, but much he merely compiled
and edited. The Four Books come from a later period and were written by
the disciples of Confucius. They are (1) the *Ta Hsio*, or *Great Learning*;
(2) the *Chung Yung*, or *Doctrine of the Mean*; (3) the *Lun Yu*, or *Sayings
of Confucius*; and (4) the *Meng-tze*, or *Sayings of Mencius*. These Four
Books consist of reports of conversations between Confucius and his
disciples, together with various maxims and doctrines of an ethical and
political nature, and make up the Chinese Bible, the guide to daily conduct.
Thorough familiarity with all of it formerly was necessary in order to hold
any official position.

Since the teaching of Confucius was not altogether original, but a
reiteration of the ideas that had developed in the centuries before him,
we cannot be sure how great a debt he owed to Lao-tzu (604–517 B.C.?).
At any rate, Taoism, or "The Path of Reason," a second Chinese philosophy for living, is associated with the latter in much the same fashion that
Confucianism is attributed to Confucius. There is a story—doubtless a
myth—that the two great sages once met, although their philosophies
remain, in essence, poles apart. The chief (and only) work attributed to
Lao-tzu, the *Tao-teh-Ching*, consists of eighty-one stanzas, or brief aphorisms, which scrutinize life and the purposes of life. A free translation of
the title reads: "The Book of the Way and the Virtue that comes there-
from." Many strange tales are told of Lao-tzu including his virgin birth,
sixty-two-year gestation, and white hair at infancy. His very name is said
to signify "Old Boy" or "Old Philosopher." His stanzas breathe contentment and preach a creative quietism.

6. The breath of life moves through a deathless valley
Of mysterious motherhood

---

[5] Arranged by Donald G. Tewksbury, Teachers College, Columbia University.
Unpublished ms.

Which conceives and bears the universal seed,
The seeming of a world never to end,
Breath for men to draw from as they will:
And the more they take of it, the more remains.

17. A leader is best
When people barely know that he exists,
Not so good when people obey and acclaim him,
Worst when they despise him.
"Fail to honor people—they fail to honor you"
But of a good leader, who talks little,
When his work is done, his aim fulfilled,
They will all say, "We did this ourselves."

33. Knowledge studies others,
Wisdom is self-known;
Muscle masters brothers,
Self-mastery is bone;
Content need never borrow,
Ambition wanders blind:
Vitality cleaves to the marrow—leaving death behind.

40. Life on its way returns into a mist,
Its quickness is its quietness again:
Existence of this world of things and men
Renews their never needing to exist.

43. As the soft yield of water cleaves obstinate stone,
So to yield with life solves the insoluble:
To yield, I have learned, is to come back again.
But this unworded lesson, this easy example,
—Is lost upon men.

56. Those who know do not tell,
Those who tell do not know.
Not to set the tongue loose, but to curb it . . .
Has attained the highest post in the world.

79. If terms to end a quarrel leave bad feeling,
What good are they?
So a sensible man takes the poor end of the bargain without
    quibbling.
It is sensible to make terms, Foolish to be a stickler:
Though heaven prefer no man, A sensible man prefers heaven.[6]

Whereas Lao-tzu pursued a policy of withdrawal and inaction, Confucius strove by writing, speaking, teaching, counseling the rulers of the provinces and state, and administration, to bring his realizations into the lives of the people. Never claiming to be an innovator or a god, he regarded himself as the conservator of ancient truth and ceremonial proprieties. While many followed his teaching, many also became adherents of Lao-tzu;

[6] From *The Way of Life according to Lao-tzu*, trans. by Witter Bynner (New York: The John Day Company, Inc., 1944), pp. 28, 34–35, 46, 53, 60–61, 75. Reproduced by special permission.

indeed it is alleged that more than a few subscribed to both doctrines, strange though this may appear to Western thinking.

Yet the differences between Confucius and Lao-tzu may be reconciled: Confucius emphasizes the qualities of the good citizen, while Lao-tzu stresses the spirit that makes the good man. It is not too much to say that these qualities should be eternally reconcilable. For we shall meet this same composed dilemma many times throughout the long history of educational thought; leaders' names may change but not this basic idea. If during this classic period in Chinese history Lao-tzu and Confucius appear as opposites, so in the classic age of Greece will Plato and Aristotle. And in medieval Europe the great nominalist controversy in which Anselm, Roscellinus, William of Champeaux, and Abelard participated eventually resulted in resolution by St. Thomas Aquinas, whose synthesis was to harmonize Christ with the Greeks.

Agencies

Most of the relationships commended by Confucius center on the life of the family; thus the locus for training under the Confucian philosophy was the home. Although the Chinese developed schools as the literary educational institution, the family continued to be the agency, much as it had been in primitive times, of the child's practical training. All practical and domestic activities were learned within the confines of the home and imposed by the sanctions of ancestral worship.

No national system was established, but private schools were encouraged and almost every village had its teacher and an elementary school. These schools were supported by tuition and frequently taught by candidates who had failed to qualify for public service posts (which will be discussed later). There were no specially erected schoolhouses; the school might be held in the house of the teacher, in the home of some wealthy patron, in a deserted pagoda or temple, or in any other available space. No attempt was made to make the schoolroom attractive or a cause for civic pride. Further, these schools were poorly attended because they prepared students only for the state civil service examinations; they did not provide training for everyday vocations. Theoretically, the village schools had the important role of selecting candidates for official positions in the civil service, for which males of all classes were eligible. But, since these schools required fees and freedom from work or other activities for an extended period, as a rule only sons of the upper classes were able to participate.

Organization

Chinese education was organized on two levels: elementary education, exceedingly formalized and rigorous; and higher education, training for the governmental examinations, which formed the highest stage of the educational process.

The child started school at the age of seven. School began at sunrise and lasted until about five in the afternoon, with an hour for luncheon about ten. School sessions were held throughout the year. Beyond the elementary level the pupil continued his education under a special teacher. At the end of higher education a series of examinations leading to degrees were conducted by the government. These degrees, with their distinctions and privileges, however, were bestowed only on the very few successful candidates. In theory, the poor as well as the wealthy received an opportunity to "leap through the Dragon's Gate," as the gaining of high public office was called.

To the mind of the Chinese truth was what had been agreed upon in the past, and virtue was the observance of those fixed ideas and customs. Morality therefore became for them merely a matter of knowledge, and thus their ethical system was the result of instruction in the ancestral traditions. As their religion was largely ancestor worship, so their education began with training the child in the path of duty, in all the minutely prescribed details of life's occupations and relationships—details which had not varied for centuries and therefore had the approval of many ancestral generations. Because ancient Chinese education was designed for the maintenance, without change or modification, of that which exists, it became the function of education to train the leaders in classical learning—all the traditional rules governing the order of society and covering the proper relationships in life—and to train the masses in the modes of conduct proper to every interest and every activity throughout their entire lives.

From a civic standpoint, the continuity of the empire was best assured by placing the official duties of government only in the hands of those who had best mastered the traditions of the past as found in the sacred books. The evaluation of such knowledge was not left to chance, but was systematically determined through the governmental program. Thus the leaders were trained in the ancient knowledge of the approved order, and common people were trained to conduct themselves in accord with the requirements of duty. Education was designed to prepare each individual to fill his place in a fixed society.

Ancient Chinese formality is revealed in the organization and conduct of the state examinations, beginning in the smaller sections of the country and culminating at the imperial capital. For example:

> The provincial examination consisted of three sessions conducted by the imperial examiners. Each session lasted three days. In the name of the emperor the chief examiner called upon the spirits to inspire or disturb the minds of the candidates according to their deserts. As he intoned this prayer, many firecrackers were set off. Thus the examination began. Locked in his cell, the student faced the stern necessity of three days of utmost concentration.[7]

---

[7] Han Yu Shan, "Molding Forces," in Harley Farnsworth MacNair (Ed.), *China* (Berkeley, Calif.: University of California Press, 1951), p. 11.

Types

That type of education outstandingly emphasized by the early Chinese was moral training, mainly in the derivative sense of *moral*, which comes from the Latin *mores*, the term for manners, customs, social conduct. So Chinese education was primarily training in customs, duties, and polite behavior. Mores could be apprehended and understood through an unlocking, or study, of the classics, which contained the proven recipes of the past. This type of education was defined by their aphorism, "Employ the able and promote the worthy." Through study one, if able, became worthy.

Vocational, domestic, civic, and military training were provided, but each fundamentally was reduced to the common basis of morality. This is to say that nothing could be considered good unless it followed the moral precepts handed down by the sages and philosophers. Perhaps the term *social training* would suffice for all of these, but today this expression has come to be used with a wide diversity of meaning.

Special schools for military training were set up from time to time; soldiers used chariots, and swordsmanship reached a high level in the period known in Europe as the Middle Ages. Archery was favored, and boxing was considered part of Chinese military training. As in India no direct provision was made for physical education, but health exercises were recommended through sitting, kneeling, bending, lying, and standing with respiratory training. Cleanliness was highly esteemed and sports of all kinds offered a training of sorts.

However, in the China of antiquity the overall emphasis was placed on the study of language and literature and the pursuits of peace rather than of war. A sound mind was reverenced more than a sound body.

Content

Although our discussion of types of classical and other training indicates some of the range of content, the true basis of all Chinese formal education—up to the new era initiated by ideological concepts produced through two world wars—was in the philosophy and teachings of Confucius, Lao-tzu, Mencius[8] and other great philosophical figures. Of these Confucius probably was the most influential, and after his death a system of thought and manners bearing his name developed. Confucianism is not a religion though, in the sense commonly accepted, for it does not offer a deity, a theological creed, or even a ritualistic worship. It is a philosophy of social and civic ethics. Confucius was the founder of a system of utilitarian morality to be inculcated into the life of each individual through the authoritative sanctions of the family and the state.[9] From his own time to World

---

[8] See Arthur Waley, *Three Ways of Thought in Ancient China* (New York: Doubleday & Company, Inc., 1956).

[9] See Lin Yutang, *My Country and My People*, rev. ed. (New York: The John Day Company, Inc., 1937), for an illuminating picture of Chinese human relations.

War I, the writings attributed to Confucius have been the principal subjects of study in all the schools of China. For the most part, these writings are an exposition of details of conduct having to do with every conceivable relationship and occasion of life. Chinese literature thus was the chief item used in testing.

The lowest examinations were held in each county, and those who successfully passed these preliminary examinations were awarded honors (*Hsiu Ts'ai*), somewhat similar to the Bachelor of Arts degree, and were elected to the ranks of nobility. Later, these scholars could take another examination conducted in the various provinces. Upon successfully passing these tests, they were awarded a degree (*Chu-jen*), somewhat similar to the Master of Arts, and they rose still higher in the social scale. The final examinations, corresponding roughly to modern doctoral examinations, continued thirteen days and were given in the capital. The successful candidate (whose attainment was called *Chin-shih*) had a right to public office at once and, if he conducted himself worthily, could rise to the great distinction of being a member of the imperial cabinet.[10]

Methods

Confucius was a master teacher. Thus he attracted pupils from far and near and bound them to himself with ties of loyalty and devotion. His methods resemble somewhat those employed by Socrates in Greece two centuries later. He walked about from place to place accompanied by those who were absorbing his views. Evidently he wished his students to reason about his teachings. "Learning without thought is labor lost," he said, "and thought without learning is perilous." He also expected practical application of his teaching. "Although a man may be able to recite three hundred odes, if he know not how to act, of what use is his learning?"

Like all great teachers, Confucius respected his students. "A young student," he said, "may be worthy of veneration. Who knows but his knowledge may yet equal mine." He also adapted his teachings to the needs and capacities of the individual. When two pupils asked whether they should immediately put into practice something they had learned, he said to one, "Ask the advice of your father and brother"; but to the other he said, "Act immediately." Asked why he gave such different answers, he said, "This first has more than his share of energy; therefore I kept him back. The second is retiring and slow; wherefore I urged him forward." And there are those who think that adjustment to individual differences is a modern method in teaching!

Another story is told of Confucius, who with his class was making a field trip. They came upon a woman weeping bitterly for her dead husband. When she explained that he had been slain by a tiger, as had his

---

[10] Han Yu Shan, pp. 11–17.

father and grandfather, Confucius asked her reasons for remaining in such a perilous location. "In this state," she replied, "the laws are just." The sage then spoke, "From this, you see, students, bad government is more to be feared than a tiger."

Modern educators who urge that children be taken out of the school-room and brought into contact with the actual conditions of life are really returning to the method of Confucius; for Confucius' teaching activity was not confined to a classroom. Another indication of his instinctive use of the principles of good teaching is that he seems to have maintained close personal relations with his pupils. He never turned away a boy who really wished to learn; all he required was a studious and virtuous spirit.

But, as we shall see again and again, the followers of Confucius soon departed from the example set by their master. Schools became formalized and meaningless. The development of reasoning was never an aim. The object of the teacher was to compel the child to remember, and thus learning became merely a laborious cramming of the memory. Direct and exact imitation was insisted upon; and discipline often was harsh. All the pupil's time was consumed in memorizing words, for he would be disgraced if he participated in labor or amusement.

The first years of a child's education were devoted to learning to read and write Chinese, a difficult process because of the intricacies of the characters used. As in India, the school was a loud school; each child repeated the passages orally until he had memorized them. Then he handed the book to the teacher, turned his back, and recited. He had to repeat the characters in exact order and at the fastest possible speed. Writing was taught by the use of tracing paper, the characters being formed with a small brush. The children first traced the characters and then tried to reproduce them.

The sacred books were committed to memory. At the higher stages some attempts were made at interpretation, and essays modeled after the sacred writings, were written. In this essay writing, the method was that of conscious imitation. The more closely the form, the construction, and the thought paralleled the original, the more highly prized was the essay.

It would be easy from these methods to conclude that language and speech literacy were mere exercises and trappings in ancient China, but this is far from the case. Sir Leonard Woolley asserts:

> In China, from the earliest period for which we have detailed informa-
> tion, the ability to read and write was expected of every member of the
> privileged aristocratic class, and the young nobles would study treatises
> on poetry and music, history and rhetoric, and writing itself was regarded
> as a fine art.[11]

---

[11] Jacquetta Hawkes and Sir Leonard Woolley, *Prehistory and The Beginnings of Civilization.* History of Mankind Series, vol. i. (New York: Harper & Row, Publishers, 1963), p. 817.

While the class bias of such an education strikes an adverse note now, the veneration of literacy even in earliest days does serve to emphasize the strength of the Chinese respect for learning.

Egypt, Gift of the Nile

The land of Egypt is, in the happy phrase of Herodotus, the Greek father of history, "the gift of the Nile, [where] perpetual summer reigns." The entire area possesses an exotic climate, which contributed to the development of another of the earliest civilizations. Settled by a Hamitic people, who inhabited the valley of this great river as anciently as 20,000 years ago, Egypt's recorded history, reaching back to the fifth millennium B.C., is one of the oldest.[12]

Its climate and the river represent chief forces in the forging of Egyptian civilization; its early culture was principally dependent on the activity of the Nile and its peculiar shaping of the life and customs of the Egyptians. Overflowing periodically and regularly from mid-August to early October, the receding waters left an alluvial deposit and a supply of moisture sufficient to produce an autumn crop.[13] To assure a summer harvest as well, the Egyptian farmers invented a system of irrigation, a development of early significance in the annals of engineering. The science of prediction, based on astronomy, and the creation of an immensely useful calendar may likewise be attributed to the effect of the Nile.[14]

A unified system of government early became a necessity for a rapidly expanding population, for the complexity of group living demanded much more organization than the simple community life which existed at first. As the primal groupings of population, or *nomes*, became inefficient to govern, they were linked into larger units, from which strong monarchies developed, both in the north at Memphis and in the south at Thebes. In 3400 B.C., a year of primary importance in Egyptian civilization, these areas were joined under the leadership of Menes. Henceforth the Pharaoh of Egypt would carry on his royal headdress the sacred cobra of the North and the Ra sun-disk of the South; following Menes, on to the period of the Roman Empire, Egypt was ruled by a series of usually indigenous dynasties of pharaoh-kings, whose power, enhanced by supernatural sanctions, was absolute.

Since Egypt was virtually surrounded by desert, invasions were fewer

---

[12] For further background see Hawkes and Woolley, pp. 110–112.

[13] A great change is presently being wrought in the Nile valley through the construction of the tremendous Aswan Dam to harness the Nile and regulate the water's flow regardless of season. What changes the dam, seventeen times higher than the pyramid of Cheops, may make in the life and culture of the United Arab Republic, remains to be seen. Coincidentally, the salvage and reconstruction of the marvelous temple and statuary of Abu Simmel, just south of Aswan, through the auspices of UNESCO and others, represents a glorious archeological achievement for both Egypt and the world.

[14] Symbolically, the Nile River resembles the lotus flower out of which the sun god, Ra, supposedly was born.

than in the other fluvial civilizations described; the Mediterranean and the Nile offered means of communication and commerce; camel trains ferried products overland from the Near and Middle East. Culture exchange undoubtedly occurred as well, with the result that a highly developed civilization appeared in Egypt—in many respects as fully evolved as that of today (without, of course, a machine culture and modern technology).

In this complex civilization both a well-organized priesthood and a strong military flourished. Control was autocratic; no popular government existed. Although the area was extensive (somewhat larger than Texas), agencies of government were not as diversified as in other imperial civilizations such as Persia. In Egypt, the personal rule of the Pharaoh, his presumed divinity, and the existence of a large bureaucracy accountable only to him and responsible for the creation of public works, the collection of taxes, and the general preservation of law and order produced a regime without the slightest tinge of democracy, although one had the right of "appeal to Pharaoh" in an adverse decision of the bureaucracy.

Correlative to the government (and a support to it) was the Egyptian religion. Again conditioned by the unique situation, the gods bore attributes relative to their geographical setting and the Egyptians' developing conceptions of morality. Although there were many gods, including those of primitive and savage origins, Re, Ra, or Amon-Ra was the chief; he was the personification, or deification, of the sun or of its influence on fruition in Egypt. His insignia, the winged sun-disk, is a familiar item in Western culture; Osiris and Isis represented respectively the Nile and the land of Egypt, thus the male and female principles; their son, Horus, was the god of day and usually was represented as hawk-headed. Osiris' evil brother, Set or Seth, appears to have been a prototype of the Judeo-Christian Satan. His domain was the desert; he also waged war against Osiris, the good. Thoth was the god of wisdom and magic—the scribe; it is said that he wrote 20,000 volumes of scientific lore and thus fostered the development of science and the arts in Egypt.

Osiris was the judge of the dead. Fanciful and elaborate ritual and custom surrounded the funeral rites of Egypt. Since the Egyptians believed in an afterlife and the existence of the *Ka* (soul), death represented for them merely an opportunity of preparation for the future. The body was carefully embalmed and usually laid to rest in a more or less elaborate tomb, depending on the circumstances of the deceased. All manner of pictures, books, and objects (sometimes including the bodies of dead slaves) accompanied the remains to the tomb. These, they thought, would be of service in the afterlife. In every possible way in Egypt the future was conditioned by the past and present; the Egyptians remembered everything, forgot nothing.[15]

---

[15] See Erich Zehren, *The Crescent and the Bull*, trans. by James Cleugh (New York: Hawthorn Books, Inc., 1962), pp. 265–269, for a more elaborate description of Egyptian mythology.

After death the deceased's soul, or double, presumably made its way to the great judgment hall of Osiris. Here certain religious texts were recited and the *Ka* was weighed in a scale against a feather, the symbol of truth. If the scales did not balance the favor of a blissful afterlife in the presence of the good Osiris was denied.

While the beauty and symbolism of this faith is apparent, it actually affected only the higher levels of society; on the lower, worship remained a superstition frequently involving degraded practices. The existence of a well-educated priesthood was a necessary concomitant to Egyptian religion, and the hierarchy learned to wield power as well. The Egyptians' preoccupation with the afterlife is revealed by the extensive remains of temples to the gods, the pyramids (which were the tombs of pharaohs), and the immense series of crypts cut into rock ledges bordering the upper Nile. Because of the unique climate much more of Egyptian antiquity has been preserved than is generally the case; both the land itself and the leading museums of the world contain vast deposits of Egyptology.

Religious texts were a necessity and these generally—as well as the business of education—were in the hands of the priests. The texts included the moral content suggested above as well as practical suggestions for behavior in this life; that religious belief and practices buttressed the power of the state and the rule of the Pharaoh, himself thought to be a descendant of Amon-Ra, is obvious. Education thus became a means for the preservation of social stability and the preservation of the status quo.

Ancient Egyptian Attitudes toward Education

Aims

Egyptian education truly represented the foundations of the autocratic state. In this it was both moral and practical. It aimed primarily at inculcating the proper respect for the gods, including the Pharaoh; secondly, the development of Egyptian civilization entailed the creation of artistic and practical forms of expression, together with the recognition of commerce and trade. Writing and account keeping were indispensable; the training of a large group of scribes for the transaction of official business likewise was an important goal. Many extant accounts suggest the respect with which Egyptians viewed writing and communication.

Scriveners were in great demand; to be a scribe was considered a responsible position: writers held preferred status in the Egyptian community. In the admonitory tale, the *Teaching of Kherty, Son of Dualf*, which dates from Mentuhotep III, 2065 B.C., a father is found advising his son to become a scribe, pointing out the advantages of this profession over all others!

> The barber shaves from morning to night; he never sits down. . . .
> The farmer wears the same clothes for all times. . . . The stonemason
> finds his work in every kind of hard stone. . . . I have never seen the

smith as ambassador. . . . If you have profited a single day at school it is a gain for eternity.[16]

The mystical and magic secrets of the priesthood were imparted to neophytes in the Temple Colleges; this practice insured the preservation and perpetuation of Egyptian society as well as the priesthood. Religious truth was a necessity for the Egyptian. If Egyptian society was not moral it certainly was bound by moral rules and regulations. The "Negative Confession" before Osiris cited many more than ten faults that had been avoided by the supplicant!

Since several systems of writing were in vogue, all had to be learned in order to communicate properly; foreign tongues and writing, including cuneiform, had to be assimilated, since Egypt played an extensive role in commerce. Systems of account keeping and all sorts of vocational and professional preparation, as well as systems of mathematics had to be mastered. In Egypt as in Sumer the rewards of learning were great.

Thus the aim of education was both cultural and utilitarian. As do all educational systems it strove to perpetuate the culture, but as in Confucian China, education was intolerant of change. It shunned innovation.[17]

Types

Many types of education were in existence but religious training and the vocational-professional predominated. There also were military schools for the sons of the nobility as well as apprenticeship for the children of the poor. Always there was training in the home. The important religious doctrines were inculcated firmly and perhaps no other country has been more successful in institutionalizing the forms of living. Spengler considered the "Egyptian" a special culture type because of the thoroughness of its integration and the rigidity of its pattern.

Training for public administration was a must since the government was but the lengthened shadow of Pharaoh, who needed many assistants to implement his will. The handing down of wonderful achievements in engineering and architecture was another necessity, as was the perpetuation of the artistic skills that embellished their temples and other public works.[18]

The education of women was largely vocational, although daughters of the aristocratic class received suitable tutoring. The social position of women was unique in the Eastern world, for the sex was placed on a higher level than in any other oriental empire—females could inherit the

---

[16] Hawkes and Woolley, pp. 467–468.

[17] Plato allegedly borrowed profusely from the Egyptian model in his creation of *The Republic*.

[18] For an anthology of plates and color pictures illustrative of the Egyptian culture and artistic representation see Christiane Desroches-Noblecourt, *Life and Death of a Pharaoh: Tutankhamen* (Greenwich, Conn.: New York Graphic Society, 1963).

throne, as did Hatshepsut and Cleopatra. And women of the poorer orders through their family association and apprenticeship, sometimes within the royal household, were provided with experience and a greater knowledge.

Content

The content of Egyptian education was both classical and vocational. Reading and writing were stressed as was the language of commerce. Both religious and secular literature was studied. In the professional and vocational spheres the content was particularly rich. Egypt's superiority in these areas was traced to the beneficence of the great god Thoth, deity of wisdom, who was presumed to have written thousands of volumes of scientific and mathematical lore, which were the basis for Egypt's advanced stage of civilization.

The duties of the apprentice were ordained by custom and time. Egypt's history was a long one, and in preliterate days much development had already occurred. The semiskilled and skilled artisans in metals and lapidary held and passed on trade secrets of the highest quality. Thus there were vocational learning of all kinds to be perpetuated, as well as the more formal content of the culture.

The actual literature is especially interesting, for many Egyptian schoolbooks have been recovered. They reveal the aphorisms, proverbs, moral judgments, and the like that comprised the fare of an Egyptian boy's copybooks. Abridgements of religious texts appeared and admonitions of the seers were included. Such an influential one was "Old Seer," Ptahhotep (2883–2855 B.C.). His advice and observations strike a parallel with those of Shakespeare's Polonius, although one is history, the other fiction. Popular accounts such as the story of an Egyptian Sinbad the Sailor were included, and songs and ballads were likewise the diet of schoolboys on the Nile.[19]

Mathematical subjects held an important place, since the annual recovery of the land from the floodwaters of the Nile presented problems to be handled through mensuration and surveying. The "Egyptian method" of computation continued in use over centuries, and even in early America arithmetic classes utilized its procedures.[20] Geometry likewise was a prominent subject. As indicated earlier, architecture and engineering were dominant in technical education, and astronomy brought aid to both religion and science. Medicine flourished, as did dentistry, in which Egyptians showed remarkable proficiency. Sports, games, and physical education assumed an important role with swimming, wrestling, and archery popular;

---

[19] Will Durant, *Our Oriental Heritage* (New York: Simon and Schuster, Inc., 1935), pp. 170–179, gives a minute description of Egyptian literature and its educational use.

[20] See V. Gordon Childe, *Man Makes Himself* (New York: New American Library of World Literature, Inc., 1951), pp. 158–159.

hunting and fishing existed as both vocations and avocations. Bathing and cleanliness, inside and out, were considered of prime importance. In the temples members of the priesthood shaved their bodies daily.

The skill and knowledge necessary for the singular accomplishments of Egyptian civilization could not have been devised by a single generation, but represent an accumulation of practical ingenuity and thousands of years of experience. These achievements were transmitted through the Egyptian agencies of education.

Music and dancing (participated in mainly by the lower classes) held a great deal of interest; musical instruction embraced drum and tambourine, cymbals, harp, lyre, and guitar. The use of castanets and clapping to rhythm likewise were in vogue. Between 1600–1400 B.C. Egypt became the military power of the ancient world; the military schools offered training in the use of the bow, battle-ax, lance, mace, and shield.

Agencies

Since the propertied and ruling classes possessed the wealth of Egypt, their offspring stood to gain most of the educational advantages. The laboring population, made up of boatsmen, tradesmen, interpreters, husbandmen, and shepherds, had little time for formal education. They worked from day to day at the favor of the rich. While others lived a life of idleness at court, the women in the poorer households led a life of drudgery, carrying water from the river or well, grinding corn, cooking, baking, making beer, carding, spinning, and weaving material for the family clothes.

But we may think first of the home as providing the basic education of the Egyptian child. Family duties as well as important precepts in the religious and moral world were impressed on young minds. Little boys played with toy crocodiles, and girls with dolls. At the age of five the boy attended (if his parents were able to pay the fees charged) reading and writing schools organized and sometimes taught by the priests. Many of these schools were located in or near the temples, and when lay teachers taught the program was under the general supervision of the priesthood.

The importance of reading and writing in Egyptian society cannot be overemphasized. As indicated above, various types of writing were utilized for different levels of thought or communication; the position of scribe was very important in Egypt, and royal scribes commanded great prestige and even power.

Apprenticeship was a frequent device for the semiskilled (and sometimes the skilled) professions. Military schools for the sons of the elite offered opportunity for practical instruction in the arts of war and perpetuated an officer class. A School of Government attached to the royal treasury trained graduates of the reading and writing schools for public administration. Commerce and industry demanded specialized education for foreign trade and account keeping. Foreign languages, including the Babylonian language and its calligraphy, cuneiform, were studied, as were the various types of mathematics. Secular teachers as well as priests were utilized, but education was under the control of religion. This was an essential part of Egyptian culture.

As noted earlier, occupations abounded in ancient Egypt: the mason, the smith, the barber, the lapidary. Thus vocational schools, not too far removed from apprenticeship, operated for the perpetuation of the simpler arts and crafts. Professional schools produced the proficiency needed in engineering, architecture, and medicine. Law was not a separate profession in Egypt; the legalities were handled by Pharaoh's corps of public officials; and law, so closely connected with religion, was in part a function of the priesthood. Astronomy likewise was largely their province. Probably the highest level of instruction in Egypt was in the temple college where, after ten or twelve years of basic preparation in reading, writing, and Egyptian literature, young men were admitted to study for the priesthood and instructed in the occult sciences and mysteries known only to it. Much of this was esoteric and forbidden to the laity and included the intense formalism of the religion and the ritual for the dead.

Organization

The home was the first school. Since women held an unusually high position in Egypt, instruction and guidance by the mother was considered important. Apprenticeship at an early age was the route taken by the poorer classes; a boy might be apprenticed under his father or with a worker in metals, stone, or lapidary.

The reading and writing school began at age five. "High schools" dealt with the professions, public service, or commerce. Military schools instructed for war. But the most significant school for the perpetuation of the Egyptian culture was the temple college. Here, at approximately age seventeen, youths entered the priesthood. Vocational schools of various types flourished.

Although the various agencies described should not be thought of as comprising an articulated system in the modern manner, the entire organization was controlled either directly or indirectly by the priesthood, since Egypt was in the final analysis a theocracy—Pharaoh himself being considered a deity.

Methods

The methods used in the Egyptian schools would have been quite familiar to European students in the Middle Ages. Dictation, memorization, and the copying of texts were the chief devices. Imitation and repetition of stories, myths, and legends firmly fixed the history of the country, along with the appropriate moral precepts from theology.[21] Observation and participation occurred in certain areas, especially physical education. These activities served a double purpose: the strengthening of the body (for possible conscription in the immense public works programs) and preparing for military service. But over and above the practical necessity for health, to the Egyptian bodily hygiene was almost of religious importance; sanitary rules and rites were memorized and strictly observed.

Cottrell, reading the Egyptian school records, gives a picture of educational practice some 4000 years ago.

> At one end of the room sits their teacher, a venerable scribe, a roll of papyrus spread out before him. . . . Each boy has in front of him a piece of potsherd, on which he is laboriously writing at the dictation of the teacher. . . . The lesson consists chiefly of learning by rote and laboriously copying out set exercises which have been used in Egyptian schools for generations.[22]

On the vocational level practice was the method. Internship as well as theory prepared for public administration and military students participated in war games which simulated actual conditions.

Among the Egyptians the inculcation of religious doctrines and precepts was of the utmost importance. Such learnings, as well as those of a secular nature, were subject to memorization. Failure to learn usually was penalized by flogging. A well-known story relates an Egyptian boy's appreciation to his teacher for what he considered to have been his opportunity for character development, "Thou didst beat my back and I didst learn."

REFERENCES

Barnes, Harry Elmer, *A Survey of Western Civilization.* New York: Thomas Y. Crowell Company, 1947.

Breasted, James Henry, *The Conquest of Civilization.* New York: Harper & Row, Publishers, 1926 and 1938. Pp. 43–110, 187–211.

Browne, Lewis, *This Believing World.* New York: Crowell-Collier and Macmillan, Inc., 1954.

Butts, R. Freeman, *A Cultural History of Western Education,* 2d ed. New York: McGraw-Hill, Inc., 1955. Pp. 6–18.

Cottrell, Leonard, *Life Under the Pharaohs.* New York: Holt, Rinehart and Winston, Inc., 1960.

---

[21] See James Henry Breasted, *The Conquest of Civilization* (New York: Harper & Row, Publishers, 1926 and 1938), pp. 85–89, for examples of Egyptian scrolls used in the schools of over 4000 years ago.

[22] Leonard Cottrell, *Life Under the Pharaohs* (New York: Holt, Rinehart and Winston, Inc., 1960), pp. 125–126. Numerous examples are given on pp. 127–141.

Creel, H. G., *The Birth of China*. New York: Reynal & Hitchcock, Inc., 1937.

De Bary, William Y. (Ed.), *Sources of Chinese Tradition*. New York: Columbia University Press, 1960.

Desroches-Noblecourt, Christiane, *Life and Death of a Pharaoh: Tutankhamen*. Greenwich, Conn.: New York Graphic Society, 1963.

Durant, Will, *The Story of Civilization,* pt. i, *Our Oriental Heritage*. New York: Simon and Schuster, Inc., 1935. Pp. 112–823.

Eby, Frederick, and Charles F. Arrowood, *The History and Philosophy of Education, Ancient and Medieval*. Englewood Cliffs, N.J.: Prentice-Hall, Inc., 1940. Pp. 36–107.

Edwardes, Michael, *A History of India from the Earliest Time to the Present Day*. New York: Farrar, Straus & Giroux, Inc., 1961.

Fairbanks, John K., *Chinese Thought and Institutions*. Chicago: University of Chicago Press, 1957.

Good, Harry G., *A History of Western Education*, 2d ed. New York: Crowell-Collier and Macmillan, Inc., 1960. Pp. 6–17.

Goodrich, L. Carrington, *A Short History of the Chinese People*. New York: Harper & Row, Publishers, 1943. Pp. 49, 116, 131, 150, 174, 194, 212, 214.

Hawkes, Jacquetta, and Sir Leonard Woolley, *Prehistory and the Beginnings of Civilization*. History of Mankind Series, vol. i. New York: Harper & Row, Publishers, 1963.

Huntington, Ellsworth, *Mainsprings of Civilization*. New York: John Wiley & Sons, Inc., 1945.

Jung, Carl G. (Ed.), *Man and His Symbols*. New York: Doubleday & Company, Inc., 1964. Pp. 104–157.

Knight, Edgar W., *Twenty Centuries of Education*. Boston: Ginn & Company, 1940. Pp. 33–40.

Latourette, Kenneth Scott, *China*. Englewood Cliffs, N.J.: Prentice-Hall, Inc., 1964. Pp. 44–100.

———, *A Short History of the Far East,* 3rd ed. New York: Crowell-Collier and Macmillan, Inc., 1957. Pp. 37–77, 78–189.

Lin Yutang, *The Chinese Way of Life*. Cleveland: The World Publishing Company, 1959.

———, *My Country and My People,* rev. ed. New York: The John Day Company, Inc., 1937.

———, *The Wisdom of India and China*. New York: Random House, Inc., 1942.

MacNair, Harley Farnsworth (Ed.), *China*. Berkeley, Calif.: University of California Press, 1951.

Mayer, Frederick, *A History of Educational Thought*. Columbus, Ohio: Charles E. Merrill Books, Inc., 1960. Pp. 28–73.

Messenger, James F., *An Interpretative History of Education*. New York: Thomas Y. Crowell Company, 1931. Pp. 17–28.

Mulhern, James, *A History of Education,* 2d ed. New York: The Ronald Press Company, 1959. Pp. 55–128.

Myers, Edward D., *Education in the Perspective of History.* New York: Harper & Row, Publishers, 1960. Pp. 32–48, 297–307, 312–313.

Nakosteen, Mehdi, *The History and Philosophy of Education.* New York: The Ronald Press Company, 1965. Pp. 23–59.

Ogg, Oscar, *The 26 Letters.* New York: Thomas Y. Crowell Company, 1961.

Pei, Mario, *The Story of Language,* rev. ed. Philadelphia: J. B. Lippincott Company, 1965.

Power, Edward J., *Main Currents in the History of Education.* New York: McGraw-Hill, Inc., 1962. Pp. 6–20, 27–29.

Smith, Huston, *The Religions of Mankind.* New York: Harper & Row, Publishers, 1958.

Smith, William A., *Ancient Education.* New York: Philosophical Library, Inc., 1955. Pp. 3–49, 50–68, 69–87.

Starr, Chester G., *A History of the Ancient World.* New York: Oxford University Press, 1965. Pp. 27–142, 164–181.

Toynbee, Arnold J., *A Study of History,* one vol. ed., abr. by D. C. Somervell. New York: Oxford University Press, 1946. Pp. 12–47.

Ulich, Robert, *Three Thousand Years of Educational Wisdom,* 2d ed. Cambridge, Mass.: Harvard University Press, 1965. Pp. 3–13, 14–28.

White, J. E. Manchip, *Ancient Egypt.* New York: Thomas Y. Crowell Company, 1953.

Woody, Thomas, *Life and Education in Early Societies.* New York: Crowell-Collier and Macmillan, Inc., 1949. Pp. 47–194.

Zehren, Erich, *The Crescent and the Bull,* trans. by James Cleugh. New York: Hawthorn Books, Inc., 1962.

SELECTED PAPERBACKS

Breasted, James Henry, *Ancient Times,* 2d ed., vol. i, *The Ancient Near East.* Boston: Ginn & Company, 1966.

Chadwick, John. *The Decipherment of Linear B.* New York: Alfred A. Knopf, 1958.

Chai, Ch'u, and Winberg Chai (Ed. and Trans.), *The Humanist Way in Ancient China.* New York: Bantam Books, Inc., 1965.

Childe, V. Gordon, *Man Makes Himself.* New York: New American Library of World Literature, Inc., 1951.

Cleator, P. E., *Lost Languages.* New York: New American Library of World Literature, Inc., 1959.

Cottrell, Leonard. *Lost Pharoahs.* New York: Grosset & Dunlap, Inc., 1961.

Desroches-Noblecourt, Christiane. *Tutankhamen: Portrait of a Pharaoh.* New York: Doubleday & Company, Inc., 1965.

Fairservis, Walter A., Jr., *The Ancient Kingdoms of the Nile.* New York: New American Library of World Literature, Inc., 1962.

———, *The Origins of Oriental Civilization.* New York: New American Library of World Literature, Inc., 1959. Pp. 71–141.

Goldberg, Isaac, *The Wonder of Words, An Introduction to Language for Everyman.* New York: Appleton-Century-Crofts, 1957.

Hollister, C. Warren, *Roots of the Western Tradition.* New York: John Wiley & Sons, Inc., 1966.

Jones, Tom B., *From the Tigris to the Tiber.* Homewood, Ill.: The Dorsey Press, Inc., 1969. Pp. 39–48, 53–62.

McEvedy, Colin. *Penguin Atlas of Ancient History.* Baltimore: Penguin Books, Inc., 1967.

Moscati, Sabatino, *Face of the Ancient Orient.* New York: Doubleday & Company, Inc., 1962.

Pei, Mario. *The Story of Language.* New York: New American Library of World Literature, Inc., 1966.

Riencourt, Amaury de, *The Soul of China,* rev. ed. New York: Harper & Row, Publishers, 1965.

Smith, Huston. *The Religions of Mankind.* New York: New American Library of World Literature, Inc., 1961.

Waley, Arthur. *Three Ways of Life in Ancient China.* New York: Doubleday & Company, Inc., 1956.

————, (Trans.), *Monkey, A Folk Novel of China* by Wu Ch'engen. New York: Grove Press, n.d.

Woolley, Sir Leonard. *History of Mankind, Cultural and Scientific Development,* vol. i, pt. ii, *The Beginnings of Civilization.* New York: New American Library of World Literature, Inc., 1965.

CHAPTER 4

Moral Training for National Ideals

By the waters of Babylon, there we sat down and wept,
when we remembered Zion.
On the willows there we hung up our lyres.
For there our captors required of us songs,
and our tormentors, mirth, saying,
"Sing us one of the songs of Zion!"
How shall we sing the Lord's song in a foreign land?[1]

A NOVEL CONCEPT OF EDUCATION

Of all the peoples of the Near East—that region lying between Mediterranean Europe and Greater Asia, between Egypt and the Black Sea—we shall have space to concentrate only on the Hebrews. The reason will not be difficult to determine. Although originally just another desert tribe, like the other wanderers of the arid bay south of the Fertile Crescent, these founders of Judaism early in recorded history began the development of a unique personality and an unmatched culture that has continued in the religion that bears their name and in the tenure of a narrow strip of land at the far eastern end of the Mediterranean. For these Jews were to permanently place their mark on human civilization, directly on its moral and religious aspects, but significantly also in salient contributions to science, medicine, the arts, and letters.

Originating in the Middle East, adjacent to the Hittite, Canaanite, and Phoenician cultures, and anchored by Sumer and Egypt, these Hebrew

---

[1] Psalm 137: 1–4, Revised Standard Version. All Biblical references or quotations are from this edition.

tribesmen surely did not match the others' imperial political and religious patterns. Indeed this unique people developed ideas and ideals that were distinctly different from all other eastern folk.[2] World civilization has received from them many contributions that have profoundly affected its educational theories and practice, as well as perceptions in the social and religious spheres that were to become the foundations of at least two other religions.

Humanity is primarily indebted to the Jews for (1) monotheism, the concept of one and only one God, a principle shared today by Jews, Christians, and Muslims; (2) the Ten Commandments, the general guide to ethical conduct that has set a standard for social living for several thousands of years; and (3) the Bible, that fountainhead of so much Western tradition and literature. Hebraic social, religious, and educational thought form important bases for modern humanitarian and pedagogical development.

Coupled with their definite achievements, a feeling of destiny greatly affected the Hebrew people. For had not their God called them his chosen nation and had he not promised to Abraham a perpetual patrimony as a reward for the strict keeping of his commandments? The Book of Genesis repeats this Jewish idea of destiny:

> [God said] And I will give unto thee, and to thy seed after thee, the land wherein thou art a stranger, all the land of Canaan, for an everlasting possession; and I will be their God.
> And God said unto Abraham, Thou shalt keep my covenant. . . .[3]

EARLY HISTORY OF THE JEWS

The story of Israel, as we now call the polity established by these nomadic Semitic tribesmen, began some 4000 years ago. Living from their flocks and herds, driven from oasis to oasis in the vast Arabian desert, the Hebrews first appear in history as a minor group that had somehow made its way to a site not far from the early civilization of Sumer. Almost primitive, their minds filled with fear—for their religion was still that of animism—their life was beset by hardship, for the desert was a cruel and bitter place. To the north and west was a goal of which they often spoke: the Fertile Crescent, reaching from the Persian Gulf to the Mediterranean, envisaged as an Eden, a Paradise, a "Promised Land." Time after time they had sought to gain a foothold in the lush lands of the Sumerians and Chaldeans, only to be repulsed.

---

[2] For a succinct presentation of the origins of the Hebrews and their religious and social customs, see Jacquetta Hawkes and Sir Leonard Woolley, *Prehistory and The Beginnings of Civilization*. History of Mankind Series, vol. i (New York: Harper & Row, Publishers, 1963), pp. 741–748.

[3] Genesis, 17:8–9.

But at a very early period they did dwell for a while in the far eastern tip of the Crescent, adjacent to the land they called Shinar (Sumer), from which it is possible they derived many myths and historical ideas. Abraham, son of Terah, is reported as living in Ur, then at Harran in the Crescent (c. 2000 B.C.) and later entering Canaan, near the eastern edge of the Mediterranean Sea.[4]

Here they again tried their fortunes, but by the time of Jacob and Joseph they were found in Egypt, at the extreme western tip of the Crescent. After they escaped through the skill of their leader, priest, and prophet, Moses, from the slavery the Egyptians imposed on pastoral peoples the Jews languished for many years in the Sinai Desert (now the Negev) until the great warrior Joshua led them again into Canaan, conquered the people of Jericho, and took lands along the river Jordan. This land, described as "flowing with milk and honey," was not agricultural, but did provide good pasturage and an abundant harvest for bees.

In Palestine they were able to remain to build an important national culture and to devise ways and means of perpetuating their ideals. A golden age, under David and Solomon, about 1000 B.C., found the Jews at the pinnacle of their affluence and secular power, which were not to endure. Dissension, apostasy, and the misrule of weak and willful kings resulted in a division of the kingdom and made it prey to more powerful neighbors. Israel, the section held by the ten northerly tribes, was seized by the Assyrians, its people dispersed and vanished from history. Judea, home of the tribes of Judah and Benjamin, was subjugated by the Babylonian successors to the Sumerians, who drove the Jews to their capital on the Euphrates. The Hebrews remained "by the waters of Babylon" until the overthrow of Belshazzar by Persian and Median arms in 539 B.C. In Babylon the prophet Daniel bested the king's Chaldean diviners, and the Hebrew children were thrown into the fiery furnace. Cyrus the Great (the Persian), however, permitted the repatriation of the Jewish remnant and the rebuilding of the temple of Solomon at Jerusalem.

Nevertheless, Hebrew fortune was at low ebb, and their small country continued largely under the political domination of stronger nations until their epic revolt brought terrible punishment by the Roman emperor Titus in 70 A.D. This brief description of an unusual people suggests the three great crises in their history: (1) the Deliverance, or Exodus, from Egypt (c. 1250 B.C.); (2) the Babylonian Exile, or Captivity (586 B.C.); and (3) the destruction of the Temple by Titus (70 A.D.) and the Diaspora.

The extraordinary character of the Hebrews began to develop about the time of the Exodus. Before that, except for their strong family structure and worship of a familial god, their social customs, religious and educational practices, differed little from those of other Eastern peoples. Moses,

---

[4] See Hawkes and Woolley, pp. 742–743; Jacob A. Rubin and Meyer Barkai, *A Pictorial History of Israel* (Cranbury, N.J.: A. S. Barnes & Company, Inc., 1958), pp. 9–14, offer a telescoped account of Jewish history.

however, was not only the great deliverer of his people from bondage but was also their lawgiver. He must be recognized as one of the decisive thinkers and reformers of antiquity. First, under his great influence and later under the thunder of the Hebrew prophets before and during the Captivity, the Jews crystallized the national, religious, and social ideals upon which they based their educational conceptions.

The cultural history of the Jewish people covers approximately four millennia, in which Jews have experienced both the joys of prosperity and the pains of adversity. But whatever their outward circumstances—whether they were exercising dominion from their splendid capital at Jerusalem or wandering among the nations—they have continued to cling with the utmost tenacity to their national feeling and to their national ideas and customs. This has had significant consequences for education.

The cultural and civic consciousness which gave this people a unity of mores and aspirations possessed by no others was built upon three outstanding concepts, or beliefs: (1) an omnipotent, righteous creator, God, who selected the Hebrews as his chosen people; (2) a coming Messiah, who would restore the Jews' exceptional position which they had lost through a period of faithlessness; and (3) holiness and obedience on the Jews' part as a condition of their restoration. The Jews believed further that such righteousness would be attained only through continuous educational emphasis. Consequently, education has been, since the day of their fall, a prime force in Jewish culture.[5]

Even in the midst of adversity, when they were humbled by imperial neighbors or by their own backsliding, history and God's promise, as renewed through prophets and teachers, stood to comfort and sustain. "I will punish you in just measure," Jeremiah says, speaking the words of the Lord, "but I will not make a full end of you."

One may well say that Jewish teaching clearly emphasized moral discipline as the most important element in education. Its greatest lesson is that a strict adherence to an educational system based on a peculiarly high religious and moral ideal preserved their unity as no political system could. The salvation of this people, at least, was due to its firm realization of the stabilizing power of education.

THE EARLY HEBREW APPROACH TO EDUCATION

Aims

The educational aims of the Hebrews mark the transition from Oriental to Occidental attitudes toward education. Although, as in all Eastern cultures, the individual was subject to an external authority, this

---

[5] James A. Michener, *The Source* (New York: Random House, Inc., 1965), offers in authentic, although popular, form the epic story of Israel's origin, rise, fall, and renaissance.

was no longer the authority of ancestor, caste, or state, but of their God, Yahweh.[6] It is this concept, more than anything else, that gives the ancient Jews their unique place in the educational history of antiquity.

As would be expected, theocracy controlled and dominated, as well as motivated, both Hebrew educational theory and practice. The chief end of education from the Mosaic period was to develop faithful and obedient servants to the personal and living God, thereby to assure harmony and cooperation in civic life and a glorious future for God's chosen people. Thus the sense of national destiny was stronger in Palestine than in Persia or even in Rome. The educational objective was to prepare the people for their destiny and to prepare each succeeding generation to fulfill faithfully its task in the great work before it.

The Bible sanctions Hebrew observance of the plan their God had covenanted:

> Did any people ever hear the voice of a god speaking out of the midst of the fire, as you have heard, and still live? Or has any god ever attempted to go and take a nation for himself from the midst of another nation, by trials, by signs, by wonders, and by war, by a mighty hand and an outstretched arm, and by great terrors, according to all that the LORD your God did for you. . . .
> Know therefore this day, and lay it to your heart, that the LORD is GOD in heaven above and on the earth beneath; there is no other. Therefore you shall keep his statutes and his commandments, which I command you this day, that it may go well with you, and with your children after you, and that you may prolong your days in the land which the LORD your God gives you for ever.[7]

Thus the dominating feature of the entire educational system was that the Jew was taught to make holiness before the Lord the aim of his daily life. Although education in Jewish principles began early in childhood, it did not end there. Throughout life a Hebrew was to consider his relationship to Yahweh his primary concern:

> Remember also your Creator in the days of your youth, before the evil days come, and the years draw nigh, when you will say, "I have no pleasure in them"; . . . Fear God, and keep his commandments; for this is the whole duty of man. For God will bring every deed into judgment, with every secret thing, whether good or evil.[8]

---

[6] The Hebrews considered the name of their God too holy to be pronounced and wrote only the Tertagrammaton *YHWH*. Certain translators added vowels changing the *Y* to *J* and the *W* to *V* (as in Latin) with the result that *Jehovah* as a name for God became current during the late middle ages. The Revised Standard Version uses Yahweh as more representative of the ancient pronunciation (which could be given by the Jewish high priest, not by common members of the tribe).

[7] Deuteronomy 4:33–40.

[8] Ecclesiastes 12:1, 13–14.

Moses Maimonides put this dedication to continuing education as follows:

> Every man in Israel is obliged to devote himself to study, be he rich or poor, of good health or afflicted by diseases, a youngster or a doddering elder; even if he be a beggar living on charity or a father burdened with a family he ought to set aside time for study by day and night. . . . Among the greatest scholars of Israel there were wood-pickers and water-carriers, even blind men. They studied nevertheless the Torah [the Law], by day and night. . . . Up to what age is one obligated to study the Torah? Unto the day of death![9]

The legacy of Abraham stood the Jews in good stead during their sojourn in Egypt, but Moses saw the need of an even stronger bond, an ethos to bind the twelve tribes into a solid national unity. Moses gave the Hebrews the concept of Yahweh as a national deity who would protect his people if they would continue to obey his commandments. It was a concept of one God, who had chosen the Hebrews alone. For other nations there might be other gods, but for the Jews there was only Yahweh. Through Moses a solemn covenant was entered into binding the Hebrews to obey the statutes of Yahweh and binding Yahweh to favor them with his divine protection. But the God of Moses was anthropomorphic, jealous, vengeful, terrible, and sometimes cruel. It was natural that at first the function of worship should be to appease and placate this Thunderer of the Wilderness.

So an elaborate ritual of religious ceremonies, social relationships, and domestic customs was arranged by Moses, assisted by the priesthood, and superimposed upon the Decalogue. This body of rules and regulations was built up and transmitted as the Torah, or essence of Jewish Law, which was developed considerably during the period of Hebrew exile. Religion became an institution; worship came to be a formalized observance of the demands of the law; and education became a training in ritualistic ordinances. But early Hebrew religion frequently resembled monolatry rather than the pure monotheism preached by Moses. And as the nation began to achieve (under Solomon and his successors) a more powerful position in international affairs, grave dangers developed. The cosmopolitanism of a regal court and the influx of imported and strange religions encouraged tendencies to neglect the Jewish heritage and to behave in too secular a fashion. Solomon's cardinal error was, oddly, his toleration of other faiths and ideologies.

But then there appeared a conservative tendency. The great prophets of Israel thundered against these aberrations, for they saw Hebrew civilization changing through the impact of new political and economic

---

[9] *Guide for the Perplexed*, trans. by Shlomo Pines (Chicago: University of Chicago Press, 1963). His *Mishneh Torah* represents the summa theologiae of Judaism—neoplatonic Aristotelism—in fourteen books.

conditions. They saw new relationships developing with the other Near Eastern nations and peoples. They realized that their own people, attracted by the sensuality of their neighbors' religions, stood in continual danger of falling from their exclusive worship of Yahweh. Blessed with charisma and courage, the prophets interpreted these otherwise evil changes as an opportunity for the teaching of new and broader ideals and hope of a more abundant life. These creative thinkers sought to restore the faith of their fathers, but ended by presenting to the Jews and the world a whole new concept of righteousness and of God: the God of justice, majesty, love— and of all nations. They presented to the Hebrews a new covenant, new commands, and strong new moral standards:

> I hate, I despise your feasts,
>   and I take no delight in your solemn assemblies.
>
> Even though you offer me your burnt offerings and cereal
>   offerings,
>   I will not accept them,
> and the peace offerings of your
>   fatted beasts
> I will not look upon.
> Take away from me the noise of your songs;
>   to the melody of your harps I will not listen.
> But let justice roll down like waters,
>   and righteousness like an ever-
>   flowing stream.[10]
>
> With what shall I come before
>   the LORD,
> and bow myself before God on
>   high?
> Shall I come before him with burnt
>   offerings,
> with calves a year old?
> Will the LORD be pleased with
>   thousands of rams,
> with ten thousands of rivers of
>   oil?
> Shall I give my first-born for my
>   transgression,
> the fruit of my body for the sin
>   of my soul?
> He has showed you, O man, what
>   is good;
> and what does the LORD require
>   of you

---

[10] Amos: 5:21–24.

but to do justice, to love kind-
    ness,
and to walk humbly with your
    God?[11]

Behold, the days are coming, says the LORD, when I will make a new covenant with the house of Israel and the house of Judah, not like the covenant which I made with their fathers when I took them by the hand to bring them out of the land of Egypt, my covenant which they broke, though I was their husband, says the LORD. But this is the covenant which I will make with the house of Israel after those days, says the LORD: I will put my law within them, and I will write it upon their hearts; and I will be their God, and they shall be my people.[12]

Through such radiant words spoke the prophets of Israel, but frequently their good seed fell upon stony ground. Hart expresses the prophet's dilemma:

A prophet is one who sees the new trend, the promise of a new life in the confusions of the present, and who is courageous enough, even at great personal peril, to teach to men the new way of life. . . . But institutions do not like prophets . . . and about all the prophet can do is to speak the speech that is in his soul and wait for the future to judge him and his work.[13]

So these religious seers and reformers set up a new goal for educational endeavor. They devoutly wished to deepen religious insight and fervor, to teach a better knowledge of God and a richer, truer righteousness. This theme is the basis for Felix Mendelssohn-Bartholdy's beautiful oratorio, *Elijah*, in which the prophet puts to rout the idolatrous priests of Baal. Obadiah sings:

Ye people rend your hearts, and not your garments; for your transgressions the prophet Elijah hath sealed the heavens through the word of God. I therefore say to ye, Forsake your idols, return to God; for he is slow to anger, and merciful, and kind, and gracious, and repenteth Him of the evil.

Then the sublime aria:

"If with all your hearts ye truly seek me, ye shall surely find me." Thus saith God. Oh! that I knew where I might find Him, that I might ever come before His presence!

Elijah sings:

    Draw near, all ye people, come to me!
    Lord God of Abraham, Isaac and Israel; this day let it be known that Thou art God, and I am thy servant!

---

[11] Micah 6:6–8.
[12] Jeremiah 31:31–33.
[13] Joseph K. Hart, *Creative Moments in Education* (New York: Holt, Rinehart and Winston, Inc., 1931), p. 110.

O shew to all this people that I have done these things according to Thy word!

O hear me, Lord, and answer me, O shew this people that Thou art Lord God, and let their hearts again be turned.

Then the women cry out:

Lift thine eyes, O lift thine eyes to the mountains, whence cometh help. Thy help cometh from the Lord, the Maker of heaven and earth. He hath said, thy foot shall not be moved. Thy keeper will never slumber.

Now, at last, the Chorus rises on a note of triumph:

And then, shall your light break forth as the light of morning breaketh, and your health shall speedily spring forth then; and the glory of the Lord shall ever reward you. Lord our Creator, how excellent thy Name is in all the nations! Amen!

But the prophets' aim was only seldom realized in the later education of the Jews; the school continued to devote most of its attention to stylized observances of the codified and institutionalized religion. Prophecy was subordinated to the Law in Hebrew education: "over and above all else was, is, and shall be ever the Law."

Types

It is difficult to decide whether to call the outstanding type of education among the Hebrews religious training or civic training, for the two were practically one: religion was synonymous with patriotism. Yahweh was the God of Israel; loyalty to him was loyalty to the Jewish nation. By teaching her children to obey the commandments of God, Israel also preserved her greatness and glory as a nation. This was moral training too, in the highest and best sense, for all customs and relationships were directed toward the common welfare.

Hence in contrast to the empirical and naturalistic style of the other peoples studied, Hebrew education was spiritual. And it was also in sharp contrast to oriental education generally, because the Jews did not have an external authority to dictate to the individual what he was to do, feel, or think. Here the authority was Yahweh, or their strong belief in Yahweh, who had covenanted with them.[14]

During the earlier period of Jewish history the chief characteristic of education was its domestic simplicity; the family was in control, a type of education that had obtained before the notion of the state became fixed. Of course, the Jews were organized in tribes, but in a sense the tribe was really one large family, an extended family, as in primitive society. Through-

[14] For a succinct story of Jewish development see H. G. Wells, *The Outline of History.* Updated by Raymond Postgate (New York: Doubleday & Company, Inc., 1961), pp. 204–217.

out history the idea of the Jews as a family—in addition to the more conventional father-mother-child relationships—has been of the greatest importance in securing unification. The family taught without some of the distractions encountered in a more complicated setting.

If the child was to become the faithful servant of Yahweh it was essential that he be taught by precept and example the moral judgments and religious beliefs of his people. It has been wisely said that

> . . . among all nations the direction impressed on education depends on the idea which they form of the perfect man. Among the Romans it is the brave soldier, inured to fatigue, and readily yielding to discipline; among the Athenians it is the man who unites in himself the happy harmony of moral and physical perfection; among the Hebrews the perfect man is the pious, virtuous man, who is capable of attaining the ideal traced by God himself in these terms: "Ye shall be holy, for I the Lord your God am holy!"[15]

Education was democratic in that all were trained upon an equal basis. The Hebrews held that education should be for everyone, regardless of class. Since all were equal before God, the Law was laid on each, and the ceremonies and sacraments were not the secrets of a class. The Hebrews not only recognized this principle in theory but put it into practice. Thus education in later Palestine was universal. It was considered essential for everyone to be educated if the nation were to survive. The ignorant man suffered civil disfranchisement and social ostracism; for the ignorant man could not be religious, and the irreligious were a detriment to the nation. It is interesting to note that the Jews were the first to insist upon the education of the whole people and were willing to establish schools for this purpose.

Vocational training was considered most essential. It was the duty of every father to teach his son a trade. "Whosoever does not teach his son a handicraft, teaches him to be a thief." Manual labor was honored, and the greatest scholars were also artisans. We may recall that Jesus of Nazareth was a carpenter, and Saul of Tarsus was a tentmaker.

These Hebrews made little provision for physical education, although the Mosaic Law included some laws of hygiene, and fathers were urged to teach their children how to swim.

Domestic training was raised to a new level. The Jews developed a much more beautiful home life than that of other countries. Woman was believed to have been created, not to be a slave to man, but as a helpmeet. The mother had a high place in the Jewish home and assisted the father in inculcating in the children their first lessons in the meaning and practice of the religious ceremonies and rites. Girls were trained by their mothers

---

[15] Quoted from J. Simon, *L'éducation et l'instruction chez les anciens Juifs* (Paris, 1879), p. 16. In Gabriel Compayre, *The History of Pedagogy,* trans. by W. H. Payne (Boston: D. C. Heath and Company, 1889), p. 7.

in all the household duties, some of which were exceedingly complex. Various foods were prescribed and had to be prepared in definite ways. Directions for the treatment of relatives, strangers, and servants were laid down minutely. A glance through the many regulations of the Law having to do with the life of the home soon reveals how necessary it was that the housewife be carefully trained for her tasks and duties.

Content

Fundamentally the content of education was the history of the Hebrew people and of Yahweh's dealings with them; the explanation of the festivals of the Passover, Shabuoth, and the Tabernacles as they recurred; the Jewish Law, the psalms, and the proverbs. Predominantly, it consisted of the Pentateuch, or Torah (the first five books of the Old Testament), and the Talmud. The latter, codified about the time of the Babylonian Captivity, came to be almost as important as the Law itself. For, by the time of their return to Jerusalem the Jews had changed from a nomadic pastoral people to an agricultural and commercial people. Partly on account of their transition to a new economy and partly because of the thundering of the prophets, the Mosaic Law had to be reinterpreted to meet new conditions and new attitudes.

These interpretations of the Law, with the commentaries upon them written later by the *sopherim*, or scribes, form the Talmud. Higher education became largely a study and knowledge of the Law, its practice and definition; primary education a review and memorization of Mosaic history. Jewish law was a blend of civil, criminal, ceremonial, domestic, and sanitary law; and instruction was based upon the assumption that all important truth had been codified in the Law, which rested partly upon revelation, and thus had only to be understood in order to meet all exigencies. Every line, word, and letter was to be submitted to microscopic investigation by scribes and rabbis in order to produce a maximum of meaning. Hence the Talmud has been the basis of all Judaic scholarship for over 2000 years. This code of endless prescription and minute ceremonial became the basis of the whole Hebrew educational curriculum and was applied to every act in Jewish daily life.

Music, sacred and common, was a part of Hebrew education. The psalms were written in rhythmic form for chanting or singing; several musical instruments were used, although Hebrew music was somewhat undeveloped. Reading, writing, and simple arithmetic were taught in the schools established in the second century B.C. The Torah was studied analytically and served as reading material. Foreign languages sometimes were added and the work was graded from six to ten. The cumbersome notational system used by the early Jews militated against the pursuit of any kind of advanced mathematics. The Talmud, not in writing until the third to sixth century A.D., was used on higher levels and with the Torah expounded in the synagogues. Education was compulsory—for boys at the elementary schools, taught by rabbis; girls at home, taught by their parents.

Agencies

In the beginning, the family was the sole educational institution, with the father acting with complete power over his children not only as patriarch and priest, but also as teacher, and with the mother sharing in the duty of instruction. Indeed, throughout Jewish history, the mother has remained her daughters' teacher. And Hebrew women have played notable roles in history. The names *Ruth, Naomi,* and *Esther* should be familiar; *Deborah, Jael,* and *Judith* may be less so, although their achievements too serve further to glorify the annals of Israel.[16]

Only boys learned to read and write in this early period. Girls were taught to spin and weave, to prepare food and to superintend the work of the household, to care for children, and to sing and dance to simple musical instruments, such as the harp, flute, drum, dulcimer, and trumpet.

Intellectual culture, in the pre-Babylonian period, was but an incident in the education of the Hebrew; since love of their country and moral and religious instruction were the major aims in Hebrew education, fathers taught their children the nation's history—emphasizing those great events that had rendered them unique—Yahweh's promise to Abraham, the Passover, the work of Moses, the Lawgiver, the building of the temple under Solomon, the safe return from Babylon; these things, they believed, marked their destiny as a chosen people.

The Babylonian exile had had a remarkable effect on the remainder of the Jewish people. (1) They saw the organized power of the Chaldeans and were, no doubt, impressed by the Chaldean general and sacred literature, the legacy of 2000 years of Tigris-Euphrates civilization. (2) They saw more clearly the necessity of preserving their own national and religious culture (which were one and the same). Back in Jerusalem, the Jewish priesthood gathered and arranged their own law and literature into three great sections: The Law, The Writings of the Prophets, and Collected Writings. Sages or *amoraim* served as interpreters.

Out of this effort and the contemplation of their history the children of Israel came to a profound conclusion, one which was to sustain them for two more millennia. As Moscati puts it: "The historical misfortunes of the chosen people are but a passing manifestation of divine disfavor, merited by the peoples' sins, and continued faithfulness will bring, in God's good time, a restoration to favor."[17] The series of events celebrated by

---

[16] For the story of Judith see the Apocrypha or the Douay Bible.

[17] Sabatino Moscati, *Ancient Semitic Civilizations* (London: Elek Books, 1957), p. 125. According to American Mormon belief, it was during such a period of disfavor under King Zedekiah that their religion's ancestors left Jerusalem.

periodic feasts renewed annually—and in which the young also participated —served to fill their hearts with gratitude toward God and to deepen their love of country.

This zeal for instruction was intensified during the Roman period and especially after the advent of Christianity. Operated under domestic auspices up to this time, now Judaic education became public. It no longer seemed sufficient merely to indoctrinate children with good principles and sound moral habits. They must also be instructed in wider areas, knowledge of the world and the learnings valuable in commercial pursuits. From the beginning of the Christian era, the Jews approached our modern ideal: that of making education compulsory and universal.

It is reported that, in the year 64, the high priest Joshua ben Gamala imposed on each town under penalty of excommunication the obligation to support a school. Moreover, there could be no technical evasion of this rule; if a town was divided by a river and there was no safe transit by means of a bridge, schools must be established on both sides. Even today we have hardly realized the rule so clearly stated in the Talmud that, if the number of children does not exceed twenty-five, the school may be conducted by one teacher; if greater than twenty-five the town must employ an assistant; and if the number of children exceeds forty, then two schoolmasters must be employed.

> Like every brave nation that has been vanquished, whose energy has survived defeat, like the Prussians after Jena, or the French after 1870 [or the Germans after Hitler], the Jews sought to defend themselves against the effects of conquest by a great intellectual effort, and to regain their lost ground by the development of popular instruction.[18]

After the Exile the scribes, whose duties had hitherto been clerical, began to assume also the duties of a special teaching class. Besides serving in a judicial capacity as interpreters of the Law, and in a priestly capacity in the synagogues as expounders of the Law, they now began to function also as teachers in the elementary schools that were being established.[19] These schools were attached to the synagogues in most of the villages, and their necessity came to be universally recognized. They were accepted as important as the synagogue itself, and to live where there was no school came to be forbidden.

Both the school and the teacher—scribe or rabbi—were regarded reverently. In the Talmud we read:

> He who studies and teaches others, possesses treasures and riches.
> He who has learned and does not impart his knowledge to others, disregards the word of God.

---

[18] See Compayre, pp. 8–9.

[19] Moscati, *Ancient Semitic Civilizations*. See also Moscati, *The Face of the Ancient Orient* (Chicago: Quadrangle Books, Inc., 1960), pp. 224–267.

It is not permitted to live in a place where there is neither master nor school.

Your teacher and your father have need of your assistance; help your teacher before helping your father, for the last has given you only life of this world, while the former has secured for you the life of the world to come.

High qualifications were required for teaching. All teachers were carefully selected, well trained, and had to be of the highest moral caliber. They were to be married, mature, and able in every respect. Most frequently scribes or priests, teachers usually pursued some other vocation as well, for they received no regular salary. Parents were permitted, however, to make gifts which were acceptable without compromise to the teacher's professional status.

Undoubtedly, the Hebrews' interest and zeal for education and their constant provision of teachers for the young carried them through the dark days of the Exile and Diaspora. Almost a hundred years ago Dittes said of the Jews:

> If ever a people has demonstrated the power of education, it is the people of Israel. . . . What a singular spectacle is offered us by that people, which, dispossessed of its own country for 1800 years, has been dispersed among the nations without losing its identity, and has maintained its existence without a country, without a government, and without a ruler, preserving with perennial energy its habits, its manners, and its faith![20]

Organization

During the long era between the Exodus and the Captivity, the organization of Jewish education was still in terms of the family, just as it had been from the earliest days in Mesopotamia. Another of the chief educational influences was the temple and its worship activities. Three times each year, at Passover, at Shabuoth, and at the feast of the Tabernacles, all males were required to visit the temple. These occasions had much the same educational result, the development of strong national feeling, upon the Jews that the Olympic games had on the Greeks.

Higher education for the training of rabbis and scribes was organized before elementary education became prevalent. Even before the Exile there arose institutions known as schools of the prophets, which helped prepare lay prophets in the historical and sacred background of Judaism. Such schools taught theological interpretation of the Law, the arts of sacred music and meter, and above all else the principles of Jewish righteousness. Much later colleges or training schools for scribes, called houses of instruction, originated in the homes of prominent scribes and were devoted to an

---

[20] Quoted from J. Dittes, *Histoire de l'éducation et l'instruction*, trans. by Redolfi (Paris, 1880), p. 49. In Compayre, p. 6. See also Lewis Browne (Ed.), *The Wisdom of Israel* (New York: Random House, Inc., 1945).

intensive analytical study of the Torah and Talmud. Such training emphasized also the virtues of charity, chastity, truthfulness, prudence, diligence, and temperance. Eventually instruction in mathematics, foreign language, astronomy, and geography was given in these schools.[21]

When formal elementary instruction was established, this organization was in terms of the synagogue or elementary school for boys and the home for girls. Work in the elementary school was arranged in three age groups: six to ten, ten to fifteen, and over fifteen. The first two levels were compulsory for all male children; and rich and poor attended and studied together. The chief text for the first group was the Pentateuch; for the intermediate group, the first part of the Talmud, the Mishna; and for the third group, the Gemara, or second part of the Talmud.

Methods

Hebrew method, as was usual in all Oriental countries because of the lack of writing materials, was largely oral. In learning to write, a wax tablet and stylus were used. Even in higher education the method was largely that of exposition by the master, with questioning and disputation afterward. This was the type of school in which Jesus of Nazareth was found by his parents at the age of twelve, "in the temple, sitting in the midst of the doctors, both hearing them, and asking them questions." There was nothing unusual about the method; the only amazing thing was the extreme youth of the pupil.

The elementary schools utilized the spoken word, with the emphasis upon memorizing. The pupils sat on the floor or on benches facing the teacher, who was supposed never to have more than twenty-five in his group. The pupils repeated the passages aloud, with careful articulation; for "to speak aloud the sentence which is being learned fixes it in the memory." Judaic teachers were skilled in the correlation of various types of memory—visual, auditory, and kinesthetic—and made extensive use of mnemonic devices. The following precepts from the Talmud show that they had some comprehension of the principles of interest, socialization, and individual differences—principles of method that are considered quite modern:

> The teacher should strive to make the lesson agreeable to the pupils by clear reasoning as well as by frequent repetitions until they thoroughly understand the matter and are able to recite it with great fluency.
>
> One learns much from the teacher, more from his school fellows, but most of all from his pupils.
>
> Only those pupils should be punished in whom the master sees capacity for learning; if they are dull and cannot learn, they should not be punished.

---

[21] For a complete discussion of Jewish training, see Eugene B. Borowitz, "Judaic Roots of Modern Education," in Richard E. Gross (Ed.), *Heritage of American Education* (Boston: Allyn and Bacon, Inc., 1962), pp. 67–101.

The school day was long, for it lasted from early morning until evening with a recess at noon, and the only vacations were the religious holidays. The discipline was somewhat rigorous, with corporal punishment recognized as a valid method of control. Severity, however, was tempered with kindliness, as is shown by the maxim, "Punish with one hand, and caress with two."

What of significance, in addition to the forms and practices of education developed by the Hebrews, can we learn from their educational history? Simply this: no civilization of importance has risen to greatness without strong emphasis on family life and training. Two reasons for the permanence of the Hebrew and Chinese forms of civilization are the dominance accorded the family and its role in education. Actually, in ancient Jewish education, the family rather than the school formed the basic social unit, and so it continues to this day. The reestablishment of Israel in 1948 serves to validate this tribute to the staying qualities of Jewish education. And to recall to the world the long history of Jewish achievement and struggle, Abba Eban, on May 5, 1949, the day of Israel's admission to the United Nations, said:

> A great wheel of history comes full circle today as Israel renewed and established offers itself with all its imperfections, but perhaps with some virtues, to the defense of the invincible human spirit against the perils of nihilism, conflict, and despair.[22]

REFERENCES

Bakan, David, *The Duality of Human Existence.* Skokie, Ill.: Rand McNally & Company, 1966. Pp. 217–221.

Barnes, Harry Elmer, *An Intellectual and Cultural History of the Western World.* New York: Random House, Inc., 1937. Pp. 78–102.

Breasted, James Henry, *The Conquest of Civilization.* New York: Harper & Row, Publishers, 1926 and 1938. Pp. 212–234.

Browne, Lewis, *This Believing World.* New York: Crowell-Collier and Macmillan, Inc., 1954. Pp. 223–253.

———, *Stranger than Fiction.* New York: Crowell-Collier and Macmillan, Inc., 1925. Pp. 1–368.

Butts, R. Freeman, *A Cultural History of Western Education,* 2d ed. New York: McGraw-Hill, Inc., 1955. Pp. 11–12, 16–18.

Compayre, Gabriel, *The History of Pedagogy,* trans. by W. H. Payne. Boston: D. C. Heath and Company, 1889. Pp. 6–11, 16.

Duggan, Stephen P., *Student's Textbook in the History of Education.* New York: Appleton-Century-Crofts, 1936. Pp. 7–13.

Eban, Abba Solomon, *My People, The Story of the Jews.* New York: Random House, Inc., 1968. Pp. 1–123.

———, *The Voice of Israel.* New York: Horizon Press, Inc., 1957.

[22] Abba Solomon Eban, *The Voice of Israel* (New York: Horizon Press, Inc., 1957), p. 44.

Eby, Frederick, and Charles F. Arrowood, *The History and Philosophy of Education, Ancient and Medieval.* Englewood Cliffs, N.J.: Prentice-Hall, Inc., 1940. Pp. 108–159.

Goldin, Judah (Ed. and Trans.), *The Living Talmud, The Wisdom of the Fathers and its Classical Commentaries.* New York: The Heritage Press, 1960.

Graves, Frank P., *Education before the Middle Ages.* New York: Crowell-Collier and Macmillan, Inc., 1909. Pp. 110–136.

Gross, Richard E. (Ed.), *Heritage of American Education,* Boston: Allyn and Bacon, 1962. Especially Eugene B. Borowitz, "Judaic Roots of Modern Education," pp. 67–101.

Hamilton, Edith, *Spokesmen for God: The Great Teachers of the Old Testament.* New York: W. W. Norton & Company, Inc., 1949.

Hart, Joseph K., *Creative Moments in Education.* New York: Holt, Rinehart and Winston, Inc., 1931. Pp. 106–120.

Hitti, Philip K., *Syria: A Short History.* New York: Crowell-Collier and Macmillan, Inc., 1959.

Knight, Edgar W., *Twenty Centuries of Education.* Boston: Ginn & Company, 1940. Pp. 40–44.

Laurie, Simon S., *Historical Survey of Pre-Christian Education.* New York: David McKay Company, Inc., 1915. Pp. 65–100.

Marek, Kurt W., *The Secret of the Hittites.* New York: Alfred A. Knopf, 1956.

Mayer, Frederick, *A History of Educational Thought.* Columbus, Ohio: Charles E. Merrill Books, Inc., 1960. Pp. 73–78.

Moscati, Sabatino, *Ancient Semitic Civilizations.* London: Elek Books, 1957. Pp. 124–166.

———, *Face of the Ancient Orient.* New York: Doubleday & Company, Inc., 1962. Pp. 235–281.

Mulhern, James, *A History of Education,* 2d ed. New York: The Ronald Press Company, 1959. Pp. 55ff.

Myers, Edward D., *Education in the Perspective of History.* New York: Harper & Row, Publishers, 1960. Pp. 316–321.

Orlinsky, Harry M., *Ancient Israel.* Ithaca, N.Y.: Cornell University Press, 1954.

Rubin, Jacob A., and Meyer Barkai, *Pictorial History of Israel.* Cranbury, N.J.: A. S. Barnes & Company, Inc., 1958.

Shaw, Charles Gray, *Trends of Civilization and Culture.* New York: American Book Company, 1950. Pp. 99–124.

Smith, Huston, *The Religions of Man.* New York: Harper & Row, Publishers, 1958.

Smith, William A., *Ancient Civilization.* New York: Philosophical Library, Inc., 1955. Pp. 197–253.

Starr, Chester G., *A History of the Ancient World.* New York: Oxford University Press, 1965. Pp. 143–163.

Ulich, Robert, *History of Educational Thought.* New York: American Book Company, 1950.

———, *Three Thousand Years of Educational Wisdom,* 2d ed. Cambridge, Mass.: Harvard University Press, 1965.

Voegelin, Eric, *Israel and Revelation*. Baton Rouge, La.: Louisiana State University Press, 1956. Pp. 111–515.

Wells, H. G., *The Outline of History*, updated by Raymond Postgate. New York: Doubleday & Company, Inc., 1961. Pp. 204–217.

SELECTED PAPERBACKS

Breasted, James Henry, *Ancient Times*, 2d ed., vol. i, *The Ancient Near East*. Boston: Ginn & Company, 1966. Pp. 217–236.

Browne, Lewis, *This Believing World*. New York: Crowell-Collier and Macmillan, Inc., 1961. Pp. 223–253.

Childe, V. Gordon, *Man Makes Himself*. New York: New American Library of World Literature, Inc., 1951.

Chouraqui, André, *A History of Judaism*. New York: Walker and Company, 1962.

Dimont, Max, *Jews, God and History*. New York: New American Library of World Literature, Inc., 1962.

Hamilton, Edith. *Spokesmen for God: The Great Teachers of the Old Testament*. New York: W. W. Norton & Company, Inc., 1949.

Hollister, C. Warren, *Roots of the Western Tradition*. New York: John Wiley & Sons, Inc., 1966.

Jones, Tom B., *From the Tigris to the Tiber*. Homewood, Ill.: The Dorsey Press, Inc., 1969. Pp. 68–76.

Josephus, Flavius, *The Jewish War*. Baltimore: Penguin Books, Inc., 1950.

Levin, Meyer, *The Story of Israel*. New York: G. P. Putnam's Sons, 1967.

McEvedy, Colin, *Penguin Atlas of Ancient History*. Baltimore: Penguin Books, Inc., 1967.

Michener, James A., *The Source*. New York: Random House, Inc., 1965.

Moscati, Sabatino, *Face of the Ancient Orient*. New York: Doubleday & Company, Inc., 1962.

Roth, Leon, *Judaism: A Faith*. New York: The Viking Press, Inc., 1900.

Smith, Huston, *The Religions of Man*. New York: Harper & Row, Publishers, 1965. Pp. 254–300.

Steinberg, Milton, *Basic Judaism*. New York: Harcourt, Brace & World, Inc., 1947.

Woolley, Sir Leonard, *History of Mankind, Cultural and Scientific Development*, vol. i, pt. ii, *The Beginnings of Civilization*. New York: New American Library, 1965. Pp. 492–500.

CHAPTER 5

The Development of Individuality

Five hundred years before Christ in a little town on the far western border of the settled and civilized world, a strange new power was at work. . . . What was then produced of art and of thought has never been surpassed and very rarely equalled, and the stamp of it is upon all the art and all the thought of the Western world.[1]

THE BIRTH OF CLASSICAL CULTURE

From Asia our review of education in the ancient world now shifts to two small nations, then on the periphery of Oriental civilization. The classic peoples of Greece and Rome were the first representatives of Western culture; and since each nation had significantly different ideals, attitudes, and practices, each made its own distinctive contribution. The Greeks contributed more elements of modern civilization than any other ancient people. They bequeathed art, drama, literature, philosophy, politics, and an embryonic science. Rome, too, has affected the world considerably. More practical of mind than the Greeks, the Romans excelled in engineering, military science, government, and law. To them we are indebted for the dissemination of the Hellenic culture throughout Western Europe.

In art, Greece produced masterpieces in sculpture and architecture that have become models for all ages; they developed the standards and forms upon which much later art has been based. The greatest classics of secular world literature have come from Greek authors or recorders; we are indebted to them for most of the accepted literary forms and types: epic and lyric poetry, oratory, the symposium, and history. Both Aeschylus' *The Persians* and Euripides' *Medea* and *The Trojan Women* plumb the human heart.[2] With literature, sculpture, and painting, Greece shows us that art is in man's nature.

---

[1] Edith Hamilton, *The Greek Way.* Copyright 1930, 1943, by W. W. Norton & Company, Inc. Copyright renewed 1958 by Edith Hamilton.

[2] See Gilbert Murray (Trans.), *The Persians* (London: George Allen & Unwin, Ltd., 1960), pp. 67–70; and Hamilton, pp. 200–203.

Greek thinkers were the first in the field of philosophy. They developed specific systems such as the Platonic, the Aristotelian, the Stoic, and the Epicurean destined to play a large part in the thought life of the world; and they formulated some basic philosophical problems which are still being speculated. Many present-day social and political theories originated with the Greeks and were applied in their efforts to develop the first democratic governments. Many of their scientific notions have long since been exploded; but the Greeks are the earliest representatives of the scientific spirit. This drive toward research and investigation is in the work of Euclid (c. 300 B.C.) in mathematics, of Archimedes (287–212 B.C.) in physics, of Aristotle (384–322 B.C.) in logic; and all are still basic elements of a science curriculum. Plato (428–348 B.C.) is famous for his blueprint of a scientifically created state, as well as for his philosophical idealism.

We may assume, then, that the educational conceptions and ideals of this virile and cultured people made important contributions to the development of educational thought. Here, for the first time, we see education conceived of as a moving equilibrium, with recognition of the desirability of the development of the individual personality. In Greece we witness a creative moment in the history of education.

With its departure from the philosophy of complacency and belief in the preservation of the status quo, we have the origins of an educational philosophy. With the acceptance of the principle of change and growth we have a recognition of education as a problem. In Greek education, for the first time, we discover a type that neither consciously nor unconsciously suppresses the individual. Indeed, here, the assertion of individuality is deemed compatible with social stability and the welfare of the state.

Just what were the conditions and influences that made such contributions to educational thought possible? What are the sources of this unparalleled Grecian people? Sometime before 1200 B.C., Indo-Europeans journeyed southward from the Pontian steppes into the peninsula called Hellas, or Greece. This rugged land and its mountains offer few passes, thus making ancient travel, transportation, and communication difficult. Consequently, the Hellenes developed isolated pockets of civilization, usually small city-states, which interacted little or not at all with each other. Such early separation of the Greek people into numerous, sometimes tiny, enclaves tended to establish a wide difference of interests. It has been alleged that the consequence of numerous centers of civic life led to that spirit of freedom and independence which is said, historically, to characterize the Greek contribution to world civilization.

Regardless of their devotion to their diminutive polities and the special interests of their various city-states, Hellenes spoke the same language and worshiped the same gods. Living in peninsular insulation from the remaining Balkan tribes and separated by the sea from Asia and

Africa, the Greeks felt distinct from all other peoples, whom they designated as barbarians, a pun on their supposedly outlandish speech. Hellenic tribal pride was thus one of the significant influences in Greek history, which, coupled with geographical setting, climate, and generally poor agricultural prospects, drove them to sea conquests and the marts of trade. Aeschylus in his *Prometheus* has this demigod say:

> And none but I devised the mariner's car
> On hempen wing, roaming the trackless sea. . . .

Here was no Nile or Euphrates, and agriculture was based on the olive and the grape; life was not easy and each small state had a port for trade, as well as the fields and grazing lands that were much later to become the chief adjuncts of manorial living. But the climate was stimulating and the need for outdoor physical exercise compelling, so the Greeks developed into a rugged, healthy folk, temperate of habit and quick to assert their fancied superiority as individuals or as a group.[3] It has been said that their own natural beauty, together with good taste, made them keen judges of beauty in other things and highly intolerant of ugliness. However this may be, two concepts did indeed govern their lives individually and collectively. *Hubris*, or overweening pride, presented a limiting factor, for it led to the destruction of the proud man, who imagined himself unique or not subject to the laws of the gods. Thus it regulated, at least theoretically, the Greek drive for excessive individuality.[4] *Arete* represented intrinsic worth; that is, everything has its own specific purpose. This could be applied, for example, to power, function, and quality. A weapon had arete; it could kill, protect, warn, or wound; a scythe had arete, as did men, beasts of burden, and ships. In Greek life, this quality meant as Ulich says, that persons and objects "must have proper structure. Their effect must not be impeded by unnecessary trifles and they must show the highest degree of adaptation to their total purpose."[5]

The Hellenic state was wholly under the city's organization, and the limits of city and state were coterminous. The port, as in Athens, usually was removed from the center because of the danger of pirates. The fields and vineyards were apart too; hence it is called a city-state to differentiate it from the modern territorial state.[6] There were several hundred small

---

[3] See André Bonnard, *Greek Civilization from the Iliad to the Parthenon*, 3 vols., trans. by A. Lytton Sells (New York: Crowell-Collier and Macmillan, Inc., 1957), vol. i, pp. 11–29; Stringfellow Barr, *The Will of Zeus* (Philadelphia: J. B. Lippincott Company, 1961), pp. 3–26, 27–47.

[4] Murray, pp. 11–12.

[5] Robert Ulich, *History of Educational Thought* (New York: American Book Company, 1950), p. 5.

[6] An interesting, although fictional, account of the rise and fall of such a Greek state is the subject of George R. Stewart's *The Years of the City* (Boston: Houghton Mifflin Company, 1955).

city-states, but gradually some combined into religious or political leagues under the leadership of the most powerful or noteworthy cities. So the original petty kingdoms of Attica were united into one city-state under the control of Athens, and Sparta became the head of a similar state located in the Peloponnesus, the southern arm of the Greek peninsula. Sparta and Athens are conveniently studied as typical of two types of Hellenic culture: Athens as the leading example of the Ionian branch, which toward the end of its history became largely democratic, and Sparta as the foremost example of the Dorian, which continued the autocratic, or totalitarian, tradition.

First, however, Greek development underwent an epic period. This was a day of small kingdoms or tribal leadership and its heroes are those recalled in Greek prehistory—Achilles, Ajax, Agamemnon, Ulysses, Menelaus, Phoenix, and many others. We can best learn of the character and customs of the heroic age from the bards, or minstrels, who traveled from court to court singing to king and nobles of the intrepid adventures of gods and heroes. These poets and singers were the authors of two great epics, the *Iliad* and the *Odyssey*, usually attributed to Homer (c. 800 B.C.). It is from these Homeric sagas that we must discern the conditions and types of education offered throughout this period.

But since Greek education changed with political and social conditions, we must study other periods as well to understand its development. Thus, our discussion will be divided as follows: (1) Homeric education, that of the archaic period, our only knowledge of which is based on saga, common to all Hellenes, extending from their beginnings to 776 B.C., the date of the first Olympiad; (2) Spartan education, from the Homeric period and continuing throughout the entire history of Greece; (3) early Athenian education, lasting from 776 B.C. to the close of the Persian Wars in 479 B.C.; and (4) the adult stage of Athenian education, generally effective until the subjugation of the Greeks by the Macedonians (338 B.C.). The initial part of this last era is often called the Periclean, or golden age of Greece, for it was then that the Greeks made signal achievements in art, drama, literature, and history.

EDUCATIONAL PRACTICES DURING THE ARCHAIC PERIOD

Aims

It can hardly be said that Greek education, in contrast to that of the Jews or Egyptians, had a religious aim. For the popular religion was founded largely on a pleasant light-hearted myth telling. When Homeric minstrels sang of the gods, they told of glorified men—gay, even lustful, brawling heroes, who dwelt on Mount Olympus and engaged in deeds of craft, cunning, and courage. Sometimes the gods descended and aided or opposed men, taking sides as in the Trojan War. These early Greeks did not particularly love their gods; neither did they always fear them. Homeric tales reveal little terror of the deities, although there is a measure of fondness, even a quality of respect. But above all else, the Greeks desired to imitate their gods, to be godlike. Their deities were like men, differing only from humans in their greater stature, strength, and immortality.[7] Although, as we have seen, the Hebrews claimed that men were created in the image of God, the Greek gods were created in the image of man.

Since the gods were only magnified men, they possessed both good and evil qualities; thus the influence of traditional religion was moral and immoral. In some tales the gods set an example of justice, kindliness, hospitality, and forebearance; but they also taught men to lie, to steal, and to kill. (It was this latter phase of Greek religion that Socrates and Plato sought to disestablish.) Nor was there a promise of a glorious reward in the hereafter, as in Egyptian and Hebrew worship, that could furnish a proper motive for right living. The realm of Hades (not to be confused with the Christian idea of Hell) was cold, dark, and lifeless; the very thought of death was hideous, while life was full of beauty, gaiety, and joy. The Greek aim was to enjoy a happy godlike earthly existence not because the gods demanded it, but because the people themselves approved this type of life. Incidentally, much as the Greeks disparaged the barbarians, they themselves retained many barbarous practices such as human sacrifice until their later cultural periods.

Nevertheless, the Homeric Greeks' ideal of the perfect man was two-fold. The first model was Odysseus, the man of wisdom. Here was a man of judgment, insight, sagacity, shrewdness, and eloquence, too—strong in counsel and a deviser of strategies and schemes. The second ideal was that of Achilles, the man of action. He exemplified the primary virtues of bravery, courage, strength, and endurance—those qualities needed for marvelous deeds and valiant exploits.[8]

The aim of Homeric education, therefore, was to develop these two ideals in each nobleman, whose action should be guided by reverence for tradition, and whose wisdom should control his appetites through reason. (No attention was paid to the menials, or countrymen, whose unskilled pursuits were fashioned by imitation of their parents or fellows, much in the manner of primitive men.)

Greek education, then, had from the first, this aim of individual excellence, *arete*, worth, often called fair-and-goodness from its com-

---

[7] But see Jane Harrison, *Prolegomena to the Study of the Greek Religion* (New York: Meridian Books, Inc., 1955), chs. vii-ix, pp. 322–477, where a more serious picture is shown. See also Bonnard, pp. 132–149.

[8] The qualities of Achilles are recounted in the *Iliad*, the Homeric epic narrating the Greek attack on Ilium, or Troy; the *Odyssey* tells of the wandering of Odysseus, or Ulysses, on his long voyage home to Ithaca following the sack of the city, entrance having been effected through Odysseus' strategy of the wooden horse.

ponent elements: perfection of body in beauty and strength; and perfection of mind in courage, temperance, justice, and wisdom—the four classical virtues. Such an aim was both practical and social, for the ideal of individual excellence was never separated from that of public usefulness. Individual worth was worth for public ends, for social and political life in peace and war. The welfare of the group was the primary consideration.

Types

Education during the Homeric period was necessarily practical and social. Through the clan, family, or service in war, the qualities, traits, and skills, requisite for tribal sufficiency were promoted. For boys and men there was training in the arts of peace and war, craftsmanship and military proficiency. For the women, training in their domestic calling included the arts of spinning, weaving, food handling, and child rearing. Of course, education was not democratic, for in archaic Greece various groups were divided into classes with different ways of life. Consequently, different types of training were needed.

Content

Since in Homer's day nobles owned the land with its agricultural plots, groves, vineyards, and pastures, slaves or hired men tended the estate while their lords lived in the villages with their peers or went on long expeditions of adventure or war. This close association of members within a class fostered intense participation in the social, political, and religious life for which they had been destined by birth. Nurtured for a higher calling, the upper classes considered themselves the brave, the high and mighty, and the best, contrasting themselves with the base, low-born, and cowardly men of the lower untrained and unskilled working classes, who led miserable and menial lives in the hinterland and performed only the rustic duties of herdsmen and farmers.

Skilled workers, or craftsmen trained in their special art, were more highly respected. In fact, lords and ladies themselves often shared in such tasks, becoming highly proficient in their métier, such as Odysseus' fashioning of bows or Penelope's weaving of robes or tapestries.[9] Occupations were varied. Among the crafts-people was the smith, forging armor and weapons; the potter, hard by his wheel, creating articles of utility and beauty; the shipwright, with his adz; the leech, curing a wound with his soothing ointment and blood letting; the seer, consulting the oracles and prophesying; the minstrel, delighting with his lyre and songs. Skilled female

---

[9] Penelope, the wife of Odysseus, has long been considered the epitome of wifely virtue. Confident of her husband's return from the Trojan War, she thwarted the many suitors for her hand and kingdom by an ingenious and amusing device. Telling them she could not remarry until she finished her weaving, she wove in the day and unraveled her work at night.

slaves were trained in making clothing, in dyeing, weaving, and embroidery. Youths and maidens were taught to dance and to play various musical instruments, adding pleasure to the life at court. Conversation was deemed an art, and men were trained to reach decisions through group discussion. A certain reverence for the gods, although mixed with human considerations, developed courage; and reason was the Homeric antidote to ungoverned passion.

Agencies and Organization

No formal educational institutions existed in Homeric days. Training was given in the family and tribe, the council of nobles, and the manorhouse of the lord. The bard taught the virtues essential to proper living through his recital of the deeds of gods and heroes; handiwork and crafts were fostered by those skilled in such arts. Participation in war taught the lessons of valor and survival.

Within the family, an extended group of clan or tribe, life was well-ordered, with roles and duties for each member. In the earliest days, women were the equals of men within the home. Matrons held authority and taught household tasks and crafts; the queen herself "sat among her serving women and appointed brave handiwork for her handmaidens."

Methods

In such a milieu educational methods depended largely upon imitation and example. Boys learned virtues through contact with the clan leaders and through listening to the tales of gods and heroes sung around the evening fire or during ceremonials or feastdays. They acquired practical skills through participation in military campaigns, the duties and crafts of the home, and attending the councils of their elders. Girls, in similar fashion, assimilated the skills of the household through close attendance to its needs and sharing in its tasks.

And, lest anyone dismiss this regimen as bucolic and antiquarian, we must note that the importance of Homeric education did not cease with the advent of later phases of Greek educational history. The virtues and ideals praised in Homer's epics were still considered appropriate for the education of the very young even in the age of Socrates, Plato, and Aristotle. This Homeric emphasis was not discarded, and is still considered in certain Greek thought the appropriate vehicle for education. Actually, Homer's eminence governed the lower schools throughout almost all of Hellas' history and was supplemented in secondary instruction with grammar, rhetoric, and mathematics.

THE SPARTAN APPROACH TO EDUCATION

Consideration of the fluvial civilizations has already shown that geography has a distinct influence in social, political, and educational history. The Spartan city-state offers an illustration. One branch of the Dorian Greeks, which we have come to call Spartan, settled south of Corinth in the Peloponnesus—the southern section of the peninsula—around the eleventh century B.C. The site of their city was a fairly level inland plain on the Eurotas River; and, unlike most Greeks, the Spartans had little interest in sea power. Their land boundaries were what they chose to make them.

Bringing under subjugation the earlier tribes of this area the Spartans had by the ninth century B.C. grown to 9000 families, surrounded by almost thirty times that number of subject peoples, known as Perioeci or Helots, who farmed, herded, and did all the menial work. The Perioeci, "dwellers-around," were the earlier occupants of adjacent lands and were subject to Spartan military duty. The Helots were outright slaves, continually under threat of oppression and death. With no natural frontier and with the constant danger of attack from without and insurrection from within the state, the Spartans called upon Lycurgus (c. 800 B.C.) to devise a constitution and develop a system of laws, which came to form the basis of the Spartan political and social system, and as such provide our best knowledge of the Spartan attitude toward education.

Aims

Lycurgus' constitution aimed at training a powerful body of soldiers and thus made Sparta a perpetual military camp or armed garrison. Education sought group welfare—the Spartan state being pre-eminent—and everything and everybody was subject to this ideal. In a way, this was in accord with the general Hellenic archetype of individual excellence for tribal advantage; but here individual excellence meant military superiority, and state usefulness meant sufficiency in time of war. We may readily note that Sparta's ideal was Achilles, the man of action, rather than Odysseus, the man of wisdom. Her aim was to develop in each person such physical perfection and complete obedience that he would make the model soldier and, consequently, the best citizen for such a state.

Even the time for marriage was fixed; should a man not marry when he was of full age, he was subject to prosecution, as was the man who married either above or below himself. Those producing three children had special immunities; those who had four were exempt from all taxes. Virgins were married without dowry, because "neither want should hinder a man, nor riches induce him," to enter into wedlock.

To develop conformity, courage, strength, cunning, endurance, and patriotic efficiency was the Spartan ideal of good citizenship. Sparta surrendered all the esthetic qualities of its people to perfect the bodily and military competency that she held necessary for her preservation and continuity. Her overall aim was to raise a nation physically invincible, with a people capable of enduring hunger, thirst, torture, even death, without flinching—a people unequaled in military skill and absolutely devoted to their state.

Spartan education—*training for conformity would be a better expression*—had a simple object: preparing Spartan citizens to defend themselves and their country at all times in domestic or international affairs. The citizen was trained to obey or command. His first and last thought was to be the interests of his native land. Personal preference had to be sublimated to the concern of all. An early example of totalitarianism, Lycurgus' system achieved the individual's mastery of himself and the mastery of the state over him.

Within its own framework, the Spartan order appeared successful (and Spartan arms eventually overcame democratic Athens). For the education based on Sparta's single-track objective continued with little or no change for over 700 years. But in all this time as a principal result of such a restricted conception of life, this great military city-state contributed nothing of cultural value to the world, except an example of rigid devotion to a single purpose that has made the term *Spartan* synonymous with a narrowly-prescribed culture and all the qualities characteristic of this same dedication to an austere or regimented habit of life.

Types

The types of education in Sparta were physical education and military training. Since both were for the general welfare, Spartan education can in its broadest sense be called social; since it mandated the preservation of the state, it can be called civic as well. Spartan moral training, a product of group living and traditional ceremonies, was but a phase of the total commitment to war. Even the minute instruction in music and dance was physical training to build an attitude for war.

Domestic training also was subordinated to the needs of the Spartan state; communal life was stressed, and family relationships were suppressed in the interest of military readiness. Moreover, most household duties were performed by Helot women. Other manual tasks were carried out by Helots or other slaves. Although slaves received some preparation for their roles, their labor was largely unskilled, technology being of a low order in Sparta. Thus, among the Spartans themselves there was no vocational training nor any need of it.

Intellectual education received little attention, being limited to the development of speech abilities, and memorization of Lycurgus' laws and a few excerpts from Homer. There was, naturally, some rehearsal or preparation for participation in public ceremonies, but this can hardly be identified as intellectual discipline.

Content

The Spartan curriculum consisted almost totally of gymnastic and paramilitary exercises, with practice in the moral and social habits essential to a life of devotion and service to the state. Boys were constrained to keep absolute control over their appetites, to be temperate in all their habits, and to be obedient and respectful to their elders. They were urged to be modest and reserved until action was demanded, when they were to behave aggressively and without fear.

Female education was not neglected, for the Spartans felt that women should be equally strong and courageous. Girls were given gymnastic exercises in order to toughen them and to prepare them to bear strong, healthy children, their greatest contribution to the state. Group activities prepared women also for the hardships of war and the rugged life Sparta admired. As boys strove to develop a reverential demeanor, stoicism under pain, and the practice of blind obedience, girls were urged to develop bodily vigor and womanly dignity.

Plutarch describes Spartan education as follows:

> As for the education of youth, which Lycurgus looked upon as the greatest and most glorious work of a lawgiver, he began with it at the very source, taking into consideration their conception and birth, by regulating the marriages. For he did not (as Aristotle says) desist from his attempt to bring the women under sober rules. They had, indeed, assumed great liberty and power on account of the frequent expeditions of their husbands, during which they were left sole mistresses at home, and so gained an undue deference and improper titles; but, notwithstanding this, he took all possible care of them. He ordered the virgins to exercise themselves in running, wrestling, and throwing quoits and darts; that their bodies being strong and vigorous, the children afterwards produced from them might be the same; and that, thus fortified by exercise, they might better support the pangs of childbirth, and be delivered with safety.
>
> In order to take away the excessive tenderness and delicacy of the sex, the consequence of a recluse life, he accustomed the virgins occasionally to be seen naked as well as the young men, and to dance and sing in their presence on certain festivals. There they sometimes indulged in a little raillery upon those that had misbehaved themselves, and sometimes they hung encomia on such as deserved them, thus exciting in the young men an useful emulation and love of glory. For he who was praised for his bravery, and celebrated among the virgins, went away perfectly happy: while their satirical glances thrown out in sport, were no less cutting than serious admonitions; especially as the kings and senate went with the other citizens to see all that passed. As for the virgins appearing naked there was nothing disgraceful in it, because everything was conducted with modesty, and without one indecent word or action. Nay, it caused a simplicity of manners and an emulation for the best habit of body; their ideas too were naturally enlarged, while they were not excluded from their share of bravery and honor![10]

Reading and writing were taught to a very limited extent, if at all; but the boys had to learn the laws of the state and the tales of the heroes of old, and to listen attentively to the conversations of their elders. Drills

---

[10] Plutarch, *Parallel Lives*. Some revised spelling and paragraphing supplied.

were given in the art of speaking without wasting words; this is the origin of the expression "laconic reply,"[11] as the territory of the Spartan city-state was called Laconia. The Spartans themselves were sometimes called Lacedaemonians after the founder of the city.

Music was taught, though the songs were always serious and moral, usually in praise of men who had died for their country; the stately Doric measures had a martial rhythm that inflamed the mind and stirred it to enthusiasm and fervor for action. Likewise, dancing was not for esthetic values or for the development of grace and beauty, but like their gymnastic exercises was designed to build bodily strength and vigor.

Agencies and Organization

The one dominant educational agency was the state, and the state controlled the education of the individual from birth until death. All family life was dictated by the state; marriage was controlled by the state and made compulsory; all children were considered as belonging to the state, and the state council decided at birth whether a child should be permitted to live.

The defective child was abandoned and exposed to the elements. Some perished or were the prey of wild beasts. A few were rescued to become slaves. A healthy boy was given to his mother for rearing until he reached the age of seven, but his education was always controlled by the demands of the Spartan state. The discipline of self-control began from the day of his birth. He was trained to overcome fear by being left alone at night; he was made hardy by fasting; he ate simple coarse food, wore scanty clothing, slept on a hard bed; he received copious out-of-doors exercise in the fresh, pure air of his Eurotas valley. At an early age he learned the habits of silence, obedience, respect, and reverence toward his elders.

When he was seven, the boy went to live in a barracks-type educational institution under the supervision of older youths and of a state official called the *paidonomus.* Until the age of eighteen, the boy remained there, under the most severe discipline and exacting rules of conduct. His bed was a pallet of straw or hay with no blankets. He received no shoes and a minimum of clothing. His food was plain and meager, and he was encouraged to steal to supplement his diet or to gain practice for the foraging of war. However, should a boy be caught in theft, he was severely punished for his lack of cleverness or skill.[12]

In these public barracks boys were rigorously trained through all

---

[11] A Spartan legend tells that the Persian king had threatened the city saying "If I come to Greece I will lay your city in the dust." The Spartan reply: "If."

[12] A famous story is that of the Spartan youth who, having stolen a fox, placed it under his tunic. During cross-examination he allowed himself to be clawed to death rather than admit the theft.

manner of games, exercises, and drills; they also participated in jumping, running, wrestling, spear throwing, and quoits, a forerunner of horseshoes. All these practical and military exercises were solely for the purpose of developing qualities serviceable in defensive or aggressive war. The *eiren*, a youth with two years' more experience than his charges, led discussion at the public dining table, to which each boy was supposed to contribute, and instructed them in moral and civic issues and in the affairs of their state. Thus they learned to express themselves in an intelligent and agreeable manner, acquiring early in life a dignity of bearing and a practical wisdom somewhat beyond their years.[13]

Between the ages of eighteen and twenty most boys were engaged in professional war training. Candidates for *eiren*, those who had demonstrated superior qualities of leadership and mind, remained in the barracks to supervise a new generation of younger boys. At twenty all took the oath of allegiance to Sparta and were dispersed to the various military posts and on war maneuvers or actual combat. At the age of thirty, each man became a full-fledged citizen and was obliged to marry and to take his seat in the public assembly or council. From time to time he was expected to visit the public barracks to serve as mentor and example to the boys in training; in this respect, every man in Sparta was a teacher!

The home was the school for girls. Except for their festival appearances, no female institution corresponded to that of the boys' barracks. Girls were, however, organized into packs as a means to insure the inculcation of group spirit, and the development through physical education of healthy bodies to bear sturdy and patriotic sons for the Spartan military state.

Methods

Education in Sparta was by training rather than by school instruction. Learning was fostered through participation in activities led by older boys, with worthy citizens acting as mentors and examples. There was nothing bookish about education; it was based wholly on activity. Periodic testing was administered, not to examine the boy's memory, but to test his moral sense and the physical capacities necessary for enduring the hardship and the strain of war.

Discipline was most severe and even cruel. Corporal punishment was utilized for moral delinquencies, inattention, and lack of alertness. Any adult citizen was expected to correct any boy caught violating a rule of proper conduct; fear of public disapproval was used as a strong motivating influence. Emulation and rivalry serve as means of stimulating learning and proficiency. Thus Plutarch, considering the goals and standards of the

---

[13] It has been suggested that Plato borrowed much from the Spartan system in the creation of *The Republic*.

Spartan people, can rightly and truthfully praise both their civic spirit and the means of its inculcation.

THE EARLY ATHENIAN ATTITUDE TOWARD EDUCATION

During the Homeric Age the Ionian, or eastern, Greeks unsophisticatedly pursued farming, vinoculture, and herding, without manufactures, commerce, or even coins. By the eighth century B.C., however (the first Olympiad was held in 776), a change began to take place. In Attica especially, industry and commerce came into fashion and tribal customs such as barter gave way to a money economy. These innovations brought about an economic, social, and political revolution; the Athenians, whose city was the capital of the Attic city-state, were enmeshed in perplexing difficulties when a respected citizen, Solon, was summoned to bring order out of the new chaos.

Solon (639–559 B.C.), like Lycurgus in Sparta, one of the great law-givers of all time, belonged to one of the noble families of Athens, and because of his insight and judgment is accounted one of the Seven Sages. No mere theorist, Solon was a clear-headed, practical-minded, sober statesman. "Nothing to excess," one of his maxims, summons a view of his character and political principles. Instituting reform in the government of Athens, Solon made it a true democracy (by the standards of the ancient world, for Greek civilization was founded on a slave economy); he drew up a set of laws that answered most of the pressing fiscal, social, and political questions of the day and guided the life of Athens for several centuries. He encouraged learning and formulated the ideals upon which it was to be based. The prosperity of the Athenian state dated from the time of Solon, and early Athenian attitudes toward education sprang largely from his influence.

Aims

Except for the simplicity of its aim and the directness with which it was to be achieved, ancient Athenian education had little in common with that of Sparta. In Athens again, the ideal of individual excellence for public usefulness was stressed; but to the Athenians individual excellence meant a fully rounded development of mind and body, and public usefulness meant the ability to take an active part in the business of state in peace as well as war. Athens emphasized the man of wisdom far more than the man of action. While Spartans aimed at strength and endurance and often developed roughness of body and manner, Athenians sought beauty and grace of body, but also knowledge and things of the spirit. Knowledge or truth did not come easily; so much more then the importance of effort. Hesiod (c. 800 B.C.) had written:

Before the gates of *excellence*
    The high gods have placed sweat.
Long is the road thereto,
    And steep and rough at first.
But, with the summit won,
    Then there is ease—
Though grievously hard
    In the winning.[14]

The Athenians believed that the best prerequisite for citizenship was a many-sided development. They conceived of education as a protection for the state; but they believed that the best preparation for citizenship was development of the individual through participation in the religious, social, political, and military activities of the state, with a rigid public opinion upholding traditional ideals of morality. Reverence, patriotism, and temperance were upheld rather than mere intellectual cleverness. The whole purpose of early Athenian education was the development of virtue, to which knowledge was to provide an introduction. The Athenians aimed to develop all aspects of individual personality useful for public welfare; their sense of proportion was evident in their education as well as in all their other concerns. In opposition to Spartan totalitarianism, the government did not attempt to control the education of its youth completely; the stronger sense of Attic individuality left more power in the hands of parents.

Although the Athenians prided themselves on their individuality, they held a special responsibility to a higher power, as Demaratus' comment to Xerxes at the time of the great Persian invasion reveals, "They are free, but not free in everything. There is over them a Master called Law, whom they fear more than thy slaves fear thee."[15] A dread of *hubris* too restrained them.

Types

Civic training was the dominant type of training in early Athenian education, and all other types were subordinated to it. Physical training was carefully organized, but was for the purpose of developing grace and harmony rather than strength and brawn. Moral training emphasized the old virtues of the Homeric heroes and also the virtues essential to the service of the state. Intellectual training was of the type needed for the activities of the assembly and the market place. Music, poetry, and dancing were taught not as a means of pleasure and amusement, but as an ennobling influence on intellect and morals; as a means of developing personality and elevating the soul, of providing a type of good cultural training. The early Athenians believed that "in union with poetry, music leads the soul to virtue and impresses it with courage." This is an Apollonian ideal.

---

14 Herodotus, book vii.
15 Herodotus, book vii.

Domestic training and vocational training were neglected. Of the half-million people of Athens, 400,000 were slaves; and practically all the manual work, despised by the free citizens, was performed by these slaves. Formal education was, therefore, a class education, limited to male citizens, the girls as well as the slaves being excluded.

Content

The Athenian boy learned to read by the alphabet method, then was taught to write through the use of a wax tablet and stylus. He learned enough arithmetic to function in the market place. Selections from Homer, Hesiod, Solon, and Aesop (c. 560 B.C.) were recorded from dictation, memorized, and chanted. Music, produced on the lyre and flute, was taught as a supplemental art to poetry; and improvisation to accompany the chanting or singing of epics and ballads was encouraged.

Gymnastic drills, accompanied by games and sports, were greatly favored. Exercises and competitions were varied and entertaining with little importance attached to merely winning. Leaping, running, jumping, wrestling, throwing the javelin, hurling the discus, and pitching quoits comprised the standard activities, with special attention given to swimming. As the boy matured he acquired military skills and learned through observation and practice the civic virtues and everything else necessary for his role as a free citizen in a democratic state. In contrast to the countries with a religious educational pattern, Athens followed the general philosophy of Hellas, "for it was man and man's life that the Greeks strove to make better."[16]

Agencies

Education in Athens was supervised by the state, but was not compulsory. The boy's development was not neglected for other reasons. First, education was a matter of family pride, a tradition to be followed; and second, by law, if a father did not give his son proper training, the son was released from supporting the father in his old age. Since there was no genuine family life in Athens, the home as an educational agency was of slight account. Unlike in Homeric days, women in the home were so poorly educated that children were rather badly brought up and formed mischievous habits. Boys could learn little at home and usually were instructed in private schools. The small training acquired by girls was sometimes given by the mother, but usually by slave nursemaids. Women were not held in as high esteem in Athens as in Sparta. The only really educated and cultured women of Athens were the *heterae*, courtesans who participated in the social life and philosophic discussions of the symposia, or gatherings of the upper-class male intelligentsia.

---

[16] Bonnard, p. 17.

The boy's school teacher held a rather low social position for reasons that follow. When very young, the youth was placed under the care of a *paidagogos* (pedagogue) and remained under his charge for his basic education. Usually an aged and trustworthy slave, this pedagogue was valet, servant, guardian, counselor, moral censor, and, in the absence of home training, the boy's chief guide to right action. Often he had been chosen for this duty because he was not fitted for anything else—in such a case, an influence hardly sound! In his later training the youth came under the supervision of state officials, who acted, usually in better stead, as drill-masters and moral guardians.

When the Athenian boy's conventional schooling ceased, the most significant part of his education began: his participation in the activities of city life. All the Athenian institutions were highly educative. The young man could learn much at the assembly, where he heard skillful debaters and learned disputants; at the courts, where he saw the laws interpreted and exercised; at the theatre, where he listened to the great works of Aeschylus, Sophocles, Euripides, Aristophanes, and other dramatists of his age and participated vicariously in the history of his people or the travails of its seminal figures; at the Olympic and other Hellenic games, where he came into contact with much of the best Greek culture, particularly its accent on harmonious development of mind and body. In Athens and its port, Piraeus, he felt the throbbing life of a great city, itself a prime agency of education. Above all, the Athenian youth learned by living.

Organization

Contrary to Spartan usage, in Athens the father determined whether his infant was to live. Until he was seven the boy lived at home, usually under the care of slaves. Despite the lack of formal educational opportunities, his childhood was easy and congenial and perhaps aided in the development of personality and poise.

From the age of seven to sixteen the boy divided his time between two schools, which he attended accompanied by his slave attendant, the pedagogue. In the *didascaleum* (music school) he learned reading, writing, arithmetic, poetry, and music. In the *palaestra* he engaged in gymnastic exercises, sports, and games. It is difficult to determine whether the boy went to the music school for the first few years and then entered the *palaestra* or spent part of each day in each school. The latter is more probable.

From the age of sixteen to eighteen the youth was freed from all literary and musical studies but continued in the public gymnasium the physical education begun in the *palaestra*. Here he associated freely with other youths and older men. He was trained in exercises, mostly athletic and military, by a state drillmaster, the *paidotribe*, and was under the supervision of a state moral censor, the *sophronist*. The censorship of his morals was quite strict in this early period of Athenian history, and the exercises and drills were more severe and rigorous than in the *palaestra*.

Having completed these two years of preliminary training, and having demonstrated to the state officials that he was physically and morally qualified for citizenship, he took the following pledge of allegiance to the state, known as the Ephebic Oath:

> I will not bring reproach upon our sacred arms, nor desert the comrade at my side, whoever he may be. For our sanctuaries and laws I will fight, alone or with others. My country I will leave, not in a worse, but in a better condition. I will at all times submit willingly to the judges and established ordinance, and will not consent that others infringe or disobey them. I will honor the established religious worship. The gods be my witness.

As an *ephebos* (a youth from the age of eighteen to twenty), the young man spent the next two years in military service. He was placed on guard at the frontier posts where he was subjected to the severest military discipline. At the age of twenty he was given the privileges of full citizenship, assumed definite duties in the assembly and on the juries, and entered fully into the pleasant and agreeable life of the city. He spent most of his time in public and in the open and was seldom at home. His female intellectual companionship was largely the brilliant *heterae* of whom we have already spoken.

Methods

The Athenian youth learned much by imitation and through the example of the living model. He imitated his master in learning to write, and his musical and physical training was largely a matter of imitating his teachers. As in Sparta, the method was one of training rather than instruction. Parts of his readings were memorized, but great emphasis was not placed upon this type of exercise. Most of his education came from participation in the activities of life.

Discipline was unusually severe. Corporal punishment was used extensively, even by the *paidagogos*. Although classes were small, there was little bond of affection between teacher and pupil. Human relationships in the early Athenian state were sacrificed to the idea that the school was "to bring up the child in the way he should go."

Plato pictures such a regimen:

> Education and admonition commence in the first years of childhood, and last to the very end of life. Mother and nurse and father and tutor are vying with one another about the improvement of the child as soon as he is able to understand what is being said to him: he cannot say or do anything without their setting forth to him that this is just and that is unjust; this is honourable, that is dishonourable; this is holy, that is

unholy; do this and abstain from that. And if he obeys, well and good; if not, he is straightened by threats and blows, like a piece of bent or warped wood.[17]

And Plato also gives what he considers the true definition of education and its philosophical origin: "Education is the constraining and directing of youth towards that right reason, which the law affirms, and which the experience of the eldest and the best has agreed to be truly right."[18] We shall return to this in the next section.

THE POSITION OF EDUCATION IN THE EMPIRE

About 500 B.C. the expansion of Persia, then the predominant Asiatic power, caused a conflict which lasted until 479 B.C., with the city-states of Greece. In this struggle Athens, which had led the loosely organized Hellenes, became an empire, a development that produced momentous change in Athenian life and educational attitudes.

Victory in that great war, the world war of its day, wrought many serious changes in the political, economic, and social life of the Athenian state and brought new ideas to bear on the content and method of instruction. As Athens had been a chief factor in the defeat of the Persians, she now became a center of Greek life as head of the Delian Confederation. Next, as imperial mistress of the surrounding states and islands, the great city began to take on a more cosmopolitan character; interchange of thought with ministers of state, traders, travelers, and other foreigners developed wider Athenian interests and a more diversified social and political life. The Greek community had grown extravagantly, and to many the older ideas seemed out of place.

These new and broader world contacts induced discontent, criticism, modification, and sometimes abandonment of older traditions and standards, seemingly sacred to an earlier Athens. The expanded activity of the trading and commercial class brought prosperity and the possibility of individual wealth hitherto undreamed of. This abundance led to the creation of an affluent society, with infinite opportunity for the pursuit of pleasure or the patronage of the arts. Greatness came to be measured by wealth and power, no longer by birth or service to the state. Political skill was no longer limited to the agora, acropolis, or assembly, but could be exercised in the larger realms of world diplomacy and imperial statesmanship. Athenian citizenship was opened to all free inhabitants, and new opportunities for personal advantage developed on every hand for the

---

[17] Benjamin Jowett (Trans.), *The Portable Plato*, ed. by Scott Buchanan (New York: The Viking Press, Inc., 1948), p. 67.

[18] Jowett, p. 659.

ambitious young men of the city. That this new dispensation removed general civic accountability and the other restraints on personal prerogative was little doubted by those who stood to profit by the new state of affairs.

Aims

With the old ideal of devotion to the public good losing its appeal, with the frequent rejection of religious and moral sanctions, and with the increasingly incessant desire for fame, fortune, and personal fulfillment, new demands were made on education. The goal for education in this new era was to prepare the individual for personal advancement through the utilization of powers of persuasion and the analysis of the new demands for success in a cosmopolitan setting. The aim of Athens' young man became the cultivation of his public image, individual excellence for individual conquest. The older objective of social service and public usefulness regardless of personal cost changed to that of selfish and rugged individualism. Youth in Athens wanted a training that would remove the hampering restrictions of the "archaic" standards of life; and would produce adeptness in the skills most useful for their personal advancement and political preferment.

Such new pragmatic demands were satisfied by the Sophists, a new group of mentors from the colonies. These revolutionary teachers brought with them—they maintained—a new type of education, adapted to the changed conditions in Athens and Hellas. They set up a new sanction for human conduct to replace the ancient external authorities of tradition—family, caste, gods, and state. Their new authority was based, they said, on the individual himself.

Protagoras (481–411 B.C.), one of the most upright Sophists, expressed the idea, "Man is the measure of all things." All knowledge comes through the senses; there are no universal principles of truth; each individual must determine for himself what should be his attitudes and conduct toward his associates, society, and state. Furthermore, as teachers of what they called practical wisdom, the Sophists aimed to prepare their students for an active and economically successful life, and especially for preferment in the realm of political and public affairs. Their philosophy was made to order for the new conditions in Athens.

The educational standards and practices of such teachers were deplored by the elder and more conservative members of the Attic community, who faithfully endeavored to stem the tide of eclectic individualism, which they were convinced was speeding Athens to her ruin, and to return the youth to the old ideal of unselfish service. Prominent leaders of the conservatives were Aristophanes (448–380 B.C.), who, through his comedies, The Clouds, and Frogs, ridiculed the Sophist idea of education; and Xenophon (434–355 B.C.), who had served as a soldier in Persia, and called attention to the Persian and Spartan dedication to their states in his

Cyropedia. But it was too late to reverse the utilitarian current; new conditions made new demands, and Athens could not turn back to the good old days. Aristophanes' parody in *The Clouds* ran:

But if you pursue what nowadays men do
You'll have—to begin with—a cold, pallid skin,
Arms small and chest weak, tongue practised to speak,
Special laws very long—the symptoms are strong—
Will show that your life is licentious and wrong!

Within this troubled period three great educational philosophers, Socrates (469–399 B.C.), Plato (428–348 B.C.), and Aristotle (386–322 B.C.) sought a solution for the ever-recurring problem of individualism and social stability. While these mediators realized that some of the older educational aims were inadequate for the rapidly changing conditions of Athens, they were equally positive that the self-serving individualism of the Sophists would not suffice as a suitable basis for either morality or education. Thus each demanded more enduring sanctions than individual self-satisfaction for uprightness, and broader and more eminent objectives for education.

Socrates found an answer by upholding a morality based upon knowledge. He believed that knowledge brings virtue, which is truth, and truth was Socrates' ultimate objective. Rejecting the Sophist position that the individual is the measure of all things and that truth is relative, he asserted the existence of universal concepts such as goodness, piety, temperance, and justice upon which all men could agree. Indeed, he stated, the reason for their agreement was that the elements of these concepts exist in the consciousness of every man and can be grasped and understood by clear and rigorous thought.

The knowledge and application of these concepts in the lives of men is virtue, and the production of virtue is the true goal of education. Thus Socrates' teaching aimed to develop the power of thinking, to enable humanity to arrive at the fundamental concepts, or moral principles, of the universe. He declared that "the unexamined life is not worth living." His maxim was "Know thyself."

Even the Athenians were not yet ready for a teaching so profound. Charged with corrupting the youth of the city, Socrates was condemned to death and, loyal to the laws of his country, drank the fatal hemlock. Plato in the *Phaedo* writes movingly of his passion and death.

But Plato, Socrates' most famous pupil, insisted that the type of knowledge demanded by his master could be had only by men of high intellectual capacity, whom he called philosophers, that is, lovers of wisdom. He maintained that this knowledge consisted of abstract ideas of universal validity, supersensual *forms*, after which all earthly existences are patterned. Not all men could grasp these abstractions; only philosophers could see behind the visible manifestation and attain the reality. Plato's ability to use vivid imagery as well as to strike a moral concerning reality and education is well illustrated by the allegory of the cave described in his chief educational work, *The Republic.*

> Behold! human beings living in an underground den, which has a mouth open towards the light and reaching all along the den; here they have been from their childhood, and have their legs and necks chained so that they cannot move, and can only see before them, being prevented by the chains from turning round their heads. Above and behind them a fire is blazing at a distance, and between the fire and the prisoners there is a raised way; and you will see, if you look, a low wall built along the way, like the screen which marionette players have in front of them, over which they show the puppets. . . . And do you see, I said, men passing along the wall carrying all sorts of vessels, and statues and figures of animals made of wood and stone and various materials, which appear over the wall?
>
> You have shown me a strange image, and they are strange prisoners.
>
> Like ourselves, I replied; they see only their own shadows, or the shadows of one another, which the fire throws on the opposite wall of the cave. . . .[19]

Plato's social system, also presented in the same volume, would be controlled by an intellectual ruling class, each individual being educated for the place in society and the kind of work for which by nature he was best suited. Plato believed that mankind possessed three dominant traits: intellect, passion, and appetite; and he would divide society into corresponding classes of rulers, soldiers, and workers, a man's place in this classification depending upon which trait was predominant in his personality. According to Plato, the aim of education is both the happiness of the individual and the good of the state; and the business of education is to achieve these ends by a determination of the social office for which each individual is fitted, by a process of selection, sifting, and testing. Plato's goal was justice.[20]

Aristotle, a pupil of Plato, declared that the purpose of education was to produce rational living. He wanted an educational system that would enable the individual, in association with others, to guide his conduct by reason. The highest function of man is to be rational in thought and

---

[19] Benjamin Jowett (Trans.), book vii, *The Republic* (Cleveland: World Publishing Company, 1946), p. 249. Plato owes a considerable debt to Pythagoras (582–500 B.C.) and his school. The Pythagoreans espoused a social order in which men were not necessarily equal, but enjoyed rights according to their merits. See Francis M. Cornford, *From Religion to Philosophy* (New York: Harper & Row, Publishers, 1957), pp. 200ff.

[20] For an interpretation of some of the superior meanings of Plato see J. A. Stewart, *The Myths of Plato* (London: Macmillan & Co., Ltd., 1905); Paul Shorey, *The Unity of Plato's Thought* (Chicago: University of Chicago Press, 1960); Adam Fox, *Plato and the Christians* (London: SCM Press, Ltd., 1957).

THE POSITION OF EDUCATION IN THE EMPIRE

conduct; the highest function of the state is to direct society in the way which effects the greatest good of mankind. Well-being and well-doing, on the basis of sound reasoning, constitute true virtue and the ultimate goal of all education. These educational ideas Aristotle set forth for the most part in his *Ethics* and *Politics.*

Aristotle's greatest goal was happiness, although this was to be reached only through the best relationship of the individual to his state and to himself. The golden mean, a realization of moderation in all things, was one of his most important concepts.

These great Greek educational thinkers, though they have had a lasting influence on the thought life of the world, had little effect upon the educational practices of their own times. Their insistence upon sanctions transcending individualism could not stem the currents of selfishness that were in a day of plebeian democracy vitiating the life of Athens. The people as a whole, though superficially acquainted with their teachings, were little influenced by them; while most of the enlightened and educated class were already thoroughly corrupted. The rascality and moral worthlessness of the so-called better class proved a greater misfortune to Athens than all its military defeats. The lack of ethical standards developed by this individualistic education ultimately brought the Athenians to ruin. The philosophers could not undo the damage done by the ambitious schemes and gross mismanagement of the politicians and the popularly controlled generals.

Types

All the educational leaders and theorists during this period were concerned with the problem of moral training. The Sophists discussed moral questions and settled them, not from a religious, social, or civic point of view, but from the standpoint of a pragmatic and utilitarian philosophy. The basis of their morality was so individualistic and rationalistic that to the conservative Greeks they seemed to be teaching immorality. Their ideas of morality placed an unprecedented emphasis upon individual choice. They taught that the individual was to determine his own ends in life, his own standards of conduct, his adjustment to group customs, and his personal service to the state.

Greatly distrustful of such individualistic solutions, Socrates, Plato, and Aristotle in turn strove to grapple with the problem of morality, which they rightly considered as the focus of the educational differences that had arisen. Was morality merely convenience? Were moral standards simply relative? Although their definitions varied, each advocated educating for virtue and goodness. Socrates urged training that would bring about the perfect life through the dispelling of error and the discovery of truth. Plato said, "Education is nurture. It can determine whether a nature should be wild and malevolent, or rich with benefits to mankind." Plato considered most essential the development of character, a disposition toward what he called the good. Aristotle believed that "the end of life, and therefore of education, is the attainment at once of intelligence and moral virtue, which bring with them the truest pleasure of which man is capable." This indeed was his idea of what constitutes true happiness, a golden mean, lacking in excess and balancing both phases of man's existence, the intellectual and personal development.

Clearly the intellectual activity of this period was of a higher type than any we have encountered so far. Although the Sophists' thought was frequently superficial, it represented an increased cleverness in attempting to meet the practical problems of life in a changing era as well as a call for increased discrimination between words. The mental vigor of an entire people was encouraged and their intellectual horizons expanded.

Unlike the Sophists, Socrates was attempting to stimulate the interior man, considering the life of the mind of the greatest consequence; he urged the cultivation of a thorough and deep intellectual discipline, and developed a type of education unsurpassed in its effectiveness. Although Plato preferred to limit intellectual training to those with natural aptitudes, he set forth a thorough procedure for this. Aristotle advocated training reason through the study of science and philosophy; he developed in his *Organon* the deductive method of reasoning, and in his *Logic* was the first to set forth a vocabulary of logic. Indeed, the activities of these three great Greeks appear all the more spectacular when contrasted with the low level of politics that followed the collapse of Athens' hegemony in the Aegean. And, in a practical sense, these philosophers' achievements confirm the supremacy of the mental over the physical world. Hamilton sums up the necessity for the intellectual life as follows: "All things are to be examined and called into question. There are no limits set to thought."[21]

Professional vocational education was now added to the older vocational training in handicrafts and manual labor. The Sophists strove increasingly to instruct in the arts of public speaking, at a time when the power to speak convincingly and persuasively was the key to positions of profit and personal advantage. Plato urged several species of vocational training, but only for craftsmen and laborers.

The emphasis upon physical, military, and civic training as a preparation for state service was lessened in actual educational practice, although the philosophers all urged these types of education as agencies for the attainment of their ideals. Domestic training for women continued to be neglected, although Xenophon advocated a system of education for girls in which for the first time a regular course of instruction in the household arts was provided. Plato recommended all types of education for women, as for men, including intellectual education and even training for the army.

Esthetic, or cultural, education during this period made much prog-

---

[21] Hamilton, p. 25. See also Aristotle, *On Man and the Universe*, ed. by Louise Ropes Loomis (New York: Walter J. Black, 1943), pp. 5–27.

ress. Literature was studied not only from the grammatical and rhetorical standpoint but also for pleasure. More leisure created a demand for esthetic enjoyment; and art, music, literature, and sports were looked upon as satisfactions of this need. This concept of education for personal enjoyment encouraged the development of new instruments and forms in music, a widening of the range of literary forms, and the utilization of sports and games for amusement and pleasure. The philosophers generally deplored the use of the arts for esthetic enjoyment and tried to elevate them again to their former place as agencies for moral education, but with little success.

Content

The content of elementary education remained generally the same as during the earlier period. Reading, writing, arithmetic, chanting of poetry, and gymnastic exercises were the basic studies of the curriculum, but with certain changes in emphasis and approach. At the higher levels, however, physical and military exercises gave way to literary and intellectual subjects. The Sophists introduced grammar, rhetoric, declamation, and argumentation, together with the study of human nature and practical rules of conduct. The core of the whole Sophist curriculum was the art of public speaking.

With the development of secondary and higher schools to take the place of the physical training and military drill of the earlier period, geometry, astronomy, drawing, grammar, and rhetoric came to be taught at the secondary level, and philosophy, mathematics, and science at the higher levels.

Socrates apparently did not believe in formal content. He himself did little, if any, reading. He believed in gaining knowledge through direct contact with people and personal observation and experience. He felt that in such ways knowledge revealed itself through the soul. Socrates thus put the emphasis upon the essential content of learning and had little interest in the forms and tools, such as the rules of grammar and rhetoric or the skills of speaking and writing.

Plato advocated, for the lower stages of training, the traditional Athenian content of reading, writing, chanting of poetry, gymnastics, and military training. For the more advanced level, he recommended four subjects which later came to be called the Quadrivium—arithmetic, astronomy, geometry, and music. For the highest stage, he advocated the study of philosophy. He held strong views concerning the importance of the study of arithmetic to liberate the slothful and to produce something intellectual. For, Plato says, "Arithmetic stirs up him who is by nature sleepy and dull, and makes him quick to learn, retentive, shrewd, and aided by art divine, he makes progress quite beyond his natural powers."[22]

---

[22] Jowett (Trans.), *Portable Plato*, p. 747.

Aristotle favored for the lower level the formation of physical and moral habits. For the secondary stages he recommended the training of the emotions through gymnastics, music, and drawing. For what would now be considered the college plane he advocated civic training and the development of reason through mathematics, logic, and the sciences. Aristotle was a prolific writer on a wide variety of subjects, especially scientific and philosophical. He sought the truth everywhere, both in the world of nature and in the world of man.

Although considered the father of deductive thought, Aristotle's use of the inductive method of discovering truth made him one of the greatest thinkers that has ever lived; he laid the foundations of logic, physics, physiology, and politics and contributed much to the curriculum of later education.

Agencies

The *palaestra* and music school continued as the agencies of primary education in the later Athenian period, but underwent certain changes in emphases and standards. In these private schools, taught by private teachers, known as grammatists in this period, emphasis was now placed upon formal literary exercises and hair-splitting discussions. New musical instruments and forms of music were introduced to give more subjective pleasurable effects. The severity of physical training was relaxed, and exercise was made esthetic.

However, it was in the agencies for higher education that the most striking changes took place. The period from the age of sixteen on, which in older Athenian education had been devoted to physical, military, and indirect political training, was now given over purely to literary and intellectual training. At first the Sophists organized no formal schools, but held informal meetings between the teacher and those who paid to hear him. Thus in private rooms, on the streets, or in the gymnasia and surrounding groves, the Sophist collected his body of adherents and gave the instruction desired.

The Sophists were well traveled and clever, and through wide contacts and careful observation of commercial, social, and political life in various parts of the world, had picked up the practical wisdom that they taught. They were non-Athenians who had been drawn to the metropolis by the opportunities to teach for high fees, and they attracted great numbers of students.

Socrates, Plato, and Aristotle taught in much the same informal manner, although they were inclined to frequent certain places more than others. Because of the fact that Plato usually taught in the grove known as the Academy, the school of philosophy later organized by his followers came to be known as the School of the Academy. Likewise, because Aristotle frequented the Lyceum, the school that developed from his teaching came to be known as the School of the Lyceum. Similar philosophical schools were developed by Zeno (336–264 B.C.), the Stoic, and Epicurus (342–270 B.C.), founder of the Epicurean school of philosophy.

Among the Sophists, Protagoras—alluded to earlier—and Gorgias (485–380 B.C.) appear to have been the most important, although Isocrates (436–338 B.C.), Prodicus, and Hippias should be mentioned also. Protagoras was a skillful teacher and is said to have received as much as 10,000 drachmas tuition for one of his courses, a fee that Plato and Aristotle viewed with horror.[23] The son of a wealthy flute manufacturer, Isocrates received an excellent education under Gorgias and Socrates, but was never a member of Socrates' select circle. Having lost his fortune as a result of the wars between Athens and Sparta, in 392 B.C. he opened a school of rhetoric, which continued successfully until his death. (The defeat of Hellas by Philip of Macedon at Chaeronea occurred in the same year.) Isocrates was famous for his *Panegyricus,* an oration extolling Hellenic unity. But, his ideas were apparently not strong enough to persuade the Greeks to present a united front against Philip of Macedon.

Thus the educational urges introduced by the new developments in Athens ultimately developed two agencies for higher education in the Mediterranean area. One stream flowed through Socrates and eventuated in the establishment of institutions known as philosophical schools; the other proceeded through Isocrates and resulted in institutions called rhetorical schools. After a few years these two bodies more or less fused, and to the organization thus formed some modern writers have given the term *University of Athens,* although at that time the word *university* certainly was not used. A similar development at Alexandria after the Macedonian conquest of Egypt gave rise to the University of Alexandria, which also became a great center of learning for hundreds of years.

Organization

Later Athenian education came to be organized into four levels: (1) home education, usually under slaves, from birth until the age of seven; (2) primary education, in private schools, from the age of seven to the age of thirteen; (3) secondary education, in private schools, from thirteen to sixteen; (4) higher education, in the rhetorical and philosophical schools, from the age of sixteen onward.

Plato advocated distinct changes in this organization.[24] He wanted a rigid system of state-controlled public education, with the slave popula-

---

[23] See Plato's parody on the Sophists through his portrayal of Thrasythmachus in book i of *The Republic.* Eric Voegelin, *Order and History,* vol. ii, *The World of the Polis,* devotes chap. 11, pp. 267–331, to a discussion of Sophistic relativity versus Platonic ethics.

[24] See book vii of *The Republic.* Plato has not always been approved. For a contrary viewpoint see Joseph K. Hart, *A Social Interpretation of Education* (New York: Holt, Rinehart and Winston, Inc., 1929), pp. 77–92. Robert Holmes Beck, *A Social History of Education* (Englewood Cliffs, N.J.: Prentice-Hall, Inc., 1965), pp. 11–16, finds much to laud in Sophistic viewpoints and even identifies Socrates as a Sophist.

tion excluded from all educational opportunities, but with women educated the same as men. The home was to be abolished, and children were to be considered the property of the state. He proposed the following divisions in the school organization: (1) from birth to ten years of age, primary education in play, exercise, games, and tales; (2) from ten to twenty years of age, secondary education in music, gymnastics, and military skill; (3) from twenty to thirty years of age, higher education in mathematics, astronomy, dialectic, and philosophy. At the age of ten those best fitted for artisans were to be eliminated; at the age of twenty those best fitted for soldiers were withdrawn; and only those fitted for ruling the others were to receive higher education. This was to continue, with periods of practical application, until the candidate reached the age of fifty. It was only then that Plato considered him a philosopher-king and ready to rule.

Aristotle suggested an organization in which home and state should each play a part. From birth to seven, the home should train in good physical and moral habits; he condemned the usual practice of relegating the child to the care of ignorant slaves. From seven to puberty, he advocated training the emotions; and from puberty to twenty-one, he prescribed a training in civic virtues and in reasoning. Both Plato and Aristotle believed that for the most intelligent few there should be a still higher education preparing for a life higher than that of civic participation: a life of study and contemplation.

Methods

The methods of the elementary schools continued very much as in the earlier period. The Sophists, however, introduced into higher education the lecture, a method most likely to develop the habit of ready acceptance rather than of individual thinking. Their discipline consisted of acquiring information and of memorizing set speeches on a variety of topics; and, even with the best of the Sophists, mere form—pretentious argument, and word quibbling—frequently played an important part. The lecture method continued as the prevailing method in the philosophical and rhetorical schools. In general, education tended to emphasize bookish and schoolroom tactics, in which rote learning or memorization was superseding the activities of the earlier period.

The greatest contribution toward the development of a theory of method was made by Socrates. Although he himself used it continuously and with great success, the method was little followed by those of his own time and is just now beginning to find wide acceptance.

As a teacher, Socrates was critical, skeptical, patient, sympathetic, and good-natured. His method was to get the pupils to think for themselves and to see things as they really are. He believed the spirit of the learner was the one thing the teacher should produce in the pupil. The teacher's function was merely that of stimulating the mental activity of the pupil, by giving suggestions and guidance. The aim of his Socratic method was to bring the pupil to the place where he would be able to see his own ignorance and acquire the attitude of the true learner. He thus applied what has come to be one of the fundamental principles of modern teaching method.

The Socratic method was designed primarily to force an individual to think in logical and rational patterns in order to arrive at the truth. When applied to the study of science, for example, the method forced the student into an either/or position: he either arrived at an absolute truth or negated his efforts entirely. So the individual might be taught to think out and solve the problems of everyday life. Happiness, or the ultimate good, could only be achieved, in the Platonic sense, by exercising the individual's mind to its ultimate capabilities.

This conversation or question method is sometimes called the dialectic method; and as developed by Socrates it has two stages: (1) the ironic,[25] or destructive, in which by interrogation the pupil is brought from unconscious ignorance to conscious ignorance; (2) the maieutic,[26] or constructive, in which by further questioning the pupil is led from conscious ignorance to clear and rational truth. Socrates called the teacher the gadfly of thought and the intellectual midwife. If only the method of Socrates had been followed by many more of the teachers who followed him!

Of course, in education, method alone is insufficient; it is not a panacea for all ills. Socrates has sometimes been accused of emphasizing method without enough attention to content and some claim that he overdeveloped mere discussion. In a way, he laid the foundations for the later development of the disciplinary concept of education. In spite of these few shortcomings, the method of the Socratic dialogue has never been surpassed as a thought-stimulating device, although the use of the parable by Jesus Christ is a similarly effective teaching method.

But in the study of Greece we are concerned with much more than the development of a teaching method, epochal though the Socratic device was. André Bonnard has written: "Ancient Greece is a living paradox which illustrates the astonishing concept of civilization and the immense difficulty primitive man had in wrenching himself out of a blind animality *in order to contemplate the world as a man.*"[27]

REFERENCES

Barnes, Harry Elmer, *An Intellectual and Cultural History of the Western World*. New York: Random House, Inc., 1937. Pp. 117–193.

Barr, Stringfellow, *The Will of Zeus*. Philadelphia: J. B. Lippincott Company, 1961.

---

[25] Ironic, from the Greek *eiron*, a dissembler in speech.
[26] Ma-ieu'tic, from the Greek *maia*, a midwife.
[27] P. 11. Italics added.

Bonnard, André, *Greek Civilization*, 3 vols. Trans. by A. Lytton Sells. New York: Crowell-Collier and Macmillan, Inc., 1957.

Beck, F. A. G., *Greek Education, 450–350 B.C.* London: Methuen & Co., Ltd., 1964.

Boyd, William, *The History of Western Education*, 8th ed. Rev. by Edmund J. King. New York: Barnes & Noble, Inc., 1966. Pp. 3–42, 43–74.

Breasted, James Henry, *The Conquest of Civilization*. New York: Harper & Row, Publishers, 1926 and 1938. Pp. 237–481.

Brubacher, John S., *A History of the Problems of Education*. New York: McGraw-Hill, Inc., 1947. Pp. 23–30, 96–106.

Butts, R. Freeman, *A Cultural History of Western Education*. New York: McGraw-Hill, Inc., 1955. Pp. 19–71.

Carpenter, Rhys, *Discontinuity in Greek Civilization*. Cambridge, England: University Press, 1966. Pp. 1–80.

Clark, Donald L., *Rhetoric in Graeco-Roman Education*. New York: Columbia University Press, 1957.

Cole, Luella, *A History of Education*. New York: Holt, Rinehart and Winston, Inc., 1950. Pp. 8–42.

Dawson, Christopher, *The Age of the Gods*. New York: Sheed & Ward, Inc., 1933. Pp. 343–361.

———, *The Dynamics of World History*. New York: Sheed & Ward, Inc., 1957. Pp. 148–166.

Duggan, Stephen P., *A Student's Textbook in the History of Education*, rev. ed. New York: Appleton-Century-Crofts, 1936. Pp. 15–50.

Durant, Will, *The Life of Greece*. New York: Simon and Schuster, Inc., 1939. Pp. 37–671.

Eby, Frederick, and Charles F. Arrowood, *The History and Philosophy of Education, Ancient and Medieval*. Englewood Cliffs, N.J.: Prentice-Hall, Inc., 1940. Pp. 160–514.

Freeman, Kenneth J., *Schools of Hellas*. London: Macmillan & Co., Ltd., 1908 and 1912.

Good, H. G., *A History of Western Education*. New York: Crowell-Collier and Macmillan, Inc., 1960. Pp. 18–41.

Hamilton, Edith, *The Greek Way*. New York: W. W. Norton & Company, Inc., 1942.

Harrison, Jane, *Prolegomena to the Study of the Greek Religion*. New York: Meridian Books, Inc., 1955. Pp. 322–477.

Hart, Joseph K., *Creative Moments in Education*. New York: Holt, Rinehart and Winston, Inc., 1931. Pp. 27–85.

———, *A Social Interpretation of Education*. New York: Holt, Rinehart and Winston, Inc., 1929. Pp. 77–92, 97, 108ff.

Jaeger, Werner, *Paideia: The Ideals of Greek Culture*, 3 vols. Trans. by Gilbert Highet. New York: Oxford University Press, 1939, 1943, 1944.

Knight, Edgar W., *Twenty Centuries of Education*. Boston: Ginn & Company, 1940. Pp. 46–71.

Kubly, Herbert, *Gods and Heroes*. New York: Doubleday & Company, Inc., 1969.

Marrou, Henri Irenée, *A History of Education in Antiquity*. Trans. by George Lamb. London: Sheed & Ward, Ltd., 1956.

Mayer, Frederick, *A History of Educational Thought*. Columbus, Ohio: Charles E. Merrill Books, Inc., 1960. Pp. 81–101.

Messenger, James F., *An Interpretative History of Education*. New York: Thomas Y. Crowell Company, 1931. Pp. 29–46.

Mulhern, James, *A History of Education*, 2d ed. New York: The Ronald Press Company, 1959. Pp. 129–177.

Murray, Gilbert (Trans.), *The Persians*, by Aeschylus. London: George Allen & Unwin, Ltd., 1960. Especially pp. 67–70.

Myers, Edward D., *Education in the Perspective of History*. New York: Harper & Row, Publishers, 1960. Pp. 71–106.

Nakosteen, Mehdi, *The History and Philosophy of Education*. New York: The Ronald Press Company, 1965. Pp. 71–90, 91–107.

Nash, Paul, *Models of Man*. New York. John Wiley & Sons, Inc., 1968.

Power, Edward J., *Main Currents in the History of Education*. New York: McGraw-Hill, Inc., 1962. Pp. 30–128.

Reisner, Edward H., *Historical Foundations of Modern Education*. New York: Crowell-Collier and Macmillan, Inc., 1927. Pp. 1–104.

Selincourt, Aubrey de, *The World of Herodotus*. Boston: Little, Brown & Company, 1962. Especially pp. 351–368.

Shorey, Paul, *The Unity of Plato's Thought*. Chicago: University of Chicago Press, 1960.

Smith, William A., *Ancient Education*. New York: Philosophical Library, Inc., 1955. Pp. 88–149.

Starr, Chester G., *A History of the Ancient World*. New York: Oxford University Press, 1965. Pp. 185–393; 413–434.

Thut, N., *The Story of Education*. New York: McGraw-Hill, Inc., 1957. Pp. 41–73.

Ulich, Robert, *History of Educational Thought*. New York: American Book Company, 1950. Pp. 1–43.

———— (Ed.), *Three Thousand Years of Educational Wisdom*, 2d ed., enl. Cambridge, Mass.: Harvard University Press, 1954. Pp. 31–89.

Voegelin, Eric, *The World of the Polis*. Baton Rouge, La.: Louisiana State University Press, 1957.

SELECTED PAPERBACKS

Beck, Robert Holmes, *A Social History of Education*. Englewood Cliffs, N.J.: Prentice-Hall, Inc., 1965.

Bowra, C. M., *The Greek Experience*. New York: New American Library of World Literature, Inc., 1959.

Breasted, James Henry, *Ancient Times*, vol. i, 2d ed., *The Greeks*. Boston: Ginn & Company, 1966. Pp. 284–810.

Bullfinch, *Mythology.* Arranged by Edmund Fuller. New York: Dell Publishing Co., Inc., 1959.

Burns, A. R., *The Lyric Age of Greece.* New York: Minerva, 1960.

Castle, E. B., *Ancient Education and Today.* Baltimore: Penguin Books, Inc., 1961.

Chiappe, Andrew, *Five Comedies of Aristophanes.* New York: Columbia University Press, 1957.

Corrigan, Robert W. (Ed.), *Greek Comedy.* New York: Dell Publishing Co., Inc., 1965.

Cottrell, Leonard, *The Anvil of Civilization.* New York: New American Library of World Literature, Inc., 1965.

Coulanges, Fustel de, *The Ancient City: A Classic Study of the Religious and Civil Institutions of Ancient Greece and Rome.* New York: Doubleday & Company, Inc., n.d.

Dickinson, G. Lowes, *The Greek View of Life.* New York: Crowell-Collier and Macmillan, Inc., Collier Books, 1961.

Dodds, E. R., *Greeks and the Irrational.* Boston: The Beacon Press, 1955.

Eckstein, Jerome, *The Platonic Method.* New York: Greenwood Publishing Corporation, 1968.

Finley, M. I., *The Ancient Greeks, Their Life and Thought.* New York: The Viking Press, Inc., 1964.

————, *The Greek Historians, Herodotus, Thucydides, Xenophon, Polybius.* New York: The Viking Press, Inc., 1959.

Graves, Robert, *Greek Gods and Heroes.* New York: Dell Publishing Co., Inc., 1960.

————, *The Siege and Fall of Troy.* New York: Dell Publishing Co., Inc., 1960.

Gutherie, W. C. C., *The Greek Philosophers.* New York: Harper & Row, Publishers, 1960.

Hamilton, Edith, *The Greek Way.* New York: W. W. Norton & Company, Inc., 1942; New York: New American Library of World Literature, Inc., 1948.

————, *Mythology.* New York: New American Library of World Literature, Inc., 1942.

————, *The Ever Present Past.* New York: W. W. Norton & Company, Inc., 1964.

Harden, Donald, *The Phoenicians.* New York: Frederick A. Praeger, Inc., 1962.

Hollister, C. Warren, *Roots of the Western Tradition.* New York: John Wiley & Sons, Inc., 1966.

Huntington, Ellsworth, *The Mainsprings of Civilization.* New York: New American Library of World Literature, Inc., 1959.

Hutchinson, R. W., *Prehistoric Crete.* Baltimore: Penguin Books, Inc., Pelican Books, 1968.

Jones, Tom B., *From the Tigris to the Tiber.* Homewood, Ill.: The Dorsey Press, Inc., 1969. Pp. 87–149, 151–180.

Kaplan, J. D. (Ed.), *The Dialogues of Plato.* New York: Pocket Books, Inc., 1955.

Kitto, H. D. F., *The Greeks*. Baltimore: Penguin Books, Inc., Pelican Books, 1965.

McEvedy, Colin, *Penguin Atlas of Ancient History*. Baltimore: Penguin Books, Inc., 1967.

Marrou, Henri Irenée, *A History of Education in Antiquity*. Trans. by George Lamb. New York: New American Library of World Literature, Inc., 1964.

Mayer, Frederick, *Foundations of Education*. Columbus, Ohio: Charles E. Merrill Books, Inc., 1963.

Muller, Herbert J., *The Uses of the Past, Profiles of Former Societies*. New York: New American Library of World Literature, Inc., 1952. Pp. 112–157.

Murray, Gilbert (Trans.), *The Persians,* by Aeschylus. London: George Allen & Unwin, Ltd., 1939, 1948, 1960.

Plato, *Great Dialogues*. Trans. by W. H. D. Rouse. New York: New American Library of World Literature, Inc., 1956.

———, *The Republic*. Trans. by H. D. P. Lee. Baltimore: Penguin Books, Inc., 1955.

Plutarch, *Nine Greek Lives*. Baltimore: Penguin Books, Inc., 1955.

Robinson, C. E., *Hellas*. Boston: The Beacon Press, 1955.

Rose, H. J., *Gods and Heroes of the Greeks*. New York: Meridian Books, Inc., 1958.

Samburdky, S., *The Physical World of the Greeks*. New York: Crowell-Collier & Macmillan, Inc., Collier Books, 1962.

Toynbee, Arnold J., *Greek Civilization and Character*. New York: New American Library of World Literature, Inc., 1953.

———, *Greek Historical Thought*. New York: New American Library of World Literature, Inc., 1963.

Warner, Rex, *The Greek Philosophers*. New York: New American Library of World Literature, Inc., 1950.

CHAPTER 6

An Accent
on Utilitarianism

*The firm edifice of Roman power was raised and preserved by the wisdom
of the ages. The obedient provinces . . . were united by laws and adorned
by arts. They might occasionally suffer from the partial abuse of delegated authority; but the general principle of government was wise, simple,
and beneficient. They enjoyed the religion of their ancestors, whilst in
civil honours and advantages they were exalted, by just degrees, to an
equality with their conquerors.*[1]

THE ROMAN CHARACTERISTIC
AND ITS WORTH

Italy has been, throughout medieval and early modern history, the
heart of the spiritual and intellectual life of the Western world. Two circumstances contributed greatly to her success, her geographical location and
the character of the Roman people. When, as Gibbon said, "victorious
Rome was herself subdued by the arts of Greece," Roman practicality
moved forward to conquer the known world. Since the days of the later
Republic and the Empire, the dissemination of Christianity, and the
flowering of the Renaissance, her adopted art and unique culture have
influenced mankind deeply.[2]

But what was the fate of wonderfully artistic and literate Greece?
We already know that internal weakness and political strife had ended its
Golden Age, despite the struggle of its great philosophers to arrest the

---

[1] Edward Gibbon, *The Decline and Fall of the Roman Empire*. An Abridgement
by D. M. Low (New York: Harcourt, Brace & World, Inc., 1960).

[2] See R. H. Barrow, *The Romans* (Baltimore: Penguin Books, Inc., 1949), ch. i,
"What Manner of Men," pp. 9–26, for a remarkable description of the Roman
ethos. Edith Hamilton's *The Roman Way* (New York: W. W. Norton & Company,
Inc., 1932) delineates the literary mode and offers pertinent profiles of Roman
leaders under the empire. Robert Lopez, *The Birth of Europe* (New York: E. M. Evans
and Company, Inc., 1967), ch. i, "Traces of the Roman Experiment," pp. 7–24,
summarizes much and delineates more concerning the achievement and special entity
of Rome.

currents of disunion and disinterest in education with justice and civic virtue. With the continued development of Hellenistic philosophical and rhetorical schools and the erection of great centers of learning at Athens, Alexandria, Antioch, Pergamum, and Rhodes, education became less concerned with building of the ideal state or developing the citizens' public responsibility. Education as a leisure pursuit or merely for profit replaced the old pattern of education for service to the polity and one's fellows.

Greek education became theoretical and the scholars of its philosophical schools remained cloistered and aloof from the concerns of daily living. Where the Hellenic philosophers had sought practical ideals for expression in life, later leaders became interested chiefly in intellectual speculation for its own sake and in the rather arcane circulation of their theories among their close communicants.

Now there was need for a new force in education—an influence to return it to the realities of life as early Hellenes had regarded them. There was need for a new civic virtue and a stronger dedication to social actualities. Indeed, patriotism and love of country were needed to establish a firmer society. Hart says, "Athens is a 'point of light in history.' But the world needs more than light. It needs a solid foundation."[3]

This new substructure was to come from the fresh and vigorous civilization of Rome, which had been developing for the past several hundred years across the Ionian Sea on the peninsula of Italy. Founded according to legend in 753 B.C. (about the time of the first Olympic Games in Greece), this tiny city-state expanded until she finally dominated the entire Mediterranean, and Romans could truly speak of these waters (not to mention the strategic lands they washed) as "our sea," *mare nostrum.*

Yet Rome did not make many intellectual or esthetic contributions to modern civilization. The achievements of the Romans were in organization, management, and administration. They were a practical people who rendered their service to mankind by erecting the institutions whereby the aspirations of other peoples might be realized. While the Western value system has been taken largely from Greek and Hebrew sources, for the institutions of modern life we are indebted largely to the Romans. Rome judged all things by their usefulness; Romans were essentially a utilitarian people. The Greeks sought to live by reason, the Romans by authority. It would be easy to compare Sparta and Rome, yet as Barr says, "the Roman Republic was not a militaristic state. . . . To a large extent Rome was forced by time and place to learn war."[4] In many ways the culture of

---

[3] Joseph K. Hart, *Creative Moments in Education* (New York: Holt, Rinehart and Winston, Inc., 1931), p. 86.

[4] See Stringfellow Barr, *The Mask of Jove* (Philadelphia: J. B. Lippincott Company, 1966), ch. i, "The Roman Thing," pp. 3–37, for a general exposition of these diversities. Ugo Enrico Paoli's *Rome, Its Life and Culture* (New York: David McKay Company, Inc., 1963) is one of the most readable books on Rome.

ancient Rome might more properly be compared to that of Homeric Greece.

The Roman genius for organization showed itself particularly in war, politics, and religion, creating institutions effective enough to permit the achievement of a world empire greater than those of Persia and Alexander. The Romans took a downtrodden and persecuted sect and gave it the closely knit administration of the universal Roman Catholic Church. The Romans organized that body of civil law which even now serves as the basis of legal systems throughout most of the Occidental world.

That Roman talent for adaptation and application was far superior to its genius for originality is manifest in Latin contributions to art and literature, although certain literary contributions—those of Cicero, Catullus, Vergil, and Horace, for example—still influence literature. In the sciences, Rome's contribution was in the field of applications, through mechanics and engineering, rather than in theoretical, or pure, science. Pragmatically, she took the mathematics and logic of the Greek philosophers and applied them to the building of aqueducts, bridges, and roads, and to the development of agriculture. Similarly, in education, although Rome contributed little that was unique or original in the development of a rationale, she was able to provide an educational pattern which—from the standpoint of organization and effectiveness in carrying on the Roman tradition—served its purpose very well.

What were the influences that produced these Roman characteristics? What made it possible for Rome to make these peculiar contributions to civilization in general and to education in particular? What were the origins of this aggressive and virile nation?

GEOGRAPHY AND ANCIENT SETTLEMENT

The Italian peninsula was settled for the most part by three groups: (1) the Italians, (2) the Etruscans, and (3) the Greeks, who colonized Sicily and the south. The Italians were composed of various Indo-European tribes who had pushed their way from eastern and central Europe across the Alps, much as the Achaeans had entered Greece. The most important Italian tribes were the Sabellians, the Umbrians, and the Latins. Ultimately they also developed city-states, with Latium, the city-state of Rome, emerging as the most powerful and significant.

Who the Etruscans were, or from whence they came, is still disputed; but they were far in advance of the Italians in all that relates to security, development, and a high culture. They produced vases and sculpture, paved roads, dug canals, built massive citadels with towers and arched gateways. They had a vigorous religion and sacred laws; and the Italians, especially the Latins, must have learned much from this astonishingly advanced Etruscan culture.[5] But, as teachers of the Italians, these Etruscans were in the end outrivaled by the Grecian colonists who, about the middle of the eight century B.C., began to migrate to these Western lands.

From the intermingling of these peoples developed the strong energetic Romans. The Italian peninsula is much longer than it is wide, and in every direction were alien states from which enemies might easily come. Thus it was a logical development for the other city-states of Italy to unite under Rome, her strongest commonwealth. Even when conjoined, the Latin state remained unsafe as long as her neighbors remained militarily powerful; consequently the desire for self-preservation eventually forced Rome to adopt the imperial career that was to have significant and lasting effect on the world's history from that time.

The Apennines, extending throughout the length of the peninsula, slope to the eastern shore; and the country is thus closed to the east and open to the west. Turning its back upon the East, with its decaying politics, ancient Rome faced the fresh vital peoples of the West and found her chief interest in giving them her institutions. It is due to the influence of Rome that the vigorous peoples of central and western Europe developed into modern nations. There is abundant reason for looking upon the Romans as the last of the ancients and the first of the moderns. Geographical conditions, climate, and the self-sufficiency of the peninsula were so advantageous that it is not surprising Dionysius, a Greek writer on Roman history, should call Italy "the best and most favored country in the ancient world."

The history of Roman development covers many periods; but from the standpoint of educational attainment we shall divide the account into two sequences: (1) the early, or purely Latin, era, extending from the foundation of the city to the destruction of Carthage and Corinth with the annexation of the Greek city-states (146 B.C.); and (2) the cosmopolitan, or Greco-Roman, period, continuing from 146 B.C. to the suppression of the pagan schools by the Christian emperor Justinian in 529 A.D.[6]

---

[5] See Raymond Block, *The Etruscans* (New York: Frederick A. Praeger, Inc., 1958), for an interesting and informative account of the Etruscans' possible origins and their considerable achievements. David Trump's *Central and Southern Italy before Rome* (New York: Frederick A. Praeger, Inc., 1965) furnishes an even more extensive elaboration and introduces further background on the earlier peoples of the peninsula.

[6] Within this latter era occurred a remarkable period which is known in history as the "Roman peace." From the beginning of the reign of Augustus (27 B.C.) through that of Marcus Aurelius (d. 180 A.D.), with the exception of border skirmishes on its far-flung frontier, the empire remained at peace. "There was nothing on which the people of the empire prided themselves more than this universal peace—the *pax Romana* as they called it. The regions devastated by the wars of the republic were restored to prosperity, commerce and industry flourished on every hand, and wealth

THE EARLY ROMAN APPROACH TO EDUCATION

Tales of the founding of Rome are undoubtedly mixtures of fiction and fact. Of the many legends, the familiar myth of Romulus and Remus was the one that the Romans chose to accept, for they wished to connect their history with that of Greece, which already had an ancient prestige and from which the Romans eventually derived so much of their culture, including many of their gods and folk legends. Actually, no one knows by whom or under what circumstances Rome began as a city. Even the traditional date of Rome's founding, 753 B.C., is approximate.

In the beginning Rome consisted of a federation of clans, or *curia,* ruled by a war chief, the king; by a senate ("old men"), composed of heads of upper-class families; and by a popular assembly, the *comitia curiata,* which included all freemen who could bear arms. Commoners were known as plebeians, the multitude, and nobles were called patricians. In 509 B.C. the kings were exiled and power transferred to the aristocratic senate, a body in which the plebeians had no representation. This led to a prolonged struggle for recognition by the commoners and provided reform in the codification of the laws by the Decemviri, elected for that purpose, into ten fundamental statutes (451 B.C.). Later, two additional canons were established, and the basic laws became known as the Twelve Tables, engraved and displayed in the Roman forum. By these laws and other political reforms, plebeians gradually won further rights, and the Roman republic became a representative democracy.

What were the attitudes of the Romans toward education during this first period, that of the rule by kings and the origin of the republic?

Aims

The aim of early Roman education was to constrain the freedom of the individual in the interest of the state—to produce a nation of brave warriors and dutiful citizens. The Roman concept of the good life was quite different from that of the Greeks. In contrast to the subjectivity of the Greeks, the Roman was objective, striving for the accomplishment of some concrete purpose lying outside his own thought—some excellence or achievement of concrete and tangible worth to his fellows. Early Roman education was distinctly a training for practical life. Its aim was the development of the *vir bonus*—the good citizen, the good soldier, the good worker.

---

increased. Never before in history had peace and contentment been so general over so large an area as during the first two centuries of the empire." (McKinley, Howland and Dann, *World History in the Making* [New York: American Book Company, 1927], p. 257.)

The *vir bonus* was the man possessed of all the virtues essential for the exercise of his rights and the discharge of his duties and obligations. The virtues chiefly prized were piety, obedience, manliness, courage, bravery, industry, honesty, prudence, earnestness, sobriety, dignity, fortitude, and gravity. Indeed, the motto of the early Roman appeared to be *gravitas* in contrast to the Greek *veritas.*

Utility rather than harmony or grace was most important to the early Romans. The Roman virtues are in sharp contrast to those praised by the Greeks: personal satisfaction, esthetic enjoyment, happiness, and intellectual activity for its own sake. The preimperial Romans looked upon the Greeks as a visionary and impractical people; for they themselves judged everything by its serviceability and effectiveness. Even religion remained a practical means of getting on in the world, a means of regulating everyday life, closely connected with the family and with political and business affairs. It consecrated love of country, hallowed the family relation, preserved the sanctity of the oath, developed a sense of duty, and gave authority and sanction to most of the goals of education. In fact the only educational aim of these early Romans was to train men to be active and efficient in daily life, to be conquerors in war, wise in politics, and to have reverence for the gods.

Types

This education was essentially practical training for the affairs of life. There was no attempt at intellectual or esthetic training; and poetry, music, and gymnastics, so prominent in Athenian education, were conspicuous by their absence. Early Rome had no use for what she thought were the passing fashions of education. Life was real, and life was earnest, and so emphasis was placed upon physical training, military training, civic training, and vocational training.

Yet the Romans held a moral view of life as well as a practical one, and most of their education had the coloring of ethical training. Moral rights and duties were clearly defined by law, and for every right there was a corresponding obligation. Youths were trained to obey the moral law, for the moral law and the civil law were, in practice, one and the same.[7]

Religious training was tied to moral and civic training. Roman religion was a religion of duty in contrast to the Greek religion of beauty. A good citizen of early Rome was obedient to authority, pious, frugal, and generally honest. His religion and morals were, however, always of a practical sort;

---

[7] Many legends or perhaps myths were used to assist in the moral indoctrination. For example there were the stories of Mucius and Cloelia, brave representatives of both sexes who so impressed an invader with their courage that he gave up the attack; of Marcus Curtius, who sacrificed himself for the city; of Camillus, the upright general; and, of course, of Cincinnatus, who willingly laid down the dictator's power; and—unnecessary to relate—of the Horatius who kept the bridge.

for, though he was willing to sacrifice his life for the good of the state, he was equally willing to enrich himself at the expense of his neighbors. Vocational education, a training for a livelihood, disdained by the Greek freeman, was given a respected place in early Rome.

Content

The content of early Roman education, therefore, was distinctly practical and moral in character. Children were taught home life, citizenship, and ancestral traditions. There were no books at first. The children memorized and chanted legendary ballads glorifying the traits esteemed by the Romans, religious songs, and the laws of the Twelve Tables.

Of the educational worth of the Twelve Tables Cicero said; "That single little book . . . if anyone look at the fountains and sources of laws, seems to me, assuredly, to surpass the libraries of all the philosophers, both in weight of authority, and in fullness of utility."[8]

The laws of the Twelve Tables formed a large part of the content of education in this early period. What the laws of Moses were to early Hebrew education, the laws of Lycurgus to Spartan education, the laws of Solon to early Athenian education, the laws of the Twelve Tables were to the early education of the Romans. These laws defined private and public relationships and made clear the human and property rights of each person under Roman control and protection. Among the rights recognized were (1) the right of a father over his children, (2) the right of a husband over his wife, (3) the right of a master over his slaves, (4) the right of one freeman over another through contract or forfeiture, and (5) the right of a man over his property.[9] The youth was ordered to memorize these laws as a practical guidance for his training in citizenship.

Children were trained in religious ceremonies and usages. Every activity of life, such as plowing and harvesting, marriage and birth, was under the auspices of some deity to whom it was necessary to give homage. In this early Roman period, the deities were conceived of as stern and inexorable; they had to be propitiated by sacrifices and ceremonies if family relations, court procedures, national campaigns, were to be well begun and fortunately carried out; religion had an intimate relation to private and public conduct. Jupiter, the chief deity, was a generalization of Roman manhood and was supreme guardian of Rome; Juno, wife of Jupiter, was the generalization of noble Roman womanhood; Janus, twin-faced, blessed the beginnings and ends of all activities; Saturn blessed seed sowing; Minerva warned "the husbandman in time of the works to be undertaken"; Mars guided the destiny of battles; Vulcan blessed the forge

---

[8] Cicero, *De Oratore*, vol. i, ch. 44.

[9] It will be noted that these Roman rights were "rights over," which corresponds to the strictness with which they viewed the social relation. They are in contrast to the obligations stressed by Confucius which represented mutual relationships.

and was the god of industry; Venus was the garden deity until identified later with Aphrodite, the Greek goddess of love. The first religious education of the child was in the home, where he gave offerings to the *Lares,* spirits of his ancestors, to the *Penates,* spirits of the household, and to the *Genius,* spirit of the father of the house. The shrine was the hearth, of which Vesta was goddess. Sacrifices were given each morning, and special ones on holidays.

In the home, the child played and romped; and games were encouraged for younger boys and girls, to help give them strength and vigor. Specific military exercises for the boys were given later in the military camps. Physical education apart from training for war was an idea unfamiliar to the mind of the Roman. As the boy grew older, he went about in the company of his father and learned the efficiencies of life from his father and the other men he met. If a patrician, he accompanied his father to banquets and to the forum, where he learned by listening to discussions of affairs of state. If a plebeian, he joined with his father in the duties of farm and shop.

The girl was trained at home by her mother in the domestic arts and the moral virtues. As in Homeric Greece she learned to spin and weave and perform the other household tasks. She too was taught to be devoted to the state and to be ready to serve it at all times. Reading and writing were little needed and so were seldom taught until late in the third century B.C., when Greek elementary schools began to be set up by private teachers.

Agencies

The family was the significant institution in early Roman life, and to its continuance as such was due largely the greatness of Rome in the best days of the republic. The father, the *pater familias,* was supreme, but the mother was also held in high esteem. The father had the right to expose weak or defective children to die, and those whom he spared usually grew up healthy and strong. Though early custom placed the wife in the power of her husband, in contrast to wives in Greek society, she moved about freely (indeed her passing on the street occasioned respect), taught her children, and sometimes assisted her husband in his career. Her position as matron of the household commanded deference from the state as well as from society in general. The phrase *Roman matron* was, in the early days, a synonym for all that was fine in womanhood. As Shakespeare said, "she was above suspicion."

The following epitaph has been copied from a gravestone dating from the second century B.C.:

> Wayfarer, come pause and read;
> My tale is short; do heed!
> This humble grave entombs the bones
> Of one most fair indeed.

> Her parents named her *Claudia*—
>   Steadfast in love was she;
> Two sons brought forth, one living yet,
>   The other lost at sea.
> She laughed and quipped—but dignified—
>   She kept her house just right;
> She span and wove efficiently.
>   That's all, my friend, *Good Night!*[10]

Both parents were equally careful to train their children in the stern simple virtues which made good soldiers and good citizens. The father had teaching as well as priestly functions in these earlier days, and the mother was his able assistant. The home, then, was a strict moral school in which youth was disciplined for private and public life. Thus the formal school played a minor part in early Rome, much education being devoted to character training, and that institutionalized in the home and family.

The military camp and the forum, as well as the farm and workshop, were agencies in the teaching of boys, but girls received all their education at home from their mothers. Toward the middle of the second century B.C., as a result of Rome's conquests, many cultured Greeks were brought to the city as slaves; they sometimes served as tutors to the offspring of wealthy Roman families. After a few years Greek teachers opened private schools in the capital and, like the Sophists, taught for a fee the rudiments of an intellectual education. Generally, however, these schools were looked down upon by the traditionally conservatively minded Romans and offered these foreign teachers little prestige.

Organization

The organization, then, was largely in terms of the home, where the mother supervised the early training of both boys and girls; and from which the boy later accompanied his father to the farm and the shop, where he learned to work, or to the forum, where he learned his future role in public affairs by hearing practical questions of state business discussed.

When the boy reached the age of sixteen, he became a citizen of the state. He now took on the *toga virilis* of manhood, in place of the *toga praetexta* of his youth, solemnized through the performance of domestic ceremonies and religious rites, temple sacrifices, and family festivals.[11] He then entered the camp, an institution for specific military training. Thus he was prepared for his duties in life, both civic and military.

---

[10] "Tribute to a Roman Matron, 198 B.C.," trans. by Kenneth V. Lottich.

[11] The *toga praetexta* had a border of purple and was shared with young boys by chief officials of towns and colonies as well as curial magistrates, censors, and dictators. The *toga virilis* was made of unbleached wool and was variously known as *toga pura*, or *toga libera*. Men standing for office treated the toga with chalk, producing a brilliantly white *toga candida*, from whence comes the term *candidate*. See Mary Johnson, *Roman Life* (Glenview, Ill.: Scott, Foresman and Company, 1957).

Methods

The method of early Roman education was mainly that of direct imitation. The Roman was convinced that the proper way to learn any activity or acquire any virtue was by imitation and practice to develop it into a habit. Great stress was placed upon habit formation. Thus education was essentially training, not instruction; to give instruction in the rational bases of habits was never even considered. The boy learned by imitating his father, the girl by imitating her mother. And they were urged to imitate the heroes of the past who had served Rome and whose exploits were recorded in song and story. Thus biography as well as living examples provided models for imitation. Plutarch's *Lives*, although written at a much later period, is typical of the form and substance of this material. These biographical stories were not usually read by the boys themselves, but were told or recited in their presence. Among them were tales of the consul Brutus, who put his own son to death for treason; the rape of Lucretia, a virtuous wife and mother; and later anecdotes concerning Hannibal, Rome's Carthaginian enemy. (Indeed, it is said that mothers for many years "shushed" their children with the admonition, "Be quiet, Hannibal will get you.") The purpose of such tales is plain, the method is one based on juvenile identification. When the father helped his boy get the little ability considered necessary in reading, writing, and counting, he did it by example and imitation. The laws of the Twelve Tables were memorized along with certain ballads and religious songs. Although the laws were recognized as a source of practical guidance for later life, they were not studied critically; the intellectual element in early Roman education was slight.

Discipline was exceedingly rigorous. Corporal punishment and even death could be inflicted by the father at will. This was possible under the power known as *patria potestas,* granted by ancient law.

ATTITUDES OF THE LATER ROMANS TOWARD EDUCATION

In the early period of Roman history educational ideals and practices were purely Roman. In the later period, however, Greek influence grew more pervasive, and education became composite and cosmopolitan. Owing to the conservative and stable nature of the Roman personality, change from the early to the later attitudes was much more gradual than in Athens; and it is difficult to fix a dividing line between the two periods.[12]

In some respects the influence of the Greeks was felt rather early. Rome drew its alphabet from Greece, and certain elements in its religion and laws were typically Grecian. But no outstanding social or educational

---

[12] Hamilton, however, suggests a change in Roman character as early as the third century B.C., especially in its regard for previously unpopular literature. The plays of Plautus, she says, define the mood.

changes were derived from Greece until about the middle of the second century B.C. In education, these changes were along the line of agencies and institutions; and the somewhat radical innovations were indebted for their acceptance to the lack of any organized system of educational institutions in Rome, although the conservative man resented them bitterly.

As Rome extended her political and military power outside the Italian peninsula, through the Punic[13] and Macedonian wars, her people came in contact with other civilizations, especially the Greek, with consequent widening of their intellectual horizon. As early as 267 B.C., cultured Greeks were brought to Rome as slaves. One of these was Livius Andronicus; after obtaining his freedom, he became a teacher of the Greek language. Andronicus translated the *Odyssey* into Latin and thus made Homer available in Roman education. Many other Greeks opened tutorial schools in Rome to teach both Greek language and literature in Latin translations. Soon, Roman youths were journeying to Greek centers of learning to study rhetoric and philosophy, and Greek philosophers and rhetoricians began to appear in Rome.

Early in this era of gradual transition, elementary schools were set up by private teachers to teach reading, writing, and counting. The name given to these schools, *ludi,* from *ludus,* meaning sport or play, indicates that their function was merely supplementary, and not considered essential to the real education of the Roman youth. In no way was the emphasis upon family training in the habits and duties of the man and the citizen lessened by these early *ludi.*[14]

These schools established under Greek influence were all private undertakings and were attended by only the children and youth of the upper classes. They were held in private homes and in certain unfrequented nooks or porches of the temples or other public buildings. Even by those who patronized them, these schools were evidently looked upon at first as diversions from the essential training of the purely Roman tradition. Indeed, the Latin word for school, *schola,* signifies leisure, and it seems the early Greek schools were so considered.

The native conservatism of Roman character made a sudden transition impossible. The leader of the opposition was Cato the Elder (234–149 B.C.), who for years strenuously opposed the growth of Greek ideas and customs, because of his conviction that the Greeks were decadent. In warning his fellow citizens against what he considered a pernicious influence, he said:

---

[13] Punic comes from Phoenician and these wars, beginning in 264 B.C. and ending with the destruction of Carthage—a Phoenician colony—in 146 B.C., completed the sovereignty of Rome in the Mediterranean.

[14] For a good description of the "downtown" Roman school, see Jerome Carcopino, *Daily Life in Ancient Rome—The People and the City at the Height of the Empire,* ed. by Henry T. Rowell and trans. by E. O. Lorimer (New Haven, Conn.: Yale University Press, 1940), pp. 103–107.

> Believe me, the Greeks are a good-for-nothing and unimproveable race. If they disseminate their literature among us, it will destroy everything; but still worse if they send their doctors among us, for they have bound themselves by solemn oath to kill the barbarians and the Romans.[15]

Through his efforts and at his instigation, the Senate in 161 B.C. decreed the expulsion of all philosophers and rhetoricians from Rome.

But with the death of Cato and, three years later, the final conquest of Greece through the destruction of Corinth (146 B.C.), the floodgates were opened to foreign influences. Shiploads of art treasures were brought in as plunder from the cities of Sicily and Greece. Without appreciation of real beauty, the wealthy nobles nevertheless took pleasure in adorning their houses and villas with stolen statues. Along with foreign art came the ideas, religions, and morals of the conquered strangers. It is not surprising that, along with other plunder, Greek scholars, Greek literature, and even complete libraries were transferred to Rome. There was also imported the system of education upon which all this culture was based, although the system was greatly improved in its organization by the institutionally minded Romans. The final triumph of the Greek influence upon Roman education was marked by the publication of Cicero's *De Oratore* in 55 B.C., for this book is the first formulation by a Roman of the Greek educational ideal. By this time, the Greco-Roman educational system was fixed as it was to remain until the close of the empire. Truly "captive Greece took captive her rude conqueror."

What were the educational attitudes prevalent during this Greco-Roman period? In what respects did Greek influence shape the aims, types, content, agencies, organization, and methods of later Roman education?

Aims

The aim of Roman education in the cosmopolitan period was chiefly capability improvement. Linguistic facility and perfection in public speaking and debate became the dominant purpose in instruction. Yet at least at first the purely Roman stress upon moral character was emphasized; the orator, who was considered the ideally educated man, was to be first *vir bonus* in his essential qualities and after that a skilled speaker. The principal function of education was to produce this good man, skilled in speaking, and thus fitted for practical service to his state. And only such a well-rounded individual could be considered the true orator. The aim was to appropriate the intellectual life of Greece to the extent that it served Roman purposes, but the Latins never quite approached the versatility or originality of the Greeks. Nevertheless, the Roman character had its own assets, and the objective in education was based on three criteria: (1) the

---

[15] Quoted by Pliny, *Natural History*, xxix, 7.14.

demand for moral character, (2) the possession of a broad if not deep knowledge, and (3) the development of an ability to speak convincingly.

The aim of the Roman-organized school system was to prepare the student for the life of public affairs. Cicero (106–43 B.C.) in his *De Oratore,* Tacitus (55–117 A.D.) in his *De Oratoribus,* Quintilian (35–100 A.D.) in his *De Institutione Oratoria,* recognized the orator as the ideally educated man. All conceived of the true orator as one who uses his learning by putting it to the practical use of public service. All agreed that he should have a wide background of basic culture and be primarily a good man.

Thus, during the republic and early empire, training for service to society was the ideal, and such training was carried on vigorously and effectively, especially in the rhetorical schools. But in the later imperial period, the three hundred years prior to Rome's loss of political sovereignty, the aim of education degenerated: the old elements—the *vir bonus* and the concept of state service—dropped out, and rhetorical training was sought for mere affectation and personal display. Indeed, this shallow interpretation of what formerly had been a rigorous and meaningful training was to remain current in education for many years after the fall of Rome.

Types

Roman education required intelligence, but was largely practical, with speech training as the outstanding type. Yet there was a unique quality about the Roman concept of the function of schools and learning. In terms of its ultimate goals, and when carried on at its highest efficiency, the education of the later period was civic training. It was based apparently on the needs of a fairly alert public and the demands of urbanization.

It is not easy to demonstrate either the standard of literacy in ancient Rome or the number of the reading public. Inscriptions were set up hastily by rich and poor, and epitaphs were presumably read. Election posters found on walls in Pompeii, shop identifications, and public notices suggest a fairly literate public. The Roman system of education must share some responsibility for this presumed general level.

We are told that the book trade flourished; copies of histories, poems, or the last oration of Cicero were sold even in the provinces, and written copies were sent from friend to friend. "Horace and Vergil became school-books in their lifetime, and appropriate quotations from Roman poets are embodied in epitaphs."[16] Caesar's *Commentaries* were written for display in the Roman Forum. Stenographers recorded public speeches, such as Cicero's "Against Catiline". Stenographers were utilized by authors such as Pliny, who dictated his notes on natural history, or St. Jerome, who was to dictate his commentary of the Bible. Barrow says, "It is probable that

---

[16] Barrow, pp. 112–113. By permission of Penguin Books Ltd., England.

in many areas a higher standard of literacy and a greater knowledge of literature prevailed at certain periods than in those same areas today."[17]

Although Roman education of this period was not democratic or universal, great men were produced under such an educational system—men who are known everywhere for their service not only to Rome but to the world. Cicero, Vergil, Caesar, Seneca, Quintilian, Marcus Aurelius—these men could think, talk, and write well, and believed that such talents should be used for the benefit of their fellow men. But it never occurred to the Roman leaders that Rome could endure only by raising the intelligence and culture of the whole mass of the people. While a few leaders were getting broad intellectual training, the great mass of the population was getting the narrowest vocational training, with less and less attention to moral training. As a result, the Roman people as a whole became more and more decadent, interested only in the material things that gave satisfaction to their senses and their appetites, and the efforts of the intellectuals went for naught in the end. Rome decayed, declined, and eventually lost the powers of government which had been the reason for her early greatness.

Yet, just before the decline, so memorialized by the historian Gibbon and others, Marcus Aurelius could still write in the best optimistic tradition of Rome:

> To the gods I am indebted
>> For having good grandfathers,
>> Good parents,
>> A good sister,
>> Good teachers and good associates,
>> Good kinsmen and friends,
>> And nearly everything good![18]

Agencies and Organization

As one would expect, the organizing genius of the Romans expressed itself in a perfected system of schools. The construction of a carefully organized educational ladder is the striking contribution of imperial Rome. The Romans appropriated the educational institutions of the Greeks, but combined them into a system the Greeks never thought of developing.

On the elementary level, the Romans developed the school of the *litterator* (teacher of letters). This was the outgrowth and successor of the earlier *ludus* and was attended by both boys and girls from the age of seven to ten. On the secondary level, they developed the school of the *grammaticus* (teacher of grammar) for boys only from ten to sixteen. This school was of two types: (1) the Greek grammar school, for the study of

---

[17] Barrow, p. 113. By permission of Penguin Books Ltd., England.
[18] Marcus Aurelius, *Meditations*, ch. i.

Greek grammar and literature and (2) the Latin grammar school, for the study of Latin grammar and literature. The Roman boy attended both, but Quintilian advocated that he should go to the Greek school first and afterwards attend the Latin school. For the higher level there was developed the school of the *rhetor* (teacher of rhetoric), providing a course of two or three years for boys aged sixteen or older.

At first there was no institution in Rome beyond the schools of the *rhetor*; and any Roman youth who wished to obtain a university education had to study abroad at Athens, Alexandria, or Rhodes. But the practice of bringing manuscripts to Rome as part of the war plunder led to the establishment of a library by Vespasian (9–79 A.D.) in 75 A.D.; and around this library there developed a center of learning called the *Athenaeum,* which was to serve the purposes of what today would constitute higher, or university, education.

Each of these schools was in the beginning privately operated and maintained by tuition fees paid to the teacher. Attendance was voluntary, and the program catered to the more wealthy. The Romans never regarded the first school, that of the *litterator,* as an important part of the system. Its teachers were held in low esteem and their fees were very irregular and uncertain. As no qualifications for teaching in this school were demanded, it usually was presided over by a simple freedman. The teaching was generally poor, as was the school's equipment. Many Roman youths never attended, but received their elementary instruction from a tutor at home. A *custos*—similar to the Greek pedagogue, but more carefully chosen—accompanied the child to and from school. As in Athens, this *custos* customarily assumed the father's role in directly overseeing his charge.[19] Ascending the educational ladder, however, the Romans held the grammatical and rhetorical schools in much higher esteem, and teachers in such schools were of a different class and received much better pay.

During the later imperial period, a movement in the direction of state control and support began—particularly for the schools of the *grammaticus* and *rhetor* and the university. Quintilian, in a lengthy argument, showed the superiority of the public school over the private school and advocated the establishment of a complete public school system. Of the emperors, Vespasian (69–79 A.D.)[20] initiated the payment of salaries out of the public treasury to Greek rhetoricians in Rome; Trajan (98–117 A.D.) provided for public scholarships in the schools; Antoninus Pius (138–161 A.D.) exempted many teachers from taxation, army service, and the obligation to support soldiers; and Marcus Aurelius (161–180 A.D.) instituted the payment of salaries to teachers in the university.

---

[19] See Carcopino, pp. 103–114, for a further description of school practices; or Johnson, pp. 54, 149–156.

[20] The dates in parentheses represent reigns rather than life-spans, a treatment designed to emphasize the continuing imperial contributions to Roman education.

Content

Even in this period elementary education included only the rudiments of reading, writing, and calculation. For a time the Twelve Tables continued to be used as reading texts, but by the era of Cicero they had given way to Latin translations of Homer and versified moral maxims from various sources. The teaching of arithmetic was very primitive because of the cumbersome Roman notation.

In the secondary school, grammar was the chief study. But the term *grammar* had a wider meaning for the Roman than it now has; it included the study of literature, prose and poetry, as well as language. Many Greek and Latin authors who reflected the newer literary attitude were read and studied for content and form; minute attention was given to the style of the works used as models for writing and speaking. Geography, history, mythology, and natural sciences were studied rather superficially to enable students to recognize such allusions in literature. In the grammar school, the practical character of Roman life was uppermost always, and only subjects of functional importance were presented.

The oldest Roman literature is an anthology of comedies by Plautus and his successor, Terence. It is alleged that the Roman expression came secondhand from a ready-made Grecian literary tradition. Although the poetic genius of Greece had flowered in Aristophanes, Sophocles, Euripides, the later Menander, perhaps circumscribed by the political conditions of his time, had produced dull safe comedies. Much of this, it seems, was appropriated by the Roman writers, but Roman sanctions demanded that comedy should reflect Roman life. Thus while literature may have suffered, clear pictures of Rome emerged, especially in Plautus.[21]

The grammar school had, however, certain limitations. Gymnastics and dancing were never introduced into these schools, for the former was emphasized in connection with the military training at the *Campus Martius,* and dancing, if taught at all, was relegated to the home. Music was often utilized as an aid to intonation in public speaking, although the Greek love of music seems not to have affected Rome greatly. Drama was not included in the grammar school's curriculum. Despite the public performances in the later republic and the empire, drama never attained the stature it did in Greece.

In the higher school the outstanding study was rhetoric, which consisted of declamation, extemporaneous speaking, and debates on points of Roman law and moral principles. At their best, these schools of *rhetor* also emphasized ethical and cultural content. Cicero insisted that the orator must not only develop his natural gifts for speaking, but must

---

[21] For clear discussions of the early Roman theatre, see Robert W. Corrigan (Ed.), *Roman Drama* (New York: Dell Publishing Co., Inc., 1966), and Hamilton. Recent American adaptations of Plautus' ribald comedy have been *The Boys from Syracuse, Fanny,* and *A Funny Thing Happened on the Way to the Forum.*

acquire knowledge in many fields as a background. He held to a high moral standard; philosophy to him was the crown of all learning, the school of virtue. Pupils must know the history of their country, he said; he cared little for natural sciences, yet he called politics the queen of sciences. In his *De Oratore* he declared that the orator must have the philosopher's knowledge of things and human nature, but must have also the power to make such knowledge effective by influencing his fellow citizens through speech.

Excluding Socrates, Marcus Fabius Quintilianus (Quintilian) may be perhaps the best known teacher of antiquity. Born in Spain, one of the most literate provinces of Rome, Quintilian was to become the acknowledged master of rhetoric, which his father also is reported to have taught. After Quintilian taught as professor of rhetoric at the metropolis for twenty years, he wrote his great works *De Institutione Oratoria* and *The Causes of the Corruption of Eloquence.*

According to Quintilian, just as the grammar school should acquaint the boy with all literature, so the rhetorical school should give him knowledge of music, arithmetic, astronomy, geometry, and philosophy. He enumerated the following as essential elements in the training of the orator: (1) a knowledge of things, (2) a good vocabulary and ability to make a careful choice of words, (3) gracefulness and urbanity of manners, (4) knowledge of history and law, (5) good memory, (6) a good delivery. He stressed ethical content in education; for, in his estimation, no one could be a good orator unless he was a good man. Practice in the schools, however, perhaps fell far short of the standards set by Cicero and Quintilian.

The curriculum of the Roman university varied from that of the Greek. Neither philosophical speculation nor pure science appealed to the practical Romans. It was science in the applied form which claimed their attention; thus in higher education there developed professional preparation for law, medicine, architecture, and mechanics. What philosophy was to the Greeks, medicine and law were to the Romans.

Methods

At the elementary level, the methods were those of memorizing and imitation. Material was meager. The pupils sat upon the floor or upon stones and rested their tablets on their knees. School hours were long, lasting from sunrise until sunset; but there was no school in summer, and holidays were numerous. The pupils were taught the names and order of the letters of the alphabet, generally without learning anything in regard to their forms.[22] All the possible combinations of syllables were then

---

[22] Quintilian, however, in book i of his *Institutes of Oratory* recommended the following: "As soon as the child has begun to know the shapes of the various letters, it will be no bad thing to have them cut as accurately as possible upon a board, so

learned by rote. Next, writing and reading were taught by means of exercises dictated by the teacher. Pronunication, enunciation, and intelligent expression received special attention. The art of writing was taught as in Greece, by copying and tracing on a wax tablet with a stylus. Counting was performed with the fingers, with pebbles, or with the abacus—a remarkable device made of wire and beads and still used in some parts of the globe. Discipline in the Roman schools was severe indeed; the conventional picture of the schoolroom depicts a boy being flogged while others look on in fear and awe.

At the secondary level, the method was largely one of exercise in good literary and moral habits. Usually there was intensive drill on the parts of speech, syntax, inflections, and other grammatical elements. There were elaborate applications of paragraphing, composition, and poetic style; a favorite process called for the *magister* (teacher) to dictate a quotation from a famous author or orator, to be reproduced verbatim and used by the student as the basis for a laborious theme, frequently organized as follows: (1) the eulogy of the figure quoted, (2) an elaboration of the thought involved, (3) an explanation and defense of the underlying principle, (4) a comparison of the thought with that found in similar works, (5) a collection of substantiating extracts or parallel incidents, and (6) a summation of the moral lesson to be drawn from the passage, with suggestions on putting the principle into practice.

At the rhetorical school, or third level, there was much declamation of approved passages, attention being given especially to articulation, modulation, emphasis, and the like. A polished delivery was considered to mark the man. Frequent debates were arranged in which the fine distinctions in Roman law and morality were stressed. The *suasoriae* were common devices through which the student learned to use his power of imagination as well as logic and dialectical skill. For example, students might be asked to elaborate on such as the following:

> Will Cicero beg mercy of Anthony?
> Will Alexander enter Babylon regardless of unfavorable oracles?
> Will Agamemnon offer up for sacrifice his daughter Iphigenia in return for a fair wind to Greece?[23]

Practice was given in all types of public speaking: funeral orations, eulogies, encomia, exhortations, and extemporaneous speech for various effects. The *rhetor* used the lecture to present the wide range of subjects considered

---

that the pen may be guided along the grooves. Thus mistakes such as occur with wax tablets will be rendered impossible for the pen will be confined between the edges of the letters and will be prevented from going astray." For a first-class biographical note on Quintilian, see William M. Smail, *Quintilian on Education*. Classics in Education, no. 28 (New York: Teachers College Press, Columbia University, 1962), pp. xiii–lvi.

[23] For further *suasoriae* and for *controversiae* see Carcopino, pp. 116–121.

necessary to the education of an orator, but exercise and practice were the important elements in rhetorical training.

While both Plato and Aristotle wrote of educational theory and Socrates taught with the greatest skill, Quintilian's *De Institutione Oratoria* is the earliest practical exposition in education.[24] It is also the first real approach to a solution for the problem of educational methodology. *De Institutione* presents the first treatment of the principles of educational procedure, and in it Quintilian anticipates many modern doctrines in teaching. In his revolutionary declarations he (1) condemns the use of physical force and emphasizes the necessity of making studies attractive and maintains that proper methods of teaching will remove the need for corporal discipline; (2) emphasizes that different natures deserve different treatments and urges teachers to study the dispositions of their pupils; (3) recognizes the importance of empathy in teacher-student relations; and (4) postulates the significance of teacher selection, setting forth just what qualities he, as a Roman, thinks the ideal teacher should possess. Obviously, each conclusion represents an educational judgment far in advance of the times. When we consider his conclusions, we readily see that Quintilian's recipe for teaching has not been realized completely even today.[25]

Perhaps *De Institutione Oratoria* reflects methods chosen by only superior Roman schools, but it represents a standard of authority for the guidance of the teacher and administrator throughout the remaining centuries of Latin history and well into the Middle Ages. Indeed, Scholasticism itself may be judged to have inherited a substantial bit of Quintilian's thoroughness. Nor should it be forgotten that the writer of these *Institutiones* was a teacher himself, not an armchair philosopher on education. In fact he was one of the most successful lay teachers of all time, having been the pioneer appointment of the Emperor Vespasian when he commissioned the state *rhetors* of Rome. Quintilian was reappointed by both Titus and Domitian, thus he served from 70 to 90 A.D. and was no dreamer but a most surprising educational artist.

Finally, although Roman utilitarian education did not rival the originality and genius of the Greeks of their golden age, it did produce in the precepts of Cicero, Terence, Seneca, and Marcus Aurelius some admirable standards for living; and through the methodology of Quintilian, together with the opportunity for moral inculcation offered by Plutarch in his justly famous *Lives,* it has influenced both the medieval and the modern world.

---

[24] For the fascinating story of the recovery of Quintilian's work, lost for centuries, see Ellwood P. Cubberley, *Readings in the History of Education* (Boston: Houghton Mifflin Company, 1900), pp. 189–191.

[25] James J. Murphy (Ed.), *Quintilian—On the Early Education of the Citizen-Orator, Institutio Oratoria Book I, and Book II, Chapters One Through Ten* (Indianapolis: The Bobbs-Merrill Company, Inc., Library of Liberal Arts, 1965), pp. vii–xxviii.

Rather fancifully, but in earnest, the Venerable Bede, a great teacher of the eighth century A.D., was to write:

As long as the Colosseum stands, Rome will stand;
When the Colosseum falls, Rome will fall; and
When Rome falls, the world too will fall!

It now becomes our goal to trace the transference of this remarkable legacy.

REFERENCES

Barnes, Harry Elmer, *An Intellectual and Cultural History of the Western World*. New York: Random House, Inc., 1937. Pp. 195–256.

Barr, Stringfellow, *The Mask of Jove*. Philadelphia: J. B. Lippincott Company, 1966. Pp. 3–37.

Block, Raymond, *The Etruscans*. New York: Frederick A. Praeger, Inc., 1958.

Breasted, James Henry, *The Conquest of Civilization*. New York: Harper & Row, Publishers, 1926 and 1938. Pp. 482–693.

Brubacher, John S., *A History of the Problems of Education*. New York: McGraw-Hill, Inc., 1947. Pp. 173–178.

Butts, R. Freeman, *A Cultural History of Western Education*, 2d ed. New York: McGraw-Hill, Inc., 1955. Pp. 72–115.

Carcopino, Jerome, *Daily Life in Ancient Rome—The People and the City at the Height of the Empire*. Ed. by Henry T. Rowell and trans. by E. O. Lorimer. New Haven, Conn.: Yale University Press, 1940.

Clark, Donald L., *Rhetoric in Graeco-Roman Education*. New York: Columbia University Press, 1957.

Clough, Shepard B., *The Rise and Fall of Civilization*. New York: McGraw-Hill, Inc., 1951. Pp. 118–162.

Cole, Luella, *A History of Education, Socrates to Montessori*. New York: Holt, Rinehart and Winston, Inc., 1950. Pp. 43–90.

Dawson, Christopher, *The Age of the Gods*. New York: Sheed & Ward, Inc., 1933. Pp. 363–384.

Durant, Will, *The Story of Civilization,* pt. ii, *Caesar and Christ*. New York: Simon and Schuster, Inc., 1944. Pp. 1–672.

Eby, Frederick, and Charles F. Arrowood, *The History and Philosophy of Education, Ancient and Medieval*. Englewood Cliffs, N.J.: Prentice-Hall, Inc., 1940. Pp. 515–577.

Gibbon, Edward, *Decline and Fall of the Roman Empire*. Abr. by D. M. Low. New York: Harcourt, Brace & World, Inc., 1960.

Good, Harry G., *A History of Western Education*. New York: Crowell-Collier and Macmillan, Inc., 1960. Pp. 42–57.

Graves, Frank P., *Education Before the Middle Ages*. New York: Crowell-Collier and Macmillan, Inc., 1909. Pp. 230–270.

Hamilton, Edith, *The Roman Way*. New York: W. W. Norton & Company, Inc., 1932.

Hart, Joseph K., *Creative Moments in Education*. New York: Holt, Rinehart and Winston, Inc., 1931. Pp. 86–105, 121–139.

Johnson, Mary, *Roman Life*. Glenview, Ill.: Scott Foresman and Company, 1957.

Knight, Edgar W., *Twenty Centuries of Education*. Boston: Ginn & Company, 1940. Pp. 72–86.

Lopez, Robert, *The Birth of Europe*. New York: M. Evans and Company, Inc., 1967. Ch. i.

Mayer, Frederick, *A History of Educational Thought*. Columbus, Ohio: Charles E. Merrill Books, Inc., 1960. Pp. 103–113.

Messenger, James F., *An Interpretative History of Education*. New York: Thomas Y. Crowell Company, 1931. Pp. 47–53.

Mulhern, James, *A History of Education*, 2d ed. New York: The Ronald Press Company, 1959. Pp. 178–212.

Murphy, James J., *Quintilian—On the Early Education of the Citizen-Orator, Institutio Oratoria, Book I, and Book II, Chapters One Through Ten*. Indianapolis: The Bobbs-Merrill Company, Inc., 1965.

Myers, Edward D., *Education in the Perspective of History*. New York: Harper & Row, Publishers, 1960. Pp. 106–116.

Nakosteen, Mehdi, *The History and Philosophy of Education*. New York: The Ronald Press Company, 1965. Pp. 111–130.

Paoli, Ugo Enrico, *Rome, Its Life and Culture*. New York: David McKay Company, Inc., 1963.

Payne, Robert, *The Roman Triumph*. New York: Abelard-Schuman, Ltd., 1962.

Power, Edward J., *Main Currents in the History of Education*. New York: McGraw-Hill, Inc., 1962. Pp. 129–151.

Reisner, Edward H., *Historical Foundations of Modern Education*. New York: Crowell-Collier and Macmillan, Inc., 1927. Pp. 105–122.

Shaw, Charles Gray, *Trends of Civilization and Culture*. New York: American Book Company, 1932. Pp. 158–186.

Smith, William A., *Ancient Education*. New York: Philosophical Library, Inc., 1955. Pp. 150–196.

Starr, Chester G., *A History of the Ancient World*. New York: Oxford University Press, 1965. Pp. 437–476, 477–499, 503–602, 669–713.

Ulich, Robert, *A History of Educational Thought*. New York: American Book Company, 1950. Pp. 44–60.

———— (Ed.), *Three Thousand Years of Educational Wisdom*, 2d ed., enl. Cambridge, Mass.: Harvard University Press, 1963. Pp. 90–123.

Wills, Garry (Ed.), *Roman Culture—Weapons and the Man*. New York: George Braziller, Inc., 1966.

Woody, Thomas, *Life and Education in Early Societies*. New York: Crowell-Collier and Macmillan, Inc., 1949. Pp. 475–756.

SELECTED PAPERBACKS

Barrow, R. H., *The Romans*. Baltimore: Penguin Books, Inc., Pelican Books, 1949. 223 pp.

Breasted, James Henry, *Ancient Times*, vol. iii, 2d ed. *The Romans*. Boston: Ginn & Company, 1966. Pp. 555–810.

Beck, Robert Holmes, *A Social History of Education*. Englewood Cliffs, N.J.: Prentice-Hall, Inc., 1965. Pp. 16–19.

Burckhardt, Jacob, *The Age of Constantine the Great*. New York: Doubleday & Company, Inc., 1956.

Carcopino, Jerome, *Daily Life in Ancient Rome*. Ed. by Henry T. Rowell and trans. by E. O. Lorimer. New Haven, Conn.: Yale University Press, Yale Paperbound, 1960.

Castle, E. B., *Ancient Education and Today*. Baltimore: Penguin Books, Inc., 1961. Pp. 106–153.

Clarke, M. L., *The Roman Mind*. New York: W. W. Norton & Company, Inc., 1968. Pp. 135–146.

Corrigan, Robert W. (Ed.), *Roman Drama*. New York: Dell Publishing Co., Inc., 1966.

Coulanges, Fustel de, *The Ancient City, A Classic Study of the Religious and Civil Institutions of Ancient Greece and Rome*. New York: Doubleday & Company, Inc., n.d.

Dudley, Donald R., *The Civilization of Rome*. New York: New American Library of World Literature, Inc., 1962.

————— (Trans.), *The Annals of Tacitus*. New York: New American Library of World Literature, Inc., 1966.

Gibbon, Edward, *Decline and Fall of the Roman Empire*, 3 vols. Abr. by D. M. Low. New York: Washington Square Press, 1962.

Grant, Michael, *The World of Rome*. New York: New American Library of World Literature, Inc., 1960.

Hamilton, Edith, *The Roman Way*. New York: New American Library of World Literature, Inc., 1951.

Hollister, C. Warren, *Roots of the Western Tradition*. New York: John Wiley & Sons, Inc., 1966. Pp. 145–216.

Jones, Tom B., *From the Tigris to the Tiber*. Homewood, Ill.: The Dorsey Press, Inc., 1969. Pp. 181–266.

Lucretius, *On the Nature of Things*. New York: E. P. Dutton & Co., Inc., 1957.

McEvedy, Colin, *Penguin Atlas of Ancient History*. Baltimore: Penguin Books, Inc., 1967.

Marrou, Henri Irenée, *A History of Education in Antiquity*. Trans. by George Lamb. New York: New American Library of World Literature, Inc., 1964.

Muller, Herbert J., *The Uses of the Past, Profiles of Former Societies*. New York: New American Library of World Literature, Inc., 1952. Pp. 216–251.

Queen, Stuart A., and Robert W. Habenstein, *The Family in Various Cultures*, 3rd ed. Philadelphia: J. B. Lippincott Company, 1967. Pp. 159–180.

Smail, William M., *Quintilian on Education*. Classics in Education, no. 28. New York: Bureau of Publications, Teachers College, Columbia University, 1962.

Warner, Rex, *The War Commentaries of Caesar*. New York: New American Library of World Literature, Inc., 1960.

CHAPTER **7**

The Christian Concept of Education

The heavenly city, while it sojourns on earth, calls citizens out of all nations, and gathers together a society of pilgrims of all languages, not scrupling about diversities in the manners, laws, and institutions whereby earthly peace is secured and maintained, but recognizing that, however various these are, they all tend to one and the same end of earthly peace.[1]

THE ROMAN PEACE

In the reign of the Emperor Augustus, when imperial Rome had brought into subjection practically all the known world (with the exception of China and India), there was born to Jewish parents in the Galilean village of Nazareth a child to whom was given the name Jesus. Rome had reached the height of its military and political power and brought her justly celebrated *Pax Romana* to her far-flung dominions. That such a magnificent creation could ever fall was undoubtedly far from the minds of most of Rome's citizens and subjects. Yet even then circumstances were developing at the frontiers that were to shake Rome's political command; and a new religion, derived from the person and deeds of the man Jesus, was to transmute Roman authority from the civil to the spiritual realm.

In Palestine the Jews, repatriated from their sojourn in Babylonia, groaned under the oppression of their Roman masters, and Jewish zealots were already fomenting the insurrections that were to lead a few years later to the Roman Titus' destruction of their temple and the Diaspora of the Hebrew nation. In such travail the Jews looked longingly for the appearance of their Messiah and a new and brighter day for the chosen

---

[1] Augustine, *The City of God*, vol. 8, *Fathers of the Church*. xix (New York: Doubleday & Company, Inc., 1958). Reprinted by permission of the Catholic University of America Press.

138

children of Israel. Meanwhile, they attempted scrupulously to follow the teachings of their rabbis and to observe the minute prescriptions of Mosaic law. By this conduct they hoped to attain the holiness and righteousness required by the God of their fathers as a condition of their release from the bonds of servitude and oppression. Into this situation and environment the lowly Nazarene, destined to become the founder of Christianity, was born.[2] His village too, held little prestige; "Can any good thing come out of Nazareth?" ran an ancient query.

Yet Christianity was to become one of the catalytic forces of history, and its influence on education can hardly be estimated. It was a new creative spirit, but suffered from its friends as well as its enemies; its idealism was frequently overcome in contact with old and powerful institutions; and its creator was to perish in ignominy.

Hart parallels Socrates' philosophy and Christianity:

> To be sure, as with Socrates, what its originator aimed at could not be accomplished; it was defeated in the lands of its professed friends, as Socrates was defeated in Athens. Humanity has not courage enough to be creative for more than a moment at a time. But even, in that moment, enough creative virus may be released to keep the old institutions on the defensive, reconstructing themselves . . . for a thousand years to come. This was the similitude—and the fate—of Christianity.[3]

For some twenty centuries this new force was to dominate the civilization and culture of the entire Western world, persistently affecting the theories and practices of its life and education. Although, many believe, it has fallen far short of its potentialities, its contribution to mankind in general and education in particular cannot be ignored.

THE MISSIONARY SPIRIT

Browne sums up the paradox in Christianity as follows:

> Though the Church of Christ may stand guilty of untold and untellable evil, the religion of Jesus, which is the little light glimmering behind that ecclesiastical bushel, has accomplished good sufficient to outweigh that evil tenfold. For it has made life livable for countless millions of harried souls. It has taken rich and poor, learned and ignorant, white, red, yellow, and black—it has taken them all and tried to show them a way to salvation.[4]

[2] See Will Durant, *The Story of Civilization*, pt. iii, *Caesar and Christ* (New York: Simon and Schuster, Inc., 1944), pp. 527–549, for a graphic account of conditions in Judea just before the advent of Jesus. G. A. Williamson, *The World of Josephus* (Boston: Little, Brown & Company, 1964), pp. 46–47, 63–64, 103–120, presents a picture of the new religion in the land of its birth.

[3] Joseph K. Hart, *Creative Moments in Education* (New York: Holt, Rinehart and Winston, Inc., 1931), p. 140.

[4] Lewis Browne, *This Believing World* (New York: Crowell-Collier and Mac-

Christianity attempted to solve the same organic dilemma that had confronted the various pagan civilizations: how to harmonize individual freedom and personal desires and aspirations with social stability in order to preserve the race or nation.

This quandary was essentially one of establishing an ethical standard for the relationship of the individual to society. The solutions offered by the Athenian mediators, Socrates, Plato, and Aristotle, were based on the intellectual nature of man and possible apparently only to the few. Stoic philosophy, which originated in Greece, but found adherents in Cato, Cicero, Seneca, Marcus Aurelius, and the intellectual class in Rome, also claimed that reason was the proper rule of life, that virtue was its own reward. It, too, was so intellectual that it satisfied only the few. What was needed was an ethical system based upon the emotions and the natural moral nature of man, a system that could touch all mankind with its inspirations to goodness and virtue. Such an ethical system was given to the world by the teachings of Christianity. Christianity, by first appealing to the emotions rather than to the intellect, entered into the lives of people of every class and of every type. Nevertheless it was a minority sect.[5]

Christianity gave to the world a new ethical force, a new motive for releasing the effective energies of all mankind, a new humanitarianism that provided a basis for the education of all and the consequent establishment of a sound social organization. The imaginative, artistic, and creative Greeks had emphasized political and personal freedom and individual initiative, and as a result had developed a literature, an art, and a philosophy that constitute one of the great heritages of modern times. The practical, aggressive, and systematic Romans had stressed law, government, and the practical arts, and as a result had imposed law and order and the institutions of government upon an unruly world. The weakness of one was the strength of the other.

Early Christianity combined and harmonized the best elements of each, and developed an ethical standard by which the claims of both personality and society could be met and satisfied. The ethical contributions of Christianity were twofold: (1) an ideal of personal morality, including such virtues as sincerity, honesty, truthfulness, and chastity; (2) an ideal of social responsibility, based upon motives of brotherly love—neighborliness, loyalty, kindness, generosity, altruism, and unselfishness. As a result of these ideals, class distinctions and racial prejudices have been lessened, womanhood has been elevated to a higher place and a new dignity, and childhood has become more sacred. Rights have come to be recognized as well as duties and obligations.

---

millan, Inc., 1954), pp. 300–301. A somewhat controversial view of early Christianity is taken in Hugh J. Schonfield, *Those Incredible Christians* (New York: Bantam Books, Inc., 1968).

[5] For a further discussion of the bases of Christianity, see Huston Smith, *The Religions of Man* (New York: Harper & Row, Publishers, 1958), pp. 266–308.

The development of the early Christian concept of education is a history of the struggle between the basic teachings of Jesus and the amplifications, constrictions—and even misapprehensions—of these teachings by his own followers. Christians, as the adherents of Jesus soon began to call themselves, found themselves in a state of confusion between the simple preachings of the Master on the one hand and the interpretations and interpolations of his disciples and apostles on the other. Indeed, within the far-flung empire a host of religions—both western and eastern—contended for priority. Christianity, at first, represented the faith of an insignificant group.

As a result the religious beliefs and practices of the ancient church were considerably altered from those of the unassuming Galilean; similar changes also occurred in educational attitudes and practices. The original gospel of Jesus was institutionalized by St. Paul and other early leaders of the apostolic and patristic periods, as well as by the converts themselves; thus elements of theological doctrine and religious ritual drawn from the Greek philosophies, the Hebrew moralities, and the various eastern mystery sects prevalent at the time were soon added. Organized Christianity is particularly indebted to Mithraism, the worship of Tammuz, and the mother-goddess cults of Egypt and Lydia. In structure the new religion borrowed much from the Roman imperial hierarchy and the Roman army, an army where Mithraism was one of Christianity's chief rivals. Thus it is not coincidental that later generations of Christians—bypassing the humility of Jesus—should commemorate the past in singing: "Onward Christian soldiers marching as to war,/With the cross of Jesus going on before"; and "Like a mighty army moves the church of God;/ Brothers we are treading, where the saints have trod."

It is our purpose, therefore, to consider the early Christian conceptions of education under two headings: (1) the educational attitudes and practices of Jesus; and (2) those of the early Christian church during the first two centuries of its existence.

JESUS' EDUCATIONAL ATTITUDES AND PRACTICES

In this study we are not concerned particularly with Jesus' contributions to the history of religion. Jesus is to be considered here as a teacher; we are not discussing him as a divine being, but simply as an educator who played his part in the tremendous drama of educational history. It is to be regretted, perhaps, that, just as the real teaching personality of that great Hindu teacher of the sixth century B.C., Gautama, the Buddha, has been distorted and obscured by later Buddhism, so the burning and magnetic personality of this penniless teacher, who wandered about the dusty sunlit country of Judea, has been sadly ignored and misrepresented.

Jesus has rightly been called the Great Teacher. He was, with Socrates and Gautama, one of the three greatest masters of the teaching art. In method his teaching resembles that of Socrates; in aim and content, it is like that of Gautama. The parable method of Jesus is as effective as the dialectic method of Socrates; the Sermon on the Mount is very similar to the Sermon in the Deer Park; the Beatitudes of Jesus approximate closely Gautama's Eightfold Path of "right views, right intentions, right speech, right action, right occupation, right effort, right mindfulness, right concentration." Each of the three had an intense consciousness of a mission to be fulfilled, and the radiant personality of the effective teacher.

In his personality, life, and teachings Jesus represented the ideal teacher. His personality was compelling, his preparation was complete, his aims were lofty, his methods were effective. He was "a man who really lived the best truth he knew, who took what he had read and thought and interpreted it to humanity by embodying it in his own life."[6] When men hereafter bow to him, it should be in recognition of a superior craftsmanship in the art of living and in the art of teaching that life to others.

Aims

The aim of Jesus' teaching may be summed up in his words, "Seek ye first the Kingdom of God and his righteousness, and all these things shall be added unto you." What Jesus himself meant by this statement and what the Christian church afterwards attributed to it for centuries to come are two different things. It was the church's interpretation which most affected our educational thought and our educational systems; it is the true interpretation of Jesus' own words that must come to influence the educational philosophy and practices of the future if the teachings of Jesus are ever to attain their highest possibilities as an influence in education. Jesus taught a new and simple and profound doctrine—the universal loving Fatherhood of God and the coming of a Kingdom of Heaven on earth, based on the principle of universal brotherhood. This is certainly one of the most revolutionary doctrines that ever stirred and changed human thoughts. The Kingdom of Heaven on earth as an ultimate objective of education has never been surpassed in its nobility and grandeur.

Jesus advanced two basic principles fundamental to this kingdom in the hearts of men: (1) respect for human personality and the rights of the individual and (2) social sensitivity in all human relationships. He aimed at giving the individual the greatest satisfactions of life, the "peace that passeth understanding." He taught that every human being is sacred in the sight of God. There are few who would deny that most of our move-

---

[6] C. F. Potter, *The Story of Religion* (New York: Simon and Schuster, Inc., 1929), p. 232. See also Bernard J. Kohlbrenner, "The Catholic Heritage," p. 104, in Richard E. Gross (Ed.), *Heritage of American Education* (Boston: Allyn and Bacon, Inc., 1962).

ments in the direction of a greater humanitarianism have been influenced by the teachings of Jesus.

But Jesus also advanced a new social gospel; he taught new principles to govern human relationships and social organization. The Golden Rule had existed before his day, but its application had been limited to the relationship of friends, relationship within families, and relationship among the peoples of one nation. Racial hatreds, national pride, fear, suspicion, antagonism, and prejudice had limited its scope. Jesus taught a new and a great commandment, "Love thy neighbor"; and, in the parable of the good Samaritan, he interpreted neighborliness in a way that few could misunderstand.

Not only did Jesus strike at the traditional conceptions of patriotism and family ties, but his teaching of God's universal fatherhood and the brotherhood of humanity clearly condemned all the artificial gradations of the economic system of his day, all personal privilege and advantage. He denounced riches and the selfishness of private ambitions. He taught not only a moral revolution in the individual but a revolution in society as well. He said that his kingdom was not one of geographical bounds ruled from a throne, but a kingdom in the hearts of men. To the extent that his kingdom was set up in the hearts of men, to that very extent would the world be revolutionized.

The problem of the wealthy young man whom Jesus advised to sell all his property, give to the poor, and follow him was different only in degree from those of his disciples. H. G. Wells shows how the broad gulf between absolute purity and the call of this world must have affected even the greatest of his admiring group:

> He was like some terrible moral huntsman digging mankind out of the snug burrows in which they had lived hitherto. In the white blaze of this kingdom of his there was to be no property, no privilege, no pride and precedence; no motive indeed and no reward but love. Is it any wonder that men were dazzled and blinded and cried out against him? . . . Is it any wonder that the priests realized that between this man and themselves there was no choice but that he or priestcraft should perish? Is it any wonder that the Roman soldiers, confronted and amazed by something soaring over their comprehension and threatening all their disciplines, should take refuge in wild laughter, and crown him with thorns and robe him in purple to make a mock Caesar of him? For to take him seriously was to enter upon a strange and alarming life, to abandon habits, to control instincts and impulses, to essay an incredible happiness.[7]

---

[7] H. G. Wells, *The Outline of History* (New York: Doubleday & Company, Inc., 1961), pp. 425–426. Reprinted by permission of Professor G. P. Wells. Darryl Chase, *Christianity through the Centuries* (Salt Lake City: Deseret Books, 1944), pp. 6–20, 21–61, offers an excellent historical view of Jesus and the work of the early Christian church.

Types

Jesus emphasized moral training in the loftiest meaning of the term; his was the highest type of ethical education. The authority for conduct was the sanction of brotherly love. The authority of ancestors, caste, state, Yahweh—all now gave way to the authority of a great moral principle in the universe, the principle of love. "For God so loved the world . . ." "As the Father hath loved me, so have I loved you; continue in my love." "This is my commandment, that ye love one another as I have loved you." "A new commandment I give unto you, that ye love one another." "Thou shalt love thy neighbor as thyself." Social education and moral education were one to him.

But Jesus was concerned also with religious training in its truest sense, the development of the right relationships between man and his God. His first and great commandment was: "Thou shalt love the Lord thy God with all thy heart, and with all thy soul, and with all thy mind." He was not concerned with teaching observance of the minute prescriptions of religious rites and ceremonies, but never ceased to emphasize the necessity of developing an abiding trust and confidence in God and a true reverence for Him. This is religious education at its best. He also recognized the obligation of citizenship, but reduced it to his fundamental principle of morality: "Render unto Caesar the things that are Caesar's."

Education based on the teachings of Jesus must of necessity be universal and democratic. He himself taught all who came to him in their need for instruction. In teaching that God is the Father of all mankind, he removed education from the fetters of national limits and racial prejudice; he swept away the distinctions of class and caste which had weighed so heavily in ancient Oriental education and in the schools of Greece and Rome. By making everyone a child of God, stamped with the divine image, he abolished all forms of slavery—slavery of workers, slavery of women, slavery of children—attached due importance to every individual, overthrew the injustices and oppressions of society, and thus stressed the necessity of and paved the way for a universal and common education for every man, woman, and child.

The teaching of Jesus emphasized the necessity of the education of the young child, elementary education. "Suffer the little children to come unto me and forbid them not, for of such is the kingdom of heaven."

Content

The essence of the teaching of Jesus is to be found in the few pages of the Sermon on the Mount. He taught his disciples not to retaliate for injuries, but to forgive as their loving Father would forgive them; not to worry about food, clothes, shelter; for if God provided for even the birds and flowers, he would care for his own children. They were to seek first the kingdom of God. He so practiced what he taught and so lived his exalted conception of what God would do if he were a man that his own life was his curriculum.

The content of his teaching had to do with human conduct, yet he was not interested in the formation of specific habits and skills, nor in the memorizing of rules and regulations. A large part of his recorded utterances is aimed against the meticulous observance of the rules of the pious and puritanical Pharisees. He flouted the habits of the formalist; he endeavored to develop in his disciples an individual and social behavior that was based on the acceptance of broad and deep general principles of human relationship.

It is noteworthy that Jesus seems to have concentrated all his efforts on teaching the essentials. Only a few things really mattered to him; he dealt only with fundamental universal truths. One finds in his program neither belles lettres nor courses in theology, and yet he was successful in inspiring the most efficient humanitarian and religious work the world has yet known.

Agencies and Organization

Jesus did not organize a school or develop any special institution for the promulgation of his teachings. The Christian church itself was organized by his later followers; Jesus himself organized no such institution. Like Socrates, he wrote nothing; he used no textbooks, although he was familiar with the literature of his people and quoted extensively from it. He merely talked to people wherever he found them. The home, the seashore, the riverbank, the highway, the hilltop, the social gathering, the religious service—all were his agencies for education. He taught whenever and wherever a situation arose of which he could make effective use.

Never did Jesus essay the role of a professional teacher. He expected no pay for his services. To him teaching was the giving of a transcendent gift of knowledge and wisdom and the setting of a noble example, and remuneration for such a service was far from his thoughts. Here was a very human, very earnest, very capable man—clearly a teacher with charisma. He attracted his disciples and filled them with wisdom, love, and courage. The most effective agency of his instruction was his own radiant personality.

Methods

The most helpful lessons that modern education can draw from the work of Jesus as a teacher are in regard to method. The teaching procedure of Jesus is, without a doubt, as effective as any yet contrived. In his manner of instructing his disciples and the multitudes that gathered around him, he set an excellent example in educational methodology. He seemed to have an intuitive grasp of the laws of learning and the principles of teaching that are now accepted as basic to teaching effectiveness.

Jesus prepared his hearers for the truth to be taught by presenting concrete examples of their application in life and in human relationships. He drew extensively upon their previous knowledge by frequent reference to the various books of the Old Testament—the Law and the Prophets. He continually adjusted his lessons to the common experiences of those he taught by referring to the familiar phenomena of nature and to the institutions and practices of social life. Without pedantry, he made effective use of the simile, the metaphor, the analogy, and the parable. The parable especially (there are fifty-three of these allegories in the Gospels), not only made the lesson concrete and interesting, but drove home the truth so that no one could miss its meaning. In these parables he made reference to such familiar experiences as sowing, shepherding, and husbandry, and such familiar objects as vines, sheep, and coins. He used concrete everyday incidents for his examples. He used the simplest language to teach the most profound truths; he used the phrases, idioms, and expressions current among the common people.

Jesus also recognized the principle of activity in his teaching. He urged his disciples to be "doers of the word and not hearers only." He encouraged questions and gently rebuked his followers for not asking questions which they had. He appealed to the imagination and made use of the power of suggestion to stimulate the thought processes of his hearers. He recognized the principle of individual differences and adjusted his teaching methods to the needs, conditions, and capacities of those with whom he came in contact. His treatment of the woman taken in adultery is different from his treatment of the rich young ruler. His approach was always determined by the nature of the teaching. His words and demonstrations were full of interest and attracted and held the attention of his listeners. The power of his motive is easily understood. The common man needs a purpose that appeals to the feelings rather than to the intellect, and this Jesus always recognized. He made no use, however, of such motives as competition and acquisition. Love was the major aim offered as a stimulus to goodness. Later a system of rewards and punishments in an eternal heaven or hell was developed from Zoroastrianism by the early church and set up as a motive for righteousness, but Jesus himself reached people by the simple motive of love—love for God and love for man.

The method of Jesus was objective, forthright, and personal. He directed attention to the external world and objective activities. He used oral instruction, either the sermon in speaking to large numbers, or the dialectic in the intimate circle of a few friends. Beyond all else, he taught by example. His own life was the best advertisement for his teachings. His obedience to authority, his observance of the spirit of the law, his humility, his mercy, his charity were continual examples set before the disciples for their guidance. He always practiced what he preached, and where can one find a better way?

EDUCATIONAL APPROACH OF THE EARLY CHRISTIAN CHURCH

The history of Christianity during the first two centuries following the Crucifixion is somewhat obscure. The record found in the Acts of the Apostles and the Epistles of St. Paul and other early Christian leaders is a patchwork, rather than a systematic account; it does, however, produce a revealing picture of the trials and tribulations of the ancient church. St. Peter, we are told, traveled to Rome and was largely instrumental in establishing the church in the eternal city. Paul likewise journeyed to Rome and to many other Mediterranean cities; he made a remarkable address at Mars Hill in Athens.[8]

Many consider Paul to be the founder of the organized religion; it was he probably more than any other who set the doctrines and worked out a system of theology. Under his inspiring leadership the movement was internationalized until it spread into every corner of the Roman world. Yet in this early period the creeds and dogma had not crystallized, and there were wide variations in tenets and practices among those who accepted the new faith.

Despite local differences in doctrine and ritual there is reason to believe that everywhere during these early days the Christians were carrying out much of the true spirit of Jesus in their daily lives and were practicing those virtues of simplicity, purity, and unselfishness that contrasted so strikingly with the vices of the pagan world. The persecutions and oppressions that the early Christians had to endure are evidence of their strength. If the faith had not been deemed a menace to government, Christians would not have been persecuted. But these persecutions, instead of weakening the church, strengthened it still more, as Constantine observed. So in 311 A.D., three years before his accession as head of the Western Empire, Christianity was legalized, that is, granted the same protection as pagan worship. Under the Emperor Constantine (272–337) it was not only tolerated but encouraged and, with his conversion, became the state religion of the Western Roman Empire.[9] This was a fine thing for the growth of the church organization, but it is an open question whether it was equally favorable to the continuation of the early emphasis upon Christlike living on the part of the whole membership of the church.

---

[8] See Durant, pp. 575–595, for a moving account of the place and influence of Peter, Paul, and John in the formation of the Christian religion. The Gospels themselves were apparently in unwritten form until the second century A.D.

[9] While a contender for the imperial crown Constantine in a vision beheld a flaming cross bearing the inscription *In hoc signo vinces,* "in this sign, conquer." Successful, he favored Christianity.

During this period certain elements from other religions and from pagan philosophies were being fused with the original teachings of Jesus. Alexandria at this time was the great melting pot of religion and philosophy, and the Alexandrian school of thought contributed much to Christianity. The Apostles and early Fathers came from different backgrounds and brought from their own earlier environment and experiences distinct contributions to the growing Christian faith. By combining with the original teachings of Christ certain elements from the ceremonies and rites of Hebrew morality, concepts from Greco-Roman philosophy—especially Stoicism and Neoplatonism—and ceremonies from some of the popular mystery religions of the eastern Mediterranean world, Christianity was gradually adapted to the temperaments and customs of the diverse peoples to whom its message was carried.[10]

Many centuries passed before the synthesis was complete and Christianity had assumed a fixed form. Bitter controversies, such as that over the nature of the deity of Jesus between the Arians, led by Arius (280–336), and the Trinitarians, led by Athanasius (296–373) (settled finally in favor of the latter by the Council of Nicaea), shook the church. It was not until the beginning of the fifth century that the structure of orthodox Christianity was completed by the work of Augustine (354–430), another great teacher and the first to build a complete and coherent system of theology for the Roman Catholic Church in his *De Civitate Dei*.

In such a formative period, Christian education was little concerned with intellectual theology, but confined itself to the training of children, converts, and clergy in the fundamental and commonly accepted doctrines and practices of the early church.

Aims

The primary aim of early Christian education was the moral regeneration of the individual. Early Christianity was distinctly a reform movement; it had as its ultimate goal the moral reformation of the world and the destruction of the corrupt society of paganism. But the church realized that the reform of society could come about only through the transformation of the individuals that make up society; so it devoted itself to the moral training of its own membership and of the converts won over to the Christlike ideal.

---

[10] Mithraism, of Persian origin, was immensely popular among the armed forces, and the sun-banner of Mithras frequently preceded the troops in battle. Mithraism had the sacraments of baptism, confirmation, and communion. It is believed that there were seven degrees, or levels, of membership: the Raven, the Hidden One, the Soldier, the Lion, the Persian, the Sun-Runner, and the Father. Founded on mysteries and allegorical interpretation, Mithraism appears to have held commonalities with the Greek Eleusinian and Orphic modes. See Donald R. Dudley, *The Civilization of Rome* (New York: New American Library of World Literature, Inc., 1962), p. 231.

The Christian protest was directed especially at the looseness and debauchery prevalent in the empire, especially at Rome. Attention to the early Roman virtues had flagged; the government was corrupt; the armies were no longer victorious. The upper classes and even the proletariat of Rome had fallen into vicious customs and habits; the abundance of slaves made it unnecessary for much of the population to work; surfeited by leisure, the common people demanded bread and circuses, which political leaders and aspirants to public office were only too glad to supply; during the second and third centuries civil war raged frequently, and barrack emperors reigned more often than not.

The Roman concept of the *vir bonus* seemed to have been forgotten in the urge to pleasure and self-gratification. Divorce became frequent and common to all strata of society.[11] Infanticide and child exposure were continued; the Roman family—the strength of the early republic—deteriorated as its members were guided no longer by the ancient morality. Cruel and bloody gladiatorial shows, public ceremonies of the most immoral type practiced under the cloak of religion, and licentiousness in private life contributed to the decay in society that the Christian viewed as an evidence of Satan's work and power.

To combat these evils, the Christian church had a new set of virtues to take the place of the vices of the pagan. Simplicity instead of luxury, purity instead of licentiousness, temperance instead of indulgence, humanitarianism instead of brutality, brotherly love instead of selfishness—these were the virtues required for entrance into the church; and in these, therefore, training must be given. For, as Augustine held:

> It is well that all should remind themselves that man is not in the world for himself, nor yet for the world, but for God; that man is not just another animal species whose function is to build civilizations, one after the other, like ants and termites endlessly laboring to build and rebuild their wonderful but fragile dwellings. [Thus] it is good, it is wholesome, to be put in mind that by all these temporary scaffoldings, which are men's works, the divine Architect is building up the City of God.[12]

To the early Christian a view such as Augustine's was not mere rhetoric, although Augustine had been a teacher of rhetoric long before he became a Christian. If he were to satify the caveats of his faith, the Christian had to reject these things: the world, the flesh, and the devil—these were the sources of evil and corruption. Men were to be taught to renounce the world, to subdue the flesh, and to escape the devil; to serve God by living pure and simple lives, and thus to obtain eventually the

---

[11] It is reported that divorce was unheard of in Rome until the Punic Wars, Rome's first large political and commercial success.

[12] Henri Marrou, *Saint Augustine* (New York: Harper & Row, Publishers, 1957), p. 76.

heavenly reward of the faithful. As the difficulty of reforming the world became more and more obvious, the Christian's aim ultimately became that of saving his own soul and the souls of as many of his fellow men as he could convert. But the early Christians of the first centuries had not yet reached these conceptions of unworldliness and otherworldliness. They still had hope of reforming the world through the regeneration of human souls. The overall aim of early Christian education was to spread *kerygma*, the "good news."

Types

To satisfy such an altruistic aim, two types of education were needed: moral training and religious training. If sufficient moral and religious training was given to prepare the child or the convert for baptism, the objective of Christian education was fulfilled.

In the beginning there was no intellectual education, for early Christianity was based on feeling rather than on reason; and at first, and particularly in the West, it was considered unnecessary to give intellectual training even to the clergy.[13] Later, especially in the East where Christianity had attracted the attention of the learned pagan world and had made converts from among the intellectual and educated classes, intellectual education was introduced if for no other reason than to train controversialists to meet the arguments of opponents from without the church and heretics from within. But even in these later schools, moral and religious training always took precedence over intellectual training.

Physical training and esthetic training were despised by the Christians, and the only musical training tolerated was in connection with the psalmody and hymnology of church worship. There was no recreational training, since sports and amusements of all kinds, because of their association with Roman life and paganism in general, were looked upon as sinful.

Content

The curriculum of early Christian education was limited by the suspicion and distrust with which Christians looked upon intellectual and worldly learning. They were bitterly opposed to the subjects taught in the pagan schools and blamed pagan culture for the vices and corruption of pagan society. To them its literature was full of impurities; its art depicted immoralities and was associated with immoral religions; its philosophy undermined and destroyed Christian faith because it led to trusting one's own wisdom. "I will destroy the wisdom of the wise and will bring to nothing the understanding of the prudent." Therefore the pagan school was the enemy of the church, and its curriculum was to be despised by all

---

[13] In I Corinthians, 19–20 (Revised Standard Version), Paul had said, "God hath made foolish the wisdom of the world," a statement taken literally by early Christians.

believers. Moreover, early converts to Christianity were from the lower classes and would have none of the learning that differentiated their masters from themselves. Physical training, literature, art, science, rhetoric, philosophy, were all eliminated from early Christian education; and subjects quite foreign to the later pagan schools, moral and religious training, took their place.

This basic instruction purposed only to fit candidates for baptism for membership in the church. The pupils were converts from Hebraism and paganism or the children of believers; so the simple elements of church doctrine and church ritual and the moral virtues of Christlike living made up the brief course of training.

But during the second century a more advanced curriculum was introduced into church education by pagan teachers who had been converted to Christianity. These teachers opened schools primarily to give elementary training in Christian faith and doctrine to prospective church leaders and workers; but grammar, literature, rhetoric, and even philosophy were taught as "handmaidens to the Scriptures." This type of curriculum flourished, particularly in the East where it first arose. For the most part, the church in Western Europe continued to oppose all pagan learning and excluded it from Christian education. It was such Greek Fathers as Clement (150–200), Origen (185–254), Basil (329–379), and Gregory (325–389) who favored the use of such studies in the training of Christian youth. They contended that if proper selection were made, pagan culture could contribute to the understanding of the Scriptures, and that it was justifiable to "spoil the Egyptians," that is, to use their learning against them. On the other hand, such Latin Fathers as Tertullian (160–230), Jerome (340–420), and Augustine, although they themselves had been deeply learned in classical literature and philosophy before their conversions, feared the effect of pagan culture on Christian morality. The *Confessions* of Augustine express this antagonism. The Western point of view finally prevailed in the church; and, at the Council of Carthage in 401 A.D., the clergy were forbidden to read pagan literature.

Agencies and Organization

Upon the death of Jesus, his followers began to come together at stated times to read, study, take communion, and plan the future of the organization of which his teachings were the seed. The church itself was thus the first agency of Christian education. The Christian home, which was far more rigid and close-knit than the contemporary pagan home, was also an efficient agency, the mother occupying an honored place and joining with the father in the moral and religious training of their children.

Very early, however, and universally throughout the church, there grew up an institution known as the catechumenal school. This school was organized for the instruction of those who desired to become members of the church, but who lacked the requisite knowledge of church doctrine and ritual and the requisite moral stability. These probationers were called *catechumens* and were divided into two groups, those who had expressed a desire to become members of the church and those who were considered to be worthy of full membership. At stated intervals these *catechumens* met in some part of the church, usually the porch, for instruction in religious discipline, moral virtue, and psalmody. The organization was informal, the teachers at first being merely able members of the local church and only later deacons and priests. Both sexes were admitted to this instruction, but no one was received into full communion or given the sacrament of baptism until he had received this training. The length of the training was usually about two years, but this was later extended to four years for the children of the believers. Such schools continued for centuries as the elementary schools of the church.

When Christianity began to make converts among the grammarians, rhetoricians, and philosophers, a new type of school was organized. At first it was private and unconnected with the church. But in 179 A.D. Pantaenus, a converted Stoic philosopher—one of the Apologists who were attempting to reconcile Christianity with Greek philosophy—became head of the catechumenal school in Alexandria. His school and those patterned after it came to be know as *catechetical* schools because of their use of the catechetical, or question-and-answer, method. They were used especially for the training of church leaders and were in a way rudimentary theological schools, but they included virtually the entire gamut of pagan studies as supplementary to the religious training.

Later in this period, when the church began to perfect its organization, and bishoprics were established, theological training schools for the education of the clergy were organized in each bishopric. These were called episcopal, or *cathedral*, schools. With the final victory of Christianity over paganism the catechetical schools disappeared, particularly in the West, and the cathedral schools remained as the higher schools of Christian learning. These schools were located in the cathedrals and were under the direct instruction of the bishop himself or of a cathedral canon delegated to that function. (The Latin term *cathedra* signifies the bishop's chair, or seat.)

Methods

The methods of early Christian education frequently fell far short of the standards set by Jesus, the Great Teacher. In the beginning, inspiration of the voice of the spirit was depended upon more than learning or instruction. Prophesying or impromptu exposition and exhortation was a common method of spreading the gospel in the early days when the church itself was the sole agency of education. In the home the method of example continued to be used.

In the schools that were established later, the catechetical method prevailed. The pupil memorized the answers to set questions and recited these answers to the teacher when the question was asked. Little attempt was made to learn meaning; it was enough if the words could be recited by rote. This method continued in use throughout the Middle Ages and is still used extensively in some parochial education.

Yet to speak of "methods" in connection with the dissemination of the teachings of Jesus seems somehow to miss the spirit of real Christianity. Those who heard the Great Teacher himself *caught* his vision. Robert Ulich has expressed this subtlety in a few simple words:

> But there inheres in Christ's gospel a deeper educational claim than can be expressed in merely didactic terms. It rests on the combination of two closely interrelated tenets of Christianity. . . . One of them is the conviction that the dignity of man imposes on him the duty of considering the human soul as an end in itself, not to be submitted to alien purposes. The other idea is that of love or charity. It springs from the same metaphysical root as the idea of dignity and ends in the same demand to respect one's fellow man.[14]

To people of a secular age, that is, the Western world of today, much of the preceding chapter may appear fanciful and irrevelant. But to early Christianity, obsessed with the image of a millennium and a desire for worldwide unity (a hope that contemporary society has not cast aside), Christian schools and methodology, added to the humanity of Jesus' teaching, suggested a way out of the despair, tribulation, and restrictions of empire. One such as Augustine believed thoroughly in such a goal; Etienne Gilson in his Introduction to a modern translation of *The City of God* shows how this could be thought possible:

> Had we religious unity, we could peacefully enjoy all other unities. . . . Philosophy, science, art and economics all can help in achieving the great work of uniting mankind, but neither individually nor collectively is it in their power to accomplish it. . . . The only possible source of future unity lies not in multiplicity, but above it. *One World* is impossible without *One God* and *One Church*.[15]

It is this interpretation of truth that motivated these early Christians and gave rise to their concept of education—and through what manner of schools it should be accomplished. Their educational wisdom was to continue virtually unchallenged for almost a thousand years.

---

[14] Robert Ulich, *History of Educational Thought* (New York: American Book Company, 1950), p. 70.

[15] St. Augustine, *The City of God*, trans. by Gerald D. Walsh, s.j., and others (New York: Doubleday & Company, Inc., Image Books, 1958), pp. 34–35.

REFERENCES

Bakan, David, *The Duality of Human Existence.* Skokie, Ill.: Rand McNally & Company, 1966. Pp. 16–101.

Barnes, Harry Elmer, *An Intellectual and Cultural History of the Western World.* New York: Random House, Inc., 1937. Pp. 267–325.

Bolgar, R. R., *The Classical Heritage.* New York: Harper & Row, Publishers, 1964.

Browne, Lewis, *This Believing World.* New York: Crowell-Collier and Macmillan, Inc., 1954. Pp. 255–301.

Butts, R. Freeman, *A Cultural History of Western Education,* 2d ed. New York: McGraw-Hill, Inc., 1955. Pp. 81–84, 94–115.

Carcopino, Jerome, *Daily Life in Ancient Rome.* Ed. by Henry T. Rowell and trans. by E. O. Lorimer. New Haven, Conn.: Yale University Press, 1940.

Chase, Darryl, *Christianity Through the Centuries.* Salt Lake City: Deseret Books, 1944. Pp. 6, 21–61.

Cole, Luella, *A History of Education, Socrates to Montessori.* New York: Holt, Rinehart and Winston, Inc., 1950. Pp. 91–111.

Danielou, Jean, and Henri Irenée Marrou, *The First Six Hundred Years.* Trans. by Vincent Cronin. New York: McGraw-Hill, Inc., 1964.

Durant, Will, *Story of Civilization,* pt. iii, *Caesar and Christ.* New York: Simon and Schuster, Inc., 1944. Pp. 552–672.

Eby, Frederick, and Charles F. Arrowood, *The History of Education, Ancient and Medieval.* New York: Prentice-Hall, Inc., 1940. Pp. 578–629.

Good, Harry G., *A History of Western Education.* New York: Crowell-Collier and Macmillan, Inc., 1960. Pp. 58–63.

Gross, Richard E. (Ed.), *Heritage of American Education.* Boston: Allyn and Bacon, Inc., 1962. Pp. 103–107.

Hamilton, Edith, *Witness to the Truth—Christ and His Interpreters.* New York: W. W. Norton & Company, Inc. 1948. Rev. ed., 1957.

Marrou, Henri, *Saint Augustine.* New York: Harper & Row, Publishers, 1957.

Mayer, Frederick, *A History of Educational Thought.* Columbus, Ohio: Charles E. Merrill Books, Inc., 1960. Pp. 115–132.

Moore, Ernest C., *The Story of Instruction: The Church, the Renaissance and the Reformation.* New York: Crowell-Collier and Macmillan, Inc., 1938. Pp. 1–91.

Mulhern, James. *A History of Education,* 2d ed. New York: The Ronald Press Company, 1959. Pp. 213–227.

Oates, Whitney J., *Basic Writings of St. Augustine.* New York: Random House, Inc., 1948.

Paoli, Ugo Enrico, *Rome, Its Life and Culture.* New York: David McKay Company, Inc., 1963.

Smith, Huston, *The Religions of Man*. New York: Harper & Row, Publishers, 1958. Pp. 266–308.

Ulich, Robert, *History of Educational Thought*. New York: American Book Company, 1950. Pp. 61–88.

——— (Ed.), *Three Thousand Years of Educational Wisdom*, 2d ed., enl. Cambridge, Mass.: Harvard University Press, 1954. Pp. 127–171.

Wells, H. G., *The Outline of History*. Updated by Raymond Postgate. New York: Garden City Books, 1961.

Williamson, G. A., *The World of Josephus*. Boston: Little, Brown & Company, 1964. Especially pp. 46–47, 63–64, 103–120.

SELECTED PAPERBACKS

Augustine, St., *The City of God*. New York: Doubleday & Company, Inc., 1958.

Beck, Robert Holmes, *A Social History of Education*. Englewood Cliffs, N.J.: Prentice-Hall, Inc., 1965.

Burckhardt, Jacob, *The Age of Constantine the Great*. New York: Doubleday & Company, Inc., 1956.

Carcopino, Jerome, *Daily Life in Ancient Rome*. New Haven, Conn.: Yale University Press (Yale Paperbound), 1960.

Castle, E. B., *Ancient Education and Today*. Baltimore: Penguin Books, Inc., 1961.

Davies, J. G., *The Early Christian Church, A History of the First Five Centuries*. New York: Doubleday & Company, Inc., 1967.

Dudley, Donald R., *The Civilization of Rome*. New York: New American Library of World Literature, Inc., 1962.

Fremantle, Anne (Ed.), *The Age of Belief: The Medieval Philosophers*. New York: New American Library of World Literature, Inc., 1950

Frend, W. H. C., *Martyrdom and Persecution in the Early Christianity*. New York: Doubleday & Company, Inc., 1967.

Herberg, Will, *Protestant, Catholic, Jew*. New York: Doubleday & Company, Inc., Anchor Books, 1960.

Hesse, Herman, *Siddhartha*. New York: New Directions, 1951.

Hollister, C. Warren, *Roots of the Western Tradition*. New York: John Wiley & Sons, Inc., 1966. Pp. 178–199.

Huxley, Julian, *Religion without Revelation*. New York: New American Library of World Literature, Inc., 1957.

Lewis, C. S., *Mere Christianity*. New York: Crowell-Collier and Macmillan, Inc., 1958.

Lot, Ferdinand. *The End of the Ancient World*, rev. ed. New York: Harper & Row, Publishers, 1961.

Marrou, Henri Irenée, *A History of Education in Antiquity*. Trans. by George Lamb. New York: New American Library of World Literature, Inc., 1964.

Marty, Martin E., *A Short History of Christianity*. New York: Meridian Books, Inc., 1959.

Muller, Herbert J., *The Uses of the Past, Profiles of Former Societies.* New York: New American Library of World Literature, Inc., 1952. Pp. 158–215.

Queen, Stuart A., and Robert W. Habenstein, *The Family in Various Cultures.* Philadelphia: J. B. Lippincott Company, 1967. "The Legacy of the Early Christian Family," pp. 181–201.

Ryan, Patrick J., *Historical Foundations of Public Education.* Dubuque, Iowa: William C. Brown Company, Publishers, 1965.

Schonfield, Hugh J., *Those Incredible Christians.* New York: Bantam Books, Inc., 1968.

Sloyan, Gerard S., *The Gospel of Saint Mark.* Collegeville, Minn.: The Liturgical Press, 1960. Pp. 3–15.

Smith, Huston, *The Religions of Man.* New York: New American Library of World Literature, Inc., 1965.

Viorst, Milton (Ed.), *The Great Documents of Western Civilization.* New York: Bantam Books, Inc., 1965. Pp. 1–14, 40–75.

CHAPTER 8

Spiritual Discipline for the Soul's Salvation

In the beginning was the Word, and the Word was with God, and the Word was God. . . . All things were made through him, and without him was not anything made that was made. In him was life, and the life was the light of men. The light shines in the darkness, and the darkness has not overcome it. . . . And the Word became flesh and dwelt among us, full of grace and truth; . . .[1]

THE MEDIEVAL CONCEPT OF EDUCATION

For over a thousand years the Roman government had continued, successfully facing many serious adversities and beginning to absorb a strange new religion. Now, early in its second millennium, a number of changes occurred that would in a few years cause Rome's decline and fall; among these were continued pressure on the frontiers, a decline in Roman vigor, failing appreciation of the *vir bonus*, and a fatal lack of an orderly law of succession. The removal of the seat of government from the city on the Tiber to Roma Nova (Constantinople) on the Bosphorus represented a symptom of the changed conditions.

Barbarian infiltration continued and the deposing of Romulus Augustulus, the Little Emperor, by the Gothic chief Odoacer (476 A.D.) is usually considered to mark the end of the Roman Empire in the West and, consequently, the passage from ancient to medieval history. For, the sovereign having been removed and the imperial regalia sent to the East in token of the presumed reunion of the Empire, the collapse of the western

---

[1] John 1:1–5, 14, Revised Standard Version.

157

sector of the great imperium of Augustus and Trajan was complete. Although there was no similar breakdown of political continuity at Constantinople, nor would there be for another thousand years, the West was henceforth to be ruled by the Teutonic invaders and their descendants. And so was initiated a new Occidental civilization, founded on the remains of Rome and modified and redirected by the vigorous influence of another successor to the imperial power, the organized and militant Christian church.

Medievalism, then, represents a fusion of three dominant elements: (1) the decaying social and moral conditions fostered throughout western Europe by the Roman government and economic structure under the later Caesars; (2) the individualistic feudalism of the Germanic barbarians who had swept down from the north and gradually undermined the power of the Roman Empire; and (3) the enterprising, formalized, and hierarchically ordered Christian church. Two of these components have already been noted. Teutonic feudalism, however, must be described, as this unique institution adds another foundation stone to the development of educational theory and practice.

The Teutons, or Germans, together with the Celts and the Slavs, belong to the same Indo-European branch of the human race to which the Greeks and the Italians belong and originated in the same regions north of the Black and Caspian seas. The Celts earlier had moved westward and occupied Britain, Ireland, Gaul, and a part of Spain, where in time they were conquered and civilized by the Romans. The Teutonic tribes too had wandered here and there over the plains of central Europe until their desire for the things of civilization impelled them to move westward and southward into the provinces of imperial Rome.

One need not doubt that these Teutonic peoples were inherently as capable as the Greeks and the Italians; in their location, however, they had fewer means of learning the arts and institutions of higher civilization. They therefore remained barbarians for a much longer time, but they were far from being savages. They had developed, but they had developed along different lines from the people of the south, with fewer intellectual complications, more personal dignity, and a more intimate contact with the rigors of wind and sky and sea. Their culture at the time they began to move in upon Rome was at the nomadic agricultural level, very similar to that of the early Hebrews under Moses. The morals of marriage and of the family were pure among them; they respected womanhood far more than the later Greeks and Romans. Their sense of personal dignity would not permit these early Teutonic peoples, as had the Spartans and early Romans, to yield their liberty to the iron discipline of a state, to make themselves an unthinking part of a social machine. Caesar, in his *Commentaries*, speaks of the Germans with great respect, and Tacitus lauds their virtues in his *Germania* and *Annals*.

Before they were Christianized, the Teutons worshiped the powers of nature—gods of war, of harvest, of the home, of waters, woods, and seasons, of various living things and natural forces. Priests attended to the public worship in sacred groves, for there were no images or temples. They were a fierce and warlike people, adventuresome and bold. Each tribe followed a hereditary king or a temporary duke elected to lead it in war or in migration. The chieftain rode in the midst of his mounted retainers, who were pledged to loyal service—this "Teutonic following," being the prototype of the lord-and-vassal relationship of the medieval feudal system.

These various Teutonic groups—the Franks, the Anglo-Saxons, the Alans, the Burgundians, the Lombards, the Visigoths, the Ostrogoths, the Vandals—were powerfully to harass the empire and eventually to establish the many petty kingdoms and principalities of feudal medievalism.

The Christian Church built of these rough but virile tribes something in the nature of a religious empire; yet the Church had inherited the general degradation of Roman civilization and now was prone to compromise and to act on expediency rather than principle. She had been turned aside from her noble aims and the higher life by a series of long devastating struggles over forms of worship, creeds, doctrines, and organization; thus uniformity of belief and practice had been secured at great price; bitter persecution of the unorthodox and heretical had left grave wounds in the body of Christianity. Furthermore, church adherents had entered into secular life and were sometimes more inclined to emphasize religious formulae than a Christlike life. The obligations of morality were often ignored, and leaders as well as laymen indulged in practices forbidden by the church of the first and second centuries.

It is not surprising that, under such circumstances, education and learning declined and the spirit of inquiry became virtually extinct. Many parish priests were only superficially trained; many church officials advanced themselves more often by intrigue than by scholarship or humanitarian service.

Yet in some monasteries in Ireland, Wales, and later Britain, the shining flame of piety and learning was preserved, a legacy that was eventually to kindle similar lights in other places; and at the monastery of Jarrow, in England, Bede the Venerable (673–735), by his saintly and stainless life and ardent love of learning, redeemed the church from the curse of absolute intellectual barrenness. Compared, however, with the earlier centuries of church history, with the distinguished leadership of a Jerome or an Augustine, much of the medieval period was characterized by a "mournful sterility of sanctified erudition."[2]

---

[2] Since little more than mention has been made of St. Jerome in this volume, the student would do well to turn to Robert Ulich (Ed.), *Three Thousand Years of Educational Wisdom* (Cambridge, Mass.: Harvard University Press, 1947), pp. 135–136, 164–171, for a profile of Jerome's scholarship. From the educational stand-

Nevertheless, out of this general lassitude, political disorganization, and occasional chaos, the Middle Ages developed four institutions which were fundamental in the evolution of modern educational concepts and practices: (1) monasticism, (2) scholasticism, (3) feudalism, and (4) the guild system. In this chapter we shall discuss the educational implications of each.

THE EDUCATIONAL IDEALS AND PRACTICES OF MONASTICISM

To begin, we should note that monasticism did not originate with, and is not confined to, Christianity. In the majority of early Oriental religions, ascetics, for personal or social reasons, chose to devote themselves to a solitary and contemplative life apart from the affairs of the world. This practice was especially common among the Hindus because of the mystic character of their religion. Undoubtedly the development of Christian monasticism was influenced by these earlier monastic practices.

In the beginnings of the church, all Christians considered themselves a people apart, a separate community within society, participating as little as possible in the political and social activities of the world which they judged evil and immoral. After Christianity was officially tolerated and became fashionable, large numbers entered the church for reasons of expediency, prompting a desire in many of the more spiritually minded to differentiate themselves from the ordinary membership. Believing that the perfection of soul necessary to eternal salvation was to be secured only by abstaining from worldly pleasures and the secular activities of society, these ascetics fled from the centers of population, subjected their bodies to rigorous discipline, and endeavored to develop the "habit of the presence of God." Even before this, many Christians, fugitives from persecution, had fled into the desert, the mountains, or the wilderness, where they could worship in safety. There were also millenarians who believed that the second advent of Christ was near at hand, and that disinterest in the life around them would better prepare them for the coming.

The term *monasticism* comes from the Greek *monos*, meaning *alone*, and the earliest form of monasticism was true to this root. From almost the very beginning of the history of the church, ascetics had retired into the deserts where, like the famous Anthony of Egypt (251–356), they lived entirely alone as anchorites, or hermits. But the social instinct eventually prevailed; and we discover that about 330 A.D. the hermit Pachomius organized a community form of monasticism on an island in the valley of the Nile. Here the monks lived apart in separate cells for contemplation and

---

point, his chief contribution is the translation of the Bible from its Greek and Hebrew sources into the Latin version known as the Vulgate.

THE EDUCATIONAL IDEALS AND PRACTICES OF MONASTICISM

mediation, but came together for meals, prayers, and religious ceremonies. This cenobitic type of monasticism was introduced into Greece by Basil about 350 A.D. and soon afterward Athanasius and Jerome transferred the idea to Rome.

For nearly two centuries, each monastery was organized under its own system of rules, which varied widely; but in 529 the organization of community monasticism became definite and uniform with the formulation of the Rule of Benedict. St. Benedict (480–543) founded the monastery Monte Cassino in southern Italy and drew up a code of seventy-three articles which covered in detail the organization and administration of the monastery and the daily life of its members. Eventually the Rule of Benedict was adopted by the monastic orders of the West; and succeeding orders have based their code upon it.

At first thought it might seem that such a movement would have but little influence upon education. And it is indeed true that the anchoritic form of monasticism made no educational contributions. The cenobitic form, however, developed the monastery as an educational institution and made large contributions not only to the Middle Ages but to later times. We owe much to the Christian monasteries for preserving and spreading learning and culture. They not only conserved ancient knowledge but they produced chronicles and religious writings of their own and made copies of the sacred writings of the early church. We rely on the works of these monks for much of our knowledge of the Middle Ages. The monasteries opposed the vice and corruption of the medieval world; and they were an influence in taming the warlike spirits and refining the rustic customs of the Teutonic peoples. Through the monasteries, Europe acquired industrial skills and a conception of the true dignity of manual labor. The poor, the sick, and the hungry found succor within their gates and at the hands of the mendicant friars. The monasteries were the schools, the libraries, the publishing houses, the literary centers, the hospitals, and the workshops of medieval times. Their educational influence was most significant.

The wide extent of the monastic schools geographically—from Scotland to the Nile—and their long life—stretching from the fourth to the sixteen centuries (with some few even in the present day)—renders generalization a difficult task. The salient features of monastic education, however, follow.

Aims

In general, the ultimate aim of monastic education was the same as the ultimate aim of monastic life—the salvation of individual souls. The primary idea of monasticism was asceticism, the disciplining of all bodily desires and all human affections and aspirations so that the mind and the soul might be devoted to the interests of the higher life. The immediate aim was physical and moral discipline.

Certain elements in the monastic ideal are not new but are to be found in the religions and philosophies of Jews, Persians, Hindus, Egyptians, and Greeks. Stoic contempt for pain and death and indifference to the vicissitudes of fortune; Pythagorean silence and submission to the forces of physical nature; Brahmanic rejection of the material world and absorption in the infinite spirit; Zoroastrian concern with the eternal struggle between the forces of good and evil—all are to be found in monasticism. Together with the Christian ideal of life based on a higher code of morality, monasticism fused all these and organized them into a system based on two principles: (1) bodily mortification and (2) renunciation of the world.

One aim of monasticism was to deny all the claims and desires of the body. The virtue of a monk was often measured by his ingenuity in devising new ways of punishing the body—by fasting or insufficient and inappropriate foods, by going without sufficient sleep, by wearing insufficient and coarse clothing, by assuming unnatural and painful bodily positions, by enduring all forms of physical torture. Any method that could produce bodily suffering was used as a subjugation of the flesh. Such physical discipline was for the sake of spiritual growth and the moral improvement of the penitent.

The second principle, world renunciation, meant denying all the claims of social and human institutions. The Rule of Benedict imposed upon the monk three vows: chastity, poverty, obedience. (1) The ideal of chastity involved giving up the family and all the human relationships and affections growing out of the institution of the home. For family ties and responsibilities were substituted religious relationships and spiritual interests, expressed in meditation and continuous devotion and worship. (2) The ideal of poverty included rejection of all the economic relationships and material interests of life. Upon entering the monastery, one surrendered his right to property and all claims to inheritance. Within the monastery all things were held in common; and, although the monastery itself could acquire property and become very wealthy, the individual monk could make no claim to any personal share in the wealth. It was because of this ideal of poverty that charity and alms giving were exalted in the Middle Ages as the highest Christian virtue, later paving the way for modern Christian philanthropy and benevolence. (3) The ideal of obedience included the renunciation of all power and rank and distinction. When one chose to enter the monastery, he had to give up all rights of personal choice, of disposing of his own time, of satisfying his own individual interests. He had to subject himself to the will of his superiors and the wishes of his brothers. He had to give up all allegiance to other institutions. This meant the surrender of his individual personality, as well as the negation of all political and social affiliations. Monasticism, then, renounced completely the three great aspects of social organization: the home, the economic structure, and the political state. The aim of monastic education was to prepare not for this world, but the next.

With the exception of this lack of interest in the political aspects of living, much of the organization of monastic life—as well as the organization of the governmental structure of the church—may be traced to Plato's picture of the ideal state in *The Republic*.

In the monastic ideal there was often an element of mysticism or transcendentalism. Most medieval mystics were also monks, though mysticism was found outside the monasteries and after the monastic period. The aim of the mystic or of the transcendentalist was to attain the highest spiritual knowledge and the purest spiritual satisfaction through appropriate training in the arts of meditation, contemplation, and inspiration. It was an attempt to grasp through intuition the ultimate reality of the "Divine Presence" and thus be in direct communication with God. To the mystic, God was an experience, not an object of reason; and there was a distinct possibility of the realization of the Divine to such an extent that the mystic could lose himself wholly in this attainment, while the material world and all human relationships became as nothing. Monastic mysticism, then, aimed at a life of contemplation and of devout and direct communion with God. To the extent that the monks were mystics, monasticism was a spiritual as well as a physical and moral discipline.

Types

With such aims, the work of the monastic schools was restricted to literary activity and manual training, both of which were looked upon as phases of moral and religious education. But, since the human relationships of the monk were so few in number, the moral education was not of a very broad character; and only in the case of the mystic was there religious education in its truest sense.

Article 48 of the Rule of Benedict declares: "Idleness is the great enemy of the soul, therefore the monks shall always be occupied, either in manual labor or in holy reading." The rule specified seven hours of manual work and two hours of reading sacred literature daily. The requirement of manual labor was to keep the monks in good physical condition and active so that they would have little time for temptation or brooding. They became skilled artisans in wood, leather, and metal; skilled farmers trained in agriculture and horticulture. Through the agency of the monasteries, swamps were drained, forests cleared, desert regions reclaimed, hillsides terraced with vineyards, and large areas developed for agriculture. The peasants were taught better methods of agriculture, provided with agricultural information, and taught various types of practical arts and crafts. In the convents for women, which corresponded to the monasteries for men and operated under similar rules, the requirement of manual labor was carried out in weaving church hangings and embroidering altar cloths and church vestments, and these arts had to be taught to the novices. Everywhere under this dignifying of manual labor, the Teutonic barbarians as well as others were raised to a new level of practical civilization.

The reading requirement led to the collection of manuscripts in monastery libraries and the copying of manuscripts to provide duplicate copies for themselves and for exchange with other monasteries. The work in the *scriptorium*, or copying room, was done to a large extent by those incapable of hard manual labor. They were allowed to spend their seven hours of work in this occupation. But the monks did not confine their literary labors to mere copying. They also produced many original (though frequently mediocre) writings of a religious, moral, or historical nature. Thus both the manual and literary training needed to carry on the activities of the monasteries were always directed toward moral and religious purposes.

Content

The subject matter used by the monastic schools was eventually incorporated into the fixed curriculum of the Seven Liberal Arts, consisting of (1) the Trivium, grammar, rhetoric, and dialectic; and (2) the Quadrivium, arithmetic, geometry, astronomy, and music. In the earlier monasteries, the educational content was very rudimentary, intended to prepare for the essential duties of the monastic life. Novices were required to learn to read in order to study the sacred books; to write in order to copy manuscripts; to sing in order to take part in the religious ceremonies; and to calculate so that they could compute the time of the church festivals.

Later, in the more advanced monasteries, certain elements from Greek and Roman classical culture were introduced. The subjects were usually studied from compendia or encyclopedias rather than from direct sources. Those most popular were Capella's *The Marriage of Philology and Mercury*; Boethius' *Consolations of Philosophy*; Cassiodorius' *On the Liberal Arts and Sciences*; and Isidore of Seville's *Origines*. It was Cassiodorus who gave to the world the term *seven liberal arts* and Isidore who first used the terms *trivium* and *quadrivium*.[3]

The content in this monastic curriculum is not well indicated by the names of the subjects as they had somewhat different meanings from those which they have today. *Grammar*, the study most emphasized in monastic education, was an introduction to literature. The pupil first acquired some skill in the rudiments of reading and then read the various Christian authors and, in some of the stronger monasteries, Vergil and other pagan authors. *Rhetoric* was largely written composition; but, besides teaching how to write various kinds of church letters, documents, and reports, it included some knowledge of church history and canonical law. *Dialectic* was similar

---

[3] See Paul Abelson, *The Seven Liberal Arts, A Study in Mediaeval Culture* (New York: Russell & Russell, 1965), for a thorough interpretation of the origins and content of these subjects.

to the formal logic of today; and, although it played little part in the curriculum of the earlier monastic schools, it later became the major subject of the trivium under the Scholastic movement, which we shall discuss later.

Arithmetic consisted at first of little more than the calculation of church festivals and holidays; but, in the tenth century, with the introduction of columnal calculation and the Arabic system of notation, its content was enlarged to include the keeping of accounts. *Geometry* at first dealt with the geometrical and geographical elements useful in surveying, architecture, and map making, but later included the complete system of Euclid. *Astronomy* was studied to determine the dates of festivals and fast days, and the proper time for planting and harvesting crops and engaging in other practical pursuits. *Music* was the study of the chants and other sacred compositions used in the church services.

Agencies and Organization

Aside from the cathedral schools, which provided very meager fare, and the parish schools, which quite superficially carried on the work of the earlier catechumenal schools, the monastic schools were the only agencies for education throughout most of the medieval era. Boys were customarily admitted to the monastic school at the age of ten and, after a course of training lasting for eight years, were admitted to the monastic order at eighteen. But in many of the monasteries and convents, particularly in the later centuries of the Middle Ages, boys and girls who did not intend to become monks and nuns were admitted as pupils. They were called *externi* to distinguish them from the *interni*, or *oblati*, who were to enter the order and take vows. The head of the monastic school was the abbot.

Monastic schools probably reached their greatest efficiency under Charlemagne (742–814) in the eighth and ninth centuries. This Frankish German warrior and Holy Roman Emperor favored all sorts of religious work including that of the monastery and of the cathedral.[4] The standards of the English monastic schools were raised by Alfred the Great (849–901), who was himself a scholar. Under such leaders the monastic schools of Western Europe multiplied rapidly and became more efficient in organization and administration.

Methods

In methods, the teachers of the monastic schools showed great interest and skill. The general method of teaching was the catechetical, or question-and-answer, technique. Since copies of authentic manuscripts were rare, teachers resorted frequently to dictation. The instructor would dictate a passage to the pupils, who would copy it for memorizing. It must be re-

---

[4] See Eleanor Shipley Duckett, *Alcuin, Friend of Charlemagne* (New York: Crowell-Collier and Macmillan, Inc., 1951), for a sensitive picture of Charlemagne's efforts to bring the dispensation of knowledge to his Frankish court.

membered that no instruction in the vernacular was given, Latin being the only language for learning; and that these schools were secondary rather than elementary. Discipline was severe, an attitude enforced by the ascetic character of cloistered life. Teachers made frequent use of the rod, individual differences being a matter of little concern to them.

In the mystic phases of monastic education, there was dependence upon the methods of quiet meditation and contemplation, since the mystics believed that the highest knowledge and the deepest experiences of life could be gained only through divine inspiration.

THE CATHEDRAL SCHOOLS AND DEVELOPING UNIVERSITIES

Late in the medieval period, that is, during the eleventh and twelfth centuries, there was a stirring of new life in Christian scholarship; and the revised beliefs and logical methods of discussion of its proponents have been termed *scholasticism*. The early Middle Ages, from the sixth to the tenth centuries, had been an era of faith, in which men had accepted without question the creeds and dogmas established by the church. But with the cessation of the barbarian invasions of the north and the east, with Europe assured a period of comparative peace and quiet, there was time for intellectual activities. With the reception into Christian Europe of Aristotelian science from Saracenic Spain, and with the return of the Crusaders from their sojournings among the Byzantine Greeks and Arabs, skepticism began to assert itself. Men speculated now on the validity of doctrines they had accepted unquestioningly. The result was that in certain monastic and cathedral schools the study of theology was pursued with new vigor; in the universities profound thinkers came to be recognized as leaders, attracting students from near and far.

There were great schoolmen before the eleventh century—Bede, Alcuin, and Erigena (John the Scot) (c. 810–880); but scholasticism received no important contributions until the treatises and teachings of Anselm (1033–1109), after 1093 Archbishop of Canterbury, often called the father of scholasticism.

Scholasticism does not refer to any one set of doctrines, but is rather a general designation for the particular methods and tendencies of philosophical speculation that were encouraged within the monasteries and cathedral schools in the eleventh century. These attained a measure of perfection in the universities in the twelfth and thirteenth centuries, and declined rapidly after the fourteenth. The most striking characteristics of scholasticism were the narrowness of its field of thought and the thoroughness of its methods. As Shaw observes:

> Scholasticism began as a movement to rationalize the doctrines of the Church; it ended in an elaborate system of civilization and culture. A vine

was planted, took deep root, and began to fill the land; the hills were covered with the shadow of it and it sent out branches unto the river and boughs unto the sea.

This scholastic vine, as we are calling it, may have been more leafy than fruitful; but it possessed life and showed itself capable of ramifying into all the nooks and crannies of Church and State.[5]

Aims

The aim of scholasticism was to support the doctrines of the church by rational argument. It was an attempt to support authority by the intellect, to justify faith by reason, to substantiate theology by logic. It was assumed that the church held possession of all final truth by divine revelation; and this "truth," diversely stated as truths, had been accepted on faith. The aim of scholastic education was to show that these truths were consistent with each other and in complete accord with reason. The origin of this aim is to be found in the fact that controversy from the East and with heretics made it necessary to promulgate this prescribed belief not on faith alone, but on the basis of reason.[6]

Up to this time, the medieval church had been hostile to the intellectual approach to theology; and when Erigena had ventured the assertion that all true philosophy was identical with church doctrine, his efforts met with little favor. It was felt that faith was sufficient and did not stand in need of any rational defense. But when, two centuries after Erigena, Anselm expressed the same attitude, his arguments met with approval. Anselm believed that reason was in accord with dogma, but maintained that faith must precede knowledge and that doubt as a preliminary to belief could not be tolerated. His motive was *Credo ut intellegam*; and in his *Monologue on the Method in Which One May Account for His Faith*, he wrote the following explicit statements:

I do not seek to know in order that I may believe, but I believe in order that I may know.

The Christian ought to advance to knowledge through faith; not come to faith through knowledge.

A proper order demands that we believe the deep things of Christian faith before we presume to reason about them.

Throughout the period of scholasticism this aim was dominant—to show the essential harmony between reason and faith.

Scholastic education sought also to develop the ability to formulate beliefs into logical systems and to defend these against any intellectual arguments that might be advanced against them. Never was any attempt

---

[5] Charles Gray Shaw, *Trends of Civilization and Culture* (New York: American Book Company, 1932), pp. 236–237.

[6] For an incisive picture of these objectives, see Edward Kennard Rand, *Founders of the Middle Ages* (New York: Dover Publications, Inc., 1928), "Boethius, the Scholastic," pp. 135–180.

made to examine critically the fundamental beliefs already formulated and accepted on authority. There was no attempt to stimulate the inquiring attitude based upon doubt and the absence of preconceived notions, which is the basis of modern scientific thinking. The chief purpose of scholasticism was to establish in a carefully organized philosophical system the theology that had been accepted as inspired. The aim of scholastic education was essentially intellectual discipline.

Types and Content

Scholasticism, as a teaching system, limited itself to religious and intellectual education, the content of which was entirely confined to theology and religious philosophy. The range of knowledge within which the scholastic mind was allowed to work was very narrow; scholars might defend only what the church held orthodox, and so applied themselves intensively to only a few subjects or questions. As a result, the scholastics subdivided and systemized their material beyond all measure. Just as the church was imposing its language and ideals upon every other activity of medieval life—architecture, music, and literature—so it set its restricting influence upon scholarship and thought. The curriculum of scholasticism, consequently, was not so much a new system of philosophy as it was a new system of philosophizing about theological beliefs.

In this task of devising a system, the scholastics divided into two camps, or schools of thought, the great controversy being the nature of universal concepts. Anselm, at Canterbury, was the chief representative of the *realists*, a term, by the way, which has a directly opposite meaning today to what it had then. Scholastic realism was based on Neoplatonism and perhaps would be better understood if we used the term Platonic idealism, which means belief in the reality of ideas. The realist believed that ideas, or concepts, are the only real entities, and that the objects known through the senses are only copies of these ideas, "specimens of the species," as it were. He contended that the human senses are deceptive, and that true knowledge can be reached only through an intellectual and abstract grasp of universals.

The year before Anselm's advancement to Canterbury, Roscellinus (1050–1122), a canon of Compiègne, had been forced to retract his heresy of nominalism; and it was to combat the effect of this heresy that Anselm put forth his argument of realism. Roscellinus had based the position of the nominalists on the philosophy of Aristotle. He insisted that universal ideas and concepts are mere convenient names, abstractions, or symbols; that individual objects as known through the senses are the only true entities. This thesis was not very favorable to such religious concepts as God, man, original sin, and salvation, nor to the concept of the church itself; and the Council of Soissons saw that the heresy was suppressed.

In the twelfth century, Peter Abelard (1079–1142), whom Weber calls "the most independent, the most courageous, and the most relentless among the schoolmen,"[7] essayed the reconciliation of realism and nominalism in a position that is sometimes called conceptualism. He argued that, although a universal concept has no objective existence, it is not merely a name out of relation to individual objects, but is an expression of the sum total of characteristics that a group of individual objects have in common. Abelard was too much interested in the practical aspects and problems of life and teaching to dogmatize with his former teacher, William of Champeaux, and Anselm in asserting that there is no reality in the individual; and yet Abelard was too sound and honest a thinker to agree with Roscellinus that only individual objects are real; so he developed conceptualism, his theory that the universal is a concept which becomes real only when it is expressed in the individual.

Abelard rescued scholasticism from becoming purely metaphysical through the extreme position of realism; but, although his position was approved by the church, his insistence that reason was antecedent to faith and could be made the foundation of doctrine brought charges of heresy against him and he was twice condemned.[8] Nevertheless, Abelard's habit of intellectual inquiry as revealed in his *Sic et Non*—a series of 158 propositions on which he was prepared to argue pro and con, for example—*1. That faith is to be supported by human reason, et contra; 122. That marriage is lawful for all, et contra; 141. That works of mercy do not profit those without faith, et contra.*—certainly stirred the medieval university and was a preview of the true spirit of university study. Abelard's students significantly called him *Rhinoceros Indomitus.*

In the thirteenth century scholasticism reached its zenith with the union of Aristotelian philosophy and Christian dogma in a logical theological system by Thomas Aquinas (1225–1274), whose *Summa Theologiae* remains the authoritative exposition of Roman Catholic theology, and was declared so by Pope Leo XIII in 1879. The resolution of the great realist-nominalist controversy was stated as follows by St. Thomas:

> The universal concept existed in the mind of God *before* the creation of the object; the universal is *implanted* in the object and the universal is comprehended by the mind of man *after* the object. Ideas do exist; they are *real*; but things also exist, they are *real*.

Agencies

The earlier representatives of scholasticism were associated with cathedral and monastic schools—Anselm at Canterbury; Roscellinus at

---

[7] Alfred Weber, *History of Philosophy*, trans. by Frank Thilly (New York: Charles Scribner's Sons, 1925), p. 224.

[8] See Helen Waddell, *Peter Abelard* (New York: Holt, Rinehart and Winston, Inc., 1933), for a penetrating picture of his personal and professional life, especially the tragic story of his great love for Heloise.

Compiègne; William, Abelard, and Aquinas at Notre Dame, Paris. They presented their ideas by both teaching and writing; students gathered at these schools to hear their lectures. Their works were widely read and copied; many were used as textbooks in the cathedral schools, especially such popular works as the *Sententiae* by Peter Lombard (1100–1160), Abelard's pupil, and Abelard's *Sic et Non* and St. Thomas' *Summa Theologiae.*

As time went on the fame of certain Schoolmen spread and brought large numbers of more mature students to the cathedral cities. These increased numbers created the need for a more flexible educational institution, and so originated the medieval university. The interest awakened in such secular studies as civil law and medicine by the Crusades and contacts with Muslim culture further stimulated the growth of universities. Almost simultaneously there developed the University of Paris for the study of theology, and the University of Bologna (1088) for the study of civil and canonical law. Although at Salerno a Saracenic school of medicine developed earlier, Bologna is sometimes considered the first of the medieval universities. *Bononia docet*, "Bologna teaches," on the university seal indicates her pride.

Organization

The organization of the monastic and cathedral schools continued as before, but there were in various lands stronger spurs to efficiency. Although he had little learning himself, Charlemagne was an ardent advocate of learning and of perpetuating the Latin culture with the Christian faith. In his desire to effect cultural unity in his Frankish kingdom, he revived learning in the north through development of his palace school. This institution for the scions of nobility was conducted at his court with the purpose of producing intelligent and knowledgeable leaders for church and state; to upgrade its leadership Charlemagne imported from the cathedral school at York, England, Alcuin (735–804), the most prominent schoolmaster of the day.

Alcuin served not only as director of the palace school but, as abbot of Tours, as head of Charlemagne's entire educational apparatus. To implement his plans Charlemagne issued official decrees, or capitularies, to the abbots of his monastic schools and to the bishops in charge of Frankish cathedral schools for a better-educated clergy and the establishment of parish schools, where they did not already exist, for children who showed special promise. The emperor's *missi dominici*, or official messengers, were also to ensure that his decrees were carried out.

In England Alfred the Great followed suit. He sent to Flanders for Grimbald, who became abbot of the monastery school at Winchester; to Corbie for John the Saxon, who became abbot of Athelney; and to the continent for other outstanding scholars to bolster England's educational effort. Alfred, himself a scholar, edited a host of religious and historical works and translated them into the vernacular; indeed, at this time, he was engaged in beginning the composition of what became the Anglo-Saxon Chronicle! Regardless of such designations as *Dark Ages* for this early medieval period, learning on certain levels was quite alive.

Around the beginning of the second millennium A.D. the university, as we have come to know it, evolved. Its structure was quite different from that of the monastic or even the early cathedral schools, although the cathedral school or setting often became the locus for the new institution. The university began as an association of teachers, in effect, a guild, which was given official sanction by a charter issued by the Pope or Holy Roman Emperor and was, therefore, more independent of local ecclesiastical authority than was the cathedral school (under the bishop) or the monastic school (under the abbot). The university was also independent of political or secular control. Many privileges, hitherto granted only to the clergy, were guaranteed to its students under the charter; among them, exemption from taxation, exemption from military service, special courts outside of civil jurisdiction, and immunity from arrest by civil authorities.

The complete organization was known as the *Universitas Magistrorum et Scholarium*, the term *universitas* being given to any chartered company or association. Thus this group was merely a corporation of teachers and students. The entire student body was the *Studium Generale*; but outside the lecture hall students grouped themselves into *nations* according to their place of origin, for they came to the university from almost every country in Europe. Each nation annually elected a councilor. Each group of masters teaching the same subject was called a *facultas*, and each of these elected annually a dean. The deans of the faculties and the councilors of the nations made up the university council, which annually elected a rector who served with delegated power as the chief executive officer of the university. In some Italian universities the rector was a student, and students virtually governed the institution.

When a student entered the university (at about the age of fourteen), he attached himself to a master under whom he studied until he could "define and determine," that is, read, write, and speak Latin. When he could demonstrate by examination that he was adequately proficient, he was declared a bachelor. He then continued his studies under several masters for from four to seven years until he could "dispute," that is, defend his thesis or masterpiece. The successful defense of his thesis entitled him to his *licentia docendi*, or license to teach. He was now admitted to the ranks of the masters and was allowed to enter into competition with the other masters for students and to charge fees for his work.

By the end of the thirteenth century, most of the universities had become fully organized into four faculties: *arts, medicine, law,* and *theology*. By the arts faculty, the Trivium and the Quadrivium of the monastic schools were taught, amplified by Euclid's geometry and Ptolemy's astronomy. Upon completing the arts course, most of the students entered the course in theology, though some entered law and medicine. Law included both canon and civil law. Medicine at first made little headway until Saracenic culture influenced European universities, bringing with it the medical texts of Jewish and Saracenic doctors.

Methods

Methods of teaching under scholasticism and in the medieval universities were designed to give students knowledge of the subject matter studied and the ability to reason and debate. Two distinct processes were utilized: first, the lecture, or reading, in which the professor imparted the original text, glosses, and annotations so that the student could make an authentic copy for study; then, disputation, in which a student, or a group of students, was opposed by another. A position, or thesis, was stated; proof was given; objections were raised and refuted; the whole proposition was treated in a minutely logical fashion.

This scholastic method of logical analysis is exemplified in the works of Thomas Aquinas and Peter Lombard. Conventionally, there is (1) a statement of the thesis or proposition; (2) its proof; (3) a citation of solutions other than that accepted, with a refutation of each; and (4) a consideration of objections to the orthodox solution, with a rebuttal of each. Actually this procedure not only emphasizes systematic arrangement, but demands precision of thought and distinct conclusions. In this sense the word *scholarly* may be said to derive from scholasticism, although scholasticism had pitfalls not usually present in modern university study.

Scholasticism sought principally to arrive at deductions drawn from general principles. The preferred form of argument was the syllogism, a form of reasoning supplied by Aristotle. The classic example is:

(1) All men are mortal.
(2) Socrates is a man.
(3) Therefore Socrates is mortal.

There are three elements in the syllogism: (1) a major premise, or large class (term); (2) a minor premise, or smaller class, or "middle term"; and (3) a conclusion, or specific case. If the middle term (minor premise) can be placed entirely within the operation of the larger term (major premise), and the specific case (conclusion) can be placed within the operation of the middle term, then the specific case comes under the operation of the larger term and is said to be valid. (However, if the premises are false, the conclusion would be valid, but untrue.)

The scholastic method was often barren in its immediate results, for it was frequently diverted to endless and fruitless quibbling over nonessentials or abstract or peripheral aspects of theology. But it stimulated mental effort and thus contributed to a wider intellectual awakening, preparing the way for the Renaissance and the advent of modern science.

The advent of the university was beneficial, even though the early medieval institution had little discipline. The many privileges granted to encourage the students sometimes made them impatient of restraint; immune to the punishment of the secular courts, students often indulged in excesses and immoralities. University rules forbade monkeys, bears, dogs, and women and prohibited witchcraft, forgery, the wearing of daggers, and stealing. Yet students retained their immunities while traveling to and from the university, so it was easily possible for them to wander from one university to another—begging, roistering, and engaging in turbulent and unconventional practices. Many Latin poems and songs, some rather unprintable, have come down to us as witness to the reckless life of these *vagantes*, or Goliards.[9]

FEUDALISM AS A TYPE OF MEDIEVAL EDUCATION

Out of the decay and demoralization of the later Roman Empire society became as fixed as it had been during the empires of Egypt and Persia. Greek ideas of democracy seemed to vanish, and the Roman concept of universal citizenship became lost. The three classes operative during antiquity again appeared: priests, warriors, and workers. Until the close of the twelfth century in Western Europe, from the Spanish border to northern Sweden, society consisted only of the Christian clergy, the feudal nobility, and the anchored-to-the-land serfs. The end of the Pax Romana and new demands for education provided some necessity for this arrangement, primitive though it may seem.

Both monasticism and scholasticism were direct outgrowths of the ascendancy of the church, whose educational agencies were primarily designed for the training of clergy, regular and secular. Little thought was then given to the education of the lower class. The medieval serf's education was both limited and plain. As in the days prior to Hellenic civilization, the serf learned by direct imitation of his elders the "tilling of the soil, the hewing of wood, and the drawing of water." The simple religious instruction needed for the rites and ceremonies of the church was given by the parish priest.

For the nobility, however, a definite system of education was pro-

---

[9] See Helen Waddell, *Wandering Scholars*, 7th ed. (London: Constable & Co., Ltd., 1949), for a definitive picture of medieval student literature and life. Noah Edward Fehl, *The Idea of a University in East and West* (Hong Kong: Chung Chi Publications, 1962), pp. 1–221, gives a thorough university picture and is sensitive to the philosophical implications of its theory as well.

vided through a new social institution which resulted directly from the needs of medieval feudalism. The age of chivalry dates from about the beginning of the ninth century to the sixteenth, from when feudalism became firmly established to when, under the new national impetus, feudalism began to decay and disintegrate.

To understand chivalry we must first understand its feudal origins. The term *feudalism* itself is not easily explained. One origin considers it a derivative of the Latin *fides* (faith); another traces its descent from the Germanic *fehu* (cattle) for, among the early Teutonic peoples, property was reckoned in terms of cattle. Concerned with both loyalty and property, feudalism has been described as organizing people's relations through the focus of land tenure and binding all, from the king to the lowest serf, together by responsibilities of defense, and mutual service, and sustenance. Since turbulent and unsettled conditions made it practically impossible for the medieval king or lord to rule an extended domain, it served his purpose to divide a portion of his estate among his military retainers, giving each one authority over his holding. In return each retainer covenanted to give military or other aid as was required to his lord.[10] Theoretically, feudalism represented a perfect system balanced among its adherents: all for one, and one for all. (Since the serfs went with the land, they were not consulted.)

Such agreements were the genesis of the institution which was general in the ninth century and a powerful political and social force in the eleventh, twelfth, and thirteenth centuries.

The feudal system developed most thoroughly in France, Germany, Italy, England, and Scotland; its cradle was the empire of Charlemagne. Charles, when merely king of the Franks, had determined to build a great Christian empire to include all the Germans; and when he was crowned by the Pope "Emperor of the Romans" (800), he had truly succeeded. Almost every sovereign of the West had become his vassal. Charlemagne's wealth was in land, not in money. So he had paid his loyal war leaders and civil governors in large grants of land and promises of protection; and they had pledged to him their own aid and service and that of their men-at-arms, as had also the nobles he had conquered. His empire had been welded by the bonds of feudalism. The method was not new with Charlemagne; it was a convenience to his Frankish predecessors and to many another landowner. But such an extensive, orderly, and effective use was new, and it established feudalism as the social system of the Middle Ages.

Feudalism developed rapidly in Europe after the breakup of Charlemagne's empire. Because of the weak successors who ruled the divided

---

[10] For a thorough interpretation of the origins and practices of feudalism, see Robert S. Lopez, *The Birth of Europe* (New York: M. Evans and Company, Inc., 1967), pp. 159–169.

empire, and because of the inroads of Saracens, Slavs, and Huns, the century after Charlemagne was an age of disorder, and all classes were glad to avail themselves of the protection the system offered. This was especially true of the subordinate classes, for the castles of the feudal nobles provided fortresses against invading lords or bands of marauding brigands. When the kings and princes gave of their lands to feudal lords who in turn granted sections to lesser lords, and so on down, the land so granted was called a fief, or feud; the grantor was called lord, or liege; and the one who received the grant was a vassal, or retainer. The vassal pledged loyalty, military service, and other aid to his lord, and the lord in turn provided his vassal with counsel and protection. The great bulk of the population were serfs, who were bound to the soil and who passed with the land when it changed masters. Thus feudalism was a system of political and economic relationship. Political feudalism centered on the relation of the landlords or nobles to one another and ultimately to the monarch; economic feudalism centered on the relation of the lord to the serfs who toiled in his domain.

The essence of feudalism was service, expressed either in tilling the land or in fighting. Those whose service was of the military type were regarded as of noble character; those whose service consisted of cultivating the soil to which they were tied were deemed of base and common extraction. Thus there developed a warrior class made up of the nobles whose sole excuse for existence seemed that of fighting. The life of the typical lord was absorbed in his castled estate, war, and the chase. But out of this crudely bold life there evolved one of the most interesting of social developments—the system of chivalry. The rules and social usages that accumulated in connection with the life of the nobility constituted chivalry, and the preparation for this life chivalric education. The term *chivalry* comes from the French *cheval* (horse), horsemanship being a basic accomplishment in the system. A noble who had gone through the prescribed training and taken the vows was made a knight; so chivalric education was largely a training for knighthood.[11]

Aims

As a system of education for the nobility, chivalry aimed to teach the best ideals, social and moral, that the Teutons could understand. Chivalry tried to take what good there was in a brutal, selfish, unprincipled fighting society, and make it over in accordance with the standards of Christianity. It sought a happy blend of barbarian warrior with Christian saint. It taught the protection of the weak, gallantry toward women, honesty in everything. Chivalry provided a definite system of training to inculcate the "rudiments of love, war, and religion." As Messenger states:

---

[11] Lopez, pp. 164–165.

The greatest virtue of the times was courage. The most useful attainment was the ability to fight. The ideals and manner of life practiced and advocated by Christ and his followers could not be comprehended [by most men]. They could understand being heroic. . . . If the courage and the fighting could be put to some good use, the world would be better. This made a good start, and it was the task of chivalry to find some virtues that would harmonize with these. The desire for glory is a powerful motive. . . . Chivalry offered something glorious to fight for. Something particular, tangible, and personal serves as an objective much better than does an abstract principle. Love, war, and religion are more spectacular than labor, thought, and morality.[12]

The ideals of chivalry were quite different from those of monasticism and scholasticism. Instead of asceticism and intellectualism, chivalry emphasized action. It was a life of high ideals and standards; the true knight was to be devoted to the service of his God, his king, and his lady. Before he could be knighted, he must take (1) the vow of religion, expressing his loyalty to the church; (2) the vow of honor, expressing his loyalty to his feudal superior; (3) the vow of gallantry, expressing his loyalty to his lady. Chivalric education had the essential aim of social discipline, to train the knight to play his part in the faithful observance of the social usages, customs, and ideals approved by his social class. The maxim by which the knight lived was, Act as if the person for whom you have the highest regard were looking on. This produced in the knight courtesy, gallantry, generosity, and good manners—all of which had their refining influence upon society, even if these actions were performed mechanically rather than from the heart.

The ideals of chivalric education are depicted in the lyrics of the troubadours of France, the minnesingers of Germany, and the minstrels of England. Chaucer, Spenser, Scott, and Tennyson have delighted in telling of knightly deeds of courtesy and courage. There was, however, much affectation and superficiality, and Miguel de Cervantes rendered a wholesome service in depicting its exaggerated sentimentality in his delightful but bitter burlesque, *Don Quixote*.

The ideals of chivalry were probably not so effectively realized in England as in an earlier France. Green, in a commentary on the introduction of the tournament in England by Edward I, speaks of "the frivolous unreality of the new chivalry," "the false air of romance," and, in connection with Edward himself, states that "chivalry exerted on him a yet more fatal influence in its narrowing of all sympathy to the noble class, and its exclusion of the peasant and the craftsman from all claim to pity."[13]

---

[12] James F. Messenger, *An Interpretative History of Education* (New York: Thomas Y. Crowell Company, 1931), pp. 78–79.

[13] J. R. Green, *A Short History of the English People* (London: Macmillan & Co., Ltd., 1929), p. iii.

Types

Chivalric education was a form of social training. It emphasized manners more than morality, but as a training in social etiquette has probably never been surpassed. It emphasized military training; in fact, it made fighting a profession and devoted a large share of its attention to the development of professional military skills. It placed emphasis upon a phase of education that both monasteries and universities neglected—that of physical training. Religious training was of a rather superficial type: the knight was trained to take part in all the religious rites and ceremonies of the church. There was some literary training, but it was mostly oral and vernacular. Chivalric education was essentially class education and was distinctly aristocratic.

Content

The curriculum was one of activity rather than intellect. The course of study consisted of physical, social, military, and religious activities. At the earlier level the content consisted of health instruction, religious instruction, training in etiquette and obedience to superiors, in playing the harp, singing, chess, and the development of skills in riding, jousting, boxing, and wrestling. Sometimes a little training was given in reading and writing the vernacular. At the higher levels, the curriculum consisted of the Seven Free Arts: (1) jousting, (2) falconing, (3) swimming, (4) horsemanship, (5) boxing, (6) writing and singing verse, and (7) chess. Girls received a thorough training in social etiquette similar to that of boys, but physical and military training was omitted from their instruction. Instead, they were given training in household duties and in such domestic accomplishments as sewing, weaving, and embroidering. Chivalric education for girls differed from convent education in that there was more emphasis upon social and less upon religious and intellectual content.

The most important change fostered by chivalry was the rapid development of vernacular literatures and the practice of them as part of the content of education. By the time of Charlemagne there were two distinct groups of spoken language, the Germanic and the Roman-derived Romance. English, a mixture of Germanic tongues slightly Latinized during the Roman occupation and more so after the Norman Conquest, told its earliest tales of chivalry in the odd conglomeration that we know as Middle English. Similarly, within other Germanic and Romance groups, differing vernaculars developed individually in different localities. The written vernacular practiced in the schools of northern France differed greatly from that of southern France. The Garonne valley from 1100 and 1300 was a land of verse and song, stimulated by chivalry. The singing poets, the troubadours, brought their own hero tales and love ballads to the court at Toulouse and, traveling over Western Europe, helped greatly in the notable ascendancy of the French language. French soon replaced Latin as the language of secular culture of the Middle Ages.

Agencies

The earliest education of the child was in the hands of his mother in the home; later the lords and ladies of the castle of his father's feudal superior were the teachers. The castle, the tournament fields, and the fields of battle, were the schools for the education of the boy; the home and the court were the schools for the girl.

We should not fail to appreciate the importance of the troubadours, minnesingers, and minstrels as agencies of education during the earlier centuries of chivalry. The medieval age was, for the most part, one in which reading was done by few but monks, scholars, and sometimes merchants; travel was slow, difficult, and dangerous; diversions, aside from eating, playing games, hunting, and fighting, were few. Then pass the traveling troubadours! They were the gazetteers, the spreaders of news, the providers of entertainment and amusement. It was their office to bear tidings from castle to castle, to sing the praises of beautiful ladies and gallant knights. They were living magazines, who acquainted the inhabitants of one district with the customs and manners evolving in another—speech, dress, methods of hunting, habits of eating, rules of courtly etiquette; and sometimes they warned of impending danger from jealous rivals or robber bands. Even those troubadours who settled in a particular castle or remained in the castle of their birth exerted appreciable influence in the education of the youth of the estate. And all the while they were circulating the new vernacular, to which each area was contributing and upon which each was drawing.

Organization

From birth until the age of seven, the children of the gentry remained at home where they were given the necessary physical, moral, and religious training by their mothers. At the age of seven, they went to the castle of the feudal overlord. (This custom probably began when the subordinate nobles sent their sons and daughters as hostages or pledges of their fidelity to the overlord.) Orphan children were sent to the castle as wards, because the overlord legally was their guardian. Girls were sent to the court by their parents with the idea of making desirable marriages. Thus the castle became the center of chivalric education.

From seven to fourteen, the boy was a page and attended a noble lady of the court, who directed his education both indoors and out. Between fourteen and twenty-one, the youth was a squire and attended a knight. He still waited upon his lady, with whom he sang, played the harp, and played chess, but his chief duty was to attend upon his lord. Many services were required of him; he served the lord at table, made his bed, groomed his horse, cleaned his armor, carried his shield. He accompanied him in tournaments and actual battle, and thus learned the arts of both peace and war.

At twenty-one his education was complete and he was ready for knighthood. He prepared himself for the ceremony by confession, fasting, and an all-night vigil. Elaborate religious rites were performed; and after promising to be faithful, to protect women and orphans, never to lie or slander, to live in harmony with his equals, and to protect the church, he received the accolade, a slight blow on each shoulder with the flat of the sword; his new sword and spurs were buckled on, and he thus became a knight.[14]

Methods

Since chivalric education was largely the acquisition of skills, the methods used were those of example and practice. Attendance upon his lady and his lord enabled the boy to develop the social behavior and accomplishments of chivalry through imitation. The color and action of court life and the desire for social approval provided motivation for his learning. Ideals were acquired through the songs of love and war, which praised beautiful virtuous ladies and gallant valiant knights, and through the pledges taken in impressive ceremonies. Discipline was maintained through the ideals of obedience and service, though at times these ideals had to be enforced by threats of mortal combat. Pupils learned by doing, were motivated by high ideals, and were restrained and controlled by an adherence to recognized social standards.

THE GUILD APPROACH TO EDUCATION

The late Middle Ages contributed other factors in the development of educational theory: the rise of the middle class, towns, and the organization of the guild system, largely as a result of the Crusades.[15]

Although the Crusades failed to wrest the Holy Land from Muslim control, unexpected results, ultimately disastrous to the system that brought them about, did occur. The insulation of feudal life was broken down, communication between countries was stimulated, new desires were kindled among those who had gone East and those who heard their wondrous tales of a different way of life. The necessity of transporting the armies of the

---

[14] See Sir Edward Strachy, "The Chivalric Inheritance," p. 347, in Grant Uden (Ed.), *A Dictionary of Chivalry* (New York: Thomas Y. Crowell Company, 1968). See also National Geographic Society, *The Age of Chivalry* (Washington, D.C.: The Society, 1969).

[15] For a comprehensive and immensely readable account of this movement see Zoe Oldenbourg, *The Crusades*, trans. by Anne Carter (New York: Pantheon Books, Inc., 1966). Although dealing with only the first three Crusades, Oldenbourg draws a fine picture of the twelfth century, especially the human aspect of society in those changing times.

Crusaders resulted in the development of seaport cities as centers of shipping, trade, and banking. Visitors to the East became acquainted with new foods, clothing, and ornamentation; with new luxuries and staples. New desires created new necessities.

As a result, a system of banking, trade, and industry to import, process, and distribute the Eastern commodities was demanded. Towns in which the new commerce and industry were centered became free cities, with feudal immunity and almost total independence from church and king. By purchase, by diplomacy, and even by force such city-states obtained the rights of self-government and so guarded their liberties. "The somber merchant on his mule won in the tilt with the gay knight on horseback."

The burghers, merchant-capitalists, established a new order, a fourth class, distinct from nobles, clergy, and serfs. The needs of this new class were quite different from those of the older classes in medieval society. Consequently, a special type of education was demanded for the burgher's children.

Much of the life of the medieval community was centered on the guild system. Guilds were organizations, or associations, of people engaged in commerce and industry. There were two types: merchant guilds and craft guilds. Merchant guilds were the first to appear and flourished from the twelfth to the fourteenth centuries, especially in England. The members all resided in the same town and were both trade merchants and artisan merchants who dealt in their own manufactures. The local guild usually held a monopoly of the retail trade in its town and exercised the privilege of taxing outsiders who brought in goods for sale.

The craft guilds were associations of manufacturers, artisans, and skilled workers such as weavers, dyers, goldsmiths, or silversmiths. Each craft banded together to maintain and advance the standards of its work.[16] Most prominent in the fourteenth and fifteenth centuries, these guilds eventually divided into two organizations: the skilled craftsmen, who were the forerunners of modern trade unions; and the owners of the shops, who formed associations of capitalist employers, which were the forerunners of modern trade associations. Types of education adapted to their needs developed around these guilds.

Aims, Types, and Content

The primary need of this new middle class was for an education of a practical type. Vocational training was necessarily emphasized, for chil-

---

[16] Lopez, pp. 22, 57, 142–144, 277–278, 280–281, 339. For the details of guild activities, see Robert J. Blackham, *London's Livery Companies* (London: Sampson Low, Marston & Co., Ltd., 1930); Sister Mary A. Mulholland, *Early Guild Records of Toulouse* (New York: Columbia University Press, 1961); and John Edgcumbe Staley, *The Guilds of Florence* (New York: B. Blom, 1967).

dren were to be prepared for the activities of commercial and industrial life. The unique contribution of this movement to education was an emphasis upon a new type of vocational training. The burghers did not want a narrow type of vocational or trade training, which neglected everything else. Elementary instruction in the rudiments of reading and writing the vernacular and in arithmetic was always required as preparation for the industrial and commercial training of the guilds. Masters were obligated to give such instruction to their apprentices and to see that they received adequate religious instruction. Although guild schools were usually taught by priests, these schools were much more secular in spirit and aim than the cathedral, monastic, and parish schools. Usually the intellectual education of the guild class was on the elementary level; yet some guild schools later expanded into Latin schools, such as Merchant Taylors' in London.

Agencies

New types of schools developed in these trading cities for the education of the burgher children. Chantry schools were founded out of bequests made by wealthy merchants or traders, stipulating that special priests be employed to chant masses for the repose of the deceased patrons' souls. Since these special priests had much time at their disposal, many such bequests provided that they devote some time to instruct children of the city in the rudiments of elementary education. Sometimes, through a union of chantry foundations, strong schools were developed in the larger towns. There were 300 chantry schools in England alone at the time of the Reformation.

Burgher schools also arose in the larger cities. These were supported and controlled by the public authorities and were often taught by lay teachers as well as priests. The usual type was the guild school, for the children of craftsmen. These were taught by the same priests who performed religious functions, such as baptism and marriage, for the guild members. Burgher schools usually provided elementary education in the vernacular, which was required as a foundation for the later vocational education given in the guilds themselves.

Organization

The only formally organized education in the guild system was this vocational training. The members of the guilds were divided into three classes: masters, journeymen, and apprentices. The masters alone were entitled to own shops, buy raw materials, and sell the manufactured articles. They bought and sold at prices established by the guild, and their establishments were supervised by the guilds so that inferior goods would not be produced. The beginners were known as apprentices. By the terms of apprenticeship the master furnished the apprentice with a home and taught him the trade. The apprentice was obligated to obey his master and to render him service as long as the apprenticeship lasted; this depended upon the trade to be learned, but usually continued for about seven years. For the apprentice's services the master was obliged to give him only board and lodging.

The second stage, that of journeyman, was more remunerative; the guild candidate now received wages from the master, as well as living quarters; he was not bound to one master, but could travel as he wished. In order to be declared a master the journeyman had to demonstrate his proficiency by constructing a masterpiece, which paralleled the thesis requirement of degree candidates in the medieval university. As soon as the journeyman became a master and amassed sufficient capital, he could set up his own business and employ apprentices and journeymen.

Methods

Nothing was particularly novel in the methods of instruction and training used in guild schools. The chantry, burgher, and trade schools operated much the same as the monastic and parish schools. The methods utilized for apprenticeship were familiar, indeed: example, imitation, and practice. In the burgher schools, dictation, memorization, and catechetical devices were most commonly used, as we shall note in the Latin grammar schools which derived from the burgher and princes' schools. Discipline was no less severe than in other medieval settings, and masters could be quite harsh in the treatment of their pupils.

Before the Reformation, guilds usually appointed members of the clergy to assist in their ecclesiastical training. And as education for work became the usual fare of the common man, some guilds offered a popular program for reading and writing not only for their members' children but also the children of other townspeople. With the addition of Latin to their programs, a few schools even became secondary institutions.

But the significant aspect of this accent on the vocational was that legislation, especially in England, developed to maintain such training programs as social policy, and these provisions found reflection in the education laws of New England and elsewhere.[17]

REFERENCES

Abelson, Paul, *The Seven Liberal Arts, A Study in Medieval Culture.* New York: Russell & Russell, 1965. Originally published as Contribution to Education, no. 11. Teachers College Press, Columbia University, 1906.

---

[17] See Bernard J. Kohlbrenner, "The Catholic Heritage," pp. 103–132, in Richard E. Gross (Ed.), *Heritage of American Education* (Boston: Allyn and Bacon, Inc., 1962).

Aries, Philippe, *Centuries of Childhood*. New York: Alfred A. Knopf, 1962.

Barnes, Harry Elmer, *An Intellectual and Cultural History of the Western World*. New York: Random House, Inc., 1937. Pp. 326–440.

Blackham, Robert J., *London's Livery Companies*. London: Sampson Low, Marston & Co., Ltd., 1930.

Bryant, Arthur, *The Atlantic Saga*, vol. ii, *The Age of Chivalry*. New York: Doubleday and Company, Inc., 1963. Pp. 238–254.

Butts, R. Freeman, *A Cultural History of Western Education*, 2d ed. New York: McGraw-Hill, Inc., 1955. Pp. 116–164.

Cole, Luella, *A History of Education, Socrates to Montessori*. New York: Holt, Rinehart and Winston, Inc., 1950. Pp. 114–200.

Daniélou, Jean, and Henri Irenée Marrou, *The First Six Hundred Years*. Trans. by Vincent Cronin. New York: McGraw-Hill, Inc., 1964.

Davidson, Thomas, *A History of Education*. New York: Charles Scribner's Sons, 1900. Pp. 151–174.

Duckett, Eleanor Shipley, *Alcuin, Friend of Charlemagne*. New York: Crowell-Collier and Macmillan, Inc., 1951.

Durant, Will, *The Story of Civilization*, pt. iv, *The Age of Faith*. New York: Simon and Schuster, Inc. 1950. Pp. 1–135, 421–1086.

Eby, Frederick, and Charles F. Arrowood, *The History and Philosophy of Education, Ancient and Medieval*. Englewood Cliffs, N.J.: Prentice-Hall, Inc., 1940. Pp. 630–815.

Fehl, Noah Edward, *The Idea of a University in East and West*. Hong Kong: Chung Chi College, 1962. Pp. 1–221.

Good, Harry G., *A History of Western Education*. New York: Crowell-Collier and Macmillan, Inc., 1960. Pp. 64–80, 88–110.

Graves, Frank P., *Education During the Middle Ages*. New York: Crowell-Collier and Macmillan, Inc., 1910. Pp. 1–39, 47–75.

Hamilton, Edith, *Witness to the Truth—Christ and His Interpreters*. New York: W. W. Norton & Company, Inc., 1948. Rev. ed., 1957.

Hart, Joseph K., *Creative Moments in Education*. New York: Holt, Rinehart and Winston, Inc., 1931. Pp. 157–185.

Knight, Edgar W., *Twenty Centuries of Education*. Boston: Ginn & Company, 1940. Pp. 87–149.

Leach, A. F., *The School in Medieval England*. London: Methuen & Co., Ltd., 1915.

Lincoln, E. F., *The Medieval Legacy*. London: Macgibbon & Kee, 1961. Pp. 11–215.

Lopez, Robert S., *The Birth of Europe*. New York: M. Evans and Company, Inc., 1967.

Marrou, Henri Irenée, *A History of Education in Antiquity*. New York: Sheed & Ward, Inc., 1956.

Mayer, Frederick, *A History of Educational Thought*. Columbus, Ohio: Charles E. Merrill Books, Inc., 1960. Pp. 133–151.

Mazzarino, Santo, *The End of the Ancient World*. Trans. by George Holmes. New York: Alfred A. Knopf, 1966.

Messenger, James F., *An Interpretative History of Education*. New York: Thomas Y. Crowell Company, 1931. Pp. 63–107.

Mulhern, James, *A History of Education*, 2d ed. New York: The Ronald Press Company, 1959, Pp. 227–293.

Mulholland, Sister Mary A., *Early Guild Records of Toulouse*. New York: Columbia University Press, 1961. Pp. i–li.

National Geographic Society, *The Age of Chivalry*. Washington, D.C.: National Geographic Society, 1969.

Oldenbourg, Zoe, *The Crusades*. Trans. by Anne Carter. New York: Pantheon Books, Inc., 1966.

Rand, Edward Kennard, *Founders of the Middle Ages*. New York: Dover Publications, Inc., 1928. "Boethius, the Scholastic," pp. 135–180.

Reisner, Edward H., *Historical Foundations of Modern Education*. New York: Crowell-Collier and Macmillan, Inc., 1927. Pp. 195–363.

Shaw, Charles Gray, *Trends of Civilization and Culture*. New York: American Book Company, 1932. Pp. 212–258.

Southern, Richard William, *The Making of the Middle Ages*. London: Hutchinson & Co. (Publishers), Ltd., 1953. Especially pp. 110–117, 154–169.

Staley, John Edgcumbe, *The Guilds of Florence*. New York: B. Blom, 1967.

Uden, Grant, *A Dictionary of Chivalry*. New York: Thomas Y. Crowell Company, 1968.

Ulich, Robert, *History of Educational Thought*. New York: American Book Company, 1950. Pp. 89–101.

——— (Ed.), *Three Thousand Years of Educational Wisdom*, 2d ed., enl. Cambridge, Mass.: Harvard University Press, 1954. Pp. 172–190.

Waddell, Helen, *The Wandering Scholars*, 7th ed. New York: Barnes & Noble, Inc., 1949.

SELECTED PAPERBACKS

Bainton, Roland H., *Early Christianity*. Princeton, N.J.: D. Van Nostrand Company, Inc., 1960.

Beck, Robert Holmes, *A Social History of Education*. Englewood Cliffs, N.J.: Prentice-Hall, Inc., 1965.

Broudy, Harry S., and John R. Palmer, *Exemplars of Teaching Method*. Skokie, Ill.: Rand McNally & Company, 1965.

Castle, E. B., *Ancient Education and Today*. Baltimore: Penguin Books, Inc., 1961.

Donohue, John W., *St. Thomas Aquinas and Education*. New York: Random House, Inc., 1968.

Fictenau, Heinrich, *The Carolinian Empire*. New York: Harper & Row, Publishers, 1964.

Francis of Assisi, *The Little Flowers of St. Francis*. Trans. by W. Heywood. London: Methuen & Co., Ltd., 1906.

Fremantle, Anne (Ed.), *The Age of Belief: The Medieval Philosophers.* New York: New American Library of World Literature, Inc., 1950.

Hamilton, Edith, *The Ever Present Past.* New York: W. W. Norton & Company, Inc., 1964.

——, *Witness to the Truth—Christ and His Interpreters.* New York: W. W. Norton Company, Inc., Norton Library, 1962.

Heer, Frederich, *The Medieval World.* Cleveland: The World Publishing Company, 1962.

——, *Intellectual History of Europe,* vol. i, *Western Thought from the Beginnings to Luther.* New York: Doubleday & Company, Inc., 1968.

Huizinga, J., *The Waning of the Middle Ages.* New York: Doubleday & Company, Inc., 1949.

Lewis, C. S., *Mere Christianity.* New York: Crowell-Collier and Macmillan, Inc., 1958.

Lot, Ferdinand, *End of the Ancient World.* New York: Harper & Row, Publishers, 1961.

Marrou, Henri Irenée, *A History of Education in Antiquity.* Trans. by George Lamb. New York: New American Library of World Literature, Inc., 1964.

Muller, Herbert J., *The Uses of the Past, Profiles of Former Societies.* New York: New American Library of World Literature, Inc., 1952. Pp. 252–282.

Painter, Sidney, *Medieval Society.* Ithaca, N.Y.: Cornell University Press, 1951.

Queen, Stuart A., and Robert W. Habenstein. *The Family in Various Cultures,* Philadelphia: J. B. Lippincott Company, 1967. "The Anglo-Saxon Family," "The Medieval English Family," pp. 202–246.

Ralph, Philip Lee, *Story of Our Civilization, 10,000 Years of Western Man.* New York: E. P. Dutton & Co., Inc., 1959.

Runciman, Steven, *Byzantine Civilization.* New York: Meridian Books, Inc., 1956.

——, *History of the Crusades,* 3 vols. New York: Harper & Row, Publishers, 1964.

Ryan, Patrick J., *Historical Foundations of Public Education.* Dubuque, Iowa: William C. Brown Company, Publishers, 1965.

Simson, Otto von, *The Gothic Cathedral, Origins of Gothic Architecture and the Medieval Concept of Order.* New York: Harper & Row, Publishers, 1962.

Viorst, Milton (Ed.), *The Great Documents of Western Civilization.* New York: Bantam Books, Inc., 1965.

Vryonis, Speros, Jr., *Byzantium and Europe.* New York: Harcourt, Brace & World, Inc., 1967.

Waddell, Helen, *The Wandering Scholars.* New York: Doubleday & Company, Inc., Anchor Books, 1960.

Wright, David (Ed.), *Beowulf.* Baltimore: Penguin Books, Inc., 1957.

CHAPTER 9

The Muslim
Approach
to Education

*The day was not far off when Catholic Europe, once again struggling to
her feet by her own efforts, would be in a position to benefit from
relations with her Moslem neighbours. But in the early Middle Ages she
was doubly far from this. Both the model of their civilization and its
fabrics were foreign to her; it was beyond her power to imitate them.*[1]

THE BIRTH OF ISLAM

Out of the Arabian desert, from time immemorial successive bands
of wanderers have shifted north, east, and west into the more fertile domains
of Egypt, Mesopotamia, and the Mediterranean littoral. We have already
noted how the ancestors of the Jews abandoned the arid Middle East to
seek a more comfortable existence in the Promised Land of Canaan; but
the Hebrew withdrawal was only one of many such Semitic migrations.[2]

Each emigration, however, left behind a nucleus of desert tribes
sufficient to raid, trade with, and exact tribute from the caravans crossing
their sandy wastes. In turn, the great empires of Egypt, Persia, Alexander's
Macedon, Rome, and Byzantium claimed sovereignty over this desert population; and, from time to time, an Arab chieftain would rise to independent
power bringing some commercial center such as Palmyra, Mecca, or
Medina into temporary prominence. In the annals of the Roman historian
Marcellinus (fourth century, A.D.) we find these desert dwellers first identified as *Saracens*, the word coming possibly from the Arabic, meaning

---

[1] Robert S. Lopez, *The Birth of Europe* (New York: M. Evans and Company,
Inc., 1967).

[2] According to the Koran, Islam's sacred book, Ishmael, the banished son of
Abraham and Hagar, found refuge in Mecca. His descendants are Muslims, while
those of Abraham's second son, Isaac, are Jews.

eastern. Its use, then, had, of course, nothing to do v
in this chapter we shall use it as an alternate for 1
of an eastern group devoted to Islam, the religion f
Mohammed in the seventh century. How can the
and its principles possibly be of interest to studen
Lichtenstedter answers and advises us:

> No culture ever developed in a vacuum. Its vitality is proved ᴜ₃
> ability to integrate new factors into the basic beliefs and ideas that were
> its original core. Islam is no exception to this rule. To understand it fully,
> we must try to determine the various strands in its fabric, the many ideas
> that eventually produced the distinct entity, "Islam."[3]

The religious movement known to the world as Islam, surrender to
God, began in Mecca and Medina in the Arabian peninsula. Mohammed
(570–632), its founder, was born in Mecca, the later focus of his faith;
the Hejira (622), or departure at the request of the Medinans to their
city, marks the advent of this young religion. Muslim educational interest
began formally about 650, eighteen years after the prophet's death, when
the Koran, the scriptures of Islam, was compiled from the notes of his
disciples; like Socrates and Jesus, Mohammed wrote nothing, but strove
through example and precept to engage his hearers in the search for a
better life.[4] And one of his cardinal means to this end was (like its Jewish
antecedent) the parallel search for knowledge.

Except for the zeal and inspiration of its founder, reasons for the
success of the Saracenic movement remain mysterious. Islam's culture
derived originally from Semitic forebears or perhaps from the history of
the Near and Middle East. Its monotheism had flourished in Israel and
for a time in Egypt; and its strong belief in an afterlife was common to
many Eastern faiths. Rising spectacularly, Islam overcame three fourths
of the Mediterranean world, and then in its medieval phase waned sud-
denly—all in the brief space of some 600 years.

The first cycle of Islamic imperialism reached its highest development
in Spain in the century prior to 1050; in those years many intellectual
Muslims, fleeing persecution by religious conservatives, had deserted
Baghdad, Damascus, and other centers of early Muslim civilization to seek
safety in the more liberal caliphates of western Africa and Iberia. Muslim
imperialism and culture came to an end in Europe about 1492, as the
Muslim authority was forced from Spain and Italy by the rising national
armies of the new European states.

But the Islamic educational concept was so distinct from the

---

[3] Ilse Lichtenstedter, *Islam and the Modern Age* (New York: Bookman Associates, 1958), p. 11.

[4] See Mahmoud Hoballah, *Muhammad, the Prophet* (Washington, D.C.: The Islamic Center, 1957), pp. 1–9, for a concise interpretation of this age of ignorance and the advent of Mohammed.

al Christian concept and so significant in its implications that it
rves a separate treatment. Indeed, no chapter in the history of edu-
tional thought is more colorful than that of the rise of Muslim culture
in Spain. Not only was this civilization an intriguing phenomenon, but it
made astounding contributions to European civilization and the modern
world as well. These contributions have, however, too often gone unrecog-
nized, as this aspect of Western culture has often been either ignored or
treated shallowly.

The Muslim culture in Spain was particularly striking because of its
contrast with contemporary conditions in the rest of Europe. While Moorish
Spain was most advanced, Christian Europe was still firmly held by repressive tendencies; the humanities had not yet replaced the divinities. To the
Muslims fell the privilege of preserving the content and spirit of ancient
learning; and to Islam goes much of the credit for leading Europe out
of medievalism.

For, as Ulich says, "much though medieval man hated the followers
of Mohammed as heretics and political enemies, he could not help but
admire parts of their culture, which in many respects was superior to his
own."[5] The great Muslim cities of Granada and Toledo in Spain, Cairo
in Egypt, and Baghdad on the Tigris (presently in Iraq) were foci of
education, leisure, and wealth. Muslim higher learning preserved the Greek
philosophical tradition; and Muslim contacts with India, which was for a
time an Islamic state, served as a cultural highway to Europe.

Not only did the Muslims preserve learning, they improved it. Their
secular greatness appears also to have been due to their ability to assimilate
what was most significant in the intellectual culture of the peoples with
whom they came in contact and to apply this heritage to their own needs;
they absorbed mathematical and medical knowledge from the Hellenistic
world; they took the notation system of arithmetic and algebraic forms
from India; they made science more than learned lore and applied it to
daily living.

The West is indebted to them for the re-creation of the scientific
spirit of investigation and experimentation and for the invention and improvement of scientific tools. They exerted a beneficent influence upon
western Europe philosophical thought. Although the Saracens developed
no new schools of philosophy, they did assimilate and elaborate those of
the Greeks. It was through the Moors that Christian scholars were led to
a revival of interest in Aristotelian science and the principles of logic.
From Spain, the scholastics gained their first complete knowledge of
Aristotle.

So it was that Muslim Spain became the cultural hub of the late

---

[5] Robert Ulich (Ed.), *Three Thousand Years of Educational Wisdom, Great
Documents,* 2nd ed., enl. (Cambridge, Mass.: Harvard University Press, 1954),
p. 193.

medieval world through a seed planted only a few centuries before in the
desert of Arabia among a scattered, simple, unlearned people, who like their
ancestors had roamed the desert bay, but had been forced only recently
to settle in walled towns near springs or wells to protect themselves from
other nomadic tribes. To begin to understand Islam and its religious,
political, and educational achievements, we must now consider the personality and history of its founder.

Although Mohammed called himself an illiterate prophet and did not
have more learning than his fellow Arabs, he surpassed them enormously
in insight. As trader and caravan guide he had traversed the neighboring
countries and come into contact with most of the prevailing religions and
philosophies. Gradually he came to believe that his people lacked "a Book
and a God." He undertook to provide them with both when convinced
that a revelation from Allah, the "Lord of the Worlds," had been granted
to him. Mohammed's doctrines were finally collected in the Koran, a strange
and remarkable volume, composed basically of a mixture of Jewish,
Christian, and other religious elements, but with an originality that was
not lost on his disciples. With the support of a small group of believers
he developed his simple but compelling message, which may be summed
up: "There is no God but Allah, and Mohammed is his prophet." Thus
the Koran's opening *sura,* or chapter, declares:

> In the name of God, the merciful, the compassionate—
>> Praise be to God, lord of the universe,
>> the merciful,
>> the compassionate,
>> ruler on the Day of Judgment.
>> Thee alone we worship; Thee alone we ask for aid.
>> Guide us in the path called straight,
>> that path of those whom Thou hast favored—
>> Not of those who have incurred Thy wrath,
>> Nor of those who go astray![6]

Mohammed (Arabic: "highly praised") began his ministry at the
age of forty, his faithful wife Khadijah being his first convert.[7] Mohammed's
message was one that Arabs could understand: a leisure-filled paradise
in a realm of many rivers, with green oases and fantastic fountains from
which flowed continually the life-giving fluid essential to the desert dweller's
existence was to be the reward of all who believed and followed the
commandments he proclaimed. For the recalcitrant, he predicted an afterlife in the midst of continual fire, burning winds, with nothing potable but

---

[6] The Qur'an (Koran), Sura I.

[7] See Hoballah, *Muhammad the Prophet*; and also Mahmoud Hoballah, *Islam
and Humane Tenets* (Washington, D.C.: The Islamic Center, 1957), pp. 8–14; see
Huston Smith, *The Religions of Man* (New York: Harper & Row, Publishers, 1965),
"Islam," pp. 217–253.

boiling stinking water. His theme that God is one, that he was the prophet God called to reform his people, and that his revelation contained the truth is repeated over and over again in the Koran:

> There is no doubt in this book; it is a direction to the pious, who believe in the mysteries of faith, who observe the appointed times of prayer, and distribute alms out of what we have bestowed on them, and who believe in that revelation which hath been sent down unto thee and that which hath been sent down unto the prophets before thee, and have firm assurance of the life to come; these are directed by their Lord, and they shall prosper.
>
> Now in the creation of heaven and earth, and the vicissitude of night and day, and in the ship which saileth in the sea, leaden with what is profitable for mankind, and in the main water which God sendeth from heaven, quickening thereby the dead earth, and replenishing the same with all sorts of cattle, and in the change of winds, and the clouds that are compelled to do service between heaven and earth, are signs to people of understanding; yet some men take idols beside God and love them as with the love due to God; but the true believers are more fervent in love towards God.
>
> There is no God but God, the living, the self-subsisting; he hath sent down unto thee the book of the Koran with truth, confirming that which was revealed before it; for he had formerly sent down the law, and the gospel a direction to men; and he had also sent down the distinction between good and evil. Verily those who believe not the signs of God shall suffer a grievous punishment; for God is mighty, able to revenge.
>
> These are the signs of the book of the Koran: and that which hath been sent down unto thee from thy Lord is the truth: but the greater part of men will not believe. It is God who hath raised the heavens without visible pillars; and then ascended his throne, and compelled the sun and the moon to perform their service; every one of the heavenly bodies runneth an appointed course. He ordereth all things.[8]

THE MUSLIM ADVANCE

The new religion had its expected effect and more. Because of its attractiveness to human nature and its satisfaction of human longings, it prospered. The nature of its faith made it imperative that its believers go forth and convert the heathen. This the Mohammedans under the unflagging and unflinching leadership of Abu Bekr, close friend of Mohammed and his successor, zealously set out to accomplish by conquest and the sword. Within ten years all Arabia was converted; and then Abu Bekr, with the faith that moves mountains, resolutely set himself to bringing the whole

---

[8] *The Koran (Alkoran)*, trans. by George Sale (New York: A. L. Burt Company, 1902), chs. i–xiii, pp. 57–211.

world to the worship of Allah. The attempt nearly succeeded; if there had been many men like Abu Bekr, it probably would have. The Muslims advanced steadily across northern Africa and into Europe through Spain until they were finally checked by Charles Martel at the battle of Tours (732).[9] Thereafter, the Pyrenees remained the western boundary of their political power, though nothing could stop their intellectual influence from filtering into Europe. (It is interesting to speculate how different the history of Europe might have been if the battle of Tours had turned out otherwise.) In the East, the energy of the Moslem advance spent itself in conquering and assimilating Persia and Turkestan; if its first successful campaigns in Syria had been continued against Byzantium, there can be little doubt that, by the eighth century, it would have entered Europe from the East as well. Wherever its conquests reached, Islam prevailed among the conquered not only because of the religious zeal of its followers but because of the social political order it offered.

As long as Islam was confined to the unlettered Arabs and remained a faith, it needed no support from learning and called for no special education. The *suras* of the *Koran* could be communicated by mouth and committed to memory, and all truth not contained in the *suras* was considered vain and to be spurned. When, however, Islam advanced into Syria, Egypt, and other centers of ancient learning, a change took place. Before Islam could hope for acceptance from the inhabitants of these countries, it had to attain the dignity of a philosophy; it had to become Hellenized, but this does not seem to have been distasteful to its sponsors. Their fresh minds and newly aroused curiosity reached out after this culture and made it their own. Special credit is due the Christian and Jewish scholars and physicians who were influential in converting the conquerors to Greek science and philosophy.

We have seen in an earlier connection that the catechetical schools of the East had shown a more liberal attitude toward Hellenic culture than had the schools of the West. But in the fifth century, the eastern church had shown itself narrowly orthodox when it denounced the Hellenized theology of Nestorius, Patriarch of Constantinople from 428 to 431, and procured his banishment to Egypt. His followers had fled to the cities of Syria—Antioch, Nisibis, and Edessa—beyond control of the church. Here they had developed excellent schools where the study of Greek science and philosophy continued. They preserved much Greek medical science, and added to it; medical skill, developed especially at their medical college at Gondesapore in Persia, made them popular with the Muslim caliphs.

The Nestorian Christians had been not the only teachers of the Arabs, however. In the various eastern cities, especially in Alexandria, the Arabs had been in contact with Jewish scholars with their distinctive literature

---

[9] Called by the French, the battle of Poitiers.

and traditions, to the mutual advantage of both Arab and Jew. Though the Muslims had on many occasions shown bitter hatred of the Jews, despoiled and exacted tribute from them, and reaped hatred in return, they could when circumstances prompted induce friendliness again; especially if the circumstances involved scholarly discussion, agreeable and advantageous to both. The Islamites, in moving up from Arabia and drawing upon the centers of learning in Syria and Egypt, had been intellectually broadened and enriched; and soon they were to find another source of ispiration in India.

These Arabs were basically assimilators rather than creators. Inspired by the cultured peoples with whom they had come in contact by travel or conquest, Muslim scholars began to translate into Arabic the Greek mathematical, philosophical, and medical writings. They applied themselves also to the mathematical lore of the Hindus. Greek libraries were established at the courts of the caliphs; and learned men—philosophers, poets, physicians, and mathematicians—were brought from the newly conquered countries to live at the courts. By the tenth century, schools rivaling the best in Syria had been established at Baghdad, Bassora, Bukhara, Cairo, Delhi, and elsewhere in the East.

The Muslim theologian Algazel, or Al-Ghazali (c1058–1111), dealt with a problem—virtually identical with Thomas Aquinas' apprehension of the paradox of mystery and reason—in *My Child*, in which he wrote:

> I have seen that each of us leans on one thing created, some on the world and money, some on gold and property, some on art and craft, and some on creatures of their own kind. Then I thought of the word of God the Highest: For him who puts his faith in God he will be all-sufficient, for God will attain his purpose, and God has assigned its destiny to everything. Trust in God, He will not mislead thee, He will reward you.[10]

Another outstanding Muslim scholar was the Persian Avicenna, or Ibnsina (980–1037), noted in Europe as a physician and interpreter of Aristotle and as the author of the *System of Medicine*. It was due largely to Avicenna's influence that a small group of savants, the Brothers of Sincerity, published the famous *Encyclopedia,* with the intention of directing Islamic higher education to a completely cogent and ratiocinative theology, and thus combating the early Islamic fanaticism and fatalism with Greek philosophy.

Understandably, efforts by Muslim scholars to rationalize the doctrines of Islam tended to arouse some uncertainty about its supernatural origin in the minds of some, especially the fanatically orthodox. Thus, those who would intellectualize Islam incurred suspicion and antagonism, which

---

[10] Hammer-Purgstall, *O Kind!* (Vienna: U. Strauss, 1838), as trans. by Ulich, pp. 197–198.

compelled them to migrate to the West, where as we have noted, they found refuge among the more liberal Muslims of western Africa and Spain. In these centers the rationalist scholars continued their work, encouraged and supported by generous caliphs.

Brilliant as Islamic civilization had been in the East, the student of educational philosophy will find the culture and scholarship of the Saracens in Spain of greater interest especially since it was the Muslims of the West who played the more important part in returning to Europe the lost spirit of learning.

The introduction of this Hellenized Islamic attitude into the peninsula brought a resplendent culture; the rulers distinguished themselves as patrons of learning and set an example of refinement in strong contrast to that of the European princes. The palaces of emirs and caliphs were luxuriously furnished when Christian lords were living in drafty and gloomy castles; religious toleration became the mode, and Cordova, Seville, Granada, and Toledo were lighted by public lamps 700 years before London; these Moorish city dwellers had paved streets centuries before the citizens of Paris.

Little wonder, then, that in a civilization so promising should be found a well-organized system of schools. Although the best example was Spain, where schooling became prevalent throughout the entire Muslim dominion, education throve in North Africa as well as in the East, providing inspiring but little-heeded examples to the Christian countries of western and northern Europe. Indeed, dedication to study became a cardinal tenet of Islamic life. As Shalabi says:

> In the history of Muslim education equalitarianism was fully recognized, and poverty was never a hindrance in the way of the gifted students. Before the establishment of schools every Muslim had free admission to the lecture of the mosque and promising students were greatly helped and encouraged to persevere with their studies.[11]

THE ISLAMIC APPROACH TO EDUCATION

Aims

Education as envisioned by the Muslims in Spain was primarily the search for knowledge and the application of scientific facts. The Moors appreciated the intellectual value of the sciences as well as their practical application; undoubtedly, they derived much gratification from the study of science as such.

The Arabian mind found special satisfaction in the pursuit of the natural sciences. The Arab's exuberant fancy, his love of wonder and

---

[11] Ahmad Shalabi, *History of Muslim Education* (Beirut: Dar-al-Kashshaf, 1954), pp. 164–165.

mystery, were intensified by an exciting and swiftly unfolding history. These factors helped to make nature an attractive subject of study.[12]

But the primary aim of education was practical and scientific. The Muslims endeavored to extend their facility with arts and crafts. Their purpose was to adapt science to their needs, to devise instruments of science for use in everyday life. Saracenic education, therefore, aimed at the assimilation and development of systematic knowledge, partly for its own sake, but especially for the services such knowledge could render man's manifold activities. The Moor did not disdain the labor of the laboratory and engaged in patient experimentation because he was working for practical results. To create artifacts that would enrich the lives of his fellow men as well as himself became an overall objective; he strove to derive and utilize scientific facts to further the development of his advancing civilization.

Here we find an education in which science was expected to play a new and important role; it was no longer to be mere intellectual gymnastics, but was to be applied to all the useful arts and crafts. Likewise, reading was not a mere accomplishment, but a necessity for the man of affairs. Their emphasis upon philosophy was a natural outgrowth of their devotion to the applied sciences. Aristotle especially interested these people because there was scarcely an aspect of the world of nature and the world of man upon which he had not thought and written. His philosophy was objective and concrete and subject to useful applications; therefore they made Aristotle their own. They stressed medicine because it was a practical art and necessary for the preservation of life—life that was interesting and worth living. Chemistry was studied because of its applications to medicine and industry. Mathematics was indispensable to mechanics and industry as well as to other sciences. Astronomy was studied as an aid to geography and navigation.

Muslim education was liberal in the truest sense, since it aimed at the development of individual initiative and social welfare. All education began with religious education, the memorizing of the Koran. It was a simple religion and for the most part easily understood. An insistence upon kindliness and considerateness in daily life was one of the main virtues of Islam, and its monotheism had none of the exclusiveness of other Semitic religions. It produced an unusual degree of tolerance, for Mohammed had also propounded that all men are brothers and equal. Except for the usual friction between liberals and conservatives, the theological hair splittings that confounded and divided Christianity were lacking, and there was no development of a hierarchical priesthood. Islam had and still has learned doctors, teachers, and preachers, but no orders of priests and no monastic

---

[12] Edward Hungerford, "The Rise of Arabic Learning," *The Atlantic Monthly,* vol. 58 (October, 1886), p. 549. See also Lopez, pp. 62, 73–76, 78–79, 80.

ranks. Consequently, except for those wishing to become teachers of philosophy, there was little need for an intensive religious training, and Muslim youth found few religious restrictions to hamper educational freedom.

Islam lacked the Christian emphasis on sin, and the afterlife was assured through simple faith. Thus education was free to devote itself to meditation, reflection, introspection, and to the possible melioration of life in this world, rather than to emphasis on the wonders of the next. Ibn-Khaldoun (1332–1406), who is judged by some historians to have been the greatest intellect of his century, in modern vein essayed the interpretation of civilization itself in terms of climatic, intellectual, and social conditions. In true Hellenistic fashion ibn-Khaldoun wrote:

> The faculty of reflection . . . uses . . . certain powers which, situated in the ventricles of the brain, seize the forms of things, turn them into comprehension, and give them new forms by means of abstraction. Reflection . . . together with the faculty of comprehension, sorts and combines the sense impressions.[13]

The Islamic call for brotherhood and the Islamic concept of righteousness is reflected in the prescription for daily life in the second *sura* of the Koran:

> It is not righteousness that ye turn your faces
>   to the East and to the West.
> But righteous is he who:
>   Believeth in God and the last day,
>   The angels, the Scriptures and the prophets;
>   Giveth of his sustenance, however cherished,
>   to kinsmen and orphans,
>   to the needy, wayfarers, and beggars
>   and to the ransom of slaves,
>   Who observeth the prayers,
>   and payeth the alms.[14]

Muslim education was eminently successful in achieving its aims. It developed leaders, and the Spanish Moors, for example, were able to improve the conditions of life on every front. They devised a system of agriculture for semiarid regions, regulated by legal codes. They introduced into Europe rice, cotton, spinach, saffron, sugar, and many fruits. They gave much attention to the breeding of fine cattle, horses, sheep, and poultry; and borrowing from the Chinese, they introduced sericulture. They adopted the Egyptian system of irrigation, with waterwheels, floodgates, and pumps. They produced paper (another Chinese invention), textiles, iron, steel, and earthenware. Their steel made the name of Toledo,

---

[13] Ulich, pp. 193–194, 199.
[14] The Koran: 2:172.

like that of Damascus, world-famous. The cities of Cordova and Morocco gave their names to the finest grades of leather. The Muslims introduced gunpowder (from China), invented cannon, other types of artillery, and the mariner's compass. In the days of their prosperity they maintained a merchant marine of more than 1000 vessels. As a result of their genius, Muslim cities and homes were, even then, equipped with many facilities and luxuries undreamed of by Christian Europe, which Lopez has said was not ready for such scientific applications.[15]

Types

It may seem strange that vocational education was stressed by the Muslims. But this education was for the professions and skilled trades and crafts; it comprised instruction as well as training. In a procedure quite different from the others we have so far encountered, such preparation skills were acquired on the basis of scientific facts and principles, not merely through imitation of skills developed through trial and error. Intellectual training in the sciences was thus made the basis for vocational training in the professions and the mechanical and commercial trades. Commercial training was emphasized, as in early Egypt and Sumer; we find the beginnings of a science of economics as a basis for business and trade.

Islam forbade the representation of human form, so the Muslims provided no art education for sculptors and painters. They did, however, offer training in architecture, artistic carving, repetitive design, and the use of color; the utilization of such skills and artistry resulted in the creation of such structural and decorative gems as the Alhambra in Spain and the Blue Mosque in Istanbul. Muslim artistic tendencies were encouraged also in the beautification of textiles, ceramics, and metal work. Religious education was generally limited to the study of the Koran, because of the simplicity of the faith and the absence of a governing and institutional priesthood.

We know less about the avocational training of the Muslims; but certainly reading was a form of enjoyment, and story telling was highly developed; observe the entertainment in *The Thousand and One Nights*— old Muslim tales of Arabia and Persia, repeated orally until gathered into a book in Egypt in the fifteenth century. There was also much extemporizing of verse—for almost every Arab would be a poet—and music and dancing, though the latter was done usually by slaves. We may count, too, falconry, which, in both the East and the West passed from a means of livelihood to a fashionable sport.

Islamic education was universal, although not entirely democratic as Mohammed had decreed it should be. The wealthy had some educational

---

[15] Lopez, p. 79.

advantages not generally available to the poor classes; but elementary education was free and open to boys and girls of all classes, and the doors of the higher educational institutions were open to all, rich or poor. Financial aid was often provided for advanced students who needed it. The great liberality which the Saracens displayed in educating their people was one of the most potent factors in the brilliant and rapid growth of their civilization; learning was so universally diffused that it was said to be difficult to find a Saracen who could not read or write.

Content

The curriculum of the Muslim schools was the most complete and most carefully organized in ancient or medieval times. At the elementary level, it consisted of reading, writing, arithmetic, religion, grammar, and elementary science. At the higher levels, it consisted of algebra, geometry, trigonometry, physics, chemistry, geography, astronomy, anatomy, pharmacy, medicine, surgery, philology, history, literature, logic, metaphysics, and jurisprudence. (In fact, the Saracens seem to have studied most of the subjects that we have in our schools today.) And not only did its curriculum include many subjects, but each subject was covered with surprising completeness.

The system of education arranged at Basra[16] by the Brothers of Sincerity in their *Encyclopedia*[17] was a marvel of completeness. This monumental outline of education comprised fifty-one treatises arranged under four heads: (1) thirteen treatises on logic, (2) seventeen treatises on natural science, (3) ten treatises on metaphysics, and (4) eleven treatises on theology. This encyclopedia claims our interest for several reasons: (1) it sums up the best thought of a long period of culture; (2) it has roots in the past of humanity and branches in its future; (3) it includes both nature and spirit, and shows that the former has its origin in the latter; (4) it attempts to harmonize reason with revelation; (5) it shows man his place in the universe, his origin, his destiny, and therefore his duty; (6) it thus furnishes a comprehensive education, enabling its recipient to lead a rational, purposeful, and free life.

The Arabians were proud of their language, and in their schools much attention was paid to the study of Arabic language and literature. Philology must have been a subject of vast interest to them. Not only grammars but great lexicons and dictionaries were produced, one of which consisted of sixty volumes, the definition of each word being illustrated. To the Arabian language we are indebted for many English nouns—*syrup, julep, elixir, admiral, alcohol, spinach, cotton, chemise,* and *chemistry.* The Saracens

---

[16] A port on the Shatt al Arab in Iraq, about sixty miles from the Persian Gulf.

[17] The *Encyclopedia* which was valued so highly by the Christian schoolmen and credited by them to the authorship of al-Farabi of Baghdad was probably this same work.

had a considerable body of literature which, in addition to the Koran and the commentaries on it, must have been studied in their schools. The first Arab writers of distinction wrote histories and biographies, and romantic fiction and the short story soon followed. Their poetical productions embraced most of the modern forms and types such as elegies, odes, and satires; but they never produced a really great epic or tragedy.

In mathematics, the Arabs built on the Greek and Hindu foundations. Arithmetic made great advances with the clumsy Roman numerals replaced by the figures the Arabs had borrowed from the Hindus. It was an Arab mathematician who first used the zero and the decimal notation and gave the digits the value of position. Algebra, although it had its beginnings in India, was virtually the creation of the Arabs. They added very little to Euclid; but they developed trigonometry, conceptualizing the sine, tangent, and cotangent.

Mathematics was applied to the study of physics and astronomy. The Arabians measured the size of the earth, calculated the angle of the ecliptic and the precession of the equinoxes. They made many applications of mathematics to the control of physical forces, for example, in hydraulics. They invented the pendulum clock. They made certain important discoveries in optics and other branches of physics, explaining refraction of light, gravity, capillary attraction, twilight, and other natural phenomena. While Christian scholars and navigators were declaring that the world was flat, Muslims were teaching geography in their schools by means of globes and studying astronomy in observatories. They constructed many astronomical instruments which are in use today. To the knowledge of the heavenly bodies they added much that we now consider elementary, but which was far in advance of a world devoted to astrology. The fate of one of their astronomical observatories in Spain is rather significant. After the expulsion of the Moors, it became a belfry because, we are told, the conquering Christians did not know what else to do with it.

Although the Arabs took the beginnings of their medical science from the Greeks, they added much to it. They kept up intensive study of diseases, diet, drugs, and various phases of physiology and hygiene. Their *materia medica* makes a large part of ours today, and their pharmacology was well begun. With some understanding of the nature of chemical changes, they could make tinctures, essences, and syrups. They had surgeons who knew the use of anesthetics and who performed difficult operations with surgical instruments of types still in use. Anatomy was studied by dissection. When in Christian Europe the diseased and crippled were seeking miraculous cures, in Saracenic Spain physicians and surgeons were practicing their healing arts with some success. An Arab physician of the 11th century supposedly used electric fish to administer shock treatment to epileptics. (Their medical university in Italy at Salerno has already been mentioned.) The Arabs also knew something of the scientific breeding of cattle and horses, and the horticultural secrets of grafting to produce new varieties of fruits and flowers.

Arabian science made strides in transforming ancient alchemy into chemistry; they discovered many new chemical substances such as alcohol, potash, silver nitrate, corrosive sublimate, nitric acid, and sulphuric acid. They applied their chemistry in many directions—to the working of metals and other substances, and to the cultivation of the soil. The former led to the development of metallurgy and ceramics. A large part of the population was engaged in contriving objects as useful as they were beautiful out of gold, silver, copper, bronze, iron, and steel, and in making and shaping glass and pottery. Their skill in manufacturing fine steel enabled them to supply not only such famous products as the Damascus and Toledo blades but also fine instruments for astronomers and navigators. Another advanced application of chemistry was in agriculture: the scientific use of fertilizers and crop rotation. Much of this practical ability and skill— necessary for the carrying out of these agricultural, industrial, and commercial advances—was undoubtedly a goal of their education.

As a combination of art and applied science, Arab workmanship reached its climax in architecture in Spain. Moorish architecture was not only elaborately beautiful, with wood and stone carvings and tile intricately patterned in colors, but it was practical and durable as well. The mosques and palaces of Cordova and Seville and that last triumph of the Moors— the fourteenth-century palace, the Alhambra, at Granada—are world-famous examples of thorough craftsmanship, along with the Taj Mahal in India.

The sciences of business and trade were not neglected, and beginnings were made in the field of economic theory.

Not only did the Moor labor in his laboratory, turning out products and deriving scientific facts; he wrote about his discoveries. There was scarcely a subject left untouched in his literature. It is said that in the library connected with the university in one of the Saracenic cities there were over 400,000 books, most of them by Muslim writers. These books were not all scientific. Many were writings on philosophy, although the Saracens, favoring as they did the philosophy of Aristotle, confined their philosophical works almost entirely to commentaries on Aristotelian thought. Chief among these philosophers was Averroes, or ibn-Rushd (1120–1198), who taught at Cordova and became the authoritative commentator on Aristotle; he was especially so regarded by medieval Christian universities, where his works were diligently translated and copied.

Agencies

The caliphs of Moorish Spain, after the example set by the rulers of the East, proceeded to foster education and scientific achievement by every means within their power and were instrumental in founding elementary schools, academies, universities, and libraries throughout their domain.

As for the East, the courts of the early caliphs might well be called educational institutions, for they were from the beginning the greatest agencies of education. The caliphs of the East surrounded themselves with groups of learned Nestorian Christians and Jews and often became ardent scholars themselves. In connection with these courts, vast libraries were fostered, with manuscripts gathered from the far corners of the earth. The caliph Haroun-al-Raschid of Baghdad, a contemporary of Charlemagne and one of the first great patrons of Muslim learning, saw the need for elementary schools and established a school in connection with each mosque, in which reading, writing, simple numeration, and the precepts of the Koran were taught. This custom was continued and became the pattern of such schools throughout all Muslim domains. The Muslims were well circumstanced to be patrons of learning in that they had become a wealthy people. Immense sums of tribute could be and were expended for the advancement of learning. Elaborate experiments could be made, and costly instruments could be constructed. Journeys were undertaken to far places, from which scholars brought back collections of rare manuscripts to be translated by learned Jews and Nestorian Christians under royal patronage. So, restrained neither by lack of means nor lack of time, the Muslim made rapid strides in assimilation of scientific knowledge and philosophical thought.

The Spanish Moors made similar expenditures to establish universities. Those at Cordova, Seville, Toledo, and Salamanca became world-famous. The best instructors to be had were employed, many of them being non-Muslim; for so completely had the Arabs become imbued with the scientific spirit that they judged the teacher by his true learning, not by his religious views.[18] Indeed, the unlettered Mohammed himself had told his followers to respect the opinions of the "people with the Book," meaning the sacred Hebrew writings; and in matters of scholarship at least this respect had persisted. The greatest of their universities, that at Cordova, had fifteen separate departments, each specializing in a different field of learning, with beautiful buildings and the most complete equipment money could buy.

Libraries profited no less than the universities from Muslim wealth and generosity. Caliphs or emirs dispatched their emissaries to all parts of the known world to collect books and manuscripts; the results of this searching and the later literary activities of the Saracens made possible the creation of voluminous libraries of meticulously copied and richly bound books. Hungerford reports that conquest too brought library rewards, the

---

[18] The position of the Jews and Christians under Muslim rule is fully discussed in David S. Margoliouth, *The Early Development of Mohammedanism*, Lecture IV, "The Status of the Tolerated Cults" (New York: Charles Scribner's Sons, 1914), pp. 99–134.

defeat of the Byzantine Emperor, Michael the Stammerer, bringing a new series of Greek manuscripts.[19]

It is reported that the library at Cordova (and its repositories in seventy other centers) contained more than half a million volumes. Nor did these books lie idle; those considered significant to Muslim students were translated into Arabic, for the students' use at will. Each university soon had an available library, and it was customary for wealthy men to place their invaluable private collections at the disposal of the scholarly.

Such a magnificent educational endowment finally attracted the attention of other Europeans, who hoped to lift themselves out of the complacency into which Christian education had fallen. When Christian schools in both eastern and western Europe were drifting into decay, Muslim schools were growing and providing eager students with facilities undreamed of in Christendom. These Moorish universities served as models for some of the early Christian centers of higher learning which sprang up in the eleventh and twelfth centuries.

Organization

The earliest educational setting was the mosque, for the Prophet had clearly shown the relationship between education and religion. Instruction was based largely on Koranic teaching, students and their leaders behaving much the same as their counterparts in Hebrew circles. Later the *kuttab* developed for the teaching of reading and writing. This school, situated in its teachers' houses, was not connected with the mosque and became prevalent around the third century of Islam. Reading and writing were taught separately, the methods being quite similar to those in the mosque.[20]

Like Confucius, al-Ghazali set a strict code for teacher-student relationships, although humanity and equity were always to be present. For example, al-Ghazali encourages the teacher to:

   1. Have sympathy with his students and treat them as if they were his own children;
   2. Follow the example of the Prophet and seek no remuneration;
   3. Be perfectly honest with the students and prevent them from presenting themselves as candidates before they are worthy;
   4. Exhort them and rebuke them for misconduct; and
   5. Guard against the teaching of matter which is beyond the comprehension of the student.[21]

The educational system in Moorish Spain was organized on three levels: elementary, secondary, and higher, or university. The early educational arrangements for the elementary school have already been men-

---

[19] Hungerford, p. 545.
[20] Shalabi, pp. 16–17.
[21] Khalil A. Totah, *The Contributions of the Arabs to Education* (New York: Teachers College Press, Columbia University, 1926), p. 63.

tioned. In Moorish Iberia, following the custom of Haroun-al-Raschid, elementary schools were especially fostered and were to be found in every city and town. These were usually attached to the mosque and were free and open to boys and girls of all classes. The children entered these elementary schools at the age of five years, remained three years if they were of the poorer classes, then went into some trade or industry. The children of the rich did not leave school until they reached the age of fourteen, after which they either entered the higher schools or traveled with a tutor. Elementary education consisted mostly of the study of reading, writing, arithmetic, grammar, religion, versification, and geography. The Koran was the chief reading text used at these lower levels.

For wealthier students, there was a type of secondary school somewhat similar to the later boarding schools of England and America. These schools were arranged in twenty-four or thirty apartments, each accommodating about four students, with a rector presiding over the school. Here learned, well-trained, and well-paid teachers—often Jews or Christians—instructed in Arabic literature, grammar, mathematics, astronomy, metaphysics, chemistry, and medicine. These schools were self-supporting.

The universities, which arose in all the chief Moorish cities of Spain, were colleges in the literal sense; for students and professors shared accommodations. Special departments, or schools, were created for the various sciences. There were medical schools with chemical laboratories, and finely equipped hospitals for clinical instruction. There were schools of astronomy which offered the use of observatories equipped with the most costly and most accurate instruments that could be constructed. Other schools specialized in mathematics, agriculture, music, navigation, physics, or some other branch of learning. The doors of these universities were open to all, rich or poor, native or foreign; and, as noted, altruistic men often provided financial aid for students who needed it.

Methods

In elementary schools the methods used were repetition and drill, basically the same *catechetical* device used in the early Christian schools. In fact, the method was also quite prevalent during the later Middle Ages and early Reformation in Western Europe. Totah shows a similarity between Muslim elementary education and that of the Jesuits much later: "What was learned yesterday, should be repeated five times over; that of the day before four times, and that of the day before that, three times."[22]

Actually, the religious emphasis in Islamic elementary education was shared with the Hebrews and Christians, and the Muslims made no particular advances beyond the methods utilized in other cultures, through memorization and imitation.

---

[22] Totah, p. 61.

It was in the higher schools that the Saracenic genius was expressed in the development of new methods of learning. Some scholars feel that the Western university grew from Muslim seedlings, or as they state, "European universities of the Middle Ages were directly modeled after their earlier Islamic counterparts."[23] The higher schools grew from mosque schools and were organized into colleges, which emphasized travel and scholarship. Although considerable use was made of the lecture method, the Muslim learned much of his science through observation and experimentation, directly exploring in an objective manner the field in which he was especially interested.

In Muslim higher education we find the origin of truly unprejudiced scientific methods. Here we find laboratories and clinics used for the first time. And chemistry, astronomy, physics, and medicine were taught by the experimental method. Undoubtedly, because of the utilization of these methods many significant scientific discoveries were made; but it is indeed surprising to the West generally to learn that the early period of Muslim intellectual and scientific activity was during their "Dark Ages," a period which we shall begin to study in the following chapter.

We shall now proceed to European humanism, but first let us repeat another verse from the Islamic scriptures, an admonition not without value in the West as well as the East:

> To seek knowledge is a duty for every Muslim man and woman. Seek knowledge even though it be in China. The Savants are the heirs of the Prophets.

REFERENCES

Barnes, Harry Elmer, *An Intellectual and Cultural History of the Western World*. New York: Random House, Inc., 1937. Pp. 494–499.

Bethmann, Erich W., *Steps Toward Understanding Islam*. Washington, D.C.: American Friends of the Middle East, 1966.

Boyd, William, *The History of Western Education*, 8th ed. Rev. by Edmund J. King. New York: Barnes & Noble, Inc., 1966.

Browne, Lewis, *This Believing World*. New York: Crowell-Collier and Macmillan, Inc., 1927. Pp. 303–334.

Butts, R. Freeman, *A Cultural History of Western Education*, 2d ed. New York: McGraw-Hill, Inc., 1955. Pp. 118, 147.

Carmichael, Joel, *The Shaping of the Arab, A Study in Ethnic Identity*. New York: Crowell-Collier and Macmillan, Inc., 1967.

Durant, Will, *The Story of Civilization*, pt. iv, *The Age of Faith*. New York: Simon and Schuster, Inc., 1950. Pp. 153–344.

Eby, Frederick, and Charles F. Arrowood, *The History and Philosophy of*

---

[23] See Ray H. Muessig and Dwight W. Allen, "Islamic Contribution to American Education," p. 153, in Richard E. Gross (Ed.), *Heritage of American Education* (Boston: Allyn and Bacon, Inc., 1962). These authors follow Totah's view.

Education, Ancient and Medieval. Englewood Cliffs, N.J.: Prentice-Hall, Inc. 1940. Pp. 668–669, 697–701, 710–711.

Fehl, Noah Edward, *The Idea of a University in East and West.* Hong Kong: Chung Chi College, 1962.

Gibb, H. A. R., *Mohammedanism.* New York: Oxford University Press, 1959.

———, and Harold Bowen, *Islamic Society and the West.* New York: Oxford University Press, 1957.

Good, Harry G., *A History of Western Education.* New York: Crowell-Collier and Macmillan, Inc., 1960. Pp. 80–89.

Gross, Richard E. (Ed.), *Heritage of American Education.* Boston: Allyn and Bacon, Inc., 1962. Pp. 133–162.

Haines, C. Grove, and Warren B. Walsh, *The Development of Western Civilization.* New York: Holt, Rinehart and Winston, Inc., 1941, Pp. 106–117.

Hitti, Philip K., *The Arabs, A Short History.* Princeton, N.J.: Princeton University Press, 1943.

———, *History of the Arabs,* 6th ed. New York: St. Martin's Press, Inc., 1956.

———, *The Near East in History.* Princeton, N.J.: D. Van Nostrand Company, Inc., 1961. Pp. 187–326.

Hoballah, Mahmoud, *Islam and Humane Tenets.* Washington, D.C.: The Islamic Center, 1957. Pp. 3–14.

———, *Muhammad, The Prophet.* Washington, D.C.: The Islamic Center, 1957. Pp. 1–9.

Hungerford, Edward, "The Rise of Arabian Learning," *The Atlantic Monthly,* vol. 58 (October, 1886). Pp. 549ff.

Knight, Edgar W., *Twenty Centuries of Education.* Boston: Ginn & Co., 1940. Pp. 157–158.

Lewes, Bernard, *The Arabs in History.* New York: Harper & Row, Publishers, 1960.

Lopez, Robert, *The Birth of Europe.* New York: M. Evans and Company, Inc., 1967. Pp. 72–81 and endpapers.

Mayer, Frederick, *A History of Educational Thought.* Columbus, Ohio: Charles E. Merrill Books, Inc., 1960. Pp. 152–160.

Mulhern, James, *A History of Education,* 2d ed. New York: The Ronald Press Company, 1959. Pp. 244ff.

Nakosteen, Mehdi, *The History and Philosophy of Education.* New York: The Ronald Press Company, 1965. Pp. 120–122, 191–208.

Nasr, Seyyed Hossein, *Ideals and Realities of Islam.* New York: Frederick A. Praeger, Inc., 1967.

Power, Edward J., *Main Currents in the History of Education.* New York: McGraw-Hill, Inc., 1962. Pp. 217–219.

Saunders, John J., *The Muslim World on the Eve of Europe's Expansion.* Englewood Cliffs, N.J.: Prentice-Hall, Inc., 1966.

Shalabi, Ahmad, *History of Muslim Education.* Beirut: Dar-al-Kashshaf, 1954.

Smith, Huston, *The Religions of Man*. New York: Harper & Row, Publishers, 1965. Pp. 217–253.

Stewart, George R., *Man, An Autobiography*. New York: Random House, Inc., 1946. Pp. 251.

Totam, Khalil A., *Contributions of the Arabs to Education*. New York: Bureau of Publications, Teachers College, Columbia University, 1926.

Ulich, Robert (Ed.), *Three Thousand Years of Educational Wisdom*, 2nd ed., enl. Cambridge, Mass.: Harvard University Press, 1954.

Watt, W. Montgomery, *The Faith and Practice of al-Ghazali*. London: George Allen & Unwin, Ltd., 1953.

———, *A History of Islamic Spain*. Edinburgh: University of Edinburgh, 1965.

———, *Muslim Intellectualism*. Edinburgh: University of Edinburgh, 1963.

SELECTED PAPERBACKS

Beck, Robert Holmes, *A Social History of Education*. Englewood Cliffs, N.J.: Prentice-Hall, Inc., 1965. Pp. 31ff.

Brockelmann, Carl, *History of the Islamic Peoples*. New York: Capricorn Books, 1960.

Castle, E. B., *Ancient Education and Today*. Baltimore: Penguin Books, Inc., 1961.

Gibb, H. A. R., *Mohammedanism*. New York: New American Library of World Literature, Inc., 1955.

Grunebaum, G. E. von, *Islam*. New York: Barnes & Noble, Inc., 1961.

Lewes, Bernard, *The Arabs in History*. New York: Harper & Row, Publishers, 1960.

Mayer, Frederick, *Foundation of Education*. Columbus, Ohio: Charles E. Merrill Books, Inc., 1963.

Pickthall, Mohammed Marmaduke (Ed. and Trans.), *The Meaning of the Glorious Koran*. New York: New American Library of World Literature, Inc., 1953.

Ralph, Philip Lee, *Story of Our Civilization, 10,000 Years of Western Man*. New York: E. P. Dutton & Co., Inc., 1959.

Runciman, Steven, *History of the Crusades,* 3 vols. New York: Harper & Row, Publishers, 1964.

Smith, Huston, *The Religions of Man*. New York: Harper & Row, Publishers, 1965. Pp. 217–253.

Smith, Wilfred Cantwell, *Islam in Modern History*. New York: New American Library of World Literature, Inc., 1957.

CHAPTER **10**

Study of the Humanities for a More Abundant Life

We must insist . . . that it was not the revival of antiquity alone, but its union with the genius of the Italian people, that achieved the conquest of the Western world. . . . The Renaissance, however, is not a fragmentary imitation or compilation, but a new birth.[1]

THE ORIGINS OF HUMANISM

Great as had been the Arabian spring and high tide of summer now Western Europe was about to burst into similar bloom, flowering once again in Italy. This new development, following the Middle Ages, marks the dawn of modern history as well as emphasizes the arrival of a novel view of God and man that has been called humanism.

Authorities generally agree that a new era began with the Renaissance; and, since education is always a reflection of its age, modern education and modern theories of education can be said to have originated in this same movement. The foundations of various theories of education were established in ancient and medieval times; but it took certain social, political, economic, and philosophical changes that occurred in Western Europe during the fourteenth and fifteenth centuries to modify these initial elements and crystallize them into the popular educational theories of recent times. The first of the modern theories of education so developed is *humanism*. Humanistic education was the distinct outgrowth of the Renaissance, but to realize its significance we must understand that the Renaissance was but one phase in the great general quickening of

[1] Jacob Burckhardt, *The Civilization of the Renaissance in Italy* (New York: New American Library of World Literature, Inc., 1961).

the Western world. As Wells says, "The Renaissance was only a part of the Renascence of Europe . . . a revival due to the exhumation of classical art and learning; it was but one factor in the very much larger and more complicated resurrection of European capacity and vigour."[2]

What were the causes of this widespread reawakening? What factors profoundly influenced the intellectual and cultural life of the new centuries and brought about the educational philosophy known as humanism?

But, first, what were the hallmarks of medieval society that now became susceptible to change? What of the universal society of Western Europe with its catholic religion; its scholarly language, Latin; its respect (and disrespect) for two great pillars of its life, Pope and Emperor? Thus, it is possible that the serenity of the age mankind was leaving also had its effect on thought and educational theory. This tribute to the medieval ethos is quietly revealed in the parable of The Castle and the Rock.

> There was, in these middle years, a valley broad and wide, well-watered and fertile whose inhabitants did indeed count themselves the most fortunate of men—men formed of the dust of the field in the image of their God. For their lives followed the rhythm of the seasons: they plowed and they sowed; they reaped and feasted; the drought came and the famine; yet the bounty of the olive tree nourished them and the vine refreshed them; and they were at peace.
>
> When the wintry blasts roared from the North, and when the scorching sirocco blew from the South they accepted these things—not gladly but hopefully for life was short and heaven held its bounty even to eternity. Thus their eyes were set on high and the two great configurations of the valley continually reassured them. For the Castle stood on its craggy eminence in the East and was ever visible though oft-times partially hidden by the mistiness of dawn and by the frosts of autumn. And, likewise, to the West, there stood the Rock, and when the morning sun first lighted the upper reaches of this great granite peak with a brilliance impossible to describe—or when in the beauty of the sunset its silhouette revealed that stairway etched in stone which stretched from earth to sky—the Rock offered a comfort that was so far beyond the simple pleasures of the soil that there is no telling of it.
>
> And from the Castle issued great retinues of men, some with bright glorious banners, others carrying the holiest of objects, and as they wound throughout the valley their progress was beautiful to behold. For at their head rode Caesar and his raiment glittered. But of the valley folk they tribute took; fat sheep and grain, one sighed but then in vain; for better they than brigands bold that dwelt beyond the plain.
>
> Yet the Rock was loftier than the Castle and indeed when one swept his gaze from the East to the West in the early dawn or rosy twilight he

---

[2] H. G. Wells, *The Outline of History,* 3rd ed., rev. (New York: Crowell-Collier and Macmillan, Inc., 1921), p. 699n. Reprinted by permission of Professor G. P. Wells.

understood their meaning and marvelled that the mystery of earth and heaven should stand exposed before him. In truth man's life was encompassed by their comforting stillness. In the morning he was born, at midday he flourished, in the evening like the somber shades that fitfully fled across the valley, he was gone. But his happy spirit dwelt forever in the shadow of the Everlasting Rock.

So these men judged (and rightly too) that this their life had meaning only in these simple observances: their soil they tilled; their toll they paid; their lives they sped. He of the Castle came and went. But the Mighty Rock did not change; it prevailed in absolute silence and solace gave to him who sought its peace. Man deemed this good, and praised the Rock; and looked to it for succor—a very present help in time of trouble![3]

MEDIEVAL SOCIETY

That medieval life was perfect is, of course, far from the truth: there was poverty and inequality, disease and death, an almost primitive economic life. Medieval symmetry lay in personal and divine relationships, the ordering of opportunities, the rootedness of life. Group activity took precedence over that of the individual; men worked, worried, worshiped, and waged war together. Life was short, but the promise of eternity assuaged its brevity. The great cathedrals of Europe bear witness to the urge for immortality—"Stone on the way to heaven," one medievalist has described them. Education was functional, geared to the absolutes and tempo of that age. Donohue writes:

> In the thirteenth century everyone received an education. It could scarcely have been otherwise, for no society regenerates itself except by transmitting its way of life to the rising generation, and were it not to educate a sizable portion of the educable, it would perish. But education, of course, is not synonymous with book learning. . . . So the peasant children learned the skills of farmer or housewife; the apprentices mastered the appropriate techniques of their craft; the nobility acquired the arts of a feudal administrat or chatelaine; and bright boys destined for civil or ecclesiastical service went to the university.[4]

Yet medieval life could not continue in isolation from other realities, when the winds of change were blowing. The achievements of the Muslim had hardly touched the common man of the Middle Ages; trade had

---

[3] Suggested by Henry Adams' appraisal of the late medieval period in *The Education of Henry Adams* (Boston: Houghton Mifflin Company, 1918). See especially ch. xv, "The Virgin and the Dynamo."

[4] John W. Donohue, s.j., *St. Thomas Aquinas and Education* (New York: Random House, Inc., 1968), pp. 47–48. There was, however, a dark side to medieval life and religion. See Jules Michelet, *Satanism and Witchcraft, A Study in Medieval Superstition* (New York: The Citadel Press, 1939).

stilled; and thought itself, if not moribund, had been rigidly circumscribed. If medieval man was happy perhaps it was because he lacked the modern concept of progress!

But then vast economic revolutions were effected. As we have noted, the Crusades had their social and commercial implications as well as religious. The growth of free cities such as Genoa, Venice, and those of northern Europe was tremendously stimulated by the business of equipping and transporting the thousands of Crusaders, who thronged to the East in the seven Crusades that occurred in the 150 years following 1095.

The Crusaders' tastes and demands were greatly enlarged by their sojourns in the Levant, where they discovered to their surprise that men possessed more to eat and wear than the medieval European had ever dreamed of. These contacts with Eastern civilization created a craving for the new products and commodities; trade blossomed and commerce and manufacturing were reanimated, particularly in the free cities. The burghers —merchants, bankers, and masters of the guilds—who supplied these new economic demands rose to the importance of a third estate, a class distinct from the medieval noble, clergy, and serf. As we observed in Chapter 8, the needs and ideals of this middle class were quite different from those of the older established classes and pointed the way to a new mode of living.

Expanding commerce sought and soon found new worlds to conquer. The discovery of additional routes to India by Marco Polo and others, and the location of the Americas by Columbus and his followers in their search for still shorter routes to the Orient, enlarged the scope of trade, and in turn changed its manner. The new commercial problems could not be handled by the free cities with their insufficient capital and military power, so trade became national in scope. This change was an outstanding factor in the rise of the nation-state in Western Europe, and a forerunner of new educational conceptions and practices. In the new Atlantic monarchies (and in some of the older European duchies and kingdoms) Princes of Trade began to supersede in prestige, influence, and power Princes of the Church.

Thus, the Crusades, the enrichment of the free cities, the rise of the burgher class, the expansion of commerce, industry, and banking, the increasing consequence of guilds and apprenticeship, the growing spirit of nationalism, the development of national languages and literatures, were all factors in the revival of interest in the things of this world.

It is easy to consider great epochs as distinct, or separate, periods, cut off sharply from those that precede and follow. We sometimes forget that all advance is evolutionary; one period grows out of previous periods. The Renaissance was the natural outgrowth of certain developments in the later medieval centuries to which we referred in the discussions of medieval and Islamic education.

The roots of the Renaissance are to be found in changed economic and social conditions. But the real meaning of the Renaissance is to be found in the new spirit of inquiry into knowledge which was undermining the structures of monasticism and scholasticism as surely as the new industry and the new trade were destroying the structure of feudalism. Scholasticism had fettered thought and engaged in a quibbling play of words until intellectual accomplishment was at a standstill; but it had supplied the foundation for intellectual advancement. It led students to see the advisability of analytical thought and furnished them with thought processes which, although at first used only to prove dogmas already accepted, later became the means by which scholasticism itself was destroyed and replaced by scientific inquiry. The universities, founded during the later years of the Age of Faith, began to stimulate a desire for intellectual achievement. With the rise of faculties of law and medicine to supplement the faculties of theology came more intellectual freedom and more dissatisfaction with institutions that restricted thought and suppressed inquiry. Muslim learning, gradually influencing Europe more and more through Spain, had prepared the way for importation from Byzantium, the storehouse of Greek culture, of the writings of the great classical authors and the teachers of the new humanities.

Many material things came into European life to aid intellectual advancement. Paper was introduced from the Muslims; printing was invented to multiply the copies of classic manuscripts discovered and brought into Europe by the early humanists. Thus the mad desire of the few to read spread to the many by the adequacy of the supply of books; and books becoming cheaper and more plentiful gave added motivation to intellectual activity.

The work of explorers and scientific discoverers quickened the spirit of inquiry and investigation. Magellan, sailing west to find the East, verified the hypothesis that the world was round. Copernicus demonstrated that the sun and not the earth was the center of the universe. So the old unity of belief, the old dogmatic authority, had to give way under the force of an inquiring attitude demanding concrete proofs instead of metaphysical abstractions.

The church itself, because of a false sense of security, had suffered a decline, and many ecclesiastical courts had become corrupted. It was not unnatural therefore that some individuals should lose trust in the church, begrudge loyalty to its leaders, and at last stand out against the powers of the ecclesiastical domination. Men became less interested in ritual and more interested in the life of the contemporary world. Their attention passed from the divinities to the humanities and was fixed upon the joys of living, the beauties and wonders of nature, the human relationships of life, and the desires, ambitions, and aspirations of individual human beings. There was less emphasis upon formalized church observances that led only to the hope of winning eternal life and escaping eternal damnation, and more on every form of art, literature, science, and commerce that made life rich and pleasant (whether it was good for the soul or not).

Thus, the thought processes developed by scholasticism, the broadening of the universities, the incoming of Muslim learning from Spain, the increased supply of books, the findings of exploration and scientific discovery, the apparent degeneration of the church, all helped to develop the intellectual freedom and individual personality that brought about the artistic, moral, and spiritual rebirth of Western Europe, and provided the genesis of its modern culture, the emancipation of its will, and an enthusiastic delight in independence of thought, speech, and action.

We have already indicated that the Renaissance was much more than a revival of learning; its influence was much more than literary; it profoundly changed the moral, social, intellectual, and artistic life of Western Europe. It should be emphasized also that the Renaissance was not limited to Italy where it began, but soon spread to every land of Europe. In Spain and Portugal the Renaissance busied itself in exploration, in colonization, and eventually in the reform of the church from within. In France the stimulative force of the movement was felt in literature and in art, in England almost entirely in literature and learning. In Germany and Holland, however, the movement took deeper root, stimulating not only scholarship and art but also the interest in moral and social reform that eventually brought on the Protestant revolt and Reformation.

In general, it is desirable to distinguish between the early Renaissance in Italy and the late Renaissance in northern Europe.[5] The Renaissance in Italy represents individual humanism: it stressed personal culture, individual freedom and development, as the best way toward full and rich lives; it produced a revival of classic learning and paganism, which eventually brought about a countermovement under Florence's Savonarola; it went back to the writers of classical antiquity to revive the long-forgotten humanistic way of living and looking at life; it was essentially aristocratic, limited to the few who had individual means for the desired culture.

On the other hand, the Renaissance in the north represents social humanism: it stressed social and moral reform as the best means of providing rich and full lives; it preserved an interest in the church and was essentially religious in spirit; it emphasized the Hebrew classics as well as the study of Greek and Latin because of its additional interest in the sources of Biblical and patristic literature; it was essentially democratic, since it aimed at rich and full lives for the masses as well as for the favored few. Therefore, in our treatment of the educational implications of humanism, it will be necessary for us to treat the subject under each of these

[5] See Wallace K. Ferguson, *The Renaissance* (New York: Holt, Rinehart and Winston, Inc., 1940), pp. 1–8.

headings. Furthermore—both in Italy and in the northern countries—humanism passed through two stages: the first a broad and true humanism; and the second a narrow and formal humanism, often designated by the term *Ciceronianism*. Because of these different aspects of humanism, we shall discuss it under two divisions: (1) Italian and (2) northern.

ITALIAN HUMANISM

Renaissance humanism began in Italy, where the quickening influences were felt earliest and more keenly than in the rest of Europe. The city-states of Italy were the first to increase their wealth and prestige as a result of the Crusades and the accompanying growth of trade and industry. Their independence, the outcome of struggles against the ecclesiastical domination of the Holy Roman Emperor, offered splendid opportunities for personal advancement and individual fortune. In Italy, the ancient home of Greco-Roman culture, the tradition of this culture had persisted more strongly than among the other peoples of Europe. It was proper that the Italians should strive with patriotic fervor to revive their cultural heritage.

Petrarch (1304–1374) and his co-laborer Boccaccio (1313–1375) may be taken as types of the early Italian humanistic scholar. Petrarch has been called the first modern scholar and man of letters. He attacked the medieval universities with their Aristotelian philosophy as "nests of gloomy ignorance"; he repudiated the otherworldly ideal of the monasteries and bitterly criticized the whole range of scholastic learning. Beginning with his first great discovery in 1333, he collected and copied ancient Latin manuscripts, taking special pleasure in the orations of Cicero. He wrote in Latin to familiarize his contemporaries with the lives of great men of antiquity; but he wrote sonnets in the Italian vernacular designed to voice the humanistic emphasis on emotional life and to give the individual, personal, and esthetic keynote to the Renaissance. He was not a Greek scholar himself, but he inspired others to revive the Greek spirit at its best. He was influential in the introduction of humanistic studies at the University of Padua.

The desire of the early humanists to be able to read the masterpieces of Greek literature caused them to turn to Byzantium for an adequate supply of the writings of the great classic authors and for good teachers to teach them how to read them. A new day dawned when Chrysoloras (1350–1415) came from Constantinople (1396) to become a professor of Greek at the University of Florence. Many distinguished humanists came to listen to this first and most famous of the émigré teachers, and they carried the seed to every university center in Italy. Chrysoloras taught at other Italian universities and wrote his *Catechism of Greek Grammar,* which became the basic text for the study of the language; he also translated Plato's *Republic* into Latin. He was the first of many Greek professors to strengthen the enthusiasm of Italian humanists for Greek culture and to spread the knowledge of Greek language and literature throughout Europe.

Humanism in Italy was fostered and strengthened by the support of those great bankers and rulers of Florence, Cosimo de' Medici (1389–1464) and Lorenzo de' Medici (1449–1492), generous patrons who founded the Medicean Library in Florence, spending large sums for the collection and copying of manuscripts, and subsidizing the endeavors of such artists as Ghiberti, Donatello, Botticelli, Raphael, and Leonardo da Vinci.

Similarly, ruling princes of other Italian city-states, including those of Milan and Urbino, and some of the popes at Rome, notably Leo X (1475–1521), were ardent patrons of humanism, supporting literary studies in the universities, the establishment of libraries, and the maintenance of court schools.

Aims

This individualistic Italian humanism provided the very foundation of modern academic freedom. Freedom of thought, self-expression, and creative activity were its fundamental bases. Such independence is the true aim of humanistic education, which strives for the fullest expression of individual personality through nature, art, music, literature, and architecture.

Versatility was made the keynote of this new concept of education. Its goal was to be versatile in order to develop individual personality to its richest extent, receive life's greatest exaltation, and be able to live the abundant life. Thus the aim of humanistic education was its design for luxuriant living; the humanist aspired to get the most possible out of life; through his contacts with the world, ancient and modern, he expected to receive the recipe for an excellent, full, rich existence.

The primary objective of Italian humanism was the Greek ideal of a liberal education: the harmonious development of mind, body, and moral sense. To the Italian humanist the archetype was represented by an individual with a development completely rounded in all the aspects of human living. The humanist's second fundamental was a renewed emphasis upon individual excellence and personal self-realization. Thus education aimed at the development of the liberal man, who, possessing individuality, would be able to appreciate the past as well as to enjoy the present. Indeed, humanism's rationale may well be stated, For God can be served, only as man is served.

Types

Italian humanistic education was literary and esthetic education. But this education was practical in the sense that it prepared the young nobles of the court for active participation in everyday affairs. It was not vocational in the modern meaning of the term, as a preparation for a definite profession. In fact, since the days of the early Greeks there has been a feeling that vocational and liberal education are antagonistic to each other. The exponents of the liberal humanistic education have usually disparaged what they consider a narrow training.

With the Italian humanists, the literary and esthetic types of education were somewhat fused. The ancient literatures of Greece and Rome were studied not only for the knowledge they gave of the institutions and ideals of the Greco-Roman world but also for their beauty and as models for new creative effort. Esthetic education was of the broadest type, aiming at appreciation not only of literature but also of art, architecture, music, and drama. This estheticism, which had been wholly absent from medieval education, was the outstanding new element in humanistic education and has always characterized it.

Another pronounced feature of individual humanism was the emphasis upon physical education not only in the form of swimming, fencing, boxing, riding, dancing, but also in matters of diet and hygiene. Social training in deportment and manners was emphasized as the most important aspect of moral education. The moral education of the early humanists was not limited to obedience to religious authority, but had a much more practical bearing upon life than did the moral teachings of the church. In practice, moral standards might often give way to license, as in the later stages of Greco-Roman civilization; but the educational writers of the Renaissance always stressed the importance of good moral training. Vittorino da Feltre (1378–1446) strongly emphasized moral and Christian influences at his palace school in Mantua.

Content

In the curriculum of the humanistic school, the humanities replaced the divinities that had so dominated the literature of medieval time. Instead of a content devoted to the otherworld, there was a turning to the things of this world. Humanism took all human interests as its province. The individualistic humanist had two outstanding characteristics: (1) variety of interest and (2) desire for light. The representatives of this movement had many and varied interests; they did many things and studied many different subjects. Leonardo da Vinci, for example, best known to the world as a great artist, was also an engineer, a musician, and a philosopher. Galileo, the famed physicist and astronomer, was also an artist and a musician. The humanist curriculum was almost as broad as life itself.

The studies of the Renaissance schools were most varied, opening up to the student three aspects of life that had remained almost unknown throughout medieval education. One of these new worlds was the vibrant life of the past, the life of the Greeks and the Romans with its variety of interest and wide knowledge. This life was reflected in the incomparable literature and arts of those who had lived it. The humanists believed that the charm of the classics lay essentially in their humanness. Hence, classical literature and classical art were sought and studied as an expression of this life and were used as models and themes for a national art of painting and sculpture and a national literature of poetry, drama, and romance; and the artistry developed soon came to rival the classic models. The humanistic course of study, when at its best, included facility in reading, writing, and speaking basic Latin; extensive study of Greek and Roman prose writers and poets; and familiarity with the life of the ancients through a reading of history and biography.

A second world opened up to the humanistic student was the subjective world of the emotions. An attempt was made to develop the joy of living and the contemplative pleasures of speculation about things of this life, to inculcate an appreciation of the beautiful, and to foster an interest in introspective observation and analysis from the esthetic and human standpoint. This was done through participation in the activities and interests of life, through self-culture and improvement, and through the appreciation and creation of literature and art.

The third world opened up to the humanistic scholar was the world of nature, a world almost unknown to the medieval scholar and in general, regardless of his veneration for Aristotle, deemed by him ignoble and debasing in its effects upon mankind.

The humanistic curriculum, however, was not limited to literary and esthetic subjects. Instruction in morals, manners, and health was included. A wide range of physical exercises was utilized, combining both Athenian and chivalric elements. Maxims of morality were drawn from both church and classical writers; and manners were taught as an essential concomitant of moral education. Dancing and music were taught not only for their esthetic but also for their social values.

Although the medieval Trivium and Quadrivium were in part retained in the universities, the shift was away from the emphasis placed upon dialectic or logic by the medieval scholars to an emphasis upon grammar, rhetoric, and mathematics.

Agencies and Organization

Humanistic education triumphed through the establishment of new schools founded in the new spirit and expressing the highest educational ideals of the humanists.

The first classical secondary schools were the court schools in Italy; they furnished models for similar schools in other countries—the *collèges* and *lycées* in France, the *Gymnasien* in Germany, the Latin grammar schools in England and the early American colonies.

The court schools were so designated because they were founded and maintained by the ruling princes and dukes of the Italian city-states. These sometimes dictatorial rulers endeavored to make their cities centers of humanistic learning, not only through the collection of manuscripts, founding of libraries, and the subsidizing of scholars and artists, but also through the establishment of schools. Famous schools were located at Florence, Venice, Padua, Verona, and other cities; but the two most outstanding were those at Mantua, under the control of Vittorino da Feltre from 1423 to 1446, and Ferrara, conducted from 1429 to 1460 by Guarino da Varona. These two great teachers, who were among the greatest scholars of the Renaissance, were thoroughly committed to the ideas of humanistic education, and were skilled in the ability to construct a curriculum and devise methods effective in achieving the aims of the new learning.

Although most of the pupils paid fees, the children of the poorer court retainers were taught free at these schools. They were like modern boarding schools in that they admitted boys at the age of nine or ten and kept them until the age of twenty or twenty-one. Girls did not attend, but studied at home under tutors. The boys lived at the school, and were educated both in and out of the classroom. The court schools at first rivaled the work of the universities which were still antagonistic to the new humanistic learning; but later, as the work of the universities became more liberal and was raised to a higher level, court schools became in some degree preparatory. Such schools as those conducted by Vittorino and Guarino, with their broad intellectual, physical, and moral training, did much to establish the type of classical humanistic secondary school that has persisted to the present day.

Methods

With the establishment of the humanistic secondary schools, new teaching methods were devised. Texts became more plentiful and were available to the students, thus obviating the necessity of continual lectures. Written themes displaced the oral disputations so common in the medieval schools. Although instruction aimed primarily at the development of linguistic ability, Latin and Greek were treated as living and not dead languages, and self-expression and self-activity were continually stressed.

For example, Vittorino, who has been called the first modern schoolmaster, made a genuine attempt to adapt the work of the individual to his particular needs and capacities, thus anticipating by almost five centuries the emphasis upon adjustment to individual differences. Vittorino, in fact, marks the advent of the professional teacher. He was the first to formulate many of the important educational doctrines. He stood for the development of interest and of the power to think; he believed that development should be well balanced, that mental activity is dependent upon physical activity, and that play is of educational significance. He contended that the subjects of the curriculum should be varied and that there should be due alternation of subjects.

The methods of discipline in these schools were mild. Punishment and threats of punishment were not needed as motives for learning, and the stern repressive asceticism of the church schools was absent. Sufficient motivation was to be found in the fact that the higher posts of honor and activity in the life of the times were open only to those who had been thoroughly trained in the humanistic manner.

HUMANISM NORTH OF THE ALPS

The spread of the Renaissance into northern Europe was facilitated by the work of a nonmonastic order, founded in Holland in 1376, called the Hieronymians, or Brethren of the Common Life. Pious and humanitarian in spirit, they devoted themselves to the copying of manuscripts and the teaching of the poor and ignorant lower classes. They also helped to support worthy but indigent scholars and were so successful in teaching backward students that existing schools were placed under their supervision and they were encouraged to open new schools of their own. In these schools they rejected the formal methods of early medieval education and attempted to satisfy the needs of their students. Their work soon spread from the Netherlands into northern France and Germany. Although their own schools were much superior to the others, the brethren were open-minded enough to seek further improvement. By the middle of the fifteenth century, when the Renaissance began to scale the Alps, they had schools in the Netherlands, France, and were being welcomed into the German states. Hieronymian scholars went to Italy to study the work of the court schools there; and wandering Italian scholars, visiting the countries of northern Europe where they were received enthusiastically by the brethren, impregnated them with the spirit of the humanistic education. Northern humanism thus came to have a dual characteristic, combining the social piety of the brethren, represented in the work of Thomas à Kempis (1380–1471), and the broad literary spirit of the Italian Renaissance, represented in the work of that other great Hieronymian scholar, Desiderius Erasmus (1466–1536). Other outstanding products of the Hieronymian movement were Johann Reuchlin, Rudolphus Agricola, Peter Luder, Jacob Wimpfeling, Philip Melanchthon, and Johann Sturm, the last of whom we shall discuss later in this chapter and the next. Juan Luis Vives (1492–1540), another famous scholar at the "dawn of the new era," lived an international life. Born in Spain and dying in Bruges at an early age, Vives held many educational posts, once serving at the court of England.[6] (Because of his

---

[6] Those impatient to read of Vives now should see Foster Watson (Trans.), *Vives: On Education* (London: Cambridge University Press, 1913).

prominence in the Realist movement, we will discuss his work in Chapter 12.)

Another influence accelerating the Renaissance in the north was the attempt of the French kings Charles VIII and Louis XII to enforce hereditary claims upon certain cities in northern Italy. From a military and political standpoint they failed, but culturally they rendered a service by bringing the French people into contact with Italian humanism at its best sources and in bringing to France humanistic scholars, who established *collèges* and libraries at such centers as Bordeaux and Paris. Guillaume Budaeus (1476–1540), the royal librarian of France under Francis I, was perhaps the greatest of the French humanistic scholars. He set up a royal press in Paris and greatly improved the *collèges* of France.

The origination of a method of printing from movable type by Johann Gutenberg (1397–1468), the fall of Constantinople to the Turks, and the geographical explorations and discoveries of Dutch and English adventurers gave additional momentum to the Renaissance in these northern countries.

Aims

The educational aim of northern humanism was different from that of the Italian; it was more social than individual. The emphasis was less subjective and esthetic and more objective and moralistic. Education was aimed not so much at the attainment of individual happiness as at social reform and the improvement of human relationships. Education in the northern countries was not directed toward a breadth of interest in human life; these northern humanists had no interest in the pleasures and riches of life beyond practical religious and social life. The selection of the classics to be translated, edited, and used in education was determined by one goal, that of eliminating the ignorance of the common people and the greed, selfishness, hypocrisy, and tendency toward exploitation of the social leaders, that is, the leaders of churches, monastic orders, universities, and governments. Wimpfeling expressed this aim when he said, "Of what use are all the books in the world, the most learned writings, the most profound research if they only minister to the vainglory of their authors, and do not, or cannot, advance the good of mankind?"

From the standpoint of the development of personal character and individual freedom, the aim of the northern education was narrow; from the standpoint of the development of the general social welfare, it was broad. Instead of aiming at a rich and full life for the individual, northern humanism aimed at a rich and full life for society as a whole. Erasmus, liberal humanist that he was, in discussing the aims of education, put piety ahead of learning, moral duty ahead of manners. Yet Vives, if anything, fundamentally more religious than Erasmus, looked upon learning in a most modern fashion—his age and the contrary movement in humanism notwithstanding. He said, "This is the fruit of all studies; this is the goal. Having acquired our knowledge, we must turn it to usefulness, and employ it for the common good. . . . We must transfer our solicitude [from princes] to the people."[7]

Types

These social-minded humanists of the north, therefore, stressed religious education, moral, and social education far more than they did esthetics. Literary training was encouraged as a means to a religious and social end, rather than for its own sake. Careful religious instruction was invariably coupled with liberal classic training. (The Italian humanists took their religion lightly; thus there was little conflict with the church.) The social humanists took their religion seriously and bitterly attacked the moral evils in the church, even though at this time they accepted the current theological doctrines.

Instead of the aristocratic class education of the Italians, we find in the north an attempt to provide a more democratic type of education. In practice, stress was placed on secondary and higher education, but there was also an attempt to improve elementary schools.

Content

The curriculum of northern social humanism united classical and Biblical literature. Erasmus provided for use in the schools a Greek edition of the New Testament, a new translation of the New Testament into Latin, and a paraphrase of the writings of such church Fathers as Jerome, in addition to editing a number of Latin and Greek textbooks. The content of the German schools consisted of the church catechism, the New Testament, and parts of Jerome, as well as an intensive study of Latin and Greek grammar, the reading of a few selected authors such as Cicero, and training in the speaking and writing of Latin after the model of Cicero. In the French collèges the Hebrew language, largely because it was the language of the Old Testament, was taught along with Latin and Greek; and Johann Reuchlin (1455–1522) introduced the same language into Germany, Thomas Elyot (1490–1546) in his *Boke Named The Governour,* an exposition of the humanistic ideal in education, advocated the study of Latin as a living language, Greek for its literature, and certain classical authors and selected parts of the Old Testament for ethical training. Erasmus urged the importance of the study of history, geography, and science as a help toward illuminating the classics. Although Elyot advocated drawing, music, dancing, and a wide range of physical exercises for the English humanistic schools, the physical training, music, and art of the Italian court schools found little place in the secondary schools of England,

---

[7] Watson, p. 278, 283.

France, and Germany at this time. Sturm and Melanchthon had little use for such subjects.

Agencies and Organization

The Renaissance in the north organized appropriate institutions to carry out its educational aims. The court schools of Italy served as patterns for the early Teutonic *Fürstenschulen,* or princes' schools, even before the first German *Gymnasium* was established by Johann Sturm (1507–1589) at Strassburg. Sturm's school was the most important school in Germany resulting from the humanistic influence, and it fixed the name and character of German secondary schools for centuries.

John Colet (1467–1519), who had studied at Florence, with the help of Erasmus founded St. Paul's School in London as the beginning of the humanistic movement in English secondary education. We have already called attention to the establishment of the French *collèges* under the influence of such great French humanists as Budaeus and Corderius.

Not only in these secondary schools but also in the universities of these northern countries, humanistic studies were encouraged by the patronage of kings, queens, dukes, and princes. In Germany the municipal authorities controlled and supported the *Gymnasien,* and this was somewhat the practice in the cities of France. The universities of France broadened their work by adding chairs of Greek; Henry VIII and Elizabeth I encouraged the colleges at Cambridge and Oxford to found royal professorships in the classics. Erasmus was the first teacher of Greek at Cambridge; and William Grocyn (1446–1514), who had studied at Florence, introduced Greek learning at Oxford. In Germany the existing universities gradually introduced humanistic studies; and new ones like Wittenberg, humanistic from the start, were founded by Philip Melanchthon (1479–1560) and Reuchlin.

There was some variation in the organization of the northern secondary schools. The grammar schools of England were usually boarding schools, but the *Gymnasien* of Germany were mostly day schools. Tuition charges were levied in all these schools; and, as a rule, the school was arranged into nine or ten classes, or forms, the beginning of the class-a-year practice still prevalent in our modern secondary schools.

These educational institutions—the humanistic secondary school and the university—were open only to boys and men (although Erasmus advocated that women should have the same educational advantages as men).

Methods

The humanistic educators of the north were concerned with the problems of method and in their writings advocated methods quite in advance of those in use. Some of the methods suggested appear very modern. Perhaps the techniques actually used in the schools fell short of the ideals of the founders; but the fact that such advanced ideas were even thought of at this time is significant.

Erasmus wrote two great educational classics in which he presented constructively his views on educational methods: *The Liberal Education of Children* and *The Method of Study*. He emphasized the importance of a careful study of the child's nature and advised continual personal and individualized care and direction of studies. He stressed the important place of plays, games, and exercise in education and the importance of keeping education in close touch with social needs and the life of the times. He discussed many of the minor details of reliable and effective method, such as the value of repetition, the mastery of small units of work at a time, and the prefacing of study by preparation. He attacked the barbarous methods of discipline used in the medieval schools and advocated a more attractive system. He favored mild discipline. Praise and reward, he said, accomplish more than threats and blows. The business of the teacher was to help his students, not to display his learning, and he especially ridiculed those narrow teachers who mistook the form for the spirit of the new learning.

As time went on, the earlier broad humanism declined into a narrower formalized humanism. From the middle of the sixteenth century on this narrower humanism was distinctly in the ascendant. In its narrowest form this tendency was called Ciceronianism.

Ciceronianism emphasized the style and sentence construction of the Greek and Roman classic writers, especially Cicero, rather than the thought and important characteristics contained in their writings. It was largely a superficial imitation; for it was based upon the idea that in order to create one must first imitate the masters of style; and few ever got beyond the stage of imitation. Erasmus expressed the narrowness of this tendency when he said, "It is an apishness in which one discovers none of the virtues that have made the glory of Cicero, such as his happy inspiration, the intelligent disposition of his subjects, his large acquaintance with men and affairs, and his ability to move those who hear him."

Juan Luis Vives made important initial contributions to the development of a psychology of education as an essential method. He urged the use of the vernacular, the broadening of the curriculum, education of women (he was the tutor of Queen Mary I of England), and recognized both the individual and social purposes of education.[8]

Roger Ascham (1515–1568), teacher of Greek at Cambridge and later tutor to Queen Elizabeth I, was the first Englishman to write a treatise on educational method in the vernacular. This book, *The Schole-*

---

[8] See Richard E. Gross (Ed.), *Heritage of American Education* (Boston: Allyn and Bacon, Inc., 1962), p. 289.

master, has been given a place in literary as well as educational history. In his discussion of method, Ascham perhaps presents the best humanistic practices of the Renaissance schools in England. He particularly advocated improved methods of teaching language; his book has been said "to contain perhaps the best advice that was ever given for the study of languages." His method of double translation, translating a passage into English and then an hour later retranslating it into the original language for comparison with the original, was a considerable improvement in linguistic method over the older method, which stressed the memorizing of meaningless forms and rules in the ancient tongue. In Ascham's method grammar was learned incidentally in connection with the translation. Like Erasmus, Ascham bitterly opposed the brutal discipline of the times and argued for more humane methods. Instead of corporal punishment, he too advocated praise. "Where the child doth well, let the master praise him and say, 'Here ye do well,' for there is no such whetstone to sharpen a hard wit and encourage a will to learning, as is praise."

In his *Gymnasium* at Strassburg, Sturm's method was more narrowly humanistic, for Sturm appears to have had a greater talent for thorough organization and careful grading of instruction than for the development of an advantageous system of teaching. His method stressed imitation and memorization, neglected the vernacular except in the lower grades, and made much use of Latin. Detailed study of words and phrases, the intricacies of grammar, syntax, and prosody, heavily burdened his students. Yet extensive use was made of pupil monitors, and classical study was motivated by the students' presentation of plays in Latin and Greek. Nevertheless, the unadulterated logical manner in which instruction was organized weakened interest, and Sturm found it necessary to resort to harsh discipline. (A sample of his scheduling will be offered in the next chapter.)

So, regardless of its original merits, humanistic education became narrow and academic in the north. Instead of including a broad reading of ancient literature, the curriculum was limited to a few selected classics. The aim of instruction was to develop a formal style, a correct mode of expression. It is strange indeed that the older scholasticism, with Aristotle as master and dialectic as content, had returned in another and a no less narrow format, with Cicero as master and linguistics as content! Erasmus, with his brilliant wit, parodied the new formalism:

> The simple folk of the golden age flourished without any armament of sciences, being guided only by nature and instinct. For what need was there for grammar when all spoke the same language, and had no other aim in speaking but that some one else should understand? What use for dialectic, where there was no battle of opinions ranged in contradiction to each other? What room for rhetoric, when no man cared to make trouble for his neighbor? . . . And now I seem to hear the philosophers disagreeing with me. But the true unhappiness, they say, is to be engrossed in folly, to err, to be deceived, not to know. *Nay, this is to live*

as a man. Why they call it "unhappy" I cannot see. It is simply that men are born thus, trained thus, constituted thus; it is the common lot of all. Nothing can be called unhappy if it fulfils its own nature.[9]

This savant from Rotterdam vividly attacked this narrowing tendency in his essay *The Ciceronians,* but his was a lone voice. It was not until the advent of the realists of the sixteenth and seventeenth centuries that one finds any really effective reaction against this stylized humanism. As Paul Monroe remarks:

> The genius of the new age had promised to lead men out of the cloister into the new world. In the end it led them only out of the cloister into the classroom. Pedantry resumed its sway under a changed form, and the present went back into the bondage of the past. Even the word "humanities" soon lost its large and generous original meaning, and shrank into a synonym for Greek and Latin learning. These two dead languages became the sole instruments of culture, and the classical scholars were accepted as the only possible type of educated men. It is necessary to lay stress upon these absurd Renaissance ideas because their evil influence was destined to be far-reaching and long-enduring and to continue indeed right down into our own modern world.[10]

REFERENCES

Adams, John, *The Evolution of Educational Theory.* London: Macmillan & Co., Ltd., 1912. Pp. 229–249.

Boyd, William, *The History of Western Education,* 8th ed. Rev. by Edmund J. King. New York: Barnes & Noble, Inc., 1966. Pp. 159–182.

Burnham, William H., *Great Teachers and Mental Health.* New York: Appleton-Century-Crofts, 1926. Pp. 1–119.

Butts, R. Freeman, *A Cultural History of Western Education,* 2d ed. New York: McGraw-Hill, Inc., 1955. Pp. 165–193.

Cantor, Norman F., *The English, A History of Politics and Society to 1760.* New York: Simon and Schuster, Inc., 1967. Pp. 278–399.

Charlton, Kenneth, *Education in Renaissance England.* Toronto: University of Toronto Press, 1965.

Clark, Donald Lemen, *Rhetoric and Poetry in the Renaissance, A Survey of Rhetorical Terms in English Renaissance Literary Criticism.* New York: Russell & Russell, 1963.

Clough, Shepard B., *The Rise and Fall of Civilization.* New York: McGraw-Hill, Inc., 1951. Pp. 163–191.

Cole, Luella, *A History of Education, Socrates to Montessori.* New York: Holt, Rinehart and Winston, Inc., 1950. Pp. 202–220.

Dickens, A. G., *Reformation and Society in 16th Century Europe.* New York: Harcourt, Brace & World, Inc., 1966.

---

[9] Desiderius Erasmus, *The Praise of Folly,* trans. by Hoyt Hopewell Hudson (Princeton, N.J.: Princeton University Press, 1941), sec. 16, pp. 43, 44.

[10] *Thomas Platter and the Educational Renaissance of the Sixteenth Century* (New York: Appleton-Century-Crofts, 1904), p. 61.

Durant, Will, *The Story of Civilization*, vol. v, *The Renaissance*. New York: Simon and Schuster, Inc., 1953. Pp. 1–728.

Eby, Frederick, and Charles F. Arrowood, *The History of Education, Ancient and Medieval*. Englewood Cliffs, N.J.: Prentice-Hall, Inc., 1940. Pp. 837–939.

Erasmus, Desiderius, *The Praise of Folly*. Trans. by Hoyt Hopewell Hudson. Princeton, N.J.: Princeton University Press, 1941.

Ferguson, Wallace K., *The Renaissance*. New York: Holt, Rinehart and Winston, Inc., 1940.

Good, Harry G., *A History of Western Education*. New York: Crowell-Collier and Macmillan, Inc., 1960. Pp. 11–138.

Guicciardini, Francesco, *The History of Italy* (1490–1534). Trans. and ed. by Sidney Alexander. New York: Crowell-Collier and Macmillan, Inc., 1969.

Hart, Joseph K., *A Social Interpretation of Education*. New York: Holt, Rinehart and Winston, Inc., 1929. Pp. 84, 130, 131–140.

Knight, Edgar W., *Twenty Centuries of Education*. Boston: Ginn & Company, 1940. Pp. 152–165.

Mayer, Frederick, *A History of Educational Thought*. Columbus, Ohio: Charles E. Merrill Books, Inc., 1960. Pp. 165–178.

Messenger, James F., *An Interpretative History of Education*. New York: Thomas Y. Crowell Company, 1931. Pp. 119–126.

Monroe, Paul (Ed.), *Thomas Platter and the Educational Renaissance of the Sixteenth Century*. New York: Appleton-Century-Crofts, 1904.

Moore, Ernest C., *The Story of Instruction: The Church, the Renaissance and the Reformation*. New York: Crowell-Collier and Macmillan, Inc., 1938. Pp. 351–397.

Mulhern, James, *A History of Education*, 2d ed. New York: The Ronald Press Company, 1959. Pp. 297–308, 328–361.

Nakosteen, Mehdi, *The History and Philosophy of Education*. New York: The Ronald Press Company, 1965. Pp. 221–249.

Power, Edward J., *Main Currents in the History of Education*. New York: McGraw-Hill, Inc., 1962. Pp. 269–304.

Quick, Robert Herbert, *Educational Reformers*. New York: Appleton-Century-Crofts, 1904. Pp. 1–32, 80–89.

Randall, John H., *Making of the Modern Mind*. Boston: Houghton Mifflin Company, 1926. Pp. 11–141.

Roeder, Ralph, *The Man of the Renaissance*. New York: The Viking Press, 1933.

Simon, Joan, *Education and Society in Tudor England*. London: Cambridge University Press, 1965.

Ulich, Robert, *History of Educational Thought*. New York: American Book Company, 1950. Pp. 102–113, 130–148, 156–161.

————, *Philosophy of Education*. New York: American Book Company, 1961. Pp. 18, 29–31, 63–64, 109–110, 153, 211.

————, (Ed.), *Three Thousand Years of Educational Wisdom*, 2d ed., enl. Cambridge, Mass.: Harvard University Press, 1954. Pp. 205–217, 250–271, 287–301.

Watson, Foster (Trans.), *Vives: On Education*. London: Cambridge

University Press, 1913. A translation of *De Tradendis Disciplinis.*
Weimer, Hermann, *A Concise History of Education.* New York: Philosophical Library, Inc., 1962.
Weiss, Robert, *Humanism in England During the Fifteenth Century.* Oxford: Basil Blackwell & Mott, Ltd., 1941.
Wender, Herbert, *The Growth of Modern Thought and Culture.* New York: Philosophical Library, Inc., 1959. Pp. 1–41.

SELECTED PAPERBACKS

Beck, Robert Holmes, *A Social History of Education.* Englewood Cliffs, N.J.: Prentice-Hall, Inc., 1965. Pp. 34–44, 49–50.
Burckhardt, Jacob, *The Civilization of the Renaissance in Italy.* New York: The New American Library of World Literature, Inc., 1961.
Caspari, Fritz, *Humanism and the Social Order in Tudor England.* New York: Teachers College Press, Columbia University, 1968.
Donohue, John W., s.j., *St. Thomas Aquinas and Education.* New York: Random House, Inc., 1968.
Ferguson, Wallace K., and others, *Facets of the Renaissance.* New York: Harper & Row, Publishers, 1963.
Gilmore, Myron P., *The World of Humanism: 1453–1517.* New York: Harper & Row, Publishers, 1952.
Heer, Frederich, *Intellectual History of Europe,* vol. i, *From the Beginnings of Western Thought to Luther.* New York: Doubleday & Company, Inc., 1968.
Leach, A. F., *The Schools of Medieval England.* London: Methuen & Company, Ltd., 1915. Pp. 277–332.
Machiavelli, Niccolo, *The Prince.* Trans. by A. Robert Caponigri. Chicago: Henry Regnery Company, Gateway Editions, 1963.
Mayer, Frederick, *Foundations of Education.* Columbus, Ohio: Charles E. Merrill Books, Inc., 1963.
Michelet, Jules, *Satanism and Witchcraft, A Study in Medieval Superstition.* New York: The Citadel Press, 1939.
Muller, Herbert J., *The Uses of the Past, Profiles of Former Societies.* New York: New American Library of World Literature, Inc., 1952. Pp. 282–294.
Santillana, Giorgio de, *The Age of Adventure: The Renaissance.* New York: New American Library of World Literature, Inc., 1950.
Viorst, Milton (Ed.), *The Great Documents of Western Civilization.* New York: Bantam Books, Inc., 1965.
Woodward, William Harrison, *Desiderius Erasmus, Concerning the Aim and Method of Education.* New York: Bureau of Publications, Teachers College Press, Columbia University, 1963.
——, *Studies in Education during the Age of the Renaissance.* New York: Teachers College Press, Columbia University, 1967.
——, *Vittorino da Feltre and Other Humanist Educators.* New York: Teachers College Press, Columbia University, 1963. Pp. 1–92, 175–250.

CHAPTER 11

Religious Moralism as an Educational Force

Although Holy Scripture contains a perfect doctrine, to which one can add nothing, since in it our Lord has meant to display the infinite treasures of his wisdom, yet a person who has not much practice in it has good reason for some guidance and direction—to know what he ought to look for in it, in order not to wander hither and thither, but to hold to a sure path—that he may always be pressing toward the end to which the Holy Spirit calls him.[1]

RELIGIOUS MOTIVATION OF MORAL CONDUCT

The educational history of the United States and all the Western countries cannot be understood without knowledge of the tremendous forces and struggles released by the Protestant Reformation and the Catholic reaction to it. The development of one of our dominant educational philosophies—the theory of education for religious moralism—can be studied only in reference to this movement. We will soon discover that many of the ideas concerning educational theory and practice held by the reformers, both Roman Catholic and Protestant, are embodied in the objectives of certain present-day patterns of education.

Contemporary American education owes a great deal to this revolutionary movement of the sixteenth century. Most traditions of a religious and ethical nature found in the United States were born of the Protestant

---

[1] John Calvin, *Institutes of the Christian Religion* (Philadelphia: The Westminster Press, 1960).

Revolt and the concomitant Catholic Reaction, and carried to our shores by early settlers, many of whom (but not all) shared religious motives. They wished to establish their own churches and schools and to maintain their own moral standards; some hoped to establish Bible states, in which they could apply their personal ideas of government and religion; some believed in general religious freedom; others were obsessed by the idea of economic gain in a new and reorganized society; but perhaps all wished to escape the struggles and persecutions that followed European ecclesiastical schisms and dynastic devolution.[2] The terrible Thirty Years' War began just at the time our Pilgrim fathers were setting sail for the New World.

The English Pilgrims and Puritans in New England, the Calvinistic Dutch of New Amsterdam, the French Huguenots of the Carolinas, the Scotch and Scotch-Irish Presbyterians of New Jersey and the Alleghenies, the English Quakers of eastern Pennsylvania, the Swedish Lutherans along the Delaware, the German Lutherans in the central valleys of Pennsylvania, the Moravians and the Baptists, the later Methodists and Disciples of Christ—all were offshoots or results from the Protestant revolt. Their influence was to determine and to fix strongly the religious and ethical ideas upon which American national life was based and toward which much of our education has been directed. Maryland was settled by Roman Catholics who also had suffered persecution in England, this time from Protestants.[3] Catholic teaching orders, particularly the Jesuits—brilliant fruits of Rome's reformation or as Protestants would say, Counter-Reformation—were a definite influence in establishing schools and colleges here and there and in fixing the religious and moral ideas of the French along the St. Lawrence and Ohio river valleys.

Glorious though present-day citizens of the United States consider the settlement period and the strong-willed founders, no other period in modern history has created such advances and discords, virtues and evils, liberties and persecutions. Many seminal and significant facts in educational development during the age of Luther and Loyola have been overlooked by those who portray a one-sided picture. (We are not concerned here with condemnation or defense; with the rightness or wrongness of ecclesi-

---

[2] See Kenneth V. Lottich, *New England Transplanted* (Dallas: Royal Publishing Co., 1964), pp. 18–29, 45–57, for further interpretation of the motives of North American colonization.

[3] The first Jesuit school in colonial Maryland was established in 1677 at Newtown and continued in operation until about 1699. Between 1745 and 1750 the Society of Jesus conducted a school at Bohemia Manor. About 1785 John Carroll, later the first Archbishop of Baltimore, proposed to his associates the erection of a college at Georgetown, on the Potomac. In 1788 the first building was ready, although 1789 is commonly considered the year of founding. Thus, Georgetown is the oldest Catholic institution of higher learning in the United States. (*General Bulletin of Georgetown University,* Washington, D.C. [1959], p. 37.) For a further discussion of Roman Catholic schools see Neil G. McCluskey, s.j. (Ed.), *Catholic Education in America* (New York: Teachers College Press, Columbia University, 1964).

astical revolt; we are concerned only with the effect of that movement upon the development of education.) Consequently, we must view the movement from each of its angles. As Eby and Arrowood state:

> The revolution of the 16th century, usually termed the *Reformation*, was the most far-reaching, many-sided, and profound awakening in the history of the western world. To think of the Reformation merely as a reform of church organization or religious doctrine, important as these were, is to misinterpret its deeper significance for human progress; no aspect of man's personality was untouched by it. The Reformation involved political, economic, religious, moral, philosophical, literary, and institutional changes of the most sweeping character; it was in fact, a Nordic revolt and reconstruction.[4]

We frequently have overemphasized the religious and ecclesiastical phases of this revolution which led directly to the breaking apart of the church. From the Protestant viewpoint, the Reformation was intended to correct abuses in the church, primarily in connection with the sale of indulgences. From the modern Roman Catholic standpoint, such a correction was thoroughly justified on moral grounds; the question is whether such a justifiable moral motive should have led to revolt and schism.[5] If the church leaders of the time had assumed a more tolerant attitude toward the tendencies of their age, the history of modern life, and particularly of educational thought, might have been different. They did not assume this attitude, however. And the truth that history records is that the Protestants did revolt, and that the church governed from Rome did reform. To what extent the revolt was a stimulant to the reform is an open question. History remains the same whether we believe that Zwingli, Luther, Calvin, and Knox were inspired men, leading the world to a truer faith, or whether we believe them to have been ambitious and selfish.

THE PROTESTANT REVOLT

In 1517, Martin Luther (1483–1546), an Augustinian friar teaching philosophy at the University of Wittenberg, criticized certain practices of the church, later defied its authority, was excommunicated, and forced into hiding. The German people, under the leadership of their princes, supported Luther in the dispute, and also revolted. The church, which had remained the great unifying force in Europe for centuries, now became permanently divided. Our chief concern, however, is with the ways in which this particular religious revolt and reform have affected the development of educational concepts.

---

[4] Frederick Eby and Charles F. Arrowood, *The Development of Modern Education* (Englewood Cliffs, N.J.: Prentice-Hall, Inc., 1934), p. 29.

[5] See "Reformation," in *The New Catholic Encyclopedia*, vol. 13 (New York: McGraw-Hill, Inc., 1967), pp. 174–180, 180–190.

For centuries the German peoples had been subjected to and awed by the ascendancy of Christian institutionalism. Their literature, their language of learning, their laws, their theological doctrines, and their religious observances had all come to them via Rome. Indigenous Teutonic characteristics had been suppressed or modified, but never completely annihilated. Under the stimulus of Renaissance humanism the native German physical vigor, moral zeal, and rustic individualism had been revitalized, imparting new power and direction to the lives and minds of these northern peoples.

Critical tendencies such as those of social humanism could not be easily stopped. The Protestant Reformation completed the work of the northern Renaissance. As Monroe points out, "This truth was put in a homely way by Luther, when he said that he but hatched the egg laid by Erasmus. To which Erasmus replied that the egg was but a hen's egg, while Luther had hatched a game cock."[6] The humanist's fervor for social reform, for the improvement of human life here and now rather than spending a lifetime in anticipation of eternity, inevitably led to criticism of the church. And even this mighty institution, which had dominated the West for over a millennium, could not escape. With the critical spirit of humanism, social and religious reformers long before Luther, had attacked the moral evils of the Church and clamored for amelioration. They had persistently demanded that the clergy, high and low, lead purer lives, that ecclesiastical leaders earn their ample incomes, that the monasteries make useful contributions to the people who supported them. However, these reformers usually made no doctrinal or theological assaults against their great mother. But with the humanistic interest in the study of the sources of Biblical literature, Greek and Hebrew, it was a foregone conclusion that interpretation, theological belief, and even ecclesiastical practice would be questioned and eventually attacked.

But not all the northern humanists went so far. Although Bugenhagen, Corderius, Melanchthon, Sturm, Ascham, and Elyot followed Luther out of the Roman Church and aligned themselves with the reformers, Colet, Erasmus, Sir Thomas More, and Jacob Wimpfeling remained within the precincts of the Church. Far from passive, however, the latter strove for more harmony within the existing framework and thus became more prominent than some of those dedicated to outright reform. While all the social humanists did not become reformers, virtually all the reformers were humanists. In a way, the new movement represented a broadening of the fusion of religion and humanism begun in the northern Renaissance.

We must remember, however, that the Protestant revolution developed because of oppressive political and economic conditions, as much

---

[6] Paul Monroe, *A Textbook in the History of Education* (New York: Crowell-Collier and Macmillan, Inc., 1933), p. 409.

as because of religious and ecclesiastical evils. The need for religious and ethical reform seems to have furnished the immediate opportunity for revolt; the need for political and economic reform was the underlying cause. The social humanists of the northern Renaissance had been religious, reformatory, critical of moral evils; and now it seemed to the Teutonic peoples that their political, social, and economic desires could best be realized by separation from the Roman Church.

The prosperous free cities of northern Europe, particularly those of the Netherlands and the north German plain, were nurseries of the revolt against the church. The political autonomy of these free towns, the indomitable spirit of individualism in their citizens, and the security of their economic independence, strengthened still further by their organization as the Hanseatic League, made these cities influences to be reckoned with in political and economic affairs. At the beginning of the sixteenth century, Germany was still divided into many petty dukedoms, principalities, and elective states, more or less independent of imperial sovereignty. Had it not been for the sympathy and protection of the free cities, the electoral princes, and the minor nobility, Luther would probably have been burned at the stake, as were the noted heretics who preceded him, and his doctrines relentlessly stamped out. Instead, the movement to which he had given such impetus spread from Germany, Switzerland, and the Netherlands to England, Scotland, and Scandinavia, where again it was a political as well as a religious revolution.

Luther's quarrel with the church began as a protest against certain economic injustices. That his protests should result in his being driven from the church and founding a new institution, he never anticipated or at first desired. Because of very effective money-raising devices, wealth had been concentrating in the control of churches, monasteries, and ecclesiastical courts for centuries. The doctrine that salvation comes from good works caused gifts, endowments, and tithes to flow into the treasuries of churches, monasteries, and ecclesiastical princes, until it is reported that two thirds of the wealth of Germany was in the hands of the church. Germany, as Charles A. Beard so aptly stated, was "the milch cow of the Papacy, which it at once despised and drained dry."

The immediate cause of Luther's challenge through the Ninety-five Theses, which he nailed on the *Schlosskirche* door at Wittenberg, was the presence of a Dominican monk, John Tetzel, commissioned by the pope to raise money to complete St. Peter's at Rome. The Germans felt that far too much of their treasure had already increased the power and the glory of the Vatican; so there quickly arose in these northern kingdoms and principalities a sympathetic and vigorous response to Luther's challenge in opposing what the people considered the economic discipline of the papacy.

Thus the movement was catalyzed through intellectual, ethical, economic, religious, and political influences. It is to be expected that an action arising from such a complexity of causes should have widespread and profound effects upon educational theory and practices. We shall now discuss these with reference first to the Protestant reformers, then to the Roman Catholic meliorators, who, in certain ways, were reformers themselves.

EDUCATIONAL ATTITUDES OF THE PROTESTANT REFORMERS

Luther, Melanchthon, and other northern reformers established basic principles with significant educational implications. Regardless of theological controversies and doctrinal divergences, they agreed upon the following fundamental conclusions: (1) the authority of their interpretation of the Bible was substituted for the authority of the church as the infallible rule of faith and moral practices; (2) individual judgment was substituted for collective judgment as sufficient for determining the truth contained in the Holy Scriptures, thereby fixing Christian duty in belief and conduct; (3) individual responsibility for salvation was substituted for collective responsibility; and (4) although the doctrine of Original Sin was accepted, only an abiding faith in God's mercy was considered the means to salvation; consequently (5) masses, penances, and works of charity, as agencies of deliverance from sin, could be dispensed with.

It has been said that in the Protestant churches preaching replaced the sacraments and music provided inspiration to all; participation in the service was a hallmark of the Protestant approach to religion. Yet the individual was vitally responsible for his own salvation. And as Eby and Arrowood state:

> Ritualism gave way to inner piety; good works, to goodwill; blind obedience, to inner faith. Holiness was held no longer to be self-renunciation or world-renunciation, but rather the benevolent spirit which lives the normal life of the human being in social relations, without yielding to sensuality or selfish interest.[7]

In the social realm the Protestant reformers demanded close cooperation between church and state, that is, religion should go with the land. The religious choice of the ruler should determine the creed of his subjects; the state should be the servant of the church in insisting upon adequate educational opportunities for the preservation of the moral and religious character of its people. Indeed, state, church, and home had to work together in the task of educating youth to serve themselves and their country.

Aims

Religious moralism as an aim for education did not originate with the Protestant reformers; the education of primitive and ancient peoples

---

[7] Eby and Arrowood, p. 178.

was primarily religious and moral, rather than intellectual. Even Greek education placed little emphasis upon literary and intellectual elements until after Socratic days. Generally the philosophers of Greece and Rome attempted to establish morality without the sanctions of religion. On the other hand, although Jesus had fused religion and morality, the church of the Middle Ages relied on an exaggerated interest in the theological doctrines and ritualistic observances. The reformers did not discontinue ecclesiastical control over education; thus they evinced their general belief in the essentially religious and moral character of education.

The object of Protestant education was the attainment of a worthy life on earth as guarantee of a glorious life hereafter. Education, therefore, provided training in the duties of home, occupation, church, and state. Luther indeed glimpsed the modern broad purpose of education, but narrowed his own aim by focusing it on religion. John Calvin (1509–1564), of Geneva, also advocated education as a training for society and the state (especially his city-state at Geneva), but added his insistence upon the necessity of education as a means to the liberty of individual conscience. Both Luther and Calvin considered religion the highest interest of life, the basis of all worthy living.

The reformers conceived an educational ideal which they hoped would prepare Christian men and women to discharge any and all duties. They realized the close interdependence of character and religion, and advocated an education that would develop physical, mental, and moral powers to bring about not only personal salvation but the moral regeneration of society. Religion, morality, and education were to be man's major interests, the "fixities and verities" of life; and the reformers deemed it impossible to consider them separately.

Luther insisted upon right training of children as a divine requirement. He was opposed to education according to the whims of parents. He wrote:

> . . . if we wish to have proper and excellent persons both for civil and ecclesiastical government, we must spare no diligence, time, or cost in teaching and educating our children, that they may serve God and the world. . . . Let every one know, therefore, that above all things it is his duty (or otherwise he will lose the divine favor) to bring up his children in the fear and knowledge of God; and if they have talents, to have them instructed and trained in the liberal education, that men may be able to have their aid in government and in whatever is necessary.[8]

Luther went so far as to say that the right bringing up of children was the straightest and most easily attained road to heaven, while hell could not

---

[8] F. V. N. Painter, *Luther on Education* (Philadelphia: Luther Publication Society, 1889), p. 117. See also Luther's "The Duty of Sending Children to School," pp. 238–249, in Robert Ulich (Ed.), *Three Thousand Years of Educational Wisdom*, 2nd ed., enl. (Cambridge, Mass.: Harvard University Press, 1954).

be more deserved than for allowing children to run about, neglected, swearing, singing shameful words, and following only the dictates of nature.

The educational aim of the Protestants attempted to combine the best ideals of the past with religious morality. Through humanism from the ancient Greek and Roman world they drew the ideals of elegant expression, rational inquiry, and public service. From chivalry, they took the ideals of good manners and social service; from Christianity the ideals of personal piety. These three ideals—intelligence, social virtue, and individual piety—were not stressed equally by all Protestant educators nor fully attained in all Protestant schools, but an integration of these three elements was attempted wherever the Protestant influence was felt.

Types

Protestant education was always religious in its ultimate aims, but varied types of training were utilized in attaining this goal.

Some Protestant educators would have called their technique character education, because its purpose was the development of Christian character. But moral training, social training, civic training, vocational training, domestic training, all played a part in the attainment of the religiously motivated moral conduct emphasized as the objective of their educational efforts.

There was little esthetic training in Protestant schools. Physical and musical training were prescribed for religious and practical reasons, rather then for artistic considerations. Protestants were educated for *work* rather than play. As Weber says:

> . . . the religious valuation of restless, continuous, systematic work in a worldly calling, as the highest means to asceticism, and at the same time the surest and most evident proof of rebirth and genuine faith, must have been the most powerful conceivable lever for the expansion of that attitude toward life which we have here called the spirit of capitalism.[9]

Practical training of professional, commercial, and the industrial types was characteristic of Protestant education. Man worked for the glory of God; he fulfilled the divine will by his exercise of the human. Revising most of the traditional Roman Catholic holidays into workdays, Protestantism sanctioned a new commerical economy to replace Jesus's injunction, of "Lay not up for yourselves treasures on earth." John Calvin wrote the first systematic treatise defending usury, or the charging of interest, which had been anathema during the Middle Ages; and Henry Van Dyke clearly expressed the Protestant ideal of work in "The Toiling of Felix":

---

[9] Max Weber, *The Protestant Ethic and the Spirit of Capitalism,* trans. by Talcott Parsons (New York: Charles Scribner's Sons, 1930), p. 172.

This is the gospel of labor
Ring it, ye bells of the kirk!
The Lord of Love came down from above,
To live with the men who work.
This is the rose he planted;
Here in this thorn-cursed soil;
Heaven is blessed with perfect rest
but the blessing of Earth is toil.[10]

Like the Protestant reformers of Europe, the Puritan forebears of New England understood well this challenge to man's energetic spirit to secure this regulated-through-work society.

The Protestant reformers advocated universal, compulsory, free education. Luther believed that all classes and both sexes should be educated, although he was in favor of a higher education not for the masses, but for those destined for the ministry and the magistracy. He advocated universal education because he realized that to fulfill the varied duties of life, different degrees of intelligence were necessary. Calvin urged that the laity be educated as well as the clergy. Both Luther and Calvin believed that if men were to save themselves by the exercise of faith and private judgment based on the reading and study of the Bible, then all must be taught to read, study, and think. In other words, there must be universal elementary education, even though higher education might continue to be selective.

Luther was the first modern educational reformer to recommend compulsory education. He not only insisted that the state authorities should establish schools or require the people to do so but also demanded that parents be compelled to send their children to school for the sake of the church and the state. In his Sermon on the Duty of Sending Children to School, he said:

> . . . I maintain that the civil authorities are under obligation to compel the people to send their children to school. . . . If the government can compel such citizens as are fit for military service to bear spear and rifle, to mount ramparts, and perform other martial duties in time of war; how much more has it a right to compel the people to send their children to school, because in this case we are warring with the devil.[11]

Content

The basic subject in Protestant elementary schools was the study of the Bible, and the basic skill imparted was the ability to read the ver-

---

[10] (New York: Charles Scribner's Sons, 1913), p. 69.
[11] As quoted in Frederick Eby, *Early Protestant Educators* (New York: McGraw-Hill, Inc., 1931), pp. 149–150.

nacular. Religion was the heart of the curriculum, and the Bible the principal textbook. As Luther said in his Address to the Nobility:

> Above all, in schools of all kinds the chief and most common lesson should be the Scriptures, and for young boys the Gospels. . . . Should not every Christian be expected by his ninth or tenth year to know all the Holy Gospels, containing as they do his very name and life? . . . Everything must perish where God's Word is not studied unceasingly.[12]

To make the Bible available to the people at large, either the people had to learn Latin, or the Bible had to be translated from the Latin Vulgate into the language of the people. A century before Luther, John Wycliffe (1320–1384), of Oxford, had asserted that everyone should be able to read and study the Scriptures as a means to personal salvation; and he partially translated the Bible into English. Jacques Lefevre (1455–1537), pioneer French Protestant, translated the Bible into the vernacular for his people. Luther's translation of the Bible not only made it available to the German public but set standards for literary German of his own and later times, just as Calvin's *Institutes of the Christian Religion* and William Tyndale's translation of the New Testament set standards for French and English prose. (The King James Version borrowed much from Tyndale.)

Luther supplemented his use of the Scriptures with other reading material, religious and moral. He published two catechisms, one for children and one for adults, and composed many hymns.[13] He translated Aesop's Fables, which he judged to be for purposes of moral instruction next door to the Bible.

The Protestant schoolmaster early developed a simple course of study for the teaching of reading. A child learning to read began with the "hornbook," a thin board on which a printed page containing the alphabet and the Lord's Prayer was glued, and covered with a fine sheet of translucent material to preserve "from fingers grubby, the letters fair." Each child learned his letters from this device until it was superseded by the primer. The earliest primer was but a simple *A-B-C* book, a sheet of cardboard folded to form four or six pages, containing an illustrated alphabet with a verse beneath each letter to stimulate the imagination or to jog the memory. From this invention developed the type of primer introduced into the American colonies, containing the alphabet illustrated with verses and pictures, the syllabarium, and short reading passages from the Psalter and the New Testament, and selected hymns. Having finally learned to read, the

---

[12] Eby, p. 150.

[13] Among Luther's hymns, "A Mighty Fortress Is Our God" and the children's Christmas carol "Away in a Manger" are especially well known in America. The origin of the latter is sometimes considered controversial, but there is no doubt about Luther's composition of "We Come Unto Our Father's God" and "Dearest Jesus, Holy Child," (1535).

child next passed to the catechism, the Psalter, and the Bible, the gamut of which constituted the entire range of reading in early Protestant schools both in Europe and America.

Singing and physical education were stressed in the curriculum of German vernacular primary schools. "Music," claimed Luther, "drives away all care and melancholy from the heart, and gymnastics produce elasticity of the body and thus preserve the health." Not since Plato and Socrates had an educator so appreciated the educational values of music. Luther created a vernacular ˙hymnology and persuaded others to do the same. The first Lutheran hymnal was produced under his direction in 1524; it allowed the public to participate in the observances of the church in a language they could understand. Luther's enthusiasm for music, especially vocal music, made it one of the chief interests of his school; many people credit to him the love of music found almost universally among the Germans.

Luther was a firm believer in vocational training as well. He insisted that every boy and girl should learn the practical arts of trade and home in order to fulfill the Protestant ethic, although he did not advocate including these subjects in the school curriculum. Most of his arguments were directed toward proving that the acquisition of such practical skills need not and must not interfere with formal school work. "My idea," he said, "is that boys should spend an hour or two a day in school, and the rest of the time work at home, learn a trade, and do whatever is desired." Similarly, in speaking of the education of girls, whom he felt should receive a brief general education, he said, "In like manner, a girl has time to go to school an hour a day, and yet attend to her work at home; for she sleeps, dances, and plays away more than that." Of course no one today would agree with him on the time prescribed; but one might agree on an education founded on work as well as on the cultural heritage.

Under the apprenticeship system, the practical arts were learned in the home. Luther and the other reformers approved this. In his discussions of practical training, Luther tried to show that schoolwork need not interfere with trade apprenticeship and home duties. He did not urge a return to the union of work and study as found in the medieval monastic schools, nor did he advocate the introduction of arts and handicrafts into the schools, which others later promoted.

Thus the curriculum for the common people, given to both sexes in the vernacular through the agencies of the primary school and the home, included religion, reading, writing, singing, physical training, trades and crafts, and household duties. This curriculum, imposed upon all by church and state, was the type found in the elementary schools established throughout northern Germany by Johann Bugenhagen (1485–1558) in carrying out Luther's educational ideas.

In the Protestant schools of England, reading, writing, catechism, manners, and morals were included in the course of study. Good manners as well as good moral conduct were greatly stressed by English teachers. Character training was a dominant feature of the English schools and was often provided for by law; the endowed schools in particular were very effective in inculcating the manners required of an English gentleman.

The curriculum of the Protestant secondary schools and universities was largely a continuation of humanistic subject matter. The alignment of such social humanists as Melanchthon and Sturm with the reformers marked the union of humanism and Protestantism in the learning of northern Europe. Luther and Calvin readily accepted humanistic studies as desirable for the training of Protestant teachers, preachers, and civic leaders. In the Protestant secondary schools, used mainly as preparatory schools for the clergy, such humanistic studies as Latin, Greek, Hebrew, dialectic, and mathematics were taught. The ancient languages, Latin, Greek, and Hebrew, were retained mainly for their aid in understanding the Bible. In the Protestant churches, one who could not read the Bible in the original tongues could not qualify as a minister. Logic, rhetoric, and eloquence were considered important as preparations for sermon construction and theological discussion.

Luther, however, had a somewhat broader view of the training of youth and urged the inclusion in the secondary curriculum of certain subjects not usually found in the humanistic schools, namely, history, mathematics, natural science, music, and gymnastics. The study of history was considered by the Protestant reformers of the greatest value in combating the claims of papal hierarchy, in understanding human nature and the growth of institutions, and as the bearer of moral lessons. "Historians," said Luther, "are the most useful of men, and the best teachers."

Since the Protestant revolt originated in the universities, it was natural that the curriculum of the northern university, at least, should be reformed. Scholastic theology was replaced by Biblical exegesis, or learned interpretation. Although the faculties of theology became of prime importance in training and examining candidates for the ministry, the faculties of law, medicine, and philosophy made advances too. The rising importance of the national state gave prominence to civil jurisprudence; and interest in philosophical and scientific studies grew.

German philosophy and science, German literature and culture, grew in the soil of Protestantism, and they may be described as the perhaps remote result of that spirit of freedom and independence of thought which the Reformation called into being.[14]

Agencies

The Protestant reformers always considered the family and home to be the basic agency for education; in their minds the family was the educa-

---

[14] F. Paulsen, *The German Universities* (New York: Crowell-Collier and Macmillan, Inc., 1895), p. 33.

tional institution of primary importance. Luther placed the Commandment, Honor thy father and mother, at the foundation of his social order. He considered good home training, parental discipline, and sound family life the very root of good government and social welfare; he bitterly criticized any lack of parental control and weak methods of home training. In Calvin's Geneva the home was supervised by the church authorities, and parents were commanded to teach children the catechism and habits of Christian living. This instruction, and even the daily conduct of parents, was strictly supervised by the local church, whose representative visited each home at least once a year in order to ascertain that regulations were being followed. All parents were obliged to see that their children attended school and received proper instruction.

One of the most significant developments of the Reformation, at least as far as Germany was concerned, was the part played by civil authorities as agents for the establishment and support of education. Luther and Melanchthon placed both school and church under the guardianship of the state, thus laying the foundation for state and national control of German education. Nevertheless, Luther hardly contemplated the secularization of education. His method was only for convenience in administration. He appealed to the German rulers on the ground that, since they derived their power from God, as God's representatives on earth they must care for their subjects' spiritual interests no less than for their material concerns.

In England, where the Protestant revolt was also political as well as religious, the civil authorities had even greater control over the schools. In Calvinistic countries, however, the church and the state cooperated. Very often, as in the Netherlands and in Puritan New England, the civil authorities acted as "servants of the church" in passing laws for the support and management of the schools. Calvin believed that the state was obliged to make laws for the organization and support of schools in accordance with the ideas of the pastors that church, state, and family must be welded into one great institution for the instruction and discipline of the entire citizenry. In other words, the state should be a theocracy, under the domination of the pastors of the church.

Where the state would not or could not serve, the church was to assume full responsibility for the support and control of the schools. John Knox (1505–1572), who carried Calvin's ideas to Scotland, recommended that each church support a schoolmaster, but if that were impossible the minister should teach the children. In the North American middle colonies of the eastern seaboard, where many sects were found, civil authorities played so small a part in education that the church-controlled parochial school was the dominant agency of education throughout the colonial period.

The importance of the teacher as an instrument of education was always emphasized by the Protestant reformers. Luther deplored the low financial status of the teaching profession. He believed that an industrious and high-minded teacher, who faithfully trained and disciplined youth, could never be sufficiently recompensed. The Protestant believed in thorough training; consequently most of their teachers were university men, as well educated as their ministers. In all Protestant countries and churches, close supervision was maintained over schoolmasters. The church leaders were held responsible for the schoolmaster's attendance at regular worship, for his orthodoxy, and for his loyalty to the government.

Organization

The Protestant school system was organized into three types of schools: the vernacular primary school, the classical secondary school, and the university. These schools, however, were not organized in a ladder sequence as they are today in the United States. They constituted rather a dual system of education, providing one type of education for the masses, and another type for prospective leaders.

The vernacular primary school was organized for popular education, and attendance was universal and compulsory. Girls as well as boys attended, although Bugenhagen's plans always included separate schools for girls. These Protestant vernacular schools were in many instances a modification and reorganization of the burgher schools that had developed in the free cities during the late Middle Ages to instruct boys of the commercial class in reading, writing, and counting. Under Protestantism, the earlier school of the middle class was more closely linked to religious instruction and became the elementary school of the common people, especially in the Netherlands. Much of the credit for the organization of the elementary school should be given to Bugenhagen, who has been called the father of the German *Volksschule*. John Knox, another firm believer in elementary education, was instrumental in establishing in Scotland, under the control of the parishes, the free elementary schools which have done so much for the enlightenment of the Scottish people. But, despite these wise and earnest organizers, many Protestant reformers and educators, being primarily interested in the development of the Latin schools, were somewhat lukewarm towards the vernacular schools.

Wherever the influence of the Protestant reformers spread, the humanistic classical school was taken over and reorganized into an instrument for training the Protestant leadership. Humanistic elements were retained, but new elements of religion and morals were added. In this reorganization of the secondary schools Melanchthon, Sturm, and Calvin played a leading part. Melanchthon was the greatest scholar among the school organizers of the German reformation. In 1527 he made a thorough survey of school conditions in Thuringia and Saxony, probably the earliest school survey ever made. As a result of this investigation, he drew up the famous Saxony plan for the reorganization of the schools of that state.

This Saxony system was the first state school system, although it dealt only with secondary school organization. According to this plan, the secondary schools were to be established in every town under the support and control of the civil authorities and were to be organized on three levels. The first level was for beginners, who were to learn to read Latin; the second level was for the study of Latin grammar; the third level was for more advanced linguistic studies, the reading of classical authors, exercises in rhetoric, and the study of logic. Sturm, in his *Gymnasium* at Strassburg, greatly improved upon this system by projecting a ten-class organization with a class a year; his plan was perhaps the first development of a graded system of school organization. Sturm's school at Strassburg was also the result of a survey of school conditions in that city, which led to the consolidation of three inefficient classical schools into one large institution. This school became the model for classical secondary schools throughout Europe and is perhaps one of the first examples of school consolidation.

Sturm's thoroughness is illustrated in the curriculum organization he perfected when taking over Strassburg's old municipal Latin school, which he headed for forty-five years. Sturm and his ten teachers operated this humanistic class-a-year institution, so that it became the most famous Latin school in Europe. Sports are quite lacking.

The accompanying patterns serve to illustrate his organizational aims:

1. *The Tenth Class*, Age 7 (the ABECEDARII or ALPHABETARII).
   Purpose: To establish a good foundation.
   Including: The form and correct pronunciation of alphabet;
   To learn declensions and conjugations in Latin;
   Make beginnings of Latin reading, writing, and spelling;
   Commit to memory the German catechism.

7. *The Fourth Class*, Age 13/14.
   Increased drill on what has been learned thus far;
   "Diligent practice" continued on style;
   Read sixth ORATION against Verres, second of Cicero's LETTERS TO FRIENDS, part of ADELPHI of Terence, and the EPISTLES and SATIRES of Horace in Latin; in Greek, read the BOOK OF EXAMPLES; Much drill on Greek grammar.
   The continued reading of Pauline epistles.

10. *The First Class*, Age 16/17.
    Logic and rhetoric extended;
    Apply to Cicero and Demosthenes; Readings from Vergil, Homer, Thucydides, and Sallust;
    Augmented translation and retranslation, write prose and poetry, and declamation; dramatic representation each week;
    Expound the EPISTLES of St. Paul (rhetorical style);
    Elementary instruction in astronomy;
    Study first book of Euclid's GEOMETRY.

John Calvin, too, had a genius for organization. He drew up plans for the religious and educational organization of Geneva into a religious city-republic. He reorganized several Latin schools into a consolidated classical secondary school, which is sometimes known as Calvin's Academy. This school had seven classes, was under the supervision of the city, but was financed by tuition fees. The basic curriculum was humanistic, resembling that of Sturm's *Gymnasium*, although much greater emphasis was placed upon religious and moral instruction. Calvin's school was one of the chief nurseries of Protestant preachers and teachers for many lands.

In England, after the Anglican revolt, the Latin grammar schools and the colleges were reendowed by private gifts and appropriations from the resources of dissolved monasteries and other ecclesiastical foundations. The Latin grammar schools, among which were some of the present public schools of England, were modeled on Colet's St. Paul's School and were humanistic-religious. By the Acts of Uniformity of 1662, all non-Anglican, or nonconformist, teachers were driven out of these schools; and religious restrictions were introduced in the universities, which could no longer grant degrees to nonconformists.

The influence of the Protestant Reformation upon educational organization was outstanding. Wherever the Calvinistic and Lutheran points of view prevailed, foundations were laid which largely determined the organization of modern state school systems. The vernacular elementary school, the classical secondary school, and the universities for the training of leadership—these educational institutions as organized or reorganized in the sixteenth century under Protestant influence have remained the general models of educational institutions in Europe and the United States.

The educational drive fostered through the philosophy of religious moralism is easily discernible in the following excerpt from Article III of the United States' great Northwest Ordinance of 1787, "Religion, morality, and knowledge . . . being necessary to good government . . ." Such an expression of the Protestant educational ideal shows how the influence of the Reformation dominated early American education.

Methods

Ciceronianism, or formal methods of instruction, which had already begun to shape humanistic teaching, was continued and extended by the Protestant schoolmasters. In elementary schools, reading was usually a routine pronunciation of words. The memorization of answers to the catechism, of passages from the Gospels and Epistles, and of hymns and psalms was substituted for the intelligent comprehension of meaning. In the secondary schools Latin grammar consisted largely of learning rules and declensions and memorizing long passages from the classics.

Many of the Protestant reformers were intensely interested in the study of the problems of educational method. In the same way that they turned to the classics to throw greater light upon their theology, rhetoric, and moral conduct, so they turned to the classics to seek information on pedagogical methods. Cicero's *De Oratore*, Quintilian's *De Institutione Oratoria*, and the educational contributions of Plato and Aristotle were rescued from the oblivion of centuries. The reformers attempted to apply many of the principles which they found to their own schools. The educational ideas of Quintilian and Cicero (or Tully, as he was sometimes called) appeared again in the writings of Luther, Calvin, Sturm, Melanchthon, Ascham, and Elyot.

Luther himself had advanced ideas concerning methods of teaching. He felt the classroom should be attractive and study made pleasant; the subject matter should be adjusted to the capacity of the child, and only the aptest pupils should go into the higher schools. There should be no lack of discipline, he stipulated, but the disposition of the individual should be considered in fixing punishment. "Our schools," he said, "are cases and tenses, and in which, with much trembling and flogging, they learn nothing."[15]

But probably because of Sturm's excessive formalism and the more severe Calvinistic theology, the Protestant classroom became a place of gloom and even terror for children. Methods of teaching became more rigid, discipline harsher, and the divorce of the life of the school from the life of the world more complete than ever before. The freedom of individual thought promised by the Protestant revolt was seldom realized in the schools. The theory that the individual was to determine his beliefs and his conduct through his own interpretation of the Scriptures did not work in practice. Through the school the church closely guided the individual's thinking, and it was easy for this guidance to become domination. Children were taught not how to think, but what to think. Religious indoctrination became the chief method of the schools.

ATTITUDES OF THE CATHOLIC REVISIONISTS TOWARD EDUCATION

The Protestant revolts were not equally successful in all countries of Europe. In Italy and Spain, all rebellion against the papacy was promptly and effectively checked. In France, the state church and the government had achieved a considerable degree of independence from Rome even before the days of the Huguenots and had forced concessions from the pope. Although the Huguenots were tolerated after the Edict of Nantes (1593), France remained predominantly Catholic. Generally speaking, Protestantism was adopted by the countries of northwestern Europe, while

---

[15] Luther's view of the strain on the instructor should be reported too: "As for school teaching, it is so strenuous that no one ought to be bound to it for more than 10 years." See Roland H. Bainton, *Here I Stand: A Life of Martin Luther* (New York: New American Library of World Literature, Inc., 1950), p. 182.

the peoples of the south, including even southern Germany, remained loyal to Roman Catholicism.

This loyalty was due in part to the Catholic Reaction, a movement within the church itself, the Counter Reformation accelerated by the Protestant Revolt. Even before Luther published his challenge to such evils as those involved in the sale of indulgences, a movement to correct the abuses had begun within the Catholic Church. The Counter Reformation was an important influence in increasing the power and vigor of the church of Rome. Abuses were swept away by reforming popes and other high church officials. The reform movement culminated in the great Council of Trent, which lasted from 1545 to 1563. This council did serious work in eliminating the most offensive abuses and in clarifying the doctrines concerning which the most controversy had arisen.

The Council of Trent enacted regulations of great importance to education. Realizing that the Protestant leaders were relying upon education as a most effective agency to advance their cause, the Catholic leaders determined to use the same instrument to root out heresy and win dissenters back to Catholicism. Teaching orders and teaching congregations were encouraged. The parish schools were reorganized; new institutions were established for the training of Catholic children; theological seminaries were developed for the training of priests.

Most of the work of educational reform in the Catholic Church was carried out by various orders established during the sixteenth and seventeenth centuries. The most important of these was the Society of Jesus, popularly known as the Jesuits, organized in 1534 by Ignatius of Loyola (1491–1558), a Spanish nobleman who had been converted to the religious life while recovering from a battle wound. Another outstanding teaching order was the Brethren of Christian Schools, established by Jean-Baptiste de La Salle (1651–1719) in 1684, and devoted to the gratuitous teaching of the poor in the vernacular. Both of these orders were concerned only with teaching boys.

Active in establishing Catholic schools for girls as well as for boys was a group of men and women sometimes called Port Royalists or Jansenists. They were followers of the Dutch bishop Cornelius Jansen (1585–1638), whose theological doctrines somewhat resembled those of Calvin. Led by the Abbé de St. Cyran, a number of Jansenists settled at Port Royal, near Versailles, and established in 1637 the famous schools known as the Little Schools of Port Royal. There were also a number of orders of Catholic sisters devoted primarily to the teaching of girls. Some of the most educationally effective of these were the Order of Ursulines, founded in 1535; the Sisters of Notre Dame, founded in 1598; and the Sisters of St. Joseph, founded in 1654. The development of education for women among the Roman Catholics was greatly stimulated by the efforts of Fénelon (1651–1715), Archbishop of Cambrai, whose treatise *The*

Education of Girls gave him first place as a modern theorist on the education of women, and whose work as supervisor of teaching at the Convent of St. Cyr gave ample evidence of his work as a practical schoolmaster.

The position of French divine-right monarchy was buttressed by the works and sermons of Bishop Jacques Bénigne Bossuet (1627–1704), who likewise undertook the education of the Dauphin, later to become Louis XV. As Armstrong states, revealing another aspect of moralism:

> For Bossuet, monarchy was a God-given form of government. Since the Holy Scriptures represented the word of God, it was, in the view of Bossuet, only necessary to read them correctly to learn in what fashion the leader of an ideal divine-right monarchy ought to comport himself.[16]

That his teaching was less than a success may be inferred from the later conduct of his royal charge; nevertheless, Bossuet exhibited a teaching aim and method somewhat comparable to Quintilian's; he believed that the king's God-given power entailed terrific responsibility, and he must be educated to be a good man and hence a good king. Subsequently, Bossuet has quite frequently been interpreted as a prop to tyranny, a conclusion far from the truth, and one which vitiates the goal and potential power of his teaching.

Aims

In its ultimate implications, the aim of the new Roman Catholic education was religious moralism. Preparation for a pious and useful life here as well as a glorious life in the hereafter was the dominant objective. The motto of the Jesuits, *Ad majorem Dei gloriam* (All for the greater glory of God), expressed the ultimate goal of their educational efforts. But, although the ultimate goals of the Protestant and Roman Catholic reformers were not dissimilar, the immediate objectives were quite different. The avowed aim of the Protestant educator was to develop a religious and moral life through the individual's interpretation of the Bible. The Catholic educator sought the same goal, but through the subjection of the individual to institutional control. The principle of the Protestant Reformation had been the elevation of individual reason and faith; the principle of the Catholic reformers remained an unquestioning obedience to the authority of the church. But since the Protestant churches did not in practice long adhere to the principle their founders had proclaimed, the methods of their schools were not very different from those of the Roman Catholic schools.

The Jesuit schools were designed primarily to train leaders to advance the cause of the church and of a pious Christian society. Men who could

---

[16] See David G. Armstrong, "Teaching the Values of the Divine-Right Monarchy Philosophy: A Study of the Methods of Jacques-Bénigne Bossuet" (Unpub. master's thesis, University of Montana, Missoula, 1967), p. 18.

read and speak Latin correctly and easily, who were disciplined and loyal to the doctrines of the church and the ideals of the order, who were competent to teach the Christian way of life, who were eager and able to perpetuate certain established ways of religious thought and moral action, they provided a high type of spiritual and moral training.

The aim of the elementary schools established by the Christian Brothers was to provide "Christian education, especially to children of artisans and the poor." These schools were impregnated with the ideals of religious asceticism. Similarly, the aim of the Jansenist schools was to bring about the spiritual salvation and moral reform of a few selected boys and girls. The aim of the convent schools was to prepare young women to perform their duties as guardians of Christian homes and as members of a Christian society. The first of these duties was to establish and maintain a chaste and pious moral character. Refined tastes and gentle manners as well as skill in the management of the home were next in importance. The professed aim of the Catholic parish schools, convents, and academies was always to prepare boys and girls to be faithful and loyal communicants of the church, to be moral and useful members of a Christian society, and to attain the salvation of their souls.

Types

In view of their aims, the Catholic schools placed religious and moral training first; every other subject was made to function through religious and moral instruction. Vocational training and domestic training were still left largely in the hands of the parents, although at school the virtues of honest labor and the ideals of a truly Christian home were impressed upon the pupils. In higher education, intellectual training was encouraged, but only in the service of church and never when it led to heresy. Among the Jesuits any type of training that prepared for preaching, mission work, pastoral duties, ministering to the sick or to the poor, or teaching was accepted as desirable. Literary work and scientific research were favored as long as the result contributed to the "glory of God and His Church."

The attention that the Jesuit teachers gave to physical training was a unique feature of their education. Their careful consideration of the health of the pupil and their encouragement of sports and games as an agency for physical welfare was unusual for this period.

One of the outstanding contributions of these Roman Catholic teaching orders was emphasis upon a better type of professional training. The Jesuits developed graduate schools of law and medicine, as well as theology. But it was in the field of teacher training that the orders rendered their greatest service to education. The Jesuits became noted for the careful selection and training of their teachers; and the Christian Brothers established normal schools, with attached practice schools, to train their members for teaching.

Content

The curriculum in the Roman Catholic schools was similar to that of the Protestants. In the elementary schools taught by the Christian Brothers, the course of study covered the four R's—reading, writing, elementary arithmetic, and religion—with the emphasis always on religion. The atmosphere of the schools was deeply pious and the natural activity of the children was severely repressed.

Of the teaching orders, the Jesuit fathers developed the broadest curricula in secondary and higher education. The course of study in their lower colleges, the *studia inferiora*, corresponded roughly to that of the German *gymnasien* and the English Latin-grammar schools; the course of study in their higher colleges, the *studia superiora*, to that of the Protestant universities. The lower college gave a humanistic-religious education similar to that of the Protestant classical secondary schools. Latin was considered the indispensable vehicle of all learning. The study of selected Latin classics was pursued in the formal manner. Greek literature was studied in Latin translations. The textbooks were prescribed, and the works of pagan authors were expurgated and supplied with notes to adapt them to the training of Catholic youth. Latin texts by Christian authors were used whenever possible. History, geography, science, and mathematics were studied only as a means of understanding the classics. The study of language, literature, and the other supplementary subjects was closely correlated with moral training and the activities and exercises of religious worship.

In the higher Jesuit colleges, the faculty of philosophy centered on the study of scholastic philosophy, with Latin classics, logic, and rhetoric added. The faculty of theology emphasized theology, with philosophy and Oriental languages included. Aristotle was the basis of their philosophy; St. Thomas Aquinas, of their theology.[17]

The Port Royalists, or Jansenists, had a curriculum somewhat more advanced than other Catholic schools. Although they neglected physical training and sciences, they went further than the Jesuit schools in the literary studies. They insisted that instruction begin with the vernacular, and they gave an introductory survey of classical literature through the use of French translations. Latin grammar was studied only as it was necessary for the reading of the classics, and a wide variety of authors was read for content rather than for style. Mathematics was taught, as well as logic, for the purpose of training the understanding. In these schools there was no specific instruction in religion or ethics: moral and religious training was through an atmosphere of piety and the continual good example set by the teacher.

---

[17] See Edward A. Fitzpatrick (Ed.), *St. Ignatius and the Ratio Studiorum* (New York: McGraw-Hill, Inc., 1933).

In the convent schools for girls, the course of study was very much the same as in the boys' schools, with some slight adaptations to the needs of women. Fénelon believed that the content of the school for girls should begin with illustrated stories in the vernacular; include writing, arithmetic, and grammar; and provide such subjects as domestic law, ancient and French history, music, art, and embroidery. Fénelon's views, unfortunately, had little effect upon the general practice, and the content of education for girls was usually much narrower and repressive than that for boys.

Agencies and Organization

The Catholic teaching orders ran three types of schools: the elementary school, the secondary school, and the higher school. The Christian Brothers confined their efforts to building up elementary schools; the Jesuits and the Jansenists were concerned with the secondary and the higher school. The elementary school was the school of the poor; the secondary and higher schools were for the education of leaders. In each case, the school was church-supported and church-controlled.

The Catholic teaching orders, especially the Jesuits, showed a genius for organization, and their schools were most effective institutions of learning. The details of Jesuit organization were worked out gradually and set forth in the constitution of the order, issued in 1556. This constitution was in ten parts, the longest of which dealt with education. In 1584, a commission was appointed to study the best educational systems of the times, Protestant as well as Catholic, and to submit recommendations for the approval of the teachers of the order. In 1599, as a final result of forty years of experience and investigation, the expanded educational section of the constitution was published as the *Ratio Studiorum.* This plan of studies provided in great detail for the administration of the schools, the courses and programs of study, the selection and training of teachers, the techniques of teaching, and the methods of discipline.

The Jesuit order is organized on the basis of a military hierarchy. At the head is the democratically elected superior general. Over each province is a provincial appointed by the general. Over each school is a rector appointed by the general, but under the supervision of the provincial in whose province the school is located. Within each school are to be found in order of their rank, the prefect of studies (appointed by the provincial), the prefect of discipline, the house prefects, the teachers, and the monitors.

The two types of Jesuit schools, secondary and higher, were both free, for boys only, and open to both *interni* and *externi.* The secondary school (lower college) was divided into five classes: three grammar classes, *Infima, Media,* and *Suprema*; a fourth class, *Humanitas*; and a fifth class, *Rhetorica.* For prospective Jesuits, this was followed by two years of spiritual preparation (novitiate). In the higher school (higher college), there was a three-year liberal arts course (faculty of philosophy), followed for prospective Jesuit teachers by two years of teacher training (juniorate) and five years of practice teaching in the secondary schools (regency). For prospective Jesuit priests, a four-year theological course (faculty of theology) followed the regency, to be followed by ordination and a final year of spiritual preparation (tertianship). Colleges were opened only when endowment funds were sufficient to support the teachers required to conduct the institution. There was close supervision over all matters of teaching, examination, and discipline. The careful selection and placing of the teachers and the close supervision of all instruction of the prefect of studies are noteworthy features of Jesuit organization. The schools, however, were large; the classes usually included so many pupils that monitors were a necessity.

The organization of the Christian Brothers' schools was set forth in the *Conduct of Schools*,[18] a manual corresponding to the Jesuits' *Ratio Studiorum*. The organization of the order roughly corresponds to that of the Jesuits: an elected general superior appointed brother visitors over each district, and brother directors over each school. From the beginning La Salle organized special training schools for teachers, and no one was permitted to teach in the elementary schools unless he had attended one of the training schools. La Salle's first training school, established at Rheims in 1685, was the earliest forerunner of the normal school or teachers' college.

Although La Salle's *Conduct of Schools* was rigidly prescriptive, it has been amended frequently. The Christian Brothers have been able to modify and expand their educational organization to keep pace with new conditions and new demands. They have expanded to include industrial schools, reform schools, commercial schools, secondary schools, and colleges. Their work has been especially successful in the United States.

La Salle's contributions not only to Catholic education but to education in general may be summarized as follows:

1. His extraordinarily fine conception of the role of the teacher (as part of Christ's redemptive scheme and as a basis for a real profession);
2. His establishment of normal schools for lay teachers;
3. His provision of a *free* education of a very high quality (for his century), and his additional idea that it should be compulsory;
4. His insistence on the use of the vernacular in primary instruction, an innovation in France, although introduced earlier in certain Protestant schools in Germany and elsewhere;
5. His use of the vernacular for psychological and educational reasons as well as religious;

---

[18] F. de La Fontainerie (Ed.), *The Conduct of the Schools of Jean-Baptiste de La Salle* (New York: McGraw-Hill, Inc., 1935).

6. His humanizing discipline as opposed to the crude and barbarous practices of the seventeenth century;

7. His use of a broad rather than narrow curriculum, even in his program for religious teaching;

8. His development of supplementary pedagogical techniques to support the change from individual to group method of teaching;

9. His emphasis on silence to create a quiet, orderly school, in sharp contrast to the riotous, disorderly schools of the day;

10. His emphasis on the importance of self-criticism in educational administration, a proto-twentieth-century idea.[19]

The Jansenists at Port Royal organized two types of secondary schools: schools for boys under the instruction of gentlemen, and schools for girls under the instruction of nuns. There was a very informal organization among the teachers, and no special preparation was required. The most unique characteristic of the Jansenist schools was their size. They were small, often called *les petites écoles*, and classes were limited to five or six pupils.

Methods

These Roman Catholic teaching orders made distinct contributions to the development of educational methods; in many respects their pedagogy was far superior to that used in the Protestant schools. The Jesuits, the Christian Brothers, the Jansenists, all used teaching devices and methods still worthy of study.

The Jesuits' methods were geared toward doing a small amount of work at a time, doing it well, and making sure it was retained. There were two steps in their teaching method: prelection and repetition. Prelection was virtually a lesson assignment: the teacher would first explain the general meaning of the lesson; then matters of syntax and grammar; then all historical, geographical, literary, and other allusions; then the rhetorical elements; and finally he would point out the moral lessons. Prelections was adapted to the abilities and interests of the pupils. In the younger classes the active participation of the pupils was enlisted by questioning; but in the higher classes the preparation was usually in the form of a lecture by the teacher.

The second step, repetition, was strongly emphasized. One of the mottoes of the Jesuits is *Repetitio mater studiorum est* (Repetition is the mother of studies). The first part of each day's class period was given to repeating the previous lesson; each week ended with a review of the

---

[19] See Edward A. Fitzpatrick, *La Salle, Patron of All Teachers* (Milwaukee: The Bruce Publishing Company, 1951).

week's work; the last month of the year was given to a review of the year's work.

The Jesuits were pioneers in the development of devices for producing motivation. Besides utilizing the pupil's desire to please parents and teachers, and his sense of duty, they developed elaborate plans for stimulating the boy's natural instinct of rivalry and emulation. Each pupil was paired with a double of about the same ability, with whom he was in continual competition; classes were divided into rival groups; schools were divided into competing camps. Honor societies were organized, and students competed for membership.

The Christian Brothers were the first to grade elementary school pupils into classes according to their ability and to adopt the simultaneous method, in which the pupil recited not to the teacher alone, but to the entire class. The Jansenists made great progress in teaching the reading of the vernacular by introducing the phonetic method of beginning with the pronunciation of the letter sound, instead of using the prevailing alphabetic method of beginning by naming the letters. The Jansenists also insisted that nothing be memorized except what was understood, and they wrote their textbooks to appeal to the reason, not solely to the memory.

The conduct of the pupils in all these schools was carefully supervised; all students were required to engage in daily public and private devotions and attend confession at regular intervals. Jesuit methods of discipline were firm, but free from the brutality so common in many other schools.[20] Corporal punishment was used only as a last resort in extreme cases of misconduct and was never administered by the teacher, but by a special official, the corrector. There was a delegation of disciplinary powers to various pupil officers, a practice anticipating student government activities.

Corporal punishment was never used in the Jansenist schools. And unlike the Jesuits, the Port Royalists, were opposed to all appeals to individual or group rivalry. They depended for motivation upon auto-emulation, or the desire to surpass one's past efforts; constant vigilance on the part of the teacher was the method of discipline. The Jansenists relied upon the affection of the child and the zeal of the teacher as the best preventive of any disorder.

In their use of corporal punishment, the Christian Brothers differed from the Jesuits and the Jansenists; but the *Conduct of Schools* minutely prescribed under what conditions and to what extent it was to be administered. Thus in each of these Roman Catholic teaching orders some signal advance in the organization and practice of educational system was achieved. These contributions were important to the development of the

---

[20] Those interested in the development of Jesuit and other teaching orders' schools in the early United States are again referred to McCluskey.

body of pedagogical theory on which today's educational decisions are made.

REFERENCES

Armytage, W. H. G., *Four Hundred Years of English Education*. London: Cambridge University Press, 1964.

Bainton, Roland H., *Here I Stand: A Life of Martin Luther*. New York: Abingdon Press, 1950.

Barnes, Harry Elmer, *An Intellectual and Cultural History of the Western World*. New York: Random House, Inc., 1937. Pp. 546–596.

Boyd, William. *The History of Western Education*, 8th ed. Rev. by Edmund J. King. New York: Barnes & Noble, Inc., 1966. Pp. 183–208.

Butts, R. Freeman, *A Cultural History of Western Education*, 2d ed. New York: McGraw-Hill, Inc., 1955. Pp. 194–217, 240–266.

Cole, Luella, *A History of Education, Socrates to Montessori*. New York: Holt, Rinehart and Winston, Inc., 1950. Pp. 221–252, 296–326.

Cubberley, Ellwood P., *The History of Education*. Boston: Houghton Mifflin Company, 1920. Pp. 287–378.

Duggan, Stephen P., *Student's Textbook in the History of Education*, rev. enl. ed. New York: Appleton-Century-Crofts, 1936. Pp. 131–155.

Durant, Will, *The Story of Civilization*, vol. v, *The Reformation*. New York: Simon and Schuster, Inc., 1957. Pp. 1–643, 751–910.

Eby, Frederick, and Charles F. Arrowood, *The Development of Modern Education*. Englewood Cliffs, N.J.: Prentice-Hall, Inc., 1934.

Fitzpatrick, Edward A., *La Salle, Patron of All Teachers*. Milwaukee: The Bruce Publishing Company, 1951.

Good, Harry G., *A History of Western Education*. New York: Crowell-Collier and Macmillan, Inc., 1960. Pp. 139–369.

Graves, Frank P., *Education during the Middle Ages*. New York: Crowell-Collier and Macmillan, Inc., 1910. Pp. 179–237.

Hart, Joseph K., *Creative Moments in Education*. New York: Holt, Rinehart and Winston, Inc., 1931. Pp. 232–237.

Knight, Edgar W., *Twenty Centuries of Education*. Boston: Ginn & Company, 1940. Pp. 166–187.

Laurie, Simon S., *The Development of Educational Opinion*. New York: Crowell-Collier and Macmillan, Inc., 1903. Pp. 86–93.

McGucken, William J., *The Jesuits and Education*. Milwaukee: The Bruce Publishing Company, 1932.

Marique, Pierre J., *History of Christian Education*. New York: Fordham University Press, 1926. Vol ii, pp. 122–162.

Mayer, Frederick, *A History of Educational Thought*. Columbus, Ohio: Charles E. Merrill Books, Inc., 1960. Pp. 180–196.

Messenger, James F., *An Interpretative History of Education*. New York: Thomas Y. Crowell Company, 1931. Pp. 127–140.

Monroe, Paul, *A Textbook in the History of Education*. New York: Crowell-Collier and Macmillan, Inc., 1933. Pp. 401–439.

Mulhern, James, *A History of Education,* 2d ed. New York: The Ronald Press Company, 1959. Pp. 308–327, 333–334.

Nakosteen, Mehdi, *The History and Philosophy of Education.* New York: The Ronald Press Company, 1965. Pp. 221–249.

Painter, Franklin, *Great Pedagogical Essays.* New York: American Book Company, 1905. Pp. 169–202.

———, *A History of Education.* New York: Appleton-Century-Crofts, 1904. Pp. 153–194.

Power, Edward J., *Main Currents in the History of Education.* New York: McGraw-Hill, Inc., 1962. Pp. 305–328.

Quick, Robert H., *Educational Reformers.* New York: Appleton-Century-Crofts, 1904. Pp. 32–62.

Randall, John H., *Making of the Modern Mind.* Boston: Houghton Mifflin Company, 1926. Pp. 143–169.

Raup, Bruce, *Education and Organized Interests in America.* New York: G. P. Putnam's Sons, 1936. Pp. 73–98.

Reisner, Edward H., *Historical Foundations of Modern Education.* New York: Crowell-Collier and Macmillan, Inc., 1927. Pp. 364–501.

Ritter, Gerhard, *Luther, His Life and Work.* Trans. by John Riches. New York: Harper & Row, Publishers, 1963.

Ryan, Lawrence V., *Roger Ascham.* Stanford, Calif., Stanford University Press, 1963.

Tawney, R. H., *Religion and the Rise of Capitalism.* New York: Harcourt, Brace & World, Inc., 1937.

Todd, John M., *Martin Luther.* Westminster, Md.: The Newman Press, 1964.

Ulich, Robert, *History of Educational Thought.* New York: American Book Company, 1950. Pp. 114–129, 149–155.

———, *Philosophy of Education.* New York: American Book Company, 1961. Pp. 165–175.

——— (Ed.), *Three Thousand Years of Educational Wisdom,* 2d ed., enl. Cambridge, Mass.: Harvard University Press, 1954. Pp. 218–249, 272–286.

Weber, Max, *The Protestant Ethic and the Spirit of Capitalism.* Trans. by Talcott Parsons. New York: Charles Scribner's Sons, 1930.

Wender, Herbert, *The Growth of Modern Thought and Culture.* New York: Philosophical Library, Inc., 1959. Pp. 41–57.

SELECTED PAPERBACKS

Aylmer, G. E., *A Short History of Seventeenth Century England.* New York: New American Library of World Literature, Inc., 1963.

Bainton, Roland H., *Here I Stand: A Life of Martin Luther.* New York: New American Library of World Literature, Inc., 1950.

———, *The Reformation of the Sixteenth Century.* Boston: The Beacon Press, 1952.

Beck, Robert Holmes, *A Social History of Education.* Englewood Cliffs, N.J.: Prentice-Hall, Inc., 1965.

Broudy, Harry S., and John R. Palmer, *Exemplars of the Teaching Method*. Skokie, Ill.: Rand McNally & Company, 1965.

Butterfield, Herbert, *Origins of Modern Science, 1300–1800*. New York: Crowell-Collier and Macmillan, Inc., Collier Books, 1962.

Dickens, A. G., *Reformation and Society in Sixteenth Century Europe*. New York: Harcourt, Brace & World, Inc., 1966.

Dillenberger, John (Ed.), *Martin Luther, Selections*. New York: Doubleday & Company, Inc., 1961.

Dolan, John P., *History of the Reformation*. New York: New American Library of World Literature, Inc., 1964.

Erikson, Erik H., *Young Man Luther, A Study in Psychoanalysis and History*. New York: W. W. Norton & Company, Inc., 1962.

Friedrich, Carl J., *Age of Baroque, 1610–1660*. New York: Harper & Row, Publishers, 1952.

Heer, Frederich, *Intellectual History of Europe*, vol. i, *From the Beginnings of Western Thought to Luther*. New York: Doubleday & Company, Inc., 1968.

Holl, Karl, *The Cultural Significance of the Reformation*. New York: Meridian Books, Inc., 1959.

Huizinga, J., *The Waning of the Middle Ages*. New York: Doubleday & Company, Inc., 1949.

James, William, *The Varieties of Religious Experience*. New York: Crowell-Collier and Macmillan, Inc., Collier Books, 1961.

Janelle, Pierre, *The Catholic Reformation*. Milwaukee: The Bruce Publishing Company, 1949.

McCluskey, Neil G., S.J. (Ed.), *Catholic Education in America, A Documentary History*. New York: Bureau of Publications, Teachers College, Columbia University, 1964.

Mayer, Frederick, *Foundations of Education*. Columbus, Ohio: Charles E. Merrill Books, Inc., 1963.

Miles, Leland (Ed.), *Sir Thomas More: A Dialogue of Complaint Against Tribulation*. Bloomington, Ind.: Indiana University Press, 1965.

Muller, Herbert J., *The Uses of the Past, Profiles of Former Societies*. New York: New American Library of World Literature, Inc., 1952. Pp. 282–294.

Rosten, Leo (Ed.), *Religions in America*. New York: Simon and Schuster, Inc., 1963.

Ryan, Patrick J., *Historical Foundations of Public Education in America*. Dubuque, Iowa: William C. Brown Company, Publishers, 1965.

Viorst, Milton (Ed.), *The Great Documents of Western Civilization*. New York: Bantam Books, Inc., 1965. Pp. 76–106.

Woodward, William Harrison, *Studies in Education during the Age of the Renaissance, 1400–1600*. New York: Teachers College Press, Columbia University, 1967.

CHAPTER 12

Preparation for Living in the World of Experience

The true method of experience first lights the candle, and then by means of the candle shows the way, commencing as it does with experience duly ordered . . . and from it educing axioms, and from established axioms, again new experiments.[1]

EDUCATIONAL REALISM AS A NEW FORCE

Educational realism came into existence as a protest against the narrowness of both the humanists and the religious reformers. As used here, the term *realism* applies to the position that education should be concerned with the actualities of life. Aristotle, a teacher with a strong sense of actuality, had preached induction (although his syllogism had been founded on and sanctified the deductive method); his *Organon,* although more deductive than inductive, was the Bible of antiquarian and medieval science. Early in the seventeenth century, Francis Bacon demanded a new objectivity based on observable facts. With this dedication to the scientific method educational realism is concerned.

Such a heightening of intellectual activity in Western Europe expressed itself along three lines: (1) the inspiration of the Renaissance, (2) the enthusiasm of the Protestant Revolt, and (3) the genesis of a new spirit of scientific inquiry and a renewed interest in the realities of existence, rather than a theorizing about the past or future. We have already inquired

[1] Francis Bacon, *Novum Organum,* ed. Fulton H. Anderson (New York: Liberal Arts Press, 1960).

into the educational consequences of the first two movements; we now examine the educational implications of the third.

This third aspect of the general renascence of European civilization, the so-called realistic movement, was in part contemporary with Renaissance and Reformation; the earliest realists were contemporaries of the humanists; the work of the reformers was still vigorous when later realists began to be heard. But where the individual and personal humanists—directed their efforts toward literary and esthetic achievements, and the social and political reformers worked toward religious and moral goals, the realists, both impersonal and nonsocial, firmly fixed their attention on the new objective determinations.

Italian humanism at its best had been overemotional and esthetic; but also its interests were narrow and sometimes superficial. Northern humanism at its best had been too engrossed in problems of social welfare and reform to the exclusion of other influences, while ecclesiastical zealots had been too insistent on the limitations of doctrinal teachings.

Many of the secondary schools that stemmed from the Renaissance and the Reformation had by the seventeenth century descended into a dreary and formal Ciceronianism, an excessive devotion to Latin linguistics and a deadening routine of word exercises. The reformers with their extreme religious fervor had not only intensified the linguistic formalism of later humanism but had added a religious sanction and authority entirely alien to the broad humanism that had been conceived at the outset of the Renaissance. It was inevitable that a reaction should occur and men should attack this sterile and narrow type of education. Ciceronianism, nevertheless, continued to dominate the schools for over three centuries more, but never without opposition from those who aimed at making education more meaningful in terms of the practical needs of life.

Realist protests were stimulated by the scientific investigations and discoveries that were being made in spite of ecclesiastical antagonism. These explorers and scientists were interested primarily in the concrete objects which make up the material universe. Their concern with the concrete and material was as old as mankind. The observation of the phenomena of nature had been an everyday experience for many Greek philosophers from Thales to Archimedes.[2]

As early as the thirteenth century, Roger Bacon had turned from the theological scholasticism of the medieval universities to experimentation and inquiries into natural phenomena. In the fourteenth century, Renaissance curiosity led Leonardo da Vinci (1452–1519) to turn his remarkable abilities as a physicist and engineer to probing science and producing concrete and valuable results. Modern science, however, really began about

---

[2] See Gordon H. Clark, *Thales to Dewey, A History of Philosophy* (Boston: Houghton Mifflin Company, 1957), especially pp. 3–144, 301–356.

the middle of the sixteenth century with the great work of Copernicus (1473–1543), which was soon followed by that of Kepler (1571–1630) and Galileo (1564–1642). The publication in 1687 of the *Principia* by Sir Isaac Newton (1642–1727), greatest vindicator of the new scientific method, laid a firm basis for physical science. What the philosophy of Aristotle was to the ancient world, and the theology of Aquinas was to the medieval world, the science of Newton was to the early modern world. These experimental scientists did not contribute directly to educational thought, yet the spirit motivating their research was identical to influencing the realists, and determined, even though obliquely, the direction of much subsequent education.

Many educational realists exercised an influence outside the schools and must be thought of as educational essayists and theoreticians rather than as actual pedagogues. Most of the realists then were concerned primarily with other interests, a reason perhaps for their objectivity. Yet during their crowded careers, each observed that education was out of touch with the realities of the new age of science and took up the problem, producing several educational classics.

The realists agreed that the schools developed by the humanists and reformers were inadequate and should be replaced by a broad new type of education which would prepare boys and girls for the concrete duties of practical living. But they were far from agreeing on the methods which would provide such preparation. As a means of understanding and evaluating their specific contributions, we will consider three categories: (1) literary, or humanistic, realists; (2) social realists; and (3) sense, or scientific, realists. Actually, the similarities among all these realists were considerably greater than any assumed differences. Thus, our arrangement is an arbitrary one, which we will utilize solely for convenience.

LITERARY REALISM

On one hand, realists desired a return to the humanism of the Renaissance; on the other, realists looked prophetically ahead to the great scientific age of the nineteenth and twentieth centuries. The earlier realists who did not entirely break away from humanism may be called humanistic, or literary, realists.

These literary realists agreed with the Renaissance that the classical languages and literature were the only objects worthy of study, the ideal means to a liberal education. They believed that the ancients had attained the highest achievements of which the human mind is capable and had included in their writings all that was worth man's attention and interest. But these realists differed widely from Renaissance humanists in their objectives. Although their curriculum was humanistic, its aims and method were realistic. Its goal was the education of the person, not merely the memorization of a body of literature or epic history.

Within this group of humanistic realists we may place (1) Juan Luis
Vives (1492–1540), Spanish scholar and philosopher, friend of Sir Thomas
More and Erasmus, teacher and author at Louvain, Bruges, and Oxford,
tutor of Mary I of England, and author of *On a Plan of Studies for Youth,
On the Instruction of Christian Women*, and *On the Teaching of the Arts*;
(2) François Rabelais (1483–1553), French monk, priest, scholar, physician, madcap, satirist, author of the *Life of Gargantua* and *Heroic Deeds
of Pantagruel*; (3) John Milton (1608–1674), English Puritan, poet, and
author of *Tractate of Education*. Each of these three writers was a typical
exponent of literary, or humanistic, realism.

Aims

The literary realists aimed at a complete knowledge and understanding
of human society, including motives, nature, institutions, and relationships
both to the world of man and to the world of nature. And with such understanding, they sought to fit the individual to his environment. Their aims,
they believed, could best be attained through knowledge of ancient civilizations, for, they believed, the most complete information on any subject of
man's endeavor would be found in classical literature. So the purpose of
these humanistic realists was to seek the meaning of classic literature not
for its own sake, but for the scientific, historical, and social instruction
which it contained. They were not concerned with diction, structure, or
style, as were the Ciceronians, nor with religious and moral precepts, as
were many of the reformers. And these realists did not look upon the
classic authors as infallible authorities, but only as convenient sources.
Those whom we call literary realists believed in the utilization of classical
literature as the best means of preparing for the realities of life.

Vives' didactic writings show that he was essentially an educational
realist, although favorable to humanistic studies. He insisted that education
should develop personality, Christian virtues, and competence in business,
while subordinating everything to religion, morality, and use. Literary
study was to be the basis of learning, the goal the development of character
and ability. Thus he wrote, "This is the fruit of all our studies. . . .
Having acquired our knowledge, we must turn it to usefulness, and employ
it for the common good"; "All things in the world as they were made by
God are good and beautiful."

Rabelais, satirically protesting against and ridiculing medievalism,
scholasticism, and formalism in education, pointed out that there is no
reason why real life values cannot be obtained from the study of the
classics. The aim of learning, he said, is "the formation of a complete man,
skilled in art and industry," "the development of the whole man, physically,
morally, intellectually."

Milton revealed his belief that education is to prepare for actual
living when he wrote, "I call, therefore, a complete and generous education
that which fits a man to perform justly, skillfully, and magnanimously all

the offices, both private and public, of peace and war." In another connection, he said, "Language is but the instrument conveying to us things useful to be known." Literary realists conceived of education as a study of words in order to understand the world in which we live and how to react to it. Many educators still hold the idea that we can best learn how to live through reading.

Types

The literary realists stressed a literary type of education, a bookish type of learning as far as agencies were concerned. But in the breadth of their aims and the scope of their subject matter advocated, we see that the literary realists had in view many forms of education. They urged a very practical type of education, since all their learning was to be put to practical use. Their education was of a much more liberal type than that of the Renaissance humanists, for the realists wished to provide intellectual, moral, social, religious, and physical education; they advocated an overall type that would develop the whole man for all the needs of life.

Content

The content of study proposed by Vives, Rabelais, and Milton was encyclopedic. These men, extensive and thorough scholars, greatly over-estimated the capacity of the average human mind for knowledge. In the completeness of the curriculum they proposed, they were at least a century ahead of their times; in many respects, our modern curriculum has not reached theirs in richness and completeness.

Although Vives believed all great knowledge was found in the Latin tongue, he felt a correct and fluent use of the vernacular was necessary for education. He said that it was the duty of the parent and the master to take pains that children speak the local language correctly, that the master had to be able to speak his pupils' mother tongue fluently and correctly if he were to teach the ancient tongues effectively; that it was the duty of every scholar to purify and improve the vernacular speech of his country. The study of the vernacular, nevertheless, he considered only incidental to the mastery of Latin, which, he believed, was necessary as a universal language to make possible (1) contacts between scholars of different lands, (2) a wide diffusion of books into many countries, and (3) the spread of the Catholic religion to all parts of the globe. In his study of the Latin language, he rejected the dialectic grammars used in the Middle Ages and advocated instead the study of grammar based upon usage. In reading books in the ancient languages, he placed the study of content and meaning ahead of the study of form and style. Works on mathematics, natural science, and physical science were to be studied, as well as works in literature and philosophy. Works on history and geography were to be included in the curriculum. In the higher schools, Vives felt the emphasis should be on technical and professional study, such as theology, law, medicine, architecture, political science, and war. For women, Vives advocated training in the vernacular, Latin, religion, moral conduct, care of children, and household management. He omitted the humanistic subjects typical for women—music, drawing, dancing—as well as mathematics, science, and history.

For the education of Gargantua and Pantagruel (his equally gigantic son), Rabelais proposed a mighty course of study! The subject matter is so extensive that he must have had in mind the mere sketching of a curriculum from each part of which selections were to be made. Rabelais presented a wide range of physical exercises, games, and sports; a rich program of Bible study and religious exercises; a long list of instrumental musical instruments; a wealth of intellectual readings from ancient authorities in science, history, mathematics, and astronomy; and a wealth of ancient literature in the Latin, Greek, Hebraic, Chaldaic, and Arabic languages. Rabelais supposed that while Pantagruel was a student in Paris, Gargantua wrote to him as follows:

> That is why, my dear son, I urge you to spend your youth making the most of your studies and developing your moral sense. You are in Paris, which abounds in noble men upon whom to pattern yourself; you have Epistemon, an admirable tutor, who can inspire you by direct oral teaching. But I demand more of you. I insist you learn languages perfectly! Greek first, as old Quintilian prescribes; then Latin; then Hebrew for the sake of the Holy Scriptures; then Chaldee and Arabic, too. Model your Greek style on Plato, your Latin on Cicero. Let no history slip your memory; cultivate cosmography, for you will find its texts helpful.
>
> As for the liberal arts of geometry, arithmetic and music, I gave you a taste of them when you were a little lad of five or six. Proceed further in them yourself, learning as much as you can. Be sure to master all the rules of astronomy; but dismiss astrology and the divinatory art of Lullius as but vanity and imposture. Of civil law, I would have you know the texts of the Code by heart, then compare them with philosophy.
>
> A knowledge of nature is indispensable; devote yourself to this study with unflagging curiosity. Let there be no sea, river or fountain but you know the fish that dwell in it. Be familiar with all the shrubs, bushes and trees in forest or orchard, all the plants, herbs and flowers that grow on the ground, all the birds of the air, all the metals in the bowels of earth, all the precious stones in the orient and the south. In a word, be well informed in everything that concerns the physical world we live in.
>
> Then carefully consult the works of Greek, Arabian and Latin physicians, without slighting the Jewish doctors, Talmudists and Cabalists. By frequent exercises in dissection, acquire a perfect knowledge of that other world, which is man.

Devote a few hours a day to the study of Holy Writ. Take up the New Testament and the Epistles in Greek; then, the Old Testament in Hebrew. Strive to make your mind an inexhaustible storehouse of knowledge. For you are growing to manhood now: soon you will have to give up your studious repose to lead a life of action. You will have to learn to bear arms, to achieve knighthood, so as to defend my house and help our allies frustrate the attacks of evildoers.

Further, I wish you soon to test what profit you gained from your education. This you can best do by public discussion and debate on all subjects against all comers, and by frequenting learned men both in Paris and elsewhere.

But remember this. As Solomon says, wisdom entereth not into a malicious soul, and science without conscience spells but destruction of the spirit. Therefore serve, love and fear God, on Him pin all your thoughts and hopes; by faith built of charity, cling to Him so closely that never a sin can come between you. Hold the abuses of the world in just suspicion Set not your heart upon vanity, for this life is a transitory thing, but the Word of God endureth forever. Be serviceable to your neighbor, love him as you do yourself. Honor your teachers. Shun the company of all men you would not wish to resemble; receive not in vain the favors God has bestowed upon you.

When you realize that you have acquired all the knowledge receive my blessing before I die.

My son, the peace and grace of Our Lord be with you. Amen.

Your father,
GARGANTUA

From Utopia, the seventeenth day of September.[3]

Milton, too, believed that the whole gamut of ancient learning should be studied. Not satisfied that the student should know the content of Latin and Greek classics, he advocated the reading of books in Hebrew, Chaldaic, Syriac, and Italian. Great literary classicist though he was, he regarded no education complete without a wide acquaintance with natural science, social science, mathematics, philosophy—all the knowledge of all the ancients. Milton condemned the study of formal grammar and the development of an elegant and ostentatious style as a waste of time. Puritan in outlook, he provided no free play or competitive games in his program, as had Rabelais; but he did advocate physical education as training for military service. Milton specified that moral and religious instruction be given not only through a pious atmosphere in the school but through the reading of ethical passages from the Bible and other ancient literature.

---

[3] François Rabelais, *Gargantua and Pantagruel—The Five Books*, translated into English by Jacques Le Clercq (New York: Heritage Press, 1942), book ii, ch. xiii, pp. 35–36. Reproduced by permission of The George Macy Companies, Inc., copyright 1936, renewed 1964.

Thus the content of the education proposed by the literary realists was to be found largely in books on all subjects and books in all languages. Although, admittedly, a bookish curriculum, it was far from narrow.

Agencies and Organization

While the literary realists were primarily concerned with the aims and content of education, they did advance widely varying proposals for the organization and arrangement of school work. Usually their suggestions were so visionary that they were practically impossible and had a minor influence, except in the case of a few exceptional teachers and schools that kept alive ideas. The work of most schools continued in the formal, artificial, perfunctory, traditional way that is always so hard to overcome. Our interest is not in the influence of these men upon the organization of the schools of their centuries, but in their advanced ideas, which we could well use today. The plans they outlined may not be, as Milton admits, "a bow for every man to shoot in," but they are rich in inspiration and practical suggestions.

Vives insisted that both parents should take part in the education of the child; the mother should be the child's first teacher, and the father should oversee and direct all the child's training. In rare instances, it might be necessary for the child to be taught privately by a tutor. When this was the case, Vives felt he should have at least one companion in his studies. Ordinarily, the boy should enter a public day school at the age of seven and live at home while attending. Vives believed that schoolmasters should be men of sound scholarship, whose training has included much practice. He advocated that schoolmasters be paid from public funds and receive no money from their pupils. Vives thought that the site of a school building should be selected with the greatest care, and that the planning, construction, and equipment of the building should be given considerable attention.

Rabelais' scheme of education is organized largely in terms of a tutorial, a private teacher who lives with the boy and makes every minute serve some educational purpose. Thus Rabelais said that "Ponocrates [Gargantua's tutor] so arranged the lad's schedule that not a moment of the day was wasted; all his time was spent in the pursuit of learning and honest knowledge."[4]

While Gargantua was being bathed, dressed, and fed, the tutor carried on his teaching. During the hours of physical games and sports, during the time spent in playing cards, during evening walks and visits under the guidance of the tutor, Gargantua was instructed. Life with all its manifold activities shared in the educative process.

Differing from both the tutorial idea of Rabelais and the public day-

---

[4] Rabelais, book i, ch. xxii, p. 67.

school of Vives, Milton's scheme is based on the idea of a single institution of learning, which he called the Academy. Milton believed that the entire education of a boy should be given between the ages of twelve and twenty-one, in this academy instead of in a secondary school and a university. He required the organizer of his academy:

> First to find out a spacious house and ground about it for an *Academy,* and big enough to lodge a hundred and fifty persons, whereof twenty or thereabout may be attendants, all under the government of one, who shall be thought of desert sufficient, and ability either to do all, or wisely to direct, and oversee it done. This place should be at once both School and University, not heeding a remove to any other house of Schollership, except it be some peculiar Colledge of Law, or Physick, where they mean to be practitioners; but as for those general studies which take up our time from *Lilly* [Lilly's Latin Primer] to the commencing [degree], as they term it, Master of Art, it should be absolute. After this pattern, as many Edifices may be converted to this use, as shall be needful in every City throughout this Land, which would tend much to the encrease of Learning and Civility everywhere.[5]

Literary realism, combined with certain other influences, eventually brought about the establishment of new educational institutions, particularly on the secondary level. The Act of Uniformity, passed in England in 1662, excluded hundreds of nonconformist ministers from their parishes and closed the Latin grammar schools and universities to nonconformists. Many of the ministers turned to teaching for a livelihood and opened private secondary schools for the children of nonconformists. Influenced probably by the description of Milton's brainchild, these schools were called academies and patterned somewhat after the educational ideals of the literary realists. But, while retaining the highly religious character of the schools of the reformers, these schools placed greater emphasis upon preparation for actual life. Latin and Greek were retained, but modern foreign languages were taught and all instruction was in the vernacular. History, geography, mathematics, and natural philosophy were other subjects of their curricula. As we shall see, this English regimen was more liberal than that to be followed in New England.

Methods

The literary realists not only attacked the narrowness of their contemporaries' methods but advocated methods far in advance of their times. Vives, in particular, had some exceedingly modern conceptions of method-

---

[5] Oscar Browning (Ed.), *Milton's Tractate of Education, A Facsimile Reprint from the Edition of 1673* (London: Cambridge University Press, 1905), pp. 8–9. See also A. F. Leach, *The Schools of Medieval England* (London: Methuen & Co., Ltd., 1915), pp. 277–332.

ology. In his writings, he drew upon the earlier educational theorists, especially Aristotle and Quintilian. He was a forerunner of contemporary psychologists in his desire to make the study of the operations of the mind the basis of teaching method. His last essay, *De Anima* (Concerning the mind), reveals a clear understanding of the function of sense perception and of the natural growth of knowledge in the individual mind.

Influenced perhaps by Quintilian, Vives advocated that masters study each pupil individually and adapt the work each pupil was to pursue to his particular interest and ability. He suggested that pupils enter school a month or so early, so that the masters might thoroughly study individual capacities. He also thought that at least four times each year all the masters should hold conferences, at which they could exchange observations concerning the progress and ability of their pupils.

In contrast to Vives, Rabelais advocated a most informal system of learning, which we would probably call an incidental method. All study was to be made pleasant; attractive rather than compulsory means were to be favored; spontaneity and interest were to be substituted for formalism and authority. Rabelais believed that learning came best through natural exuberant activities engaged in spontaneously in the open air; that knowledge was attained best by following natural interests. He thought reference books should be used to clarify discussions; and careful observation of nature and direct contact with the everyday activities of life should supplement and vitalize the reading of the classical authors. Rabelais substituted reasoning for rote memorizing and observed, "Learning truly becomes, not the drudgery of imprisoned schoolboys, but the sport of kings."

Milton bitterly condemned the existing grammar schools because of their excessive emphasis upon grammatical drill and the writing of compositions in imitation of classical Latin and Greek models. He mocked, "These are the fruits of misspending our prime youth at the schools and universities as we do, either in learning mere words or such things chiefly as were better unlearned."

The basis of Milton's method was reading widely and thoroughly for content, not for syntax and grammar. This reading was to be vitalized through discussions with the teacher and through explanations and lectures on all subjects, by authorities, who were to be brought to the academy for conferences with the boys. The education in the academy was to be supplemented by the students' travel in England and abroad.

THE SOCIAL REALISTS

The social realists joined the literary realists in their attacks upon classical learning; but whereas the literary realists protested chiefly against the narrowness and formalism of such rote learning and imitation, the social realists protested against its utter uselessness in preparing the individual for his life among other human beings; the social realists attacked its failure to fit the individual for social living and social adjustment. Most social realists were aristocrats or members of the upper classes, men of affairs interested in training their sons for active participation in public life. They sought an education that would develop the gentleman, the man of the world; and they believed that such an education could be had best by direct contact with people and social activities, not through books. They had little patience with the bookishness of the literary realists, who, they said, were preparing young men for the life of the past.

Michel de Montaigne (1533–1592), French aristocrat, Mayor of Bordeaux, lawyer, outstanding essayist, tolerant epicurean, and admirable gossip, was the most truly representative exponent of the educational position we have called social realism. His educational views are set forth in detail in his famous essays "On Pedantry" and "On the Education of Children."

Aims

Social realism was another reaction to Ciceronianism and was another step toward sense realism. The aim of the social realist was not to produce a scholar or a professional man, but to prepare the aristocratic youth for the life of a gentleman in the world of affairs. Montaigne held that education was the art of forming men rather than specialists. To him education meant pragmatic utilitarianism. Like the better Sophists of Greece, he advocated a highly individualistic education that would prepare the youth for individual efficiency and success in the social life of his day. Montaigne's immediate aim was to develop in the youth a sound and practical judgment of men and affairs. Instead of cramming the memory with facts, education was to provide the basis for making sensible choices and decisions, to enable the individual to get along efficiently with his fellows and enjoy his leisure hours. Actually, the predominant objective was to prepare the aristocratic youth for a successful and pleasurable career. As Montaigne wrote in "On the Education of Children":

> For a child of noble family who seeks learning not for gain (for such an abject goal is unworthy of the graces and favor of the Muses, and besides it looks to others and depends upon them), or so much for external advantages as for his own, and to enrich and furnish himself inwardly, since I would rather make of him an able man than a learned man, I would also urge that care be taken to choose a guide with a well-made rather than a well-filled head; that both these qualities should be required of him, but more particularly character and understanding than learning; and that he should go about his job in a novel way.[6]

So social adjustment, fitting the individual for an efficient and pleasant

---

[6] Montaigne, Michel Eyquem de, *The Complete Works of Montaigne*, trans. by Donald M. Frame (Stanford, Calif.: Stanford University Press, 1958), p. 110.

life with other individuals, was the educational aim of the social realist. The development of a practical judgment and a social disposition was the best means to that end for the art of living was the goal of learning; the pupil was to live what he learned.

Types

The social realist advocated a practical type of education, but not utilitarian in the sense of being vocational or professional. He was not interested in preparing for a specialized trade or profession, but was concerned with developing the practical man of affairs, the versatile man of the world. This was social education in the broadest meaning of the term: the development of the ability to get along smoothly and harmoniously with other people in all the activities of life. Montaigne proposed a broad education that included physical, moral, and intellectual training. His physical training had in it a suggestion of the hardening process later developed more fully by Locke and Rousseau; his moral training was an adaptation to the social customs of the gentleman, including such abilities as drinking gracefully and making love romantically; his intellectual training consisted of developing sound practical judgment and discrimination.

Montaigne's conception of education was essentially aristocratic. He was concerned only with training the upper classes and paid little attention to the other classes. He was satisfied to have the apprenticeship system and the workhouse provide the education of the poor.

Content

Montaigne advocated the use of an activity curriculum and scorned the idea that a mere study of books would provide an adequate education. To him experience was much more important than words and books. When books were used, he maintained that the most important result was the reader's vicarious participation in the experience of others. Montaigne approached history as a study of the experiences of the past, and he considered philosophy the study of human conduct and man's offices, or duties.

Montaigne demanded the addition of new subjects to the curriculum. He favored retaining Latin as part of the education of a gentleman, but he rejected the humanist overemphasis on Greek, which he considered as the mere equipment of a scholar. Actually, he felt French and contemporary foreign languages, because they were the languages for conversation with people at home and abroad, were much more important than Latin and Greek.

Like Milton, Montaigne stressed travel as an effective means of education and as the best agency for gaining experience and becoming familiar with people and customs. Contact with people and places he considered much more valuable than reading about them. The world was Montaigne's curriculum, for he said:

This great world, which some multiply as several species under one genus, is the true mirror wherein we must look in order to know ourselves, as we should. In short I would have this to be the book my young gentleman should study with most attention. Many strange humours, many sects, many judgments, opinions, laws, and customs teach us to judge rightly or our own actions to correct our faults, and to inform our understanding which is no trivial lesson.[7]

Agencies and Organization

Montaigne had little use for schools and colleges as agencies of education. In speaking of the product of these institutions, he said:

> Do but observe him when he comes back from school, after fifteen or sixteen years that he has been there; there is nothing so awkward and maladroit, so unfit for company and employment; and all that you shall find he has got is, that his Latin and Greek have only made him a greater and more conceited coxcomb than when he went from home.[8]

Instead of the conventional institutions as agencies for education, Montaigne urged the use of a tutor was the most important and most difficult duty of the parents. This private tutorial system, under which the education of the boy at home and abroad was closely directed and supervised, was adopted not only by many of the noble families of France but also became popular in England and later in the American South. The narrow classical formalism of the Latin grammar schools and the growing acceptance of the idea that the grand tour was an indispensable part of a gentleman's education brought about the adoption of tutorial training in the British upper classes.

Although Montaigne favored private tutors, a few social realists demanded new types of schools to carry out their aims. So some French aristocrats demanded a school which should turn out gentlemen instead of pedants, and such schools were ultimately established under the name *academies.* Instead of the classics and religion, which had been stressed in the Renaissance and Jesuit colleges, these academies emphasized modern languages, mathematics, good manners, and military arts.

The development of such schools for the upper classes was much more pronounced in Germany. The Thirty Years' War (1618–1648) enhanced the position of the nobility and developed an antagonism between the bourgeoisie, or burgher class, on the one hand, and the aristocracy, on the other. Social differentiation led to educational differentiation. The sons of the noblemen were withdrawn from the classical *Gymnasien,* and schools, called the *Ritterakademie,* were established for the nobles' exclusive use. The character of this school was determined not only by the desire

---

[7] Montaigne, p. 116.
[8] Montaigne, p. 125.

of the nobleman for a school that would prepare for civil and military affairs but also by the influence that French court life was beginning to have upon the German nobility. French language and literature, physical training and social accomplishments, political history and geography, mathematics and military science, formed the backbone of the curriculum.

The schools that developed under the influence of social realism which survive today are the finishing schools and military academies attended by the sons and daughters of the wealthier classes in American life, and the public schools of England.

Methods

The gist of Montaigne's conception of method is his famous saying, "To know by heart only is not to know at all." He believed in a method that emphasized understanding and judgment rather than mere memorization: knowledge should be assimilated, facts used, actions imitated, ideas applied in conduct. Latin should be learned through usage; foreign languages should be learned by traveling through foreign countries and conversing with the people; information should be obtained through direct social contacts rather than from books. For, Montaigne asserted, "What a man knows directly, that will he dispose of without turning to his book or looking to his pattern."

Montaigne urged that learning should be pleasurable and attractive to the child. He condemned the harsh measures so often used in the schools of his day to secure attention and diligence, and he observed and instructed:

> Some never cease brawling in their scholar's ears to follow their books; yet is their charge nothing else but to repeat what has been told them before. I should have a tutor [show the pupil] how to choose and distinguish, without the help of others, sometimes opening him the way, other times leaving him to open it by himself. I would not have [the tutor] invent and speak alone, but suffer his disciple to speak when his turn comes. . . . "Most commonly the authority of them that teach, hinders them that would learn". . . . I would not only have him demand an account of the words contained in his lesson, but of the sense and substance thereof, and judge of the profit he hath made of it, not by the testimony of his memory, but the witness of his life. . . . I would have him make his scholar narrowly to sift all things with discretion, and harbour nothing in his head by mere authority, or upon trust.[9]

Thus Montaigne advocated a method that is in accord with the best principles of modern teaching; he encouraged discrimination, independent thinking, and application on the part of the pupil, and he condemned too much authority and activity on the part of the teacher.

---

[9] Montaigne, p. 110.

SENSE REALISM

Although the contributions of each member of the realist group is important, the movement in education culminates in the sense realists, who brought to fruition the seeds sown by the literary and social realists. Instead of a reality found in books or experienced in everyday human relationships, the sense realists postulated a basic reality, the reality found in the forces and laws of nature. Their position has been called scientific realism, and marks the beginning of the scientific movement in education.

The realistic movement was the outgrowth of the scientific discoveries of the sixteenth and seventeenth centuries: Copernicus' heliocentric theory of the solar system, Kepler's exploration of the motions of the planets, the discovery of the moons of Jupiter through Galileo's invention of the telescope; the development of logarithms by Napier, analytical geometry by Descartes, and calculus by Liebnitz; Newton's discovery of the law of gravitation; Boyle's theories of gases and of the vacuum; Harvey's theory of the circulation of the blood; Torricelli's invention of the barometer; and Malpighi's invention of the compound microscope. All these achievements were the results of a new type of intellectual activity far removed from the traditional learning of the schools and paving the way for a new conception of education. Practical men looking upon these fruits of the new methods of observation and reasoning, of independent thinking and of free judgment, determined that such training should find a place in the schools. They advocated a type of education which introduced scientific content and utilized the scientific method.

Four great educational philosophers may be taken as typical exponents of sense realism: (1) Richard Mulcaster (1531–1611), headmaster of the Merchant Taylors' School and St. Paul's School in England, author of two texts on education, *Positions* and *Elementarie*; (2) Francis Bacon (1561–1626), English statesman, philosopher, scientist, and author of *Advancement of Learning, The New Atlantis,* and *Novum Organum*; (3) Wolfgang Ratke (1571–1635), German founder of experimental schools, author of *Methodus Nova*; (4) John Amos Comenius (1592–1670), Moravian bishop, prophet of modern education, philosopher, educator, textbook writer, and author of *The Great Didactic, Gate of Tongues Unlocked, The Vestibule, The School of Infancy,* and *Orbis Pictus* (The World in Pictures).

Aims

The ultimate aim of the sense realists was to develop a harmonious society, working in accord with sense perception. Universal conditions and natural universal laws, which they considered the only true realities, were the goals of the sense realists' education. Mulcaster said that education does not attempt to repress the natural tendencies and activities of childhood, but the "aim of education and training is to help nature to her perfection." Bacon believed that the ultimate goal of education is to give man dominance over things, to increase human power through the utilization of scientific knowledge. Knowledge of the natural environment, its phenomena and its processes, was to be utilized as the new foundation for a practical and useful life. As Bacon observed, "Man is but the servant and interpreter of nature; it can be commanded only by being obeyed; thus do human knowledge and human power really meet in one." The chief purpose of education was to learn nature's laws and to control the universe for the benefit of man. Bacon was a realist in making the end of scientific inquiry practical, not metaphysical.[10] He believed that learning had as its aim the mastery of things in order to extend man's control over nature. He optimistically foresaw the use of the scientific method for human welfare; he believed that the scientific study of nature was basic to all human progress. *The New Atlantis,* his plan for a model state, included the establishment of a research institution, a clearinghouse for scientific investigation, called Solomon's House, which would apply its findings to advance human welfare. In popular speech Bacon believed that "Knowledge is power."

Bacon was not alone in his dream of a social order brought about through a new type of education. The scientific inventions and discoveries of the sixteenth century had fired many enlightened men to attempt the transformation of human society through education. Most of the writers who presented their seventeenth-century schemes for the reform of society agreed with Bacon that education was the essential agency for the betterment of both society and the individual. Although novel for that century, the idea was not really new; Plato in *The Republic,* 2000 years earlier, had looked upon education as a means for reforming society and state. Yet somehow Bacon's ideas appeared more practical. Cowley's often-quoted ode (to the Royal Society) runs:

Bacon, like Moses, led us forth at last,
The barren wilderness he past,
Did on the very border stand of the blest primis'd land;
And from the mountain's top of his exalted wit,
Saw it himself, and shew'd us it.

Comenius, with his combination of religious zeal and passion for knowledge, represents a bridge between the religious moralists and the

---

[10] Although romanticized to some degree, Catherine Drinker Bowen's *Francis Bacon, The Temper of a Man* (Boston: Little, Brown & Company, 1963), offers an interesting profile of the man and his work.

sense realists. His ultimate goal of education was "eternal happiness with God." But this, he believed, could come about only through the right kind of earthly living. Comenius was a firm believer in the power of education to regenerate human life and insisted that the best way to raise the standards of sunken humanity was through the proper education of the young. This, he felt, could be accomplished only through pansophic teaching. The aim of education should be the teaching of all things to all men; he said, "Charity bids us not niggardly to withhold from mankind what God has intended for the use of all, but to throw it open to the whole world." Although eternal happiness with God was the ultimate goal of education, the immediate aim of his school was to prepare for the activities of life through the utilization of a wealth of knowledge. As Comenius stated:

> In this *palaestra* they "will learn, not for school, but for life," so that the youths shall go forth energetic, ready for everything, apt, industrious, and worthy of being intrusted with any of the duties of life, and this all the more if they have added to virtue a sweet conversation, and have crowned all with the fear and love of God. They will also go forth capable of expression and eloquence, and that not merely in their own tongue, but in the Latin, Greek, and Hebrew.
>
> For the attainment of these great results three instruments are necessary: good books, good teachers, and a good method.[11]

Sense realists aimed at the discovery and advancement of new knowledge rather than mere learning from books. They sought their aims in the realm of nature, but they did not seek information about nature as an end in itself or only to satisfy curiosity. They sought power with which to utilize nature's forces for the welfare of mankind. The sense realists, like the practical scientists of today, aimed at the discovery and utilization of the secrets of the universe for the real and practical benefits they could bring to man in his everyday work.

Nor did the sense realists limit their search for natural laws to the external world. They believed that the inner operations of the mind were also governed by the laws of nature. The immediate aims of Ratke and Comenius were to discover the laws of nature that governed the learning process. They aimed at an educational system that would be in accord with the natural order followed by the mind of a child learning. Bacon's immediate aim was the development of a scientific method to discover and organize scientific knowledge; the immediate aim of Ratke and Comenius was the development of a scientific method to inculcate that knowledge.

---

[11] S. S. Laurie, *John Amos Comenius—Bishop of the Moravians—His Life and Educational Works* (London: Cambridge University Press, 1904), p. 233. See also David G. Scanlon, *International Education*, Teachers College Classics in Education, no. 5 (New York: Bureau of Publications, Teachers College, Columbia University, 1960), pp. 2, 33–52.

Types

The sense realists, like the other realists, emphasized a practical type of education as far as purposes were concerned. From the standpoint of content, most of them placed stress on the scientific type of training. Their education was liberal to a much greater degree than most of that which had preceded them, for they were interested in a pansophic curriculum, which included practically all knowledge. Yet religious and moral types of training were still stressed, especially by Comenius; and linguistic and intellectual types of training were considered essential as tools for gaining knowledge.

One striking characteristic of the sense realists was their emphasis upon democratic education and the vernacular. Comenius in particular had a profound sympathy for the common people and was a champion of education for all in the same schools. He stipulated that "As far as is possible, all should be educated together, that they may stimulate and urge on one another." Mulcaster thought that education should be widely diffused and adapted to the needs of all. Both Bacon and Comenius firmly believed that if knowledge were properly organized, it could be grasped by the common man.

Content

Most sense realists advocated a comprehensive curriculum. Even Mulcaster, who had perhaps the narrowest conception of content in the group, contended that learning should be wide in scope and adapted to the needs of each student. In Mulcaster's planned six-year elementary school, children of both sexes were to be taught reading and writing as a necessary equipment for all citizens; and the vernacular, English, was to be given first place, both as the sole medium of instruction and as a subject. With reading and writing, drawing and music were to become the education for all. And these subjects were the only offerings related to sense training or object study, for Mulcaster made no provision for the study of natural phenomena, the basic characteristic of sense realism and the one from which it derives its name. The conventional emphasis of other sense realists upon the universe as an object of study was not a part of Mulcaster's educational theorizing, although he did insist that all his pupils should participate in physical exercise and group sports.

The German Ratke was more interested in developing a spontaneous method of teaching than in discovering the essential qualities of man. Like Luther, he placed great emphasis upon the languages of the Bible, Latin, Greek, and Hebrew, and expected his students to acquire these as rapidly as possible. In Ratke's lower three grades the German vernacular was taught; in the upper grades the classical languages were approached through German. Ratke hoped to develop teachers able "to impart to their pupils a thorough, good, and fluent knowledge of any language—especially

Hebrew, Greek, and Latin, in less time . . . and also with less pains." In addition to language, Ratke stressed music, arithmetic, and religion. As far as the content of his instruction was concerned, he could hardly be called a true sense realist.

Francis Bacon was convinced that only a universal knowledge could be real and fruitful; thus, he felt, natural phenomena were the backbone and the sole subject matter worth presenting in school. His greatest desire was to advance knowledge rather than to leave it (on the part of both teacher and student) at the same stage that it had been found. The true educator, he said, "should labor as the bee, gathering where he can and working into a single structure all that he gathers." The teacher, by whom he meant anyone working to further existing knowledge, should turn to nature and contrive experiments which would reveal the cosmic secrets. The teacher should observe and weigh his observations, and collate his discoveries most carefully. From such scientific inductive investigations averred Bacon, come generalizations that make up the authentic perceptions of natural laws and their applications, which should be the true content of learning.[12]

In Solomon's House, the most distinctive feature of Atlantis, Bacon contrived to set up a high-level research institution, devoted to scientific investigation of all natural appearances, discovery of physical and biological laws, and harnessing the universe in the service of man. Of Solomon's House, Bacon wrote, "The End of our Foundation is the Knowledge of Causes, and Secrett Motions of Things; and the Enlarging of the bounds of the Humane Empire, to the Effecting of all Things possible. The Preparations and Instruments are these . . ." He then gave ten pages to describing the laboratories, experimental grounds, and equipment he judged necessary to discover the knowledge as yet unknown to mankind.

According to Bacon the greatest task of education is to learn the laws of nature, and the most important subject of education is science. Instead of superstition and false notions, the "idols" as he called them, of scholasticism and humanism, he planned to fill the curriculum with the true knowledge that comes from an inductive study of nature.[13] Bacon was more interested in educational content than in educational method. He concerned himself with the problem of discovering and classifying knowledge; he said that he had "taken all knowledge to be his province," nevertheless.

---

[12] Will Durant, *The Story of Civilization,* vol. vii, *The Age of Reason Begins* (New York: Simon and Schuster, Inc., 1961), pp. 173–176.

[13] Renowned for his advocacy of the inductive method, and thus the spirit of scientific investigation, Bacon is famous likewise for his conception of the "four idols," bars to clear and rigorous thought. These erroneous preconceptions in thinking Bacon labeled Idols (1) of the Tribe (human lack of objectivity); (2) of the Cave, or Den (ethnocentric, national, or other group inhibitions); (3) of the Marketplace (self-interest, the commercial aspects, or simply specious ignorance); (4) of the Theater (the mode, climate, or special context wrongly invoked).

Bacon's greatest weakness was his failure to appreciate the place of mathematics in science. He rejected the work of Copernicus largely because he did not understand its mathematical implications.

Comenius proposed an even wider curriculum than Bacon's. As had many other realists, Comenius overrated the capacity of the human mind for knowledge. He proposed a curriculum—all-comprehensive and encyclopedic in scope. Since he considered it the aim of education "to know all things, to do all things, to say all things," every subject was to be taught in his schools. He accepted Bacon's principle of utility and demanded that all useful knowledge should be taught, if not in all its details, at least in its general outlines. He included all the older subjects of the Trivium and Quadrivium—grammar, rhetoric, dialectic, arithmetic, geometry, astronomy, and music—and in addition included physics, geography, history, morals, and religion. He especially emphasized the value of history as "the most important element in a man's education, the eye of his whole life, as it were." He was especially insistent that manual and industrial arts and play activities be included in the curriculum, and he was the first to recognize play as an agency for building a healthy body and a normal mind. He even advocated the use of humor and wit as a part of the content of education.

In regard to linguistic content, Comenius emphasized the vernacular, but advocated the study of foreign languages for the sake of conversation with neighbors. He included Latin, Greek, and Hebrew in his secondary and higher schools, but was not too enthusiastic about most classical authors. The languages were never to be learned as ends in themselves, but always as means for the discussion of scientific and practical subjects. Latin was to be used as a supplement to the vernacular in acquiring a knowledge of the arts and sciences. In all his linguistic education, he shifted the emphasis from words to things.

In Comenius' "School of the Mother's Knee," the content was to be drawn from the various areas of the child's interest in things, manipulation, language, people. In Comenius' vernacular and Latin schools, these interests were to be further utilized: the interest in things was to lead to a study of natural phenomena, the interest in languages to the study of the mother tongue and then the Latin, the interest in manipulation to the study of the practical and fine arts, the interest in people to the study of history and literature. Thus Comenius' principle of curriculum organization was one of continuing at each higher level the studies begun in the level below.

Agencies

All these sense realists, with the exception of Bacon, were practical schoolmasters interested in the development of schools as the ideal agency of education. Even Bacon, who wrote little about the applications of his theories to concrete educational practice, devotes a section of *The New Atlantis* to a description of Solomon's House, his model educational institution for scientific investigation, a forerunner of the modern research university.

Mulcaster believed that education in schools was much more effective than education by tutors and insisted on the education of girls as well as boys. Although himself a secondary school headmaster, he contended that as much attention should be given to the development of the elementary schools as to the development of secondary and higher schools. He drew up a detailed plan for a six-year vernacular elementary school open to all. He was particularly interested in having school buildings situated to furnish plenty of light and air, and he favored ample playground space for every school.

Ratke, through the generosity of Prince Ludwig of Kothen, was able to demonstrate his educational theories in a model school. The state furnished him with a building and all the equipment necessary to try out his ideas with about 500 boys and girls. The school was doomed to early failure, but furnished a pattern for many of his followers to imitate.

Comenius also advocated schools as the best agency for education. He believed that educational objectives could be realized only by a carefully organized and clear-cut system. His was composed of four: (1) the School of the Mother's Knee, in every home; (2) the vernacular school, in every hamlet; (3) the Latin school, in every city; and (4) the university, in every province. He also mentions a "College of Light," similar to Bacon's Solomon's House—to be established for advanced research.

Comenius was a firm believer in the value of the textbook as an agency of instruction. Up to his time handbooks were scarce and expensive, and there was a serious lack of uniformity. Most schools were still following the medieval custom in which each pupil reproduced his own text from dictation by the teacher. But Comenius wanted all pupils to have a uniform text, covering the entire subject matter of the course. One of his greatest contributions to education was the development of textbooks; he prepared manuals for his School of the Mother's Knee and the vernacular school, but is best known for his many Latin texts.

All sense realists emphasized the importance of the teacher as an agency in education. They believed a trained instructor could study children and master the natural laws underlying sound educational practice. Mulcaster advocated the establishment of training schools, associated with the English universities. He insisted that teachers of young children should be especially well trained and well paid, since their work required the greatest teaching skill. Ratke and Comenius devoted most of their efforts to developing methods of teaching, so that educators might be more efficient in their work. They believed that the *method* of classroom instruction used by the teacher was the most important factor in educational success.

Early in the eighteenth century, certain new educational institutions were established in Germany embodying the conceptions of sense realism. The development of these supplemental agencies for sense realism was largely due to the Pietists, dissenters from the Lutheran faith, and their chief educational representative, August Hermann Francke (1663–1727). Francke developed a group of institutions at Halle, including the newly founded university, which emphasized scientific studies; a pedagogical seminar for the training of teachers for the new *Volksschule*; the *Pedagogium*, a secondary school combining the study of science and modern language with the older Latin and Greek classics. In Berlin Julius Hecker (1707–1768), established the *Realschule*, a secondary school in which the classics received little stress and in which pure and applied sciences dominated. This was the first of the *Realschulen* established throughout Germany, which even now offer an alternative to the classical *Gymnasien* in preparing German students for university studies.

Organization

The sense realists believed that school organization should be based upon the natural capacities of pupils and should follow the sequence of child development. They advocated, for the first time, a ladder system of organization. Mulcaster was in favor of a six-year vernacular elementary school for children from the ages of six to twelve. He insisted that this first stage of learning was most important and that all children were able to profit from elementary training in the vernacular. Since reading and writing, at least, should be the common right of all people, he urged coeducational universal attendance in these schools. But he did not think that all could profit from higher education in the classical languages; only those who were fitted for such education should attend the secondary schools and university. But by Mulcaster elementary education was considered of as much if not more value than higher education, and he believed that the study of the vernacular should precede both in time and importance the study of Latin. Those who were to continue in the Latin grammar schools and the university, as well as those who were not, should be thoroughly trained in the use of their native tongue, he felt.

Ratke's experimental school at Kothen was also organized on a six-year plan. This school represented a fusion of elementary and secondary education. It was divided into six classes. In the first three classes the vernacular was taught, in the fourth class the study of Latin was started, and in the sixth class the study of Greek. Ratke believed that the vernacular should be the medium of all instruction and that all other languages should be approached through it.

Of all the sense realists, Comenius made the foremost contribution to the theory of school organization. He suggested a complete graded system based upon the natural psychological development of the pupils, a consistent ladder plan of organization, with each school leading to the next. According to his scheme, there should be four educational periods, each of six years, starting with the instruction given in the home, or in the school of infancy, the School of the Mother's Knee. Comenius antedated the modern conceptions of preschool education by two centuries and set forth in detail what should be done in training the child during these formative years. For the next six years of childhood, from seven through twelve, Comenius advocated for all children a vernacular elementary school situated in every hamlet. For those who aspired to occupations higher than that of farm or workshop, the next six years, thirteen through eighteen, were to be spent in a Latin school, one of which was to be established in every city. The vernacular school was to train the senses and to give sensory experience; the purpose of the Latin school was to train the pupil to understand and systematically organize the information he had collected in the earlier period. The Latin school was not to be limited to the learned or higher classes, but was to be open to all who had the will and ability to profit by its instruction. Those who were of high moral character and could pass rigid examination were to be admitted to the university for six years, from nineteen through twenty-four, and a university was to be established in each province. Like Bacon, Comenius believed that scientific research could best be achieved through the cooperation of the learned men of all nations. He therefore urged the establishment of a research institution, the College of Light, somewhere at a strategic world center, where the great scientists of all countries could assemble and carry on their investigations. He believed that university graduates of superior ability should not only attend the College of Light but should also travel widely to have direct contact with human nature and institutions.

In the matter of administrative organization, Comenius' recommendations were equally advanced. He insisted that all schools should begin on the same date each year and that children should not be admitted except on the opening day. He believed in a very systematic organization of the schedule of classwork; each year, month, week, day, and hour was to have a definite task assigned to it. Each class was to have a separate room, a separate teacher, and separate textbooks. The schoolday was to be organized in agreement with child development. Older children were to study six hours a day; younger children were to study four. There was to be no homework and a half-hour period of relaxation was to follow each study period. Morning hours were to be devoted to intellectual subjects; afternoon hours were to be given to physical and esthetic subjects.

Comenius envisaged an educational ladder similar, though more superior in its organization, to the one that developed in American education more than two centuries later. He anticipated many contemporary principles of classroom organization and administration. For these and other reasons he has been called the father of modern education.

Methods

Of the sense realists' contributions to educational theory, the most noteworthy are those concerning methods of teaching. The sense realists believed that natural laws which could be discovered and formulated underlay the processes of learning; and they paved the way for later developments in child study and educational psychology. They insisted that knowledge comes through the senses and that the order of learning must be "things, thoughts, words."

Mulcaster urged that children be studied and their innate abilities respected. His psychological analysis of the three natural powers of children, "wit to conceive, memory to retain, discretion to discern," was not very penetrating, but was in the right direction. His desire to make use of the natural tendencies and activities of childhood through the use of games, plays, and exercises was sound.

As far as classroom methods were concerned, Bacon had nothing better to suggest than the successful practice of the Jesuits. His prescription, however, of the inductive method for the advancement of learning was of great educational significance. Bacon did not invent the inductive method, which had been practiced by Aristotle and really is as old as the human mind. What Bacon did was to state the procedure under which inductive reasoning operates: the removal of prejudices, the thorough observation by the senses, the careful tabulation of cases, study of exceptions as a check, the formulation of the generalization. In his *Novum Organum*, Bacon justified the use of this inductive method as the only true source of knowledge. Although Sir Francis himself did not apply the inductive method to school procedures, his thought paved the way for the use of observation and experimentation as classroom procedures; for the study of facts to formulate a hypothesis; for the selection, comparison, and classification of examples and instances; and for placing the emphasis upon the problem.

Ratke was the first educator to attempt to determine the natural order in which the mind develops. Although both Ratke and Comenius erred in basing their conclusions concerning the growth and development of children on mistaken analogies, they firmly established the concept that the true basis of educational method is the process of natural growth. Ratke undertook the shaping of an overall teaching method based on the following principles:

1. Everything in its natural order;
2. Teach only one thing at a time;
3. Let each thing be repeated often;
4. Teach everything first in the vernacular;
5. Teach everything without compulsion;
6. Let nothing be learned by rote;

7. Teach similar subjects in the same way;
8. First the *thing*, afterwards the explanation of the *thing*;
9. Everything to be taught through induction and experimentation.

Ratke was convinced that if his rules were followed the fruits of education would appear in a much shorter time.

Comenius, too, reasoned largely by analogy and based his psychology on the accepted modes of the seventeenth century. But perhaps he improved on Ratke's formulae, if only in terms of organization; and his principles of method are amazingly modern. The basis for all his teaching was the imitation of "nature's method." He observed:

> It is now quite clear that the order, which is the dominating principle in the art of teaching all things to all men, should be, and can be, borrowed from no other source but the operations of nature. As soon as this principle is thoroughly secured, the processes of art will proceed as easily and as spontaneously as those of nature. . . .
>
> Following in the footsteps of nature we find that the process of education will be easy
> (i.) If it begin early, before the mind is corrupted.
> (ii.) If the mind be duly prepared to receive it.
> (iii.) If it proceed from the general to the particular.
> (iv.) And from what is easy to what is more difficult.
> (v.) If the pupil be not overburdened by too many subjects.
> (vi.) And if progress be slow in every case.
> (vii.) If the intellect be forced to nothing to which its natural bent does not incline it, in accordance with its age and with the right method.
> (viii.) If everything be taught through the medium of the senses.
> (ix.) And if the use of everything taught be continually kept in view.
> (x.) If everything be taught according to one and the same method.[14]

Such were the principles and rules of method set forth by Comenius in his eminent educational classic, *The Great Didactic*. He was not only a theorist but a practitioner. He successfully applied his methods to classroom procedure and embodied them in his textbooks. His *Orbis Pictus* (1658), was the first illustrated school textbook, and his *Janua Linguarum Reserata* applied his new and better methods to the teaching of Latin.

---

[14] John Amos Comenius, *The Great Didactic*, ch. xiv, p. 7, ch. xvii, pp. 74–75, trans. by M. W. Keatinge in *Comenius* (New York: McGraw-Hill, Inc., 1931), p. 53. See also *John Amos Comenius, Selections,* introd. by Jean Piaget (Paris: United Nations Educational, Scientific and Cultural Organization, 1957), pp. 11–31. This work includes many passages from Comenius' less-familiar *The Labyrinth of the World and the Paradise of the Heart* (1623) as well as *The Great Didactic, The Pampaedia,* and *The Panorthosia*.

Comenius believed that his methods would make school a place of happiness and joy instead of drudgery and gloom, and that interest in work instead of the rod would become the agency of good discipline. He recognized the distinction between moral infractions and backwardness in studies and believed that the latter should be dealt with only through rebuke tempered with encouragement. Ratke also believed in a mild form of discipline. There was to be no constraint in his school; the teacher was to devote his wholehearted efforts to teaching; and the pupils were to keep order and good discipline.

There is an interesting story that Comenius was offered the presidency of Harvard College, founded a generation earlier in the American colonies of Great Britain, but this conceivably is myth.[15] It is clear, however, that the educational methods advocated by the Moravian bishop were greatly in advance of those of the religious moralists of colonial New England and that Harvard could have greatly benefited through Comenius' pansophism.

Another European-American tie of this realist period was the development of the new American secondary school, the public academy. Perhaps influenced from abroad (although this is debatable), this practical school first appeared in the colonies at the end of the seventeenth century. In 1751 the most famous of these was founded by Benjamin Franklin (1706–1790) in Philadelphia;[16] and within a few decades the academy, rapidly replacing the Latin grammar schools, became the prevailing type of secondary education for the American school system. These academies were at first designed to prepare for the activities of life and not for college, and were patronized by those desiring a nonclassical education leading to participation in business and trade. Franklin's academy, which became the nucleus of the University of Pennsylvania, was heralded enthusiastically in an advertisement published in the *Pennsylvania Gazette* on December 18, 1750:

> NOTICE is hereby given, That the Trustees of the ACADEMY of Philadelphia, intend (God willing) to open the same on the first Monday of January next; wherein Youth will be taught the Latin, Greek, English, French and German Languages, together with History, Geography,

---

[15] Yet no less an authority than Cotton Mather has recorded in his *Magnalia Christi Americana* (Hartford, Conn.: Silas Andrus, 1820), vol. ii, p. 10, the following memorial and tribute: "That brave old man, *Johannes Amos Commenius*, the *fame* of whose worth has been *Trumpetted* as far as more than *three* languages (whereof everyone is endebted unto his JANUA) could carry it, was indeed agreed withal, by one Mr. *Winthrop* in his travels through the *Low Countries*, to come over into *New-England,* and illuminate their *Colledge* and *Country*, in the quality of a *President*. But the solicitations of the *Swedish* Ambassador diverting him another way, that incomparable *Moravian* became not an *American*." The date was 1654 and the occasion the resignation of President Dunster.

[16] See James Mulhern, *A History of Secondary Education in Pennsylvania* (Philadelphia: The Author, 1933), pp. 174–216, for a complete account of the academy's founding.

Chronology, Logic, and Rhetoric; also Writing, Arithmetic, Merchants Accounts, Geometry, Algebra, Surveying, Gauging, Navigation, Astronomy, Drawing in Perspective, and other Mathematical Sciences; with Natural and Mechanical Philosophy, & c., agreeable to the Constitutions heretofore published, at the rate of Four Pounds per annum, and Twenty Shillings entrance fee.

First, we are struck by the multiplicity of offerings and breadth of the program of instruction; second, we remember that by 1750 academies had already been organized in several of the colonies.[17] Thus, the Philadelphia Academy was not the first of a new type of school, as its backers suggested, but institutionalized the movement, being chartered and perhaps instituted on a stronger basis than some of its predecessors. Furthermore, because of Franklin's connection with this school, perhaps wider publicity surrounded its inception. The pragmatic methodology, too, undoubtedly attracted.

Academies were usually open to both sexes and were private educational institutions, although many were supported by generous endowments, gifts, or state subsidies (as in New York). Their curricula were broad, as indicated by the Philadelphia example, and generally included modern languages as well as English grammar and composition, the sciences, drawing, mathematics, history, and many practical arts. Most importantly in our own study, until the establishment of normal schools for teacher preparation (the first started in 1827) these academies were almost the sole educational institutions for elementary teachers in the United States.

REFERENCES

Bacon, Francis, *Novum Organum.* Trans. by William Wood. Chicago: Henry Regnery for Great Books Foundation, 1949.

——, *Novum Organum.* Trans. by Fulton H. Anderson. New York: Liberal Arts Press, 1960. Pp. 33–268.

Barnes, Harry Elmer, *An Intellectual and Cultural History of the Western World.* New York: Random House, Inc., 1937. Pp. 669–705.

Boyd, William, *The History of Western Education,* 8th ed. Rev. by Edmund J. King. New York: Barnes and Noble, 1966. Pp. 46–48, 222–223, 234–237, 240–244, 269–271.

Browning, Oscar (Ed.), *Milton's Tractate of Education, A Facsimile Reprint from the Edition of 1673.* London: Cambridge University Press, 1905. Pp. 8–9.

Burnham, William H., *Great Teachers and Mental Health.* New York: Appleton-Century-Crofts, 1926. Pp. 141–187.

---

[17] For a painstaking account of the founding of academies in the United States generally see Theodore R. Sizer (Ed.), *The Age of the Academies* (New York: Teachers College Press, Columbia University, 1965).

Butts, R. Freeman, *A Cultural History of Western Education,* 2d ed. New York: McGraw-Hill, Inc., 1955. Pp. 217–239, 267–299.

Cantor, Norman F., *The English, A History of Politics and Society to 1760.* New York: Simon and Schuster, Inc., 1967. Pp. 400–449.

Clough, Shepard B., *The Rise and Fall of Civilization.* New York: McGraw-Hill, Inc., 1951. Pp. 191–216.

Cole, Luella, *A History of Education, Socrates to Montessori.* New York: Holt, Rinehart and Winston, Inc., 1950. Pp. 328–355, 356–397.

Cubberley, Ellwood P., *The History of Education.* Boston: Houghton Mifflin Company, 1920. Pp. 379–427.

Durant, Will, *The Story of Civilization,* pt. vii, *The Age of Reason Begins.* New York: Simon and Schuster, Inc., 1961. Pp. 166–183, 399–415, 582–583.

Eby, Frederick, and Charles F. Arrowood, *The Development of Modern Education.* Englewood Cliffs, N.J.: Prentice-Hall, Inc., 1934. Pp. 200–288.

Gide, André, *The Living Thought of Montaigne.* New York: Longman Green & Co., 1939 (W. C. Black Edition).

Good, Harry G., *A History of Western Education.* New York: Crowell-Collier and Macmillan, Inc., 1960. Pp. 170–200.

Graves, Frank P., *Great Educators of Three Centuries.* New York: Crowell-Collier and Macmillan, Inc., 1912. Pp. 1–51.

———, *Peter Ramus and the Educational Reformation.* New York: Crowell-Collier and Macmillan, Inc., 1912.

Gross, Richard E. (Ed.), *Heritage of American Education.* Boston: Allyn and Bacon, Inc., 1962. Pp. 288–301.

Knight, Edgar W., *Twenty Centuries of Education.* Boston: Ginn & Company, 1940. Pp. 188–209, 343–346.

Mayer, Frederick, *A History of Educational Thought.* Columbus, Ohio: Charles E. Merrill Books, Inc., 1960. Pp. 199–221.

Messenger, James F., *An Interpretative History of Education.* Thomas Y. Crowell Company, 1931. Pp. 141–155.

Monroe, Paul, *A Textbook in the History of Education.* New York: Crowell-Collier and Macmillan, Inc., 1933. Pp. 442–502.

Montaigne, Michel Eyquem de, *The Complete Works of Montaigne.* Trans. by Donald M. Frame. Stanford, Calif.: Stanford University Press, 1957. Pp. 110ff.

———, *The Complete Essays of Montaigne.* Trans. by Donald M. Frame. Stanford, Calif.: Stanford University Press, 1958. Pp. 106–131.

Mulhern, James, *A History of Education,* 2d ed. New York: The Ronald Press Company, 1959. Pp. 328–372.

Nakosteen, Mehdi, *The History and Philosophy of Education.* New York: The Ronald Press Company, 1965. Pp. 271–301.

Power, Edward J., *Main Currents in the History of Education.* New York: McGraw-Hill, Inc., 1962. Pp. 329–363.

Quick, Robert H., *Educational Reformers.* New York: Appleton-Century-Crofts, 1904. Pp. 63–79, 103–171.

Rabelais, François, *Gargantua and Pantagruel—The Five Books*. Trans. by Jacques Le Clercq. New York: Heritage Press, 1942.

Ulich, Robert, *History of Educational Thought*. New York: American Book Company, 1950. Pp. 162–199.

——, *Philosophy of Education*. New York: American Book Company, 1961. Pp. 63–64, 112, 208, 215.

—— (Ed.), *Three Thousand Years of Educational Wisdom*, 2d ed., enl. Cambridge, Mass.: Harvard University Press, 1954. Pp. 305–346.

Wender, Herbert, *The Growth of Modern Thought and Culture*. New York: Philosophical Library, Inc., 1959. Pp. 59–82.

SELECTED PAPERBACKS

Bacon, Francis, *Selected Writings*. Ed. by Hugh G. Dick. New York: Random House, Inc., 1955.

Beck, Robert Holmes, *A Social History of Education*. Englewood Cliffs, N.J.: Prentice-Hall, Inc., 1965.

Comenius, John Amos, *Selections*. Introd. by Jean Piaget. Paris: United Nations Educational, Scientific, and Cultural Organization, 1957.

Hampshire, Stuart (Ed.), *The Age of Reason: The Seventeenth Century Philosophers*. New York: New American Library of World Literature, Inc., 1950.

Jones, Richard Foster, *Ancients and Moderns, A Study of the Rise of the Scientific Movement in the Seventeenth Century*, 2d ed. Berkeley: University of California Press, 1965.

Montaigne, Michel Eyquem de, *The Essay*, vol. i. Trans. by John Florio. New York: Oxford University Press, 1924.

——, *Selections from the Essays of Montaigne*. Trans. and ed. by Donald M. Frame. New York: Appleton-Century-Crofts, 1948.

More, Sir Thomas, *A Dialogue of Comfort Against Tribulation*. Ed. by Leland Miles. Bloomington, Ind.: Indiana University Press, 1965.

——, *Utopia*. Trans. by Peter K. Marshall. New York: Washington Square Press, 1960.

Morris, Edward E. (Ed.), *Milton, Tractate of Education*. London: Macmillan & Co., Ltd., 1895.

Muller, Herbert J., *The Uses of the Past, Profiles of Former Societies*. New York: New American Library of World Literature, 1952.

Piaget, Jean (Ed.), *John Amos Comenius on Education*. New York: Teachers College Press, Columbia University, 1967. Text similar to 1957 UNESCO publication.

Sizer, Theodore R. (Ed.), *The Age of the Academies*. New York: Bureau of Publications, Teachers College, Columbia University, 1965.

Viorst, Milton (Ed.), *The Great Documents of Western Civilization*. New York: Bantam Books, Inc., 1965.

CHAPTER 13

Formal Discipline and the Appeal to Reason

It will perhaps be wondered that I mention reasoning with children: and yet I cannot but think that the true way of dealing with them. They understand it as early as they do language; and if I misobserve not, they love to be treated as rational creatures sooner than is imagined.[1]

TWO NEW DIRECTIONS

The Renaissance humanists, maintaining that it had little value for actual life, had rejected the theological dialectic of scholasticism. And they turned to the classical literature of Greece and Rome as "the humanities replaced the divinities." In these classics they found a content they judged sufficient to enrich their lives and bring a new knowledge of the human activities and institutions that had in ages past contributed to the rich and full careers of statesmen and philosophers, of archons and emperors. But the study of classical languages and literature in a short time degenerated into Ciceronianism, and the liberal spirit of the older broad humanism was lost.

Consequently, the first half of the eighteenth century was characterized by two reactions: (1) the rise of the doctrine of formal discipline and (2) the development of a coterie devoted to the defense of reason. Formal discipline in education arose to defend classical humanism against the advances of realism; an aristocracy of reason appeared and, as rationalism became its educational goal, checked the movement toward a democratic and universal system of education as advocated by Comenius and others. There were, however, good and sufficient reasons for this about-face.

---

[1] John Locke, *Some Thoughts on Education*, abridg. and ed. by F. W. Garforth (Woodbury, N.Y.: Barron's Educational Services, Inc., 1964).

Although the great humanist leaders of the Renaissance and pre-Reformation had viewed classical education as the accepted means of training in secondary and higher schools, to the seventeenth-century mind, this linguistic and literary curriculum was justified only by two centuries of use and by the details of classroom procedure and techniques for instruction which had developed to such a high degree of perfection.

It had not been difficult for the sense realists to demonstrate that linguistic training in the classical languages had little practical value. Among the Protestant churches Latin had ceased to be the language of religion. Services were conducted and the Bible and other religious books were read in the vernacular, although the clergy continued to use Greek and Hebrew in their study of original Biblical sources. Latin was retained as an official language only by the Roman Catholic Church. By the end of the seventeenth century Latin had ceased to be the sole language of the universities; it had become less and less the medium for scientific discussion and was no longer the only approach to the knowledge of human achievement and human thought. Latin literature was rapidly being replaced by a new interest in the vernacular. Therefore, classical education could no longer be justified on the basis of practical values. If it were to survive, it had to find a new justification and a new defense. Such a defense was found in the doctrine of disciplinism, or formal discipline.

Both the reformers and the realists had been instrumental in advancing the cause of popular and universal education. While Luther had insisted on special classical training for those who were destined to serve state and society as preachers, doctors, teachers, and civil magistrates, he had also demanded religious and vocational training for the masses. The Calvinists had insisted upon elementary education for the common people. In the cities and towns of the Netherlands especially, public efforts were made to make elementary education compulsory for all children; and upon the civil authorities was laid the duty of establishing schools where children of every class of society might learn to read. Among both Protestant and Catholic reformers, the movement for universal popular education was growing slowly but surely, and the realist philosophy added momentum. Comenius advanced the most democratic conception of education formulated until recent years in his demands for the education of all children, "Not the children of the rich and the powerful only, but of all alike, boys and girls, both noble and ignoble, rich and poor, in all cities and towns, villages and hamlets, should be sent to school."

The movement for popular education found support not only among the Protestants but also among some of the Catholic teaching orders. Impelled by a sense of duty and piety and a desire to build Christian character, philanthropic societies were organized and missionary teachers sent out to educate the masses. The Protestant Pietists of Germany took great pains to educate the poor and give religious instruction to all classes. In England, the Society for the Propagation of the Gospel in Foreign Parts (Episcopal) carried popular education into the North American colonies, and La Salle's Brothers of the Christian Schools performed a similar function for Roman Catholics.

It is hardly surprising that these democratic conceptions were opposed by some in positions of power in government and church. The blunt point of view held by the aristocratic opponents of popular education was succinctly expressed by Governor William Berkeley of the British colony Virginia (1671) when he said, "I thank God there are no free schools nor printing; and I hope that we shall not have these for a hundred years; for learning has brought disobedience and heresy. . . . God keep us from both." This class view was presented also by Cardinal Richelieu, French statesman and cleric, who laid the foundation of power for Louis XIV, in similar words:

> Although the knowledge of letters is eminently necessary for a country, it is certain that they need not be taught to everybody. . . . If letters were profaned for all types of mind, one would see more people ready to raise doubts than to solve them; and many would be more ready to oppose truth than to defend it.

The rationalists advanced another aristocratic conception of education; yet the aristocracy they espoused was not one of lineage or breeding, but an aristocracy of brains and talent. Creating such a group was a meritorious idea, but it implied a Platonic type of social order dedicated to seeking and developing individual capacity and, hence, the creation of a society in which the elite should rule; those thought inferior would not necessarily be discriminated against, but would remain in positions of little prestige or power. Obviously, a hard and fast line cannot be drawn between disciplinism and rationalism.

In considering the two conservative movements of formal discipline and rationalism, we shall give particular attention to the work of the English Puritan, John Locke (1632–1704), philosopher, political economist, and educational theorist, whose thought merged so many currents that it is often called eclectic.[2] In recommending an encyclopedic curriculum he resembled the literary realists; in his distrust of existing schools and his recommendation of the tutorial system and travel, he resembled the sense realists. Yet in his most effective contributions to education he wrote along the lines of conservatism and rationalism. From Locke's *Essay Concerning the Human Understanding,* his *Some Thoughts on Education*, and his *Conduct of the Understanding* we can select his contributions to the conservative and ratiocinative movements of the late seventeenth and

---

[2] For profiles of both Locke and his contemporary Sir William Petty, see Robert Ulich (Ed.), *Three Thousand Years of Educational Wisdom*, 2d ed., enl. (Cambridge, Mass.: Harvard University Press, 1954), pp. 347–382.

eighteenth centuries. These contributions were almost as important in America as in Europe.

EDUCATIONAL ATTITUDES OF THE DISCIPLINISTS

It is most desirable that considerable attention be given to the disciplinary conception of education, for it dominated schools from the time of Locke and Petty through the mid-nineteenth century and is still very much in evidence, especially at the secondary and higher levels, and in private preparatory or high schools. (We should realize, however, that Locke is not responsible for all that developed within his century; some of his views support disciplinism and some do not.)

The doctrine of the efficacy of formal discipline is based on habituation, the ideas that practice makes perfect and one is shaped by his habits, and stressed the value of processes of learning, rather than the value of the things learned. In this respect disciplinism was but a revival and a new defense of the formalism of medieval scholasticism and Ciceronianism. This new justification of narrow classical humanism was welcomed by those who looked upon education from a religious viewpoint. The leaders of the Church of Rome, and the Protestant moralists as well, had considered the realistic movements, especially sense realism, irreligious and atheistic; and we find in this antagonism the beginning of opposition by some theological sources to scientific education. The church was glad to have a new defense for the subject matter which extreme realism sought to displace. The church was familiar with the idea of discipline in all its aspects: monasticism had been a moral discipline, mysticism a spiritual discipline, scholasticism an intellectual discipline, chivalry a social and physical discipline. By emphasizing education as the eradication of man's essential evil and as the development of high moral character, religious thought provided a parallel background for the educational theory of disciplinism.

The disciplinary concept of education was also in accord with the traditional psychological theories current at the time. Aristotelian faculty psychology, still accepted in the seventeenth century, held that the mind was made up of certain "faculties" such as attention, memory, observation, and reason. One who had trained his faculties well could use them effectively. Education consisted of habituating the faculties of the mind by appropriate disciplines or exercises.

The disciplinary concept of education has always been popular with many people; church leaders have liked it because it adheres closely to their religious doctrines, classical scholars because it justifies their favorite subjects, teachers because it provides them with a simple technique and a definite goal, parents because they understand it and think its results are salutary for their children. Even many psychologists liked disciplinism until faculty psychology was dethroned by modern psychological investigations.

Whether Locke pioneered the doctrine of formal discipline has been debated. Some writers give Locke credit for the disciplinary theory and claim he formulated and elaborated it, and it seems that this many-sided thinker did develop and support certain aspects of the theory. But he was by no means responsible for many of the ideas and practices that have been advocated under the name of formal discipline. Many who claimed to be followers of Locke carried his educational doctrines to ridiculous extremes.

Aims

The ultimate aim of disciplinism was the formation of character in its broadest sense. This involved the cultivation of the whole man—moral, physical, mental. Locke, for example, believed that the development of the body was an essential concomitant of the development of mind and morals. Like the Greeks, his motto was, "A sound mind in a sound body." Physical, mental, and moral prowess result from rigorous exercises of body, mind, and self-control, he believed. The immediate aim of education is to provide these exercises, Locke stated:

> The great work of a governor is to fashion the carriage and to form the mind, to settle in his pupils good habits and the principles of virtue and wisdom . . . to give him vigor, activity and industry. The studies which he sets him upon are but, as it were, the exercise of his faculties . . . to teach him application and accustom him to take pains.[3]

The theory of formal discipline, therefore, maintained that it is not the thing learned, but the process of learning that is the important aim of education. Locke stood for the belief that mental power is more important than knowledge acquired through study. Thus he set up as the aim of mathematics the making of rational creatures, as the aim of reading the development of discrimination. He believed that all intellectual capacities were the result of practice, which he considered analogous in body and mind: "As it is in the body, so it is in the mind."

The aim of disciplinism was to provide the exercise, or disciplines, for training the mind as well as for hardening the body and for developing self-control. The disciplinist sought to develop by exercise desirable physical, moral, and mental habits. His whole plan of education was to habituate his pupils to effective and desirable ways of thinking and acting. He believed that the mind of the child at birth is a blank tablet, a *tabula rasa*, and

---

[3] John Locke, *Some Thoughts on Education,* The Library of Education, vol. i (Boston, 1830), par. 88. See also Peter Gay (Ed.), *John Locke on Education,* Classics in Education, no. 20 (New York: Bureau of Publications, Teachers College Press, Columbia University, 1964).

development comes only through the formation of habits through discipline. For the disciplinist, the work of education is to form specific habits and to develop intellectual capacities through exercise; the educative process is to increase the powers of the individual, rather than to enlarge his stock of knowledge.

Types

Locke emphasized three major types of education: physical, moral, and intellectual. He accordingly advocated (1) vigor of body, (2) good breeding and wise conduct, and (3) mental power. He stressed character education, or education of the whole man. Locke believed in a broad type of education and never confused education with mere instruction. But there is a great divergence between Locke's view and the views of the later disciplinarians, who thought of education only as an intellectual discipline. Locke himself started all education with bodily exercises. The first paragraphs of his *Thoughts Concerning Education* are devoted to a discussion of physical education:

> Thus I have done with what concerns the body and health, which reduces itself to these few and easy observable rules; plenty of open air, exercise, and sleep, plain diet, no wine or strong drink, and very little or no physic, not too warm and straight clothing, especially the head and feet kept cold, and the feet often used to cold water and exposed to wet.[4]

After physical education, Locke placed moral education, the control of the desires by reason. He speaks of virtue as "the hard and valuable part to be aimed at in education." Intellectual education was placed last in order of importance by Locke, whereas the later disciplinarians have advanced it to a place of first if not sole importance.

Content

The exponents of formal discipline were usually satisfied with a limited curriculum. They contended that the intellectual powers of memorizing and reasoning, developed through the study of the right kind of subject matter, could be used in mastering other subjects or in meeting the experiences of daily life. Since they were confident that the classical languages and mathematics were best adapted to training the mental powers of memory and reasoning, they considered it unnecessary to teach other subjects. They alleged that the student who developed his mind through the study of these subjects could readily master of his own accord the easier practical subjects and meet all the demands of vocational, political, and social life. The disciplinarian built his curriculum on the theory that these few well-organized linguistic and mathematical studies, with their

---

[4] Gay, pp. 25–26, par. 30.

orderly arrangement of parts, their universality of principles, their perfected techniques of method, were sufficient for a liberal education.

Locke certainly would not have favored the curriculum that the later disciplinarians advocated. In his discussion of the content of education in *Thoughts on Education*, he is in agreement with the realists, especially in the matter of the intellectual subjects. The content he recommended was quite different from that of the grammar school curriculum of his day. He considered intellectual study of less importance than physical and social training. Although he considered Greek essential to the scholar, he thought it quite unnecessary in the education of a gentleman. While Locke advocated the retention of Latin, he did not do so on disciplinarian grounds; such a justification was advanced by his followers. He was opposed to the linguistic exercises the humanists used in their teaching of Latin; he was more concerned with developing the ability to read Latin than to speak or write it. Locke emphasized the value of being able to speak and write the English vernacular; he said that French, as well as Latin, should be learned by the conversational method. He suggested additions to the curriculum such as drawing, geography, history, anatomy, ethics, dancing, and a few practical and fine arts as hobbies and recreations. In view of such recommendations, it is difficult to see how the later disciplinarians used Locke to justify their narrow formalized curriculum. Yet Locke really discussed the curriculum from two points of view. In his *Thoughts on Education* he considered the kinds of information needed in the education of an English gentleman, and he spoke as a utilitarian and a realist; in his *Conduct of the Understanding* he discussed the kinds of exercises and drills needed to train and develop the mind, and here he advocated disciplinism.

Locke's discussion of the place of mathematics in the curriculum justifies calling him a disciplinarian and probably had the greatest influence upon the later advocates of formal discipline. Locke repeatedly emphasized the value of mathematics in the training of the reasoning faculty; for example, he asked:

> Would you have a man reason well, you must . . . exercise his mind. . . . Nothing does this better than mathematics, which, therefore, I think should be taught to all those who have the time and opportunity; not so much to make them mathematicians, as to make them reasonable creatures . . . that having got the way of reasoning, which that study necessarily brings the mind to, they might be able to transfer it to other parts of knowledge, as they shall have occasion.[5]

Such statements led those who wished to keep the classic languages in the schools to use the disciplinarian theory to retain their hold upon

---

[5] John Locke, *The Works of John Locke*, vol. iii, *Of the Conduct of the Understanding*. New ed. in 10 vols., reprint of 1823 ed. (Germany: Scientia Verlag Aalen, 1963), pp. 220, 222.

education. In the study of Latin and Greek they saw the same training in reasoning and transfer of reasoning power that Locke seemed to see in mathematics. The justification that Locke used for the inclusion of mathematics in the curriculum, the classicists used for the linguistic study of Greek and Latin. Even the later scientific realists came to defend the place of scientific studies in the curriculum in terms of their value in the development of the mental powers.

In the elementary schools, the disciplinary concept gave a new stimulus to drill subjects such as spelling, arithmetic, and formal grammar, and postponed the addition of content subjects such as history, geography, and the elementary sciences. Instead of considering these drill subjects for their value in the development of useful and practical habits, the disciplinarians valued them for their contributions to the development of the general powers of the mind.

Agencies and Organization

Formal discipline gave few new agencies or organizations of education; it tended to preserve the traditional organization of the existing schools. The fact that great minds had been developed by these traditional means provided a sufficient excuse for their continuation; and the established schoolmasters seized upon this reason to perpetuate themselves and their institutions. The grammar schools of England and America, the *Gymnasien* of Germany, and colleges and universities everywhere found in this doctrine a defense for the continuation of their traditional organization and practices.

Locke distrusted the existing schools and, like the social realists, advocated the tutorial system as the best agency for educating the young gentleman. He had the typical attitude of the English aristocrat toward the education of the common people. Like Montaigne, he believed that any training the masses received could best be obtained in the workhouse or by apprenticeship.

Locke's recipe emphasized the proper selection of a tutor, and he advised:

> To form a young gentleman, as he should be, it is fit his governor should himself be well-bred, understand the ways of carriage, and measures of civility, in all the variety of persons, times, and places; and keep his pupil, as much as his age requires, constantly to the observation of them. This is an art not to be learnt, nor taught by books: nothing can give it but good company and observation joined together. . . . Breeding is that which sets a gloss upon all his other good qualities, and renders them useful to him, in procuring him the esteem and good will of all that comes near. Without good breeding, his other accomplishments make him pass but for proud, conceited, vain, or foolish.[6]

---

[6] Locke, vol. ix, *Some Thoughts Concerning Education*, p. 78.

But it was not the tutorial system that became the great instrument of disciplinism; it was the humanistic secondary school and college and the religiously motivated church elementary school. These schools were organized entirely in terms of physical, moral, and intellectual discipline well into the nineteenth century. In the English secondary schools, the whole course of from six to nine years was given to Latin and Greek prose composition and to the writing of Latin verse.

The extent to which the early American Latin grammar school and college were organized and articulated by the disciplinarian philosophy is indicated in the following statement of admission requirements for Harvard College in 1642:

> When any scholar is able to understand Tully [Cicero] or such like classical author extempore, and make and speak true Latin in verse and prose . . . and decline perfectly the Paradigms of Nouns and Verbs in the Greek tongue, let him then, and not before, be capable of admission into the College.

Until 1850 at Oxford and until 1851 at Cambridge, the subjects for entrance examination had to be chosen only from the classics and mathematics.

The disciplinary conception was exemplified by the German *Gymnasien* until the twentieth century, by the great public schools of England until the end of the nineteenth century, by the Latin grammar schools in America until the nineteenth century when popular academies replaced them. Even today in many countries schoolmasters help preserve the theory of formal discipline by defending the old formal grammar, Latin, algebra, and geometry as the most important subjects in the curriculum, on the grounds that they produce great minds through training in logical thinking.

Methods

As a rule, the disciplinarians continued the formal methods of the Ciceronians; for formal discipline provided new justification for these monotonous and uninteresting devices of learning. Locke's disciplinism is more clear in the area of methods than in aims and content. He based all his educational procedure on the laws of habit formation; his educational techniques were devised to habituate pupils to desirable ways of thinking and acting. Learning, to Locke, was thus largely a matter of exercise and drill, whether physical, moral, or intellectual.

Nevertheless, Locke had a much broader conception of the educational process than did the later disciplinarians. He recognized three distinct steps in learning: (1) sensation, (2) memory, and (3) reasoning; and his idea of drill was an exercise of all three of these faculties. He believed sense impressions formed the basis of learning, and so sense training was of the first importance. He claimed that although sense impressions and experiences make up the content of knowledge, they must be retained through memory to be of value. He urged that memory training be stressed, since retained knowledge is the raw material for the higher and more important mental processes involved in reasoning. Reasoning he considered the most important aspect of the educational process.

Later disciplinarians overlooked the importance of sense training and concentrated on drill in formal memorizing and formal reasoning. They retained the emphasis upon habit formation, but restricted their efforts, at least in the intellectual field, to forming habits of rote memorizing and logical associations. Instead of drilling with useful material, they concentrated on subject matter that was merely difficult. They confused the uninteresting with the difficult, and took it for granted that a subject painful to the student was valuable as an exercise in developing memory and reasoning. Locke himself had urged that the educational process be made as pleasant as possible for the child, and was opposed to severity. He suggested pleasurable methods of study and play devices to make drills interesting. He never implied that a subject had disciplinary value just because it was hard and dry.

The disciplinary schools and schoolmasters, however, soon developed a severe authoritative methodology. They believed that physical and mental powers, and powers of moral control would result only from rigorous exercises of body, mind, and conduct. The work of the schools became a process of physical, mental, and moral gymnastics, by which the body, mind, and conscience were to be strengthened and trained in the right directions. The body was to be trained by hardening exercise, the conscience by the constant checking of natural desires, the mind by continual exercises in memorizing rote material and reasoning with abstract and logical material.

In all schools dominated by the disciplinary concept, authority was exerted with the utmost severity. Corporal punishment was used extensively for even the slightest offenses and deficiencies. Not only did the masters themselves rule with the utmost severity but fagging and hazing developed, in which the older boys undertook to discipline the younger.

Locke believed in utilizing the motive of approval rather than the motive of fear. He advocated the use of praise and censure, the former to be administered in public, but the latter only in private. Corporal punishment was to be resorted to only in cases of obstinacy, which he considered the root of many later evils.

With Robert Ulich, "One might ask how it came about that for two centuries or more the ideas of the Commonwealth educators [William Petty, John Durie, Samuel Hartlib, and John Milton, for example] and of Comenius were condemned to oblivion, whereas John Locke's treatise . . . became a classic."[7] The simplest answer is Ulich's, "that

---

[7] *History of Educational Thought* (New York: American Book Company, 1950), p. 200.

Locke provided for the educated Englishman of the eighteenth century the right mixture of progress and conservatism."[8] Locke's prestige in political science and philosophy secured a wider reading of his *Thoughts Concerning Education*. Locke provided just the image of the English gentleman eighteenth-century England was seeking, an image close in many respects to the Greek and Roman equivalents of the Hellenistic age and that provided by Plutarch.

RATIONALISM AS AN EDUCATIONAL PHILOSOPHY

Rationalism was originally intended to offer a protest against arbitrary authority in church and state. Its ultimate results, however, led to a reaction against the newly awakening forces of democracy and universal education and against the rise of downtrodden or neglected classes. In its appeal to reason rather than the hampering restrictions of tradition and authority, the ratiocinative movement was praiseworthy; in its disregard of the needs of the masses and the right of the common man, it was reactionary.

Yet such a movement was sorely needed. The early eighteenth century was a period of bigotry in religious and social life and despotic absolutism in government. After the first flush of the Reformation had paled under the hatreds of the religious wars, worship among both Protestants and Catholics had settled down to a rigid conformity to dogmas and practices, from which no divergences were allowed. Religious creeds and social conduct were based upon supernaturalism and revelation; the authority for all phases of life rested upon precedent rather than reason.

Government by divine right was in the hands of sovereigns who ruled as benevolent despots at their best and absolutist tyrants at their worst. England alone had achieved a limited constitutional monarchy through its Bill of Rights, but this was a victory for Parliament and not for the common people. In Prussia, Austria, Russia, and Spain, legislative assemblies rarely met; but the benevolent despots in power, although they ruled autocratically, did make an attempt to improve the conditions of the masses in the interest of their nationalistic ambitions, giving expression to the oft-quoted statement, "Everything for the people, but nothing by the people." In France, absolutism shorn of all benevolent interests in the common people bore its most terrible fruits. The magnificent and luxurious court at Versailles, infested by hypocritical sycophants and extravagant idlers, rested on an impoverished, overtaxed, submerged population.

Two powerful social institutions, an arrogant church and a despotic state, joined together to check the individual freedom that had been the fruit of the Renaissance, and to curtail the recognition of the needs of the

---

[8] Ulich, *History*, p. 200.

common man first made by the reformers. What was needed was a force powerful enough to break the bonds of an autocratic authority based largely upon custom and traditions, and to secure for the common man the right to think and act for himself. Rationalism provided such a force, but in limiting reasoning power to the aristocratic few, it failed to realize fully its possibilities. Rationalism succeeded in attacking political absolutism and the dogmatism of the contemporary Christian church, but it neglected the needs of the peasants and workers. Essentially an aristocratic movement, its goals were limited to the attainment of rational freedom for the few.

Not a new conception, this questioning of all sanctions other than that of the intellect, or "autonomy of thought," had proceeded from Stoicism and Cynicism through Cicero and the medieval gadfly, Peter Abelard. Its essential view was that reason alone possessed the capability for discerning all truths, religious and moral as well as mundane; thought could perceive, by its own volition and without assistance from supernatural agencies or sense perception, a system of eternal verity.

Modern rationalism first arose in England. Herbert of Cherbury (1583–1648) began a movement critical of revelation, which was later espoused by Locke and Newton and led to the growth of English deism. In Germany Christian Wolff, Gotthold Lessing, Moses Mendelssohn, and Hermann Reimarus shared in rationalistic activities leading to the *Aufklärung*, a northern revival of interest in self-realization, general education and culture, and emancipation from prejudice, although Baron Gottfried Wilhelm von Leibnitz (1646–1716) is perhaps the best-known German rationalist philosopher of this period. Baruch Spinoza (1632–1677) in the Netherlands accepted pantheism and, somewhat earlier, René Descartes (1596–1650) in France had used reason as a buttress for religious truth in the realm of faith.

In England, while rationalism fostered deism, its influence was largely political. Although Locke never renounced Christianity, he upheld reason as the chief faculty to be developed. In his zeal for the development and use of the individual's mind, he emphasized that rational freedom makes possible a reign of reason, and in this respect he was the first rationalist. His views influenced Hume and Berkeley in their philosophical speculations and advanced the development of English skepticism and deism.

It was in France, however, that the worship of reason reached its zenith. Influenced by Locke's empiricism and the rationalistic philosophy of Descartes, which had glorified the supremacy of reason and provided an exact method of verifying truth and discovering the invariable laws of nature, François Voltaire (1694–1778) headed the movement at Paris where it received a warm welcome. The rationalistic theory was more completely elaborated by a group of men known as the Encyclopedists. Their leader was Denis Diderot (1713–1784), editor of the French *Encyclopedia* then being written; other prominent members of the group were Helvetius,

Holbach, Montesquieu, Turgot, Condillac, and La Mettrie. These French rationalists called themselves *illuminati*; hence the rationalistic movement is often spoken of as the Enlightenment. In America rationalism founds its chief vehicle in Thomas Paine's *Age of Reason.*

Aims

The rationalistic aim of education was to train those capable of reasoning so that they could throw off the "binding shackles" of religious, political, and social authority which they maintained restricted their intellectual freedom. Their objective was to enable men to think for themselves, to test all things human and divine by the power of reason. The ultimate purpose was to free the individual intellect from all repression.

Rationalism aimed at developing an individual who could control all the aspects of his life by means of a coldly critical reason and who could suppress all spontaneous enthusiasm and feeling. The rationalist realized that this aim was attainable by few individuals; and so the rationalistic philosophy of life and aim in education were applied only to the upper classes. In a sense, rationalism aimed at the education of the young gentleman as much as did disciplinism. Rationalism was directed toward teaching the youth to think for himself, control his passions by reason, avoid all display of vulgar feeling, and live the reasonable life of a highly artificial society. Thus philosophy aimed at the intellectual education of the few so that reason might replace tradition and dogmatism among those who controlled society, and the educated classes as a whole might be dominated by reason. The aim of the rationalist was to build a new aristocracy of intelligence to replace the old aristocracy of family, position, and the church, a new aristocracy of talent to replace the old aristocracy of blood.

Thus, the aims of Voltaire and the *illuminati* were in many ways negative and destructive. While they attempted to prevent dogmatism, tradition, superstition, prejudice, passion, injustice, ecclesiastical privilege, and absolute despotism from adversely affecting the lives of intelligent people, they did little to develop the reasoning power, which they praised so highly, to a point where it would become a guide to better living and a means for solving the problems of private and institutional life. The movement had more the nature of a religious and political revolt than of a constructive attempt to remove social inequities.

Types

The education resulting from rationalist aims was aristocratic. Voltaire and his coworkers were as unapproachable as their opponents, the aristocrats of the old regime. They did not believe that the masses were amenable to reason, and they could not accept the idea that the lower classes were educable. Voltaire himself referred to the masses as *canaille*, needing a god and a king to keep them under control.

The Encyclopedists had a similar attitude. They had only an academic interest in the woes of the common man and no desire to share with him their intellectual knowledge and reasoning powers. These advantages of the Enlightenment were only for the *illuminati*, the higher classes endowed with the intelligence they exalted. The rationalists had no use for universal education.

Almost the entire emphasis of rationalistic education was upon intellectual training. Physical, esthetic, and vocational education were neglected. Social education was recognized as essential, but it was formal, stilted, and artificial. Manners, language, and taste were developed and refined to the highest degree; but this so-called culture was heartless and artificial. Cleverness, brilliance, and wit were glorified; sparkling conversation, polished manners, and elegant taste were exalted. Training in manners took the place of moral training. Never were morals at a lower ebb.

Content

The content of rationalistic education consisted of everything that was "reasonable," and everything considered unreasonable was cast aside. The curriculum included the truth that was to make men free: philosophical and scientific knowledge was the subject matter of greatest value. The textbooks of rationalism were found in the ever-increasing tide of political, philosophic, economic, and scientific pamphlets and books, often written in a satirical as well as a critical vein. Scientific and philosophical arguments became the rage among the French intelligentsia. Aristocratic ladies discussed the latest theories in their boudoirs and salons. The natural laws discovered by scientists were supplemented by the human laws discovered by philosophers. Enlightenment replaced old traditions as the content of learning. Superficial though it was, the intellectual subject matter of the Enlightenment was more comprehensive than any since that of the ancient Greeks. Although sensual, materialistic, and atheistic, it had universality.

The rationalists' educational content included philosophy, science, art, literature, and social refinement. There was no place for religion or for the actualities of the workaday world. Polished manners, formal etiquette, and codes of self-interest were substituted for ethics and morality. The old moral virtues were replaced by sexual looseness, immodesty, conjugal infidelity, voluptuousness, and extravagance, all adorned to be sure by wit, sophistication, and elegance. Manners became an art, and the traditional virtues of morality were looked upon as "unreasonable" and worthy only of contempt. The artificialities of a coldly calculating society made up a large part of the individual's training.

Agencies and Organization

The rationalists were not schoolmasters; they contributed no new constructive agencies and organizations of education. What they had to say about schools and schoolmasters was largely destructive. They criticized every educational institution that hampered freedom of thought, and gave colleges and schools their share of abuse. Since rationalism was opposed to all that was arbitrary and organized, it gave little thought to building educational institutions and organizations. Rationalism seemed to imply a self-education through the reading of tracts and pamphlets and through discussions in fashionable salons. The goal of the *illuminati* in compiling their new *Encyclopedia*, a monumental work embodying all the knowledge of science and philosophy discovered to that time, is an indication of the type of agency the rationalists considered most helpful in the attainment of their ends.

Such a society utilized the secondary and higher schools developed under the earlier humanistic movements. The dancing master seems to have been the chief agency for the education of the child of the aristocracy, whom he instilled with the artificialities of drawing-room society and attempted to convert into a miniature adult.

Methods

Since the chief aim of rationalistic education was to develop the reason, the rationalists applied the doctrines of sensationalism and disciplinism. Materialistic in their views, they believed that man was a machine, whose higher mental processes were the result of impressions made by objects upon his physical sense organs. They felt nothing could be known except what appeared to the senses; therefore, all reasoning had to proceed according to Bacon's inductive method. The rationalists left no place for revelation, imagination, or feeling, but approached everything through critical analysis.

Characteristic of the rationalist method was the application of the cold light of reason to every phase of human life and to every human institution, and the cynical rejection of everything that apparently could not stand this test. As a result of their exclusive concern with the reasoning process, they neglected the emotional side of life and tossed aside all faiths and institutions as enemies of clear and logical thinking. Reason as the sole means of enlightenment was exalted to the extent of fanaticism. In the following chapter we shall note the reaction of Jean-Jacques Rousseau, a contributor to the *Encyclopedia* and friend of Diderot, to such sophistication.

REFERENCES

Axtell, James L., *The Educational Writings of John Locke*, A Critical Editing with Introduction and Notes. London: Cambridge University Press, 1968.

Browning, Oscar, *A History of Educational Theory*. New York: Harper & Row, Publishers, 1905. Pp. 102–118.

Butts, R. Freeman, *A Cultural History of Western Education,* 2d ed. New York: McGraw-Hill, Inc., 1955. Pp. 281–299.

Demiashkevich, Michael, *An Introduction to the Philosophy of Education.* New York: American Book Company, 1935. Pp. 227–228.

Duggan, Stephen P., *Student's Textbook in the History of Education,* rev. enl. ed. New York: Appleton-Century-Crofts, 1936. Pp. 182–198.

Durant, Will, and Ariel, *The Story of Civilization,* pt. viii, *The Age of Louis XIV*; pt. ix, *The Age of Voltaire.* New York: Simon and Schuster, Inc., 1955, 1963.

Eby, Frederick, and Charles F. Arrowood, *The Development of Modern Education.* Englewood Cliffs, N.J.: Prentice-Hall, Inc., 1934. Pp. 386–440.

Good, Harry G., *A History of Western Education.* New York: Crowell-Collier and Macmillan, Inc., 1960. Pp. 181–189.

Graves, Frank P., *Great Educators of Three Centuries.* New York: Crowell-Collier and Macmillan, Inc., 1912. Pp. 52–66.

Hart, Joseph K., *Creative Moments in Education.* New York: Holt, Rinehart and Winston, Inc., 1931. Pp. 246–252.

Jeffries, M. V. C., *John Locke, Prophet of Common Sense.* London: Methuen & Co., Ltd., 1967. Pp. 20–109.

Locke, John, *The Works of John Locke,* 10 vols. Reprint of 1823 ed. Aalen, Germany: Scientia Verlag, 1963.

———, *Some Thoughts Concerning Education.* Abridg. and ed. by F. W. Garforth. Woodbury, N.Y.: Barron's Educational Services, Inc., 1964.

Mayer, Frederick, *A History of Educational Thought.* Columbus, Ohio: Charles E. Merrill Books, Inc., 1960. Pp. 222–230.

Messenger, James F., *An Interpretative History of Education.* New York: Thomas Y. Crowell Company, 1931. Pp. 156–163.

Monroe, Paul, *A Textbook in the History of Education.* New York: Crowell-Collier and Macmillan, 1933. Pp. 505–529.

Mulhern, James, *A History of Education,* 2d ed. New York: The Ronald Press Company, 1959.

Noble, Stuart G., *A History of American Education,* 2d ed. New York: Holt, Rinehart and Winston, Inc., 1954. Pp. 339–362.

Painter, Franklin, *Great Pedagogical Essays.* New York: American Book Company, 1905. Pp. 278–290.

———, *A History of Education.* New York: Appleton-Century-Crofts, 1904. Pp. 230–238.

Quick, Robert H., *Educational Reformers.* New York: Appleton-Century-Crofts, 1904. Pp. 219–238.

Ulich, Robert, *History of Educational Thought.* New York: American Book Company, 1950. Pp. 200–210.

———, *Philosophy of Education.* New York: American Book Company, 1961. Pp. 31–34, 112, 127–129, 265.

——— (Ed.), *Three Thousand Years of Educational Wisdom,* 2d ed., enl. Cambridge, Mass.: Harvard University Press, 1954. Pp. 347–382.

Wender, Herbert, *The Growth of Modern Thought and Culture*. New York: Philosophical Library, Inc., 1959. Pp. 83–112.

SELECTED PAPERBACKS

Beck, Robert Holmes, *A Social History of Education*. Englewood Cliffs, N.J.: Prentice-Hall, Inc., 1965.

Becker, Carl L., *The Heavenly City of the Eighteenth-Century Philosophers*. New Haven, Conn.: Yale University Press, 1959.

Berlin, Sir Isaiah (Ed.), *The Age of Enlightenment: The Eighteenth Century Philosophers*. New York: New American Library of World Literature, Inc., 1950.

Crocker, Lester G., *Diderot, The Embattled Philosopher*. New York: The Free Press, 1966.

Ford, Franklin L., *Robe and Sword, Regrouping of the French Aristocracy after Louis XIV*. New York: Harper & Row, Publishers, 1965.

Garforth, Francis W. (Ed.), *John Locke's Of the Conduct of the Understanding*. New York: Bureau of Publications, Teachers College, Columbia University, 1965.

Gay, Peter (Ed.), *John Locke on Education*. New York: Teachers College Press, Columbia University, 1965.

Hampshire, Stuart (Ed.), *The Age of Reason: The Seventeenth Century Philosophers*. New York: New American Library of World Literature, Inc., 1950.

More, Sir Thomas, *A Dialogue of Comfort Against Tribulation*. Ed. by Leland Miles. Bloomington, Ind.: Indiana University Press, 1965.

Muller, Herbert J., *The Uses of the Past, Profiles of Former Societies*. New York: New American Library of World Literature, Inc., 1952.

Paine, Thomas, *The Age of Reason, Being an Investigation of True and Fabulous Theology*. New York: The Thomas Paine Foundation, Inc., undated.

Tocqueville, Alexis de, *The Old Regime and the French Revolution*. Trans. by Stuart Gilbert. New York: Doubleday & Company, Inc., 1965.

Viorst, Milton (Ed.), *The Great Documents of Western Civilization*. New York: Bantam Books, Inc., 1965.

Woodward, William Harrison, *Studies in Education during the Age of the Renaissance, 1400–1600*. New York: Teachers College Press, Columbia University, 1967.

CHAPTER **14**

Education as Harmony with Nature

I know my heart, and I know men. I am not made like any of those I have seen; I dare to believe that I am not made like any of those who are in existence. If I am not better, at least I am different. Whether Nature has acted rightly or wrongly in destroying the mould in which she cast me, can only be decided after I have been read.[1]

THE ANCIEN RÉGIME IN FRANCE

France in the mid-eighteenth century presented the height of paradoxes; the shining court of the Sun King and his long-lived successor, reflected in the great mirrors at Versailles, was a triumph of artificiality; the nobility who, in Dickens' rhetoric, were soon to be driven to their tombs, like their king had learned nothing and forgotten nothing; the philosophers, wonderfully brilliant and learned figures, cared neither socially nor intellectually for any beneath them; the clergy, from conviction or ignorance, asserted the primacy of divine right; the people, *canaille* to the upper classes, lived in poverty and illiteracy. It was the time for a new philosophy of education.

But philosophies come from men; and in 1712 life began for one of the strangest men in history, a man half-child and half-genius, who espoused a retreat from artificiality and a return to Nature. And catalytic though his contributions were, it is difficult to determine whether Jean-Jacques Rousseau was saint or devil, madman or giant, savior or corruptor of the educative process.

---

[1] Lester G. Crocker (Ed.), *The Confessions of Jean-Jacques Rousseau* (New York: Washington Square Press, Inc., 1965).

NATURALISM

But before we discuss Rousseau's unique contributions, let us return to his epoch and its needs. His educational philosophy, *naturalism*, was both an outgrowth and continuation of certain aspects of sense realism, and, at the same time, an antecedent and forerunner of the psychological developmentalism of the next century. Naturalism, Rousseau stated, is "education in accord with nature." But this definition is not simple, since *nature* is so general a term that it can easily lead to confusion, especially in discussions concerning education.

Nevertheless, we must give particular attention to naturalism not only because of its influence upon current educational theory and practice but also because the concept of natural rights is the basis for the American political and economic structure. And historically and philosophically naturalism was the most influential educational movement of the eighteenth century. The development of educational theory owes much to the doctrine of naturalism, which prevailed to the close of that fruitful century not only in educational thinking but, as we have noted, in economic, political, and social thought.

To educate according to nature could mean the discovery, formulation, and application of natural laws to the educational process, as well as a simple imitation of nature; this first possible aim was in the minds of the sense realists, although they did very little to achieve it in practice. Bacon, Ratke, and Comenius believed that educators should "diligently observe nature and learn of her," studying her methods and basing their own upon hers. Although these educational thinkers are not ordinarily considered as naturalists, in their advocacy of the following of nature they were indefatigable. Their naturalistic theory failed because it was based upon faulty reasoning by analogy.

Second, to educate according to nature could mean education in accord with the natural laws of human development. To educate an individual, one would have to understand the nature of his growth. Both the end and the process of education would be determined by a study of the nature of the pupil. This type of naturalistic approach to education, later designated as the "paidocentric" attitude by G. Stanley Hall, had been accepted by Plato, Quintilian, Ascham, and Comenius. Although the idea did not reach its full expression until the late nineteenth century with the work of the developmentalists, the eighteenth-century naturalists deserve credit for first popularizing this doctrine in the educational world.

Third, to educate according to nature could mean a return to the natural, as opposed to all that is artificial. This was the naturalists' greatest contribution to educational thought, and it is in this sense that we shall use the term *naturalism*. The target of the naturalistic movement was the highly affected life of the upper classes. Naturalism attacked especially the training of children in these artificialities; it condemned the repression of the child's natural spontaneity, the treatment of children as manikins, and the hothouse type of development, all of which were the dancing master's stock in trade. It deplored the absence of a simple home life and the prevailing tendency to relegate the care of children to nurses, governesses, and tutors. To its advocates naturalism meant a return to the simple life of the peasant home and to the family's rearing of the young.

Like rationalism, naturalism emphasized the rights of the individual and rejected the absolute authority of the state and the dogmatic authority of the church; but in other respects the two movements were quite different. As we have already pointed out, the rationalistic revolt of Voltaire and the Encyclopedists was aristocratic and aimed at setting up an aristocracy of reason to replace the aristocracy of birth and power. The naturalistic movement, on the other hand, was a revolt not only against the aristocracy of blood but also against what the naturalists considered the cold and heartless oligarchy of intellect. Naturalism opposed both autocratic and intellectual pretensions. Unlike rationalism, it rejected not only the medieval institutions of authority but also all the conventions and artificialities of a cultured society based on reason. The naturalists desired a return to an unaffected stage ruled simply by natural feelings. While the rationalist glorified the intellect, the naturalist worshiped feeling. And since feeling is an element common to all men, the doctrine of naturalism was essentially democratic. Actually naturalism was not a philosophical system, but a tendency to look upon nature as the origin and basic source of all existence. Thus its adherents sought to explain everything in terms of natural phenomena. It began with Thales in Greece in the sixth century, B.C.[2]

The outstanding champion and exponent of eighteenth-century naturalism was Jean-Jacques Rousseau (1712–1778). This great French thinker and writer had tremendous influence not only upon education but upon the course of modern civilization itself. His writings on government, society, religion, and marriage revolutionized the prevailing ideas of his day; and his doctrines have profoundly modified modern political and social life. His great work *The Social Contract* provided the basis of modern democratic political theory; his *Confession of Faith of a Savoyard Vicar* influenced the development of a religion based on nature and the rejection of the doctrine of Original Sin; his *The New Hèloïse* put forth the idea of marriage based upon romantic love and conjugal fidelity. Yet it is his influence upon education with which we are concerned, and certainly this was not the least of his potent contributions to modern life. His educational views were set forth in *Émile* (1762), one of the greatest and most influential educational classics. At its first appearance, the book was a

---

[2] Gordon H. Clark, *Thales to Dewey, A History of Philosophy* (Boston: Houghton Mifflin Company, 1957), especially pp. 3–29.

sensation. It attracted the hostile attention of Catholic and Protestant leaders, who regarded it as the most godless and impious book of its day; but others read it with pleasure and profit, greatly impressed with its doctrines. We cannot give here the fascinating details of Rousseau's life; but we must note that his convictions and ideas were largely determined by the tragic and quixotic events of his controversial career.

Rousseau's *Confessions* (which despite his claims of objectivity should be taken with several grains of salt) reveals resolution if not self-confidence. The furor in Paris, Switzerland, and elsewhere upon the publication of *Émile* was intense. Fleeing apparently for his life, Rousseau befriended and then offended his benefactors and moved on; he finally arrived in England, only to quarrel with his host, David Hume, and to return to Paris, where in his old age he was no longer attacked. From the *Confessions* it appears that Rousseau considered the *Traite de l'Education* his masterpiece.

Rousseau himself was not a school practitioner; he was a theorist. He never attempted to put into practice any of his own educational theories and principles. Himself an orphan, he placed his children in foundling homes when they were born, and gave them no further attention. Like so many other educational theorists, he probably would have discovered the inconsistencies and weaknesses in his ideas had he tried them out. Others who attempted to apply his theories soon discovered that certain modifications had to be made in his program if teaching success was to be assured.

The first to put Rousseau's naturalistic doctrines into practice was Johann Bernard Basedow (1723–1790), a German schoolmaster who was profoundly affected by reading *Émile*. Basedow raised enough money through writing *An Address to Philanthropists* in 1768 to establish a school, the *Philanthropinum*, in which he attempted to put a naturalistic plan into practice. In 1774, as a result of his experience, he published *Das Elementarwerk* and *Das Methodenbuch*, in which he set forth his modification of Rousseau's ideas. Both of these books were received with considerable enthusiasm, and together with *Émile* they laid the foundation for the development of an educational philosophy based on naturalism. Basedow and the Philanthropinists gave physical education an important role in the new curriculum; they also called for industrial training, although for its motor activity rather than for its vocational worth. While Basedow's own *Philanthropinum* was short-lived, its reputation stimulated the establishment of similar schools and opened the way for further reforms in elementary education.

NATURALISTIC EDUCATION

Aims

The doctrine of naturalism developed by Rousseau in *Émile* aimed at the preservation of the natural goodness and virtue of the individual, and the formation of a society based upon the recognition of natural individual rights. Rousseau's ultimate end for education was the attainment of a social order in which the principles, or primitive virtues, of simplicity, liberty, equality, and fraternity would be realized by all its members.

"Everything is good as it comes from the hands of the Creator; everything degenerates at the hands of man." These ringing words with which Rousseau opened the first book of *Émile* immediately reveal the basis of Rousseau's educational aims. The Author of Nature, God, has created perfection; man alone has sullied it. We must needs go back to our primeval stage of Adamic purity.

And just how may this be accomplished? Rousseau conceived of education as a negative process, a matter of *laissez faire*, a hands-off affair. He wished to ward off the evils of artificial society so that the natural goodness of the child would be free to unfold itself in all its spontaneity. He proposed to give the child free play to develop his natural endowments, to cultivate his individual nature and his own natural capacities and inclinations. Since, in Rousseau's judgment, the child at birth is intrinsically good, his instincts, inclinations, and feelings should be given full, free, and spontaneous expression.

Yet it is erroneous to suppose that the author of *The Social Contract* was opposed to social organization; he aimed, indeed, at the creation of a new type of social order. He believed that the traditional organization of society had created in the France of 1762—as he saw them—artificial inequalities which made it impossible for man to realize his true self. He advocated a society based upon the return to Nature. His objective was to prepare the individual to enter enthusiastically and effectively into all the human relationships of a society adjusted to his natural traits and capacities, a society in which he could live to the fullest degree the life of a "natural man."

This Swiss-born Frenchman did not want to abolish all the institutions of civilization; he merely hoped to change the church, the state, the family, the school, in order to bring them into closer harmony with what he considered the fundamental principles of nature, to adapt them to the needs of the natural man. In all of his social dogma he contended that personal liberty and equality belong to man as an inherent right.

Yet the educational program set forth by Rousseau in *Émile* was directed toward the upper classes. The poor man, he contended, had no need of education, since he was so close to nature that he was saved from the false and artificial training to which the children of the higher classes were submitted. The very nature of the peasant's life had developed in him all the natural virtues of equality, spontaneity, and unaffectedness, according to Rousseau. It was the children of the upper classes who had to be protected from the artificialities and insincerities of their society. Instead of an education to adjust the child to the existing social conventions, attitudes, and accomplishments, Rousseau proposed to remove the child from all such artificialities and take him into the country, where his natural inclinations could have free rein. (Some authorities feel that the child and his tutor were to be placed on an island.)

Rousseau's educational aim, therefore, was highly individualistic. He desired an education that would emancipate man from the trammels of an artificial society as well as from the restraints of human authority. For Rousseau, education was not a procedure to be imposed from without; it was a process of natural individual development, or growth. The ultimate goal of education was to be the maintenance of a natural stage wherein the rights of the individual, as found in the laws of his own nature, would be preserved; wherein the simple tastes and wants of the untutored masses would dominate; wherein the natural desires and interests of the individual would not be hampered, freedom would not be lost, and the artificial arts and sciences of civilization would be undeveloped and despised.

Types

Naturalistic education was general rather than specialized. Rousseau was opposed to the education prevalent in his day which aimed at producing workers, citizens, and members of society. He saw that the training in specialized powers and the building up of specialized occupations involved the subjection of certain individuals to others and the dependence of one upon others. Education, Rousseau felt, in making a worker or a citizen, made him less a man. He pleaded for a generous and liberal cultivation of all the child's natural endowments; he urged a development of the whole man instead of what he believed was a cramping, distorting specialization.

Not only did he consider the direct vocational type of training unnecessary and unwise, but he despised the direct civic type as well (except as a finale to Émile's adult development). He observed that:

> Education by Nature will restore the natural unsophisticated man, whose sole function is to be a man. In the natural order of things, all men being equal, their common vocation is manhood; and whoever is well trained for that, cannot fail to perform any vocation connected with it. Whether my pupil be destined for the army, the church, or the bar, is of small consequence. Regardless of the calling of his family, Nature calls him to human life. To live is the craft I desire to teach him. When he leaves my hands, I admit he will be neither magistrate, soldier, nor priest; he will be, first of all, a man; all that a man may be, he will be able to be, as well as any one.[3]

While Rousseau did advocate that everyone learn an industrial trade, he did not suggest this be done for a vocational purpose. Émile, though an

---

[3] J. J. Rousseau, *Émile*, p. 5, as quoted in Thomas Davidson, *Rousseau and Education According to Nature* (New York: Charles Scribner's Sons, 1898), pp. 102–103.

upper-class boy, learns a trade because it is the best preparation for understanding social relationships, raises him above any danger of parasitism,
and overcomes any tendency to despise those who work with their hands.
For similar reasons, Basedow recommended handicrafts for all in his
Philanthropinum.[4] Under naturalism, the pupil was not to be trained for
a definite vocation and a definite social position or class. He was to be made
adaptable, so that he could adjust himself to the changing fortunes of
industrial life and the changing environment of society.

The naturalist stands for a democratic and universal type of education. Rousseau declared that education is the privilege of all freemen, one
of their natural rights; and he declared, "Since all children, by the constitution of the state, are equal, they should be educated together and in the
same way." Basedow also insisted that rich and poor should be educated
together.

Naturalism particularly emphasized the importance of physical education and health training. The aim was to make the child a healthy little
animal, and that was accomplished best by letting nature take its course.
Rousseau laid down many sensible, though mostly negative, health rules.
The young child must not be swaddled, confined, or rocked, but must be
allowed the utmost freedom of limb and voice. Clothing was to be loose
and comfortable and limited to that which is necessary. The child was to be
nursed and tended by his own mother, not by a foster nurse. The child
must be exposed to a reasonable amount of cold, heat, and risk, in order
that he would be hardened into a robust and courageous individual; and
medicines and doctors were to be avoided. All restraint on physical freedom should be removed; and the child should be allowed to run, jump,
climb, and swim at will, playing naturally in the open country.

Although Rousseau recognized the need for moral education, he
specified that it, too, be acquired naturally. Rational moral training was
tabooed; ideas of right and wrong were not to be imposed, because he felt
the child was unable to understand them. Moral instruction through the
use of precepts, history, fables, and similar devices was to be avoided
because these methods demanded moral judgments of which the child,
being amoral, is incapable. Rousseau advocated moral training through
natural punishment, the natural consequences of a child's acts serving to
inhibit those that are unnatural and therefore undesirable, and to cause a
repetition of those that are natural and therefore desirable. Moral education
was to be a matter of experience rather than of instruction. Basedow likewise contended that formal moral instruction was of little value and insisted
that all practical instruction was moral in that it led to the natural life.

---

[4] For an excellent depiction of Basedow's school and his educational philosophy
see Luella Cole, *A History of Education, Socrates to Montessori* (New York: Holt,
Rinehart and Winston, Inc., 1950), pp. 398–433.

Intellectual education Rousseau limited to the informal training of the senses, the development of sense discrimination, the free expression of the child's ideas, the acquisition of knowledge through natural curiosity and interest, the opportunities for training in scientific observation, investigation, and inference. Books were to have little place in education; affected speech and the use of meaningless words were to be carefully avoided.[5]

Religious education was to be postponed until the child was past fifteen. Rousseau felt that until that age the child was unaware of any deity and that he should learn of divinity through its manifestation in nature. Rousseau advocated a natural rather than a revealed religion. He favored a deistic, naturalistic explanation of life, stressed reverence instead of creeds and dogmas, and insisted that every individual should be allowed to develop his own theology. He objected to the teaching of ritualistic forms and ceremonies, which he thought made good sectarianism, but did little to develop reverence for God or love for one's neighbors. Religion to the naturalist is a matter of heart rather than head; it is to be felt.

Content

Since Rousseau's program relied chiefly on nature, the task of those in charge of education was mostly to keep the traditional subject matter away from the pupil. The curriculum consisted of natural phenomena, presented in the order in which they become manifest to the child. Instead of the conventional habits and ideas of an artificial society, the curriculum consisted of the budding activities and interests of the pupil's own nature. The habitual responses and skills of civilization and the body of knowledge and information accumulated by humanity through the centuries was to be consistently avoided. The program of education was to be the natural unfolding of the child's powers to meet his natural needs. The activities which spring naturally from the needs of life were to make up the curriculum in Rousseau's plan.

In place of the books which played so prominent a part in the traditional Enlightenment curriculum, Rousseau advocated the informal exercises of the senses, the muscles, and the tongue. Rousseau was opposed to the three Rs because they dealt with artificial symbols. He hated books because, he said, "they merely teach us to talk of what we do not know [and they] come between the child and the things of nature." He approved *Robinson Crusoe* as the only desirable textbook because it alone pictured the unfolding of a human being under natural conditions and emphasized the advantages of simple living. The work of Basedow inspired the writing of the *Swiss Family Robinson*, conceived in the same vein and used for the same purpose. This novel was the forerunner of a new type of children's

---

[5] See R. L. Archer (Ed.), *Rousseau on Education* (New York: David McKay Company, Inc., 1912).

literature different from the fairy tales and the fables which had been used for centuries. Rousseau also opposed the study of foreign languages. The child, he felt, should learn to use only his mother tongue in a natural, un-affected manner. Reading, writing, language, literature, history were sub-jects that he would rigorously avoid.

The educational program of Émile as a young child consisted of sensory and motor activities motivated by his own curiosity. His physical activities of running, jumping, climbing, and swimming were encouraged. His sense discrimination was developed by counting and weighing things, measuring distances, drawing objects, and singing. Speech and drawing were used as means for the free expression of Émile's own ideas. Agricul-ture and carpentry were introduced; and the child learned to use the spade, the hoe, the lathe, the hammer, the saw, the plane and all the other tools of the common trades as a means to develop his sense perception and practical judgment. Arithmetic and geometry were taught not as formal studies, but as experiential activities in the pupil's natural life.

As Émile grew older, intellectual subject matter was included in his educational program. The phenomena of nature, however, rather than the facts of human relationships were to absorb his attention. He studied astronomy and geography not from books, but directly from nature. He made his own apparatus from the study of the natural sciences; and he learned geography from the topography of the neighborhood, instead of from the customary maps and globes. Meanwhile, he continued the activi-ties of agriculture and of the manual arts and trades.

Knowledge of human nature and social institutions was not given to Émile until he reached the age of fifteen. At that time, he began his contact with actual social situations. He visited prisons, workshops, and hospitals, where human beings were grouped. He participated in play groups, where social characteristics were manifested. History, in the form of biography, was introduced as a means of teaching him how to live with his fellows. As Émile reached maturity, he took up a careful theoretical study of the physical sciences, previously studied concretely. He learned ancient lan-guages to obtain a more thorough knowledge of his native tongue; and he now approached ancient literatures, with a glance at modern literature as well. Philosophy, ethics, and religion Émile studied to develop the right kind of social-minded conduct and to be able to play his part in bettering society.

Rousseau's conception of the educational curriculum for women was retrograde. His model woman, Sophie, had no individuality; her duty was to please man; and her whole life was supplementary to that of man. She was made physically strong in order to bear strong children. She was taught singing, dancing, embroidery, and designing in order to please man and be able to contribute to his comfort. She received an early education in morals and religion so that she could provide a good home for her family. But she was never to be trained to think for herself.

But it was not Rousseau's attitude toward woman, but his views on religion in the curriculum that drew upon him the universal condemnation and opposition of both Catholic and Protestant churchmen. *Émile* was burned in Paris with Voltaire's *Philosophical Dictionary*; the Genevans too burned *Émile*.

Rousseau believed that in trying to give children an idea of divinity when they were young, teachers gave them a conception of God which was "mean, harmful, grotesque, and unworthy." Rousseau thought that only when the youth approached maturity should he be given a religion, a deistic belief, which discovered in the constitution of the universe a logical morality and a dynamic impulse to serve his fellows.

Basedow and his followers had much the same ideas of the content of education as did Rousseau. In Basedow's curriculum the early training of the child was dominated by motion and noise; that is, by activities. Physical exercises and games were employed for physical training and bodily development. Nature study and excursions were used to train the senses. The vernacular, rather than the classical languages, was the chief instrument of learning; and, when Latin was taught, conversational or natural methods were used. Every child learned a handicraft for educational and social reasons; and arithmetic, geography, physics, and geometry were taught from a practical standpoint.

Agencies

Under the naturalistic theory of education, those who are to take charge of the child's education act chiefly to protect the child from the dangers of an artificial society. Rousseau said that the father and mother, as the natural tutor and nurse of the child, must "stand guard over him from the moment he comes into the world, take possession of him and not leave him till he is a man." Rousseau asserted that the parents must combine all their efforts to develop their child's inherent qualities. Rousseau's insistence on the duty of parents in the education of their children, was admirable, although he himself did not furnish a very good example.

While glorifying the parents as the most effective agency of education, Rousseau did not insist that all education was in their hands. Some have claimed that Rousseau was inconsistent in sometimes advocating education as a family function and at other times as a public function. But Rousseau probably would not have admitted any contradiction; he favored the agency best suited to achieve his purposes in the conditions in which the pupils had to live. In his model state, education would begin in the family and then be taken over by public authorities.[6] In the *Discourse on Political Economy* he advocated a universal system of public education that he believed would

---

[6] This position is particularly evident in his tract *Considerations on the Government of Poland and on the Reformation of It Projected in April, 1772*. See William Boyd (Tr. and Ed.), *The Minor Educational Writings of Jean Jacques Rousseau* (New York: Bureau of Publications, Teachers College, Columbia University, 1962), pp. 94–101.

result in causing children to "learn to cherish one another, as brothers," asserting:

> L'éducation publique, sous des règles prescrites par le Gouvernement, . . . est donc une des maximes fondamentales du Gouvernement populaire ou légitime. Si les enfants sont élevés en commun dans le sein de l'égalité, s'ils sont imbus des lois de l'État et des maximes de la volonté générale, s'ils sont instruits à les respecter par-dessus toutes choses, s'ils sont environnés d'examples et d'objets qui leur parlent sans cesse de la tendre mère qui les nourrit, . . . ne doutons pas qu'ils n'apprennent ainsi à se chérir mutuellement comme des frères. . . .[7]

In his discussion of the function of the family and the state as agencies of education, Rousseau was concerned with the ideal family and the ideal state; in these circumstances education was to begin in the family under close supervision and then be taken over by public authorities.

In *Émile*, Rousseau confronted a different situation. Émile is the scion of wealth and aristocracy, and his problem is far removed from that of a child brought up in a natural family or a state of nature. It is necessary to isolate Émile from his family relationships and the artificial society into which he was born. Yet Rousseau declared that even for Emile the father is the natural teacher, as the mother is for girls; he asserted that Émile would be "better educated by a judicious though ignorant father" than by the most skillful teacher in the world. But Émile is an orphan; and so Rousseau used another type of educational agency, the tutor, as the imagined practitioner of his educational theories. This model tutor is young not only in years but in tastes and feelings, and he is above accepting pay. Rousseau expressed his high opinion of the teaching profession in these words, "There are professions so noble, that no one can pursue them for money without showing that he is unworthy to pursue them."[8]

The tutor had to be loyal to his task and remain with his pupil for twenty-five years, for any change of tutors would affect the education of the pupil. The tutor was to choose for his ward a nurse who was willing to remain with the child as long as she was needed. The tutor and the nurse were to be in complete accord, and both had to follow the laws of nature. For, Rousseau declared, "The child at birth is already the pupil not of the tutor, but of Nature. The tutor merely understudies this first teacher and prevents her efforts from being balked."

Although Rousseau had little to say about the education of teachers,

---

[7] C. E. Vaughan (Ed.), *The Political Writings of Jean Jacques Rousseau*, 2 vols. (New York: John Wiley & Sons, Inc., 1962), vol. i, pp. 256–257. See also Introduction, pp. 1–38.

[8] Rousseau disclaimed the role of teacher for himself, saying, "I knew myself unfit and I refused. Instead of the difficult task of educating a child, I now undertake the easier task of writing about it." See William Boyd, *The Émile of Jean Jacques Rousseau, Selections* (New York: Teachers College Press, Columbia University, 1962), pp. 19–20.

Basedow placed strong emphasis upon training teachers in the methods of naturalism; and teachers from the *Philanthropinum* at Dessau ultimately dispersed all over Germany, proving effective agents in the promulgation of the naturalistic aims and methods.

It must be remembered, however, that whether the naturalist accepts as agencies of education the parents or tutor in the home, on the one hand, or teachers in private or public schools, on the other, the one great agency and authority of education is Nature. Under this philosophy, Nature is supreme; all other agencies are merely instruments for carrying out her purposes and program.

Organization

Naturalism entails a careful and systematic organization of educational procedures. Although Rousseau was not a schoolmaster and therefore was not concerned with the organization of a school system, he outlined a thorough gradation of education into definite periods, or stages. He rejected the traditional attitude that education must be uniform in character throughout its course, that the child should be treated throughout his training just as an adult would be. He firmly believed that the development of the pupil proceeded through sharply defined periods having little connection with each other, and that the education of the child was to be determined by these various stages of development. Each of these stages, he felt, had its own characteristic and dominant trait, which became the dominating factor in organizing the learning of that period.

Rousseau was the first to develop the recapitulation theory as the basis for educational organization. He believed that the child, in his progress from birth to maturity, lives again the epochs through which the race passes in its progress from savagery to civilization, that ontogeny repeats phylogeny. The child is first an animal, then partly civilized, then a solitary Robinson Crusoe, then a rational being, and finally a social being. Rousseau was also the first to advance the saltatory theory of development, that certain faculties arise with a leap at certain stages of the child's development. Education at each stage must be adapted to these newly awakened characteristics and functions, he maintained.

The education of Emile was organized into four stages, and each of the first four books of Rousseau's great classic is devoted to one of these periods: (1) infancy, (2) childhood, (3) boyhood, (4) adolescence. The first period lasts from birth to five years, during which the infant, being in a state of nature, is an animal with few needs, mechanical actions, no power to reason, and feelings dominant but simple. The second period lasts from five to twelve years, and during this period—says Rousseau—the child is in a stage of savagery, nonmoral and nonsocial, with his needs still few and feelings active and dominant. The third stage lasts from twelve to fifteen years, during which the boy is in a Robinson Crusoe state of solitude, still amoral and asocial, with less dominant feelings, emerging reason and judgment, and curiosity driving him to seek the meaning of things. The last period is from fifteen to twenty years, during which the adolescent becomes a social being, unable to satisfy his wants by himself, with the emergence of a sex life resulting in marriage, with abstraction arising, and with imagination and reason developing. For each of these stages, Rousseau proposed a special curriculum and a distinct methodology. (A fifth level, Émile's civic life, lies beyond the scope of this section.)

Methods

The supreme contribution of naturalism to educational method lies in its emphasis upon making the child the center of the process. The study of the nature of the child was to be the determining factor in all educational procedures. "Observe nature and follow the route which she traces for you," was Rousseau's slogan. In his insistence upon observing and obeying the laws of nature in all instructional methodology, he followed the lead of the sense realists.

The child's nature and the child's growth were to determine the processes and techniques of teaching, Rousseau felt. Nature to him meant the native instincts and predispositions of the child as opposed to the habits and conventions acquired through drill and social contacts. Rousseau demanded an educational process which would consist of the unhampered and unrestrained growth of the pupil's native powers and capacities. Nature rather than nurture was his keynote. All the conscious processes of instruction were to be based upon a study of the child's native equipment, instincts and interests, and resulting natural expressions and activities.

Rousseau's analysis firmly established three modern principles of teaching: (1) the principle of growth, (2) the principle of pupil activity, (3) the principle of individualization. These fundamental laws lay at the heart of the reforms of Pestalozzi, Herbart, Froebel, and later developmentalists.

It is easy to misunderstand and misjudge Rousseau. Many have insisted that he advocated a soft pedagogy, and certain of his followers have adopted the easygoing methods of allowing the pupil to do exactly as he pleases. Some of Rousseau's statements seem to support this interpretation. Émile does not follow any set program; he is subjected to no regimen and no arbitrary commands; he is relieved of the harsh yoke of the conventional system of education. But Rousseau, in advocating the overthrow of the rigorous rule of the pedagogical martinet, did not go to the extreme of a *laissez-faire* policy in education. He merely substituted the commands and necessities of nature for the demands and compulsions of what he considered an artificial society. To Rousseau, the driving powers of human development are the natural needs of life; the human faculties are developed through functioning to supply these needs. The order of nature is (1) need, (2) activity, (3) experience, (4) knowledge. The process of education should follow the same order, he asserted. The work of the teacher is not to drive, but merely to guide in such a way that learning follows the natural sequence.

Nothing must be done for the pupil that he can do for himself is the great principle of pupil activity. Since the child is educated through his own activity, not what the teacher does, but what the pupil does is the important factor. Rousseau said, "Do not give your pupil any sort of verbal lesson, for he is to be taught only by experience."[9] Again Rousseau said, "Without doubt we derive much clearer and more accurate notions of things which we learn for ourselves than of that we gain from the instruction of others." A basic principle of the naturalistic method, therefore, was that nothing should be learned on the authority of others. Rousseau placed Émile in circumstances where he was obliged to rely upon himself to an ever-increasing degree, to form his own thoughts, and to reach his own conclusions; Émile is told nothing that he can discover for himself. He must construct his own apparatus for learning: he must make his own charts, maps, and globes, his own apparatus for the study of scientific and philosophical phenomena when his development requires them.[10]

Another basic principle of Rousseau's was that each child be allowed to develop according to his own nature. The interests and needs of the individual must be placed above those of society; individuality must not be sacrificed for social stability, he declared. The child's individuality was not to be crushed by forcing him into the mold of social conformity. Man was not to be fitted for his station in life; his station was to be fitted to him. In the same way, the child was not to be adjusted to his education; his education was to be adjusted to his needs. Rousseau says: "Do not save time, lose it."

Naturalism placed the authority of the school upon an entirely new foundation. Rousseau expressed his attitude toward traditional methods of discipline as follows, "Discipline, the restraining of curbing of the natural impulses, is what confuses, degrades, and blasts human nature." Instead of attempting to control the conduct of the pupil through scolding or whipping or through praise and reward, Rousseau merely permitted the pupil to suffer the natural results of his own acts. This doctrine of natural punishment has been discussed widely in connection with school discipline, and its advantages and disadvantages have been ably presented. Such a procedure removes the human element in discipline, and the child feels no resentment to the teacher or parent. Furthermore, when the child is old enough to reason, the recognition of the law of cause and effect is indeed valuable. On the other hand, there are many objections to natural punishment: it is sometimes too severe and sometimes not severe enough; it applies in vary-

---

[9] An excellent interpretation of *Émile* is in Gabriel Compayre, *The History of Pedagogy*, trans. and ed. by W. H. Payne (Boston: D. C. Heath and Company, 1885), ch. xiii, "Rousseau and the *Émile*," pp. 278–310.

[10] Boyd, *Émile*, pp. 33–68.

ing degrees to different individuals, so that the "just are often punished with the unjust"; it often punishes others more than the child; finally, it may result in the development of a negative morality of mere expedience. This lack of an absolute standard is only one of the many dilemmas associated with naturalism.

Furthermore, the idea of education as affording only opportunities for natural reaction and natural growth is not one a person who realizes the complexities of modern life can hold. Perhaps it would be theoretically desirable as some claim to return to a simpler and more natural way of life, under which instinctive impulses and reactions would regain their original usefulness; but this is practically impossible. We must recognize the complexities of modern civilization and adjust the child to its artificialities.

Rousseau maintained that when men join together in a social state, they do so by a mutual contract; thus, he said, they endeavor to "find a form of association that will defend and protect with the whole common force the person and goods of every associate, and in which each, while uniting himself with all, may still obey only himself and remain as free as before." He aimed at the development of a social order in which all cooperated for protection without any loss of individual liberty.[11] But perhaps the author of *The Social Contract* failed to consider the power and sanction of culture itself. Although sociologists still debate the domination of culture (see Chapter 1), if one accepts it as the significant force, the compulsive power of society, that is, the culture into which an individual is born, can hardly be described better than by Peter Berger:

> Society not only controls our movements, but shapes our identity, our thought and our emotions. The structures of society become the structures of our own consciousness. Society [culture] does not stop at the surface of our skins. Society penetrates us as much as it envelops us.[12]

Thus, we may raise several dissents to naturalism as an educational philosophy, while keeping firmly in mind its remarkable assets in regard to the child's nature, growth, and development. If a civilization desires to preserve itself, it must eventually train children in ways that are not natural to them. Self-direction, self-control, and originality are not possible to children unless they are developed through a carefully controlled education. Complete freedom may not train an individual in the inhibition of natural but undesirable responses; and such training is essential if the individual is to play his part in the cooperative improvement of human

---

[11] See M. A. Cobban, *Rousseau and the Modern State* (London: George Allen & Unwin, Ltd., 1934), pp. 15–44, for a trenchant analysis of Rousseau's political conceptions.

[12] *Invitation to Sociology—A Humanistic Perspective* (New York: Doubleday & Company, Inc., Anchor Books, 1963), p. 121.

society. But that, it seems, regardless of his method, was Rousseau's ultimate objective.[13]

REFERENCES

Adams, John, *The Evolution of Educational Theory*. London: Macmillan & Co., Ltd., 1912. Pp. 250–282.

Archer, R. L. (Ed.), *Rousseau on Education*. New York: David McKay Company, Inc., 1912.

Boyd, William (Trans. and Ed.), *The Émile of Jean Jacques Rousseau, Selections*. Classics in Education, no. 101. New York: Teachers College Press, Columbia University, 1962. Pp. 198ff.

Butts, R. Freeman, *A Cultural History of Western Education*, 2d ed. New York: McGraw-Hill, Inc., 1955. Pp. 290–291.

Château, Jean, *Jean-Jacques Rousseau*. Paris: Librarie Phil. J. Vrin, 1962.

Cobban, M. A., *Rousseau and the Modern State*. London: George Allen & Unwin, Ltd., 1934.

Cole, Luella, *A History of Education, Socrates to Montessori*. New York: Holt, Rinehart and Winston, Inc., 1950. Especially ch. on Basedow.

Crocker, Lester G., *Jean-Jacques Rosseau*, vol. i, *The Quest: 1712–1758*. New York: Crowell-Collier and Macmillan, Inc., 1968.

Davidson, Thomas, *Rousseau and Education According to Nature*. New York: Charles Scribner's Sons, 1898.

Duggan, Stephen P., *Student's Textbook in the History of Education*, rev. enl. ed. New York: Appleton-Century-Crofts, 1936. Pp. 203–219.

Durant, Will, and Ariel, *The Story of Civilization*, vol. ix, *The Age of Voltaire*. New York: Simon and Schuster, Inc., 1965. Pp. 283, 322, 323–324, 345, 755–756.

————, vol. x. *Rousseau and Revolution*. New York: Simon and Schuster, Inc., 1967. Pp. ·3–37, 152–170, 171–188, 189–214, 881–892.

Eby, Frederick, and Charles F. Arrowood, *The Development of Modern Education*. Englewood Cliffs, N.J.: Prentice-Hall, Inc., 1934.

Good, Harry G., *A History of Western Education*. New York: Crowell-Collier and Macmillan, Inc., 1960. Pp. 201–224.

Graves, Frank P., *Great Educators of Three Centuries*. New York: Crowell-Collier and Macmillan, Inc., 1912. Pp. 77–121.

Hart, Joseph K., *Creative Moments in Education*. New York: Holt, Rinehart and Winston, Inc., 1931. Pp. 252–261.

————, *A Social Interpretation of Education*. New York: Holt, Rinehart and Winston, Inc., 1929. Pp. 142–144.

Knight, Edgar W., *Twenty Centuries of Education*. Boston: Ginn & Company, 1940. Pp. 347–356.

---

[13] See Phillipe Aries, *Centuries of Childhood* (New York: Alfred A. Knopf, 1962), for verbal and visual pictures of childlife and rearing before and after the age of Rousseau.

Mayer, Frederick, *A History of Educational Thought*. Columbus, Ohio: Charles E. Merrill Books, Inc., 1960. Pp. 231–244.

Messenger, James F., *An Interpretative History of Education*. New York: Thomas Y. Crowell Company, 1931. Pp. 164–181.

Monroe, Paul, *A Textbook in the History of Education*. New York: Crowell-Collier and Macmillan, Inc., 1933. Pp. 535–585.

Mulhern, James, *A History of Education*, 2d ed. New York: The Ronald Press Company, 1959. Pp. 411–422.

Nakosteen, Mehdi, *The History and Philosophy of Education*. New York: The Ronald Press Company, 1965. Pp. 302–318, 389, 440.

Parker, Samuel C., *History of Modern Elementary Education*. Boston: Ginn & Company, 1912. Pp. 161–206.

Power, Edward J., *Main Currents in the History of Education*. New York: McGraw-Hill, Inc., 1962. Pp. 377–388, 420.

Roberts, Roy W., *Vocational and Practical Arts Education*. New York: Harper & Row, Publishers, 1957.

Quick, Robert H., *Educational Reformers*. New York: Appleton-Century-Crofts, 1904. Pp. 239–289.

Ulich, Robert, *History of Educational Thought*. New York: American Book Company, 1950. Pp. 211–224.

———, *Philosophy of Education*. New York: American Book Company, 1961. Pp. 214–218.

——— (Ed.), *Three Thousand Years of Educational Wisdom*, 2d ed. enl. Cambridge, Mass.: Harvard University Press, 1954. Pp. 383–425.

Weimer, Hermann, *A Concise History of Education*. New York: Philosophical Library, Inc., 1962.

Woody, Thomas (Ed.), *Educational Views of Benjamin Franklin*. New York: McGraw-Hill, Inc., 1931.

SELECTED PAPERBACKS

Beck, Robert Holmes, *A Social History of Education*. Englewood Cliffs, N.J.: Prentice-Hall, Inc., 1965. Pp. 77ff.

Becker, Carl L., *The Heavenly City of the Eighteenth-Century Philosophers*. New Haven, Conn.: Yale University Press, 1959.

Berger, Peter, *Invitation to Sociology—A Humanistic Perspective*. New York: Doubleday & Company, Inc., Anchor Books, 1963.

Berlin, Sir Isaiah (Ed.), *The Age of Enlightenment: The Eighteenth Century Philosophers*. New York: New American Library of World Literature, Inc., 1950.

Boyd, William (Trans.), *The Minor Educational Writings of Jean Jacques Rousseau*. New York: Bureau of Publications, Teachers College, Columbia University, 1962.

——— (Trans. and Ed.), *The Émile of Jean Jacques Rousseau, Selections*. New York: Bureau of Publications, Teachers College, Columbia University, 1962.

Crocker, Lester G. (Ed.), *The Confessions of Jean-Jacques Rousseau.* New York: Washington Square Press, 1965.

Mayer, Frederick, *Educational Foundations.* Columbus, Ohio: Charles E. Merrill Books, Inc., 1963.

Rousseau, J.J., *The Reveries of a Solitary.* Trans. by Gould Fletcher. New York: Brentanos, 1927.

Strickland, Charles E., and Charles Burgess (Eds.), *Health, Growth, and Heredity: G. Stanley Hall on Natural Education.* New York: Bureau of Publications, Teachers College, Columbia University, 1965.

Viorst, Milton (Ed.), *The Great Documents of Western Civilization.* New York: Bantam Books, Inc., 1965.

CHAPTER 15

Education for Patriotic Citizenship

Nationalism is first and foremost a state of mind, an act of consciousness, which since the French Revolution, has become more and more common to mankind. . . . The modern period of history, starting with the French Revolution, is characterized by the fact that, in this period, and in this period alone, the nation demands the supreme loyalty of man.[1]

THE RISE OF NATIONALISM

The principle of nationalism has had without doubt the most consequential influence on education in the entire history of pedagogical thought. Its prominence followed the American and French revolutions of the eighteenth century, for, immediately subsequent to their parallel declarations of the rights of man, two new educational ideas became increasingly prevalent and persuasive. The first of these was the nationalistic, or patriotic, theory which we are about to discuss; the second was the doctrine of developmentalism, to which Chapter 16 will be devoted. Although developmental influences were related chiefly to the internal aspects of education, the influence of nationalism was felt in both the internal and external organization of school systems.

While some forms of nationalism had existed prior to the French Revolution, this critical convulsion catalyzed nationalism's widening influence as nation after nation sought to establish its separate and significant individual identity. Thus nationalism greatly stimulated the genesis and growth of state-controlled and state-supported public school systems, now almost universal. Wherever there has been the effect of a strong nation-

---

[1] Hans Kohn, *The Idea of Nationalism* (Crowell-Collier and Macmillan, Inc., 1951).

alistic spirit, "schools and the means of education" have been warmly encouraged and utilized as powerful agencies for the inception, preservation, and perpetuation of nations. Even the few remaining monarchies, like the democracies, have accepted the establishment and maintenance of public schools, usually free up to certain levels, as an essential national policy.

Indeed, the nationalization of education has occurred similarly under republican and totalitarian governments. Totalitarianism has promoted education to produce tractable, efficient, and ideologically proper subjects; republicanism has fostered education to make its people responsible and literate citizens, with the faith in their institutions and representatives necessary for the functioning and perpetuation of their society. In each instance, the nation-state is considered the supreme expression of the group's political and/or social ideology.

The nineteenth century was the era in which the first clear-cut and nominally effective national school systems were built, although nationalism had been the guiding spirit in the political development of Europe for several centuries.[2] Actually, the embryo of nationalism was in ancient civilizations; this growing spirit, which eventually flowered into national and even chauvinistic consciousness, had a tenuous evolution and was the result of many influences.

Early Egypt developed under the joint authority of religion and royalty: pharaoh was considered divine and an object of national reverence. In ancient Persia and Sparta the military was dominant, and devotion to country was the supreme virtue; the Jewish people represent an interesting variant, for obedience to the commandments of their God was an imperative of patriotic citizenship. Civic responsibilities and virtues reached a peak in ancient Athens and republican Rome; in the latter, patriotism and loyalty to the state took the place of religion. These examples imply a devotion to the state perhaps more evident "and more common to mankind," in Kohn's phrase, in later centuries when nationalism became *the* reigning political motive; but throughout antiquity group loyalty was invariably a strong factor in survival and stability, and treason was considered a most serious offense.

Nevertheless, during the medieval era secular power was radically weakened, and the authority of the church rose in the name of Christendom, an international, or ecumenical, concept. With few exceptions the power of kings and princes was sublimated to that of the church. Ecclesiastical approval represented a stronger sanction than any civil authority. Feudal lords, though maintaining power over their retainers in temporal matters, were themselves under the suasion of the pope in all events of

---

[2] See Kohn, pp. 10–12. Kohn's conception emphasizes revolutionary rather than evolutionary aspects.

great importance. Nor was such a condition completely detrimental to medieval life; despite local wars and sanguine conflict among rival nobilities, the European world achieved, within this much-debated epoch, a higher degree of brotherhood and unity than at any other period.

But with the revival of commerce and the rise of cities in the eleventh and twelfth centuries, ambitious and sometimes unscrupulous kings were able to reestablish their authority over their petty feudal lords and, with the growing debate over ecclesiastical power, eventually to challenge the authority of the church. In consequence of the Protestant and other concomitant revolts, the influence which the papacy had held over the secular activities of medieval man became fragmented. The church's "seamless garment" was rent.

By the beginning of the sixteenth century, the era of discovery, exploration, and Copernicus, several princes of new national states were able to achieve supremacy over the claims of the international church-state. The seventeenth and eighteenth centuries saw the emerging nation-state, with a compact area and strong economic and military resources, become the dominant organization in Europe. And these states began to acquire colonies all over the globe. The French Revolution, a supreme expression of nationalism, assured the power of the patriotic movement. The nineteenth century saw the unification of Italy and Germany, the birth of the French Republic, and the sudden rise of Japan, as well as the evolution of Latin America. The twentieth century has witnessed the emergence of the African states.

In recent years many influences have fanned the spirit of nationalism. The growing economic problem of finding food, clothing, and shelter for the enormously increased world population has brought into existence an industrial and commercial conflict which has subtly intensified earlier national animosities and envies. The ideological wars of the twentieth century have smoldered into overt military action and declared warfare.

Nations obtained new areas only at the expense of enmity with rival nations, or by dispossessing or exploiting the original habitants. The development of commerce and industry through modern science has furthered the interests of nationalism. Interchange of raw materials and world markets for finished goods intensified the economic rivalries of powerful nations and the exploitation of weaker ones. Traditional economic theory recognized the nation as the basic unit in an economic policy of manufacturing raw materials at home and selling the finished products abroad in order to maintain a favorable balance of trade. Such expansionist and nationalistic tendencies have led to international rivalry and have been one of the causes of the world wars and nervous tension in our times.

Economic rivalries added to ideological enmities make the condition of any nation precarious. Military preparedness is not a sufficient guarantee of security. It is not surprising that in all nations schools have been used to stimulate loyalty to the nation and to prevent defection from its aims and ideals. Public education was early recognized as one of the most effective agencies of national defense. Even some of the benevolent despots of the eighteenth century realized that the economic and military prosperity of a nation depended in the long run upon the welfare and understanding of the common people, and attempted to improve their educational system.

Early in the nineteenth century, nationalism became dominant in education, and countries began the establishment of systems of schools to help achieve their national aspirations. It will suffice for our purpose to take three nations as typical of this movement—France, Germany, and the United States. These were the nations that first responded to this tendency, and the other states have duplicated their procedures. The great exponents of nationalism in education have been citizens of these nations, but the influence of these leaders has been felt in countries other than their own. La Chalotais, Roland, Diderot, and Condorcet in France; Francke, Hecker, and Fichte in Germany; Jefferson, Webster, and Barnard in the United States, stand out as advocates of nationalistic conceptions of education.

Nationalistic conceptions of education were influenced by earlier educational, political, and social theories. The naturalism of Rousseau gave rise to a deeper recognition of the rights of the individual and of the significance of human personality. The rationalism of the Encyclopedists and the physiocrats had weakened the authority of the church and had developed a new idea of sovereignty, as providing intelligent and benevolent rule for the benefit of the people. The pietism and philanthropism of Francke and other German philosophers led to the realization that the greatness of a nation depends upon a happy, contented people. These theoretical considerations as well as the more practical considerations of benevolent or intelligent rulers led to the widespread acceptance of national education as a beneficial thing.

HOW NATIONALISM AFFECTED EDUCATION

The ultimate objective of nationalism is the glorification and preservation of the state, which is conceived as a society organized primarily to protect its members from the dangers of external attack and internal disintegration. The state is composed of those who govern, or administrate, and those who are governed. Although the government in a democracy is different from that of an autocracy or a limited monarchy, in each case government is the instrument set up within the state to administrate it. Thus, the nationalist regards education as one of the most effective agencies for assisting the state in the performance of its governmental responsibility. The nationalist considers the maintenance and utilization of public education as a requisite and patriotic duty. From this assumption it follows that education may be used to develop military preparedness and aggressiveness, national wealth and economic independence, and national unity, through common traditions and ideals. Proponents of nationalism recognize that education is an instrument which the state can use to maintain itself and to achieve its national ideals. Nationalists believe that the state must rely upon education to safeguard itself against disintegration. The efficiency of a national policy of education in promoting national ends is rarely questioned. And the policy of education generally varies little under the various forms of nationalistic government. To demonstrate this, we will now consider the educational policies of several representative countries whose historical development and nationalistic urges during the eighteenth and nineteenth centuries had tremendous effects on their expanding educational systems. Although we might as conveniently have chosen other nations, we shall center on France, Prussia (the antecedent of modern Germany), and the United States.

THE GREAT FRENCH REVOLUTION

Although not the country in which the oldest alliance between nationalism and education is to be observed, France offers an excellent example of the concentrated power of such a union. Here the conception of education for the national security arose as a defense reaction of a badgered people. Following the French Revolution of 1789 (the year the United States Constitution went into effect), Frenchmen had to defend their newly won freedom against a combination of foreign powers. As the kings of other European countries saw in this revolution threats to their own power, a grand coalition of their armies marched against the French Republic with the hope of restoring the *ancien régime* and insuring their own survival as monarchies. This attack on their liberties aroused strong patriotic fervor, which was expressed in the inspiring French national anthem, "The Marseillaise." With its watchwords, *liberty, equality, fraternity,* and its stirring call, "Ye sons of France awake to glory," the masses took new courage and drove the invaders from their country. Then their revolutionary leaders, realizing the necessity of keeping these patriotic impulses alive, recognized the desirability of establishing a state system of education through which the people might be informed of the benefits of the republican form of government and instructed in their rights and privileges under the new social order, as codified in the Declaration of the Rights of Man. The revolutionary government saw immediately that in the education of children it had an effective agency of social control and a potential guarantee of stability and permanence.

Although successive regimes of the French Revolution did not succeed in establishing a workable system of state education, the various reports that were made to the assemblies, the bills that were introduced, and the laws that were passed set forth the aims and purposes that were to dominate national school systems during the entire nineteenth century. Although little was actually accomplished, the Revolutionary Convention gave much attention to the possibility of establishing a national system of lay education. The numerous Jesuit colleges had been suppressed in 1764, and in 1792 the National Convention confiscated the schools of other religious orders. Such actions left the French people virtually without schools. From 1763 to the close of the century, such educational reformers as La Chalotais, Roland, Diderot, and Condorcet, and such political leaders as Talleyrand and Mirabeau formulated and presented plans for systems of national schools to replace the suppressed teaching orders of the church. These aimed at the centralization of all learning under public control for the sake of improving the state and maintaining the government. La Chalotais in his *Essay on National Education* (1763), Roland in his *Report on Education to the Parlement of Paris* (1768), Diderot in his *Provision on Education* (1791), recommended new educational systems dedicated to the purposes of national solidarity and to the service of the state. La Chalotais was especially influential in shaping subsequent political theory and prompting action regarding this relationship of education to the state. He believed that education was essentially a civil affair; that the real purpose of education was to prepare loyal citizens of France; that the government should make citizens efficient as well as content by educating them for their sphere in life. Roland said, "Education cannot be too widely diffused, to the end that there may be no class of citizens who may not be brought to participate in its benefits. It is expedient that each citizen receive the education which is adapted to his needs."

Condorcet's *Report on Behalf of the Committee on Public Instruction* (1792) proposed an educational system through which "each individual is to be taught to direct his own conduct and to enjoy the plenitude of his own rights and to insure the perpetuation of liberty and equality." Schools were to be organized in each village with 200 children.

In the philosophy of these French liberalists, the objectives of education were completely and radically changed from what had been accepted in earlier centuries. Education was understood as aiming at civic virtues rather than the traditional religious and humanistic virtues. These intrepid thinkers believed and asserted that instruction was a civil affair, aiming at the development of a national spirit, the ability to guard one's rights, and the proficiency to serve the state in civil offices.

THE FORCE OF PRUSSIAN NATIONALISM

Yet the French revolutionary assemblies contributed more to the objectives of nationalistic education than they did to actual accomplishments. Condorcet's great plan was not implemented. It remained for Prussia to effect the first embodiment of the nationalistic concept of education in a comprehensive state system of schools. Here again the recognition of the nationalistic function of education came in a time of crisis.

It was even easier for the nationalistic concept to flower in the Protestant states of Germany. From the time of the Protestant revolts, the church and its religiously motivated schools had received encouragement and support from civil rulers. Although the rulers of the German states during the seventeenth and eighteenth centuries did not recognize the possibilities of the schools in the development of a patriotic loyal citizenship, they did feel that it was part of their duty as benevolent despots to maintain schools for the teaching of literacy and religious faith, as a phase of the internal improvement of their realm. In 1642, near the close of the Thirty Years' War, the German Duke Ernst of Saxe-Coburg-Gotha issued his remarkable *Schulmethodus*, a program of school reform which aimed at the restoration of universal training in the four *R*s under church supervision, but by the authority of the state.

In Prussia particularly, the rulers had exhibited considerable interest in educational affairs, and the state had long exercised authority over the establishment of schools and had shown itself interested in their maintenance and improvement. As early as 1717, Frederick William I (1713–1740) had issued decrees requiring compulsory school attendance and prescribing conditions for the building of schoolhouses, the support of teachers, the payment of tuition and fees, and administrative aid. Frederick the Great (1740–1786), believing that the child belonged to the state and not to the family, laid the real foundation for a state system of public elementary education. Frederick, who is known as one of the most tolerant and humane of the eighteenth-century European despots, issued in 1763 the epochal *General Land-Schule Reglement* (General Regulations for Village Schools) as a part of his policy of internal improvement. These regulations aimed at securing "an education both scientific and Christian in true fear of God and in other useful things . . . to the end that ignorance so dangerous and unbecoming to Christianity may be prevented and remedied." These ordinances provided for the compulsory attendance of children, the maintenance of a complete school term each year, the curricular requirements, methods of instruction, and the education and compensation of teachers.

Although the rulers of eighteenth-century Prussia accepted the principles of Francke and Hecker that it was the obligation of the state to foster and maintain schools, their aim was largely that of religious moralism, and the actual supervision of the schools was still left to the church leaders and the local pastors. Nationalism as the principal function of education did not dominate the schools of Prussia until after the defeat of the Germans by Napoleon at Jena in 1806. Yet it is true that as early as 1794 the twelfth chapter of the *General Civil Code,* drawn up by the commission of eminent jurists appointed by Frederick the Great to codify the Prussian law, asserted the supremacy of the state over all education in these words:

> Schools and universities are state institutions, charged with the instruction of youth in useful information and scientific knowledge. Such institutions may be established only with the knowledge and approval of the state. All public schools and educational institutions are under the supervision of the state and are at all times subject to its examination and inspection.

Nevertheless, Frederick's successor, Frederick William II, continued to appoint clergymen to positions of educational leadership and supervision; and the schools were secularized without eliminating the religious aim.

The crushing defeat administered by Napoleon revealed to Prussia the inadequacy of its social and economic order, the corruption of its government, the selfishness of its nobility, and the indifference of its oppressed people. With the nation prostrated, Frederick William III inaugurated a series of reforms to bring it back to new life and vigor. In this effort he was assisted by liberal and able advisers, infused with the principle of nationalism. Among these no one was more influential than Johann Gottlieb Fichte (1762–1814), a philosopher who saw education as the most effective of all national regenerative forces. In 1807–1808 he delivered a series of fourteen *Addresses to the German Nation,* in which he set forth the following ideas:

> . . . individualism and self-seeking among the citizens and classes of Germany were the causes of her defeat and humiliation. Only when the individuals of the country were drawn together in common loyalty and service to a social organism could they discover the true meaning of their existence. For all Germans, the society in which each person had to find his larger self, and to which he owed full loyalty and love, was the German nation, which had been placed upon the earth as a part of the divine plan and had a destiny to fulfill. The only way in which the individual could realize his complete selfhood was through identifying himself with the nation by serving and improving it. The subordination of self to society for the sake thereby of realizing a richer individual life was to be accomplished through love of the fatherland. . . . In order that all may be made to realize this sentiment, which was a necessary condition for the development of the moral nature of the individual, schools had to be established in which children could be separated from the reigning social habit of self-seeking and nurtured in the atmosphere of social service and co-operation. If Germany was to be saved, the nation must be taken as the unit of social organization. Germany must know its character and destiny, and through a conscious control of education it must liberate all the potentialities—moral, intellectual, physical,

vocational—for national service, that existed within the children of all people.[3]

With these stimulating words Fichte conveyed the conception of nationalism as the dominant aim of education, and the sentiment that the school's function was that of strengthening and preserving the national welfare. To implement this objective in the quarter of a century following the Treaty of Tilsit, Prussia enacted a series of laws establishing a thoroughly efficient national system of education headed by a national Department of Public Instruction, under the Ministry of the Interior, with Wilhelm von Humboldt (1767–1835) as its chief.[4] In a general order issued by one of Humboldt's successors, the Baron von Altenstein, we find a succinct statement of the nationalistic aim that was to characterize Prussian or, after 1871, German education for almost 150 years:

> And, to sum up all very briefly, [that the people] may know how to serve and wish to serve God, the king, the fatherland, and themselves, with strong, skillful bodies, awakened intelligence, and good conscience.

Another illuminating statement of the ideology of Prussian education is found in a *Sketch of a General Education Law for Prussia*, prepared in 1819:

> Loyalty to king and nation and unqualified obedience to the laws and legal ordinances are essential aspects of moral character. It is thereby declared that to awaken and strengthen these qualities in the youth and through all the means at the command of the school to work toward that condition when every school will be a nursery of blameless patriotism, is made the most sacred duty of all schoolmasters and mistresses.

NORTH AMERICAN NATIONALISM

A nationalistic concept of education has prevailed in the United States of America almost from the beginning of its history as an independent country. Throughout the 170 years of its colonial period the only real motive for the maintenance of schools was the religious idea, which sprang largely from the Reformation and Counter-Reformation. The vocational, or apprenticeship, aim, directed toward those not intending professional, religious, or governmental service, was largely secondary to the religious motive. For the colonists, whether situated in New England, the Middle colonies, or the South, believed that religious influence was a necessary requisite to a stable society.

---

[3] Abstract of Fichte's *Addresses* in Edward H. Reisner, *Evolution of the Common School* (New York: Crowell-Collier and Macmillan, Inc., 1930), pp. 218–219.

[4] The University of Berlin, now situated in East Berlin, capital of the German Democratic Republic, has been renamed in honor of Prussia's first head of Public Instruction.

With the demand for independence, which began about 1750 and resulted in the American Revolution and the Declaration of Independence, this religious motive began to wane. But it required at least another half-century before ecclesiastical influence and, in some cases, control gave way to the creation of the democratic, secular, public school. The theories upon which the American public school system was eventually erected were inherent in the political philosophy held by the Founding Fathers and expressed in the Declaration of Independence and the Constitution. The leaders of the American polity (a new order for the ages, as the Great Seal read, to be controlled by the people and for the people) recognized education as an absolute necessity. But independence gave a new motive to American education: the individual had to be educated not only to save his soul, as Puritan Massachusetts had held, but also to save his country. If the people were to rule, they must be taught the prerequisites of rule. As Hansen has written in defense of Noah Webster, America's great prophet of nationalism, "To continue the form of education that had largely prevailed while the states had been colonies under a monarchical form of government that bred on aristocracy and class divisions was to miss the very spirit of the declaration of independence."[5]

These leaders of the American Revolution held a philosophy of government derived largely from the teachings of the French *philosophes*. In the Declaration of Independence they asserted that "all men are created equal" and "endowed by their Creator with certain inalienable rights"; that "to secure these rights Governments are instituted everywhere, deriving their just powers from the consent of the governed." They also claimed that human life is susceptible of infinite improvement, and that government exists to effect this improvement; they believed that man had natural rights such as "life, liberty, and the pursuit of happiness," and that a government should be instituted which would assure to the people the enjoyment of these rights. Generally they agreed that education was the principal means to assure a government able to secure the heritage and to protect the general welfare of all the people.

The two conflicting political theories then prevalent led to two different conceptions of the relationship of government to education. The Federalists argued that government should be highly centralized, and insisted that the federal government prepare its citizenry through a strong national educational system. Anti-Federalists, called variously Jeffersonians, Republicans, Democratic-Republicans, held that individuals and communities should manage their own affairs; they urged that education satisfy local needs, instead of being administered and controlled as a single system by a powerful central government.[6]

---

[5] Allen Oscar Hansen, *Liberalism and American Education in the Eighteenth Century* (New York: Crowell-Collier and Macmillan, Inc., 1926), p. 235.

[6] See Charles S. Sydnor, *American Revolutionaries in the Making. Political Prac-*

And when the federal Constitution was ratified in 1788, education on a national basis had not been achieved in any European country. In the former thirteen colonies, other matters of state held priority; and education was one of the concerns left for future consideration and therefore not mentioned in the Constitution.[7]

This is not to say that the national importance of education was not recognized, but that the means of providing it were viewed in a different light for, though France and Prussia formed national systems, these were not created until 1802 in France and 1819 in Prussia.

Thus, it was not until 1791 when the Bill of Rights, the first ten Amendments to the federal charter, was accepted that the legal status of education in the new country was defined. For the Tenth Amendment stated clearly that "all powers not delegated to the United States by the Constitution nor prohibited by it to the States, are reserved to the States respectively, or to the people." Under the provision of this amendment, education (along with marriage and divorce, suffrage, and certain police powers) remained the province of the state, to be maintained as each saw fit. It was expected that the separate states would adopt systems best adapted to their local, historical, and regional needs.

In the year that the federal Constitution was written, the Ordinance of 1787 (as cited in Chapter 11) provided for the organization and government of the federal territory north of the Ohio River and east of the Mississippi, and revealed a dedication to general literacy. It emphasized the necessity for "religion, morality, and knowledge," and encouraged "schools and the means of instruction."[8]

For very early in American history outstanding leaders of state and nation confirmed their acceptance of the nationalistic conception of education. Again and again they expressed belief in citizenship as the new motive for education. The leaders in the Confederation and the Union all voiced the realization that preparation for civic responsibilities in a republic is the primary aim of education:

Thomas Jefferson, in a letter to James Madison, in 1787:

> Above all things, I hope that education of the common people will be attended to; convinced that on this good sense we may rely with the most security for the preservation of a due degree of liberty.

---

tices in Washington's Virginia (New York: Crowell-Collier and Macmillan, Inc., Collier Books, 1962), pp. 15, 17–18, 61, 112–115.

[7] For a fuller account see Newton Edwards and Herman G. Richey, *The School in the American Social Order*, 1st and 2d eds. (Boston: Houghton Mifflin Company, 1947, 1963), pp. 237–240 in 1st ed., pp. 214–217 in 2d ed.

[8] For further background on the ordinance, settlement, and schools in the Northwest Territory, see Kenneth V. Lottich, *New England Transplanted* (Dallas: Royal Publishing Co., 1964), pp. 18–91.

George Washington, in his First Message to Congress, 1790:

> Knowledge is in every country the surest basis of public happiness. In one, in which the measures of government receive their impression so immediately from the sense of the community, as in ours, it is proportionately essential.

John Hancock, as Governor of Massachusetts, in 1793:

> Amongst the means by which our government has been raised to its present height of prosperity, that of education has been the most efficient; you will therefore encourage and support our Colleges and Academies; but more watchfully the Grammar and other town schools. Should the support of such institutions be neglected, the kind of education which a free government requires to maintain its force would be very soon forgotten.

Alexander Hamilton, himself a brilliant student, urged the establishment of a national university to be supported by federal funds. On September 4, 1796 he wrote to Washington:

> As to the establishment of a university, it is a point which, in connection with the military schools . . . I meant agreeably to your desire, to suggest to you as parts of your speech at the opening of the session.[9]

George Washington, in his Farewell Address, September 19, 1796, failed to heed Hamilton's advice, but reinforced his own earlier demand for the creation of public knowledge:

> Promote, then, as an object of primary importance institutions for the general diffusion of knowledge. In proportion as the structure of government gives force to public opinion, it is essential that public opinion should be enlightened.

John Jay, in a letter to Dr. Benjamin Rush:

> I consider knowledge to be the soul of the Republic; and as the weak and the wicked are generally in alliance, so much care should be taken to diminish the number of the former as of the latter. Education is the way to do this, and nothing should be left undone to afford all ranks of people the means of obtaining the proper degree of it.

Thomas Jefferson, to Colonel Benjamin Cudworth Yancey, in 1816:

> If a nation expects to be ignorant and free in a state of civilization, it expects what never was and never will be. There is no safe deposit

---

[9] Hamilton's request did not bear fruit, however, and the federal Military Academy for national service was not established until 1802, to be followed by academies for the Navy, 1845; Merchant Marine, 1876; Coast Guard, 1938; and Air Force, 1955.

for the functions of government but with the people themselves; nor can they be safe with them without information.

James Madison, as President of the United States:

> A popular Government without popular information, or the means of acquiring it, is but a Prologue to a Farce or a Tragedy, or, perhaps, both. Knowledge will forever govern ignorance: and a people who mean to be their own Governors, must arm themselves with the power which knowledge gives.

Daniel Webster, at Plymouth, Massachusetts, in 1822:

> We do not, indeed, expect all men to be philosophers and statesmen; but we confidently trust, and our expectations of the duration of our government rest on that trust, that by the diffusion of general knowledge and good and virtuous sentiments; the political fabric may be secure, as well against open violence and overthrow, as against the slow but sure undermining of licentiousness.

De Witt Clinton, as Governor of New York, in 1826:

> The first duty of government, and the surest evidence of good government, is the encouragement of education. A general diffusion of knowledge is a precursor and protector of republican institutions, and in it we must confide as the conservative power that will watch over our liberties and guard them against fraud, intrigue, corruption, and violence. I consider the system of our common schools the palladium of our freedom, for no reasonable apprehension can be entertained of its subversion as long as the great body of the people are enlightened by education.

Abraham Lincoln, in a letter to the [Illinois] *Sangamon Journal,* 1832:

> Upon the subject of education, not presuming to dictate any plan or system respecting it, I can only say that I view it as the most important subject which we as a people can be engaged in. That every man may receive at least a moderate education, and thereby be enabled to read the histories of his own and other countries, by which he may duly appreciate the value of our free institutions, appears to be an object of vital importance.

Thaddeus Stevens, to the Legislature of Pennsylvania, 1835:

> If an elective republic is to endure for any length of time, every elector must have sufficient information, not only to accumulate wealth and to take care of his pecuniary concerns, but to wisely direct the Legislatures, the Ambassadors, and the Executives of the Nation; for some part of all these things, some agency in approving or disapproving of them, falls to every freeman. If, then, the permanency of our government depends on such knowledge, it is the duty of government to see that the means of information be diffused to every citizen. This is a sufficient answer to those who deem education a private and not a public duty.

Daniel Webster, at Madison, Indiana, in 1838:

> On the diffusion of education among the people rests the preserva-
> tion and perpetuation of our free institutions. I apprehend no danger to
> the country from a foreign foe. . . . Our destruction, should it come
> at all, will be from another quarter. From the inattention of the people
> to the concerns of government—from their carelessness and negligence—
> I must confess that I do apprehend some danger. I fear that they will
> place too implicit a confidence in their public servants, and fail properly
> to scrutinize their conduct. . . . Make them intelligent and they will be
> vigilant—give them the means of detecting the wrong, and they will apply
> the remedy.

Abraham Lincoln, in 1837, a year of panic and frustration:

> Let reverence for the laws . . . be taught in schools . . . and in
> colleges. . . . Let it be preached from the pulpit, proclaimed from the
> legislative halls and enforced in the courts of justice. . . . Let the old and
> the young, the rich and the poor of all sexes and tongues and colors and
> conditions, sacrifice unceasingly upon its altars.

The sentiments expressed above have been accepted by a large proportion of the American people, and today no motive is more prevalent in
education than this desire to utilize schools to prepare youth for state and
national citizenship. In a brilliant editorial Henry Steele Commager calls
public education "the American religion," for he notes, "it is in education
that we have put our faith. . . . Even in architecture we have proclaimed
our devotion, building schools like cathedrals."[10]

Yet even as early as 1790 Noah Webster had cautioned that new
schools for the people would be necessary if the new nation were to survive
as workable democracy. Of existing schools, he said:

> This appears to me a most glaring solecism in government. The con-
> stitutions are *republican*, and the laws of education are *monarchical*. The
> *former* extend the civil rights to every honest and industrious man; the
> *latter* deprive a large portion of the citizens of a most valuable privilege.[11]

The American problem, then, was to redevelop its educational provisions to harmonize with both the dictates of nationalism and the demands
of rising democracy. A distinction should be made between educational
systems, in which the public schools aim simply to develop responsible
citizenship and national feeling, and those totalitarian systems, which in
supernationalistic fashion ultimately foster war through school indoctrination. Thus evaluation of nationalistic education presents obvious difficulties,
for some of its results have been very good and some have been indescrib-

---

[10] "Our Schools Have Kept Us Free," *Life*, vol. 29, no. 16 (October 16, 1950),
pp. 46–47. This piece has been reprinted often.

[11] As quoted from Noah Webster's *Essays*, 1790, p. 24, in Hansen, *Liberalism*.

ably evil. Reisner presents an objective analysis in his discussion of education for national purposes:

> Mass nationalism has meant competition among nations, all the keener because it involved the best resources of economic and military strength which the nations have possessed. It has produced wars, probably not so many as occurred in the seventeenth and eighteenth centuries, but certainly bigger wars, and besides it has kept nations stirred up to a tension of military preparedness which is bad enough in itself. On the spiritual side, it has fostered intense, restricted loyalties for their own country and unreasoning suspicion and violent hatred of other nations in the individual citizens. In this way the fact and the attitude of nationalism have operated against the development of co-operative relationships within the whole social order, embracing all national groups.
>
> On the other hand, it must be observed that national interest has provided the effective dynamic of social reform and better human husbandry. In the interest of pack strength the individuals had to be made more intelligent, more productive, more loyal, and better contented. On the spiritual side it must be credited with a positive enlargement of human personality. The citizen, conscious of his identity with an historical tradition and a living cause and willingly devoting himself to his country's need, is more of a person than the peasant who knows nothing and cares for nothing beyond his immediate local and personal affairs. To lift the individual to the vistas of national consciousness and loyalty was a great human accomplishment. Perhaps it ought to be regarded as the necessary halfway station on the upward road to a lively consciousness of human kind.[12]

THE NATIONALISTIC APPROACH TO EDUCATION

Aims

The nationalistic aim in education, developing earliest in France, Prussia and the United States, now directs the educational thinking of practically all nations, especially the new emerging countries, in existence since World War II.[13] Prior to this conflict, Italy, Germany, and Japan were usually considered as salient examples of the extreme nationalist and totalitarian position in education. In these countries effective dictatorships utilized the schools and universities as indoctrination agencies respectively of Fascism, Nazism, and Shinto, and created powerful youth movements as well. (Soviet Russia's use of education as a prop to Communist ideology will be discussed in Chapter 21.)

Wiggin, a contemporary writer of educational history, might well be

---

[12] Reisner, pp. 230–231.

[13] See Andreas M. Kazamias and Erwin H. Epstein (Eds.), *Schools in Transition* (Boston: Allyn and Bacon, Inc., 1968), especially pp. 126–140, 327–334.

paraphrasing Webster when she speaks of the aims of the "half-mystic" nationalistic state:

> . . . all citizens must come under its influence if the state is to survive . . . the people who are at its base must be educated either to participate effectively in its development or to accept the fact of being manipulated by leaders in its behalf. . . . No longer is it conceivable that schooling be limited to scholars or leaders or specialized personnel.[14]

Thus the modern state, in contrast to ancient kingdoms or feudal governments, exists either through the zeal of an actively participant citizenry, or the acquiescence of a debased and slothful people.

Types

The exercise of nationalistic principles requires certain types of education, which we have described as national systems. Generally, these systems were based on history, ideology, or religion and sought to achieve unanimity through the inculcation of common ideals and practices. The nationalistic archetype emphasized secular and civic education. When religious and moral types were preserved, these were considered agencies in promoting loyalty and patriotism. Every nation has recognized law-abiding morality as an essential element in patriotic citizenship. Countries have varied, however, in their attitude toward pietistic education. In Germany, religious instruction has been retained as a part of civic training. The German church has been subordinate to the state since the Reformation, when its leaders had to depend on the support of German princes for survival. In France the schools are completely secularized. From the revolutionary period, French liberals have believed that the schools should be taken from the church and controlled wholly by the state, with lay instructors instead of religious orders. As a result, religion has seldom played the part in French nationalism that it did in the Prussian and German. Nevertheless, in pre–World War II Germany Adolf Hitler fostered a distinct movement toward a thorough-going secularization.[15] The issue of religious versus secular schooling was revived when his totalitarian government inaugurated a semiofficial campaign to destroy both Roman Catholic and Protestant schools.

The conditions under which the United States was founded, including its multiplicity of religious sects, made it impracticable if not impossible to erect a national school system on a religious base. The framers of the Constitution handled this problem in perhaps the only intelligent manner possible; they provided for religious toleration. The result was that religious

---

[14] Gladys A. Wiggin, *Education and Nationalism—An Historical Interpretation of American Education* (New York: McGraw-Hill, Inc., 1962), p. 13.

[15] See Gregor Ziemer, *Education for Death, The Making of the Nazi* (New York: Oxford University Press, 1941), or Douglas Miller, *You Can't Do Business with Hitler* (Boston: Little, Brown & Company, 1941).

education was left to the different churches, the public schools confining themselves to secular instruction.

In Communist Russia, although churches still exist, political ideology is the real religion; and the Union of Soviet Socialist Republics has actualized the efficacy of a national policy of education in promoting national ends by establishing for its 300 million people a system of education that seeks to make the Marxist concept of the state universal. The blueprint developed by the Kremlin includes thorough indoctrination in the theories of government cherished by the Soviet state and a rigid exclusion of all conflicting theories. All teachers must be approved politically as well as academically; and the curriculum is closely controlled.

The curriculum has invariably been judged one of the most significant features in nationalistic education; and physical education is an essential element in such a system. For example, under Frederick the Great of Prussia, the final authority over national education was placed in the Ministry of Religion, Education, and Public Health. The German schools have always placed heavy emphasis upon training for health, dexterity, and physical vigor. In the United States, particularly since two world wars uncovered gross physical defects in young American men and women, both state and federal governments have encouraged more and better physical training.

National governments have also emphasized vocational training, especially for their nonprofessionals, who must be made vocationally efficient if the country is to survive its economic and military struggles with other nations. National figures in both Europe and the United States have stressed the necessity of having a body of well-adjusted citizens as a guarantee of public stability. David Snedden (1868–1951), an American educational sociologist, spent his life in an attempt to determine valid criteria for curricula appropriate to both the professional and the "rank and file" members of the American social order.[16]

Largely as a result of the opinions of leading statesmen, the extension of suffrage, the associations of workingmen, and the efforts of such educational reformers as Horace Mann (1796–1859) and Henry Barnard (1811–1900), the United States in the mid-nineteenth century established free and universal elementary education.[17] This was later extended to the

[16] See Walter H. Drost, *David Snedden and Education for Social Efficiency* (Madison, Wisc.: University of Wisconsin Press, 1967).

[17] For a well-integrated account of the activities of Mann, Barnard, and others, see Edwards and Richey, pp. 344–356 in 1st ed., pp. 310–319 in 2d ed. Louis Filler (Ed.), *Horace Mann on the Crisis in Education* (Yellow Springs, Ohio: The Antioch Press, 1965), conveys the enthusiasm of this great Massachusetts educational crusader. Mention should be made also of similarly great leaders in other American states: Thaddeus Stevens in Pennsylvania, Samuel Lewis in Ohio, Calvin Wiley in North Carolina, Caleb Mills of Indiana, and Isaac Crary, whose activities in Michigan will be reported later in this chapter. Vincent P. Lannie's "Samuel Lewis and the 'People's Colleges,' " *School & Society*, December 9, 1967, pp. 493–498, offers an interesting portrait of this Ohio crusader.

secondary and higher levels, so that a complete system of public education, free and open to all, was developed.

Nationalistic education is conventionally universal, compulsory, and free, although seldom common in the true sense of the word. The revolutionary French reformers proclaimed that education must be universal. Roland said, "Education cannot be too widely diffused, to the end that there may be no class of citizens who may not be brought to participate in its benefits." Most of the French revolutionists believed that instruction should be relatively free even for professional training and for adults. Condorcet recommended that education be absolutely free. These Gallic liberals also maintained that schooling should be compulsory and attendance mandatory.

Aided by the census required for her general military service, Prussia very early succeeded in persuading her children to attend schools regularly. Unbroken school attendance became a national habit in Germany half a century earlier than in England and three quarters of a century earlier than in the United States.

Although the United States has not yet actually provided equal educational opportunities, the principle of a common school system organized on the ladder pattern has been accepted as the American ideal. The "American Dream" mandates equal opportunity for all the children of all the people at all levels of education. This ideal is quite different from the dual type of education generally prevalent in the older established countries or in the nations that have sprung from their colonization. In Germany, France, and other European countries, a parallel system of folk and secondary schools developed, with a wide social and economic gulf between those in the free elementary schools and those in the secondary and higher schools, which required the parents to pay a fee. The European tradition has provided for a type of public elementary school designed to serve the needs of the working class; secondary schools and universities are maintained for the development of leaders from the more favored classes. In the United States the single track, favoring the rise of individuals from even modest circumstances and minimizing social stratification, has evolved. Thus the American educational system is more common than are those of the older European countries.[18]

Content

One of the most important steps in the development of nationalism is the creation of a common culture and a unity of attitude. Nothing con-

[18] In recent years, however, some dissent has been raised about the existence of social stratification in the United States and the school's responsibility in this direction. Sociologists such as William Lloyd Warner, The Yankee City series (New Haven, Conn.: Yale University Press, 1941), and August B. Hollingshead, Elmtown's Youth (New York: John Wiley & Sons, Inc., 1949) have been conspicuous in this debate.

tributes more to this end than a common language spoken by all the elements in a nation's population. The leaders of the French Revolution realized this; and so their plans for education called for the teaching of standard French in all the schools in order to eliminate as far as possible the use of other tongues and local dialects by the inhabitants of certain regions. They further emphasized the necessity of teaching French language and literature in the secondary schools and colleges, where Latin had always been the language of first importance. Likewise, in Prussia, special attention was given to German language and literature. In Germany, not only the *Volksschulen* but the secondary schools and universities as well were required to teach the German language and literature as a subject in the curriculum; German was, as a rule, the medium of teaching; and teachers and pupils were expected to use German as the extra-class language. In the teacher-training schools it was the patriotic duty of the prospective teacher to give special attention to the study of the German language and literature. In the United States, great emphasis has been placed on the teaching of the English language and English and American literature.

One of the most important developments of the nineteenth century in both England and the United States was the rise of English grammar as a leading subject in the curriculum. Such original texts as Lindley Murray's *English Grammar* were used extensively in both England and America and rapidly replaced Latin grammars in importance. In the years during and immediately after World War I, the Americanization movement stressed the teaching of English to foreign-born immigrants who had continued the use of their native tongues. This movement providing for the training of illiterate adults in the English language, as well as in the principles of democracy and the duties of citizenship, was an obvious outgrowth of a nationalistic conception of education.

Next in emphasis to the teaching of the national language and literature comes the teaching of history and geography. The French revolutionists advocated instruction in the history and geography of their country, and these subjects still represent required units in the curriculum of the French secondary schools. In the Prussian elementary schools, geography and history were taught, not only in their general implications, but with special reference to the German nation. As Reisner observes:

> If the child was to be made conscious of his country, he needed to know its body—its towns and cities, mountains and plains and rivers, the make-up of its population, its products, its occupations, and its historic places. Thus to cause the child to connect the whole extent of his country with the little valley or the single town in which he lived and to identify his fortunes and his physical heritage with that of the millions of his fellow citizens, was an indispensable condition to the enlargement of his thinking to the national scale.
>
> But this latitudinal extension of his interests was not sufficient. It was

necessary that he should identify himself with the generations dead and gone and become conscious of membership in a social group that had a history and was to live on in the future. He must be made to see himself as the custodian of a whole heritage of heroism, suffering, and effort, which it was his duty to conserve and enrich. To this end, he learned the story of battles lost and won, and heard tales of heroic adventure and unselfish devotion to his country's cause. He came to revere the names of great men and of kings bold and good, the shepherds of the people. Likewise he learned to know the enemies of his land and to hate them for the suffering and death which they had brought to his own.[19]

The central feature of most nationalistic courses of study is government and the duties of citizens. The leaders of the French Revolution insisted that the Declaration of the Rights of Man and the Citizen be memorized, just as the United States has frequently emphasized the phrases of the Declaration of Independence and the Preamble to the Constitution. These political doctrines were expected to replace the earlier stress on religion in the pupils' interest. In Germany, emphasis was still placed upon training for a moral and Christian life; but the pupils were also taught to love their rulers and their fatherland; to be informed, according to the needs of their social position, of the social institutions and laws of their country; to be contented with their social status and happy in their work.

In the United States the teaching of civics has not only been emphasized but required by law. No subjects have been made the object of legal requirement as extensively as have the subjects of civics and American history. Most states provided by law for the study of United States history and that of the state itself. For example, the state of Nevada enacted legislation as follows:

> It is hereby made the duty of all school officers in control of public high schools in the State of Nevada to provide for courses of instruction designed to prepare the pupils for the duties of citizenship, both in times of peace and in time of war. . . . It shall be the aim of such instruction to inculcate a love of country, and a disposition to serve the country effectively and loyally.

Similarly, a Connecticut statute of 1930 requires that the "duties of citizenship, including the knowledge of the form of national, state, and local governments, shall be taught in all elementary schools." And Iowa demands that "each public and private school teach the subject of citizenship in all the grades." The state of Maine stipulates that all youth shall be taught in the elementary schools:

---

[19] Reisner, pp. 228–229. See also Kenneth V. Lottich, "Extracurricular Indoctrination in East Germany," *Comparative Education Review*, vol. 6, no. 3 (February 1963), pp. 209–211, for a profile of an extreme form of ideological education, not the norm in the West.

338　EDUCATION FOR PATRIOTIC CITIZENSHIP

. . . the cost, the object, and the principles of our government, the great sacrifices of our forefathers, the important part taken by the Union army in the war of eighteen hundred sixty-one to eighteen hundred sixty-five, and to teach them to love, honor, and respect the flag of our country that cost them so much and is so dear to every American citizen.

The true spirit of such legislative requests is clearly shown by a New York enactment just a few days after the American entry into World War I:

In order to promote a spirit of patriotic and civic service and obligations and to foster in the children of the state moral and intellectual qualities which are essential in preparing to meet the obligations of citizenship in peace or in war, the regents of the state of New York shall prescribe courses of instruction in patriotism and citizenship, to be maintained and followed in all of the schools of the state.

A number of western states including Arizona, California, Kansas, and Oklahoma require that candidates for teaching certification be examined in both the United States and State constitutions (unless they have had college courses in them).

Coupled with knowledge of country and institutions, the nationalistic curriculum invariably includes physical training designed to secure the health, vigor, and physical soundness of the people. In Prussia physical exercises were given a previously unheard of emphasis because of their hygienic and military value. Religion was also utilized with the emphasis now placed upon moral earnestness, self-sacrifice, and obedience to authority rather than the earlier stress on the catechism and church doctrine.

Social studies, portions of the social sciences adapted for school use, represent the chief area in nationalist instruction. But such instruction is not necessarily jingoistic. The social studies lend themselves admirably to the creation of worthy life patterns, regardless of nationalism. The Educational Policies Commission of the National Education Association has listed four main categories, relating to everyday life, that convey the themes of nationalist desire and personal efficiency:

1. The objective of self-realization;
2. The objective of human relationship;
3. The objective of human efficiency; and
4. The objective of civic responsibility.[20]

Music, too, receives emphasis in nationalistic education. Patriotic songs and martial orchestration particularly are used. Music was emphasized as a preparation for participation in the German patriotic singing societies and festivals which were organized at the time of the uprising of

---

[20] *The Purposes of Education in American Democracy* (Washington, D.C.: National Education Association, 1938), pp. 39–123.

Prussia in 1813. The singing of patriotic songs is not only a definite part of the exercises of all schools in the United States but generally is prescribed by law. In Maryland, for example, it is mandatory that "any grammar school, high school, preparatory school, college, or university who have morning, afternoon, or evening exercises, open such exercises . . . with the singing of 'The Star-Spangled Banner.' "

Agencies

Those who subscribe to the nationalistic concept of education believe in the public school as the foremost agency of instruction. As a standard they usually favor measures for establishing a system that is publicly supported, publicly controlled, free, universal, and nonsectarian. While they may not always attain this ideal in practice, they accept its characteristics as basic for the school systems they build. As we have noted, such public school systems developed early in the nineteenth century in France, Prussia, and the United States; and toward the close of the 1800s in England, Italy, Denmark, and other countries. These public school systems, although not usually the sole educational agencies, are recognized as the appropriate agencies of nationalistic education.[21]

In France before the present century the contest between the church and the secular-minded waxed hot indeed. King reports an argument on this issue that ended with the ecclesiastically inclined protagonist's bitter reproof that "A demand for compulsory schooling is to be expected from a secularist, just as tyranny is to be expected from a usurper."[22]

As early as 1792, Condorcet, in his *Report to the Legislative Assembly of the Committee on Public Instruction*, proposed the establishment of a completely democratic system of public schools. This report called for a primary school in every village, higher primary schools in the principal towns, secondary *collèges* in the larger cities, and secondary *lycées* in nine principal centers of France. The National Society of Sciences and Arts was to crown this public educational system. Although Condorcet's proposal was not put into effect, it became the basis for the gradual development of a French state school system, and had an important influence upon similar developments in other countries. (It is interesting to compare Condorcet's plan with that of Jefferson's for "the greater diffusion of education in Virginia," made thirteen years earlier.)[23]

In 1802, Napoleon appointed the Comte de Fourcroy (1755–1809) as Director of Public Instruction, and by legislation laid the foundations for

---

[21] See Frederick Eby, *The Development of Modern Education*, 2d ed. (Englewood Cliffs, N.J.: Prentice-Hall, Inc., 1952), pp. 532–545.

[22] Edmund J. King, *Other Schools and Ours*, rev. ed. (New York: Holt, Rinehart and Winston, Inc., 1963), p. 45.

[23] For the provisions of Jefferson's bill see Gordon C. Lee (Ed.), *Crusade against Ignorance, Thomas Jefferson on Education* (New York: Teachers College Press, Columbia University, 1961), pp. 82–92.

a general organization of public instruction. Although the law provided that primary schools be established in every district, with a schoolhouse and a teacherage, the government gave no financial support to these schools and attendance was not compulsory. Napoleon was not particularly interested in primary schools, but in *lycées* for the training of youth of superior ability for the executive duties of his autocratic government. The law of 1802 placed emphasis upon secondary and higher education with a high degree of uniformity and centralized control. In 1808, Napoleon established the University of France, not an institution for instruction, but a governing, examining, supervising, and disbursing body to control all educational institutions, public or private, primary, secondary, or higher.

Victor Cousin (1792–1867), Director of the Higher Normal School of France, was sent to study the school system of Germany in 1831. Upon his return he published his famous *Rapport sur l'état de l'instruction publique . . . en Prusse*, which was translated into English and published in London and New York where it had great influence upon British and American educational thinking. Based upon this report, a law of 1833 laid the foundations of French elementary public schools and strengthened the public secondary and higher schools. Under this law, provision was made for teacher certification and school inspection. These beginnings proved effective and France gradually developed a complete system providing universal education at public expense and under close state supervision and control.

As early as 1713, under the administrative genius of Frederick William I of Prussia, the foundations of a centralized state school organization were laid; and the sponsorship, centralization, and control of education by the state was still further developed by Frederick the Great. Frederick William's Regulatory Code of 1713 and Fundamental School Law of 1737, with Frederick the Great's General School Regulations of 1763 and General Civil Code of 1794, offered beginnings in the inception of a system of publicly supported and administered schools. Although the last-named code did not provide a free system, it prescribed rates of tuition and state subsidies for those whose parents were unable to pay. This code also provided for a high degree of central state control and fines upon parents who neglected to place their children in school. Teachers were required to maintain accurate records, teacher qualifications were stipulated, uniform texts were designated, and annual clerical inspections demanded. In 1808 the Department of Public Instruction was created as a branch of the Ministry of the Interior.

In 1834 a system of "leaving" (graduation) examinations, the *Abitur*, was established for *Gymnasium* completion. Success in these interrogations was a requirement for entrance to the university and for almost all branches of the civil service. The closest analogy to this plan in the United States is the system of Regents Examinations in New York State, and similar completion examinations in the various provinces of Canada. In addition, the College Entrance Board Examinations have been strongly influenced by this German device.

Such requirements tended to unify the Prussian elementary and secondary schools and university system into a centralized governmental operation, and so evolved a German public school system existing for the express purpose of preparing German subjects for faithful and efficient service to their state on professional and nonprofessional levels.

When the American federal government established its Bureau of Education in 1867, it too made this agency a branch of the Department of the Interior, but with vastly more limited authority. In 1817 the Prussian Department of Public Instruction became a ministry, something that has not occurred in the United States, despite some agitation for it. The American Bureau of Education (now the Office of Education) lacks a great deal of departmental status granted in other countries to similar offices, which are headed by cabinet officers. The reason, quite obviously, is the unique relationship between the states and the federal government in the United States, a relationship that has changed considerably in the past twenty years. The Office of Education itself has been placed under the Department of Health, Education and Welfare rather than the Interior, and, through its opportunity to disburse federal allotments, has gained a certain power and leverage over the nation's schools.

It took almost a half century of discussion and conflict before the issue of public education was settled in favor of publicly provided schooling for all children. Although practice has still to follow completely the principle agreed upon, by 1850 proponents of state public schools had won their fight. A public school system had been established as an instrument of American national policy. There had been numerous battles for tax support, to eliminate sectarianism, to establish state supervision, and to eliminate the pauper school idea, among others; but at the middle of the nineteenth century victory appeared to be won. The terrible Civil War in the next decade wiped out many elements of progress, but under the leadership of Abraham Lincoln the concept of "one nation, indivisible" survived. Indeed the war served to enhance the idea of universal, free education in both the North and South.

Yet almost from the beginning of the nation's history, steps had been taken in the direction of the public secular school. In 1779, Virginia Governor-to-be Thomas Jefferson (1743–1826) advocated a universal education for his state, on the assumption that a moderate education for all and special advanced education for the most capable should be offered at public expense. He proposed the establishment of free elementary schools in each hundred, or township, a number of secondary schools throughout the state, and a university as the crown of the state's school system. Jefferson's plan was too advanced, apparently, for his time and was not adopted (nor did it succeed when resubmitted in 1817, long after Jefferson's term as President). However, in 1810 Virginia established a permanent fund to subsidize the education of the poor; and, again through Jefferson's efforts, the University of Virginia was created in 1819.

Napoleon's University of France was patterned after the University of the State of New York (1784), its closest parallel in the United States. Neither institution, however, is a university in the familiar sense, but represents the authority of the state in educational matters. Alexander Hamilton drafted the legislation authorizing the New York institution and was especially interested in the problems of higher education, particularly the affairs of Columbia University, his alma mater. In his writings to James A. Bayard he described advanced curriculum matters and gave a table of his requirements, as a trustee, for the office of Columbia's presidency.[24]

In 1812 New York became the first state to designate a state officer with authority to supervise its schools. In that year a law providing for state aid to its schools and establishing the office of State Superintendent of Common Schools was enacted. The first holder of this position, Gideon Hawley (1785–1870), was apparently too efficient for his constituents and was removed by the politicians, his office for a time abolished.

Michigan was the pioneer state in establishing permanently a state office for school supervision. Under the influence of Cousin's report, Isaac Crary (1804–1854) and other leaders of the constitutional convention in 1835 secured provision for this state's school system and the State Superintendent of Public Instruction. John D. Pierce (1797–1882), the first to hold the office, did much to make this position a permanent one in American education; the post eventually being established in each of the states. Pierce revealed the origin of his belief in the efficacy of the state as an educationalizing agency as follows:

> About this time, Cousins' report on the Prussian system came into my hands and was read with much interest. Sitting one pleasant afternoon upon a log, General Crary and myself discussed for a long time, the fundamental principles which were deemed important for the constitutional convention to adopt, in laying the foundations of a new state. The subject of education was the theme of special interest. It was agreed, if possible, that it should be a distinct branch of government, and that the state Constitution ought to provide for an officer who should have the whole matter in charge.[25]

---

[24] See Richard B. Morris (Ed.), *The Basic Ideas of Alexander Hamilton* (New York: The Pocket Library, 1957), p. 438.

[25] For further illustration of Pierce's dedication to the concept of a statewide system of instruction at all levels, see Allen S. Whitney, *A History of the Professional Training of Teachers at the University of Michigan for the First Half-Century* (Ann Arbor, Mich.: George Wahr Publishing Co., 1931), pp. 1–11.

The offices for state supervision were created to enforce the state requirements set up for securing special funds from the growing state school funds, which had been accumulated largely under the stimulation of the landgrant policy of the federal government. The Northwest Territory, from which the States of Ohio, Indiana, Illinois, Michigan, and Wisconsin were carved, was divided by Congress into townships and sections, and land sold to the settlers or dedicated to the public interest. When Ohio was admitted to the Union in 1803 the United States reserved the sixteenth section of each township for school use, with the understanding that the state should not tax unsold school lands.[26] With few exceptions, such grants were made to all states later admitted, and grants of public lands in the West were made to the older states in the East, where public lands were no longer available.

The first State Board of Education in the United States originated in Massachusetts in 1837, largely as the result of the efforts of James G. Carter (1795–1849), an outstanding leader in the struggle for an American public school system. This state board was empowered to appoint an executive secretary to act as state school officer, and an excellent man was chosen for the post. Events moved similarly in Connecticut, but agitation, propaganda, and even legislation are not sufficient to insure educational reform. Men must be found and supported to undertake the delicate task of putting ideas into practice and through persistent effort making reform a reality. Horace Mann and Henry Barnard, chosen as secretaries in Massachusetts and Connecticut, were outstanding. Above all others, they did most to establish a workable public system, which became a model for emulation throughout the country. Both deserve the highest honors as pioneers in the effort to establish a pattern of free schools for all the children of all the people. Samuel Lewis in Ohio, Calvin Wiley in North Carolina, and Caleb Mills in Indiana played similar roles in their respective states.

By 1861 there were ex-officio state school officers in nine, and regular school officers in nineteen states. Ten states had also provided the office of county superintendent of schools, and twenty-six cities employed local superintendents for their public schools.

In the first half of the nineteenth century, state funds were used to defray the cost of schooling only for orphans and paupers. Those who could afford to pay did so through tuition and rate bills. In state after state battles were fought to eliminate these charges and to make the schools free to all. Several influences made it easier to achieve this result. For a number of years the taxpaying public had become accustomed to subsidize the education of the indigent, or poor, through membership in such philanthropic

---

[26] Lottich traces the development of public schools in Ohio's Western Reserve and in the Northwest generally.

educational agencies as the Sunday School Society, the Infant School Society, and various city school associations such as that of New York, which was made prominent through the leadership of De Witt Clinton (1769–1828), governor and Erie Canal builder.

These philanthropic associations, founded on the idea that since education contributed to the general welfare, it should be supported by public gifts, paved the way for an increased willingness to have tax monies used to support the schools. But another influence from abroad, which curiously rested on the public's hope of getting something for almost nothing, called attention to the idea of public support for their schools.

This was the monitorial school, developed about 1800 by Andrew Bell (1753–1832) in India and Joseph Lancaster (1778–1838) in England. Lancaster is said to have offered to educate one child for one year for one dollar.[27] These schools were imported to the United States during the early nineteenth century because of their intriguing methodology and undoubted cheapness; and perhaps they helped to develop a public willingness to further support education.

In 1821, in Boston, the first public secondary school, later called a high school, was established. This new type of institution spread through the country as the successor of the earlier Latin-grammar school and the public academy. Then a Massachusetts law of 1827 made the establishment of public high schools mandatory. And in Michigan the decision in the Kalamazoo Case (1874) affirmed the legal status of the tax-supported secondary school.[28]

In 1787 provision had already been made for state universities in Ohio, where land was set aside for the support of Ohio University (Athens) and Miami University (Oxford). In order to create state universities quickly, a few misguided attempts were made to convert existing denominational colleges into public institutions. But such efforts were checked by the Supreme Court of the United States in the well-known Dartmouth College Case in 1819.[29] By 1860, however, sixteen states had established state universities, the majority aided by federal landgrants. A further stimulus to the creation of state-controlled higher education was the Morrill Act of 1862, which offered 30,000 acres for each of its Congressmen and Senators to any state interested in providing state colleges of agriculture and mechanical arts for their citizenry.

Admittedly, enthusiastic nationalists have sometimes endeavored to stretch the power of the state beyond its limits. A half century ago, Oregon

---

[27] For one of the best accounts of the Lancaster-Bell era and its unique methodology, see Phil E. Hagar, "Nineteenth Century Experiments with Monitorial Teaching," *Phi Delta Kappan*, vol. xxxx, no. 4 (January, 1959), pp. 164–167.

[28] Charles E. Stuart et al. v. School Dist. No. 1 of the Village of Kalamazoo, 30 Michigan 69 (1874).

[29] Dartmouth College v. Woodward, 4 Wheaton 518 (1819).

sought to give its public schools a monopoly in the education of the children of the state. The legislature enacted a law requiring all children to attend the public schools, so that all other agencies, including parochial bodies, would be eliminated. An appeal was carried to the United States Supreme Court, which in 1925 in a historic decision declared that while states have the right to determine the minimum educational standards to be enforced, parents have the right to decide by which agencies these standards are to be enforced.[30] Across the Atlantic, France closed all convent schools in 1904, giving the national government a virtual monopoly in primary education. While several other nations have moved in the same direction, such action has seemed incompatible with the American conception of democracy, as guaranteed by the Constitution.

Nationalism recognizes the teacher as the most important factor in achieving its purposes. Cubberley, one of the most nationalistic of the middle generation of American educators, has proclaimed, "Education in a democratic government such as ours is the greatest of all undertakings for the promotion of the national welfare, and the teacher in our schools renders an inconspicuous but a highly important national service."[31]

In all national school systems, provision must be made for the careful selection and training of teachers. Thus, teacher-training institutions have been established under state control, and systems for the examination and certification of teachers have been developed. The Prussian government realized early that the success of its public schools depended more on the quality of the teachers than on any other single factor. A private seminary for training teachers was established as early as 1738 by Hecker and became, under Frederick the Great, the Royal Teachers Seminary, with a strong state subsidy. By 1800 there were already a dozen or so of these pedagogical seminars.

In 1809, as a result of Pestalozzian influence, a teachers seminary was set up at Leipzig, the first to be established as an integral part of the state school system. Now Prussia led the way among all European states in providing competent teachers, thoroughly trained in a teachers seminary, which was located in each administrative unit. The qualifications of Prussian school teachers were determined by examination, and no teacher could be given a post unless he received royal ratification of his nomination. In practice, only teachers who had been trained in the approved seminars were selected.

The Superior Normal School of France, established by the National Assembly in 1794 was abandoned in a short time, but reestablished by Napoleon in 1808. The normal school, a French development, has been a

---

[30] Pierce v. Society of Sisters of the Holy Names of Jesus and Mary, 268 U.S. 510 (1925).

[31] Ellwood P. Cubberley, *Public Education in the United States*, rev. enl. ed. (Boston: Houghton Mifflin Company, 1934), pp. 763–764.

significant influence in providing teachers in empathy with the aspirations of the nation. Since 1870 there has been a normal school in each of the provinces, or *départments* of France, in addition to the Superior Normal School in Paris.

In the United States, New York State made the earliest provision for training teachers, and granted aid to academies which included teacher training in their curriculum. The first state Normal School was established at Lexington, Massachusetts, in 1839 under the inspiration of James G. Carter and headed by Cyrus Peirce (1790–1860). A second was opened at Barre in 1839 and a third at Bridgewater in 1840. The normal school movement spread and at the beginning of the Civil War there were at least a dozen, one as far west as Minnesota. Although they are no longer called normal schools, public teacher-training institutions exist in each of the fifty states, as we will note in Chapter 19.

Teachers Institutes, first organized by Henry Barnard in Connecticut (1839), multiplied rapidly and became the strongest educational device for updating and inspiring public school teachers. These institutes were temporary training centers, lasting from several days to a week, at which leading administrators and professors of education lectured or demonstrated methods current in the field. In-service training has largely taken the place of such convocations, and certification requirements now usually demand the taking of additional courses at a teachers college or university. Every state in the Union has a system of teacher certification, although procedures vary widely in administration and requirements. There is no reciprocity among states.

All nationalistic governments have endeavored to see that the teachers in their public school systems are loyal and patriotic servants of the state. For example in the United States, several states have passed laws providing for the study of civics, United States history, and state and national constitutions, by all students in teacher-education institutions. A number of states have also passed laws requiring teachers on various levels to take an oath of allegiance to support the constitutional form of government.

Organization

The tendency in all national systems of education is toward a highly centralized organization with a hierarchy of administration and supervision. The system is invariably headed by a national or state school officer, with authority delegated downward through minor officials. In practically all countries, educational organization is centralized in a minister of education, who is a member of the cabinet.

France still has the most completely centralized plan for education in Western Europe. At the head of the entire system is the Minister of Public Instruction. He is assisted by an advisory council, known as the Higher Council of Public Instruction, and by three directors, one each for higher, secondary, and primary education. At the head of each of the districts, or academies, into which the country is divided, is a rector assisted by an academic council. The rector has authority over all three levels of education in his district with the exception of the appointment of teachers, which is in the hands of the prefect of the department. The efficiency of the entire system is assured by the maintenance of a complete corps of state and district inspectors, assisted by local school committees. Through this highly centralized organization, teachers are appointed, salaries fixed, pension systems maintained, curriculum and method controlled, and private instruction supervised. It has been said facetiously that at a given time each child in France will rise and spell *cat*.

Prussia, the forerunner of modern Germany, appointed a national school head with the educational reforms adopted by Frederick the Great. In 1817 the Bureau of Education was elevated to an independent ministry; and in 1825 the organization of a centralized state system of public instruction was completed by the establishment of provincial school boards, responsible to the Minister of Education, and intended to replace the church consistories in the local control of education. However, many of the members of the district school boards, which operated under the administration of the provincial boards, and many of the local school inspectors were clergymen; and this continued through the formation of the German empire in 1871, its defeat in 1918, and until after the adoption of the new federal constitution of the Weimar Republic. Yet in spite of the opposition of church officials and conservative Germans, every school regulation issued in Germany from the establishment of the Ministry of Education to the end of World War II was in the direction of more thoroughly centralized national control. Recognizing nationalistic education as the principal support of the nation, not only Prussia but other German states adopted centralized school systems.

Hitler organized the German schools even more thoroughly on a militaristic basis as a means of solidifying his government, preserving the ancient culture, and satisfying the demands of the new industrial and economic life of the nation.

A similar tendency toward supernationalism occurred in pre–World War II Italy. Here, under the spell of another totalitarianism, leaders of education attempted, beginning in 1922, to develop nationalistic patterns in accord with Fascism. The clearest statements of their ideology were made by Giovanni Gentile (1875–1944), Mussolini's Minister of Education and author of the *Reform of Education*. Gentile believed that the practical aim of education is nationalism; that the means of education are the spiritual products of the past relived in the present. He asserted that the state, representing universal will or reason, is as a whole over and above the citizen. The state is universal and continuous, and the individual good must be identical with the state's good or else be sacrificed for the good of the state, he asserted. The individual is an instrument of the state. The state has rights, but the individual only duties. The individual participates in the benefits of government, but not in the government. Education, by giving the pupil the common national language, history, and culture, evokes the common will. Thus developed a Fascist conception of education—a nationalistic type even more pronounced than those of the monarchies and democracies already discussed. The schools of Fascist Italy were radically reorganized and strictly controlled.

An idealist, Gentile maintained that the teacher "must transfuse the pupil with something of himself, and out of his own spiritual substance, create elements of the pupil's character, mind, and will." Although his Fascist leanings at first pleased Mussolini, after a two-year term Gentile was dismissed.[32] When Mussolini fell, Gentile was slain by partisans.

In the United States there has never been a national centralized school organization. And even in the states no move to substitute a strongly controlled state school organization for local autonomy has succeeded. Although the central government had been making landgrants for educational purposes to the states for almost 100 years, it was not until 1867 that Congress made any effort to enable the federal government to do more about education than subsidize it. In that year, as we noted, Congress created the Department of Education (without cabinet rank) for the purpose of "collecting facts, statistics, and information as to schools and school systems to aid the different states in the establishment and maintenance of efficient school systems and otherwise promote the cause of education generally throughout the country." Henry Barnard, former head of the Connecticut system, was the first commissioner. In addition to his fact-finding role, he was to report annually to Congress. Thus, the American government adopted a policy of investigation and inspiration, rather than one of administration and control on the models of France and Prussia.

The placing of the Office of Education under the Secretary of Health, Education, and Welfare only indicates the decentralized role of education under the United States Constitution. Since the establishment of the office Congress has carefully contrived to retain control of most of the educational activities of the federal government, rather than delegate them to the Commissioner of Education. When the Smith-Hughes Vocational Education Act was passed in 1917, setting up a national system of vocational training, administration of the act was placed in the hands of the federal Board of Vocational Education. Many other federal educational activities are scattered throughout various federal departments. When in 1935 Franklin D. Roosevelt set aside 50 million dollars for a national youth

---

[32] See George F. Kneller, "Education in Italy," pp. 245–298, in Arthur H. Moehlman and Joseph S. Roucek (Eds.), *Comparative Education* (New York: Holt, Rinehart and Winston, 1952).

movement, the administration of the fund was placed under the Treasury Department. During the 1950s and 1960s, however, the Office of Education has gained more power through its opportunity to distribute large grants of federal funds made available after Sputnik and during the civil rights controversy.

Although the organization of the school system varies considerably in the different states, there is still a great deal of uniformity. Each state has a chief school officer, known variously as the superintendent of schools, superintendent of public instruction, or commissioner of education. He is usually elected or appointed by the state governor or a state board of education. The majority of states have boards of education, which differ considerably in their scope and functions; but some states apportion educational control among different boards. In all the states there is a greater or lesser degree of local autonomy, something vastly prized in the United States. In some states the school district is the smallest local unit; in some, the town or township; and in others, especially in the South and West, the county. There has been a strong movement toward reorganization of schools on a county basis; and since the Great Depression there has been a distinct tendency to centralize educational support and control in the hands of the state government in order to provide a more thorough equalization of educational opportunities.

City school systems often operate under special charters, independent of state authority. States conventionally delegate administrative responsibilities to county, township, district, and city boards of education. In some states county superintendents are the executive officers of county boards of education, but more often they are elected by the people and operate directly under the state board or department. City superintendents, unique in the United States, are appointed by city boards of education as their professional executive officers, but in a few cities administrative responsibility is divided between the superintendent (for instruction) and the business manager. Thus the general direction in American education, especially in the larger centers of population, seems to be towards a larger and more "efficient" type of organization. In the 1960s, however, because of local conditions, especially in regard to the civil rights movement, the desire for local autonomy became active again as citizens' groups demanded extreme forms of local control.

The trend in organization of the levels of instruction has been towards the ladder plan, as advocated by John Amos Comenius. Unfortunately, however, the arrangement of levels has followed the route of administrative convenience rather than being based on a careful study of child growth and development.

Let us trace briefly the pattern and form of education in the countries we have used as examples of nineteenth-century trends in school organization. In France, the child first enters the *école maternelle* and remains there until he enters the *école primaire* at six years. The primary school is compulsory until fourteen. After the *école primaire* is the *école primaire supérieure*, with a three-year course devoted to practical work of a vocational nature. There are also continuation schools, supported by the various districts and subsidized by the state, for agricultural and industrial education. The secondary schools are *lycées*, national schools supported partly by the state, and *collèges*, originally maintained by the districts with some aid from the state. Children may transfer to these secondary schools from the primary school at the age of eleven, but sometimes are prepared instead in the preparatory departments of the *lycées* and *collèges* themselves. The completion of secondary education is crowned by a rigorous state examination, the *baccalaureate*, a prerequisite for entrance to the university or the professions.

Following World War I a movement developed in France to establish a common school for all, the *école unique*. This plan was to give all children the same schooling from six to thirteen. The brighter pupils were to receive a secondary education from fourteen to seventeen, and finally a few selected students would at the age of eighteen be admitted to the institutions of higher education. All of this education was to be without expense to the student. But French progress was imperiled by World War II, when education under German occupation stagnated, as Nazi attempts to revise the curriculum were only partially successful. Upon the liberation of Paris in August 1944, the French government empowered Dr. Paul Langevin and Dr. Henri Wallon to suggest modifications in keeping with the *école unique* idea. The new organization (only parts of which were enacted into law) calls for two levels that follow a single pattern. Three cycles make up the lower level: (1) personal development, at ages seven through eleven; (2) orientation, eleven through fifteen; (3) determination, fifteen through eighteen. Higher education for those who qualify begins at age eighteen.[33]

In Germany before 1919 there was no sign of the educational ladder as it has come to be in the United States. The children of the masses were educated in the *Volksschule*, which provided an eight-year course, ending at fourteen and not leading to any secondary school. It was impossible for a graduate of the *Volksschule* to enter a secondary school even if he could pay the necessary fees. The only avenue open to him was common labor or attending the *Fortbildungschule* (continuation school) to become skilled in a trade. The prerequisites required for entrance to the secondary schools, the *Gymnasium*, the *Realgymnasium*, or the *Realschule*, were provided by private tutors or a *Vorschule* (private preparatory school), although many did go to the *Volksschule* for three years and then transferred to the sec-

---

[33] See Kneller, pp. 190–244.

ondary school. Secondary schools were for the children of the higher classes, who were destined for the universities, the professions, and higher civil service.

The Constitution of the 1919 Republic abolished this dual organization. The Common School Law of 1920 provided that a "public school system be constructed as an organic whole, the Middle and Higher schools to be extensions of a common school." A public four-year elementary school known as the *Grundschule*, was organized as a common school for all. The *Mittelschule* took pupils from the fifth year and carried them through the ninth or tenth years. In addition to the older patterns of secondary schools, two new types were established: the *Deutsche Oberschule* (vernacular high school) and the *Aufbauschule* (rural high school).

The general plan (although each *Land*, or state, had a separate system) was for a *Grundschule*, occupying from four to six years; a *Volkschule*, taking from two to five years; and a *Gymnasium*, for those capable of secondary school work (about 15 percent). *Gymnasien* were entered at age ten or eleven and continued for six or eight years.

In Germany, as in France, a single track or *Einheitsschule* had been considered since 1919; but only lately has there been substantial progress. Following Hitler's defeat in 1945 and the subsequent occupation, the schools of the Western Zone, that is, the German Federal Republic, and West Berlin were modified somewhat. In the Eastern Zone, occupied by the Communists, and now called the German Democratic Republic, they were modified also, but in the direction of Marxist education. (Soviet education and recent changes within the Federal Republic will be discussed in Chapter 21.)

In the United States, the traditional ladder system was organized on an 8–4–4 basis. The eight-year elementary school was followed by a four-year high school and this in turn by a four-year college. Beyond this came the graduate and professional schools. Since 1910 certain interesting reorganizations have taken place.

As early as 1892 national committees were urging the reorganization of the 8–4 plan. Urging economy of time it was commonly thought that if the high school could begin at the seventh grade rather than the ninth, students could be prepared for college and university somewhat earlier, thus allowing entrance into the professions at a more advantageous age. This idea was first furthered by offering high school subjects at lower levels, but in 1910 a clear break was made with the older organization in the creation of the junior high school, generally the seventh, eighth and ninth grades.

The idea of economy of time soon was lost, however, and thus the junior high school came to be looked upon as a setting for orientation and academic and vocational guidance. Many arrangements were offered but the usual brackets were 6–3–3, 6–2–4, or 6–6. Following World War II, a new organization, the middle school, was advocated and tried. It generally included the sixth through the eighth or ninth grades, although other variations were offered.[34]

The expansion of the public junior college at about the same time convinced many Americans that they had indeed achieved a democratic single ladder in education. The popularity of the comprehensive high school, which housed several tracks including academic, business, technical, agricultural, mechanical, and the like did little to dispel a notion revered by the world's leading democracy.[35]

Methods

The nationalist conception of education has done little directly in pioneering and developing new methods of instruction, unless we consider the consolidation and correlation of those subjects thought to favor the inculcation of patriotic and indigenous frames of mind a method. Legislation, as a rule, has not concerned itself with matters of methodology, being usually content with prescribing the schools' curriculum and organization. Nevertheless, almost as a by-product of their interest in nationalization, with the advent of the scientific movement and the growth of interest in the findings of psychology (see Chapters 16 and 17), the lines between organization and method have become somewhat blurred.

Early in the nineteenth century, the Prussian government sent a number of young men to Pestalozzi's institute at Yverdon to observe the methods and try to catch the spirit of the Swiss schoolmaster; and upon their return they "Pestalozzianized" the state teacher-training system and thus introduced the new methods into their national system of instruction.[36] Victor Cousin's *Report on the Conditions of Public Instruction in Prussia* described the methods as well as the organization; but it was the latter that attracted the greatest attention and had the most influence.

Conscientious state and national school officials in the United States have always tried to keep teachers in their school systems to the highest standards of pedagogy. Although Horace Mann confessed in his diary that he had never read a book on pedagogy at the time he was appointed secretary of the Massachusetts State Board of Education, he did much to familiarize his teachers with the best methods developed up to his time. Through his annual messages—especially the Seventh Annual Report dealing with European schools—he familiarized the teachers of Massachusetts with the

---

[34] For some pros and cons of middle school organization, see Paul Gastwirth, "Questions Facing the Middle School," *The Clearing House*, vol. 41, no. 8 (April, 1967), pp. 472–475.

[35] But see Robert Ulich, "The Legend of the 'Single Ladder,'" *School and Society*, vol. 65, no. 1675 (February 1, 1947), pp. 73–75.

[36] The work of Pestalozzi and other developmentalists is discussed in Chapter 16.

best methods of instruction available. Henry Barnard's idea of teachers' institutes developed into a popular state agency for the dissemination of information about new teaching methods. His powerful *American Journal of Education* was another strong influence. Placed in charge of early state normal schools, educators like Cyrus Peirce at Lexington, and David Page (1810–1848) at Albany, gave considerable thought to the question of the improvement of instruction. Peirce's *Lectures on the Art of Teaching* and Page's *Theory and Practice of Teaching* were outstanding among the books presenting practical suggestions for the conduct of schools under the district system. State normal schools were instrumental in introducing the actual use of Pestalozzian and Herbartian methods into the United States.

State departments of education and the United States Office of Education, through their bulletins and reports have familiarized local schools with the latest educational methods and have been instrumental in the exchange of instructional experiences. The states, by requiring teachers to take professional courses before they can secure certificates, are doing much to improve instruction in American classrooms.

Frequently those in charge of national school systems are not in sympathy with experimentation and innovation in methods of teaching, although they do encourage the adoption of methods that have been proved safe, practical and efficient. Most pioneering in method has been done in private schools by dedicated teachers like Pestalozzi, Froebel, and Parker, and through the encouragement of associations of teachers.

On the other hand, supernationalist philosophy regards a paramilitary spirit and organization as conducive to the development of the proper academic attitude, that is, minds receptive to the prevailing ideology of the state and indoctrination in the current presentation of whatever "facts" or interpretations have been determined by the ruling clique. This entails the use of special methods or organization for its effectiveness; a rigorous discipline is enforced; and social or paramilitary youth groups are formed at appropriate age levels both within and outside the school. Such devices were much in evidence in pre-World War II Italy, Germany, and Japan, and currently flourish in Communist-controlled areas, especially in the Soviet Union, East Central Europe, and mainland China with her satellites.[37]

While nationalistic education does not necessarily lead to totalitarianism, its potential monolithic character is most clearly revealed through such examples. And in each phase of nationalism, whether historical origins are merely utilized as unifying devices (with the hope of strengthening the national fiber) or education is considered merely another branch of politics,

---

[37] For a thorough discussion of educational philosophy and method in East Europe and Communist China, see Joseph S. Roucek and Kenneth V. Lottich, *Behind the Iron Curtain, The Soviet Satellite States—East European Nationalism and Education* (Caldwell, Idaho: Caxton Printers, Ltd., 1964).

discipline is an essential ingredient in school practice. National school authorities usually favor a condition of system, order, and obedience. They are seldom in sympathy with permissive doctrines or authentic student self-government. Under extreme nationalism (totalitarianism), the school and its students are mere supports to national ideology.

REFERENCES

Arrowood, Charles F., *Thomas Jefferson on Education*. New York: McGraw-Hill, Inc., 1930.

Boyd, William, *The History of Western Education*, 8th ed. Rev. by Edmund J. King. New York: Barnes and Noble, Inc., 1966. Pp. 330–378.

Butts, R. Freeman, *A Cultural History of Western Education*, 2d ed. New York: McGraw-Hill, Inc., 1955. Pp. 267–337.

Cantor, Norman F., *The English, A History of Politics and Society to 1760*. New York: Simon and Schuster, Inc., 1967. Pp. 450–499.

Cubberley, Ellwood P., *Public Education in the United States*, rev. enl. ed. Boston: Houghton Mifflin Company, 1934. Pp. 163–281.

Curti, Merle, *Social Ideas of American Educators*, rev. ed. Totowa, N.J.: Littlefield, Adams and Company, 1959. Pp. 101–168.

Doughton, Isaac, *Modern Public Education, Its Philosophy and Background*. New York: Appleton-Century-Crofts, 1935. Pp. 380–459.

Drost, Walter H., *David Snedden and Education for Social Efficiency*. Madison, Wisc.: University of Wisconsin Press, 1967.

Eby, Frederick, and Charles F. Arrowood, *The Development of Modern Education*, 2d ed. Englewood Cliffs, N.J.: Prentice-Hall, Inc., 1952. Pp. 540–617.

Edwards, Newton, and Herman G. Richey, *The School in the American Social Order*. Boston: Houghton Mifflin Company, 1963.

Filler, Louis (Ed.), *Horace Mann and the Crisis in Education*. Yellow Springs, Ohio: The Antioch Press, 1965.

Fontainerie, François de La, *French Liberalism and Education*. New York: McGraw-Hill, Inc., 1932. Pp. 29–169, 311–378.

Good, Harry G., *A History of American Education*. New York: Crowell-Collier and Macmillan, Inc., 1956. Pp. 81–170.

———, *A History of Western Education*. New York: Crowell-Collier and Macmillan, Inc., 1960. Pp. 292–295, 318–325, 344–356, 367–433.

Gross, Richard E. (Ed.), *Heritage of American Education*. Boston: Allyn and Bacon, Inc., 1962. Pp. 233–313.

Hansen, Allen Oscar, *Liberalism and American Education in the Eighteenth Century*. New York: Crowell-Collier and Macmillan, Inc., 1926.

Kandel, Isaac L., *Comparative Education*. Boston: Houghton Mifflin Company, 1933. Pp. 1–22.

King, Edmund J., *Other Schools and Ours,* rev. ed. New York: Holt, Rinehart and Winston, Inc., 1963.

Knight, Edgar W., *Education in the United States,* 2d rev. ed. Boston: Ginn & Company, 1941. Pp. 192–407.

Kohn, Hans, *The Idea of Nationalism.* New York: The Macmillan Co., 1951.

Lee, Gordon C., *Education in Modern America,* rev. ed. New York: Holt, Rinehart and Winston, Inc., 1957. Pp. 3–54, 272–294.

Lottich, Kenneth V., *New England Transplanted.* Dallas: Royal Publishing Co., 1964. Especially chs. ii–iv.

Mayer, Frederick, *A History of Educational Thought.* Columbus, Ohio: Charles E. Merrill Books, Inc., 1960. Pp. 247–262, 291–304.

Moehlman, Arthur H., and Joseph S. Roucek, *Comparative Education.* New York: Holt, Rinehart and Winston, Inc., 1952.

Mulhern, James, *A History of Education,* 2d ed. New York: The Ronald Press Company, 1959. Pp. 422–435, 494–568.

Pounds, Ralph L., *The Development of Education in Western Culture.* New York: Appleton-Century-Crofts, 1968. Pp. 191–224.

Raup, Bruce, *Education and the Organized Interests in America.* New York: G. P. Putnam's Sons, 1936. Pp. 40–72.

Reisner, Edward H., *Evolution of the Common School.* New York: Crowell-Collier and Macmillan, Inc., 1930. Pp. 225–257.

Rippa, S. Alexander, *Education in a Free Society.* New York: David McKay Company, Inc., 1967. Pp. 84–127.

Roucek, Joseph S., and Kenneth V. Lottich, *Behind the Iron Curtain, The Soviet Satellite States—East European Nationalisms and Education.* Caldwell, Idaho: Caxton Printers, Ltd., 1964.

Ulich, Robert, *The Education of Nations,* rev. ed. Cambridge, Mass.: Harvard University Press, 1967.

————, *History of Educational Thought.* New York: American Book Company, 1950. Pp. 225–257.

———— (Ed.), *Three Thousand Years of Educational Wisdom,* 2d ed., enl. Cambridge, Mass.: Harvard University Press, 1954. Pp. 426–479.

Wiggin, Gladys A., *Education and Nationalism—An Historical Interpretation of American Education.* New York: McGraw-Hill, Inc., 1962. Pp. 1–503.

Ziemer, Gregor, *Education for Death.* New York: Oxford University Press, 1941.

SELECTED PAPERBACKS

Aiken, Henry D. (Ed.), *The Age of Ideology; the Nineteenth Century Philosophers.* New York: New American Library of World Literature, Inc., 1950.

Bailyn, Bernard, *Education in the Forming of American Society.* New York: Random House, Inc., Vintage Books, 1960.

Beck, Robert Holmes, *A Social History of Education.* Englewood Cliffs, N.J.: Prentice-Hall, Inc., 1965.

Bohannan, Paul, *Law and Warfare.* Garden City, N.Y.: Natural History Press, 1967.

Boorstein, Daniel J., *The American Colonial Experience.* New York: Random House, Inc., Vintage Books, 1964.

Broudy, Harry S., and John R. Palmer, *Exemplars of Teaching Method.* Skokie, Ill.: Rand McNally & Company, 1965.

Carlton, Frank Tracy, *Economic Influences upon Educational Progress in the United States, 1820–1850.* New York: Teachers College Press, Columbia University, 1967.

Cassirer, Ernst, *The Myth of the State.* New York: Doubleday & Company, Inc., 1955.

Cremin, Lawrence A. (Ed.), *The Republic and the School: Horace Mann on the Education of Free Men.* New York: Teachers College Press, Columbia University, 1957.

————, *The Wonderful World of Ellwood Patterson Cubberley.* New York: Teachers College Press, Columbia University, 1965. Pp. 1–52.

————, *The Genius of American Education.* New York: Random House, Inc., 1966. Pp. 3–116.

Fellman, David (Ed.), *The Supreme Court and Education.* New York: Teachers College Press, Columbia University, 1958.

Franklin, Benjamin, *Autobiography.* Introd. by Verner W. Crane. New York: Harper & Row, Publishers, 1956.

Hall, David D. (Ed.), *Puritanism in Seventeenth-Century Massachusetts.* New York: Holt, Rinehart and Winston, Inc., 1968. Pp. 14–25, 55–60.

Lee, Gordon C. (Ed.), *Crusade Against Ignorance: Thomas Jefferson on Education.* New York: Teachers College Press, Columbia University, 1958.

Mayer, Frederick, *Foundations of Education.* Columbus, Ohio: Charles E. Merrill Books, Inc., 1963.

Morris, Richard B. (Ed.), *The Basic Ideas of Alexander Hamilton.* New York: The Pocket Library, 1957.

Rippa, S. Alexander, *Education in a Free Society.* New York: David McKay Company, Inc., 1967. Pp. 84–127.

Roucek, Joseph S., and Kenneth V. Lottich, *Behind the Iron Curtain: The Soviet Satellite States—East European Nationalism and Education.* Caldwell, Idaho: Caxton Printers, Ltd., 1969.

Sizer, Theodore R. (Ed.), *The Age of the Academies.* New York: Teachers College Press, Columbia University, 1967.

Starkey, Marion L., *The Devil in Massachusetts.* New York: Doubleday & Company, Inc., Dolphin Books, 1949.

Sydnor, Charles S., *American Revolutionaries in the Making. Political Practices in Washington's Virginia.* New York: Crowell-Collier and Macmillan, Inc., Collier Books, 1962.

Tyler, Alice Felt, *Freedom's Ferment. Phases of American Social History from the Colonial Period to the Outbreak of the Civil War.* New York: Harper & Row, Publishers, 1962.

Viorst, Milton (Ed.), *The Great Documents of Western Civilization.* New York: Bantam Books, Inc., 1965.

Wright, Louis B., *Culture on the Moving Frontier.* New York: Harper & Row, Publishers, 1961.

CHAPTER **16**

The Foundations of Child Development

Every child, dependent as he is on the help of the community, finds himself face to face with a world that gives and takes, that expects adaptation and satisfies life. . . . He realizes at an early age that there are other human beings who are able to satisfy their urges more completely, and are better prepared to live.[1]

DEVELOPMENTALISM

While the nationalists were engaged in the organization of educational agencies that would be effective in the attainment of patriotic ideals, another group of thinkers and teachers, from the late eighteenth century into the twentieth century, concerned themselves with reforming the educational process and bringing it into greater accord with the laws of human development. This endeavor is usually known as the psychological movement, since it is concerned primarily with the nature of the mind and its workings. It is based upon a child-centered point of view, and its findings grew out of a careful study of the child.

Especially in its later stages, the psychological movement was greatly stimulated by the theory of evolution, as developed by Lamarck, Darwin, and Huxley, and was for that reason sometimes designated as evolutionism. However, since its chief characteristic was the belief that education is control of the child's development from within, instead of an imposition of adult standards from without, the term *developmentalism* is perhaps preferable and will be used here.

---

[1] Alfred Adler, *Understanding Human Nature* (New York: Greenberg Publishers, Inc., 1946).

The following definitions by later developmentalists present their point of view.

> *Education is the process of developing which goes on in the individual human being as the result of his activity in and his reaction upon the environment and which by giving meaning to experience progressively increases his power to direct subsequent experience.*[2]

The work of teaching is to produce and to prevent changes in human beings; to preserve and increase the desirable qualities of body, intellect and character and to get rid of the undesirable.

Using psychological terms, the art of teaching may be defined as the art of giving and withholding stimuli with the result of producing or preventing certain responses.[3]

The aim of the teacher is to produce desirable and prevent undesirable changes in human beings by producing and preventing certain responses. The means at the disposal of the teacher are the stimuli which can be brought to bear upon the pupil,—the teacher's words, gestures and appearance, the condition and appliances of the schoolroom, the books to be used and objects to be seen, and so on through a long list of the things and events which the teacher can control. The responses of the pupil are all the infinite variety of thoughts and feelings and bodily movements occurring in all their possible connections.

The basis of educability lies in the striving of the child to compensate for his weaknesses. A thousand talents and capabilities arise from the stimulus of inadequacy. . . . [But] the situations of individual children are extraordinarily different.[4]

These men were concerned primarily with the child and his development, a development which results only through the child's continual interaction with his stimulating environment. The complete conception and full significance of this idea evolved gradually through the contributions of many educational philosophers and experimenters, but its implications are now almost universally accepted. The developmentalists have brought about changes in the curriculum and in the organization and administration of educational agencies, as well as a revolution in the methodology of teaching, better teacher training, and a better understanding of the whole educational process. Indeed, it was in the effort to provide just such a departure from the earlier disciplinary methodology that the developmental movement arose.

Rousseau's naturalism may be considered the antecedent of develop-

[2] Isaac Doughton, *Modern Public Education—Its Philosophy and Background* (New York: Appleton-Century-Crofts, 1935), pp. 134.

[3] Edward L. Thorndike, *The Principles of Teaching Based on Psychology* (New York: A. G. Seiler, 1906), p. 7.

[4] Adler, p. 35.

mentalism's proclamation that education is a matter of the free and un-restricted development of the individual's natural powers and inclinations. Naturalism was a distinct reaction against the belief that the individual, by nature, was bad and had to be fashioned by nurture into a different being. Naturalism condemned all that was artificial, and looked negatively upon any school procedures that attempted to shape the individual to the institutions of human society. Developmentalism is a reconciliation of two extremes: education as a matter of human *nurture*, and education as a matter of natural *growth*. The psychological developmentalist conceived of education as a natural process of growth, an unfolding of native capacities; but he believed also that this development, or organic growth, could be hindered or helped, and thus guided in desirable directions, by the methods with which the natural capacities and activities were treated.

The work of the psychologists was influenced considerably by the spread of the theory of materialistic monism. As long as the dualistic con-ception of mind as distinct from body prevailed, discussion of mental phenomena necessarily remained in the realm of philosophy. But with the growing conviction that the body and mind are one, metaphysical specula-tion gave way to inductive observation and experimentation. One of the chief characteristics of developmentalism was this belief that observation and experimentation would lead to the discovery of psychological principles upon which educational procedures could securely rest. Late in the nine-teenth century, developmentalism became linked with scientific determin-ism in its insistence that all educational procedures should be based upon a careful scientific study of the mind. As a result of scientific study, a new dynamic biological psychology replaced the older faculty psychology as a basis for educational theory and usage.

The influence of developmentalism was felt first in the elementary school. The earlier psychologists gave most attention to the study of the young child and to the beginning years of his development. They felt that if education were a process of development, the primary stages in this evolution were of greatest importance. As a result of this emphasis upon early growth, elementary education supplanted secondary education as the chief interest of those concerned with educational thinking and practice. Thus, the reforms in educational procedures resulting from the psychologi-cal movement were confined for almost a century to elementary school instruction.

Developmentalism had many contributors, but in this chapter we shall consider those who made the most outstanding contributions. The phases of the movement to which we shall give most attention are (1) Pestaloz-zianism, (2) Herbartianism, (3) Froebelianism, (4) the child study move-ment of G. Stanley Hall, (5) the development of educational psychology under the leadership of William James and Edward Lee Thorndike, (6) behaviorism, and (7) later, or contemporary, developmentalism.

PESTALOZZI AND HIS SUCCESSORS

Johann Heinrich Pestalozzi (1746–1827) was born in Zurich, Switzerland. Unlike Rousseau, he received a careful rearing in a good home environment. His mother, when Pestalozzi was only five years old, was widowed, but still able to send him through the local Latin school and to the University of Zurich. As a youth he became greatly interested in the plight of the poor. Influenced by his grandfather, the pastor in a nearby town, he first studied briefly for the ministry, and then studied law to prepare himself as a champion of the neglected Swiss peasants. His revolutionary ideas brought him into conflict with the government, and ended his legal career.

In 1769 he married and bought a farm, which he called Neuhof; here he launched an experiment to improve the dismal conditions of the Swiss farmers through education. He read *Émile* and tried to rear his young son according to Rousseau's principles of naturalism. This experience convinced him that in practice naturalism needed many modifications; and so he took a group of ragged vagrant children and attempted to instruct them in the rudiments of reading, writing, and counting, as well as in religion and morals, while they supported themselves by industrial work under the influence of a good home environment.[5] The experiment was an educational success, but a financial failure, which had to be abandoned when the reformer became bankrupt.

The next eighteen years of Pestalozzi's life were times of extensive literary production. In 1781, he wrote his great didactic novel and educational classic, *Leonard and Gertrude*. Later he published a sequel, *How Gertrude Teaches Her Children*. In these works and in *The Evening Hour of a Hermit* (1780), he explained his educational ideas and described the methods for realizing them. (*The Evening Hour* gives the clearest picture of Pestalozzi's philosophy.)

In 1798, Pestalozzi again was given the opportunity to turn from the pleasant task of theorizing about education to the more thrilling and difficult task of teaching. The Swiss government asked him to establish a school in an old convent at Stanz and entrusted him with the task of educating about eighty war orphans. Here he began the experiments in educational methods which were later continued at Burgdorf, where he first acted as assistant to the head teacher in the village school and later established his own school. With the aid of several loyal and efficient assistants, he continued his experimentation; and now he was able by the aid of voluntary contributions and government subsidies to open an institute for training

---

[5] For an unusual profile of Pestalozzi, with an American reference, see Hugh C. Black, "Pestalozzi and the Education of the Disadvantaged," *Educational Forum*, vol. xxxiii, no. 4 (May 1969), pp. 511–521.

teachers in his new methods. In 1805, the institute was moved to Yverdon where for twenty years he continued his inspired teaching and the teacher-training work begun at Burgdorf. As the fame of the institute at Yverdon spread, students and visitors were attracted from many other countries; Pestalozzian philosophy and methods were carried to other nations, particularly Germany, France, England, and the United States.

Yet in his native country, Pestalozzi's pedagogy was slow in gaining recognition. The most notable fruit of Pestalozzianism in Switzerland is to be found in the works of Phillip M. Emanuel von Fellenberg (1771–1844), who established a school at Hofwyl designed to give a combined industrial and intellectual education. Fellenberg's institution was very successful and attracted wide attention; his modification of Pestalozzianism found ready acceptance in educational institutions beyond the borders of Switzerland.

Pestalozzianism was especially influential in Germany, for German teachers were among the first to study at the institute at Yverdon. Under the influence of Fichte, the Prussian government early recognized the value of Pestalozzi's work, sent able young men to Yverdon to study, and placed Pestalozzian-trained men in charge of the public school system.

In France, progress was made toward the adoption of Pestalozzianism, especially in the training of teachers, after the publication of Victor Cousin's *Report on the Conditions of Public Instruction in Prussia*, which attributed the remarkable educational progress of Prussia to the use of Pestalozzian methods. Pestalozzianism was introduced into England by Charles Mayo and his sister Elizabeth, who spent three years at Yverdon where they absorbed the mechanics of the methods, but it is alleged not much of the philosophy and spirit. The Mayos opened a private school in London for wealthy children, in which formalized Pestalozzian methods were used. And their manual for teachers, *Lessons on Objects*, was greatly popularized by its adoption by the philanthropic Home and Colonial Infant School Society. This society, although it established model schools and a training college for teachers which had great influence in spreading the movement, fostered an anglicized Pestalozzianism which was quite different from the German model and quite lacking in the true spirit of the great reformer.

The first attempt to introduce Pestalozzian methods to the United States was made as early as 1809, when a wealthy eastern philanthropist brought Joseph Neef, an associate of Pestalozzi, to Philadelphia to establish a school. The effort met with little recognition, and after Neef joined the communistic group at New Harmony, Indiana, his influence waned. Actually, educators in the United States first learned of Pestalozzianism through the publication of Warren Colburn's *First Lessons in Arithmetic* in Boston in 1821; and the bringing of Arnold Guyot and Hermann Krusi from Switzerland to lecture in the Massachusetts state normal schools, attracted some attention to Pestalozzian principles and methods. Articles in Woodbridge's *American Annals of Education* and William Russell's *American Journal of Education* also aroused some interest; but it was not until after 1860 that American schools really began to be Pestalozzianized.

It was the so-called Oswego movement that put Pestalozzianism into practice in American schools. Edward A. Sheldon (1823–1897), superintendent of the schools at Oswego, New York, visiting Toronto, across the lake in Canada, in 1859, happened upon an exhibit of materials used for object lessons by the British Home and Colonial Infant School Society. Greatly interested, he secured books and materials for this object study and persuaded Miss Margaret Jones, one of the Society's teachers, to come to Oswego and train his faculty in the new object-lesson teaching. A year later, he was able to employ Hermann Krusi, who spent the next twenty-five years in the new Oswego Normal School infusing American teachers with the spirit as well as the form of Pestalozzian method. The Oswego Normal School became the center of the movement, and the enthusiasm of its students carried the new methods to every state in the Union.

Johann Friedrich Herbart

Johann Friedrich Herbart (1776–1841) was a native of Oldenburg, in northwestern Germany. He, too, came from a well-to-do family; his father was a learned public official, and his mother was a woman of exceptional intelligence, who carefully supervised the early rearing and education of her gifted son. Between the ages of twelve and eighteen, Herbart attended the *Gymnasium* of his home city, from which he was graduated with the highest honors. He entered the University of Jena to prepare for the practice of law. Studying under Fichte, he was deeply influenced by the new humanism which was beginning to prevail there and by his associations with a brilliant group containing such creative geniuses as Herder, Goethe, and Schiller. Finding that he now had little taste for the study of law, Herbart left the university to become private tutor to the three sons of the Governor of Interlaken, in Switzerland. While in Switzerland, he visited Pestalozzi's school at Burgdorf and wrote sympathetically of what he observed. From 1802–1808 he lectured on education and philosophy at the University of Göttingen, where he published his famous *Science of Education*. For the next twenty-six years, he held the chair of philosophy formerly occupied by the great Immanuel Kant, at the University of Königsberg in the former German province of East Prussia. Here he founded a pedagogical seminar, a practice school for teacher training and experimentation in methods of teaching, and in 1835 published *The Outline of Educational Doctrine*, a clear and practical exposition of his educational ideas.

In Germany, the influence of Herbart was carried into the second half of the nineteenth century by Tuiskon Ziller (1817–1882), who headed the pedagogical seminar at the University of Leipzig, founded the Association for the Scientific Study of Education, and extended the Herbartian methods to elementary school instruction; and by Rein, a pupil of Ziller, who became head of the pedagogical seminar and practice school at the University of Jena, and made it the chief center of German Herbartianism.

The Herbartian movement did not reach the United States until almost the close of the century. A group of young men from the Illinois State Normal School at Bloomington studied at Jena and returned with the new science of educational method. Charles Degarmo's *The Essentials of Method* (1889) and *Herbart and the Herbartians* (1895), Charles A. McMurry's *General Method* (1892), and his brother, Frank M. McMurry's *The Method of the Recitation* (1897) were great contributions to American pedagogical literature.[6] In addition, the McMurrys published books on the special methods of teaching the various subjects stressed by the Herbartians. In 1892, the National Herbartian Society was organized in the United States, the name of the society being changed ten years later to the National Society for the Study of Education. Most American normal schools, particularly in the Midwest, were soon won over to Herbartian principles and, through the teachers they sent to every section of the country, greatly influenced the practices of the elementary schools. American Herbartianism became, at the turn of the century, the significant movement in education.

Friedrich Wilhelm Froebel

Friedrich Wilhelm Froebel (1782–1852) was born in the mountains of Thuringia in southern Germany. His father was the overworked pastor of an extensive parish; and when Froebel's mother died in his infancy, Friedrich was left under the unsympathetic control of a harsh stepmother. This unhappy environment made him deeply introspective and developed his tendency toward mysticism. Deprived of parental affection and congenial playmates, he turned to nature for companionship. From ten to fourteen, young Froebel spent his few happy years with a kindly uncle, attending the parish school, where he received the only systematic instruction of his life. At fifteen he was apprenticed to a forester and for the next eight years engaged in a variety of occupations, none of which

---

[6] Degarmo's small volume, *The Essentials of Method* is a living testament to Herbart and American Herbartianism. The revised edition of 1893 published in Boston by D. C. Heath and Company, is subtitled, *A Discussion of the Essential Form of Right Method in Teaching—Observation, Generalization, Application.* It is generally supposed that this influential book was first written in 1892, but the Widener Library of Harvard University in 1968 listed a copy on its shelves published in "Boston. 1889."

gave him satisfaction. In 1799, at the age of seventeen, he visited his brother who was studying medicine at the University of Jena, where, greatly impressed with the intellectual activity centered there, he conceived a lasting interest in teaching. By a happy accident he was invited to teach drawing in a Pestalozzian school at Frankfurt; and three years later he was engaged as a private tutor and spent most of the time with his younger charges at Pestalozzi's institute at Yverdon, where he studied the methods of the Swiss teacher and became one of his most enthusiastic disciples.

At the age of twenty-four, after a careful study of the works of Rousseau, Basedow, and Pestalozzi, Froebel opened an experimental school at Keilhau, in his native Thuringia. This as might be expected, was a pedagogical success, but unfortunately a financial failure. During the next few years he taught in various schools in Switzerland, and in 1826 published his epochal work *The Education of Man*, which contains the best exposition of his educational philosophy. He was attracted to the writings of Comenius, whose description of the School of the Mother's Knee confirmed Froebel's belief that the earliest years of childhood were the most important in education. In 1837, he opened the first *kindergarten*, his School for Little Children, in the mountain village of Blankenburg. The remainder of his life was spent in developing games, plays, and songs for young children, founding other kindergartens, training kindergarten teachers, and further elaborating his methods.

Froebel's preoccupation with early childhood education and his mystical nature alienated certain Germans, and a reactionary ministry prohibited kindergartens, a shattering blow which led to his death in 1852. But Froebel's ideas were taken up by Baroness Bülow-Wendhausen and in 1860 kindergartens were permitted to reopen in Prussia. In England the infant school, and in France the *école maternelle* were influenced by the spirit of Froebel. In the United States, the first private kindergarten was established in 1855 by Mrs. Carl Schurz for German-speaking children at Watertown, Wisconsin. The first English-speaking school was founded in 1860 by Elizabeth Peabody, sister-in-law of Horace Mann, in Boston. The first American public kindergarten, taught by Susan Blow, was opened in 1873 as part of the St. Louis public school system by Superintendent William T. Harris. In more recent years the Froebelian influence has been extended into the first and second grades of the elementary school in the new unified kindergarten-primary organization of early childhood education.

William James

William James (1842–1910), one of the most influential American philosophers and psychologists, was born in New York City, but spent most of his youth in Europe. His early education was irregular and intermittent, partly because of constantly changing residence, and partly because of his wealthy father's desire that he should develop from within rather than undergo the formal education of the time. Thus, young James acquired the fragments of a liberal education in schools and under private tutors in Switzerland, France, England, and America. In his international travels, in addition to his formal schooling, he stored a fund of impressions which nourished his mind and stimulated his imagination. After a year engaged in the study of art, he was convinced that he could not distinguish himself in that field; so in the fall of 1861 he entered the Lawrence Scientific School at Cambridge, Massachusetts, thus inaugurating a career in science and the connection with Harvard that continued until his death.

For thirty-five years, he taught at Harvard University. He was instructor of physiology and anatomy for seven years, professor of philosophy for nine years, then professor of psychology until the last decade of his teaching, when he returned again to the teaching of philosophy. He was a prolific and gifted writer in the fields of philosophy, psychology, and education; and his influence upon the transformation of education in America was exceptional. His greatest and most influential work *The Principles of Psychology* (1890) soon became a classic. His concepts of education and his views concerning the work of the teacher are best summed up in his *Talks to Teachers and Students* (1900). Through their popularity, these books exerted a powerful influence upon a whole generation of teachers.[7]

G. Stanley Hall

G. Stanley Hall (1844–1924) was born in Ashfield, Massachusetts. Although not professional, young Hall's family was one of unusual culture and intellectual superiority, with the financial resources to give him an extensive education at Williams College, Union Theological Seminary, and the universities of Bonn and Berlin in Germany. For four years he taught English literature and philosophy at Antioch College, in Ohio. Resigning this position, he spent two years as a graduate student at Harvard studying under William James, the functional psychologist, and received his Ph.D. in 1878. He went to Germany again to study physiology at the University of Berlin, and psychology, under structuralist Wilhelm Wundt (1832–1920), at Leipzig. His unusually comprehensive education thus included specialization and study in theology, philosophy, psychology, physiology, anthropology, biology, anatomy, and neurology under the most noted teachers of Germany and America. In 1880 in Boston he wrote his famous study *Contents of Children's Minds on Entering School.*

---

[7] See William James, *Talks to Teachers and Students* (New York: Holt, Rinehart and Winston, Inc., 1900); for a vivid impression of James as a teacher, see "Beloved Psychologist," ch. xvi, in Houston Peterson (Ed.), *Great Teachers* (New Brunswick, N.J.: Rutgers University Press, 1946), pp. 223–228.

Next Dr. Hall taught psychology and pedagogy for six years at Johns Hopkins University, and then for thirty years was the president of Clark University at Worcester, Massachusetts, one of the most unique and influential institutions of higher education in the United States during his administration. Here a small group of selected students, stimulated by Hall's scholarship and scientific spirit, explored hitherto unknown regions of genetic psychology, the laws of human development, and the laws of growth and learning. Clark University became the acknowledged center for the study of child nature and development. Hall set forth his educational theories in fourteen volumes, notable among which are *Adolescence, Educational Problems,* and *Youth, Its Education, Regimen, and Hygiene.* In 1891, he initiated the publication of the *Pedagogical Seminary,* devoted to articles on child study and education from this new point of view.

Edward Lee Thorndike (1874–1949), eminent pupil and follower of G. Stanley Hall and William James, was born at Williamsburg, Massachusetts, and attended Roxbury Latin School. His undergraduate and graduate work was done at Harvard University, and his first teaching appointment was at Western Reserve University, in Ohio. In 1899 he became an instructor of genetic psychology at Teachers College, Columbia University, where he remained and played a leading part in the emergence of that institution as one of the foremost educational centers of the world. Although his greatest contributions were to the scientific movement, which we shall consider in the next chapter, his early work as a dynamic psychologist carried the developmentalist movement to its zenith. His *Principles of Teaching* (1905); his outstanding *Elements of Psychology,* published in the same year; and his monumental *Educational Psychology* (1914), with its three gospels, "original nature," "individual differences," and "laws of learning," have had a profound influence on teaching practice.

James McKeen Cattell (1860–1944), with James and Hall, studied under Wundt in Germany. Born at Easton, Pennsylvania, he graduated from Lafayette College before becoming the first assistant to the German structural psychologist. Returning to America, Cattell taught at the University of Pennsylvania from 1888 to 1891, here publishing his famous *Mental Tests and Measurements* (1890). At Columbia from 1891 to 1917, Cattell became associated with Thorndike, with whom he had much in common. Considerably important in American psychology and extremely influential in spreading the influence of applied psychology and testing, Cattell utilized both laboratory and statistics in his psychological excursions. He served as editor of *School and Society, Science,* and *Scientific Monthly.*

John Broadus Watson (1878–1939) shared the popularity which psychology enjoyed in early twentieth-century America. A native of Greenville, South Carolina, Watson took his Ph.D. at the University of Chicago, where he taught from 1903 to 1908. Named Director of the Psychological Laboratory at Johns Hopkins he retained the post until 1920, when he entered private business. Relying heavily on Pavlov's conditioned reflex findings, Watson became the father of behaviorism, describing action in terms of psychological response to stimuli and rejecting the concept of conscious or unconscious mental activity. Celebrated for his work with infants, Watson relied on three instincts, or unconditioned, unlearned responses, fear, love, rage, and believed implicitly in the supremacy of conditioning. "Give me the baby," he is reported to have said, for with this raw material he was confident that he could shape an intelligent, well-adjusted person. Watson wrote *Psychology from the Standpoint of the Behaviorists* (1919), *Behavior* (1925), and *The Psychological Care of Infant and Child* (1928).

Maria Montessori (1869–1952) was the first woman to be granted an M.D. by the University of Rome. Talented and blessed with drive and decision, she soon developed theories concerning education based on her contacts with certain groups of defective children. In 1898, as a result of a series of lectures by Dr. Montessori, a school for defective children was established; now her teaching was augmented as she reentered the university for courses in psychology and anthropology. In 1907 she staffed and supervised a series of tenement schools for average, normal children, and her great success soon made her an international celebrity. Her *Casa dei Bambini* were constructed with conditions approximating actual life, rather than as retreats; but with the unsettled times in Europe after 1914 her methods lost some followers.[8] Since World War II, however, there has been a revival of Montessorianism, although on a rather limited scale.

Karl Spencer Lashley (1890–   ) was a pupil and disciple of Watson at Johns Hopkins. Born at Davis, West Virginia, Lashley taught after graduation at Hopkins, Chicago, and Harvard. His experimentation on the structure and function of the brain is perhaps among the most significant carried on in the United States. Through brain surgery with rats, Lashley determined that habits are not dependent upon specific neural pathways. He concluded, however, that the amount of uninjured brain tissue possessed by the subject is important and governed its action. This struck at the main thesis of the connectionists. Following his tenure at Harvard, Lashley became Director of the Yerkes Laboratory of Primate Biology at Orange Park, Florida.

---

[8] For a fine discussion of Montessori's contributions to modern education, see Luella Cole, *A History of Education, Socrates to Montessori* (New York: Holt, Rinehart and Winston, Inc., 1950), pp. 563–590.

Significant for his role and influence in the reconstruction of the laws of child development was Arnold Gesell (1880–1961). Born in Salina, Wisconsin, Gesell studied at Clark University under G. Stanley Hall and won his doctorate in 1906. After some preliminary teaching at Los Angeles, he moved to Yale in 1911, where he remained until 1948 as Director of the Clinic of Child Development of the Medical School. Upon retirement he organized and headed the Gesell Institute of Child Development in New Haven, perhaps the world's foremost child study center. Gesell's studies were concerned with the development of children from birth through age sixteen, and his observations and conclusions were largely instrumental in breaking the rigidity of former child-rearing methods. Gesell's writings include *The First Five Years of Life* (1940), *Studies in Child Development* (1948), and *Infant Development: The Embryology of Early Human Behavior* (1952).

Meanwhile, in Europe, at Geneva, Jean Piaget (1896–   ) had initiated a psychological study of child play and a thorough inquiry into child thought analysis. His cognitive research, published in 1926, dealt with a young subject's awareness of self and his lingering coming to grips with the actual realities of the world. The *Language and Thought of the Child*, of course, stimulated American research in this area, as well as forwarded the study and teaching of what may now be called the sociology of knowledge.

Piaget sees cognitive development as the child's gradual advance toward a more thorough and intelligent adaptation to his environment through his systematic collating of different points of view, as they appear to him from his various experiences or from his verbal contact with adults.[9]

Called the world's foremost behavioral psychologist, Burrhus Frederic Skinner (1904–   ), has been extremely influential in the attempt to determine just how people learn. "We know a great deal," this Harvard professor says, "Learning is merely a change in the behavior of an organism." Skinner's works include *The Behavior of Organisms* (1938) and his controversial *Verbal Behavior*. Skinner is also author of the Utopian novel *Walden Two*, which depicts, rather glowingly, a society perfectly controlled through psychological principles, and *Science and Human Behavior* (1953).

With this brief introduction to the personalities who have contributed most to the movement of psychological developmentalism, we are now ready to analyze those theories that are pertinent to the various phases of educational practice.

---

[9] See William Kessen and Clementina Kuhlmann (Eds.), *Thought in the Young Child*. Monographs of the Society for Research in Child Development, vol. xxvii, no. 2, ser. no. 83 (Lafayette, Ind.: Child Development Publications, 1962).

EDUCATION AS PSYCHOLOGICAL DEVELOPMENT

Aims

The psychological developmentalists were concerned more with the immediate individual aims of education than with ultimate social objectives. They aimed at making the child the center of the educational process, and so applied themselves to the primary task of discovering the psychological laws of learning. They believed that teaching should direct itself toward the development of the child from within, and not toward an imposition of adult standards. Since education was a matter of directing and controlling growth and development, they insisted that there must be continual observation and experimentation to determine the psychological principles upon which the educational process could securely rest. Since they recognized the early stages of the child's progress as important factors in determining his later development, the developmentalists aimed particularly at a careful control of the child's elementary schooling.

Pestalozzi believed that the genuine reform of society must begin with the reformation of the individual, and that the individual can be elevated only by putting into his grasp the power of helping himself. Pestalozzi felt that the only sure means of attaining the end sought is through the process of development. His aim was to secure a happier and more virtuous life for every individual, and the process by which he hoped to achieve this end was "the natural, progressive, and harmonious development of all the powers and faculties of the human being." He felt that these powers were latent in every child, merely awaiting an opportunity to unfold; education must furnish the opportunities for their unfolding. Pestalozzi liked to compare the education of the child with the development and growth of a plant. He wrote, "Man, formed from the dust of the earth, grows and ripens like a plant rooted in the soil." Pestalozzi's main purpose was to discover the natural laws underlying the development of the child's head, heart, and hand. Education was to provide the conditions under which this development could occur naturally and harmoniously.

Pestalozzi's ultimate goal was the social regeneration of humanity. He said that his sole end was to eradicate the sources of the misery in which he saw the people around him. "I lived like a beggar," he said, "in order to learn how to make beggars live like men." He desired to improve the desperate conditions under which humanity existed, but instead of depending upon new forms of religion, new types of government, or new systems of economic organization he turned to education for he believed that it was possible to improve society by changing the individuals that make up society.

This idea of Pestalozzi marks a striking change in aim. In the schools of his day teaching meant giving information. To Pestalozzi teaching meant developing the child in accordance with his inborn faculties. To Pestalozzi, education meant continuous development and, thus, the sum total of the natural and spontaneous exertion of the mind.[10]

Fellenberg, in his agricultural and industrial institute at Hofwyl, endeavored to carry out the Pestalozzian idea of developing the hand as well as the head and heart. This ideal of the simultaneous development of muscle, mind, and morals was brought to the United States and prevailed in our earlier manual-training shops and schools, in the self-help institutes of the Middle West, and later in the YMCA and YWCA vocational movements. With Fellenberg, these American institutions aimed at educating the children of rich and poor together in order to develop a mutual sympathy and understanding.

According to Herbart, the ultimate goal of education should be the development of moral character. He regarded dependable moral personality as the highest aim of humanity and, consequently, of education. Herbart rejected Rousseau's idea of allowing free expression to the native capacities of the child; he also rejected Pestalozzi's idea of harmonious development of all the child's faculties and powers. Herbart believed that the ultimate goal of moral personality could be attained only through the development of a group of desirable, abiding, many-sided interests. The aim of education, he felt, should be to analyze the interests of man to discover which are best for individual and social living, and then to teach him to develop and apply these interests in the various situations of life. By producing a number of well-balanced, many-sided, and worthy interests, Herbart asserted, education endeavors to develop the will to be good and the desire to make sound moral choices, resulting in a high degree of personal character and social morality.

Medieval and Reformation educators aimed at teaching morality through the use of preaching, precept, and the memorizing of moral maxims. Herbart believed that moral conduct must be based upon the development of the will, and that will-attitudes depended upon the accumulation of experiences, organized for free and consistent expressions as intelligent moral decisions. "We *will* what we know; we cannot *will* what we do not know," is Herbart's justification for his aim of many-sided interests. He maintained that the salient purpose of education is the growth and development of ideas in the mind of the child, brought about in conformity with psychological laws.

Herbart differed from most developmentalists in aiming at the de-

---

[10] For an original account of Pestalozzi's childhood and youth and the formation of his educational ideas, see Hans Ganz, *Pestalozzi, Leben und Werk* (Zurich: Origo Verlag, 1956), pp. 20–71.

velopment of the adolescent, rather than of the child, and concerning himself more with secondary than with elementary education. Most of his followers, however, applied his philosophy and method to primary education.

Froebel shared Pestalozzi's and Herbart's belief that the aim of education is the development of the child. But he differed in his conception of the nature of this development. According to the father of the kindergarten, the aim of education is the development of the child's inborn capacities, the latent powers of the individual. However, his conception of original nature was quite different from Rousseau's pure naturalism. Froebel was the first educational evolutionist; he believed that education is an essential element in cosmic evolution and that education is the process by which the race and the individual evolve to an ever higher level.

Froebel insisted that the underlying power in the universe is the Absolute, the original, active, energizing, creative, intelligent, self-conscious source of all being, which manifests itself as force in nature and as consciousness in man. Creation is a continuous process of productive activity, he held, and the source of all created objects (including the child's nature) is this universal power, that is, God. The forming crystal, the growing tree, the developing child all are different manifestations of God's plan of creation, Froebel believed. Therefore, any study of changes in the evolution of nature will throw light upon the nature of the development of man. All that man is ever to be lies hidden, however slightly revealed, in the being of the child. The educator is to control the growth of the child into a man, just as the gardener is to control the growth of a plant to its full flowering and fruition. The aim of the teacher is to see that the child's development is in accord with the original and logical course of human development. Failure in education, according to Froebel, consists of neglecting or preventing the development of certain sides of the child's personality, and thus causing "the distortion of originally good human powers and tendencies by arbitrary and willful interference."

If the child's nature has been marred it must be redirected into the original course of development; if the child displays activities contrary to the true principle of growth these must be observed and corrected in order to keep the development progressing along the right lines. Thus, according to Froebel, education must be controlled development by which the individual comes into realization of the life of the all-encompassing unity of which he is but a part, a development by which his life broadens until it has related itself to nature; until it enters sympathetically into all the activities of society; until it enters, as Froebel said, into the achievements of the race and the aspirations of humanity. Education is but the realization in the individual human being of the highest stage of the evolutionary process, Froebel asserted; the work of the teacher is to bring about this unified evolutionary development.

Hall, James, and Thorndike

G. Stanley Hall agreed with European developmentalists that the aim of education is the development of the child's own nature, activities, capabilities, and interests. He, too, believed that education should be many-sided and lead to a well-balanced normal personality; but he based his fundamental theories of development upon the principles of biological evolution rather than philosophy. He devoted his life to the study of genetic psychology, the evolution of mind, in order that an educational method could be perfected which would enable the child to realize his highest possibilities. Hall's fundamental thesis were that mental and physical life are always parallel; that there is "no psychosis without neurosis"; that mind and body evolve together; that throughout the process of evolution mental life develops along with the body and its biological activities. Hall attempted to trace the history of physical life; his aim was to educate the individual in such a manner that through him the race would continue its upward climb.

Earlier developmentalists believed that the human race had passed through certain stages which the unfolding life of the individual repeated, both physically and mentally. This theory of Rousseau, designated by the Herbartians as the culture-epoch theory and by the biologists as the recapitulation theory, was accepted and elaborated by Hall as a basic principle in his educational aims. Hall was firmly convinced that "ontogeny repeats phylogeny" in mental as well as physical life. The teacher must discover through the study of genetic psychology the stages in the mental development of the race, and then construct the curriculum and build methods so that the growth of the child is in accord with the order of development. Hall urged educators to "develop nature's first intention and fulfill the law of nascent periods, or else not only no good, but great harm may be done." He believed that the teacher must, above all else, see that education does not obstruct, but facilitates, natural evolution. Education, he felt, should make the individual the fittest possible instrument for racial improvement.

On the surface Hall's recapitulation theory, although aiming at individual development, may seem retrograde in its social and racial outcomes. Nor does it aim at the "regeneration of society" or at the "process of cosmic development." Actually, Hall's theory is more concerned with the development of the individual child as an end in itself.

Similarly, William James was essentially an individualist. Nowhere in his *Talks to Teachers* does he speak of education as a social function. To him education aims merely at "the organization of the instinctive tendencies of behavior and the acquired habits of conduct and action to fit the individual to his environment." Developmentalism he defined as an organization of the elements of mental experience in order to prepare the individual effectively for the struggle of life. This concern with instinct and habit was a natural outgrowth of James' study of animal psychology and the doctrine of biological evolution.

James' great emphasis upon instincts and the place he gave them in education led many of his disciples to the belief that one of the important ends of education was to allow the child to follow his instincts. Thus there came into educational theory the maxim, Work with the instincts and not against them. The more careful could find in James' writings support for the modification of some instincts, but James undoubtedly was more concerned with arguing that the associationist psychologists had failed to recognize the power of instincts in human life.

James' doctrine of habit was highly individualistic and conservative in its implications. In spite of his admission that habits could be changed, his principles seem to imply an "iron law of habit" and a belief that the main purpose of teaching is the early development of individual and class habits in order to produce a more integrated society. As James says:

> Habit is thus the enormous fly-wheel of society, its most precious conservative agent. It alone is what keeps us all within the bounds of ordinance, and saves the children of fortune from the envious uprisings of the poor. It alone prevents the hardest and most repulsive walks of life from being deserted by those brought up to tread therein. . . . It dooms us all to fight out the battle of life upon the lines of our nurture or our early choice, and to make the best of a pursuit that disagrees, because there is no other for which we are fitted, and it is too late to begin again. It keeps different social strata from mixing . . . the man can by-and-by no more escape than his coat-sleeve can suddenly fall into new sets of folds. On the whole, it is best he should not escape. It is well for the world that in most of us by the age of thirty, the character has set like plaster, and will never soften again.[11]

Thus, James maintained that the basis of all education is the fund of native instincts with which the child is endowed, and that the purpose of education is the organization of the individual's acquired habits in such a way as to promote the individual's personal well-being.

Thorndike, on the other hand, distinguished between the *ultimate* and *proximate* aims of education. He looked beyond the immediate psychological changes that the school was to produce in the individual to the ultimate social goals of education. Nevertheless, he insisted that one cannot change society without assuring the proper development of the individuals that make up society.

> Education as a whole should make human beings wish each other well, should increase the sum of human energy and happiness and decrease the sum of discomfort of the human beings that are or will be,

11 William James, *Principles of Psychology* (New York: Holt, Rinehart and Winston, Inc., 1890), p. 121.

and should foster the higher, impersonal pleasures. These aims of education in general—good will to men, useful and happy lives, and noble enjoyment—are the ultimate aims of school education in particular. Its proximate aims are to give boys and girls health in body and mind, information about the world of nature and men, worthy interests in knowledge and action, a multitude of habits of thought, feeling and behavior, and ideals of efficiency, honor, duty, love and service.[12]

According to Thorndike, education aims at satisfying the wants of all in order to give each individual the fullest realization of his own desires. For Thorndike the chief aim of education is to realize the fullest satisfaction of human wants.

Thorndike, more than any of the earlier developmentalists, emphasized the importance of aiming at the development of the child not only for adult life and work but also for the life of childhood itself. He held that we should strive more at making children succeed with the problems and duties of childhood and less at fitting them for the problems and duties of twenty years after.

Types

We can readily see, from the statement of their aims, that the majority of developmentalists emphasized individual education rather than social education. They were concerned primarily with the child himself; it was the child as an individual, not as a unit of society, that primarily interested them. To them education was basically a matter of individual approach and individual growth. Social education they left for another and later group of reformers.

Generally developmentalists conceived of education as having broad scope. Pestalozzi, with his aim of the "harmonious development of all the faculties," was concerned with (1) intellectual education, "the training of the head"; (2) moral education, "the training of the heart"; and (3) industrial education, "the training of the hand." The Fellenberg movement was especially effective in connection with industrial and agricultural types of education. Neither Pestalozzi nor Fellenberg considered these three types of training as entirely separate and distinct forms, but rather as phases as closely related as the three aspects of life for which they trained. Both advocated a humanistic approach with general education for all, but they insisted that this general cultural education should not neglect training in practical activities. Practical education was not to be narrow vocational preparation nor job training. It was to be a broad training in practical power, creativity, productivity—a "skill, readiness, or capacity for performance, for execution, or for production." Education was to prepare man not only to think and feel but also to act. The three types of education

---

[12] Thorndike, pp. 3–4.

emphasized by Pestalozzi and Fellenberg were those that developed the intellect, the moral-religious nature, and practical power.[13]

Herbart and the Herbartians emphasized intellectual education above all else, without disregarding the broad scope of life for which education must prepare. Unlike the faculty psychologists, however, the Herbartians did not consider it necessary to provide for the separate cultivation of the intellect, the emotions, and the will. They did not believe in distinct forms of education, intellectual, moral, and practical. Instead, the central idea of Herbartian psychology is that the true foundation of the whole structure of education is intellectual instruction, the growth and development of ideas in the mind of the child. All mental nature is a unity, they claimed, and therefore there is only one type of education, education by instruction, or, more properly speaking, educative instruction. Development of the intellect results in controlled emotions and a purposeful enlightened will power that expresses itself in desirable action and performance, the Herbartians asserted.

While Froebel also carefully insisted that man is a unity, he made productive activity the central factor in this unity. Therefore, he emphasized what might well be called creative education. It is a mistake to say that Froebel was concerned only with motor training, that is, only with the development of the manual, vocal, or general muscular activities. He contended that in any creative activity the memory, the imagination, the perception, the reasoning, the will, and the feelings all cooperate with the sense organs, the nerves, and the muscles. Since all these elements are exercised in unity, he considered the development of productive or creative activity the one important type of education. Froebel turned to his religious concepts for a still more powerful sanction for his emphasis upon creative education; and he declared, "God is the original unity from which the entire universe has evolved by virtue of His own creative self-expression." To develop the child's creative self-expression is to develop the most nearly divine attribute of the child, he held.

Hall was interested in every type of training, every aspect of human growth. His own widespread education and his many-sided specialization gave him comprehension and insight that enabled him to study education with considerable range and detail. He emphasized every phase of human development: physical and emotional growth, moral and religious growth, and growth of the will and social nature. But he emphasized emotional training as the most important. He believed that the emotional life is far more fundamental than the intellectual, that intelligence is a comparatively late development, while emotion is as old as life itself. He believed that the emotions motivate the development of the intellect; that all thought owes its origin to the universe. Hall also stressed play as an important type of education. Play is the best kind of education, he held, because it exercises

---

[13] The relationship of these types to the principles of 4-H Club work is obvious.

powers of mind and body which in our highly specialized civilization would never otherwise have a chance to develop.[14]

James and Thorndike, with their interest in habits and instincts, were primarily concerned with the development of behavior and conduct. Their emphasis, was upon dynamic education, training for manifold activities of life. They urged physical training, intellectual training, and emotional, or moral, training, but they, too, conceived of the individual as a unit and not as a collection of faculties. Their emphasis, however, was upon practical training as the central feature of development. As Thorndike said:

> With respect to the amount of emphasis upon different features . . . the best judgment of the present rates practical ability somewhat higher. . . . No sensible thinker about education now regards the ability to support oneself as a mean thing. Every one must gain power at school as well as at home to pull his own weight in the boat.
>
> The best judgment of the present gives much more weight . . . to health, to bodily skill and to the technical and industrial arts. The ideal of the scholar has given way to the ideal of the capable man— capable in scholarship still, but also capable in physique and in the power to manipulate things.[15]

Thus the developmentalists concerned themselves with as many types of education as there were aspects of the individual organism to be developed. Although all of the later developmentalists consider the individual as a unit, with the various types of training dependent upon each other, they emphasize one phase or another as the central factor in human development.[16] For this reason, there is a disagreement over which type of training should be made central. We have seen, however, that the developmentalists generally neglect no part of the growth of the individual. What ever neglect there is in the scope of their educational theory is along the lines of social education and the development of society as a whole.

Methods

Since the educational philosophy of the psychological developmentalists emphasized the child and his growth as the central factor of education, methodology played a larger part in their thinking than any other aspect of education. With them, content, organization, and agencies were all secondary to and dependent upon method. For that reason, in this chapter we consider method before we deal with other phases of education.

The period from Pestalozzi to Watson was marked by the development of new psychologies of learning. Pestalozzi based his method upon

---

[14] G. Stanley Hall, "Play and Dancing for Adolescents," *The Independent*, vol. 62, pp. 355–356.

[15] Thorndike, pp. 4–5.

[16] James, *Talks to Teachers*, illustrates his basic principle, "No reception without reaction, no impression without correlative expression."

the principle of pupil activity. There were two steps in his procedure, impression and expression; and both of these had to be performed by the child himself. Pestalozzi said, "Sense impression of nature is the only foundation of human instruction, because it is the only true foundation of human knowledge." He firmly believed that observation must be the basis of all learning. For this reason his instruction of children, especially in the early stages, consisted largely of having them observe, count, analyze, and name objects. He made use of the object lesson, where learning comes through sense experience rather than through words. He insisted that all subjects be taught orally.

Like Rousseau, Pestalozzi believed that the child should not be taught from a book; the teacher was not to hear the child's recitation. The child's expression activities should come from the impressions he gained from observing actual objects. Language expression, both oral and written, should grow out of the observation of objects presented to the child's various senses. So it was with drawing. Geographical expression consisted of such activities as the modeling of landforms perceived on field trips. Arithmetical expression consisted of counting and measuring exercises, such as counting the windows in the room and measuring the distance across the room. Moral expression grew out of the problems which arose in the children's daily lives.

Pestalozzi likewise abandoned the older deductive methods, in which teaching began with rules and abstractions, for inductive methods, in which children began with simple elements of experience which they combined into larger meaningful wholes. He recognized the principle that learning must proceed from the known to the unknown, which to him meant from the simple to the complex. He bitterly criticized the then prevalent method of "teaching the unknown by means of the uncomprehensible." He reduced all subjects to their simplest unanalyzable elements (their *ABC*s), and then taught them carefully in graded steps. He specified that nothing was to be learned which was not readily understood and easily mastered. The application of this principle to the teaching of reading, drawing, and music was not very effective, but its effect upon the teaching of arithmetic, language, geography, and elementary science was most significant.

The principle which formed the core of the Pestalozzian method was that of proceeding from the concrete to the abstract, from the particular to the general. (This was, of course, not the method of Comenius.) Pestalozzi protested vehemently against teaching the child generalized ideas in the form of meaningless words. He insisted that the child express his own ideas as the result of the impressions gained from concrete observation and experiences. Pestalozzi's great contributions to the new educational methods were (1) the study of real objects, (2) learning through the various senses, (3) individual expression of ideas. One of his main limitations was that his efforts were spent in perfecting the elementary steps of instruction. The second was that he knew nothing about the psychological control of mental organization, which went on between impression and expression. It was along these lines that Herbart was to make his greatest contribution.

The English version of Pestalozzianism, achieved by Charles and Elizabeth Mayo with their textbook *Lessons and Objects*, missed the spirit of Pestalozzi's method completely. The lessons were bookish, formal, analytical, and far beyond the comprehension of children.[17]

For example, if common salt were the "object" of the lesson, the class would be expected through a small sample to learn its chemical structure, its uses, how and where it is found in nature, how it is mined and refined, that its crystalline form is cubical, that it varies in color from white to bluish and reddish, that it is transparent to translucent, that it is soluble in water and saline in taste, that it imparts a yellow color to flame.[18]

Charles Dickens satirized such formal memorizing of object lessons in the following passage abstracted from his *Hard Times*:

> Sissy Jupe, Girl No. 20, the daughter of a strolling circus actor, whose life, no small share of it, has been passed under the canvas; whose knowledge of horse, generic and specific, extends back as far as memory reaches; familiar with the form and food, the powers and habits and everything related to the horse; knowing it through several senses; Sissy Jupe has been asked to define horse. Bewildered by the striking want of resemblance between the horse of her own conceptions and the prescribed formula that represents the animal in the books of the Home and Colonial Society, she dares not trust herself with the confusing description, and shrinks from it in silence and alarm.
>
> "Girl No. 20 unable to define horse," said Mr. Gradgrind.
>
> Girl No. 20 is declared possessed of no facts in reference to one of the commonest of animals, and appeal is made to one red-eyed Bitzer, who knows horse practically only as he has seen a picture of a horse or as he has, perhaps, sometimes safely weathered the perils of a crowded street-crossing.
>
> "Bitzer," said Thomas Gradgrind, your "definition of a horse!"
>
> "Quadruped, Gramnivorous. Forty teeth, namely: twenty-four grinders, four eye teeth, and twelve incisors. Sheds coat in the spring; in marshy countries sheds hoofs too. Hoofs hard but requiring to be shod with iron. Age known by marks in mouth." Thus, and much more, Bitzer.
>
> "Now, Girl No. 20," said Mr. Gradgrind, "you know what a horse is."

---

[17] See Robert Potter, *The Stream of American Education* (New York: American Book Company, 1967), pp. 275–277; or Newton Edwards and Herman G. Richey, *The School in the American Social Order* (Boston: Houghton Mifflin Company, 1963), pp. 583–641.

[18] Ellwood P. Cubberley, *Public Education in the United States*, rev. enl. ed. (Boston: Houghton Mifflin Company, 1934), p. 353.

Pestalozzi was opposed to the harsh, brutal discipline which for ages had characterized the schools, and tried to substitute for it a discipline of sympathy and love. He wanted to reproduce as far as possible the gentle and refined atmosphere of a good Christian home. When a father visited his school and said, "Why, this is not a school, but a family," Pestalozzi was very pleased. His doctrine of "thinking love" was a natural outgrowth of his conception of education as the development of the child, rather than the pressing of the child into molds of adult behavior that was the concept of most educational practice in his day.

The basic principle upon which Herbart's methods were based was the "doctrine of interest." He believed that interest is of first importance in good instruction; only that knowledge which is acquired within the warm glow of genuine interest will affect the will of the learner and pass into appropriate action. He maintained that skillful teaching is marked by the ability to secure interest without resorting to force or "sugar-coating." Herbart's whole philosophy is, in a sense, a summation of ways in which interest, the sine qua non of "educative instruction," could best be aroused.

Herbart emphasized the principle that learning must proceed from the known to the unknown and elaborated it into the doctrine that new knowledge is always assimilated in terms of what the learner already knows. If the child is to be interested in new experience, he must already have something in his mind which will cause him to listen. The pupil must be in the proper frame of mind to accept the new experience and must have a stock of related ideas which will enable him to interpret and respond to the new situation. Since Herbart termed these related revived experiences *apperceptive masses*, this precept is known as the doctrine of apperception.

Herbart insisted that only large connected units of subject matter are able to arouse and keep alive the deep interest of the child's mind. He devised a principle of teaching known as the doctrine of concentration. Effective reactions of will and conduct come only when the whole consciousness has been focused on a single unit of thought. He also supplemented this doctrine with the doctrine of correlation, which makes one subject central in the focus of attention, but organizes the learning situation so that precepts, concentration, and correlation play a prominent part in clarifying his conception of the principle of interest.

Herbart was the first to formulate an educational method based on psychological principles. He was the first to set forth a theory of the stages of procedure which presumably enable the teacher to control all the child's learning processes, including the process of mental organization and the processes of impression and expression. Herbartians recognized five steps as essential in the procedure of instruction. These, usually designated as the Five Formal Steps, were as follows:

1.   Preparation, or the process of reviving in consciousness the related ideas from past experience which will arouse a vital interest in the new material and prepare the pupil for its rapid understanding and assimilation;

2.   Presentation, or the exhibiting of the new material in concrete form (unless there is already ample sensory experience), and in such a way that it is closely articulated with the apperceptive mass, or past experience;

3.   Association, or the process of assimilating the new experiences, by using analysis and comparison to point out points of likeness and points of difference between the new and the old, thus enabling the new idea to take its true place in the mind's understanding;

4.   Generalization, or the process of forming general rules, laws, and principles from the analyzed sensory experiences, thus developing general concepts in addition to sensations and perceptions in the mind's structure;

5.   Application, or putting the generalized idea to work, sometimes merely to test it, sometimes to deepen the impression by expression, and sometimes to use it in a purely utilitarian sense.

John Dewey later was to challenge these formal steps on the ground that thinking occurs only when the problem is real. The special weakness of the Herbartian method, however, was its attempt to use the formal steps in planning all types of teaching—in the lesson for skill and in the appreciation lesson, as well as in the thought lesson. Yet credit is still due Herbart for developing a more complete organization of educational psychology and technique of classroom instruction than had existed. His system has led to a better understanding of educational psychology and method.

Froebel considered education to be the process of creative self-development, which he believed came from an "inner unfolding," and was brought about by means of the pupil's spontaneous self-activity. Froebel based his methodology on this principle of self-activity. He insisted that a child really develops only when he is actively creating, only when he is "making the inner outer," as he put it. Like Pestalozzi, Froebel contended that the child must learn by doing, but where the former depended upon natural objects from without to stimulate impressions, the latter endeavored to draw out of the child, by means of self-prompted activities, every potentiality of his nature. Froebel did not believe that these activities should result from outer stimulation or from an instinct to emulate, but from a process of natural evolution like the unfolding of the leaves of a plant. This principle of evolutional self-activity is succinctly expressed in his *The Education of Man:*[19]

---

[19] Friedrich Froebel, *The Education of Man*, trans. by W. N. Hailman (New York: Appleton-Century-Crofts, 1887), pp. 68, 279.

> . . . all the child is ever to be and become, lies—however slightly indicated—in the child, and can be attained only through development from within outward.
>
> . . . For the purpose of teaching is to bring evermore *out* of man rather than to put more and more *into* him; . . .

According to Froebel, educative activity is to take place only when the child is ready for it, and has a "certain felt need" for it. But this readiness is a condition of the child's inner nature and not of curiosity, interest, or past experience, Froebel asserted. The teacher must plan so that the child has the opportunity to engage in the activity when the "budding point" is reached.

Froebel was the first educational philosopher to perceive the significance of socialization as a basic principle of teaching. He maintained that the inner nature of the child impels him to cooperative activity with others. This was part of his central doctrine of unity in creative evolution. The "morning circle" in his kindergarten, where the teachers and all the children stood in a ring and joined hands for song, prayer, and play, was a splendid method of socialization, a method of instilling a unity of feeling and group purpose. Froebel felt that it was the duty of the school to make possible the expression of cooperative social activity so that children would develop better forms of social living.

In his insistence that educational method should follow the natural course of the evolution of the child's innately stimulated activities, Froebel did not offer illuminating information regarding the true nature of this inner urge; nor did he give much definite information as to how one should proceed in later developments of the child's life. His conceptions were drawn largely from a metaphysical symbolism which other teachers found rather difficult to put into practice especially after the kindergarten level.

Hall rendered a service in clearing away some of the eccentricities of Froebelian methodology. From his knowledge of biology, anthropology, and child study and development, he formulated more definitely than either Herbart or Froebel the cultural epoch theory and the law of recapitulation. Hall interpreted the inner urge in terms of simple instincts or tendencies inherited from the past of the race. He contended that these innate traits were not connate, that is, operative at birth, but under normal conditions had a definite order of appearance. He thought that although the neural connections are fixed at birth, the stimuli that set up the excitations do not appear until later. (In some cases, the reacting mechanism must await development, if not full maturation, he said.)

According to Hall, the appearance of these delayed instincts follow the same order as the appearance of similar forms of activities in the history of the race, so that "ontogeny repeats phylogeny" in mental life as well as in physical. He claimed that there was a fixed period, or nascent stage, for each form of activity, corresponding to similar periods in the successive development of animals from lower to higher forms, and of man from savagery to civilization. He advised that the teacher must strike while the iron is hot, "and arrange that the child engages in the appropriate activity when the nascent stage for that activity is reached."

A startling aspect of Hall's theory, with important bearing upon school discipline, is his doctrine of catharsis, the doctrine that innate tendencies must be allowed to run their course when they appear naturally in childhood, even though they would be considered harmful in later life. For, he claimed, being allowed to pass through their normal and natural development, they would discharge themselves and disappear. Thorndike later showed that this theory was opposed not only by common sense but by science, when he advanced abundant evidence that a capacity becomes more deeply ingrained through exercise! Other discoveries in the conditioning of reflexes and the sublimation of instincts have led educators to the view that undesirable tendencies can, and must be, weeded out as soon as possible.

Although psychologists disagree with him and question the reliability of his methods of research, Hall deserves credit for (1) stimulating the study of child nature and (2) inspiring an intelligent sympathetic treatment of children. Largely as a result of his efforts, we now realize that the teacher can do his best work only when he understands fully the nature of his pupils. Methods must be determined by that understanding; the school at each level must provide the type of activity best suited to the nature of children at that level; the school must provide methods and facilities which will enable children to behave normally and naturally and to learn by means of that behavior.

The most influential contribution of William James to educational method was in connection with habit formation. He says:

> The great thing, then, in all education, is to *make our nervous system our ally instead of our enemy*. It is to fund and capitalize our acquisitions and live at ease upon the interest of the fund. *For this we must make automatic and habitual as early as possible, as many useful actions as we can,* and guard against the growing into ways that are likely to be disadvantageous to us, as we should guard against the plague. The more of the details of our daily life we can hand over to the effortless custody of automatism, the more our higher powers of mind will be set free for their own proper work.[20]

In discussing the methods of habit formation, James set forth four basic principles:

1. Launch yourselves with as strong and decided an initiative as possible.

---

[20] William James, *Psychology—Briefer Course* (New York: Holt, Rinehart and Winston, Inc., 1892, 1920), pp. 144–145.

2. Never suffer an exception to occur till the new habit is securely rooted in your life.

3. Seize the very first possible opportunity to act.

4. Keep the habit alive by a little gratuitous effort every day.

Thorndike developed these principles further and applied them to all forms of associative learning in his famous laws of learning.

1. The law of readiness. The start of learning must be enthusiastic and motivated.

2. The law of exercise. The more frequently a bond is exercised, the stronger it becomes.

3. The law of effect. There must be some measure of progress so that the learner can gauge his success and thus gain a feeling of satisfaction.

Thorndike was even more influential than James in formulating and applying the principles of functionalist psychology. Through his elaboration of laws of learning he, more than any other psychologist, convinced teachers that learning consists of effecting changes in the individual's nervous system, that development comes with the building of neural connections. His educational psychology is based upon the well-known Stimulus-Response Hypothesis, which states that when a given stimulus has been followed by a certain reaction or response under satisfying conditions, a bond is created between the two. Learning is viewed as the result of the formation of these bonds, and development comes with the multiplication of these bonds into patterns of behavior. The teacher's work is to control the formation of these bonds. In the case of undesirable natural behavior, the teacher must either withhold the stimuli or so modify the neural organization that the stimuli will evoke responses different from those prompted by nature. The ideal teaching methods, therefore, are those that develop within the child the neural organization that produces desirable responses.

In developing this methodology, Thorndike elaborated upon (1) the principle of self-activity, (2) the principle of apperception, and (3) the principle of motivation, which had been formulated by earlier developmentalists. He added, however, an important fourth principle, that of individual differences. As he observes:

> Common observation shows that children differ greatly in their mental make-up. . . . The practical consequence of the fact of individual differences is that every general law of teaching has to be applied with consideration of the particular person in question. . . . The responses of children to any stimulus will not be invariable like the responses of atoms of hydrogen or of filings of iron, but will vary with their individual capacities, interests and previous experience.[21]

---

[21] Thorndike, pp. 68, 83.

Maria Montessori's three principles of education were (1) adaptation to the individual child, (2) freedom for both teacher and student, and (3) thorough training of the senses, for, she noted, "the education of the senses has as its aim the refinement of the differential perceptions of stimuli by means of repeated exercises."

Thus developmentalist conclusions have led to the formulation of five basic principles of teaching, with psychological bases and procedural applications:

1. The Principle of Pupil-Activity (Self-activity)
    a. Psychological basis: Learning comes from the pupil's own responses to stimulation.
    b. Law of procedure for teacher: Control the activity of the pupil in the right direction.
2. The Principle of Motivation (Interest)
    a. Psychological basis: The intensity of the learning response depends upon interest.
    b. Law of procedure for teacher: Reveal interests in the stimulating situation.
3. The Principle of Apperception (Preparation and Mental Set)
    a. Psychological basis: The nature of the learning response depends upon past experience and present frame of mind.
    b. Law of procedure for teacher: Present stimuli adapted to the experience and mental set of the pupils.
4. The Principle of Individualization
    a. Psychological basis: Learning responses are determined and limited by individual differences in ability.
    b. Law of procedure for teacher: Adapt instruction to individual differences.
5. The Principle of Socialization
    a. Psychological basis: Every response has its social implications, "No one lives unto himself alone."
    b. Law of procedure for teacher: All learning responses must be developed in natural social settings.

Developmentalists as a matter of consistency consider these principles applicable to all teaching situations and to all levels of instruction. The later Gestalt, or field, psychologists see learning somewhat differently; their contribution to educational psychology will be considered in Chapter 18.

Behaviorism

Before considering developmental content, we must note the position of behaviorism, which during the second quarter of the twentieth century assumed a prominent position in structural and functional psychology. The American phase of this movement, an extreme development of functionalism, dates from the publication of John B. Watson's *Behavior: An Introduction to Comparative Psychology* (1914). Watson adopted the conditioned reflex principle made famous by the experiments of the Russian physiologist and psychologist Ivan Petrovich Pavlov (1849–1936), which stressed the mechanistic foundations of life.[22] Watson and his followers rejected both introspective methods and the concept of consciousness; they maintained that "scientifically valuable data cannot be obtained by introspective observations [such as Hall's] but are a strictly private affair."

The behaviorists, Meyer in Germany and Watson and Lashley in the United States, emphasized stimulus and response, the concept of the conditioned reflex (or response)—as had Thorndike's experimental use of connectionist psychology. They were interested chiefly in the processes and activities related to the organism's motor (muscular and glandular) responses to environmental stimuli. But the proponents of this school frequently disagreed in their premises and conclusions and behaviorism soon reached its zenith, at least in the United States. Its effect on American educational methodology was not great, as two authors note:

> . . . Despite Behaviorism's exaggerated claims, few of its theses have been scientifically disproved. What conditioning can do was demonstrated in the educational practices of Nazi Germany and Fascist Italy and it is being utilized to the hilt presently in the entire Communist world. But Behaviorism denies the existence of the soul, mind, and consciousness, and the American mentality does not favor a doctrine holding that behavior should be placed on a purely mechanical, stimulus-response, conditioning basis, and that only those aspects of human behavior which can be observed and analyzed should be studied.[23]

Content Determined by Method

One of the obvious results of the educational theories of the psychological developmentalists was the broadening of the curriculum, especially at the elementary level. While some of the newer subjects were not included in their conception of education, and had to be introduced as a result of more recent movements, the curriculum that the psychological developmentalists developed was much more extensive than any which had preceded them. Moreover, many of the older subjects were changed to such an extent that they were scarcely recognizable.

In general terms Pestalozzi believed that the essential elements of an elementary education were language, number, and form, and that all the materials of instruction could be brought under this threefold classification. The Pestalozzians retained the traditional names of the various subjects in

---

[22] See Boris P. Babkin, *Pavlov: A Biography* (Chicago: University of Chicago Press, 1949).

[23] From an unpub. paper by Joseph S. Roucek and Kenneth V. Lottich.

the elementary curriculum, but modified each according to their theory. Some of the subjects were changed for the better and some were not, but all came under their influence.

As a result of the Pestalozzian emphasis upon oral object teaching, certain subjects were emphasized more than others and were greatly improved in character; arithmetic, geography, elementary science, and language were so enhanced. But as a result of the radical application of Pestalozzi's principle of proceeding from the simple to the complex, other subjects did not fare so well; drawing, music, reading, and writing suffered.

In connection with the teaching of object lessons, Pestalozzi and his followers used many materials employed later in the teaching of the natural sciences. They usually designated such instruction by the term *object teaching*, the phrase *elementary science* coming into use later, and the phrase *nature study* still more recently. Object teaching was at first rather informal, the teacher making use of materials in the children's environment in order to enlarge the scope of their impressions and provide the basis for language expression. Later, this objective teaching became more scientific and quite highly systematized. Collections of physical, chemical, mineralogical, botanical, and zoological specimens were made available for observation by the children, who had to learn to describe them in scientific terms. Finally, especially among the English and American Pestalozzians, these lessons in elementary science were looked upon as essential preparation for the advanced study of natural science and history in the secondary schools.

No subject in the curriculum was more completely changed by the Pestalozzian influence than geography. Before the time of Pestalozzi, geographies were mere compendia of facts, arranged in encyclopedic manner. Even after the development of Pestalozzianism this dictionary-encyclopedic type of geography continued to be taught in many localities, and it is not uncommon to find traces of it in geographies today. This fact-geography involved memorizing all kinds of astronomical, physical, natural, and political data, which was usually presented in a catechetical, or question-and-answer, form. Pupils learned definitions, statistics, boundaries, capitals, products, exports and imports, population figures, and so on; and the teacher heard the pupils recite these memorized facts.

The application of oral object teaching to geography changed all this. A new study of home geography was introduced, based on the principle of proceeding from the simple and known to the complex and unknown. Karl Ritter (1779–1859), a German pupil of Pestalozzi, moved the emphasis from political and statistical geography to physical and human geography, with much attention to out-of-door observation and the study of landforms. Arnold Guyot (1807–1884), a pupil of Ritter, who came to America as an institute lecturer for the Massachusetts State Board of Education, wrote a geography textbook on the Pestalozzian plan; his purpose, he said, was "to fill the young with vivid pictures of nature in such regions of the globe as may be considered great geographical types." Francis W. Parker, in his *How to Teach Geography*, and Alexis Frye, in his textbook series, improved the earlier Pestalozzian content.

The third subject that was greatly improved as a result of Pestalozzian theory was arithmetic. Earlier arithmetic consisted largely of figuring, and was commonly known as ciphering. Rules were memorized and examples solved according to these fixed rules. Pestalozzi replaced such processes with rapid mental calculations in counting and measuring objects. He tried to develop "number ideas," instead of meaningless words about numbers. Such number ideas were gained by counting, measuring, grouping, and arranging concrete objects and lines. This type of arithmetic was popular until the end of the nineteenth century. Mental arithmetic was the first of the Pestalozzian subjects to be introduced into the United States. In 1821 Warren Colburn published his *First Lessons in Arithmetic on the Pestalozzian Plan*, a book which represents the only phase of the Pestalozzian curriculum to receive any attention in the United States before the beginning of the Oswego movement in 1860.

Pestalozzi made oral language one of the outstanding features of his curriculum. He was the first to introduce the oral language lessons which became a prominent phase of elementary school study. Children were encouraged to tell what they had experienced after they were filled with sense impressions through their observation of objects. Thus language came to be a free oral description based on sensory experience (perhaps the first "show and tell") rather than a reproduction of words read in a printed text; and correct speech usage came to be stressed, instead of the formal rules of grammar.

Writing, drawing, and music should have been developed by Pestalozzi along with oral language as agencies for free expression. But these subjects in his course of study were influenced unfavorably by his principle of procedure from the simple to the complex. Because he attempted to reduce each of these subjects to its elements and to present it logically, each was presented in a mechanical, lifeless, and ineffectual manner. Children started to learn to write by means of drills on lines, curves, and muscular movements. Years were spent on angles, geometric figures, and forms in preparation for drawing. In music, children were drilled on notes, scales, and tones.

Insofar as he taught reading, Pestalozzi was satisfied to continue in the traditional manner, beginning with drills on the alphabet, and then proceeding through drills on syllables and words to phrases and sentences. As a result of the work of later educational psychologists, the phrase or sentence is considered the simplest element to the child, and many begin the teaching of reading with these elements. Even arithmetic came under the influence of Pestalozzi's principle. German Pestalozzians reduced arithmetic to its "elements," and with intense thoroughness spent days teaching each. This idea was introduced into the United States by Louis Soldan, a teacher in the St. Louis public schools, and surprisingly found a wide acceptance in the last decade of the nineteenth century.

Pestalozzi's early use of industrial and agricultural activities found little place in his later work at Burgdorf and Yverdon. In fact, he never particularly stressed these activities as a form of vocational preparation. Even the Fellenberg institutes seldom used training in these activities for any other purpose than self-support while engaged in the study of academic subjects. Pestalozzians looked upon manual training as a form of developmental expression, as a part of the "harmonious development of the faculties," and the early manual-training movement in this country and much of the handwork in our elementary schools were in accord with this point of view.

Herbart outlined the materials of instruction in his doctrine of interests, classifying all subject matter in terms of "typical" human concerns. Man's interests, he said, were derived from two sources: (1) his contacts with the real things of his environment, or sense impressions; and (2) his contacts with other human beings, or social intercourse. Herbart believed, therefore, that the content of education should consist of two types of studies: (1) studies about things, such as sciences, mathematics, and fine arts; and (2) studies about people, such as languages, history, and literature—a forerunner to the social studies concept.

The Pestalozzians, as indicated above, had already emphasized and developed the first group of subjects. Of the second group, however, Pestalozzi had concerned himself only with oral language. It remained for Herbart and his followers to offer and foster history and literature as subjects of preeminent importance in the curriculum. Herbart was concerned primarily with the application of his theory to the study of languages, literature, and history in the secondary schools. Ziller, seeing the value of Herbartian-taught history and literature as a means for developing the child's morals, made narrative material from history and literature the basis of the content of his elementary curriculum. The Herbartians favored history as a study of primary importance in developing good human relationships and good citizenship. Partly as a result of the influence of the American Herbartian Society and its successor, the National Society for the Study of Education, history and literature have become important subjects in American elementary courses of study. Literature, originally used as models for expressions and taught by means of a few selected classics, is now taught for its moral and esthetic values with material drawn from the whole range of children's publications.

Froebel's curriculum was an activity curriculum. His content included all types of self-expression activities. He encouraged language as the earliest and most fundamental means by which unfolding occurs, for he believed that language must accompany all other educational language, song, gesture, and constructive activity. He included drawing and rhythm among the activities of the school, for he considered these as opportunities for expression, an aid to further impression. Handwork Froebel looked upon as an opportunity for expression, an aid to further impressions, a training of the mind through the hand. Nature study, instead of being a mere review of classified specimens, became with him the examination of living and growing plants and animals.

Above and beyond everything else, Froebel emphasized play as the most valuable form of self-expression. He was interested in its social and intellectual implications rather than in its health values. He organized his play apparatus systematically and designated them "gifts" and "occupations." These he developed gradually, manufactured, and sold for school purposes. Such materials as balls, spheres, cubes, cylinders, small blocks, sticks, and paper for folding were included for the stimulation of motor expression on the part of the child. Froebel also developed many types of cooperative play and group games and minutely and systematically set forth the songs and movements involved in each. While the idea that a spiritual meaning is intuitively grasped by the child from every gift and occupation may be somewhat fanciful, we must admit that Froebel enriched the curriculum, especially at the early elementary level, with a vast amount of valuable educational material.

Hall was particularly influential in organizing the curriculum by the stages of the child's development. First, he said, the child should be trained in the use of his own physical endowments, walking, talking, and the movements and activities essential to comfort and self-preservation. Next, he stipulated, attention should be given to training the child's senses, through activities of sensory observation and sense impression. Sensory activity should give way to imaginative activity when the child reached the proper stage. Then, Hall advised, reading of myths and poetic fancy should be encouraged, and the child's imagination extended into the past and out over the world.

Next should come drill, memorization, and order, for acquisition of the fundamental habits needed for adaptation to an integrated society. At this stage the subject matter should be made up of the rudiments, the essential habits of daily life. Finally, Hall specified, at the adolescent stage the child should learn to appreciate and understand the "whole world of nature and of man," by being brought into touch with the cultural subjects of a civilized people. Even if we feel that Hall was wrong in organizing the curriculum into fixed periods, we must admit that he advocated a most extensive and complete educational content.

The dynamic psychologists, under the leadership of James and Thorndike, although they retained somewhat the organization of the stages-of-development curriculum, were more inclined to classify and discuss the subjects of instruction in terms of types of teaching and learning. As a result of their influence, familiarity with the psychology of elementary and secondary school subjects came to be considered an essential part of the teacher's preparation. Subjects were approached from the standpoint of their psychological aims, and the content of the curriculum was analyzed in terms of skills, appreciations, and knowledge.

Thorndike, for example, said that the first six years of school should be given to the development of (1) physical training and protection against disease; (2) knowledge of the simple facts of nature and human life; (3) skill in gaining knowledge through reading and in expressing ideas through spoken and written language, music, and other arts; (4) interests in the concrete life of the world; (5) habits of intelligent curiosity, purposive thinking, modesty, obedience, honesty, helpfulness, courage, justice; and (6) ideals and appreciations proper for children. From twelve to eighteen, he said, school should be given to the development of (1) physical skills; (2) knowledge of general laws of nature and of human life, and of the opinions of the wisest and best; (3) skill in the effective use of the expressive arts; (4) interests in the arts and sciences and in human life as directly experienced and as portrayed in literature; (5) powers of self-control, accuracy, steadiness and logical thought, technical and executive abilities, cooperation, and leadership; (6) habits of self-restraint, honor, courage, and justice; and (7) the ideals and appreciations proper for youth.[24]

The Montessori Method

Professor Luella Cole gives Montessori gold stars in the eleven "fundamental ideas about education" she lists in *A History of Education, Socrates to Montessori*. (Both content and method are determined by her emphases.)

1. Materials adapted for children
2. Attention to individual differences
3. Discipline based on love and interest
4. Personal bond with pupil
5. Analysis of abilities
6. Classification of pupils
7. Education to be fun
8. Development of both mind and body
9. Education as guidance of native abilities
10. Education as a science
11. Emphasis upon moral growth[25]

Only Pestalozzi does as well on Cole's scorecard!

---

[24] See R. Freeman Butts and Lawrence A. Cremin, *A History of Education in American Culture* (New York: Holt, Rinehart and Winston, Inc., 1953), pp. 336–339, for a good interpretation of the contributions of Thorndike.
[25] (New York: Holt, Rinehart and Winston, Inc., 1950), p. 637.

Agencies

As a rule psychological developmentalists set up few new agencies of instruction, but made use of existing institutions. The welcome that was given to their ideas by nationalists made it unnecessary for them to break away and found new schools outside the national school systems. But the new types of schools fostered by the developmental movement were the Fellenberg institutes, the Froebelian kindergartens and Montessori's *Casa dei Bambini*.

Even the kindergarten was not an entirely new institution. The idea that attention should be given to the education of preschool children is at least as old as Comenius, who advocated the School of the Mother's Knee. Jean Oberlin (1740–1826) had already founded the first *école maternelle* in France, and Robert Owen (1771–1858) had initiated infant schools in Great Britain. But both of these institutions were the result of a philanthropic desire to ameliorate conditions arising from social and economic maladjustments. Froebel was really the first to give a philosophical and psychological basis to such an institution for children. Montessori's purpose, likewise, is clear.

Developmentalists considered the teacher to be the only truly effective agency for education. As an obvious corollary of their belief that teaching was a matter of psychological methodology, they continually emphasized the careful training of teachers in their methods. We cannot say that the first teacher-training schools were started as a result of this movement, for we have already called attention to earlier institutions of this type. There is no question, however, that the psychologists, more than any other group, stimulated the establishment and growth of teacher-training facilities as educational agencies. From the establishment of Pestalozzi's institute at Yverdon, to the pedagogical seminars of the Herbartians, to the foundation of teachers' colleges in the United States, the psychologists have been instrumental in building thriving and effective teacher-education institutions. Not only have these schools presented the theories of developmentalism, but in their model and practice classes they have made it possible for teachers to put child development, as well as later concepts, into practice.

Organization

The earlier developmentalists made no recommendations for changes in the established organization of the school system, either in regard to administrative control or to levels of instruction. Pestalozzi was so closely concerned with elementary education, Herbart with secondary education, and Froebel with kindergarten, that they gave little attention to the problems of articulation and reorganization. It remained for Hall to make the first start in this direction, although in Italy Montessori established her *casa* in her efforts to fit the child to life.

Hall believed that educational development proceeds in distinct stages

with somewhat abrupt breaks at certain points. (This is known as the saltatory theory of development, as opposed to the gradual theory.) He also
believed that different phases of development begin at different stages
rather than develop side by side. (This is known as the serial theory of
development, as opposed to the concomitant theory.) As a result of these
theories, Hall suggested that there should be distinct levels of schools,
organized on the basis of the changes in the child's life and his development. He divided this development into four general stages: (1) infancy,
(2) childhood, (3) youth, (4) adolescence. Some of his later followers
expanded this into a fivefold division: (1) infancy, (2) early childhood,
(3) later childhood, (4) early adolescence, (5) later adolescence.

According to Hall, infancy is the period from birth to about four
years of age; childhood extends normally from about four to eight years
of age; youth is the prepubescent period, from eight to twelve or thirteen
years of age; and adolescence begins with puberty and extends to full
physical maturity at twenty-two to twenty-five years.

This theory concerning stages in the development of the child has
been one of the most influential factors in bringing about such reorganizations of the American school system as those represented by the establishment of the kindergarten-primary, the junior high school, the junior college
and, currently, the middle school. These changes have come about largely
as a result of attempts to bring the child's passage from one level to another more closely into accord with the changes in his psychological nature.

REFERENCES

Adler, Alfred, *Understanding Human Nature.* New York: Greenberg
    Publisher, Inc., 1946.
Boyd, William, *The History of Western Education,* 8th ed. Rev. by Ed-
    mund J King. New York: Barnes and Noble, Inc., 1966. Pp. 379–398.
Burnham, William H., *Great Teachers and Mental Health.* New York:
    Appleton-Century-Crofts, 1926. Pp. 189–247.
Butts, R. Freeman, *A Cultural History of Western Education,* 2d ed.
    New York: McGraw-Hill, Inc., 1955. Pp. 383–406.
————, and Lawrence A. Cremin, *A History of Education in American
    Culture.* New York: Holt, Rinehart and Winston, Inc., 1953. Pp.
    343–347, 496–499.
Cole, Luella, *A History of Education, Socrates to Montessori.* New York:
    Holt, Rinehart and Winston, Inc., 1950. Pp. 454–540, 563–590.
Cremin, Lawrence A., *The Transformation of the School.* New York:
    Alfred A. Knopf, 1961.
Cubberley, Ellwood P., *Public Education in the United States,* rev. enl.
    ed. Boston: Houghton Mifflin Company, 1934. Pp. 340–366, 449–
    467.
Curti, Merle, *Social Ideas of American Educators,* rev. ed. Totowa, N.J.:
    Littlefield, Adams and Company, 1959. Pp. 396–498.

Drost, Walter H., *David Snedden and Education for Social Efficiency.* Madison, Wisc.: University of Wisconsin Press, 1967.

Eby, Frederick, and Charles F. Arrowood, *The Development of Modern Education.* Englewood Cliffs, N.J.: Prentice-Hall, Inc., 1934. Pp. 619–678, 755–855.

Good, Harry G., *A History of Western Education.* New York: Crowell-Collier and Macmillan, Inc., 1960. Pp. 225–291.

Graves, Frank P., *Great Educators of Three Centuries.* New York: Crowell-Collier and Macmillan, Inc., 1912. Pp. 122–233.

Kessen, William, and Clementina Kuhlmann (Eds.), *Thought in the Young Child.* Monographs of the Society for Research in Child Development, vol. xxvii, no. 2, ser. no. 85. Lafayette, Ind.: Child Development Publications, 1962.

Knight, Edgar W., *Twenty Centuries of Education.* Boston: Ginn & Company, 1940. Pp. 356–369.

Mayer, Frederick, *A History of Educational Thought.* Columbus, Ohio: Charles E. Merrill Books, Inc., 1960. Pp. 264–287.

Messenger, James F., *An Interpretative History of Education.* New York: Thomas Y. Crowell Company, 1931. Pp. 182–227.

Montessori, Maria, *The Absorbent Mind.* Trans. by Claude A. Claremont. New York: Holt, Rinehart and Winston, Inc., 1967.

Mulhern, James, *A History of Education,* 2d ed. New York: The Ronald Press Company, 1959. Pp. 462–481, 490–493.

Noble, Stuart G., *A History of American Education,* 2d ed. New York: Holt, Rinehart and Winston, Inc., 1954. Pp. 220–237.

Parker, Samuel C., *History of Modern Elementary Education.* Boston: Ginn & Company, 1912. Pp. 273–484.

Potter, Robert, *The Stream of American Education.* New York: American Book Company, 1967.

Pounds, Ralph L., *The Development of Education in Western Culture.* New York: Appleton-Century-Crofts, 1968.

Power, Edward J., *Main Currents in the History of Education.* New York: McGraw-Hill, Inc., 1962.

Silber, Kate, *Pestalozzi, The Man and His Work.* London: Routledge and Kegan Paul, Ltd., 1960.

Sizer, Theodore R., *Secondary Schools at the Turn of the Century.* New Haven, Conn.: Yale University Press, 1964.

Ulich, Robert, *History of Educational Thought.* New York: American Book Company, 1950. Pp. 258–291.

———— (Ed.), *Three Thousand Years of Educational Wisdom,* 2d ed., enl. Cambridge, Mass.: Harvard University Press, 1954. Pp. 480–576.

SELECTED PAPERBACKS

Backman, Carl W., and Paul F. Secord, *A Social Psychological View of Education.* New York: Harcourt, Brace & World, Inc., 1968.

Beck, Robert Holmes, *A Social History of Education.* Englewood Cliffs, N.J.: Prentice-Hall, Inc., 1965.

Bruner, Jerome, *Toward a Theory of Instruction.* New York: W. W. Norton & Company, Inc., 1966.

Curti, Merle, *Social Ideas of American Educators,* rev. ed. Totowa, N.J.: Littlefield, Adams and Company, 1959.

Darwin, Charles, *Voyage of the Beagle.* New York: Doubleday & Company, Inc., Anchor Books, 1962.

Ganz, Hans, *Pestalozzi, Leben und Werk.* Zurich: Origo Verlag, 1956.

Grattan, C. Harley (Ed.), *American Ideas about Adult Education.* New York: Bureau of Publications, Teachers College, Columbia University, 1959.

Gutek, Gerald Lee, *Pestalozzi and Education.* New York: Random House, Inc., 1968.

Joncich, Geraldine M. (Ed.), *Psychology and the Science of Education: Selected Writings of Edward L. Thorndike.* New York: Bureau of Publications, Teachers College, Columbia University, 1960.

Jones, Howard Mumford (Ed.), *Emerson on Education, Selections.* New York: Teachers College Press, Columbia University, 1966.

Jones, L. Charles, *Learning.* New York: Harcourt, Brace & World, Inc., 1967.

Mayer, Frederick, *Foundation of Education.* Columbus, Ohio: Charles E. Merrill Books, Inc., 1963.

Rippa, S. Alexander, *Education in a Free Society.* New York: David McKay Company, Inc., 1967. Pp. 158–174, 207–230.

Robison, Lloyd E., *Human Growth and Development.* Columbus, Ohio: Charles E. Merrill Books, Inc., 1968.

Stephens, J. M., *The Process of Schooling, A Psychological Examination.* New York: Holt, Rinehart and Winston, Inc., 1967.

Strickland, Charles E., and Charles Burgess (Eds.), *Health, Growth, and Heredity: G. Stanley Hall on Natural Education.* New York: Teachers College Press, Columbia University, 1966.

CHAPTER **17**

The Rise
of the Scientific
Movement
in Education

It is manifest that we must consider the ideal man as existing in the ideal social state. On the evolution hypothesis, the two presuppose one another; and only when they co-exist can there exist that ideal conduct which Absolute Ethics has to formulate, and which Relative Ethics has to take as the standard by which to estimate divergences from Right, or degrees of Wrong.[1]

SCIENTIFIC DETERMINISM

The educational theories of the psychological developmentalists were formulated largely as a result of simple empirical and speculative thinking. At their best these theories were too often based upon the trial-and-error experiences of one education reformer; and frequently they were educational pronouncements founded upon nothing more than philosophical speculation. Although they added much to educational progress, such findings and surmises lacked the reliability and adequacy which the inductive method had brought to the pure and applied sciences during the critical advance of the latter half of the nineteenth century.

This great century was characterized by tremendous developments in the pure sciences of astronomy, biology, chemistry, physics, and physiology, and by the applications of science to agriculture, manufacturing, transportation, and almost every other phase of practical life. As the 1800s drew to a close, a new industrial stage appeared, most prevalently in the United States and Germany. In America novel progress was characterized

---

[1] Herbert Spencer, *The Data of Ethics* (New York: Hurst and Company, 1879).

by the advent of an age of electricity, created by Steinmetz and Edison, and by the introduction of mass production, fostered by Ford and others. In Germany chemistry reigned supreme as perfumes, extracts, fats, fertilizers, and explosives began to emerge from test tubes, while steel fabrication and armaments dominated heavy industry, and Benz and Daimler built the automobile, itself soon to create a new world. In the rest of Europe, France, England, Belgium and Sweden also prospered; and in the Far East, Japan, the England of the East, gave the Orient a new thrust.

Although the awakening in the sixteenth and seventeenth centuries had been reflected in the sense-realistic movement in education; and a new impetus had been given to scientific curriculum content by Rousseau and Pestalozzi, inductive studies and scientific methods were introduced into the schools only slowly and against vociferous opposition. Now, however, two men, Spencer in England and Comte in France, were to suggest a more rapid application of the findings of science to education. Since Spencer was more directly concerned with the problems of education and of what knowledge is of most worth, we shall because of lack of space consider only him.

In his century Herbert Spencer (1820–1903) was perhaps the most influential in stimulating the demand that the new scientific content and the new scientific method be given a more conspicuous place in schools and universities. In *Education, Intellectual, Moral, and Physical* (1860), he urged the introduction of the exact sciences into the curriculum, not only for their content but also for their method values. But even after their introduction and the consequent dedication to the scientific method, education was far from becoming a science; its aims, content, organization, and methods were still a long way from scientific determination.

By 1900, however, the spirit of inquiry and scientific experimentation began to penetrate the professional thought of educators and to make some significant contributions to educational progress. Within a few years the older empirical and speculative thinking of educational leaders had given ground to inquiries in a more rigid format and pursued by more accurate and precise inductive methods.

The educational mind now developed a new sensitivity to suggested reforms based on scientific inquiry, and became increasingly skeptical of proposals not so founded. This scientific approach to the problems of education was especially emphasized in the United States in the graduate schools of education such as those at Chicago, Columbia, Harvard, and Stanford universities. For each of these centers had been in turn influenced by individual and group researchers in Germany, England, and France.

The scientific method was first applied in psychology's attempt to determine data concerning the working of the mind. As early as 1879 Wilhelm Wundt established the first psychological laboratory at Leipzig, Germany. Other Teutonic psychologists, notably Weber and Fechner, began the development of a series of psychophysical measurements, and by the end of the nineteenth century various psychological yardsticks, chiefly limited to the fields of sensation and perception, were being developed in Germany. In England, Francis Galton and Karl Pearson developed statistical methods of research and measurement in biology, eugenics, heredity, sociology, and psychology. Although these men were not engaged in educational work as such, they pioneered the statistical methodology and originated the statistical principles adopted by educators and later used extensively in educational testing and research. The contributions of Alfred Binet of France will be noted later in this chapter.

Predicated upon the research and discovery just cited, the scientific determinist in education demanded that all instructional problems be approached with a scientific attitude, that educational practices and procedures be determined by investigation conducted scientifically by the inductive method. In essence, this meant that inquiry should be (1) objective, (2) impartial, (3) mathematically precise, and (4) subject to independent verification by any competent observer. Education, said the determinists, should draw not only upon the basic sciences for data, both facts and general principles, but should also copy the statistical investigative procedures of the exact sciences.

EARLY LEADERS

In the United States, James McKeen Cattell and Edward Lee Thorndike were early advocates of applying the scientific method to educational problems. Cattell came under the influence of the new anthropometry, or biometry, which had grown out of the statistical work of Galton and Pearson, and in 1890 at the University of Pennsylvania published his *Mental Tests and Measurements*, which heralded the first such use of these terms (Cattell is also described in Chapter 16).[2]

Thorndike was the creator of "educational statistics" and the first to apply the methods of quantitative research to pedagogical problems. In 1902 at Columbia he offered the first course in educational measurement and two years later published his seminal *Mental and Social Measurement*. In the Preface Thorndike wrote modestly: "It is the aim of this book to introduce students to the theory of mental measurements and to provide them with such knowledge and practice as may assist them to follow critically quantitative evidence and argument and to make their own researches exact and logical."

A vivid teacher, Thorndike stimulated his students to shape devices for the scientific measurement of the results of instruction. Although called by some the father of this American movement, he actually was not the

---

[2] A. J. Poffenberger, *James McKeen Cattell, Man of Science,* 2 vols. (Lancaster, Pa.: The Science Press, 1947), offers in vol. ii, pp. 7–20, Cattell's description of Wundt's psychological laboratory.

first to attempt it. The American measurements movement itself really began with the work of Dr. J. M. Rice, who in 1894 made a famous study of the spelling attainments of over 30,000 children in various city and village schools.[3] Using a single list of fifty words, Rice made the striking discovery that those who spent fifteen minutes a day on spelling were able to spell as well as those who spent forty minutes. His findings attracted great attention, but gained few adherents in school circles. Contemporary school authorities, still largely dominated by the doctrine of formal discipline, asserted that it was foolish to determine the value of the teaching of spelling by measuring the spelling ability of pupils! Thus the principal importance of Rice's pioneer study was that it focused attention on the feasibility of using standardized tests for the objective and exact measurement of educational attainment. It is just this end that Cattell and Thorndike sought.

And a complete program of scientific educational measurement did spring from Thorndike's genius. Utilizing Cattell's equal-distance theorem, Thorndike devised a scale unit for the measurement of educational achievement. Stone's Arithmetic Reasoning Tests, developed under the direction of Thorndike in 1908, represented a transition from the Rice comparative exercise to the scaled tests advocated by Thorndike. The Thorndike Handwriting Scale (1909) was followed by the publication of work by several of his students, for example, the Hillegas Composition Scale, the Buckingham Spelling Scale, the Trabue Language Scale, and the Woody Fundamentals of Arithmetic Scale. Meanwhile, in Detroit, Stuart Courtis had been successful in experimenting with standardized tests, and was appropriately chosen to direct the testing in the first formal survey where scientifically constructed devices were used, the New York City survey of 1911.

Other problems that could be studied statistically soon began to attract the attention of those interested in quantitative research. Thorndike's *Elimination of Pupils from School* appeared in 1907. Two years later Leonard P. Ayres published *Laggards in Our Schools,* a study of retardation and elimination in city school systems; and in 1912 Harlan Updegraff's *Study of Expenses of City School Systems* was published. These three studies were pioneer attempts to measure by precise and rigid statistical methods just what the schools were accomplishing and what they cost. In 1913 Thorndike, in collaboration with George D. Strayer, published *Quantitative Studies in Educational Administration,* in 1915 Harold Rugg published his *Statistical Methods Applied to Education,* and in 1918 Charles H. Judd published his *Introduction to the Scientific Study of Education.*

---

[3] For an excellent account of Rice's contribution to education, see Lawrence A. Cremin, *The Transformation of the School—Progressivism in American Education, 1876–1957* (New York: Alfred A. Knopf, 1961), pp. 3–8, 358–359.

Yet, the results obtained from the measurement of achievement did not have much significance until these results could be interpreted. The scales for measuring school accomplishment had to be supplemented by scales for measuring intellectual ability before any great progress could be made in the solution of educational problems. The beginning of objective mental testing had been made in 1905 when Alfred Binet (1857–1911), a French psychologist at the University of Paris, devised a scale for the measurement of general intelligence in terms of mental age. The intelligence quotient, which offered a yardstick for mental testing, was developed in 1910 by William Stern. Binet's scale was revised in 1908 and again in 1911. Translations of the Binet Scale were made and used in the United States by Goddard and others; but it was the revision and adaptation of the tests, made by Lewis M. Terman (1900–1960) and several assistants at Stanford University and published in Terman's *The Measurement of Intelligence,* that gave the intelligence-testing movement its impetus in this country. During World War I a group of psychologists devised the Army Alpha Group Intelligence Scale for classifying soldiers for vocational purposes and for officer training; thus was demonstrated the significance of measuring the intelligence of large groups. Following the war, Otis, Terman, Haggerty, and others constructed similar group tests for measuring the intelligence of elementary school, secondary school, and college students.[4]

In recent years, the study of the child has become more and more scientific. No longer is dependence placed upon the enthusiastic but random observation and introspective questioning used by G. Stanley Hall and others. Thousands of scientific experiments and research studies have been made to determine the nature not only of the child's intelligence but also of his physiology, his personality, his emotional responses, his social responses, and his growth and development along intellectual, physical, emotional, and social lines. With the aid of endowment funds, systematic growth studies have been initiated, notably that at Harvard University under Walter F. Dearborn, at Yale under Arnold Gesell, and at the State University of Iowa under Bird T. Baldwin. The day has long passed since psychologists considered the child a lump of clay to be molded by parents and teachers in the shape demanded by the current fancy.

The school survey was a natural outgrowth of the scientific movement in education. Each survey made use of all the methods of quantitative research developed up to the time it was made. The first of these was made in 1910 in Montclair and East Orange, New Jersey. The reports on these

---

[4] Lewis M. Terman and others, *Genetic Studies of Genius,* 5 vols. (Stanford, Calif.: Stanford University Press, 1925, 1926, 1930, 1947, 1959). In these works Terman and his associates, over a thirty-eight-year period, prepared this series; its titles indicate the content: *Mental and Physical Traits of a Thousand Gifted Children; The Early Mental Traits of Three Hundred Geniuses; The Promise of Youth: Follow-Up Studies of a Thousand Gifted Children; The Gifted Child Grows Up: Twenty-five Years' Follow-Up of a Superior Group; The Gifted Group at Mid-Life, Thirty-five Years' Follow-Up of the Superior Child.*

surveys were composed largely of the personal observations and opinions of one experienced educational expert, Paul H. Hanus, of Harvard University. In 1911, Hanus organized a staff to conduct a comprehensive study of the school system of New York City, in which Courtis used standardized tests for the first time in a school survey. Within a short time surveys became objectively oriented and were based upon precise statistical research methods. The first of this type was the survey of the schools of Butte, Montana, conducted by Strayer. By 1915, when the extensive Cleveland survey was made by a staff under the direction of Charles H. Judd, the technique had become standardized. The survey was financed by the Russell Sage Foundation and published in twenty-two monographs.

Educational experimentation under scientifically controlled conditions developed rapidly. Scientific curriculum construction and scientific determination of teaching methods have become accepted techniques of administration. George D. Strayer, of Columbia University, was most influential in the application of scientific methods to the solution of the problems of school administration and organization.

Beginning with New York City in 1913, bureaus of investigation and research were established in school systems. The National Association of Directors of Educational Research was formed in 1916, the name later being changed to the American Educational Research Association, now an active and extensive department of the National Education Association. The work of these research specialists has rapidly expanded, from that of a general survey of accomplishment and of the conducting of testing programs, to include a wide diversity of scientific studies dealing with such problems as pupil placement, retardation, curriculum reorganization, salary schedules, school finance, legislation, and even school publicity and public relations. During the postwar years and the resulting great increase in school construction, school building scales and scorecards were developed, and school architecture and school construction were placed on a more exact and scientific basis.[5]

The schools of education at The Ohio State University and at Harvard likewise were particularly active in this area. Phillip J. Rulon at Harvard and Ralph W. Tyler at Ohio State were prominent in statistical analysis. T. C. Holy, of Ohio State, conducted school organization surveys in a number of states, especially Oregon in 1955.

BIRTH OF THE TEACHING MACHINE

Sidney L. Pressey, at The Ohio State University, may be called the Columbus of mechanized teaching. In December, 1924, he presented the pioneer version of the teaching machine at the Washington, D.C., meeting

---

[5] William Clark Trow, *Scientific Method in Education* (Boston: Houghton Mifflin Company, 1925), reports these early developments quite carefully.

of the American Psychological Association and he read a paper. Two years later he published a description of the first instrument, with diagrams indicating its operation and a number of psychological justifications for its use.

Strange to say, Pressey's article, "A Simple Apparatus Which Gives Tests and Scores—and Teaches," drew little interest. His instrument was about the size of a portable typewriter and was geared to present a series of questions to the student, multiple choices being revealed through the hole at the front; four levers (only two of which were to be used when true or false questions were posed) were attached; following the student's choice on a given question, the machine automatically unrolled another question. Behind the basic mechanism there was a fifth lever, which when pressed, revealed the correct answer. The psychologist had likewise provided his machine with a feature that rewarded the efficient pupil and hopefully stimulated him to continue the exercises. Pressey described it thus:

> . . . there is an additional attachment which drops in a little container before the subject a small piece of candy, if he makes the number of correct responses for which the experimenter has set the "reward dial." With this attachment, the apparatus thus does one thing further; it automatically rewards the subject as soon as he reaches whatever goal the person giving the test may set for him.[6]

It is obvious that the inventor, at first at least, considered his work and the apparatus as experimental: he writes of *the experimenter, the reward dial, subjects*; but, later as is indicated in the title of his paper, he apparently began to think of the device as a teaching machine. Pressey appears to reflect the emphasis of the behaviorists and their debt to Pavlov; Pressey, it seems, remained a psychologist at heart, although one with a strong interest in education. Apparently he was somewhat amazed that his device in operation parallels Thorndike's learning laws, for he observed:

> The somewhat astounding way in which the functioning of the apparatus seems to fit in with the so-called "laws of learning" deserves mention in this connection. The "law of recency" operates to establish the correct answer in the mind of the subject, since it is always the *last* answer which is the right one. The "law of frequency" also cooperates; by chance the right response tends to be made most often, since it is the *only* response by which the subject can go on to the next question. Further, with the addition of a simple attachment the apparatus will present the subject with a piece of candy or other reward upon his making any given score for which the experimenter may have set the device; that is, the "law of effect" also can be made, automatically, to aid in the establishing of the right answer.[7]

---

[6] Sidney L. Pressey, "A Simple Apparatus Which Gives Tests and Scores—and Teaches," *School and Society*, vol. 23, no. 586 (March 20, 1926), pp. 373–376.

[7] Pressey, p. 375.

The lack of attention to Pressey's "box" and his interpretation seems odd today, when such hardware has become commonplace; but in the 1920s a high economic prosperity coupled with the development of the "activity school" may partially explain such disinterest; then the economic debacle of the thirties made even the smallest educational expense anathema. To continue the teaching-machine story we must turn thus to other investigators.

B. F. Skinner, mentioned in the preceding chapter, brought Pressey's work to a further conclusion. Attempting to distinguish between *elicited* behavior (Pavlov's conditioning resulting from unobservable stimuli such as drives) and *instrumental* conditioning, he developed a "conditioning box." With this invention the learning situation can be so arranged that a hungry animal may receive food only when moving a lever at the identical time some other set stimulus, a gong, bell, or buzzer, is activated. He found that given these conditions a rat learned to depress the lever only when it heard the noise.

In 1954 Skinner's paper, "The Science of Learning and the Art of Teaching,"[8] filled the gap in Pressey's observations and demonstrated the relevance to education of such experimental work on the control and modification of behavior. Karpas states the fundamental difference between Skinner's method and that of Pressey:

> The major identifying feature of the Skinner format as opposed to Pressey's, is insistence upon a freely constructed response on the part of the learners. Instead of being offered a selection of several possible answers or responses, the student must actually write in the missing words or, depending upon the nature of the device, make some other appropriate but constructive response. Skinner's program proceeds, more or less like others, in the Socratic fashion, leading students to pursue the complete identification of knowledge that they already possess.[9]

A third pioneer in the area is Norman A. Crowder. In 1955, while developing a method for training electronic engineers in trouble shooting, Crowder became involved in the production of programmed learning devices. His contribution was the "scrambled textbooks." Not only must an engineer choose the correct answer from a series of multiple choice responses, but he must be given adequate reasons why a wrong choice is not permissible. Basically, Crowder's plan (when applied to verbal material) was as follows:

> . . . the student is given the material to be learned in small logical units and tested on each unit immediately. The test result is used to

---

[8] *Cumulative Record,* enl. (New York: Appleton-Century-Crofts, 1961), pp. 145–157.

[9] Melvin R. Karpas, "Automatic Teachers—Or Human?" *V.O.C. Journal of Education* (Tuticorin, India), vol. 3, no. 2 (August, 1963), p. 14.

automatically conduct the material that the student sees next. If the student passes the test question, he is automatically given the next unit of information and the next question. If he fails the test question, the preceding unit of information is reviewed, the nature of the error is explained to him, and he is retested. The test questions are multiple choice questions and there is a separate set of correctional materials for each wrong answer that is included in the multiple choice alternative. The technique . . . is called "intrinsic programming."[10]

Crowder refers to *wash back* and *wash ahead* procedures but does not mention *branching,* the term now most frequently applied to Crowder-related programs; the constructed response programs currently are identified as (1) linear and (2) branched.

Edwards judges that Crowder makes use of redundancy features:

. . . i.e., if insufficient evidence is provided for a student to choose the correct alternative, more information is provided. This extra information consists of an explanation of error plus a restatement of the original information, which increases the redundancy. If he still fails to make the correct response, more information is given, followed again by a reading of the original information. The amount of redundancy must now be sufficient for the reception of a perfect 'message.' More recently, in reply to attacks by Skinnerians, Crowder has claimed that his method is based on differential psychology.[11]

To sum up the distinction suggested above, in the Pressey and Skinner regimens the learner is constantly informed as to the rightness of his responses, but is never given the reasons for the correctness or incorrectness as he is in the Crowder format.

This brief review of the development of a scientific approach to the development of pedagogical thought and usage is only indicative of the vast quantity of educational research initiated during the past seventy-five years, and refers to only a few of the leaders active in the various areas of investigations. (For lack of space we concentrate almost solely on the United States, summarizing in Chapter 21 the educational situation in present-day Europe and mainland China.) We will now develop in greater detail the implications and effects of this doctrine of scientific determinism

---

[10] Norman A. Crowder, "Automatic Teaching by Intrinsic Programming," p. 286, in A. A. Lumsdaine and Robert Glaser, *Teaching Machines and Programmed Learning: A Sourcebook* (Washington, D.C.: National Education Association, 1960).

[11] Reginald Edwards, "Teaching Machines and Programmed Instruction," *Canadian Education and Research Digest*, vol. 3, no. 4 (December, 1963), p. 265. For further discussion of machines and programs, see Kenneth V. Lottich, "The Programmed Textbook or the Teaching Machine," pp. 41–56, in Joseph S. Roucek (Ed.), *Programmed Teaching* (New York: Philosophical Library, Inc., 1965); William W. Brickman and Stanley Lehrer (Eds.), *Automation, Education, and Human Values* (New York: School and Society, 1965); Harry Kay, Bernard Dodd, and Max Sime, *Teaching Machines and Programmed Instruction* (Baltimore: Penguin Books, Inc., 1968).

as it has related to the aims, types, content, agencies, organization, and methods current in the American educational system of the late nineteenth and most of the twentieth centuries.

EDUCATIONAL ATTITUDES OF THE SCIENTIFIC DETERMINISTS

Aims

Science, as we have used the term here, is not particularly concerned with the ultimate goals of education. The scientific determinist's chief interest lies in the measurement of educational achievement and the measurement of capacity to achieve, goals which have tended to divert him from an analysis of fundamental social aims and from prolonged consideration of the ultimate objectives of education. There is little question, however, that the scientific determinist contemplates a universe and social order operating in harmony with universal natural laws, which, he believes, can be discovered by accurate and, if necessary, painstaking experimentation and research. For him, the ideal social order is one in accord with the principles and laws that have been formulated by science; therefore he looks upon science as the prime guarantor of social progress. This is what Spencer is talking about in this chapter's prologue.

Thus it is hardly difficult for the scientifically minded educator to agree with Karl Compton (1887–1954), prominent scientist and former head of the Massachusetts Institute of Technology, who said that the future safety and prosperity of the country depended upon the adoption of a national program based on scientific research and scientific principles; that the United States should rigorously attack problems of agricultural overproduction; that a scientific base for industrial functioning should be found; and that we must develop our natural resources so that scientific usage replaces prodigal extravagance.

After he has accepted this concept of the social order, the scientific educator sets up as his educational aims the development of (1) a coterie of skilled scientists who would discover, formulate, and apply these principles; and (2) a body of enlightened citizens who would accept such scientific findings and adjust their lives to them.

Thomas H. Huxley (1825–1895), along with Spencer active in promulgating the scientific point of view in the England of the last century, expressed this concern precisely:

> Education is the instruction of the intellect in the laws of nature; under which name I include, not merely things and their forces, but men and their ways; and the fashioning of the affections and the will into an earnest and loving desire to move in harmony with those laws.[12]

---

[12] *Science and Education* (New York: Appleton-Century-Crofts, 1910), p. 83.

Yet there are those who question the adequacy of such a concept as the final goal of education. They believe that, in attacking social problems, especially those involving intricate human relationships, complex social motives, and varied individual personalities, it is necessary to employ philosophy, not just scientific induction. Nevertheless, there has been a strong tendency to neglect older fields of philosophical speculation in favor of an almost exclusive dependence upon unrelieved science. Ross L. Finney, an American sociologist, points out what he calls the error of this aim:

> Devotees of science, in their ardor to promote the prestige of their deity, are wont . . . to select problems for the solution of which there is a prospect of demonstrable conclusions, eschewing such problems as promise slight prospect of that sort. But such eclecticism is what leaves large fields uncultivated. The cultivation of these neglected fields is what remains. . . . Their claim to recognition and respect lies however, in the obvious fact that . . . most of the problems of life are still left in the gray shadows of partial conjecture, despite the amazing growth of scientific knowledge in many fields.[13]

A positive aim of education should be, therefore, to supplement the present findings of science with the findings of synthetic reasoning; to utilize not only factual scientific research but also that other method of investigation which consists of a careful, critical, systematic formulation of beliefs, with the aim of making them represent the highest degree of probability in the absence of adequate and complete scientific proof. Naturally, dogmatic statements, flimsy generalizations, a priori "certainties," and unwarranted conclusions are to be discouraged; but the extreme scientist in condemning all that cannot be scientifically determined is clearly limiting the scope of his educational objectives.[14]

But there is yet another point to be considered. The scientific process is dependent to a large degree upon tedious and sometimes painful experimentation. A formula which looks well on paper or works well under laboratory conditions may not apply with equal success to human affairs. Scientists, of necessity, are patient people, willing to try a system and see how it works, to accept disappointments as they come and use them as stepping-stones to hoped-for ultimate success. The general public, however, is not so tolerant, and is likely to be particularly impatient with scientists pursuing scientific methods. It wants quick results, and failing to secure them, it wants to start all over again with something entirely different. To get the world's affairs placed on a scientific basis we must first get the

[13] *A Sociological Philosophy of Education* (New York: Crowell-Collier and Macmillan, Inc., 1928), pp. 3–5.

[14] Lecomte du Nouy, *Human Destiny* (New York: David McKay Company, Inc., 1947), shows the futility of scientific thinking without a recognition of its intrinsic weaknesses.

world in a truly scientific frame of mind. And that is an educational objective that is big enough to engage the efforts of the best of the scientific determinists.

The scientific educator has aimed at making education a *science,* and it is along this line that he has accomplished most. Both Thorndike and Judd insisted that the chief duty of the critical student of education is to form the habit of rigorous study and to learn the logic of statistics. Their predominant interest was the application of the scientific method to education. Their influence in establishing and popularizing the fact-finding, statistical, and empirical technique in education was tremendous, for, inspired by their leadership at Columbia and Chicago, graduate students and administrators throughout the United States have aimed in their formal papers and theses, and also in practice, at answering scientifically the question of how individuals may be changed through education.

One of the scientific determinist's basic purposes has been the determination of educational processes and consequences quantitatively, so that by careful measurement of school and pupil populations they could formulate standards of efficiency, time-and-effort evaluations of instruction, and standards of accomplishment. These would serve, in turn, as measuring sticks of schools everywhere and at all times to determine scientifically the economy or waste, efficiency or inefficiency, of their educational work.

William A. McCall, another Thorndike disciple, in his *How To Measure in Education,* whose first edition appeared in 1922, offered the following theses in justification of his aim. In brief form, McCall's hypotheses may be stated as:

1. The ultimate test of all things is the happiness they yield.
2. It is proper for most tests to measure secondary traits.
3. The alleged conflict between measurement and Gestalt psychology is equivalent to the conflict between secondary criteria and the ultimate criterion.
4. Measurement is essential to the maintenance and increase of each generation's capacity to learn.
5. Tests perform a vital service to governments.
6. "Whatever exists at all, exists in some amount."
7. Anything that exists in amount can be measured.
8. Measurement in education is in general the same as measurement in the physical sciences.
9. All measurements in the physical sciences are not perfect.
10. Measurement is indispensable to the growth of scientific education.
11. Measurement in education is broader than educational tests.
12. To the extent that the pupil's initial abilities or capabilities are unmeasurable, a knowledge of him is impossible.
13. To the extent that any goal of education is intangible, it is worthless.

14. The worth of the methods and materials of instruction is unknown until their effect is measured.

15. Measurement of achievement should precede supervision of teaching method.

16. Measurement is no recent educational fad.

17. Teachers should cooperate in all testing and should be allowed to administer and score intelligence and educational tests and interpret results.[15]

In aiming at such objectives, some philosophers say, the scientific determinist should take certain precautions. In the first place, he should remember that we cannot expect to perfect our measuring instruments in this world of intellect, emotions, and social relations in a few decades. In the second place, he should not conclude that only those things have value that can be measured objectively and concretely, and that we can safely ignore the work of the educational philosopher. In the third place, he should never depersonalize and mechanize the work of the schools, and allow the child to degenerate into a mere tally in a frequency distribution or a number in a case study. Scientific measurements and statistical studies should never become ends in themselves, but should always be used as a means toward the more effective education of children.

A prominent aim of the scientific determinist is to make use of his measuring instruments in classifying and placing the schoolchild in the vocational or professional world. Although efficiency appears to be at stake here, not all are agreed that such classification can be done without some sacrifice of individual pupils. William C. Bagley, more than a generation ago, in 1900 addressed the National Education Association to this effect; his speech "Democracy and the I.Q." bitterly assailed this aspect of the hopes of determinists. Making a formidable attack upon determinist use of general intelligence tests for classification and vocational placement purposes, Bagley asserted that such scientists, by emphasizing the presumed intellectual limitation of the masses and by openly disregarding the possibility of securing individual and social progress by environmental means, cast a long shadow across democratic hopes.

Recent conceptions of the significance of IQ testing tend to consider the results simply as measures of opportunities lost or as an indication of potential school success, rather than as a definitive prediction for the individual's life-potential. Thus, fitting the round peg in the round hole and

---

[15] Abstracted from William A. McCall, *Measurement—A Revision of How to Measure in Education* (New York: Crowell-Collier and Macmillan, Inc., 1939), ch. i, "A Philosophy of Measurement," pp. 3–26. McCall acknowledged his debt to Thorndike for thesis 6 by putting it in quotation marks and citing his source as "E. L. Thorndike, *The Seventeenth Yearbook of the National Society for Study of Education, Part II*, p. 16; Public School Publishing Co., Bloomington, Ill."

the square peg in the square hole appears not to be the comfortable task the earlier scientific determinists judged it to be.

But in 1969, in spite of reams of evidence to the contrary, Arthur R. Jensen, at the University of California, Berkeley, asserted that the success of people of different races is based on what he calls inherent inferiorities.[16]

Types

The type of education predominantly favored by the scientific educator is utilitarian in character. Like Bacon's sense realism and Rousseau's naturalism, it must face the pragmatic test, Of what use? The scientist is particularly concerned with efficiency in education, and he cannot consider any education efficient if it does not contribute to the attainment of a practical end, the utility of which has been scientifically determined. By careful and precise measurements, he attempts to discover exactly what directly affects conduct, improves life, and benefits man individually or socially. Because of this emphasis upon a utilitarian type of education, the scientific tendency has become a much more effective reaction against disciplinism than either the naturalistic or the developmentalistic movements.

There are some who claim that the scientific movement, because of this emphasis upon utility, is inclined to favor a narrow vocational type of education. The truth is that prominent scientific educational leaders advocated an education much more truly liberal and cultural than that urged by those who called themselves liberal educators. The narrow curriculum pursued in the traditional academic course in high school and college and labeled as a liberal-culture course of study, is, in reality, perhaps "vocational" in that it prepares only for a few selected occupations, and in no sense fits the student for the whole of modern life. Scientists, with their interest in the natural and social sciences, consider those subjects cultural and liberal that develop the judgment and understanding, enlarge the vision and extend the intellectual horizon, broaden the human sympathies, train for efficient living, stimulate ambitions for individual and social progress. They believe that such subjects as human and economic biology, astronomy, economics, industrial chemistry and physics, commercial and industrial history, government and sociology, domestic science and household finance, can be as truly liberal and cultural as the traditional languages, literature, mathematics, and history so often looked upon as the only "cultural"

---

[16] "How Much Can We Boost I.Q. and Scholastic Achievement?" *Harvard Educational Review*, vol. 39, no. 1 (Winter, 1969), pp. 1–123. In contrast to Jensen, Robert Rosenthal, Harvard University, conducted a study which indicated that "children performed just as teachers had been led to expect based on rigged I.Q. scores." A news report of February 1, 1969, indicated the banning of IQ tests in the primary grades of the Los Angeles City school system.

subjects. Indeed, the scientist believes that any subject can be either liberal or vocational, according to the use to which it is put by the individual student.

Scientific determinists are confident that they are providing types of education that are truly universal and democratic. By scientific job analysis of the needs of life, by scientific curriculum building, and by scientific classification of pupils, they feel that they are presenting education fitted to the needs of every individual. Differentiation of instructional content and method, they think, provides the most democratic type of education whereby each individual is enabled to attain the maximum of his potentialities with the least emotional disturbance and the least expenditure of time and effort. Thus they believe they are opening the door of opportunity to every child.

On the other hand, some such devices as ability grouping and differentiated curricula are viewed as examples of undemocratic class discrimination. Some maintain that the propaganda of the intelligence-testers and the resulting glorification of the IQ has led the schools to cater still further to the superior child, with a consequent neglect of the average and underprivileged. Others claim that the scientific emphasis upon the study of handicapped children—the blind, the deaf, the crippled, the physically weak, the feeble-minded, and other types of defectives—has led to a serious neglect of the gifted child.

Content

The rapid increase in scientific knowledge during the later decades of the nineteenth century and the constantly growing interest in scientific investigations and applications brought about many additions of scientific subject matter to the curriculum. Herbert Spencer, especially, was influential in adding the natural and physical sciences to the course of study. In his discussion of *What Knowledge Is of Most Worth?*, he insists that there are five types of knowledge which are of supreme importance:

> 1. Knowledge which leads directly to self-preservation and produces physical well-being, including the knowledge to be obtained along these lines from such sciences as physiology, hygiene, biology, physics, and chemistry.
> 2. Knowledge which leads indirectly to self-preservation through the building up of sufficient vocational capacity to secure food, clothing, and shelter, including the vocational knowledge obtainable from the sciences of mathematics, physics, chemistry, and the various practical and applied sciences.
> 3. Knowledge which leads to parenthood and the rearing of offspring, including the knowledge valuable for these ends to be secured in such sciences as biology, physiology, and psychology.

4. Knowledge which leads to the proper use of leisure and the enjoyment of the finer things of life, including the knowledge that is to be found in the sciences underlying the fine arts, such as physiology, physics, and psychology.

5. Knowledge which leads to citizenship and which helps one to become a good neighbor and a useful member of the community, including primarily the political, social, and economic sciences, but not neglecting the knowledge to be obtained from psychology.[17]

Spencer emphasized the fundamental importance of the natural sciences and gave them precedence over both the social sciences and the humanistic arts. Both Spencer and Huxley urged the abandonment of much of the traditional in favor of a more useful scientific curriculum.

Yet there were many so-called scientific subjects in the curriculum of elementary school, secondary school, and higher schools in the United States and abroad, before the development of modern laboratory science at the close of the nineteenth century. Such studies, however, were quite bookish and speculative. The most commonly taught subjects were known as natural history and natural philosophy. Scientific study did not really shift from the bookish-demonstration type, as developed by the sense realists and the Pestalozzians and Froebelians, until the very end of the nineteenth century. Actually the present curricular offerings in the natural and physical sciences have had their greatest development in the last half century. (The earlier scientific studies, as taught in the colleges and universities, and academies, and *Realschulen*, and even the elementary schools, were often justified on the basis of the disciplinary conception of education and defended because of their difficulty rather than their usefulness.)

Germany has been a pioneer in the introduction of modern experimental science in the curriculum. The scientific spirit developed by Francke at the University of Halle as early as 1695, and by Hecker in the *Realschule* in Berlin in 1747, was never lost, and eventually flowered into the modern scientific methods and techniques which made the Germans the early leaders in applied science. Laboratory experimentation was probably first begun about 1826 by Liebig at Giessen. As early as 1823, technical schools were established in Nuremberg, with scientific and mathematical subjects taught as the bases for the applied sciences. In 1852 the *Realschulen* began to teach physics, chemistry, mineralogy, and physical geography with a new emphasis upon the use of scientific material as a basis for industrial activity.

In the United States, laboratory experiments were not performed by the students themselves, even in universities, until after 1850, and not

---

[17] Abstracted from *Education, Intellectual, Moral, and Physical* (New York: Appleton-Century-Crofts, 1860), pp. 32–96.

412   THE RISE OF THE SCIENTIFIC MOVEMENT IN EDUCATION

until the close of the century in the high school. It was not until the 1850s that laboratory methods were introduced into the universities of England; even now in both England and France, superior scientific work is done in the technical and special schools rather than in the older universities and colleges. In all countries, however, the various physical and natural sciences are included in the curriculum of at least some of the schools at practically every level of instruction, and taught with an ever-increasing recognition of the true scientific spirit and of the precise scientific methods of controlled experimentation.

Scientific educators would include science in the curriculum as a core subject for every pupil. They believe that the facts of science and the scientific spirit and method should be imparted to all citizens. Bode, of The Ohio State University, has said:

> The development of science is evidence that man can control his physical and social environment for his own ends. There is every reason to believe that this control will become more extensive and more complete as time goes on. Science with all its triumphs is still in its infancy. The prophets and seers of the race have seen visions and dreamed dreams; we look to science for the means by which these visions and dreams will be brought to fruition. The cultivation of science, therefore, is a collective enterprise, a common concern.[18]

The influence of science upon the curriculum, however, has gone far beyond the inclusion of the sciences into the course of study. Its greatest contribution has been along the lines of an intensive study of the curriculum and scientific curriculum construction. Up to the beginning of the twentieth century, the curriculum had altered slowly. Additions had been made by force of opinion and authority, or by the fortuitous accumulation of knowledge. Very little had ever been subtracted once it had become a part of the educational offering. Even when a subject had outgrown its original usefulness, it was kept in the curriculum because of the force of custom, or because teachers wanted to teach it, or because parents felt that their children should be taught what they themselves had learned.[19]

The scientific movement in education brought about a systematic objective analysis of curricular materials in order to determine scientifically just what should be taught to satisfy the actual needs both of the individual and of society. David Snedden, Frederick G. Bonser, Werrett W. Charters, and Franklin Bobbitt were early representatives of this movement for scientific curriculum reconstruction.

---

[18] Boyd H. Bode, *Modern Educational Theories* (New York: Crowell-Collier and Macmillan Inc., 1927), p. 288.

[19] See Harold Benjamin [J. Abner Peddiwell], *The Saber-tooth Curriculum* (New York: McGraw-Hill, Inc., 1960), for a delightful parody on this aspect of educational history.

Snedden made the scientific determination of the sociological objectives of education the basis of his concept of curriculum construction. He furthered development of a fully worked-out science of educational objectives, made up of a series of scientifically validated specifications for the school curriculum based on a scale of social values objectively determined by the techniques of sociological science. His scientific procedure consisted of the following:

1. The scientific determination of social objectives.
2. The scientific determination of the social objectives that could be attained by education—the educational objectives.
3. The scientific determination of the educational objectives that could be attained by the school—the school objectives.
4. The scientific determination of the kinds and amounts of subject matter that could be utilized to attain the school objectives—the curricular objectives.
5. The scientific determination of the differentiation needed to enable each individual to attain the maximum potentialities of his intellectual capacity and his specific talents—the pupil objectives.[20]

Snedden considered all the objectives of education in terms of the needs of adult life, physical, vocational, civic, and cultural. These needs are to be considered both from the standpoint of the producer and performer, and from that of the consumer and enjoyer—all the general objectives to be scientifically analyzed into specific goals of knowledges, habits, powers, and interests.[21]

Particularly interested in the construction of the elementary curriculum, Bonser was concerned with the scientific determination of the integrating habits and skills, attitudes and appreciations that every individual must have in order to bring about a unified, harmonious, and stable social order. Through a process of scientific job analysis, he would construct an elementary curriculum made up of such integrating activities.

Charters emphasized the scientific analysis of the ideals, activities, and ideas of efficient social living. He set forth four essentials in scientific curriculum building:

1. The scientific determination of the ideals that sway socially efficient individuals.

---

[20] *Foundations of Curricula, Sociological Analyses* (New York: Teachers College Press, Columbia University, 1927), pp. 146–169.

[21] Walter H. Drost, *David Snedden and Education for Social Efficiency* (Madison, Wisc.: University of Wisconsin Press, 1967), offers a thorough tracing of the origins and development of Snedden's educational ideas, with the final rather controversial judgment: "his own story of upward social mobility, based upon hard work and keen intellect in the best tradition of the "American Dream," is more eloquent in its message than his own proposals of education for social efficiency" (p. 198).

2. The scientific determination of the physical and mental activities that are needed for a socially efficient life.

3. The scientific determination of the ideas that control the specific activities of socially efficient living.

4. The scientific determination of the order in which these ideals, activities, and ideas are to be presented to the pupils.[22]

Bobbitt's book, *How To Make a Curriculum,* was the forerunner of many others on the subject and has had great influence upon school practice. Bobbitt believes that scientific curriculum making should begin with a careful analysis of the shortcomings of children and adults, or a human survey, as he calls it. And through objective scientific studies he would determine the general fields of human life and action and analyze these major areas into ever finer units. Thus the school, provided with detailed lists of socially desirable activities drawn from life, and with scientific knowledge of skillfully diagnosed individual deficiencies, would be able to select, from a rich store of experiential knowledge, suitable remedies psychologically matched to the age and ability of the pupils.

It is a recognized principle of scientific curriculum building that three types of experts should cooperate in the selection of subject matter for school use. First, there should be an expert on the subject, with a complete history of the subject, who should be responsible for the reliability and truth of the facts that make up the content of the subject. Second, there should be an expert supervisor or administrator, with a sound sociological training and point of view, who should be responsible for the selection of subject matter necessary for the satisfaction of community needs. Third, there should be the expert teacher, with a thorough knowledge of child psychology and the individual child, who should be responsible for the selection of subject matter adapted to the age, capacity, and interests of each pupil. In scientific curriculum building these three experts would reject:

1.   Irrelevant and obsolete details, and facts that are unreliable or questionable.

2.   Materials that are not related to the real needs of life.

3.   Materials that are not within the child's comprehension and that do not appeal to the child's interests.

Ernest Horn (1882–1956) pointed out that it is rather difficult to make any adequate scientific analyses of the real values of life; thus, since we must necessarily limit our analysis largely to the functioning of particular subjects in life outside the school, most of the practical work in scientific curriculum revision has been along the lines of adapting existing

[22] W. W. Charters, *The Teaching of Ideals* (New York: Crowell-Collier and Macmillan, Inc., 1920). Abstracted from ch. iii, pp. 44–78, "The Selection of Ideals."

school subjects more closely to the needs of life.[23] Ayres' study of the frequency of use of words and the frequency of misspelling of words as a basis for the spelling curriculum, Charters' study of grammatical errors as a basis for the language curriculum, and Wilson's study of the arithmetical calculations actually used in home, store, and shop, as a basis for the arithmetic curriculum, are examples of this practical type of scientific curriculum building. Yet this was one of the weaknesses of the whole movement; too much of the work in curriculum making was directed toward an analysis of society as it is instead of toward an analysis of society as it ought to be.

Agencies

Those interested in the teaching of the sciences have usually succeeded in introducing their subjects in the existing schools, and few new schools have been established primarily for scientific instruction at the elementary and secondary levels. In some cases, technical schools have been introduced at the secondary level for the purpose of providing instruction in pure and applied sciences that could not be obtained in the conventional schools. At the college and university level, separate scientific schools have been more common, because of the hesitancy with which the traditional colleges introduced scientific subjects before the World Wars and Sputnik.

The earliest special scientific school in the United States at the collegiate level was the Rensselaer Polytechnic Institute, founded at Troy, New York, in 1824, which has been the pattern for many similar institutions. The charter of this school provided that the students were not to be taught by seeing experiments and hearing lectures according to the usual methods, but were to experiment under the immediate direction of a professor or competent assistant; thus they were to become practical scientists. The Lawrence Scientific School was organized in connection with Harvard College in 1847, to provide instruction in science leading to the Bachelor of Science degree. A similar institution, the Sheffield Scientific School, was organized at Yale in 1860. The Morrill Act of 1862 brought about the establishment in each state of either a separate college or a branch of the existing state university in which the sciences were to be studied in their application to the agricultural and mechanical arts. One such institution, Cornell University, at Ithaca, New York, founded in 1867, has been especially active in scientific and technical research.

The movement to make education a science furthered the establishment of a number of schools of education in connection with the leading universities in the United States. It is in these schools or colleges that the

---

[23] See his *Methods of Instruction in the Social Studies* (New York: Charles Scribner's Sons, 1937), for an evaluation of the necessary social teachings.

scientific study of education has been most successfully carried on, and the most effective research in educational problems has been developed. The influence of these schools has been felt not only in our own country but also in many foreign lands; indeed, students from other countries come to them in order to train themselves for service in scientifically attacking the educational problems of their homelands.

One of the most influential of these institutions has been Teachers College, founded in 1887, and now a part of Columbia University in the City of New York. The University of Chicago had its Department of Education from the time of its establishment in 1892. A decade or so later the School of Education was formed, with Charles H. Judd as director, and here some of the most outstanding scientific research work in silent and oral reading, arithmetic, and penmanship was carried out. Other prominent centers of scientific research developed at the School of Education of Stanford University with Ellwood P. Cubberley as Dean, and the Graduate School of Education at Harvard University under the leadership of Dean Henry W. Holmes. At present most large universities maintain professional schools for the scientific study of education. In addition, the normal schools, now usually designated teachers colleges or sometimes state colleges, also have become imbued with the spirit of scientific research in the study and practice of education.

The Graduate School of Education at Harvard also has the distinction of pioneering the professional doctorate in education. With the belief that the Doctor of Philosophy degree does not lend itself to preparation for teaching or careers in the schools, the Ed.D. was developed as the professional degree. Differing from the Ph.D. primarily in its broader scope, the Ed.D. requires candidates to present "such special preparation in foreign languages, mathematics, or other tools of research, as may be necessary for proper handling of the thesis problem."

The scientific movement in education has been marked by the appearance of the educational research specialist. Directors of research are found in many of the larger school systems and most of the state departments of education, and national and state research committees are constantly at work on a great variety of scientific studies in various educational fields.

Such functions are being carried out by the various committees of the National Education Association, especially the American Association of School Administrators, the American Association for Educational Research, the National Society for the Study of Education, the National Society of College Teachers of Education, and similar organizations. Various surveys conducted under the auspices of the United States Office of Education are also steps in the same direction. Yet the educational laboratories of the larger universities remain the centers for most of the scientific experimental work in education.

Many educators believe that each educational worker should be equipped with the tools of scientific research, and schools of education generally require at least one course in tests and measurements, and, on the higher degree level, a course or two in statistics. For, as McCall pointed out, experimental education cannot expect to cope with its self-appointed task until superintendents, principals, and teachers are equipped to solve their own problems. Thus scientific educators suggest that every teacher should be a scientist and every classroom a laboratory. The scientific determiners would gear the school to the methods of business efficiency.[24]

The teaching machine and programmed learning are contemporary examples of the inductive scientific approach. Peters, Burnett, and Farwell list six types of machines, which do not necessarily oppose, but frequently aid programmed learning, particularly in the Crowderian Scrambled Textbook plan. These six machines are:

1.   The Automatic Rater;

2.   The Auto Score, same as the Automatic Rater but with items presented on a plate;

3.   The Cardboard Mask, a cardboard folder containing a mimeographed sheet that presents one line at a time, as the sheet is drawn upward;

4.   The Chemo Card, a specially prepared answer sheet for multiple-choice items;

5.   The Card Sort Device, multiple-choice teaching machine that presents cards one at a time to the student; and

6.   Skinner's Disc Machine, a write-in type of teaching apparatus.[25]

The precept of the scientific group has been that administrators and teachers have the responsibility not only to constantly examine critically and scientifically their own practices but also to lead or help in the discovery and organization of scientifically determined procedures. That is, educators should be consistently alert to the developments in their field and systematically search for better routes to efficiency in school operation and pupil progress. The scientific determinists say that every superintendent, supervisor, and teacher should cultivate the habit of scientific thought. As McCall wrote when the movement was new:

> The practice of scientific experimentation in a school or school system pays in terms of an altered attitude on the part of the entire staff,

---

[24] These scientific determinists were undoubtedly influenced by Taylorism, the doctrines of Frederick W. Taylor (1856–1915), called the father of scientific management, much in vogue during the early part of the twentieth century. See Frank Barkley Copley, *Frederick W. Taylor* (New York: Harper & Row, Publishers, 1923).

[25] Herman J. Peters, Collins W. Burnett, and Gail P. Farwell, *Introduction to Teaching* (New York: Crowell-Collier and Macmillan, Inc., 1963), p. 145.

a willingness to consider new proposals, and an alertness for new methods and devices. Experimentation plows up the mental field.[26]

Organization

The scientific movement, having begun over a half century ago, is still strong. It has led in the United States to many reorganizations of the school system, each designed to adjust the school more carefully to the needs of the individual pupil. Such reorganization has been supplemented by many extensions to the older, basically nineteenth-century, school arrangement. Solicitude for individual differences has led to flexible grading systems, ability grouping, differentiated courses, individualized laboratory plans, qualitative instead of quantitative symbols for marking, progress reports, socialization indexes, and the like. Reorganizations of the school machinery have led to the development of the ungraded school, the middle school, and the comprehensive high school.

New functions have been assumed in the recognition of student activities as an integral part of the program, the supervision of playground use, and the better supervision of health programs. Special rooms have been provided for problem cases. Special classes have been established for pupils who are overage, non-English-speaking, mentally slow, mentally gifted, speech-defective, and retarded. Open-air rooms have been provided for those profiting by such an environment. Special state schools have been established for the feeble-minded, the deaf, the blind, the handicapped, and the neglected. The incorrigible have been given more ample opportunity for rehabilitation. Scientific study has made possible the organization of a system of special education adapted to the needs of these exceptional cases, and progress has been made in their scientific treatment.

The study of school architecture has brought about many changes in school buildings and equipment. Buildings have been made fireproof; heating, lighting, and ventilation have been standardized according to scientific principles, and toilets and drinking fountains are now constructed according to scientifically determined laws of sanitation. Custodial service has become a science in itself, and the construction and maintenance of school buildings are based on scientifically determined rating scales, such as those devised by Strayer and Englehardt, of Teachers College, Columbia University. Even the financial support of the schools has felt the impact of science. Under the leadership of such research workers as F. H. Swift and Paul R. Mort, the problems of school taxation and school budgeting have been approached scientifically.

One of the most important results of the scientific study of education has been the reorganization of the units of the educational system. The traditional 8–4–4 organization of elementary school, secondary school, and

---

[26] William A. McCall, *How To Experiment in Education* (New York: Crowell-Collier and Macmillan, Inc., 1923), p. 3.

college, has been broken into new units. The nursery school, the middle school, the junior high school, the senior high school, the junior college, the senior college, are units of school organization developed largely as a result of attempts to adjust the school system to the findings of educational research in human growth and evolution.[27]

Scientific determinism has added a new branch to the organization of education, a division responsible for carrying out the inspectorial function. The school survey movement was the first attempt to perform this function in a scientific manner. It was an effort to evaluate in terms of objective standards and scientific principles the various factors involved in educational labors. It aimed at analyzing the school organization and its activities into specific elements and measuring the efficiency of each of these elements. There is a permanent need for the performance of such a task. The need will continue for what the survey attempts: a stock-taking of results, an inspection of each factor in education to see whether it should continue or not, and if not, by what it ought to be replaced.

The functions of educational organization have come to be divided into three classes: (1) legislative, (2) administrative, and (3) inspectorial. In the organization of the general civil government as well as in the organization of the schools, the third function has appeared. To anyone who has followed closely the recent tendencies in governmental policies, it is clear that a new regulatory function has been added to the traditional legislative, administrative, and judicial functions, and that this function of government is becoming of greater and greater importance as is evidenced by the innumerable investigation committees that have sprung up through the force of public opinion.

In the development of the school system, the school board came first; the superintendent came later. More recently, within the past fifty years, the supervisor of special subjects has appeared. A later development in this evolution of school organization is the bureau of research, with inspectorial functions of scientific investigation and appraisal. As Wilds notes, the responsibilities of school government are now shared by these three groups:

1. The legislative body in school affairs is the school board. It is the policy-determining body. It determines the conditions under which the educational work must be carried on. It determines the educational needs of the community and fixes educational policies to meet these needs. It appropriates and distributes the school funds. The board is not to administrate, but gives over this task to those who are skilled in the doing of what it has decided must be done.

2. The administrative and executive labors are performed by the

superintendent and those under his direction, the business manager, the principals, the supervising heads.

3. The board must, in some way, scientifically determine whether the work is being done efficiently and according to their wishes and policies. Accurate and reliable inspection must be had to determine the adequacy of the work. This inspection is of two sorts: first, antecedent inspection of what is to be done before work is started, as in the cases of plans for buildings, or of records of prospective teachers; and second, subsequent inspection of results after the work is done. Research workers measure the adequacy of conditions, the waste or inadequacy of financial outlay, the efficiency of instruction in the various subjects, and many other factors similarly important. There are three ways in which this inspectorial function has been performed: (1) by a specially employed outside survey staff, from national or state departments of education, or from higher institutions of learning; (2) by a permanently established Bureau of Research within the local school system; or (3) by a self-survey committee of supervisors, teachers, and others within the school system, working under the direction of the superintendent in addition to their regular administrative and instructional duties.[28]

The scientific movement in education has greatly increased the number of administrators and supervisors in the school system. Specialists of all kinds have been added to the administrative staff, especially in the various state and city school organizations. The American school superintendency, in many ways quite analogous to the position of executive or manager in the industrial world, occupies a unique status in the organization and functioning of the school. In its origin it is perhaps one of the most American educational developments, probably arising from the creation of the district system in Massachusetts and Connecticut.

When this (likewise strictly American) method for handling the needs and wishes of the smallest local school entity was legalized in 1766 in Connecticut and 1789 in Massachusetts, the stage was set for the creation of the new office of superintendent. With the fragmentation of towns because of the advent of industrialism and the increasing population it sometimes happened that as many as ten or twenty such local divisions might exist within a given corporation limit. In order to produce a certain desired uniformity for the town or city it was deemed advisable to place an official over the districts in order to preserve the identity as well as the common purposes of the town or municipality. Such an administrative official, although an educator, did not teach or even associate with the pupils of the various schools as did the headmaster or principal, positions imported from the continental schools. The superintendent's business was that of regularizing and coordinating the activities of those placed under his jurisdiction as

---

[28] Elmer H. Wilds, "The Inspectorial Function," *Wisconsin Journal of Education*, vol. li, no. 1, pp. 12–16.

well as serving as director of the financial phase of the operation and personnel manager. He acted, of course, in liaison with the board of education or the school trustees and was responsible to them.

In the United States, New Orleans is said to have provided such a city director as early as 1826. Buffalo, New York, is generally credited with the first city superintendent as of 1837. The date of the establishment of the state school superintendency has been credited to New York (1812) and the first county superintendent was authorized in Delaware (1829). Louisville and Lexington in Kentucky provided superintendents in 1838, as did Providence, Rhode Island. St. Louis followed suit in 1839 and Springfield, Massachusetts, in 1840. The movement spread rapidly, paralleling its march with that of the great post–Civil War era of new industrial growth.

That this imitation of big business (actual or fortuitous) has caused some question, there is no doubt. While on the one hand there is common agreement on the necessity of providing for an efficient and well-articulated method of regularization, on the other there has been some feeling that the schools have become big business themselves and that the contact, at least theoretically valuable, between the parts of the organization are being largely lost. The hierarchical nature of the superintendency with its growing staff and special structure is in some situations viewed as not a real part of the actual educational effort. Conflicts of loyalty are suggested and the superintendent's relationship to the board of education does not seem to parallel relationships among the teachers, students, and lesser officials.

Campbell, in a recent analysis of this problem of the ambivalent position of the American school superintendency, suggests that the analogy between administration in business and the schools may be forced:

> To the extent that personal needs-disposition are affected by professional values, superior intelligence, and by articulate communication, it seems clear that administration in schools must pay greater attention to personal needs-disposition than administrators in factories; conversely, school administrators can rely less on standard operating procedure than administrators in industrial plants can.[29]

This is a welcome diagnosis to those who fear the depersonalization of some forms of business management in the area of public education. Campbell remarks further that this judgment should apply in the case of the schools because they are public rather than private and because an operation "highly visible at all times must be sensitive to its many publics."

---

[29] Roald F. Campbell, "Educational Administration: Is It Unique?", *The School Review* (Winter, 1959), pp. 461–468, especially pp. 465–466; for a complete summary of the rise of school administration as a profession, see Theodore L. Reller, *The Development of the City Superintendent of Schools in the United States* (Philadelphia: The author, 1935), especially pp. 8ff. and table, p. 81.

Methods

Research (at the beginning of the century the very sound of this word appalled the teacher) aims simply at the solution of a problem on the basis of facts; and the scientific method in education is no more or less than a procedure of answering educational questions by means of the statistical and experimental technique.

In the discussion of sense realism, we pointed out how Francis Bacon and John Amos Comenius reintroduced the method of inductive reasoning into the solution of problems. The scientific educator, like any other scientist, merely makes use of this same empirical process, which resolves uncertainties through the formulation of hypotheses leading to generalizations based on data pertaining to concrete and specific cases. In order to develop sound generalizations, it is necessary to gather facts and to organize them into usable form. The gathering of data usually involves careful quantitative measurement, and the organization of data involves statistical tabulation and treatment. The scientific method of educational research, therefore, has particularly emphasized *quantitative measurement* and *statistical manipulation*.

Most of the workers in the fields of educational research have been captivated by the mathematically precise quantitative techniques of the inductive process, and have concentrated most of their effort on measurement and statistical analysis. As a result, since World War I, they have set forth an almost complete quantitative description of American education in all its phases. The zeal for quantitative measurement and tabulation has brought about the collection and classification of facts concerning such educational factors as:

1.   School buildings—standards of design, materials, equipment, and arrangement-unit costs;
2.   School finance—sources, budgeting, expenditures, accounting systems;
3.   Teaching staff—personality, training, experience, salary schedules, and tenure;
4.   School curriculum—content of textbooks and courses of study, appraisal of results;
5.   School population—social and economic background of pupils, distribution by age, grade, sex, retardation, and elimination;
6.   Pupil achievement—skills, knowledge, appreciations, marking and promotional systems;
7.   Pupil traits—physical, emotional, intellectual, and social, anatomical, physiological, and mental growth.

The advances in the field of educational measurement have been particularly striking, Instead of the traditional measurement by the methods of subjective judgment of teachers, various types of scientifically constructed and standardized tests are now in use. An examination of the lists of such pioneer test publishers as the World Book Company and the Public School Publishing Company will reveal the large number of such measuring devices.

Most schools and teachers are utilizing objective achievement tests, either in the standardized and published form or in the homemade form, as these have been constructed and are available for practically all subjects. By means of standardized achievement tests, we are able to determine the pupil's educational age (EA) and educational quotient (EQ), the latter being the ratio between educational age and chronological age (CA). Thus:

$$EQ = \frac{EA}{CA}$$

Many different scholastic aptitude or intelligence tests, both of the verbal and of the nonverbal or performance types, have been made available; some of these must be administered individually while others can be administered to a group. From these tests the pupil's mental age (MA) and intelligence quotient (IQ) can be determined. The IQ is usually expressed in terms of 100 (the quotient for the normal child) and is computed as follows:

$$IQ = \frac{MA}{CA} \times 100$$

It is also possible to measure the pupil's effort by obtaining the ratio of his educational quotient to his intelligence quotient, a result which has been somewhat misnamed the achievement quotient (AQ). Hence:

$$AQ = \frac{EQ}{IQ}$$

Work has been done likewise in the development of methods for measuring both general and special aptitudes. The Stenquist Mechanical Aptitude Tests and the Thurston Clerical Aptitude Tests are examples of the general type; and the Rogers Prognostic Tests in Mathematics and the Wilkins Prognostic Tests in Foreign Languages are examples of instruments for measuring special aptitudes and talents.

Attempts have been made, with some success, to develop methods for measuring personality and character traits. The Downey Will Temperament Tests and the Allport A. S. Reaction Tests are examples of personality tests; Hartshorne and May, and Voelker pioneered in the construction of character tests, of which the Haggerty-Olson-Wickman Behavior Rating Scales are good examples. Some progress is also being made in the development of techniques for the measurement of the pupil's anatomical, physiological, and social growth.

Every scientific worker must keep an accurate record of his data.

Educators now realize this, and efforts have been made to develop comprehensive and cumulative records and report systems, for the accumulation and preservation of facts essential to scientific investigation and experimentation. The scientific educator takes the position that a large proportion of the school's time, energy, and resources should be expended in the careful study of the pupil and in organizing this information into readily accessible records and reports, before the school's energy and resources can be used effectively in teaching.

Quantitative facts are meaningless unless they are treated statistically. Harold Rugg's *Statistical Methods Applied to Education* (1917) was the first of a series of books designed to familiarize school administrators and teachers with the statistical techniques available for the organization and interpretation of quantitative facts. The normal frequency curve has appeared so frequently on the blackboards of classes in education that someone has facetiously called it the coat-of-arms of the teachers college. Measures of distribution, measures of central tendency, measures of deviation, measures of reliability, and measures of correlation have all been applied in educational statistics. Most school workers of today are familiar with such terms as *median, quartile deviation, standard deviation, probable error,* and *coefficient of correlation.* Progress in the collection of quantitative facts and in the statistical treatment of these facts has reached goals undreamed of only a few decades ago.

Striking advances have also been made during the last few decades in the field of educational experiments. The experimental laboratory methods of the basic sciences have been taken over by educational workers. The physical and chemical scientists have developed a scientific method of experimental problem solving consisting of the following steps:

1.   The realization and recognition of the problem;
2.   The venture of an inference or tentative hypothesis;
3.   The testing of this inference or hypothesis;
4.   The modification of the hypothesis in the light of the findings of the testing;
5.   Further testing and modifications until a valid theory is established;
6.   A verification of the theory and its acceptance as a verified law, rule, or principle;
7.   The application of the accepted generalizations to all relevant situations.

Educational experimenters have developed and established techniques in connection with each of these steps. By means of these techniques experimental investigations have been carried out to evaluate practically every aspect of educational method, educational materials, and educational aims. One or the other of two methods of attack is usually followed. The first is to start with one or more causes (the experimental factor or factors) as the hypothesis, and then determine the absolute or relative effects upon the situation involved in the problem. The second is to start with some desired effect, and then determine whether the hypothetical causes are the real causes, and just how much each of several hypothetical causes contributes to produce the desired effect. In all such experimentation the experimental factor must be isolated and its effect carefully measured, or the experimental method will be unreliable. Experimental conditions must be controlled, or false conclusions may be reached.

Those engaged in educational research must remember that the obvious purpose of scientific measurement and experimentation is problem solving. All too frequently research workers in education stop with the collection of data by survey or experimentation, and fail to interpret these data or to apply them to the solution of a problem. The three processes, (1) diagnosis, (2) interpretation, and (3) verification, are much more important steps in the scientific method than the mere collection, tabulation, and manipulation of data.

One of the most fruitful results of this scientific study of educational problems has been the improvement of teaching methods. Classroom method is no longer a matter of guesswork, but has been carefully determined on the basis of its effectiveness in directing the learning of the pupils. As a result, the quality of teaching methods has been greatly improved, with a corresponding decrease in the time expended in the process. Experimentation in teaching method has brought about an increased recognition of the fact that specific method is more important than general method; that each subject has a special methodology that must be utilized. This has placed a new emphasis upon the psychology of the school subjects, and the method used in practically every subject of the curriculum has been undergoing continual experimentation and revision during recent years.

The scientific movement has increased the attention given by teachers to the problem-solving methods of teaching. The development lesson, the problem lesson, and the project method are emphasized and given a prominent place in all schoolwork. Laboratory methods play a large part in all scientific instruction and are being extended even to the social studies. Exercises in reflective thinking and problem solving have a definite place in almost every subject. John Dewey's *How We Think* had an immense influence upon educational methodology. Improved drill techniques have made possible a quicker formation of the essential integrating habits, giving the pupil more time for vital problem solving; improved reasoning techniques have made possible the reduction of more of the pupil's immediate problems, thus preparing him for the solution of his problems in later life. Scientifically determined educational psychology has produced considerably improved and effective teaching methods.

As we noted earlier in this chapter, the teaching machine represents one of the fruits of psychological experimentation. Like programmed learning, the machine makes use of known principles of teaching and learning. But the machine does not displace the teacher, who, as in the Dalton and Winnetka plans (devices relying on individual progress through what might now be considered programmed material, popular in the 1920s and 1930s),[30] must be even more knowledgeable and more technically educated. The teacher's abdication is out of the question, for, with the advent of "hardware" or with the adoption of scrambled textbooks, and other programmed learning media, the teacher becomes more indispensable than ever. In fact, the teaching task becomes doubly demanding: first, in determination of individual needs; and second, in the provision of the adequate media for the satisfaction of these requirements. Concomitantly, the teacher now requires a great deal of special training in the workings and mechanics of these new devices.

As far as methods of discipline are concerned, traditional formulas governing classroom management and pupil conduct have given way to treatment of problem cases on the basis of thorough scientific study of the physical, emotional, and social nature of the individual pupils. The rod is being replaced by guidance, a burgeoning new professional field. The detention period and bugbear of "a trip to the principal's office" have given way to the clinic and the psychological laboratory of the psychiatrist.

Yet actual teaching method has a long way to go if each child and/or each group is to have the equal educational opportunities and the experiences that should be the legacy of all. Psychologist B. F. Skinner has said, "the present educational process is one in which methods of imparting knowledge have changed scarcely, if at all."[31] The development of teaching machines and other media of individual instruction plus the partial reorganization of the school ladder suggest at least a partial modification of this judgment. Philosophy of education, too, can offer some significant aid in the creation of optimum settings for learning. It is this philosophical area that we next consider.

REFERENCES

Bode, Boyd H. *Modern Educational Theories.* New York: Crowell-Collier and Macmillan, Inc., 1927.

Brickman, William W., and Stanley Lehrer (Eds.), *Automation, Education and Human Values.* New York: School and Society, 1965.

---

[30] Adolphe E. Meyer, *The Development of Education in the Twentieth Century* (Englewood Cliffs, N.J.: Prentice-Hall, Inc., 1956), pp. 488–494.

[31] The Technology of Teaching (New York: Appleton-Century-Crofts, 1968), p. 3.

Butts, R. Freeman, *A Cultural History of Western Education,* 2d ed. New York: McGraw-Hill, Inc., 1955. Pp. 554–584.

Clough, Shepard B., *The Rise and Fall of Civilization.* New York: McGraw-Hill, Inc., 1951. Pp. 217–254.

Cole, Luella, *A History of Education, Socrates to Montessori.* New York: Holt, Rinehart and Winston, Inc., 1950. Pp. 548–562.

Cremin, Lawrence A., *The Transformation of the School—Progressivism in American Education, 1876–1957.* New York: Alfred A. Knopf, 1961.

Crowder, Norman A., "Automatic Teaching by Intrinsic Programming," in A. A. Lumsdaine and Robert Glaser (Eds.), *Teaching Machines and Programmed Learning: A Source Book.* Washington, D.C.: National Education Association, 1960.

Drost, Walter H., *David Snedden and Education for Social Efficiency.* Madison, Wisc.: University of Wisconsin Press, 1967.

Edwards, Reginald, "Teaching Machines and Programmed Instruction," *Canadian Education and Research Digest,* vol. 3, no. 4 (December, 1963), pp. 562–578.

Good, Harry G., *A History of American Education.* New York: Crowell-Collier and Macmillan, Inc., 1956. Pp. 313–341.

———, *A History of Western Education.* New York: Crowell-Collier and Macmillan, Inc., 1960.

Gross, Richard E. (Ed.), *Heritage of American Education.* Boston: Allyn and Bacon, Inc., 1962. Pp. 423–476.

Karpas, Melvin R., "Automatic Teachers—Or Human?" *V.O.C. Journal of Education* (Tuticorin, India), vol. 3, no. 2 (August, 1963), pp. 14ff.

McCall, William A., *How To Experiment in Education.* New York: Crowell-Collier and Macmillan, Inc., 1923.

———, *Measurement—A Revision of How To Measure in Education.* New York: Crowell-Collier and Macmillan, Inc., 1939. Pp. 3–26.

Mayer, Frederick, *A History of Educational Thought.* Columbus, Ohio: Charles E. Merrill Books, Inc., 1960.

Meyer, Aldophe E., *The Development of Education in the Twentieth Century.* Englewood Cliffs, N.J.: Prentice-Hall, Inc., 1956.

———, *An Educational History of the American People.* New York: McGraw-Hill, Inc., 1957. Pp. 291–313.

Monroe, Walter S. (Ed.), *Encyclopedia of Educational Research.* New York: Crowell-Collier and Macmillan, Inc., 1941.

Mulhern, James, *A History of Education,* 2d ed. New York: The Ronald Press Company, 1959. Pp. 435–446, 510–523.

Myers, Alonzo F., and Clarence O. Williams, *Education in a Democracy.* Englewood Cliffs, N.J.: Prentice-Hall, Inc., 1937. Pp. 122–158.

Nakosteen, Mehdi, *The History and Philosophy of Education.* New York: The Ronald Press Company, 1965. Pp. 540–557.

Noble, Stuart, G., *A History of American Education,* 2d ed. New York: Holt, Rinehart and Winston, Inc., 1954. Pp. 468–482.

Pounds, Ralph L., *The Development of Education in Western Culture.* New York: Appleton-Century-Crofts, 1968. Pp. 125–162.

Pressey, Sidney L., "A Simple Apparatus Which Gives Tests and Scores—and Teaches," *School and Society,* vol. 23, no. 586 (March 20, 1926), pp. 373–376.

Reller, Theodore Lee, *The Development of the City Superintendency of Schools in the United States.* Philadelphia: The author, 1935.

Roucek, Joseph S. (Ed.), *Programmed Teaching.* New York: Philosophical Library, Inc., 1965.

Sizer, Theodore R., *The Secondary School at the Turn of the Century.* New Haven, Conn.: Yale University Press, 1964.

Terman, Lewis M., and others. *Genetic Studies of Genius,* 5 vols. Stanford, Calif.: Stanford University Press, 1921–1959.

Trow, William Clark, *Scientific Method in Education.* Boston: Houghton Mifflin Company, 1925.

Ulich, Robert, *A History of Educational Thought.* New York: American Book Company, 1950. Pp. 337–349.

Valentine, P. F., *Twentieth Century Education.* New York: Philosophical Library, Inc., 1946. Pp. 155–326, 327–371.

Wender, Herbert, *The Growth of Modern Thought and Culture.* New York: Philosophical Library, Inc., 1959. Pp. 115–179.

Wiggin, Gladys A., *Education and Nationalism, An Historical Interpretation of American Education.* New York: McGraw-Hill, Inc., 1962. Pp. 40ff.

Woelfel, Norman, *Molders of the American Mind.* New York: Columbia University Press, 1933. Pp. 81–118, 178–200.

SELECTED PAPERBACKS

Alexander, William M., and others, *The Emergent Middle School,* 2d rev. ed. New York: Holt, Rinehart and Winston, Inc., 1969.

Backman, Carl W., and Paul F. Secord, *A Social Psychological View of Education.* New York: Harcourt, Brace & World, Inc., 1968.

Beck, Robert Holmes, *A Social History of Education.* Englewood Cliffs, N.J.: Prentice-Hall, Inc., 1965.

Benjamin, Harold (*pseud*) [J. Abner Peddiwell]. *The Saber-tooth Curriculum.* New York: McGraw-Hill, Inc., 1960.

Bode, Boyd H., *Modern Educational Theories.* New York: Random House, Inc., Vintage Books, 1964.

Cremin, Lawrence A., *The Transformation of the School—Progressivism in American Education, 1876–1957.* New York: Random House, Inc., Vintage Books, 1964.

Cross, Barbara M. (Ed.), *The Educated Woman in America. Selected Writings of Catherine Beecher, Margaret Fuller, and M. Carey Thomas.* New York: Teachers College Press, Columbia University, 1960.

Curti, Merle, *The Social Ideas of American Educators,* enl. ed. Totowa, N.J.: Littlefield, Adams and Company, 1959.

Grambs, Jean Dresden, *Schools, Scholars, and Society.* Englewood Cliffs, N.J.: Prentice-Hall, Inc., 1965.

Kay, Harry, Bernard Dodd, and Max Sime, *Teaching Machines and Programmed Instruction*. Baltimore: Penguin Books, Inc., 1968.

Kazamias, Andreas M. (Ed.), *Herbert Spencer on Education*. New York: Teachers College Press, Columbia University, 1964.

Lee, T. E., *Psychology and the Science of Education*. New York: Teachers College Press, Columbia University, 1962.

Mayer, Frederick, *Foundations of Education*. Columbus, Ohio: Charles E. Merrill Books, Inc., 1963.

Piaget, Jean, *The Origins of Intelligence in Children*. New York: W. W. Norton & Company, Inc., 1963.

Rippa, S. Alexander, *Education in a Free Society*. New York: David McKay Company, Inc., 1967. Pp. 158–174.

Robison, Lloyd E., *Human Growth and Development*. Columbus, Ohio: Charles E. Merrill Books, Inc., 1968.

Tyack, David B. (Ed.), *Turning Points in American Educational History*. Waltham, Mass.: Blaisdell Publishing Company, 1967.

White, Morton (Ed.), *The Age of Analysis: Twentieth Century Philosophers*. New York: New American Library of World Literature, Inc., 1950.

CHAPTER 18

The School
and Society

The school has the function also of coordinating within the disposition of each individual the diverse influences of the various social environments into which he enters. One code prevails in the family; another, on the street; a third, in the workshop or store; a fourth, in the religious association. As a person passes from one of the environments to another, he is subjected to antagonistic pulls. . . . This danger imposes upon the school a steadying and integrating office.[1]

THE SOCIAL MOTIVE

The most commonly accepted educational theories and practices of the first half of the twentieth century were strongly influenced by sociology. During the closing decades of the nineteenth century, psychology reigned as the dominating factor in educational thinking; with the turn of the century, however, the contributions of the sociologists were added to those of the psychologists. Thus developed an educational sociology as well as an educational psychology, both characterized to a considerable degree by the spirit and methods of the scientific determinists. Although Auguste Comte, the founder of modern scientific sociology, gave little specific attention to education, his followers have had much to say about its place in social organization and social progress. The new educators concerned themselves with the social implications and social outcomes of education; they approached the study of educational issues from the standpoint of their social, political, and economic significance.

Yet the point of view of the educational sociologist is not necessarily antagonistic to that of the psychological developmentalist and the scientific determinist. The psychological movement and the sociological movement in education complement each other. The difference in the two tendencies

---

[1] John Dewey, *Democracy and Education* (New York: Crowell-Collier and Macmillan, Inc., 1916).

is a difference in emphasis. The psychologist is concerned with education and the development of the individual; the sociologist and indeed the social anthropologist are concerned with both the individual and his relationship to the social structure; they are interested in education and its contributions to the preservation and progress of society. Each needs to realize, however, his dependence upon the other. For the development of the individual is conditioned by his social environment; cultural integration and social progress depend upon the habits, skills, attitudes, and reasoning powers that have been developed in the individuals who compose the society.

Nor is there any conflict between the sociological tendency and the scientific tendency in education. The sociologist is eager to adapt the techniques of the natural and physical sciences to social science, just as the psychologist was willing to use scientific methods in the development of a psychological science. The scientific method is barren unless it is directed toward the attainment of psychological and sociological objectives. The scientific worker in education errs when he thinks that his scientific technique is supreme and fails to realize that it is only a tool. Thus, the three most recently developed tendencies in educational thinking, the psychological, the scientific, and the sociological, or cultural, must be synthesized in building a complete and adequate educational philosophy.

Comte anticipated Dewey in his emphasis on methodology, although Comte was interested in humanity as a whole, while Dewey favored individualism. Comte was concerned with social progress, and he asserted:

> The progress of the individual mind is not only an illustration, but an indirect evidence of that of the general mind. The point of departure of the individual and the race being the same, the phase of the mind of the race was the same. [Each man] was a theologian in his childhood, a metaphysician in his youth, and a natural philosopher in his manhood.[2]

Comte confidently expected social progress through scientific education.

Sociological educators consider the ultimate aim of education as social rather than individualistic. Few believe that the school's purpose is to prepare the individual merely for the attainment of his own security, welfare, happiness, or power. Socializers distrust the idea that human beings have become dependent upon one another for good or for harm, to an unprecedented degree. This interdependence is increasing, not lessening, and must be taken into account by education. We must not only educate individuals to live in a world where social conditions beyond the reach of any one individual will affect his security, his work, his achievement, but we must—for educational reasons—take account of the total

---

[2] Auguste Comte, *The Positive Philosophy*, trans. by Harriet Martineau (London: G. Bell & Sons, Ltd., 1896), p. 4.

incapacity of the doctrine of competitive individualism to work anything but harm in this state of interdependence in which we live.[3]

But in our earlier history, conditions favored "rugged individualism" and competitive acquisitiveness. The individualistic ideal of the early nineteenth century, which asserted the right of individuals to equality of opportunity and freedom of action unhampered by social control, was an understandable doctrine. The prevailing economic conditions supported the belief that social welfare and social progress were best advanced by the personal choice, personal initiative, and personal action of the individual.

In many areas population was sparse and land abundant and available. Enormous stores of unappropriated natural resources invited human exploitation. New continents were still to be conquered, an opportunity presenting a challenge to all but the most indolent. Under such conditions, it seemed desirable to educate individuals to win the race of life through the development of their own competitive ability and industry. Furthermore, under these earlier economic conditions, individual prowess and success seemed to go hand in hand with the satisfaction of society's needs. Those who discovered new lands, cleared forests, cultivated fields, built roads, developed cities, and invented machines were conscious that they were rendering a service to society as well as to themselves. Personal success was not a private affair; it was a contribution to social welfare and progress. Educating a pupil for success in life was automatically considered a service to society, even though no study was made of social needs, no thought given to social objectives. Preparation for the attainment of personal rewards and satisfactions brought with it a sense of service to society. According to Curti it was just such a conception of American life that catalyzed John Dewey's thought on education.[4]

Because of changed economic and industrial conditions during the last few decades, training for acquisitive individualism has lost some impetus; in World War II the all-out effort to build an "arsenal for democracy" emphasized cooperation and teamwork. And a new climate of opinion which regards group judgment as generally superior to that of one man or woman likewise has served to recondition educational thinking.

But the social goals of education are not new. Primitive education was socializing in its adjustment of the child to group characteristics. Oriental educational systems were devised for the preservation of social stability. The ancient Hebrews, Greeks, and Romans saw the social significance of education. Jesus presented a most advanced social goal, a goal that many of his followers lost sight of. In the twentieth century,

---

[3] John Dewey and John L. Childs, "The Social-Economic Situation and Education," ch. ii, p. 68, in William H. Kilpatrick (Ed.), *The Educational Frontier* (New York: Appleton-Century-Crofts, 1933).

[4] Merle Curti, *The Social Ideal of American Educators*, rev. ed., enl. (New York: Pageant Books, Inc., 1959), pp. 501ff.

however, a new and more pronounced interest has been aroused in education for social purposes; progressive thinking has concerned itself with the nature of social organization and social needs and the ways in which education can serve them. As Courtis writes:

> Leaders in world thought are coming to see clearly that in spite of the inadequacy of the individual man, there is a way out. In the arithmetic of cooperation, an I.Q. of 100 added to an I.Q. of 100 makes a combination which by teamwork can solve problems which demand an I.Q. of 125. Singly, each man proves to be hopelessly inadequate and fails. Jointly, men may form a larger, more powerful individual who can triumph over material limitations. Today the major issues of life have far outstripped the powers of individuals to cope with them successfully; modern civilization must master a new technique of co-operative thinking and action or die.[5]

DEWEY AND HIS LABORATORY SCHOOL

Largely as the result of the work and writings of John Dewey (1859–1952), sociological objectives and actual socializing techniques came to be emphasized as never before. When Dewey left the University of Michigan in 1894 to become head of the Department of Philosophy and Education at the newly established University of Chicago, he found himself in a position favorable to the inauguration of a new movement in education, at a time when it was greatly needed. In 1896, he established his Laboratory School, now often spoken of as the Dewey School,[6] where he was able to put into practical experimentation his theories of a socializing education. Here between 1896 and 1903, he crystallized his social philosophy of education. The practices and experiments of this pioneer venture in socialized education, and others both earlier and later, had more to do with giving impetus to the new movement than any other previous endeavor.

Out of his work in this school, Dewey developed the ideas presented first in that influential educational classic *The School and Society* (1899) and later in his epochal work *Democracy and Education* (1916), which is the most complete statement of his educational philosophy.[7] Dewey had many disciples, among the most influential of whom were William H. Kilpatrick, Boyd H. Bode, Thomas H. Briggs, Ross L. Finney, and George

---

[5] S. A. Courtis, "Achievement of the Impossible," *Michigan Educational Journal*, vol. 8, no. 5 (January 1930), p. 211.

[6] K. C. Mayhew and A. C. Edwards, *The Dewey School* (New York: Appleton-Century-Crofts, 1936); see also Lawrence A. Cremin, "John Dewey and the Progressive Education Movement, 1915–1952," *The School Review*, vol. 67, no. 2 (Summer, 1959), pp. 160–173, for a new interpretation of Dewey's place in the movement.

[7] John Dewey, *The School and Society* (Chicago: University of Chicago Press, 1899); *Democracy and Education* (New York: Crowell-Collier and Macmillan, Inc., 1916).

S. Counts. These so-called "Molders of the American mind" have not been in complete agreement in all phases of their thinking, but they have shared an emphasis on a social philosophy of education.

Dewey's Laboratory School was the forerunner of many other such schools. In Europe blossomed such experimental agencies as the German country-home schools of Herman Lietz, the French *Ecole des Roches* of Edmond Demolins, and the Belgian progressive schools founded by Ovide Decroly. In the United States, appeared the Francis W. Parker School of Chicago, the Meriam School at the University of Missouri; the Menomonie School, Wisconsin; the Lincoln School and the Speyer School at Columbia University; the Fairhope (Alabama) School. These were just a few of the great number of experimental schools. The Progressive Education Association in the United States and the New Education Fellowship in Europe were organized to further the cause of this new type of socializing school.

Of course, in the interpretation of the school's ultimate social goal, there is still considerable confusion and wide variation of opinion. In setting up the social objectives of education, four possible alternatives have been suggested:

1.   Education should prepare for the status quo, for social life and institutions as they now exist, by integrating the pupils into the established social order and indoctrinating them in the accepted traditions of their inherited culture;

2.   Education should attempt to anticipate the changed social conditions that come about through a natural drift along the paths of least resistance, and prepare the pupils for these anticipated new needs;

3.   Education should accept the vision of a new social order in all its details, mold the pupil for this preconceived society, and, through propaganda, help bring about this preconceived society; or

4.   Education should prepare thinking individuals to play an intelligent part in a cooperative social planning toward an ever-improving social order, only dimly conceived in its vague outlines by farseeing prophets.[8]

In reviewing these alternatives, we find that the first three involve what could be called social adjustment, whereas the fourth involves social guidance. Education for the first three demands introduction and propaganda; for the fourth, training the intelligence for problem solving and social responsibility is needed.

In discussions of the social implications of education, the principal conflict is between those who would train for the accepted social standards

---

[8] For a thorough account of the new experimentalism, see Lawrence A. Cremin, *The Transformation of the School* (New York: Alfred A. Knopf, 1961), pp. 143–153.

and those who would educate toward a solution of debatable (and controversial) mutually exclusive social issues. Since the two points of view are not necessarily opposed, it is desirable to arm the pupil for both the constants and the variables of society. For convenience and clearness, however, we shall discuss these two concepts, (1) social traditionalism and (2) social experimentalism, separately.

THE DOCTRINE OF SOCIAL TRADITIONALISM

Tradition is the record of man's accomplishments and the accumulation of human experience. Each individual comes into the world with a social as well as a biological inheritance. Each generation acquires and transmits the collective cultural tradition of the past, and makes an effort to preserve the continuity of the common social tradition.

There is no question that much of this social inheritance is extremely desirable. Survival usually is a test of value. Traditional ideas, customs, and institutions are considered by many as valuable today as when they first developed. It is possible, however, for an idea, a custom, or an institution to outlive its usefulness and become ill-adapted to changed conditions. Unquestionably, certain things are permanent in society, social constants; while other things change in society, social variables. The careful educational thinker must learn to distinguish between the constant and the variable, between the universally accepted and the ephemeral. He must learn to make the distinction between the task of adjustment and the task of guidance.

Aims

The social traditionalist aims at giving all pupils an insight into their social inheritance, into the ideals, institutions, conditions, and customs of society. He aims at arousing a knowledge of, an interest in, and a sympathy toward all branches of society. He aims at giving practice in social communication and social service. He aims at developing social efficiency and adapting the individual to society. The traditionalist agrees with William James that "There is 'no impression without expression.' Children thus must be taught under democratic conditions to exercise democratic attitudes." Or as Nicholas Murray Butler, former President of Columbia University, put it, "Education [must] mean a gradual adjustment to the spiritual possessions of the race. The child is entitled to his scientific, literary, esthetic, institutions, and religious inheritance."

William C. Bagley continuously advanced the doctrine that the development of the socially efficient individual is the ultimate aim of education. He would complete well-roundedness through:

1.   Economic efficiency, or ability to "pull one's own weight" in economic life;

2.   Negative morality, or willingness to sacrifice one's own desires when their gratification would interfere with the general social efficiency;

3.   Positive morality, or the willingness to contribute directly or indirectly to social efficiency.

Such educators would adjust the child to his social heritage chiefly for the benefit of the child himself rather than for the benefit of society. Other writers, however, disparage this individualistic use of social tradition. Dewey asserted, ". . . social efficiency as an educational purpose should mean cultivation of power to join freely and fully in shared or common activities."[9] Thorndike holds that the socially efficient individual is one who (1) leads a useful and happy economic, civic, and domestic life, (2) has good will towards others, and (3) engages in harmless enjoyments.

Emmett A. Betts said that the socially efficient person has:

1. A spirit of artistry in work and achievement;
2. A spirit of social good will and service;
3. A capacity for fine appreciations.[10]

Undoubtedly most child developmentalists would agree with these objectives. The aim of Pestalozzi, Herbart, and perhaps Arnold Gesell would surely be in harmony with the goal of these social educationalists.

There have been many attempts to analyze this ultimate goal of social efficiency into specific social objectives. Perhaps the most familiar of these enumerations is that adapted from Spencer in 1918 by the Committee on Reorganizing the Secondary School and known generally as the Cardinal Principles of Education:

1.   Health;
2.   Command of fundamentals;
3.   Citizenship;
4.   Worthy use of leisure;
5.   Vocations;
6.   Worthy home membership;
7.   Ethical character.

A more complete and consistently expressed enumeration listing is the following:

1.   Physical efficiency;
2.   Vocational efficiency;

---

[9] Dewey, *Democracy and Education*, p. 144.

[10] Former Director of the Betts Reading Clinic, Haverford, Penn. See his *Foundation of Reading Instruction*, rev. ed. (New York: American Book Company, 1957).

3. Avocational efficiency;
4. Civic efficiency;
5. Domestic efficiency;
6. Social efficiency;
7. Moral efficiency;
8. Religious efficiency.

Franklin Bobbitt has suggested ten types of social activities to which the pupil must be adjusted:

1. Language activities, social communication;
2. General social activities, meeting with others;
3. Health activities;
4. Citizenship activities;
5. Parental activities;
6. Religious activities;
7. Mental and emotional activities, mental hygiene;
8. Spare-time activities;
9. Unspecialized practical activities;
10. Practical activities of one's calling.[11]

Thus, the social traditionalist conceives the aim of the school as a preparation for all the phases of social life, for a balanced and effective participation in all social institutions. He believes that social welfare depends upon men and women finding and filling their places in all phases of life.

The social traditionalist is primarily interested in social integration and seeks social efficiency through social harmony. One of his purposes of education is the formation of the common habits of social life, so that the individual can participate smoothly and harmoniously with his fellows. The more one has acquired the universally accepted habits and attitudes of his social group, the less friction there will be in his social relationships. One cannot object seriously to such an aim, providing these common habits are not socially undesirable. We may criticize, however, any limitation of education to this sole integrating function.

There are certain social standards that the sociologist would have education help maintain, by training the pupil to adjust to them. The child should be educated away from crime, poverty, drugs, disease, unemployment, and all such recognized social evils. The social traditionalist as an educational sociologist believes that will maintain standards, safeguard traditions, and preserve society's institutions. He defines education as the

---

[11] *The Curriculum* (Boston: Houghton Mifflin Company, 1918), pp. 189–204. See also his *How To Make a Curriculum* (Boston: Houghton Mifflin Company, 1924), pp. 7–62.

preeminent process of developing in the individual the power of adaptation and adjustment to his social environment.

Types

Those who are interested in the adjustment of the child to the accepted standards and institutions of society have much to say, of course, about social education; but some confusion is likely to arise in the use of the term. *Social education* in its broadest sense covers all types of education that prepare the pupil for living with his fellows; in its specific meaning it refers to the formation of the skills of social communication through language, and the building of the etiquette of harmonious and frictionless human relationships. In this latter sense social education is merely one of many types of training including physical training, vocational training, civic training, domestic training, avocational training, moral training, and religious training, all of which are considered essential in the development of complete social efficiency.

The results of the medical examinations of conscripted men during American participation in World War II stimulated intensified interest in physical education. The appalling number of physical defects and the low standard of health revealed by these examinations aroused demands for health education and physical training in the schools. Industrial accidents led to the passage of workingmen's compensation laws in many states. Manufacturers joined with the insurance companies in a campaign to teach safety in the schools. In recent years, the phenomenal increase in automobile accidents has strengthened the movement. The National Safety Council, and the American National Red Cross, through its Junior Red Cross, have enlisted the cooperation of the schools in an extensive program of accident prevention.

Vocational education has been particularly emphasized by the social educator. With the development of modern manufacturing methods in all parts of the world and the breakdown of the old apprenticeship system, a new demand arose that the schools should train industrial and agricultural workers as well as those who were to go into business and the professions. Germany, France, and Denmark led the way in building schools for the teaching of the practical arts. The United States was slow in responding to this new need, largely because of the influx of technically educated workers from Europe. With new immigrants furnishing both cheap unskilled labor and technically trained workers, the schools continued to devote themselves to preparation for white-collar jobs.

During the past half-century, however, we have at last turned attention to the vocational training of factory and farm workers. The National Commission on Vocational Education, set up by Congress in 1913, made a comprehensive study that ultimately resulted in the passage of the Smith-Hughes Bill in 1917. This act provided for a Federal Board of Vocational

Education to cooperate with the states in furthering high school instruction in industrial trades, agriculture, home economics, and commerce. With the growth of vocational high schools and the introduction of prevocational courses in the elementary schools, vocational education in the practical arts is now being provided for the large proportion of our population that will engage in industrial, agricultural, clerical, and domestic occupations.

Closely connected with vocational education has been the development of vocational guidance. Not only are students to be trained for jobs, but they are also to be placed advantageously. The movement began in this country in 1907, when a bureau was opened in Boston for the placement of youth in vocations best fitted to them. This grew into the Bureau of Vocational Guidance, which later was taken over by Harvard University. Through the influence of its director, John M. Brewer, this bureau became the center of the movement, which spread rapidly to every section of the country. The study of occupations became a part of the curriculum in almost all schools.

Recreational training also has received a new emphasis. Especially since the Great Depression new attempts have been made to train the pupil for his leisure hours. Even courses in the practical arts have been increasingly given, not as training for vocations, but as training in hobbies and leisure occupations. Play and playground activities have been encouraged, as have been all forms of wholesome recreation.

Much has been done in the training for a better home life. In addition to the teaching of the household arts, instruction is being given in sex hygiene, infant care, and other phases of marriage and parenthood. Sex education and parental education have been assumed by many schools as a definite part of their responsibility. And instruction in some schools includes the dangers of drugs and drug addition.

The attempts to introduce more civic, moral, and religious education into the schools have met with difficulties, because of the controversial issues involved. The social traditionalist is inclined to follow the lead of the nationalist in respect to the content and methods of civic education. He stresses conformity to American ideals of democracy, Christianity, and capitalism. As a result, his teaching may easily become indoctrination based on allegiance.

Since social efficiency demands the adjustment of each individual to the social organization, social traditionalism is committed to a policy of universal education, which is, however, differentiated to meet the needs of the various groups in the social structure. Because they consider education in terms of its benefits to the social order, the traditionalists are as insistent upon compulsory education as are the nationalists, and they have been active in extending the compulsory attendance limits to higher levels. In a few states the leaving age has been increased to eighteen years, although the usual limits are fourteen and sixteen.

Content

John Dewey opined that the school is not a preparation for life, but is life itself. Therefore, he said, the school curriculum must be made up of the activities of real social living; the school cannot be a preparation for life except as it presents the conditions of social life. This point of view has led to the present emphasis upon the "activity," or project, curriculum, consisting of exercises and problems drawn from the fields of actual social conduct. The social motive in education demands that all the materials of the school be drawn from the varied activities of social, political, and economic life, rather than from what social educators consider the abstractions of an academic world far removed from actuality.

There seems to be general agreement that the elementary school should provide the essential tools of social living and the common integrating habits of human relationships; that the intermediate school should present opportunities for the exploration of the world of nature and the world of man so that the pupil can find himself and his place in society; that the secondary school must provide specialized training for the individual's specific needs once they have been determined.

The elementary schools perform their function by drills in the essential integrating habits of arithmetical calculation, oral and written language, hygiene, and social manners, supplemented by much constructive and cooperative work, together with music, art, and other forms of esthetic appreciation and recreational participation.

Most junior high schools attempt to give an exploration of the various aspects of life through courses in general science, general mathematics, general language, social studies, general fine arts, general practical arts, and such exploratory agencies as general shop, tryout courses, and classes in occupations. Exploration is the basic function.

The most satisfactory program, according to some social educators, would be to have the middle grades curriculum organized in terms of social objectives. Instead of courses in mathematics, science, English, and history, they suggest courses in vocations, health, moral conduct, home life, leisure occupations, educational opportunities, and social communication, with accompanying tryout opportunities.

As a result of this new emphasis, there has been a growing tendency for the high schools to retreat from a narrow propaedeutic curriculum, dominated by college entrance requirements, and to offer a curriculum fitting boys and girls directly for life. Vocational subjects have gained an importance akin to that of the academic subjects. Even in the colleges the social sciences, such as history, government, economics, and sociology, and the applied sciences are encroaching on the domains of the humanities and pure sciences.

Many colleges and universities are moving away from the traditional academic curriculum by requiring that a part of the student's time be given to socially useful work, travel, and study. Such developments have been especially noteworthy at Antioch, Bennington, Olivet, Sarah Lawrence, the General College at Minnesota, and the New College at Columbia University; Chapman College even offers a travel year through the "University Afloat." High school and college curricula are being better adapted to the satisfaction of social needs.

One of the most striking results of the social emphasis in education has been the recognition of the place of extracurricular activities in the school program. These activities, once looked upon with indifference if not with open hostility by teachers and administrators, are now accepted as valuable educational assets. Although these activities have been carried on by pupils for generations, only lately have they been taken over as part of the school's educational program.

Extracurricular activities, when properly controlled and directed, are of the utmost value in providing experiences through which training may be obtained for the various phases of life. These activities are effective instruments for the achievement of the social objectives of education. Some activities contribute to each objective, and some contribute to many or even all. Moreover many of these educational contributions come only through these activities, in which may be recognized values not ordinarily found in the routine of the classroom. Such activities are an effective means of training young people to live together on the highest plane. Social training, vocational training, civic training, training in leadership, moral training, training for leisure, are all provided through participation in the extracurricular program.[12]

Athletic activities, public-speaking activities, dramatic activities, journalistic activities, musical activities, school councils, dances and parties, clubs, assemblies, homeroom activities, are providing fruitful sources of training for the various aspects of social life. They are furnishing an adjustment that is seldom secured through traditional school subjects.

The content of the traditional subjects, the social educationalists feel, can be socialized and enriched by the addition of new materials. Much deadwood can be removed from the curriculum; much can be replaced by content drawn from the experiences of life. Vocational life, home life, community life, should be the sources of a functional curriculum that adjusts the child to his environment and satisfies his assured immediate and future needs, they suggest.

Agencies

Within the experimentalist philosophy the school is looked upon as the primary agency for adjusting the individual to his place in society. When-

---

[12] See a pioneer in the field, Elmer H. Wilds, *Extra-Curricular Activities* (New York: Appleton-Century-Crofts, 1926), pp. 17–35. A later text in this area is Robert W. Frederick, *The Third Curriculum* (New York: Appleton-Century-Crofts, 1959), and seems to indicate an increasing popularity for this guidance field in the 1960s.

ever and wherever other agencies have failed to prepare the child for any of the aspects of social life, the school, and particularly the public school, must assume this task as its proper function. This point of view has given to the school a new importance as a social institution. Since society will be harmed by failure to adjust the child to his social environment, a new obligation is placed upon society to fully support the school by public taxation. Society must contribute to the support of public schools in order to protect itself from maladjusted individuals.

This recognition of the social responsibility of the school has brought about many extensions of public education, particularly at the secondary and college levels. The former college preparatory emphasis has given way either to the comprehensive high school with its multiple curricula or to a system of specialized higher schools in which each school prepares the pupil for a particular career. The junior college has been established to extend secondary education over a longer period. At the University of Minnesota, the General College was founded for students who do not have the capacity or inclination to follow the traditional college curriculum. During the Depression many states established junior colleges in local communities for young people who were unemployed and unable to receive a higher education. In most countries, there has been an extensive increase in technical and professional schools to fit young men and young women more adequately for the various trades and professions.

Since it is usually difficult for public schools to secure up-to-date machines and other industrial and commercial equipment, many educators are now advocating that much of our vocational training be turned over to factory schools, store schools, and corporation schools. In recent years, there has been a great increase in such schools. The National Factory School Association is active in promoting this type of vocational education. These schools may be desirable agencies for vocational education, as long as any tendencies toward the exploitation of youth for the profit of the corporations are promptly checked.

One of the striking developments of recent years has been the provision of opportunities for adult education. Schools have been established for both the employed and the unemployed. Evening schools have existed for many years. Originally they were established to give vocational education that would lead to promotion or to a better job. More recently, evening schools have devoted themselves to the task of providing general education to the employed to enrich their lives and make them better members of society. The Folk Schools of Denmark have led the way in this movement to raise the people's cultural level.[13]

---

[13] See Robert E. Belding, *Worker Education in Denmark*, reprint series, no. 19 (Iowa City, Iowa: Center for Labor and Management, 1968).

During and immediately after World War I, adult education in the United States was largely confined to the Americanization movement, through which the foreign-born was taught the use of English in his native speech, and prepared for naturalization by training in the history and principles of American government and the traditions and standards of American life. The widespread unemployment of the Depression and the increased amount of leisure time intensified the demand for new types of adult education. There was an increased effort in this direction; the federal government made a large appropriation for the establishment of adult education forums to be conducted in various cities under the direction of the United States Office of Education. Public lectures, motion pictures, and radio programs were used as agencies of adult education. A wider use of the school plant made the school a community center for adult education and recreation. The city of Flint, Michigan was especially successful here.

Nation, state, and localities assumed a new responsibility for the education of out-of-school youth. The educational work of the Civilian Conservation Corps was a demonstration of what could be done. The National Youth Administration made it possible for many to attend school who otherwise could not have. States established short unit courses and correspondence and extension courses, even for those in penal institutions. Guidance bureaus and placement offices undertook the task of readjusting and reeducating youth already at work.

The social motive in education not only developed new agencies of education but brought about a cooperation between the school and other institutions and organizations. The YMCA and YWCA, the scouting organizations, and similar youth groups are active in the work of adjusting youth to their social responsibilities. The National Congress of Parents and Teachers has organized parent-teacher associations throughout the country as active and effective educational agencies. Women's clubs, chambers of commerce, and the various service clubs have added educational activities to their programs.

The task of adjusting the child to social living makes necessary a new type of teacher, one with social vision; the effective preparation of pupils for the opportunities and responsibilities of social participation demands a teacher with broader preparation than is required for the dispensing of knowledge. The teacher must have a broad background of social knowledge gained largely through his varied contacts with life. In teacher education new emphasis is placed upon the social studies. A knowledge of biology, social psychology, sociology, economics, and government is considered as essential for the teacher as an acquaintanceship with the subjects he teaches and the methods he employs. The two-year normal school has given way to the four-year teachers college, with professional subjects postponed until the prospective teacher has been given a broad general background; graduate schools of education are requiring a broad general education as a prerequisite to specialization in education. If the teacher is to be a social agent, he must have a thorough knowledge of social institutions and social organization.

The new socialized school is much less dependent upon books than were the older schools. Visual materials, in the form of photographs, transparencies, and motion pictures, give the child a vicarious contact with life. Television and radio programs bring the child close to the activities of life and give him a clearer picture of social institutions.[14] School excursions and trips give him actual contacts with different community endeavors. The curriculum, especially at the elementary level, is growing less bookish. Life is now the book from which the pupil reads.[15]

Organization

The increasing interdependencies of social living have made necessary the organization of education on a much larger scale. When each little community was self-sustaining and self-contained, the organization of the schools on a small district basis was satisfactory. The ease with which people today can move from place to place has made a larger group consciousness of the problems of education inevitable. Lack of educational opportunity in any locality is likely to reflect on any other part of the state or nation; educational benefits flow over a wide expanse of territory. In order to satisfy local needs, it is now not necessary to have a school unit smaller than the trade area surrounding a town or village.

If larger educational opportunities are to be provided for communities, school finance likewise must be organized on a statewide or even a nationwide basis. The social motive has led to increased state aid to schools. Because certain states are unable to finance the type of education needed to maintain desired social standards, demands are being made upon the federal government to appropriate large sums to the states on the basis of need. Unless additional sources of support are found, schools in many areas will lag behind the better-financed schools, and the nation as a whole will be unfavorably influenced. The problem is to secure equalizing centralization of support without hampering centralization of control.

Methods

The methods used in teaching the child to live with others are those of social communication, social cooperation, and social service. The socializing method gives experiential education in social groupings. The teacher

---

[14] See William B. Levenson and Edward Stasheff, *Teaching Through Radio and Television* (New York: Holt, Rinehart and Winston, Inc., 1954), pp. 2–27.

[15] See Harold Rugg, *American Life and the School Curriculum* (Boston: Ginn & Company, 1936), pp. 215–237, for a thorough exposition of this social and progressivist educational philosophy.

works with the various social interests of the pupils such as gregariousness, cooperation, altruism, and emulation. Informal conversation, group discussions, group assignments, dramatizations, and construction projects are used as socializing devices to develop social virtues and to eliminate antisocial tendencies. Socialized school management, through the use of student participation in school housekeeping and government, is an effective aid in training the pupils for social life. The various school enterprises and extracurricular activities, if conducted in the proper social spirit, provide plentiful opportunities for initiative, leadership, responsibility, and cooperation.

Children are encouraged to work for each other rather than for themselves. They are taught to face the class instead of the teacher and to have a lively sense of communication. They are given many opportunities to work together in helpful cooperation, and individual pupils and small groups are held responsible for definite contributions to the class.

Teachers have little difficulty in perfecting a technique for the development of the social virtues. The difficulty is in determining what the social virtues are. The social traditionalist is inclined to be overzealous in preserving the social heritage; he is likely to try to standardize children in accepted social patterns. The pupils' immaturity and the authoritative position of the teacher make the method of domination over social activity much easier than guidance in social choice. The plasticity of youth stimulates the use of the methods of indoctrination and coercion. But the teacher's direction, which is necessary in the rapid and accurate formation of integrating skills, can easily be extended into the realms of alternatives and controversial questions.

Conformity to officially approved social behavior is often considered the acme of social virtue, and youth is not encouraged to examine critically the approved social order. Few teachers are able to strike a balance between coercion and coddling. They either give the child so much freedom that it becomes license, or they swing to the other extreme of domination, regimentation, and indoctrination in order to make sure that the child is adjusted to the approved social patterns. They are inclined to support a school discipline that brings the pupil into conformity to law and order.

These traditionalist principles are indeed those of the twentieth-century essentialism, although essentialists generally require a more rigid program than did the social traditionalists of the Depression and early postwar era (see Chapter 20).

SOCIAL EXPERIMENTALISM — EARLY PROGRESSIVISM

The social traditionalist is primarily concerned with the adjustment of the individual to the existing social order. At his best, he uses the school to adapt the pupil only to the elements in social organization that are universally accepted; in extreme form, he seeks to perpetuate all traditional social beliefs and practices by pupil indoctrination and coercion. Social traditionalism is not concerned fundamentally with social change. In its failure to meet the necessities of progress, it falls short of the complete socialization of the individual desired by experimentalists.

In recent years—particularly between the two world wars and during the worldwide Depression—there developed the growing realization that the social order changes, and that change is necessary and desirable. Although some adhere to a philosophy of permanence and believe that "this is the best of all possible worlds," and some insist that the traditional institutions of the established social order are essentially valuable and infallible, many groups in various parts of the world are convinced that the developments of modern science and modern technology have made certain old customs, traditional beliefs and standards, and inherited institutions ill adapted to modern times. They represent the group, here labeled *experimental.*

Social, economic, and political institutions must change and are changing. The social order continues to change. The society of tomorrow will be different even from the society of today. What is to be the attitude of education toward such inevitable social change? Surely, the experimentalists say, the school can never be satisfied with preparing the child for his assured immediate needs. His future needs under changed social conditions must also be considered.

Some contend that change evolves naturally, that nothing can be done about change except to let it occur. They claim that we live in a genetic society haphazardly mutating through the chance reactions of its elements. Thus they would have the school anticipate this social drift and prepare its pupils for a drifting society. In attempting to adapt the pupils to this naturally changing situation, the teacher would have to play the role of a clairvoyant. To anticipate and chart such a drift would be difficult and would require real discernment.

Under the spell perhaps of the social science of Spencer and Comte or of the mathematical certainties of Cattell and Thorndike some would map out an ideal social order in all its details, and use education to help achieve it. It would undoubtedly be possible to achieve a preconceived society, but the school would have to use the same methods of indoctrination and coercion that are used to preserve an existing society. The schools can change society by changing the individuals who make up society. During the Great Depression several works appeared whose purpose was to blueprint the shape of a new and better society. George S. Counts', "New Social Order," and Harold Rugg's "Great Technology" are not the first "total visions" to be revealed; more recently Theodore Brameld has offered, as a reconstructionist philosophy, a design for a new school and method of education which had, as its inception, the necessity for remaking the social order.[16] Many utopian societies have been projected, from Plato to H. G. Wells. Are educators willing to adopt one of these as a universal goal? For a preconceived society can be looked upon by some as bad and by others as good; it can be the object of condemnation as well as praise.

The social experimentalist believes he is attempting to steer a course between the Scylla of social traditions and the Charybdis of social preconception. He tries to cling firmly to a doctrine of progressive democracy in the midst of appeals from reactionaries on the one hand and ultraliberals on the other, each promising shortcuts to social perfection.

More than a generation ago Glenn Frank, President of the University of Wisconsin, predicted danger to the school from extreme forms of social experimentalism:

> Until recently few, if any, Americans could be found who did not think the enslavement of the schools to a formula was utterly dangerous. Lately, however, from the widely separated quarters of the Right and the Left have arisen Americans who demand that the schools be made agencies of propaganda. Those on the Right want the schools to become agencies of propaganda for their particular conservative concept of the traditional social order. Those on the Left want them to become agencies of propaganda for their particular brand of a new social order based on some measure of collectivism.[17]

Aims

Social experimentalists believe that the task of the school is to prepare for a progressive structuring of the social order. Both Dewey and Kilpatrick insisted that the environment of the school should direct the pupil in learning to meet the progressively developing demands of a changing society, and should develop in the pupil a social motive and a social intelligence that will enable him to play his part in solving the problems of a changing civilization. They, and their followers, are called instrumentalists because they believed that social institutions and science should be used only as instruments in the development of new and better ways of life.

---

[16] George S. Counts, *Dare the School Build a New Social Order?* (New York: The John Day Company, Inc., 1932). Harold Rugg, *The Great Technology* (New York: The John Day Company, Inc., 1933), and his *Now Is the Moment* (New York: Duell, Sloan & Pearce—Meredith Press, 1943). See also Theodore Brameld, *Patterns of Educational Philosophy* (New York: Harcourt, Brace & World, Inc., 1950), pp. 569–620; and his *Toward a Reconstructed Philosophy of Education* (New York: Holt, Rinehart and Winston, Inc., 1956).

[17] From an address at St. Louis on February 20, 1936.

THE EXPERIMENTALIST APPROACH

The social experimentalist believes that the school can play an effective part in a telic society, which purposively directs itself to a better social order, even though it can only dimly perceive the exact nature of the ultimate achievement. As examples, Henry W. Holmes has advocated for many years a social policy in education that would set as its goal the creation of a purposive society, and Ross L. Finney, in his *Sociological Philosophy of Education,*[18] has urged the adoption of a teleological function in education. Both believe this is the only aim possible if we are to preserve a true democracy, in which each one contributes freely and to the maximum of his powers to the general welfare. Dewey pointed out that the national democratic tradition includes the following:

> In spite of all limitations, however, the earlier conceptions contained the core of that democratic idea which forms the distinctive ethical tradition of the United States. It includes the political aspect of democracy; this was definitely limited in the first part of the history of the republic but broadened out later to include the right and duty of every mature citizen of the country to participate in the government of his locality, state, and nation, on the ground that such participation both made the individual a better citizen and helped ensure that government would serve the public good. The democratic idea included also broader moral ideas, such as the equal right of every individual for opportunity to make his own career and develop his own personal being; moral individualism, which asserted the right of all to personal freedom of development without allowing fixed classes and castes to develop; faith in the possibility of an abundant life for all, not only materially but culturally; belief that government is an affair of voluntary organization for the common good, so that the people have the right to change their institutions when they find that they are failing to meet the common need, Jefferson and Lincoln agreeing that this right extends even to revolutionary action; faith in individual inventiveness and adaptability; an attitude which welcomes change as an omen of future good rather than resists it as a sign of degeneration from a superior past.[19]

Can the school help to insure the preservation of these rights? It has been said that "society cannot be made better until the schools are made better." This statement sounds like a hopeless enigma of lifting ourselves by our own boot straps, but there is some truth in it, especially with the present restrictions placed upon publicly supported and controlled schools. For if a few strong thoughtful leaders can envisage needed steps in the

---

[18] (New York: Crowell-Collier and Macmillan, Inc., 1928).
[19] Dewey and Childs, pp. 42–43.

direction of an improved society, and if our teachers can produce thoughtful citizens ready to evaluate, accept, and put into practice these improvements, and can also develop additional leaders for the future, then there are strong prospects for the survival of democracy and the Judeo-Christian ethic, according to the experimentalists.

Social, economic, and political leaders mark the general goals toward which society must gradually move. A committee of the National Education Association enthusiastically set forth the following (somewhat abridged) as the "Social-Economic Goals of American Education":

> 1. Hereditary strength—everyone has a right to be well-born under conditions which will conserve his innate strengths and capacities.
>
> 2. Physical security—everyone has a right to protection from accident and disease.
>
> 3. Participation in an evolving culture—everyone has a right to share the skills, standards, values, and knowledge of the society.
>
> 4. An active flexible personality—everyone has a right to conditions which foster the development of initiative, ability to weigh facts, resist prejudice, and act cooperatively.
>
> 5. Suitable occupation—everyone has a right to whatever joy the most fitting work can bring.
>
> 6. Economic security—everyone has a right to a minimum income that will provide a reasonable standard of living.
>
> 7. Mental security—everyone has a right to trustworthy information from unprejudiced, unbiased sources.
>
> 8. Equality of opportunity—everyone has a right to the fullest possible development.
>
> 9. Freedom—everyone has a right to the widest sphere of freedom compatible with the equal freedom of others.
>
> 10. Fair play—everyone has a right to expect others to act in conformity with the highest good of all.[20]

Types

Social experimentalists would include in the schools all the types of education included by the social traditionalist, but with different emphases. Training for intelligent cooperative social planning in all phases of human activity makes certain types of education particularly significant.

The social experimentalists raise intellectual training again to a place of prominence. The pupil must be trained in the intellectual processes indispensable to the cooperative functioning of society. He must learn the sources of factual information about the realities of social conditions and social problems; he must gain skill in selecting, checking, and verifying

---

[20] See *Curriculum*, 31st Yearbook of the American Association of School Administrators (Washington, D.C.: NEA, 1953), p. 8, for basic philosophy of these goals.

these sources for their authenticity and reliability. He must be taught to discover and state the various sides to controversial issues; he must develop skill in weighing and evaluating these issues through group discussion and thinking. To be effective, the pupil must be taught to think, to make wise decisions in his choice of alternatives and sound conclusions in reference to controversial issues. In the training of the emotions, emphasis must be placed upon the elimination of fear, prejudice, and the mob emotions that lead to unintelligent and irresponsible social action.

Social-moral, or character, education the experimentalists place on a new basis, the motive of social service. It involves the development of a love for the good, an appreciation of the clean and beautiful, a disposition toward law and order. There must be created in the pupil a desire and a will to use his knowledge and reasoning powers for beneficial social results, the experimentalists assert.

In the new type of civic training, emphasis is placed upon intelligent participation and cooperation in civic affairs, instead of a blind national patriotism or party loyalty. The social experimentalist believes that instead of training yes-men to take orders from headquarters, the school must develop thinking citizens who will critically examine every proposal and act on the basis of social intelligence rather than social emotionalism, on the basis of fact and reason *rather than mass demonstrations and propaganda.* Education must develop citizens who are willing to adhere to the democratic principles of having matters decided by the majority, and giving minorities the advantages of free speech, free press, free instruction, so that each minority may use every legitimate device for becoming the majority. Viscount Bryce's (1838–1922) definition of the good citizen is pertinent:

> The good citizen is one who will have sense enough to judge of public affairs; discernment enough to choose the right officers; self-control enough to accept the decisions of the majority; honesty enough to seek the general welfare rather than his own at the expense of the community; public spirit enough to face trouble or even danger for the good of the community.[21]

A liberal conception of vocational training has been developed by the social experimentalists. They assert that pupils must be trained for much more than the "automatic repetitiousness of machines." Vocational education must be broad and comprehensive and integrated with the cultural and intellectual education, so that, in the inevitable monotonous work hours, the imagination may be able to feed upon the interesting materials of art, literature, and science—instead of being, as Dewey stated, "frittered away upon undisciplined dreamings and sensual fancies." The pupil must be taught the importance of his task and its place in the general scheme

---

[21] *Promoting Good Citizenship* (Boston: Houghton Mifflin Company, 1913), p. 3.

of industrial and social life. Beyond all else, he must be trained for the social relationships of his job. Brewer has pointed out that most discharges in industry are due, not to failures in performing vocational tasks, but to failures in human relations. The social experimentalist, it is clear, is not without an idealistic streak.

Content

The social experimentalist devotes his attention largely to the development of the part of the curriculum that includes the social studies. During the Depression the report of the Hoover Commission on Recent Social Trends and the work of the Commission on the Social Studies of the American Historical Association aroused the educational world to a new interest in the social studies.[22] In 1932, a committee of the Department of Superintendence of the National Education Association was appointed to prepare a yearbook on the social studies curriculum, which was published in 1936 as the fourteenth yearbook of that department.

Experimentalists feel that particular emphasis should be placed upon the teaching of controversial issues. Differences of opinion and clashes of interest are common in all phases of economic, social, and political life. The presentation of these differences must necessarily be a part of the social studies curriculum. Instead of limiting social studies to history and geography, the social life of the "past and the far-away," current social issues and the social problems of the pupil's own community are emphasized. History and geography textbooks are reinforced by the current issues of newspapers and magazines, by films and the electron tube.

The social, economic, and political activities of the local community are used as materials of instruction. Actual community experiences are considered far superior to vicarious experiences. Through extensive programs of field trips and directed classroom study, the pupils can engage in an analysis of the social structure of their community and gain a better understanding of the problems and issues of community life. It is even possible for the pupils to participate in certain of the simpler aspects of community social planning.

The extracurricular activities of the school also furnish abundant opportunities for training in social planning if they are properly administered, but teachers must avoid domination in their sponsorship of these exercises, which should be generally pupil-initiated, pupil-planned, pupil-organized, pupil-conducted, and pupil-evaluated. Cooperative school activities should be substituted for the recent excess of competitive contests, the experimentalists advise. To prepare pupils for social planning, the school

---

[22] The report of the Hoover Commission on Recent Social Trends was published by McGraw-Hill, Inc., 1933; and the Report of the Commission on the Social Studies was published in sixteen volumes by Charles Scribner's Sons, 1932–1940.

must educate more in the direction of cooperation and less in the direction of competition. Cooperative activities could be substituted for competitive activities even in interschool relationships, they specify. The National High School Orchestra and Band, all-state orchestras and bands, the National High School Chorus, Boys' and Girls' State, music festivals, decisionless debates, playdays and athletic festivals, all-school student councils, press conferences, and school tours have all been developed; and their success offers much in the direction of interschool cooperative planning. In such activities students of different schools work with each other, instead of against each other, for the benefit of others as well as themselves. Thus, say the experimentalists, the motif of interschool relationships can cease to be competition for personal and institutional renown and become instead, cooperation for community and social service.

Agencies

Social experimentalism strongly supports a free public school system as the only safe agency for education. It is distrustful of any school that is likely to exploit pupils for the benefit of a privileged class or to indoctrinate the pupils in the dogmas or prejudices of a single group. The social experimentalist, however, would extend the public school system to include the general education of adults.

Such a conception of education demands a free teacher in addition to a free school. One of the concluding volumes to appear in the American Historical Association's Commission on the Social Studies, Howard K. Beale's *Are American Teachers Free?*[23] raised grave questions in regard to the academic freedom of American teachers, as well as their personal freedom under certain circumstances. The National Education Association, through annual conventions and various subsidiary bodies, attempts to provide the same type of protection for public school teachers that the American Association of University Professors furnishes college personnel.

During the Great Depression (and again after World War II), the question of academic freedom became prominent. In 1935 at the Denver meeting of the NEA, stirred by the passage of the so-called gag laws in state after state, and by the efforts of certain newspapers and patriotic organizations to pin a "red" label upon many classroom teachers, the liberal delegates determined to commit the association to a strong declaration for academic freedom and to the protection of teachers unjustly accused of subversive teaching. The resulting resolution placed the association squarely on record in affirming a policy of academic freedom.

---

[23] (New York: Charles Scribner's Sons, 1940). Dr. Beale's conclusions (although restrictive, have merely changed in the past generation) are as pertinent for the sixties and seventies as they were in the 1940s. Every teacher or potential teacher should read this book.

The National Education Association believes that administrators, teachers, and schools should have full opportunities to present differing points of view on any and all controversial questions in order to aid students to adjust themselves to their environment and to changing social conditions.

Among the activities which the NEA set itself to perform in this connection were the following:

1. To make known to teachers and other friends of education any proposed legislation against freedom in teaching, and to take necessary steps to combat such legislation.

2. To investigate and to report upon cases of discharge of teachers in violation of the principle of academic freedom.

3. To cooperate with other reputable and recognized national organizations which are actively engaged in maintaining the principles of academic freedom.

In 1941 the National Education Association organized the National Commission for the Defense of Democracy Through Education to help develop understanding of the important relationship between a better education for all and the maintenance of the American democracy and way of life, and to bring to the teaching profession greater strength and unity in working for increased democracy through education. The functions of the National Commission for the Defense of Democracy Through Education, as stated in 1958 by the Representative Assembly, are:

1. To defend teachers, schools, and the cause of education against unjust attacks; to investigate controversies involving teachers, schools, educational methods and procedures justly, fearlessly, and in the public interest; to issue appropriate reports of its activities.

2. To gather information about the various individuals and groups who destructively criticize or oppose education, and to make résumés of their activities.

3. To investigate alleged subversive teaching and to expose any teacher whose actions are found to be inimical to the best interests of our country.

4. To develop among members of both the teaching profession and the public a better understanding of the issues and problems in the area in which the Commission operates.

Academic freedom places an important obligation upon all teachers in service and all prospective teachers in training. One of the most sincere and sensible objections to this freedom is that the ordinary teacher is not sufficiently prepared to use it wisely. Some fear that the inadequately educated teacher will merely substitute propaganda or new and untried theories for the customary interpretations of accepted political, social, and economic theories. True academic freedom implies that the teacher be permitted to teach the whole truth, not just a factional selection of the truth; this means that teachers must have a broad background of social information and experience.

Another volume in the American Historical Association's Commission on the Social Studies series, Merle Curti's *The Social Ideas of American Educators*,[24] confirms the necessity for a truly social education and for social thinking on the part of American teachers and administrators. Curti believes that in many cases educational leaders have not really led, but have been too influenced by economic and political considerations to be able to give an objective appraisal of the real goals of education in American democracy.

In order to prepare pupils for social planning, it is necessary to have teachers who have come out of their sheltered academic cloisters. Teachers must be more familiar than they generally are with the social sciences. In addition to the usual state educational requirements for a teacher's certificate, thorough training in current events should be required. Teachers should also be encouraged to participate in the various social, economic, and political activities of their community, state, and nation. In this way they would study at first hand the controversial issues of the day and secure practice in the cooperative social planning needed to meet them.

Experimentalism suggests that schools and teachers alone cannot furnish all the education needed to prepare for social planning. The community must be used as a laboratory. Some plan of cooperation should be worked out between the school and the community by which the pupils can be given a larger share in the responsibility of solving local problems. The practice of withholding the rights of citizenship until the age of twenty-one is a survival from the period when adults ran the world, and the periods of childhood and youth were supposed to be spent in preparing for adult citizenship. We realize now that citizenship can be developed only through practice. Many opportunities should be offered for young people to participate in the responsibilities of community life. High school and college students can certainly make many contributions to the solution of social problems. Every age level should be allowed to play its part, however slight, in this enterprise of cooperative social thinking. Many commencement speakers now suggest to their graduating classes that, at age eighteen, they are ready to vote. Indeed a constitutional amendment to lower the voting age has been proposed.

Organization

Social education teaches that in order to prepare for a democratic society, it is necessary to have a democratic school organization. Authori-

---

[24] Rev. ed., enl. (New York: Pageant Books, Inc., 1959).

tarian and dictatorial methods of administration and government are out of place in a school that seeks to develop democratic ideals. The hierarchical system of organization should give way to a cooperative government in which all concerned play a part. Student councils should be able to justify their vows to give impartial objective justice.

Teachers are participating in the administrative problems of school organization to a greater degree than ever before. The National Education Association and the various state education associations have taken steps to place classroom teachers on a par with administrators in the management of association affairs. These organizations, representing American teachers, are, therefore, in a position to speak for the teaching profession of the United States.

School government by boards of education and superintendents is being superseded by systems of administration in which teachers and even pupils participate. Faculty and student councils are becoming more common. A still more democratic scheme would provide a school council in which students, teachers, administrators, parents, and citizens, every group concerned with the school, would be represented. Here practice could be obtained and an example set in intelligent cooperative social planning.

In democratic social planning and action, it is necessary to have the cooperation of two types of people: inventive leaders and intelligent followers. Experimentalists suggest the school be organized so that all would be provided with the equivalent of sixteen years of education. During these years the school would guide the pupil in (1) the discovery, development, and control of his mental, physical, and emotional tools; (2) the formation of commonly accepted habits, skills, and attitudes; (3) the acquisition of sensory and perceptive experience and the broadening of his horizons; (4) the interpretation of the world of nature and the world of man, thus developing insight, wisdom, and a philosophy of life. In addition, they feel a higher school should be organized for those capable of leadership. This school would guide its students in the mastery of some specialized form of expert leadership, preparing them to discover and formulate new laws and principles and invent new devices and institutions for the social welfare. Such a system of education, they claim, could bring about intelligent social action, through popular mass understanding and cooperation with expert leadership.

Upon his retirement from the faculty of the Graduate School of Education at Harvard, Dean Henry W. Holmes joined Dr. John W. Mahoney in establishing the Civic Education Center at Tufts University (1948). Their view that "education for citizenship in a democracy must remain faulty and inadequate unless it results in serious attention on the part of young people in school to the problems that democracy must work at and try to solve," implemented through the activities of the Civic Education Center, did much to make civic education a major concern in

American high schools. Under their direction, the center published *The Living Democracy,* a series dealing with social, economic, and political issues, which has been used extensively in American schools. Holmes and Mahoney also played a part in effecting the appointment of the Director of American Citizenship in the Massachusetts State Education Department.

Methods

If the goals of the social experimentalist are accepted, some traditional classroom methods will be abandoned; and teachers will have to educate their pupils for intelligent and cooperative participation. For, the experimentalists feel, teachers must accept the responsibility of developing intelligent and willing participants in a work of social cooperation. The method to be used, both in the classroom and in extracurricular activities, is guidance. Guidance means helping pupils to solve their own problems, to make intelligent choices when presented with alternatives. Guidance means helping pupils to find all the available facts, and helping them to develop the reasoning powers needed to use these facts wisely in solving social problems. Above everything else, teachers must teach facts rather than a partisan selection of facts, teach how to think rather than what to think. The work of the school should be cooperative. Values are implicit in a society where cooperative action directed toward social security for all molds the basic characteristics of living. Pupils must be alerted to the facts of social situations, the experimentalists urge. Teachers must fit their pupils for an intelligent planning together of democratic procedures. This can best be done by pupil-planned and pupil-executed exercises and activities in the school. Teachers must develop in their pupils methods of thought and action which reevaluate and reconstruct traditional theories as changing conditions demand new attitudes and procedures. The social experimentalist's program covers a broad area.

He believes that social guidance should be substituted for discipline as a method of establishing order and good behavior in the school. Pupils should be taught to see that they can best satisfy their own legitimate desires by refraining from any action that will thwart the legitimate desires of others. Self-control should be established by development of the social motive, by substitution of the cooperative for the competitive basis of action. Recognition of the rights of others is the surest source of good conduct, the experimentalists assert. When a pupil refrains from a certain act because he sees that it is inimical to the welfare of the group, he is well on the road to good behavior outside the school as well as in it.

The objective of guidance is to set in motion, through the progressive development of individual intelligence, the unlimited play of group intelligence in a progressive cooperative planning for world betterment. Some of our social problems may never be solved, but most are more likely of solution if attacked by men and women who have been trained to think honestly and intelligently, who have been given both the ways and the will for cooperation, who have been taught to believe in the greatest good for all.

At the beginning of the Dewey era in educational transformation a splendid note was struck by President Glenn Frank, of the University of Wisconsin. It is still applicable:

> In a democracy the major business of the schools is to train the exceptional man for leadership and to cultivate in the vast and seething majority a capacity for understanding the trends of the time and sensing the human meaning of the policies that leaders propose. Democracy falters only when leadership is laggard and popular understanding is darkened.[25]

REFERENCES

Bode, Boyd H., *Modern Educational Theories*. New York: Crowell-Collier and Macmillan, Inc., 1927. Pp. 73–139, 223–266.

Bonser, Frederick G., *Life Needs and Education*. New York: Bureau of Publications, Teachers College, Columbia University, 1932. Pp. 69–219.

Boyd, William, *The History of Western Education*, 8th ed. Rev. by Edmund J. King. New York: Barnes & Noble, Inc., 1966. Pp. 398–411.

Brubacher, John S., *A History of the Problems of Education*, 2d ed. New York: McGraw-Hill, Inc., 1966. Pp. 130–134, 581–611.

Butts, R. Freeman, *A Cultural History of Western Education*, 2d ed. New York: McGraw-Hill, Inc., 1955. Pp. 338–382.

———, and Lawrence A. Cremin, *A History of Education in American Culture*. New York: Holt, Rinehart and Winston, Inc., 1953. Pp. 461–499.

Curti, Merle, *The Social Ideas of American Educators*, rev. ed. Totowa, N.J.: Littlefield, Adams and Company, 1959. Pp. 499–591.

Dewey, John, *Democracy and Education*. New York: Crowell-Collier and Macmillan, Inc., 1916. Pp. 94–129.

———, *How We Think*. Boston: D. C. Heath and Company, 1910.

———, *The School and Society*. Chicago: University of Chicago Press, 1899.

Doughton, Isaac, *Modern Public Education, Its Philosophy and Background*. New York: Appleton-Century-Crofts, 1935. Pp. 345–365.

Faunce, Roland C., and Nelson L. Bossing, *Developing the Core Curriculum*. Englewood Cliffs, N.J.: Prentice-Hall, Inc., 1958.

---

[25] Frank, address at St. Louis. For an interesting picture of this colorful university president of an earlier generation, see Lawrence H. Larson, *The President Wore Spats: A Biography of Glenn Frank* (Madison, Wisc.: University of Wisconsin Press, 1965).

Ferrière, Adolph, *The Activity School*. Trans. by F. Dean Moore. New York: The John Day Company, Inc., 1928.

Finney, Ross L., *Sociological Philosophy of Education*. New York: Crowell-Collier and Macmillan, Inc., 1928. Pp. 116–131.

Good, Harry G., *A History of American Education*. New York: Crowell-Collier and Macmillan, Inc., 1956. Pp. 345–407.

Hart, Joseph K., *Creative Moments in Education*. New York: Holt, Rinehart and Winston, Inc., 1931. Pp. 449–463.

Justman, Joseph, *Theories of Secondary Education in the United States*. Contributions to Education, no. 814. New York: Bureau of Publications, Teachers College, Columbia University, 1940.

Larson, Lawrence H., *The President Wore Spats: A Biography of Glenn Frank*. Madison, Wisc.: University of Wisconsin Press, 1965.

Mayer, Frederick, *A History of Educational Thought*. Columbus, Ohio: Charles E. Merrill Books, Inc., 1960. Pp. 351–366.

Mead, Margaret, *The School in American Culture*. Cambridge, Mass.: Harvard University Press, 1951.

Meyer, Adolphe E., *An Educational History of the American People*. New York: McGraw-Hill, Inc., 1957. Pp. 314–329.

Mulhern, James, *A History of Education*, 2d ed. New York: The Ronald Press Company, 1959. Pp. 633–667.

Myers, Alonzo, F., and Clarence O. Williams, *Education in a Democracy*. Englewood Cliffs, N.J.: Prentice-Hall, Inc., 1937. Pp. 164–227.

Nakosteen, Mehdi, *The History and Philosophy of Education*. New York: The Ronald Press Company, 1965. Pp. 597–619.

Noble, Stuart G., *A History of American Education*, 2d ed. New York: Holt, Rinehart and Winston, Inc., 1954. Pp. 482–493.

Potter, Robert E., *The Stream of American Education*. New York: American Book Company, 1967. Pp. 422–440.

Pounds, Ralph L., *The Development of Education in Western Culture*. New York: Appleton-Century-Crofts, 1968. Pp. 191–220.

Randall, John H., *Making of the Modern Mind*. Boston: Houghton Mifflin Company, 1926. Pp. 594–638.

Raup, Bruce, *Education and Organized Interests in America*. New York: G. P. Putnam's Sons, 1936. Pp. 179–229.

Rugg, Harold, *Now is the Moment*. New York: Duell, Sloan & Pearce—Meredith Press, 1943.

———, *American Life and the School Curriculum, Next Steps toward Schools of Living*. Boston: Ginn & Company, 1936. Pp. 5–29, 215–237, 441–457.

Russell, Bertrand, *Education and the Good Life*. New York: Liveright Publishing Corporation, 1926. Pp. 1–83.

Shaw, Charles G., *Trends of Civilization and Culture*. New York: American Book Company, 1932. Pp. 368–394, 596–653.

Snedden, David, *Sociological Determination of Educational Objectives*. Philadelphia: J. B. Lippincott Company, 1921.

Tugwell, Rexford G., and Leon H. Keyserling, *Redirecting Education*, vol. I. New York: Columbia University Press, 1934. Pp. 2–112.

Ulich, Robert, *History of Educational Thought*. New York: American Book Company, 1950. Pp. 315–336.

———— (Ed.), *Three Thousand Years of Educational Wisdom*, 2d ed., enl. Cambridge, Mass.: Harvard University Press, 1954. Pp. 577–614.

Valentine, P. F., *Twentieth Century Education*. New York: Philosophical Library, Inc., 1946. Pp. 3–155, 372–456.

Wender, Herbert, *The Growth of Modern Thought and Culture*. New York: Philosophical Library, Inc., 1959. Pp. 183–213.

Wingo, G. Max, *The Philosophy of American Education*. Boston: D. C. Heath and Company, 1965. Pp. 197–304.

Zachery, Caroline B., and Margaret Lighty, *Emotion and Conduct in Adolescence*. New York: Appleton-Century-Crofts, 1940.

SELECTED PAPERBACKS

Archambault, Reginald D. (Ed.), *Dewey on Education, Appraisals*. New York: Random House, Inc., 1966.

Bayles, Ernest E., *Pragmatism in Education*. New York: Harper & Row, Publishers, 1966.

Beck, Robert Holmes, *A Social History of Education*. Englewood Cliffs, N.J.: Prentice-Hall, Inc., 1965.

Belding, Robert, *Worker Education in Denmark*. Reprint series, no. 19. Iowa City, Iowa: College of Business Administration, Center for Labor and Management, 1968.

Bode, Boyd H., *Modern Educational Theories*. New York: Random House, Inc., Vintage Books, 1964.

Broudy, Harry S., and John R. Palmer, *Exemplars of the Teaching Method*. Skokie, Ill.: Rand McNally & Company, 1965.

Crane, Theodore Rawson (Ed.), *The Colleges and the Public, 1787–1862*. New York: Bureau of Publications, Teachers College, Columbia University, 1963.

Curti, Merle, *The Social Ideas of American Educators*, enl. ed. New York: Pageant Books, Inc., 1959.

Demerath, N. J., III, *Social Class in American Protestantism*. Skokie, Ill.:Rand McNally & Company, 1965.

Dworkin, Martin S. (Ed.), *Dewey on Education*. New York: Bureau of Publications, Teachers College, Columbia University, 1957.

Frankena, William K., *Three Historical Philosophies of Education*. Glenview, Ill.: Scott, Foresman and Company, 1965.

James, William, *Pragmatism and Other Essays*. New York: Washington Square Press, 1963.

Jones, Howard Mumford (Ed.), *Emerson on Education*. New York: Teachers College Press, Columbia University, 1966.

Krug, Edward A. (Ed.), *Charles W. Eliot and Popular Education*. New York: Teachers College Press, Columbia University, 1960.

Lee, Dorothy, *Freedom and Culture*. Englewood Cliffs, N.J.: Prentice-Hall, Inc., 1959.

Mayer, Frederick, *Foundations of Education*. Columbus, Ohio: Charles E. Merrill Books, Inc., 1963.

————, *Introductory Readings in Education*. Belmont, Calif.: Dickinson Publishing Company, Inc., 1966.

Pulliam, John D., *History of Education in America*. Columbus, Ohio: Charles E. Merrill Books, Inc., 1968. Pp. 81–111.

Rippa, S. Alexander, *Education in a Free Society*. New York: David McKay Company, Inc., 1967. Pp. 175–206.

Rudolph, Frederick, *The American College and University, A History*. New York: Random House, Inc., 1965. Pp. 355–372.

Tyack, David B. (Ed.), *Turning Points in American Educational History*. Waltham, Mass.: Blaisdell Publishing Company, 1967.

Ulich, Robert, *Education in Western Culture*. New York: Harcourt, Brace & World, Inc., 1965.

Van Waters, Miriam, *Youth in Conflict*. New York: Republic Publishing Company, 1925.

CHAPTER **19**

American Progressivism in Depression and Recovery

No educational discovery of our generation has had such far-reaching implications. It has a two-fold significance: first, that every child is born with the power to create; second, that the task of the school is to surround the child with an environment which will draw out this creative power.[1]

NEW DIRECTIONS IN EDUCATION

Both the psychological revolution and the scientific movement led directly to a new conception of the child and the learning process. These new realizations, based on the work of Hall, Gesell, and Piaget continued the advance sparked by Rousseau, Pestalozzi, and Froebel. Now the child was to be viewed not as a miniature adult, but as a person and personality in his own right, with childhood itself as a definite area in human development.

Coupled with the idea of childhood as a valid realm was the advancing doctrine of permissive rearing of infants and children advocated by a number of pediatricians in the early middle twentieth century. From the educational standpoint this new direction in child development thought ushered in what has popularly been called the child-centered school. For Philippe Ariès recently explained that "our society has passed from a period which was ignorant of adolescence to a period in which adolescence is the

---

[1] Harold O. Rugg and Ann Shumaker, *The Child-Centered School* (New York: Harcourt, Brace & World, Inc., 1928).

favourite age. We now want to come to it early and linger in it as long as possible."[2] Thus, the changed institutional orientation.

But, before we deal especially with this virtually new institution, we must pause to review the economic, and also educational, dilemma that befell the United States in the 1930s.

EDUCATION AND ADVERSITY

This debacle which burst with startling suddenness on the United States in the fall of 1929 was part of a world economic collapse which had its roots in the disruptions growing out of World War I. It was felt more deeply here than elsewhere because it had been preceded by a postwar boom of great prosperity. Probably because of this era of good times and the confidence and faith of the American people in education, the results of the Depression did not affect the schools at once.[3]

By 1931, however, the severe economic dislocation had begun to have serious effects upon the country's cultural agencies, including the schools. Educational appropriations were greatly cut, teachers' salaries were drastically reduced, building programs were abandoned, teaching load and size of classes were increased, school terms were shortened (in many cases from ten months to six), and educational economies of all kinds were attempted.

But more serious than the slashing of educational budgets and the resulting crippling of educational efforts was a new wave of criticism that swept over the schools and their work. Public authorities seized upon the few instances of squandered public school funds, expensive and ornate public school buildings, fads and frills in educational practice, as excuses for "intelligent economy" in education. Even teachers and administrators, failing to realize that the lessening of financial support for education was due to the three *D*s, debt, deficit, and depression, accepted a sense of guilt and feared that perhaps all this was a punishment for their educational sins. The schools were criticized not only by press and pulpit from without but by certain leaders in education. Educational theories and practices were questioned as never before. As Knight describes it:

> . . . the educational hired men and women of the community were severely censured by the high priests in education—those who set the pedagogical styles for school-teachers and managers. These professional

[2] *Centuries of Childhood*, trans. by Robert Baldick (New York: Alfred A. Knopf, 1962), pp. 10–11, 30.

[3] See Dixon Wecter, *The Age of the Great Depression* (New York: Crowell-Collier and Macmillan, Inc., 1948), for a comprehensive and penetrating account of the various aspects of this unique period in American history. Lawrence A. Cremin, *The Transformation of the School—Progressivism in American Education, 1876–1957* (New York: Alfred A. Knopf, 1961), is perhaps the definitive work related to school progress.

educational experts condemned, often out of hand, about every feature of the democratic theory and practice of public education which had so long been one of the proud boasts of the United States. The elementary school was attacked for its low standards of discipline and the chaos of its curriculum, as well as its inadequately trained teachers and the fact (apparently only then discovered) that most of them were women. The secondary school was assailed as an educational fetish and an arid and purposeless luxury, which was every year costing the American public immense sums.

Higher education was condemned as positively degenerate.[4]

The educational misery of the country was reflected in the discussions at state and national educational meetings, and in the appointment of various educational councils, commissions, and committees to deliberate on policies and practices. Many earnest efforts not only to end the financial problems into which the schools had fallen but more importantly to place education upon a surer and sounder foundation developed.

The criticism and lack of faith in education were perhaps a reflection of the existing worldwide confusion regarding the aims of life. The resultant confusion in educational thinking indicated the absence of a consistent philosophy from which to derive educational aims. These educational commissions, therefore, attempted to formulate an educational philosophy and to establish educational policies adapted to the impaired economic and social conditions.

Wecter's *Age of the Great Depression* capsules in kaleidoscope the history of this uncomfortable period as shown in this vignette of social reorientation during adversity:

> The Hoover beliefs in laissez faire, the gold standard, individual enterprise, and the profit motive are contrasted with Roosevelt's program, including creation of government financed work, codes used in industry for raising of employment and wage rates, crop restriction and direct benefit payments to raise prices in agriculture, and government spending on a huge scale to "prime the pump" of prosperity. The resulting impingement by government upon the life of the citizen in taxing, lending, spending, building, setting quotas and conditions of employment, and controlling commerce is shown as a new concept of American democracy.[5]

In 1932 the National Education Association established its Joint Commission on the Emergency in Education. This agency inaugurated a program designed to meet the educational difficulties growing out of the Depression. It undertook to exert the full force of the million teachers and the millions of citizens interested in the preservation of the idea of free public education and of making that idea increasingly valid by improving

---

[4] Edgar W. Knight, *Education in the United States*, 2d rev. ed. (New York: Ginn & Company, 1941), pp. 580–581.

[5] Student summary, 1965.

schools and colleges. The work of this commission was most effective in stimulating sound thinking about educational problems.

The Department of Superintendence (later called American Association of School Administrators) in its 13th Yearbook (1935) reiterated its faith in education as an indispensable instrument of social progress. Under the heading "The Meaning of Social Change," this organization spoke as follows:

> In the swirl of social change which threatens at present to engulf mankind, education must strive with double diligence to keep both its balance and its sense of direction. . . . Where there once was mutual participation in common values, there is now much of the blighting effects of competition for private pecuniary gain. Where once there was well-nigh universal faith in democratic institutions as the effective guarantee of a freer and nobler life, interests which now largely control public opinion increasingly decry that faith.

Ten trends, of special significance to education, are detected:

> I. Mechanical inventions make possible increased time freed from the production of goods and services required for the maintenance of a given standard of living.
>
> II. Society is today characterized by serious strains due to the failure of many of our institutional forms and practices to keep pace with the rapid rate of industrial change.
>
> III. The increasing amount of specialization and division of processes has increased the interdependence among individuals, communities, and nations, and is resulting in an increase of cooperative action.
>
> IV. The growing complexities of modern life are resulting in an increase of large-scale, long-time planning.
>
> V. The machine age renders the direct personal relationship between producers and consumer and thus tends to increase our dependence upon forms of social control.
>
> VI. With the increasing complexity of society, the source of control of a social agency tends to become more remote from its individual beneficiaries.
>
> VII. The intricacies of social relationship have resulted in the increased use of expert knowledge and trained leadership.
>
> VIII. The growing recognition of individual differences is resulting in greater differentiation of the provisions made available to people in a democracy.
>
> IX. The dynamic character of industrial society, the diversity of culture patterns in modern life, the wider diffusion of knowledge, and the rise of the scientific attitude are tending to weaken authoritarian and conventional controls over human conduct.
>
> X. The development of social cleavages, both horizontal and vertical, is deepening the strains and tensions in American life.[6]

---

[6] 13th Yearbook, Department of Superintendence, National Education Association (Washington, D.C.: National Education Association, 1935), pp. 9–13, 13–24.

In December 1935, the Educational Policies Commission was established by joint action of the National Education Association and the Department of Superintendence. This commission was empowered to hold meetings, call conferences, conduct studies, issue pronouncements, and adopt such procedures as would be necessary for the accomplishment of its purposes. The work was financed by a grant from the General Education Board. Upon its organization the commission formulated the following objectives:

> 1. To stimulate thoughtful, realistic, long-term planning within the teaching profession, looking toward adaptation of education to social needs.
> 2. To appraise existing conditions in education critically and to stimulate desirable changes in the purposes, procedures, and organization of education.
> 3. To consider and act upon recommendations from all sources for the improvement of education.
> 4. To make the best practices and procedures in education known throughout the country and to encourage their use everywhere.
> 5. To develop understanding and cooperation among all organized groups interested in educational improvement.[7]

The Educational Policies Commission sought through cooperative means to develop long-term policies for American education, which would merit the support not only of the profession but of all citizens.

Many sincere and able efforts to adapt education more effectively to the needs of a world in a period of great change were made by an organization known as the Progressive Education Association, and later called the American Education Fellowship. Actually this group was part of a worldwide association of educational liberals whose goal entails development of the newer methodology and a life-centered curriculum. They have held international conferences in such widely scattered places as Heidelberg, Locarno, Elsinore, and Ann Arbor. (In the United States the movement began in 1919 with the establishment of the Progressive Education Association.)

According to Stanley the membership of the American Education Fellowship was drawn largely from nontraditional tuition schools and from public schools in wealthy communities. Disbanded in 1957, the fellowship emphasized the child's total personality, stressing his activity and self-direction. The John Dewey Society, while not a lineal descendent of the American Education Fellowship, pursues somewhat the same aims.[8]

---

[7] See 14th Yearbook, Department of Superintendence (Washington, D.C.: National Education Association, 1936), p. 369; *NEA Journal*, vol. 24, no. 9 (December 1935), p. 304.

[8] See William O. Stanley and others, *Social Foundations of Education* (New York: Holt, Rinehart and Winston, Inc., 1956), p. 597, for a concise statement of the history and purposes of the American Education Fellowship.

These organizations grew out of the success of a number of experimental schools in both Europe and the United States. In its early years, the child-centered movement was confined largely to private schools and had only negligible influence on public education. But during the Depression decade, the influence of these organizations as agencies for improving the schools to meet the world emergency was quite pronounced. The child-centered movement made rapid progress in the public schools, especially in the wealthy suburbs of large cities. It throve on the attacks of its opponents, especially after the meeting of the American Association of School Administrators in Atlantic City in 1938, when the controversy between the progressives and the essentialists first broke into the open; now proponents of progressivism felt called upon to defend their theories and practices before the bar of public opinion.

In an attempt to adapt education to the needs of a world in depression and war, two seemingly conflicting philosophies of education emerged from the thought and discussion of educational leaders. In a way, the collision between the philosophy of totalitarian education and the philosophy of democratic education, which was discussed in the chapter on nationalism, continued. But this older conflict, based on differences of political ideology, appeared to be less violent than the newer controversy raging in the ranks of education between what we shall call naturalistic progressivism and realistic essentialism. With the world in the throes of economic depression, progressivism seemed to be in the ascendancy. But with the advent of World War II, especially after the entrance of the United States in December, 1941, essentialism gained ground.

This reversal was not without hazard, however; the gravest danger that confronts a democracy in the exigencies of war or, more recently, cold war is that the people may lose their right to utilize their mature intelligence in determining what the experience of the race has demonstrated as the "essentials" in which youth is to be trained, both for war and for peace.

CHALLENGES TO DEMOCRATIC EDUCATION

The American Association of School Administrators meeting in Atlantic City in February, 1941, had already stressed the growing concern of educational leaders for the cause of democracy and national defense. The general theme was "provision for the common defense, the promotion of the general welfare, and the safe-guarding of the blessings of liberty." Convention members agreed that the safety and welfare of the nation was:

> . . . largely dependent upon the success to which our young people are taught to be loyal to our institutions and freedoms, upon their understanding of democracy, its strengths, weaknesses, and enemies, upon the

efficiency of their vocational training and upon their willingness to sacrifice for the common good.[9]

Yet who is to determine the essentials for which training is to be given? In totalitarian nations the dictatorial leaders determine these essentials on the basis of their own interpretation of experience. The Soviet system of Russia, the Fascist system of Italy, the Nazi system of Germany, were advanced by their authors as utopias. Each of these nations educated its children for and into a preconceived social structure. Is such a goal desirable for a democracy?

In a democracy, it is the responsibility of education not only to provide training in the essentials but also to help develop a realization by all that these types of education are essential, and thus to produce a willingness to enter voluntarily into the needed educational training. If democracies are to resist the might of totalitarian powers, they must do more than develop the skills that make resistance possible. They must arouse a spirit that will inspire resistance by making evident the background of the struggle, the underlying causes, and, above all, the aims that are to be attained. When this is done, training is not only initiated but its results are used with a conviction based upon understanding rather than emotion. *It is* essential to know what is essential, and providing this knowledge is the task of education in a democracy.

Thus, the prosecution of the war entailed grave dangers. Would it be possible to organize and indoctrinate for victory and yet not lose the democratic spirit which had begun to characterize the schools during and after the Great Depression? This was the challenge.

As one democracy after another in Europe and Asia lost its sovereignty and was enslaved by the onward march of the totalitarian powers, Germany, Italy, and Japan, educational leaders became more and more concerned with the phases of education essential to the preservation of what they called the democratic way of life. Even isolationists, who wanted America to remain neutral and to take steps only for its own defense, advocated an education that would build and preserve a true democracy, that would shine as a light in a darkened world. During the early months of World War II the emphasis in educational discussions was on education for democracy. The NEA's Educational Policies Commission published a series of books and pamphlets under such titles as *The Unique Function of Education in American Democracy, The Purpose of Education in American Democracy, Education and the Defense of American Democracy, The Education of Free Men in American Democracy,* and *Learning the Ways of Democracy.* The commission also held a series of regional conferences early in 1941 devoted to the discussion of ways in which youth could be better educated for the responsibilities of American citizenship.

---

[9] *NEA Journal,* vol. 30, no. 3 (March 1941), pp. 99–100.

With the adoption of the lend-lease policy and the resolution to make the United States the arsenal of democracy, schools began to realize that the greatest need in the emergency was for realistic training in the essential skills of industrial production. Farsighted educational leaders saw clearly that our national policy was tending inevitably towards actual participation in a shooting war, and the educational slogan became "Education for National Defense." Education now concerned itself with the basic essentials of an all-out war effort. In the autumn of 1940 the impact of the immense rearmament program began to be felt in the schools. Congress established the National Defense Training Program under the direction of the Federal Security Agency; and public schools, the NYA, and state employment agencies cooperated in inaugurating within and outside the schools defense training classes devoted to the development of essential industrial skills.

The United States Office of Education issued a variety of publications on this theme and urged the schools to incorporate elements essential to education for democracy into their curricula and to stress these essentials as steps in the forward march of democracy.

The year 1941 was a difficult one for schools and colleges. The Selective Training and Service Act had been passed, and colleges were uncertain as to the policy they should follow in connection with the deferment of students to complete their education. Schools found it difficult to harmonize the instructional needs of their pupils with the demands of governmental agencies for defense training. The majority, still concerned not only with the defense of the nation but with the defense of democracy as well, wished to preserve not only America but also the American way of life. Many feared that in a war to save democracy the United States might lose its own heritage. They felt that it was not enough to train our people to repulse aggressor nations who would destroy the democracies by force, but that we must educate our people to understand democracy, to love and to practice it.

At Pearl Harbor, on December 7, 1941, this period of uncertainty and ambiguity ceased. By December 11, Congress had committed the nation to war with all of the Axis powers. With this action the conflict between usual education and defense training for the war effort ended. The schools and colleges through their leaders quickly pledged all educational resources to the prosecution of the war and the attainment of victory.

Since progressivism had become the leading educational philosophy in the period directly preceding the return to war, it is appropriate to turn now to a more specific discussion of the progressive movement and its relationship to the new essentialism before, during, and immediately following World War II.

Concern with the development of personality is a cardinal principle of progressivism, for its primary regard is wholesome human growth and development, whereas, essentialism is concerned primarily with the preservation of a way of life and the adaptation of education to the maintenance of established institutions and practices. Which is to be the dominant philosophy of the future, history alone can tell. Here we can merely analyze these opposing points of view, as revealed in recent events, and examine their effects on the various aspects of education.

NATURALISTIC PROGRESSIVISM

It has been said that progressive education is not so much a philosophy of education as a philosophizing about education. Within the membership of the prewar Progressive Education Association there were wide differences of position and conviction. Progressive education is at once a protest and a vision. In its beginnings it was a protest against the deadening subordination of the individual to mass methods of education, the regimentation of minds, and the standardization of education through efficiency methods stimulated by the determinism and mechanism of educational science.

Critiques of progressivism (and, to some degree, of its offspring, reconstructionism) have generally alleged that this doctrine has no distinctive philosophy of its own; that although it purports to be child-centered and speaks in terms of the training of the whole child, in reality it represents merely an opposition to traditional methods and philosophies; in this sense, they claim, it presents a negative rather than a positive approach to education.[10]

Many critics have assailed the movement as being neither progressive nor educational. Others have charged that harm has been done to the pupils; that progressive education is soft; that it is responsible for the relaxation of discipline in American life; that it allows too much freedom to children who need careful adult direction; and that it develops egotism, cockiness, impertinence, and disregard for the feelings of others.

One of these critics has written as follows:

> One thing that makes it difficult to reach an understanding with certain proponents of the "new education" is their apparent unwillingness to stick to the point or to come out with any thoroughly clear statement of position. On the negative side, we understand that they are against whatever can be stigmatized as "formal," "conventional," "traditional," or "subject-matter," but with all candor and good will it is sometimes difficult to see just what they stand for positively. Thoughtful and honest examination of the common general principles as set forth by Mr. Kilpatrick will show how constantly the philosophy of the new education takes refuge in obscurity. . . . It seems clear to some of us that

---

[10] See Pedro J. Orata, "Progressive Look at Progressive Education," *Educational Administration and Supervision*, vol. 24 (November 1938), pp. 570–580.

it is not really new; that it is not education and that—whatever else it may be—it is certainly not in the best sense philosophy.[11]

One of the deeper roots of progressivism reaches back to the seminal philosophy of Jean-Jacques Rousseau; another (and there are many) takes us to Russia of the nineteenth century. Although not frequently considered a part of the mainstream of progressive education Count Leo Tolstoy (1828–1910) was intimately concerned with the learning process and the education of his children and serfs (indeed, of downtrodden men everywhere). When he put his great intelligence to the task the results were, by most standards of evaluation, progressive.

No doubt, his efforts gained more publicity than usual because of his literary reputation and political importance; but, vastly disenchanted with conventional methodology, he sought to change its lockstep. Busy with the education of his thirteen offspring in an out-of-the-way rural setting, he developed Rousellian ideas that appear not too dissimilar from those of other European and American progressivists.

The count spent a great deal of time with his children; he read to them regularly and attempted to teach them arithmetic by a method of his own, now called base five. He wrote an educational volume entitled *The Alphabet.* He became famous, or (from the viewpoint of the Russian nobility) infamous, for his attempts to teach the children of his peasants, and even the serfs themselves. He experimented with the monitorial system, using his own children as guides for peasant youngsters. In 1862 Tolstoy published an educational journal, *Yasnaya Polana* (named after his country estate). Coming to an Émile-like conclusion, he maintained that "it was a gross error for intellectuals to attempt to teach peasants. They, in their simplicity, should be engaged to teach aristocrats!"[12]

Having considered some roots of progressivism, we now turn again to America and the developments which led to the creation of a climate favorable to the creation of an ideology congenial to the early child-centered school. Lester Dix, in 1939, in the Foreword to his *A Charter for Progressive Education*, gave his optimistic appraisal of the future of the progressive ideology in glowing terms and predicted the realization of "that democratic education which is not yet, but destined to be, both the invigoration and decoration of the great American society which will ultimately emerge on this continent."[13]

---

[11] Lewis Foley, "The Philosophy of the New Education: A Reply to Professor Kilpatrick," *School and Society,* vol. 55, no. 1411 (January 10, 1942), pp. 33, 37.

[12] For further material on the life of Tolstoy and his educational realizations see *Tolstoy on Education,* trans. by Leo Wiener (Chicago: University of Chicago Press, 1967). See also Henri Troyat, *Tolstoy,* trans. by Nancy Amphoux (New York: Doubleday & Company, Inc., 1967), especially pt. iii, ch. 4, "Arbiter of the Peace and Schoolmaster," pp. 219–240.

[13] (New York: Teachers College Press, Columbia University, 1939), p. iii.

His conception of the foundation of this motive, as well as a partial definition of progressive education, is revealed in the imperatives he set for progressivism. First, said Dix, this education will be organic; "it completely abolishes the old separation of mind and body, and robs of reality any assumed separation of physical, emotional, and intellectual activities"; next, this education must be evolutionary, for "the best things that man can know and do have not all been done; his behavior may continue to evolve without limit into more efficient, more satisfying, and more beautiful forms"; third, "It will be dynamic. . . . Life, growth, and learning do not proceed in the absence of actual activity on the part of the individual, and they cannot go on in the absence of purpose and choice"; and, finally, and perhaps most significantly, the modern conception will view learning as life and growth: "One cannot live without learning and growing. [Young people] will learn what they do, not what they are told, or what they see others do."[14]

As illustrated by Dix's interpretation, the progressive movement was at first dominated by those who wished to move from regimentation and mechanization to free child-centered activities in real life situations. Many of its early leaders, influenced consciously or unconsciously by the basic theories of Rousseau, Pestalozzi, Herbart, Froebel, and Hall, advocated an educational procedure based on the "natural inner urge of growth," the "unfolding of self," and the child's "immediate interests"; they did not always distinguish carefully between these elements and childish whims and caprice. Naturalism is one of the characteristics of the movement, for one of the familiar slogans of progressivism is, Work with and not against the pupil's instincts.

Since naturalism is still popular, it is well that we attempt an evaluation of this conception, particularly in its application to present-day conditions and in the light of its contemporary meaning. The modern psychologist admits that the child comes into the world with natural biological and psychological predispositions; but he insists that these are modifiable by processes of conditioning and sublimation, and even subject to elimination and substitution. It is true, as the naturalists have contended in their protests against meaningless formalism in education, that the child is educated only by his own responses to stimulation. No doubt the child would be educated by being left free to respond to natural situations in the environment. But there is a desirable education and an undesirable one, and certainly many of the child's natural reactions would be socially undesirable and would educate in socially undesirable directions.

The modern exponents of naturalism and freedom praise the qualities of self-direction, self-control, and creative originality. These are most desirable goals. The mistake is in thinking these characteristics are "nat-

---

[14] Dix, pp. 25–28.

ural," for children find it tiresome and confusing to have their own way at all times. The fallacy of the doctrine of freedom in education is revealed by the remark of a child in one of the ultramodern progressive schools, who reportedly asked, "Teacher, do we have to do just what we want to all day?"

There is a distinct place for the school and the teacher as controls of stimulation. Elementary psychology teaches that the teacher has a responsibility to present stimuli that will produce desirable responses and withhold stimuli that will introduce undesirable responses.[15] Complete freedom would undoubtedly result in many undesirable instinctive and habitual responses, which were once useful, but are no longer in modern civilized conditions. Thus, in practice, the natural has to be seriously modified.

This naturalistic earlier stage of the progressive educational movement, however, had a great influence on education throughout the world. It helped to change the school from an institution concerned with teaching the facts of a narrow curriculum and developing a few basic skills, to an institution devoted to developing the whole child, both as a psychological and a social organism.

ORGANISMIC PSYCHOLOGY

American psychology, as noted in Chapter 16, owes much of its impetus and inspiration to European sources. During the second quarter of the twentieth century this debt was to be doubled with the arrival from Germany of four outstanding practitioners of the experimentalist group. Their researches were destined to be among the most significant in furthering organismic teaching and in reorganizing American educational psychology during and after the Depression.

The influence of Max Wertheimer (1880–1943) was barometric in the development of organismic, or Gestalt psychology. From professorships at Berlin and Frankfurt, Wertheimer came to the United States in 1933, where he held positions at Columbia and at the New School for Social Research. He had discovered (1910–1912) the phi phenomenon (which concerns the illusion of motion) and thus may be considered the father of Gestalt psychology. His approach to the study of psychological problems has been called macroscopic, as opposed to microscopic. The latter years of his life were devoted to the study of the problem of learning, and in 1945 his *Productive Thinking* was published posthumously.

Kurt Koffka (1886–1941) was born in Germany and secured his

---

[15] But James D. Koerner in *The Miseducation of American Teachers* (Boston: Houghton Mifflin Company, 1963), p. 37, says that the "inferior intellectual quality" of educationists is a fundamental limitation to practice.

Ph.D. at Berlin. After serving as visiting professor at Cornell and the University of Wisconsin, Koffka remained permanently in the United States at Smith College in 1928. In company with Wertheimer and Wolfgang Kohler he contributed much to the development of Gestalt psychology. Koffka's *Growth of the Mind* (1924) dealt with organismic principles and created considerable interest. He published *Principles of Gestalt Psychology* in 1935.

Wolfgang Köhler (1887–   ), another product of the University of Berlin, served as professor of psychology at Göttingen and at Berlin. His experience as director of the anthropoid station at Tenerife in the Canaries resulted in his famous *Mentality of Apes* (1925). His relationship to Wertheimer and Koffka has already been suggested; and Köhler's interpretation of field, or organismic, psychology appeared as *Gestalt Psychology* in 1929 (revised in 1947). In America he took a post at Swarthmore (1935–1955) and, after that, became affiliated with the Institute for Advanced Study of Princeton University, New Jersey.

Kurt Lewin (1890–1947) was born at Mogilno, Prussia, and graduated in 1914 from the University of Berlin, where he taught before coming to the United States. After holding posts at Stanford (1932–1933) and Cornell (1933–1935), Lewin became affiliated with the University of Iowa. In harmony with his connection with Wertheimer, Koffka, and Köhler, he was interested in experimental, theoretical, and social psychology. Lewin was perhaps foremost in the area of group dynamics and his *A Dynamic Theory of Personality* (1935) and *Principles of Topological Psychology* (1936) represent salient contributions to American psychological literature.

Various psychologists have been interested in linguistics, the child's apprehension of language, and the significance of language in distinguishing man from animals. As Noam Chomsky notes, complete adherence to transformationalism suggests an organizing power within the brain denied by earlier psychologists.[16]

Gestalt (from *Gestalten*, visual shapes) psychologists interpret phenomena as organized wholes, rather than as masses of distinct parts. Their theoretical and experimental contributions have buttressed the more progressive educational methodology, sustaining as they do the view that the whole child is involved in every educational process. In maintaining that "the whole is greater than the sum of all of its parts," the Gestalt approach to motivation offers an excellent basis for projects which begin with the child's natural, unpracticed, spontaneous interests, and serves also as a rationale for educational routines which proceed from the general to the particular.

As noted earlier, the movement began in Germany and passed to the

---

[16] See his *Syntactic Structures* (The Hague: Mouton & Co., 1966).

United States with the arrival of four leading gestaltists about 1930. In addition to Wertheimer, Koffka, Köhler, and Lewin, Gestalt in America has been espoused by George W. Hartmann, Robert M. Ogden, and Raymond H. Wheeler. Its central feature rests on the whole and unitary aspect of organismic behavior and considers insight as the salient factor in learning. Gestalt maintains that perception and memory are invariably concerned with the wholes which determine the meaning of their parts.

Two underlying laws have been adduced by the gestaltists: (1) each element of a pattern, or configuration, through dynamic participation, alters its individuality; and (2) the dynamic attribute of self-fulfillment permits small gaps or incompletions which may properly be ignored through perception of the whole. Gestalt criticism of the mechanistic stimulus-response interpretation of behavior has greatly encouraged changes in teaching practices which abet the unity, or integratedness, of experiences. Although Gestalt psychology was not concerned exclusively with educational method, its advent served to stimulate reevaluation of pedagogical practices and to reemphasize the necessity for a consideration of the whole child, both physically and mentally. Thus, Gestalt aided the progressive movement.

After Dewey the most influential champion of the progressive doctrine was William Heard Kilpatrick (1871–1966). He was more instrumental than anyone else in formulating its philosophy and developing its practices. As a distinguished professor of education, lecturer, writer, and editor, he popularized the movement among classroom teachers as well as educational leaders. He taught at Teachers College, Columbia University, from 1909 until his retirement in 1938. He was a guiding force in the Progressive Education Association and the John Dewey Society for the Study of the School and Culture. He wrote such influential and popular books as *Foundations of Method, Education for a Changing Civilization*, and *Education and the Social Crisis*. And he edited *The Educational Frontier* and *Frontiers of Democracy*, organs of the progressive movement. A review of his books, magazine articles, and editorials is perhaps the best avenue to an understanding of the philosophy of progressivism and its implications for the various aspects of education.

With the death of Dewey in 1952, progressive education lost its strongest accent although, of course, Kilpatrick still was vocal. George Counts and Harold Rugg, as well as Harold Hand and Lester Dix, continued the crusade, yet the spark seemed gone. The tide of essentialism was running stronger and at the University of Illinois, long a center of progressivist activity and the headquarters of the journal, *Progressive Education*, Arthur E. Bestor maintained his (for a time) one-man vendetta against the progressive movement.

The most common complaint against progressive education has been that it glorifies the means at the expense of ends. Yet the fact that the essentialists adopted many of the methods of the progressives and grafted them on their system indicates that the means frequently were very good.[17]

Leadership in the progressive movement over the last half-century has included Boyd H. Bode, William H. Burton, George Counts, Lester Dix, Harold Hand, Sidney Hook, Gordon Hullfish, Alice Keliher, William H. Kilpatrick, Doris and J. Murry Lee, Harold Rugg, W. Carson Ryan, Harold Taylor, V. T. Thayer, William Van Til, Carleton Washburne, and Carolyn Zachery. Although differing moderately among themselves, all have adhered to the principles enunciated in Dewey's writings and to William James' pragmatic spirit.

Although in the 1950s and 1960s some loss of allegiance to the progressivist cause occurred, it should be remembered that during the doldrums of the Great Depression it was the dynamic force of progressive education that gave much of the strength and meaning to community life. Critics, in their zeal to disestablish progressivism, frequently forget that the progressive attempt to counteract the effects of those lean years by fostering an education aimed at developing the human personality and individual character was not entirely unsuccessful.

EDUCATIONAL ATTITUDES OF PROGRESSIVE LEADERS

Aims

The progressive education movement, influenced as it was by followers of Dewey's social philosophy, has always been conscious of the social implications of education, but has never been limited to an exclusive concern with the child-centered concept. The serious threat of economic depression and the rise of totalitarianism in the world, however, brought social concern to the forefront in progressive thinking. Faced with the serious economic evils of the Depression, the Progressive Education Association in 1933 appointed a Committee on Social-Economic Problems which formulated a policy entitled, *A Call to the Teachers of the Nation.* Teachers were asked to recognize the corporate and interdependent character of the contemporary economic order and to transfer the democratic tradition from individualistic to cooperative economic foundations, to a productive and distributive system managed in the interests of all who labor, to a society dominated by the ideal of guaranteeing to every child the fullest opportunities for personal growth. The continuation of depression conditions, the spread of totalitarian thought, and the reappearance of

---

[17] For a good analysis of progressive education and its post–World War II problems, see Frederick L. Redefer, "What Has Happened to Progressive Education?" *School and Society,* vol. 67, no. 174 (May 8, 1948), pp. 345–349.

world war caused progressives to turn to the possibilities of designing an education that would lead to the creation of a society nearer to man's dreams and desires.[18]

In 1941, with democracy facing extreme danger if not destruction, the Progressive Education Association attempted a new formulation of its philosophy in a report entitled, *Progressive Education: Its Philosophy and Challenge*. In this summation, the association rejected not only the idea of education based solely on the natural growth and interests of the child but also the concept of education for a planned society. It set forth its educational aims in these words:

> The committee holds that the dominant ideals of our democratic culture, continuously reinterpreted and defined, provide the direction for education. . . . Democracy is not a mere association of individuals whose purposes and acts are individualistic in the laissez-faire sense. It is an intelligent use of co-operative means for the progressive attainment of significant personalities. Significant personalities cannot be unfolded from within; they must be acquired by individuals in union with other individuals intent upon a similar quest.[19]

These are the aims and purposes of progressivism: the development of significant human personalities through the means of social democracy. Two ideals, respect for human personality and cooperative social participation, are envisioned and recognized as reciprocal. The more we respect human personality, the more we will organize social institutions to promote personality development; and the more we share in the activities of our cooperative social institutions, the more we will enhance the development of individual personalities.

Progressive educators, as a rule, advocate a personalistic philosophy of education. They insist that education cannot be effective in the development of the individual and of society unless it facilitates growth in all phases of the pupils' lives. Personalism is an evolutionary philosophy which emphasizes the individual pupil and his all-around development as a person, not just his intellectual training. Its proponents are in accord with the point of view of a long line of educational philosophers from Protagoras to Dewey. They believe that the basic purpose of education is to assist individuals in achieving that whole personality which is within the range of complexities of modern industrial-social organization. Progressivism demands the education of the whole man, the development of a personal character that includes physical, emotional, and social worth as well as intellectual. Progressives talk much of human growth and development; they are interested in attitudes, emotions, and interests, the nonintellectual

---

[18] The earlier aims of progressive education are fairly represented in Rugg and Shumaker.

[19] Harold Alberty and others, *Progressive Education: Its Philosophy and Challenge* (New York: The Progressive Education Association, 1941).

as well as the intellectual aims of education. They believe that significant personalities are whole personalities.

Types

Progressivism, in its recognition of the pupil as a complete, dynamic, living organism, emphasizes the necessity of a continual use of every type of education. Progressives feel that the child is always a unity, and they recognize the dangers involved in a preoccupation with only one aspect of growth or one phase of behavior. They know that there are both physical and cultural requisites for healthy growth into individually satisfying and socially valuable personalities. They believe that education results from the interaction between the individual and the culture in which he lives, and therefore must include every element in a changing dynamic culture. Schools must make use of every type of growth-inducing experience and activity to be found including the principles of gestalt psychology, they assert.

Progressive education recognizes, as has seldom been recognized before, the dominant role that emotion plays in human life, and emphasizes the great need for an education of the emotions and feelings. Progressives believe that education of the emotions is as essential as education of the intellect. Emotions, however, are not conceived as separate and distinct elements, but as aspects of the organism's various biochemical and biophysical processes. Emotional education, therefore, is not something apart from mental and physical education; all three are considered phases of the unitary functioning of the organism.[20]

The earlier progressives believed to a greater or less degree in the doctrine of naturalism. They held that the goal of education is an adherence to "natural" law; they insisted that education is for the benefit of nature, to provide opportunities for and to remove all hampering influences and restrictions from natural growth, thus furthering the natural evolution of the individual and of the human race. Preaching a gospel of freedom in education, they were exponents of the naturalistic movement initiated by Rousseau, refined and elaborated by the early educational psychologists, and popularized by John Dewey and his followers.

Later progressives give social education and individual education equal consideration. Their concept of the interaction of the individual and his culture prevents any exclusive or excessive preoccupation with either the individual and his desires or the culture and its patterns. These later progressives are equally concerned with the development of the individual who will fulfill his potentialities for social contribution, and the development of a social culture that will provide the fundamental requisites for the

---

[20] A sympathetic account of this phase of progressive education is found in Ernest E. Bayles and Bruce L. Hood, *Growth of American Educational Thought and Practice* (New York: Harper & Row, Publishers, 1966), ch. xi, pp. 219–243.

best possible growth and functioning of the individual. They argue the futility of viewing social and individual values as antagonistic.

In attempting to achieve their aim of developing significant whole personalities, progressives neglect no type of education. They emphasize the necessity for work experiences and the development of occupational skills and proper work attitudes. But they also recognize the need for the rich and full development of the nonfinancial aspects of life. They give attention to training for adequate recreational and leisure activities, the development of hobbies and abiding esthetic interests. They place emphasis on the sports and recreational pursuits that have continuing value. Education, they hold, should be pleasant; mutual enjoyment they consider as important as pure academic training. The expressive activities associated with esthetic interests they feel should be a vital part of education. Most of the work of the progressive schools and much of their pupils' activity have been devoted to the development of interest in creative and esthetic achievement.

Progressivism in education has emphasized functional activity. It does not merely teach items of knowledge or fix habits of response. It strives to provide its students with opportunities for concrete experiences. It provides opportunities for expression. Practical experiences and activities, esthetic experiences and activities, and social experiences and activities are emphasized equally with intellectual experiences and activities, and are considered agencies for the development of the personality.

To be sure, certain educational liberals have taken positions further to the left than most progressives. This is especially true of the reconstructionists. Headed by Theodore Brameld, this movement retains many of the attributes of early progressivism, particularly the emphases developed by Counts (*Dare the Schools Build a New Social Order?*) and Rugg (*Now is the Moment*). Reconstructionism is indebted also to naturalism and stands much in the same relationship to progressivism and pragmatism as essentialism does to idealism.

To paraphrase Brameld, reconstructionism directs its chief attention to the future, and thus is indebted to the best in utopianism. The potential in American and world culture is the reconstructionist goal. It projects its thinking well beyond our accustomed ways of living, for it strives with "imagination and audacity to design novel cultural patterns upon the solid basis of scientific knowledge of nature and man";[21] it strives also to develop workable methods of achieving them. The guiding goal of reconstructionism is, then, the enunciation of beliefs demanded by the revolutionary age in which we live. At the same time, these beliefs are to be both concretely grounded in experience and attainable in practice.

While many reconstructionists tolerate the more conservative progres-

---

[21] Theodore Brameld, *Patterns of Educational Philosophy* (New York: Harcourt, Brace & World, Inc., 1950), p. 397. Brameld now alleges that he is *not* a reconstructionist!

sivism, they generally reject and frequently denounce the educational ideologies of the right, essentialism and classic idealism, or perennialism.

Content

Progressivism insists upon a curriculum of life experiences; it abandons the idea that educational content consists of the words and ideas provided by a textbook or a professor's lectures. Learning takes place when any part or phase of experience, once it has been lived, stays on to affect pertinently further experience; we learn what we live and in the degree that we live it. In his definition of progressivism John S. Brubacher emphasizes the fluidity of naturalistic pragmatism. He says: "to ensure a maximum of freedom for each individual, the pragmatic progressive favors a pluralistic view of society. . . . By preventing any one agency such as the state or the church, from obtaining a monopoly over education, society ensures freedom for the individual."[22]

Progressives condemn the older curriculum which was made in advance and handed to teachers who in turn assigned lessons to pupils. Its bookish content was divided logically into separate subject-matter areas, airtight compartments, often remote from the rapidly changing world and the pupil's actual life. Students memorized the information contained in lessons and repeated it in oral recitations and written examinations, success being determined by the degree to which the pupil returned what had been given to him. Progressives maintain that when the pupil did succeed in retaining this mass of organized information, its value usually was established as purely pedantic.

The progressive curriculum, on the other hand, consists of the experiences of actual living. What the child actually lives he builds into his character and personality; the progressive school is established to foster the kind of living which encourages the building of good character and personality. This curriculum cannot be constructed in advance and handed down to teachers and pupils. The progressive curriculum seeks to convey both a richness of life and all-aroundness; it includes "distinctions made, knowledge used, consideration for others sensed, responsibilities accepted"; it includes all the aspects of daily living, practical, social, moral, vocational, esthetic, and intellectual.

Progressivism accepts the newer organismic psychology which rejects the idea that only the child's mind is educated and insists that whenever any learning takes place the whole organism learns. Learning does not come about through repetition, but through the interaction of the individual organism and the culture in which he moves, according to this belief.

Field theory psychologists reject the mechanistic views of the func-

---

[22] *Modern Philosophies of Education* (New York: McGraw-Hill, Inc., 1969), pp. 333–334.

tionalists. Insight, for them, is the central factor in learning. This concept is also central to later progressivist thought. Mayer has stated the significance of configuration as follows:

> Gestalt psychologists like Wertheimer, Lewin, and Kohler are correct when they point to pattern as the fundamental fact of existence. The whole does determine the structure of the parts. Our achievements, in part, are products of the Zeitgeist, the spirit of our times.
>
> Humility implies both a recognition of the importance of reason and what Santayana calls "the wisdom of the heart." *Thus we see knowledge, not as a possession, but as a process; not as an entity, but as a quest; not as an achievement, but as an adventure.*[23]

The task of the school is to make available all the elements of the culture for this process of interaction. This interaction between the individual and his environment has three results: expansion, differentiation, and integration. Children are expanding, differentiating, integrating individuals. The expanding individual, as he reacts to his environmental culture, is continually absorbing experiences. The growing organism continually participates in activities, but he is not progressively advancing unless he is differentiating and integrating these separate experiences toward a meaningful and purposeful goal. This, assert the gestaltists, is the only true learning; the older subject-matter curriculum destroys this wholeness, say progressives, and actually disintegrates the individual. The progressive curriculum preserves and promotes integration by providing the pupil with rich and varied opportunities to select and engage in his own goal-seeking activities. But progressives realize that the school can provide only part of the materials of an integrating curriculum, only part of the work can be done in the classroom.

The educational sociologists attempted to break away from the traditional subject-matter curriculum in the direction of a curriculum adapted to social needs by moving first toward a course of study made of broad fields of learning, such as general mathematics, general science, general language, and so on. Then they advocated the core curriculum, and took the position that a core of common materials was necessary for all children in a given school period. In the elementary school, the whole curriculum was a core; nothing was to be put in that was not needed for social ends. In the secondary school, the core consisted of those subjects or experiences required by society; subjects of individual interest were designated electives. Both of these approaches to curriculum building involved a concern with *objectives, scope,* and *sequence,* terms carried over from the subject-matter curriculum and the authoritarian educational philosophies.

---

[23] Frederick Mayer, *Philosophy of Education for Our Time* (New York: The Odyssey Press, Inc., 1958), p. 18. See also I. N. Thut, *The Story of Education* (New York: McGraw-Hill, Inc., 1957), pp. 267–282, 327–350.

Progressives moved even further away from subject matter by organizing the curriculum in terms of what they called units of work, based on the structure of society and its aims. Units of work were built around the major functions of social living and the structures and processes through which these functions were carried out. Society has such institutions as the government, the family, and the church, and their functions include protection of life and property, food getting, and reproduction, and worship; the processes involved are economic, political, and social. Attempts were made to vitalize the curriculum and make it more functional by organizing units of work around such topics. The Virginia curriculum program, the Wilmington, Delaware, program, and the unit-of-work program of the Horace Mann–Lincoln School are examples of attempts in this direction. Here again, as in traditional treatments, concern with aims, scope, and sequence in curriculum building is found.

The experience-integrating curriculum of present-day progressivism generally does not attempt to analyze or set up aims in terms of social objectives. The true progressive fears that if he sets up specific aims they may become static. He believes that the child himself should determine the scope and sequence of experience getting. As the child integrates his experiences into a meaningful whole, we have what Dewey calls relevancy; and as the child expands and grows purposefully, we have what the progressives call continuity. Thus instead of the scope and sequence of the subject-matter curriculum, the integrating curriculum has relevancy and continuity.

The curriculum according to progressive educators, should be made up of all the child's activities, the sum total of his experiences; its scope is the extent of human living. Its function is to integrate experiences so that the child will have an opportunity to expand and grow into a significant personality, with attitudes and ways of conduct that make his life individually satisfying and socially desirable.

Agencies

In developing personalities, the schools have been found insufficient, especially when they attempt to work alone. The serious plight of American youth, particularly during the Depression, was revealed by many studies, including the notable one by the American Council on Education in 1938.[24] These reports revealed that without assistance from other organizations, schools could not meet the economic, social, recreational, and health needs of American youth; thus many agencies would have to cooperate in solving the problem.

Progressives stress education's need to cooperate with other social agencies, which also provide educative experiences useful in the develop-

---

[24] Howard M. Bell, *Youth Tell Their Story* (Washington, D.C.: American Council on Education, 1938); see also Wecter, especially ch. ix, "Youth in Search of a Chance," pp. 178–199.

ment of character and personality, and frequently operate in areas not commonly served by the school's program of activities. Adult education groups, churches, leisure-time and recreational groups, the YMCA and the YWCA, and many other agencies are positive educational forces with which the progressive schools seek to ally to bring educational efforts into a more unified pattern.[25]

In 1933 the federal government started to participate in meeting the needs of American youth with the establishment of the Civilian Conservation Corps (CCC) which was organized (1) to relieve distress through the employment of young men on constructive conservation projects, (2) to aid in the rehabilitation of youth, and (3) to assist in the general administrative drive for economic recovery. In 1935, the National Youth Administration (NYA) was established as an independent division of the Works Progress Administration (1) to provide funds for the part-time employment of needy students, whether high school, college, or graduate students, sixteen to twenty-four years of age, so as to enable them to continue their education; and (2) to provide funds for the part-time employment of youth of relief families on work projects designed not only to give young people valuable work experiences but also to benefit their communities. These governmental agencies were designed not only to give financial aid to needy youth, but also to improve their morale and help them develop into useful workers and well-rounded personalities.[26]

Progressive education, however, has maintained that, of all the agencies of education, the teacher is the most important. Through its annual national meeting and its various regional meetings, the Progressive Education Association made every effort to imbue teachers with its philosophy and to instruct them in the techniques of personality development.

Teachers, of their own accord, have done much to clarify their philosophies and improve their methods, in spite of conditions that would have discouraged a less loyal and conscientious group. During the Depression, many teachers demonstrated their loyalty to the cause of education. Their salaries pared to the bone and thousands unpaid, they worked at their tasks patiently, even attempting improvements in the face of discouraging difficulties. In spite of their own financial plight, they retained their belief in the importance of the education of boys and girls. Having seen how easy it is for material possessions to slip away, they came to believe as never before in the worth of their job of developing imperishable and indestructible human personalities. The materialistic philosophies that had swayed them in the prosperous era following World War I were stripped away and were replaced by a dedication that invested their work with a new meaning. Teachers, through their organizations, began to formulate

---

[25] Wecter, pp. 178–199.
[26] Wecter, ch. ii, "New Design for Living," pp. 25–40.

for the emergency a philosophy which expressed a new belief in the improvability of the human character and destiny.

Teacher-training institutions underwent a process of redirection and reorganization. Under the leadership of such organizations as the American Association of Teachers Colleges and the National Society of College Teachers of Education, teacher education took a new direction. The multiplication and duplication of courses in teachers colleges which developed during the postwar decades has been checked. Closer ties have evolved between departments of education and academic subject-matter departments for the better training of teachers. Courses in education have been more closely integrated with the social sciences so that teachers might see the relationship of education to the social order. Educational sociology and cultural anthropology have been added to the curriculum. Teachers colleges have been renamed state colleges.

In 1938, the American Council on Education projected a study of teacher education in the United States. This undertaking was made possible by grants from American educational foundations. The Commission of Teacher Education, set up by the Council, with Karl Bigelow as director, inaugurated a far-reaching study of teacher education. The underlying principles of this study, as set forth by the directors, were based on the assumption that the adequate education of teachers was a social obligation of increasing importance:

> What teachers are, what they know, and what they do, will be factors of critical importance for individuals and society alike. Teachers should be viewed as human beings and attention should be paid to their needs as men and women and citizens as well as their needs as teachers. The good teacher must first be a good human being.

Reports from the cooperating institutions revealed that improvements had been projected in the education of both in-service and prospective teachers along lines of guidance and personnel work, general education, and professional education.

The Progressive Education Association took the lead in the development of a new agency for the training of teachers, known as the summer workshop. The first was held at The Ohio State University during the summer of 1936, under the auspices of the Commission on the Relation of the Secondary School and College of the Progressive Education Association. Thirty-five teachers, carefully selected by the staff of the commission and by local educational authorities, attended. In the summer of 1937, a workshop was held at Sarah Lawrence College, Bronxville, New York, and attended by 126 teachers from a wide range of subject-matter fields. In 1938, the Progressive Education Association held four workshops in four different sections of the country, attended by over 500 teachers. In 1940, the Commission on Teacher Education organized workshops for college and university teachers who were cooperating in the study of teacher education. By the following year the establishment of summer workshops had spread widely throughout the country, almost every teacher-training institution having organized one or more. In Michigan alone, thirteen were in operation.

Basically, a workshop is a group of teachers working under flexible laboratory conditions on their immediate and practical problems and those of the schools they represent. A workshop differs from a course in that a course is prearranged and provides a systematic overview of a certain area, while a workshop is organized around the problems which its participants furnish. Each member of the group takes as his special task the solution of a problem or the completion of a project related to his own teaching or administrative position. The major part of his time is spent in individual conferences on his problem with staff members, or in small seminars or conferences of those working on similar problems.

The characteristics and values of the workshop techniques are as follows:

1.   The participant brings a specific interest or problem which has arisen out of his experience as a teacher or administrator, and is afforded an opportunity to make an intensive study of the interest or problem at a place where superior library, advisory, and other resources are available to aid him.

2.   The participant may have not only easy access to the services of various staff members and consultants representing a variety of kinds of assistance related to his problem, but a ready contact with other members of the group who have problems akin to his own.

3.   The participant has formal and informal association with those of varied background; this association contributes to his thinking on his specific problem, broadens his general professional orientation, and provides training in cooperative social thinking and action.

4.   The participant's total experience as he studies his specific interest or problem tends to prepare him for future solution of other professional problems.

5.   The participant, through the workshop's supplementary program of social and recreational activities, is given opportunities to improve himself as an individual personality in addition to opportunities to solve his professional problem.[27]

The beginning teacher is usually inclined to teach as he has been taught, unless teacher-education institutions promote the inclusion of new

[27] K. L. Heaton, W. G. Camp, and P. B. Diederich, *Professional Education for Experienced Teachers: The Program of the Summer Workshop* (Chicago: University of Chicago Press, 1940).

areas of social education in their preparation of teachers. The progressives urge that the educational experiences of teachers include contacts with many community undertakings, and that provision be made for responsible participation by teachers in various community activities. They maintain that opportunities for contacts with children should be a dominant part of the teacher-education program, so that through knowledge and experience the teacher may acquire an understanding of the principles of human growth and development.

Organization

Since the primary concern of progressivism has been the growth and development of the individual as an integrated human personality, from his prenatal stage to maturity, the progressives have discouraged organization of the school into distinctly separate units and levels. They agree that a certain degree of organized division of responsibility is necessary for administrative convenience, but they fear that too frequently the mechanics of organization interfere with the real function and purpose of the school. Under the influence of the progressive movement, the rigid system of school organization, with its emphasis upon distinct stages of development, was broken down and replaced by a close articulation of the units and levels of the school organization and a preview of the ungraded school. The overemphasis upon the division of education into preschool, early elementary, later elementary, junior high, senior high, junior college, and senior college levels has been checked, and the only divisions now recognized in many quarters are between elementary, secondary, and higher education. Even in this division, progressives have urged greater articulation, attempting to bridge breaks in the pupil's continuous development.

Progressives do recognize certain differences in the task of educating youth. As Goodwin Watson says:

> In childhood are laid foundations for emotional poise or instability, for social adjustment or isolation and for life-long patterns of behavior. . . . During the years of adolescence new strengths, new hungers, new associations, new insights and new social demands bring a Renaissance to personality. Sometimes the childhood patterns persist; usually they are modified; occasionally they are transformed for better or for worse.[28]

But progressives insist that the elementary and the secondary school must work most closely together in this total task of personality building.

The most unique contribution of the Progressive Education Association was the work of its Commission on the Relation of the Secondary School and College, which began in 1932 an eight-year experiment with

---

[28] Goodwin Watson and Ralph B. Spence, *Educational Problems for Psychological Study* (New York: Crowell-Collier and Macmillan, Inc., 1930), pp. 1–4, 128–150.

thirty secondary schools and a large number of colleges, under the direction of Wilford M. Aikin. Twelve public schools, twelve private schools, and six university schools were included in the experiment. The purpose was to determine whether the graduates of secondary schools that had not followed a set college preparatory curriculum could succeed as well in college as those from traditional schools. Two hundred and fifty colleges and universities agreed to waive their technical requirements for admission for graduates of the thirty schools and to enroll these students on the basis of scholastic aptitude and intelligence plus achievement in a broad field. The thirty schools were left free to revise their curricula on the basis of what they considered the interests and needs of the students.

The results of this extensive investigation, published in 1942,[29] revealed that preparation for a fixed set of entrance requirements was not the only satisfactory means of fitting a student for college success; and that the stimulus and initiative which the less conventional approach to secondary education afforded produced better student material for the colleges than there was in the past. In 1937, the Southern Association of Colleges and Secondary Schools initiated an experiment, similar to that of the Progressive Education Association, in which schools and colleges agreed to modify their instruction to meet more closely the abilities and needs of youth. Such experiments illustrate the way in which schools and colleges have been stimulated to bring their organizations closer together, each giving up some of its cherished prerogatives.[30]

Another educational trend growing out of the Great Depression was the emphasis placed upon the community school. The community school may be defined as a school that recognizes the partnership concept in public education, the continuity of the educational process through the adult level, and the integration of the school with the community of which it is a part.

In 1937, the Committee of Secondary Schools of the Society for Curriculum Study issued a report,[31] in which it recommended that the school be organized as a definite and integral part of the community, and that the school be the agency for the organized participation of teachers and pupils in the life of the community. The community school increases

---

[29] Wilford M. Aikin, *The Story of the Eight-Year Study* (New York: Harper & Row, Publishers, 1942). For several relevant evaluations of the Eight-Year Study see Kenneth V. Lottich, "Democracy Begins in Progressive High School Classrooms," *The Social Studies*, vol. 42, no. 4 (April, 1951), pp. 162–166. The writer questions the technique of the study as well as the significance of its conclusions, while defending the necessity for and purpose of the experiment.

[30] See R. Freeman Butts, *A Cultural History of Western Education*, 2d ed. (New York: McGraw-Hill, Inc., 1955), pp. 569–584, for a thorough-going review of progressive practices and professional activities on each educational level.

[31] Samuel Everett, *The Community School* (New York: Appleton-Century-Crofts, 1937).

the amount of community responsibility in education; it obligates all members of the community to participate in the work of developing the children of the community; it brings greater reality into the classroom. Progressive educators urge that the whole community organize a program for the education of children and youth, with the goal of seeing that every young person gets the help he needs in developing physical strength, getting a job, enjoying leisure, participating as an intelligent citizen in the affairs of the world, and, most of all, developing a well-adjusted personality. The Committee on Adolescence of the Progressive Education Association, the Regents' Inquiry in the State of New York, the American Youth Commission, and similar organizations issued reports emphasizing the necessity of such organized community effort for the education of American youth in self-realization as well as social service.[32]

Although the community school movement flourished during the decade of World War II in such diverse settings as Holtsville, Alabama; Kings Ferry, New York; and the Desert Queen School, located in the San Bernardino Mountains of California; its uniqueness and drive now seem to have been absorbed into the regular curriculum or into adult education programs. Yet the idea of school and community working in harmony and sharing educational experiences offers infinite possibilities for an educational and cultural renaissance.

The immense publicity received by the life-adjustment movement,[33] which sought to turn curriculum requirements from a more formal program to certain immediate needs, was sparked by the Prosser resolution of May, 1947, which described the conventional high school curriculum as "unrelated to the everyday needs of life." Prosser's statement served to crystallize public opinion and to divide the progressive and essentialist camps more sharply. The most persistent criticism of progressive education is that it neglects the essentials of training needed for the realities of actual living, that is (in essentialist terms), the traditional subjects. As we noted earlier, some critics claim that the progressive movement is intangible and indefinite; that it is far removed from the realities of life; and that it is therefore difficult to know what it actually stands for or accomplishes. Others charge that progressivist aspirations are merely utopian dreams, while progressivist practices often increase the evils.

According to Potter, life adjustment recognized "the importance of the fundamental skills" of arithmetic, reading, writing, listening and speak-

---

[32] See Edward G. Olson, *School and Community Programs* (Englewood Cliffs, N.J.: Prentice-Hall, Inc., 1949), and Richard Waverly Poston, *Small Town Renaissance, a Story of the Montana Study* (New York: Harper & Row, Publishers, 1950), for illustrations of an interesting approach to community education.

[33] See *Life Adjustment Education for Every Youth*, Bulletin no. 22 (Washington, D.C.: Federal Security Agency, Office of Education, 1951).

ing; its demise came as a result of warfare between various philosophical factions. Its basic purpose had been to equip more high school students for life, not really a bad idea![34]

Methods

The progressive classroom, like the socialized classroom, provides for the participation of each individual in group activities and situations, and requests the contribution of each member of the group. But these activities are selected in terms of the extent to which they enable each individual through his interaction with others to cultivate personal as well as social status and growth; the exercises of the classroom are centered on and directed toward the individual as an organized personality; the methods are socialized in order to bring each member of the group progressively toward the acceptance and skilled use of dynamic procedures, as the truly democratic way of protecting individual interests. Progressive education emphasizes conference, consultation, planning, and participation as special elements of a teaching procedure that provides maximum learning.

The methodology of progressivism is experiential as well as social. Abundant and varied opportunities must be provided, and students must be given the chance to express themselves in more than verbal ways in order to attain their complete status as persons, the progressive urge. Practical experiences, social experiences, esthetic experiences, emotional experiences, as well as intellectual experiences should be emphasized and evaluated in terms of their capacity to bring about the highest development of each individual. The basic principle of progressive method is that vital personalities are developed best through active participation.

The basic premise of progressive learning is often called the wholeness of method.[35] Learning is one whole experience, a single thing that branches and grows. Skill comes from experiences in original writing and creative expression in the arts. Knowledge is the fruit of experience with a world of things. Understanding comes through the experiences of social living. Experiences are "learned" when they fuse into the wholeness and goodness of an individual's life, personality, and character.

Progressives accept the principles of motivation and apperception as formulated by the earlier psychological developmentalists, but express them in newer and simpler terms. Kilpatrick says:

> I learn each response in the degree that I feel it or count it important, and also in the degree that it interrelates itself with what I already know. All that I thus learn I build at once into character. . . .

---

[34] Robert Potter, *The Stream of American Education* (New York: American Book Company, 1967), pp. 464–466.

[35] A. Gordon Melvin, *Method for New Schools* (New York: The John Day Company, Inc., 1941).

The presence of interest or purpose constitutes a favorable condition for learning. Interest and felt purpose mean that the learner faces a situation in which he is concerned. The purpose as aim guides his thought and effort. Because of his interest and concern he gets more wholeheartedly into action; he puts forth more effort; what he learns has accordingly more importance to him and probably more meaningful connections. From both counts he is better learned.[36]

The progressive's first requisite for learning is a pupil who recognizes that he cannot do what he wants until he possesses further knowledge or skill. All learning leads to some goal. Thus the teacher must analyze the pupils he teaches; he must know what values these individuals subscribe to, what cultural deficiencies they bear, what driving interests now motivate them, what personal conflicts they must overcome. The progressive teacher, to be effective, must discover and understand the uniqueness of each child.

The progressivist method of instruction is largely that which was earlier called the project, the carrying-on of pupil-needed, pupil-planned, pupil-organized, and pupil-evaluated activities, with situations created through which pupils can learn to gain control of themselves and of the conditions they face. The test to be applied in the selection of experiences is whether the pupils need them in order to live fully developed and integrated lives. The principles of Gestalt psychology are commonly used.

The common criticism of the progressive classroom is that it lacks discipline, that pupils are spoiled. This is the same criticism that was raised against socialized education. It is perhaps justified in cases where teachers misunderstand progressive principles and allow liberty to degenerate into license, with whim and caprice followed instead of purpose and interest. A school where children are living and working together in order to develop in themselves and each other wholesome personalities and good character can be nothing but a well-disciplined school; this discipline is positive rather than negative. The basic characteristics of a disciplined democracy are a love of justice and a respect for human personality; these can best result from more student responsibility in school activities.

It is in this last feature that the reconstructionists feel that their planning and organization is superior to that of the conventional progressives. Governed by the urge to develop a utopian society, they consider their motivation more purposeful and self-directive.

Harold Hand, in a manual for school evaluation, suggested that the community's interest and stake in the school must be analyzed in social terms and that "thumbs-up" and "thumbs-down" groups are its vital concern. Under such headings as "How Parents Feel about the Way Their Children Are Treated by the Other Pupils" and "How Pupils Feel about

---

[36] William H. Kilpatrick, "The Case for Progressivism in Education," *Journal of the National Education Association*, vol. 30, no. 8 (November, 1941), pp. 232.

the Help They are Getting with Their Personal Problems," Hand attempted to show how the social setting influences the tone and work of the school.[37]

Nevertheless, for reasons we have mentioned earlier in this chapter, the progressive movement in America appears to have lost much of its early drive. The necessities of conflict, the growth of essentialism, and the Cold War have contributed greatly to its decline. Yet many of its methods, and much of what it preached, were assimilated by schools which carried a traditional label and by leaders who chose to consider its ideas their own.[38]

IS PROGRESSIVE EDUCATION DEAD?

Cremin has epitomized the decline of the progressive movement and the death, in 1955, of the Progressive Education Association, as the "end of an era in American pedagogy":

> Somehow a movement which had for half a century enlisted the enthusiasm, the loyalty, the imagination, and the energy of large segments of the American public and the teaching profession became, in the decade following World War II, anathema.[39]

Perhaps his judgment is too severe; yet interest in the "movement" did wane and the journal *Progressive Education* suspended operation in 1957. However, and this in no way disagrees with Cremin's thesis, two pertinent factors must be mentioned here. First, the progressive movement was much more diffuse than usually considered, and to equate progressivism largely with the activities of the Progressive Education Association compounds this error. As part of the general reform movement in the

---

[37] Harold Hand, *What People Think about Their Schools* (New York: Harcourt, Brace & World, Inc., 1948), pp. 96–99, 111–114. For a delightfully visionary approach to the relationship of two mythical communities to their schools, see the Educational Policies Commission's report *Education for All American Youth* (Washington, D.C.: National Education Association, 1944), pp. 23–170, 171–338. See also Theodore Brameld, *Ends and Means in Education: A Midcentury Appraisal* (New York: Harper & Row, Publishers, 1950).

[38] David Lawson, "Two Views of the Child's Education for Freedom," *The Educational Forum*, vol. xxiv, no. 3 (March, 1960), pp. 345–350, attempts reconciliation of the presumed differences between the naturalists and the idealists. His arguments are well chosen and pertinent to the progressivist controversy.

[39] Lawrence A. Cremin, "What Happened to Progressive Education?" *Teachers College Record*, vol. 61, no. 1 (October 1959), pp. 23ff; also Cremin, "The Progressive Movement in American Education: A Reappraisal," *Harvard Educational Review*, vol. 27, no. 4 (Fall, 1957), pp. 251–270; and his "John Dewey and the Progressive Education Movement, 1915–1952," *The School Review*, vol. 67, no. 2 (Summer, 1959), pp. 160–173; William H. Kilpatrick, "Personal Reminiscences of Dewey and My Judgment of His Present Influence," *School and Society*, vol. 87, no. 2159 (October 10, 1959), pp. 374–375, emphasizes the indigenous features of Dewey's educational philosophy.

United States following its coming of age at the turn of the century, progressivism appears to be as natural a development as movements for slum clearance, purer food and drugs, and municipal reform. To attribute solely to John Dewey that which to a large degree resulted spontaneously is unhistorical and oversimplified.

Second, although the movement has subsided, progressiveness in education is anything but dead. Still very much in evidence are its famous methods: the use of problems and projects, unit teaching, provision for individual differences, the guidance function of education, and the reorganization of the school to accomplish these things. So, too, is the utilization of an organismic psychology of education.

The British Summerhill and its imitations in the United States appear to have caught the vision repudiated by postwar essentialism.[40] Perhaps, then, to borrow from Mark Twain, the death of progressivism has been greatly exaggerated!

Yet is progressivism dead? Let us turn to several recent developments which may, in many respects, be considered "progressive." Two new programs have been established by the United States to aid in the reduction of illiteracy and thereby, hopefully, poverty both at home and abroad. The Peace Corps, originated during the administration of John F. Kennedy, seeks to accomplish its mission wherever wanted throughout the globe. "Since 1961, a new kind of teacher has staffed classrooms throughout the developing world," says a recent report of this unique organization. "He (or she) is a college or university graduate with a baccalaureate degree in science or humanities. Before Peace Corps training, he had never taught a class or planned to spend two years of his life teaching. [Now] after three months of Peace Corps preparation, he serves as a full-fledged faculty member in an over-seas primary or secondary school." The same source states that, in 1968, volunteer teachers were to help educate more than 700,000 school children and help train 55,000 teachers. Peace Corps volunteers serve in sixty countries, from Afghanistan to Uganda, and from Colombia to Ethiopia. Upon return, many teach in the less attractive sections of the United States. The Peace Corps publication cited above states that:

> Conventionally trained teachers are fleeing from slum-area schools in favor of neat, clean, comfortable suburbs. Peace Corps returnees have no such abhorrence of poverty and cultural differences. They have participated with distinction in Cleveland's PACE and Washington, D.C.'s Cardozo High School Programs.[41]

---

[40] See A. S. Neill, *Summerhill: A Radical Approach to Child Rearing* (New York: Hart Publishing Company, 1960).

[41] *From Rote to Reason* (Washington, D.C.: The Peace Corps, 1968), p. 16.

Volunteers in Service to America (VISTA) serve within the United States. Some are concerned with anti-poverty programs, community development, migrant adjustment, senior citizen activities, and so on, while others teach.

A VISTA publication gives an example of dedication on the part of young Americans working under VISTA:

> "We're having a one-year poverty honeymoon together," announced Larry and Elena Jones, newly-married VISTA Volunteers now serving in Tulare County, California.
>
> The couple met during their VISTA Training Program at Camp New Hope, near Chapel Hill, N.C. They were married just two hours after graduating from their six-week VISTA Training Program.
>
> Larry and Elena are now living and working in a small migrant settlement called Toneyville near the town of Lindsay, California. Their house lacks windows and needs certain other repairs, but the couple is quite happy with their VISTA home. They are pleased to have a living room large enough to use as a classroom for a pre-school program and for English classes for the migrant families who spend some nine months of every year in the small settlement at Toneyville.[42]

Former President Lyndon B. Johnson, in greeting the first VISTA volunteers at the White House on December 12, 1964, summed up their role:

> Your pay will be low; the conditions of your labor will often be difficult. But you will have the satisfaction of leading in a great national effort and you will have the ultimate reward which comes to those who serve their nation and who serve their fellow man.

Such words and actions, of course, spring from the basic American belief in the rightness and necessity for universal education.

REFERENCES

Alberty, Harold, and others, *Progressive Education: Its Philosophy and Challenge.* New York: Progressive Education Association, 1941.

Ariès, Philippe, *Centuries of Childhood, A Social History of Family Life.* Trans. by Robert Baldick. New York: Alfred A. Knopf, 1962.

Bayles, Ernest E., *Democratic Educational Theory.* New York: Harper & Row, Publishers, 1960.

————, and Bruce L. Hood, *Growth of American Educational Thought and Practice.* New York: Harper & Row, Publishers, 1966.

Beard, Charles A., *The Unique Function of Education in American*

---

[42] *Vista: An Exciting Adventure* (Washington, D.C.: Published for Volunteers in Service to America, n.d.), p. 4.

Democracy. Washington, D.C.: National Education Association, 1937. The report of NEA's Educational Policies Commission.

Bode, Boyd H., *Progressive Education at the Crossroads*. New York and Chicago: Newson and Co., 1938.

Brameld, Theodore, *Patterns of Educational Philosophy*. New York: Harcourt, Brace & World, Inc., 1950. Pp. 167–208, 508–526.

Brubacher, John S., *Modern Philosophies of Education*, 4th ed. New York: McGraw-Hill, Inc., 1969, Pp. 3–25, 73–91.

Butts, R. Freeman, *A Cultural History of Western Education*, 2d ed. New York: McGraw-Hill, Inc., 1955. Pp. 569–584.

———, and Lawrence A. Cremin, *A History of Education in American Culture*. New York: Holt, Rinehart and Winston, Inc., 1953. Pp. 515–562.

Carr, William G., *The Purposes of Education in American Democracy*. Washington, D.C.: National Education Association, 1938. Another report of the Educational Policies Commission.

Counts, George S., *The Education of Free Men in American Democracy*. Washington, D.C.: National Education Association, 1942. A third report of the Educational Policies Commission.

———, *The Social Foundations of Education*. New York: Charles Scribner's Sons, 1934. Pp. 1–30, 252–282.

Cremin, Lawrence A., *The Transformation of the School—Progressivism in American Education, 1876–1957*. New York: Alfred A. Knopf, 1961.

Edwards, Newton, and Herman G. Richey, *The School in the American Social Order*, 2d ed. Boston: Houghton Mifflin Company, 1963.

Good, Harry G., *A History of Western Education*. New York: Crowell-Collier and Macmillan, Inc., 1960. Pp. 536–606.

Hand, Harold C., *What People Think about Their Schools*. New York: Harcourt Brace & World, Inc., 1948.

Justman, Joseph, *Theories of Secondary Education in the United States*. New York: Teachers College Press, Columbia University, 1940. Pp. 12–54.

Kandel, I. L., *Conflicting Theories of Education*. New York: Crowell-Collier and Macmillan, Inc., 1939.

———, *The New Era in Education, A Comparative Study*. Boston: Houghton Mifflin Company, 1955.

Knight, Edgar W., *Education in the United States*, 2d rev. ed. Boston: Ginn & Company, 1941. Pp. 576–669.

———, *Twenty Centuries of Education*. Boston: Ginn & Company, 1940. Pp. 583–608.

Levine, Daniel, *Varieties of Reform Thought*. Madison, Wisc.: State Historical Society of Wisconsin, 1964.

Mason, Robert E., *Educational Ideals in American Society*. Boston: Allyn and Bacon, Inc., 1960.

Mayer, Frederick, *Philosophy of Education for Our Time*. New York: The Odyssey Press, Inc., 1958.

Melvin, A. Gordon, *Method for New Schools*. New York: The John Day Company, Inc., 1941.

Meyer, Adolphe E., *The Development of Education in the Twentieth Century*. Englewood Cliffs, N.J.: Prentice-Hall, Inc., 1939. Pp. 1–124.

———, *An Educational History of the American People*. New York: McGraw-Hill, Inc., 1957. Pp. 396–426.

Myers, Alonzo F., and Clarence O. Williams, *Education in a Democracy*. Englewood Cliffs, N.J.: Prentice-Hall, Inc., 1937. Pp. 228–360.

Nakosteen, Mehdi, *The History and Philosophy of Education*. New York: The Ronald Press Company, 1965. Pp. 505, 515–516, 519–520, 560–564.

Neill, A. S., *Summerhill: A Radical Approach to Child Rearing*. New York: Hart Publishing Company, 1960.

Park, Joseph (Ed.), *Selected Readings in the Philosophy of Education*. New York: Crowell-Collier and Macmillan, Inc., 1958. Pp. 55–150.

Potter, Robert E., *The Stream of American Education*. New York: American Book Company, 1967. Pp. 441–471.

Pounds, Ralph L., *The Development of Education in Western Culture*. New York: Appleton-Century-Crofts, 1968. Pp. 166–187.

Raywid, Mary Anne, *The Ax-Grinders, Critics of Our Public Schools*. New York: Crowell-Collier and Macmillan, Inc., 1963.

Rugg, Harold, *Foundations of American Education*. New York: Harcourt, Brace & World, Inc., 1947.

Tolstoy, Count Leo, *Tolstoy on Education*. Trans. by Leo Wiener. Chicago: University of Chicago Press, 1967.

Trubowitz, Sidney, *A Handbook for Teaching in the Ghetto School*. Chicago: Quadrangle Books, 1968.

Ulich, Robert, *History of Educational Thought*. New York: American Book Company, 1950. Pp. 315–345.

——— (Ed.), *Three Thousand Years of Educational Wisdom*, 2d ed. enl. Cambridge, Mass.: Harvard University Press, 1954.

Valentine, P. F., *Twentieth Century Education*. New York: Philosophical Library, Inc., 1946. Pp. 42–68, 89–113, 482–654.

Washburne, Carleton, *A Living Philosophy of Education*. New York: The John Day Company, Inc., 1940.

Weber, Christian O., *Basic Philosophies of Education*. New York: Holt, Rinehart and Winston, Inc., 1960. Pp. 239–285, 303–322.

Wecter, Dixon, *The Age of the Great Depression*. New York: Crowell-Collier and Macmillan, Inc., 1948.

SELECTED PAPERBACKS

Backman, Carl W., and Paul F. Secord, *A Social Psychological View of Education*. New York: Harcourt, Brace & World, Inc., 1968.

Beck, Robert Holmes, *A Social History of Education*. Englewood Cliffs, N.J.: Prentice-Hall, Inc., 1965.

Bell, Howard M., *Youth Tell Their Story*. Washington, D.C.: American Council on Education, 1938.

Conant, James B., *Slums and Suburbs*. New York: McGraw-Hill, Inc., 1961.

Cremin, Lawrence A., *The Transformation of the School—Progressivism in American Education, 1876–1957*. New York: Random House, Inc., Vintage Books, 1964.

Curti, Merle, *The Social Ideas of American Educators*, rev. ed. Totowa, N.J.: Littlefield, Adams and Company, 1959.

Duker, Sam, *The Public Schools and Religion. The Legal Context*. New York: Harper & Row, Publishers, 1966.

Education for All American Youth. Washington, D.C.: National Education Association, 1944. A report of NEA's Educational Policies Commission.

Education and Economic Well-Being in American Democracy. Washington, D.C.: National Education Association, 1940. A report of the Educational Policies Commission.

Fiedler, Leslie A., and Jacob Vinocur, *The Continuing Debate, Essays on Education for Freshmen*. New York: St. Martin's Press, Inc., 1964.

From Rote to Reason. Washington, D.C.: The Peace Corps, 1968.

Goldston, Robert, *The Negro Revolution*. New York: New American Library of World Literature, Inc., 1968.

Greene, Maxine, *The Public School and the Private Vision*. New York: Random House, Inc., 1965.

Hofstadter, Richard, *The Progressive Movement, 1900–1915*. Englewood Cliffs, N.J.: Prentice-Hall, Inc., 1963.

Johnson, Robert H., and John J. Hunt, *Prescription for Team Teaching*. Minneapolis: Burgess Publishing Co., 1968.

Koerner, James D., *The Miseducation of American Teachers*. Boston: Houghton Mifflin Company, 1963.

Life Adjustment for Every Youth. Washington, D.C.: Federal Security Agency, Office of Education, 1951.

Mayer, Frederick, *Foundations of Education*. Columbus, Ohio: Charles E. Merrill Books, Inc., 1963.

———, *Introductory Readings in Education*. Belmont, Calif.: Dickinson Publishing Company, Inc., 1966.

Nash, Paul, *Models of Man. Explorations in the Western Educational Tradition*. New York: John Wiley & Sons, Inc., 1968.

Neill, A. S., *Summerhill: A Radical Approach to Child Rearing*. New York: Hart Publishing Company, 1960.

Phenix, Philip H. (Ed.), *Philosophies of Education*. New York: John Wiley & Sons, Inc., 1961.

The Purposes of Education in American Democracy. Washington, D.C.: National Education Association, 1938. A report by the Educational Policies Commission.

Remmling, Gunter W., *Road to Suspicion, A Study of Modern Mentality and the Sociology of Knowledge*. New York: Appleton-Century-Crofts, 1967.

Rippa, S. Alexander, *Education in a Free Society*. New York: David McKay Company, Inc. Pp. 233–257, 258–282.

Rugg, Harold, and William Withers, *Social Foundations of Education*. Englewood Cliffs, N.J.: Prentice-Hall, Inc., 1955.

Tyack, David B. (Ed.), *Turning Points in American Educational History*. Waltham, Mass.: Blaisdell Publishing Company, 1967. Pp. 314–351.

The Unique Function of Education in American Democracy. Washington, D.C.: National Education Association, 1937.

CHAPTER 20

American Education in the War Decades

One stumbling block [to universal schooling] has been the inevitable impoverishment in the results of education when the process is made available for the masses at the cost of being divorced from its traditional cultural background. The good intentions of Democracy have no magic power to perform the miracle of the loaves and fishes. Our mass-produced intellectual pablum lacks savor and vitamins.[1]

AN UNCERTAIN VICTORY

Victory for the West in World War II implied that the democratic idea (and education in democratic principles) had prevailed. With the cessation of hostilities in 1945 the totalitarian governments in Germany, Italy, and Japan were overthrown and republican regimes instituted. The educational systems also were revised in accordance with democratic principles, although in each case the organization was somewhat more class-oriented than in the United States. Toynbee's comment, given in the first flush of victorious excitement, proved only a slight immediate hazard, but it held some grave implications for the future.

In Europe and Asia the danger from totalitarianism was far from vanquished. By the end of the war's European phase the Soviet Union had moved its army and institutions into ten countries in East Central Europe and (although under the terms originally agreed upon by the Grand Alliance) occupied the eastern sector of Germany, erecting another

---

[1] Arnold J. Toynbee, *A Study of History* (New York: Oxford University Press, 1946).

people's democracy, a carbon copy of the Soviet system. Communist totalitarian education was imposed in each of these settings.[2]

Politically the situation worsened steadily and by as early as 1947 the cold war, between the Soviet-controlled bloc and the Western democracies, was in effect. When the former Republic of China (with the exception of the island of Taiwan, or Formosa) became Communist and adopted Marxist collectivism, the peril increased.

Indeed, many educational thinkers in the United States felt that the aims fostered in the stress of World War II were the only guarantee against softness and inefficiency should a deteriorating international situation result in another appeal to arms, a terrifying third world war.

The resurgence of the Communist advocacy of a world-state, especially since the Soviet seizure of East Europe and the emergence of mainland China as a world power, has led to a certain apprehension, at least among conservatives, in the United States. Curti notes the "great gulf between Communism and the western form of democracy" that has produced the cold war:

> This in turn has been in part responsible for the conservative mood of America in the post-war era. It has expressed itself, so far as education goes, in many ways. One has been the closer relations between American business and education . . . but the chief example of the relation between the conservative mood of the country and education has been the retreat of the idea that the school can and should take the lead in initiating and implementing social reform.[3]

Explicit reference to the social experimentalists who, at the time of the Great Depression, suggested that the school act as an advance agent for social and political blueprinting clearly indicates the changed educational climate of the immediate postwar years. That other events might shake this certainty was not apparent in 1959 when Curti wrote.

Although World War II had been fought to obliterate totalitarianism and thought-control tactics, the upsweep of Communism which followed presented an ominous picture. By the end of 1949 all of mainland China had come under Communist control, a Soviet-type people's republic had been established, and in 1950–1953 the Korean conflict occurred as the Chinese attempted to drive the United States and United Nations forces

---

[2] See Winston S. Churchill, *Triumph and Tragedy* (Boston: Houghton Mifflin Company, 1953). The overrun countries in East Central Europe, the so-called Iron Curtain countries, are Estonia, Latvia, Lithuania, Poland, Czechoslovakia, Hungary, Romania, Bulgaria, Albania, and Yugoslavia (although the last frequently operates independently of Moscow). The Soviet-occupied section of Germany has likewise been designated a Communist satellite, the German Democratic Republic.

[3] Merle Curti, *The Social Ideas of American Educators*, enl. ed. (New York: Pageant Books, Inc., 1959), pp. xxxii, xxxiii.

from that peninsula. A somewhat similar confrontation was to occur in Vietnam in the 1960s.

Students of education must grasp the threat of Communism to objective truth and to democratic education as the West understands it. For grave though the political aspect of Communism appears, this menace is far greater in its attacks on the mind as well as the body. The so-called brain-washing tactics heavily utilized during the Korean affair are well known to students of psychology; that this species of thought-control is inherent in Leninism-Marxism and in its system of education is less well known.

In order to visualize the power of this Communist drive through the senses one must review the materialist origins of the Marxist-Leninist movement. Although indebted to Karl Marx (1818–1883), the German political and economic writer, author of *Das Kapital* and, with Friedrich Engels, *The Communist Manifesto*, the groundwork for a Communist state to be constructed on utopian lines had already been conceived by nineteenth-century Russian revolutionary leaders. Its necessity was a new man "possessed neither of patriotism nor of pity; his only faith in the revolution itself, and in this fanatic . . . a man who regarded himself as expendable, who followed blindly the leader and the party line, and who if need be would lie, cheat and murder to gain his objective."[4] Communism, then, became and remains a secular faith and from this fact springs its power.

Ivan Sergeyevich Turgenev, the Russian novelist, has put this peculiar fascination of Marxist extremism into words:

—To you who desire to cross this threshold, do you know what awaits you?
—I know, replied the girl.
—Cold, hunger, abhorrence, derision, contempt, abuse, prison, disease and death!
—I know, I am ready, I shall endure all blows.
—Not from enemies alone, but also from relatives, from friends.
—Yes, even from them. . . .
—Are you ready to commit a crime?
—I am ready for crime, too.
—Do you know that you may be disillusioned in that which you believe, that you may discover that you were mistaken, that you ruined your young life in vain?
—I know that too.
—Enter!
—The girl crossed the threshold and a heavy curtain fell behind her.

[4] Alan Moorehead, *The Russian Revolution* (New York: Harper & Row, Publishers, 1958) p. 33.

—Fool! said someone gnashing his teeth.
—Saint! someone uttered in reply.[5]

Communism thus assumes the status of a religion to its followers; since the education systems of the Communist bloc are designed for the perpetuation of Marxist principles and world revolution, the West faces a grave threat. This, as noted earlier, has already partially conditioned educational thinking away from its prewar emphases on progressivism and child-centeredness.

THE ROAD TO ESSENTIALISM

In the United States following World War II, opposition to progressivist and popularist tendencies made greater headway. A new group of critics appeared and venerable Harvard produced a lengthy study indicating the need for stemming the tide of popularism.[6] The two forces in American education are sometimes designated as Jeffersonian (the more traditional, idealistic, and academic tendency) and Jacksonian (the pragmatic, vocational, and popular at its most extreme stage). In general the essentialists may be called Jeffersonian, and the progressives Jacksonian.[7]

Jacksonianism, far from dead, was especially visible in the vogue for life adjustment, a development originally fostered at the close of the war by the division of vocational education of the United States Office of Education. Charles A. Prosser, a member of one of the groups called for the purpose of formulating the platform and objectives of the movement, introduced a resolution indicating that the consensus of the conference was that at least 60 percent of the students of secondary school age could not find opportunity for the training they needed in the conventional schools. This appeared to demand an entirely new program for secondary education; at a later time the use of percentages was dropped, and the request for "Life Adjustment Education for Every Youth" was made general.[8]

---

[5] As quoted by Moorehead from *The Threshold*. B. P. Yesipov and N. K. Goncharov, *I Want to Be Like Stalin*, trans. by George S. Counts and Nucia P. Lodge (New York: The John Day Company, Inc., 1947), ch. ii, "For Bolshevik Character," pp. 42–52, stresses the development of the Communist mentality.

[6] *General Education in a Free Society* (Cambridge: Harvard University Press, 1945).

[7] *General Education in a Free Society*, pp. 27–35, expresses the view that the Jeffersonian-Jacksonian terminology is perhaps "unfair to Jefferson's express interest in the citizen-farmer and artisan" but goes on to emphasize his attachment to selection of the ablest through education as revealed in his famous plan for Virginia proposed in 1779.

[8] See *Life Adjustment Education for Every Youth*, Bulletin no. 22 (Washington, D.C.: Federal Security Agency, Office of Education, 1951); also Harl R. Douglass (Ed.), *Education for Life Adjustment: Its Meaning and Implementation* (New York: The Ronald Press Company, 1950).

The concept life adjustment called forth mixed and formidable reactions. In one camp Prosser and his group were accused of favoring whittled-down, Mickey Mouse courses for the majority of American high school students; in the other it was as strongly argued that life adjustment meant a solidly pragmatic vocational curriculum geared to individual life-expectancy needs, a naturalistic personally-effective approach with no frills or deferred goals.

This is not to say that Jacksonianism had again gained the ascendancy. Life adjustment, however, won enough adherents to serve as an agency for crystallizing educational thought and thus contributed to the necessity for a thorough reappraisal of American educational practice.

A second result of pressure from without (although this direction may indeed owe much to the social doctrination of the earlier depression years) was the new accent on anti-individualism and conformity. Curti notes that "in becoming increasingly corporate in character American life and values stressed the importance of teamwork, of conformity to the group norm, of reducing conflict in personal and group relations . . . summed up in such slogans for 'other-directedness,' 'the organization man,' and 'togetherness'."[9]

Simply put, the thesis of this new direction, first cited by David Riesman[10] several years ago, is this: Three stages in value formation may be detected throughout the past 1000 or so years of Western civilization. The first, tradition-centered, lasted until around 1500; it was replaced by an inner-directed urge based on individualism and inner compulsion (this appears to have been the wellspring of Puritanism, and the Calvinistic ethos); however, within recent years, reported Riesman (and this may have incubated during the Depression or in the early postwar era at the latest), a third orientation has gained ground. This is "other-directedness," seemingly a reversal of the value formation index of earlier American life.

Riesman is not alone in his perception of other-direction, especially as applied to the business world in the United States; this is revealed by the spate of contemporary novels and motion pictures which deal with these phenomena in realistic fashion. The reader is directed to the offerings of John P. Marquand, Cameron Hawley, Sloan Wilson, Frederic Wakesman, William H. Whyte, and others for this contemporary view.

This philosophy, which undoubtedly owed a debt of some kind to one of the various existential movements, found favor with the younger

---

[9] Curti, p. xxxvi.

[10] David Riesman, Nathan Glazer, Reuel Denney, *The Lonely Crowd, A Study of the Changing American Character* (New Haven: Yale University Press, 1950). David Riesman and Nathan Glazer, *Faces in the Crowd* (New Haven: Yale University Press, 1952); David Riesman, *Constraint and Variety in American Education* (Lincoln, Neb.: University of Nebraska Press, 1956).

adults and some adolescents. The presence of the world-owes-me-a-living type, the Beatnik, inhabitant of the Blackboard Jungle, the general feeling of "living for today" prevalent in certain sectors of American life in the sixties seems to corroborate Curti's diagnosis.

That other-directedness has already conditioned American schools is not admitted, although the recent vogue for so-called life adjustment courses rather than the conventional elements of the more formal curriculum may be submitted as evidence of a tendency to anti-individualism.

There are, nevertheless, new American educational leaders who view education from the strictly Jeffersonian vantage point. And in the present mood of conservation and caution their advice may be followed.

James B. Conant, former President of Harvard, and Paul Woodring, of Western Washington College and formerly with the Ford Foundation, offer plans for the reorganization of American public education.[11] In deference to the broadness of the essentialist definition they too may be placed in this camp. Woodring's design is far to the right and Conant, too, would remove many of the soft electives in the high school through a stricter series of required subjects and prerequisites. Arthur E. Bestor's Council for Basic Education, organized in 1956, stands even further to the right and would, in effect, revive most of the curriculum and practices of the early twentieth century.

Leadership of the essentialist camp (comprising, for our purposes, both idealists and realists) has included William C. Bagley, Arthur E. Bestor, Franklin Bobbitt, William W. Brickman, Thomas H. Briggs, Harry C. Broudy, James B. Conant, Harold Clapp, Michael John Demiashkevich, Hermann Harrell Horne, Robert M. Hutchins, Charles H. Judd, Isaac L. Kandel, Henry C. Morrison, Robert Ulich, and Paul Woodring.[12]

ESSENTIALISM AND PERENNIALISM

While it is easiest to identify the opponents of progressivism (and reconstructionism) as traditionalists, a sharper definition would characterize those at the extreme right as perennialists and the moderate traditionalists as essentialists, and this would recognize their philosophical position

---

[11] James B. Conant, *The American High School Today* (New York: McGraw-Hill, Inc., 1959). Paul Woodring, *A Fourth of a Nation* (New York: McGraw-Hill, Inc., 1957). See also his *Let's Talk Sense about Our Schools* (New York: McGraw-Hill, Inc., 1953).

[12] Although Bagley was perhaps the most prominent of the *essentialists*, credit for the origination of the term (in 1935) usually is granted to Demiashkevich. For an excellent interpretation of these basic American educational positions, see James C. Stone and Frederick W. Schneider, *Commitment to Teaching*, vol. i, *Foundations of Education* (New York: Thomas Y. Crowell Company, 1965), pp. 25–48, 217–239.

as well. By the older terminology, both moralists and disciplinists would be included with the traditionalists; naturalists, of course, would share the progressives' position on the more liberal left. The *Jeffersonians are the traditionalists* and the *Jacksonians are the advocates of popularism in education.*

Progressivism was strongest before and during the Great Depression. With the threat of war, essentialism appeared to gain ground. Thus, when war actually began in Europe in the fall of 1939 and the democracies were threatened with destruction by the totalitarian powers, the doctrine of essentialism was greatly strengthened and given new support.

William C. Bagley (1874–1946), who was recognized as the leader of the essentialists in education in 1938 when the controversy between the progressives and essentialists first appeared in national discussion, championed his position as a necessity for a nation faced with possible ruin from the strongest combination of powers yet to oppose the democratic tradition. Bagley said:

> The essentialists are sure that if our democratic society is to meet the conflict with totalitarian states, there must be a discipline that will give strength to the democratic purpose and ideal. If the theory of democracy finds no place for discipline, then before long the theory will have only historical significance. The essentialists stand for a literate electorate. That such an electorate is indispensable to its survival is demonstrated by the fate that overtook every unschooled democracy founded as a result of the war that was 'to make the world safe for democracy'. . . . Essentialism provides a strong theory of education; its competing school offers a weak theory. If there has been a question in the past as to the kind of educational theory the few remaining democracies of the world need, there can be no question today.[13]

Bagley, though far from being a reactionary or an extreme conservative, stood in opposition to radical and extreme tendencies in American education. In an earlier chapter we noted that he was influential in checking the extremes of the scientific movement. He was respected and followed because of his long years of educational leadership and accomplishment. He was Professor of Education and Dean of the School of Education at the University of Illinois from 1908 to 1917, and at Teachers College, Columbia University, from 1917 until 1940, when he retired from active teaching. He is the author of such influential books as *The Educative Process, Classroom Management, Educational Values, School Discipline, Determinism in Education, Education, Crime, and Social Progress,* and *Education and the Emergent Man.* Bagley was editor of the Modern

---

[13] William C. Bagley, "The Case for Essentialism in Education," *The Journal of the National Educational Association,* vol. 30, no. 7 (October 1941), pp. 201–202.

Teachers' series published by The Macmillan Company, and was for many years editor of *Educational Administration and Supervision*. In 1939, he was instrumental in the organization of the Society for the Advancement of American Education, becoming its secretary. He was the editor of its official publication, *School and Society*, and a member of its Essentialist Committee.

Although picking up strength during and following World War II, the essentialist cause suffered serious losses in leadership with the deaths of Bagley, Judd, and Horne in 1946; Morrison had preceded this illustrious trio in 1945. Influential men remained, in Kandel, Hutchins, and Robert Ulich of Harvard, but for a few years opposition to progressivism did not flourish. In the next decade, however, the former controversy burst forth with a vengeance.

Among those who sought to indict what they felt were contrary currents in the schools, especially the fad for life adjustment courses, were Albert S. Lynd, Mortimer Smith, John Keats and Bestor. Lynd's account, "Quackery in the Public Schools," drew a great deal of attention; Smith wrote *And Madly Teach;* Keats deplored *Schools Without Scholars*. Bestor, then Professor of History at the University of Illinois, attacked in several new directions: the "certification racket," by which he meant required education courses; the growing hierarchy of administrative personnel in the public schools; and he cited instances of poor teaching and subject-matter dilution.[14]

In the last instance Bestor followed the lead of the generally accepted essentialist philosophy. While, as could be expected, significant variations in philosophy exist among the essentialists they are as one in prescribing the following rubrics for their educational program:

1.   A fixed curriculum;

2.   Certain minimum "essentials": literature, mathematics, history, and so on;

3.   Preconceived educational values;

4.   Education as individual adaptation to an absolute knowledge which exists independently of individuals.[15]

---

[14] See Arthur E. Bestor, *Educational Wastelands* (Urbana, Ill.: University of Illinois Press, 1953); *The Restoration of Learning* (New York: Alfred A. Knopf, 1955). See also William W. Brickman, "Essentialism Ten Years After," *School and Society*, vol. 67, no. 1742 (May 15, 1948), pp. 361–365, a plea for rejuvenated leadership in the essentialist cause. In opposition, Mary Anne Raywid, *The Ax-Grinders, Critics of Our Public Schools* (New York: Crowell-Collier and Macmillan, Inc., 1963), presents profiles of the attackers and describes in detail cases of aggression at Tenafly, N.J. and in Montgomery County, Md.

[15] According to Raywid, the "critics of our public schools" disagreed most vehemently with progressives' attitudes (in the following order) toward curriculum, costs, aims, values, methods, professional organization, administration, teacher education, and textbooks.

Although it will be easily seen that items three and four especially identify the idealistic wing of essentialism, the realists, by no means, eschew inherent values, although they usually choose to emphasize content and organization.

The interpretation of realism as supplied by Harry S. Broudy (which he calls classical realism) may be noted here, for it provides considerable assistance in producing an understanding of what has been labeled Essentialism in this text. Broudy's emphasis "accepts as regulative principles the idea of a truth independent of the knower, and the idea of structures in the universe, man, and society that are normative for man's striving toward the good life and for the education that will help him achieve it"; its foundation, "the fundamental notions about the structure of human personality, its goals, and its destiny are adaptations of the theories of Plato and Aristotle." Broudy maintains that "this role does not point to the traditional school, but rather to a curriculum, organization, and methodology that tries to take account of the contributions of psychology, the science of education, and the more basic contribution of Dewey's Instrumentalism."[16]

Perhaps this identification serves as well as any to pull together the various interpretations and positions of those we have denominated essentialists.[17] Clearly the differences in orientation are of much less significance than their agreements.

One of the most vocal opponents of American education as it developed during and after the Great Depression was Vice Admiral H. S. Rickover; his suggestions for improvement included the rigid program advocated by all essentialists plus tougher courses and teaching procedures. Rickover, in order to strengthen the program still further, called for the imposition of "national standards," a device quite foreign to conventional American thinking.[18] Bestor was vocal too and most influential in founding the Council for Basic Education, an organization devoted to disseminating the ideas of Bestor, Mortimer Smith, and others. Its recent president, James D. Koerner, in a symposium participated in by Woodring and T. M.

---

[16] Harry S. Broudy, *Building a Philosophy of Education* (Englewood Cliffs, N.J.: Prentice-Hall, Inc., 1954), p. viii.

[17] See Christian O. Weber, *Basic Philosophies of Education* (New York: Holt, Rinehart and Winston, Inc., 1960), ch. 3, "Essentialism and Traditionalism," pp. 35–45; also Robert E. Mason, *Educational Ideals in American Society* (Boston: Allyn and Bacon, Inc., 1960), pp. 41–51; for a thorough discussion of the currents of American educational philosophy during the years which followed World War II, see *School and Society*, vol. 87, no. 2145 (January 17, 1959). Especially valuable are accounts by Ernest E. Bayles, Theodore Brameld, J. Donald Butler, Harry S. Broudy, and Foster McMurray.

[18] See H. S. Rickover, "European vs. American Secondary Schools," *Phi Delta Kappan*, vol. 40, no. 2 (November, 1958), pp. 60–64, *Education and Freedom* (New York: E. P. Dutton & Co., Inc., 1959), and his *Swiss Schools and Ours* (Boston: Little, Brown & Company, 1962). Rickover gives curriculum samples and lists of examination questions.

Stinnett attempts to clarify the role of education in modern American society. He prefaces his own words by quoting Susanne Langer:

"To determine the aims of education is probably the most urgent philosophical problem in the whole pedagogical field today; and it cannot but draw in vast further questions of the aims of human societies, the ultimate values that set up these aims, our basic ideas of society and individual life. . . ."

Then Koerner himself says:

. . . the crisis of American education is at bottom a philosophical one. It is a crisis of purpose, of the definition of goals, and we should not avoid this fact in any talk about contemporary teacher training. . . . We might look again at the four fundamental positions that have been taken in America about universal education. . . .

[First, there is the Jeffersonian view echoed today] in the writings of James Bryant Conant and of many academicians. . . .

[Then there is the Deweyan] view of education as "process" and indiscriminate "growth" [which] is still strongly held, I believe, by very large numbers, perhaps the majority, of professional educators.

At the other end of the spectrum is the [traditionalist] view best represented and most eloquently set forth by Albert Jay Nock. . . .

Finally, there is the view, best represented perhaps by Robert Maynard Hutchins, that almost all children are capable of sustained academic study and that it is the proper business of a public school system to give this study to them through the medium of what Matthew Arnold called "the best that has been thought and said in the world." In this system all students run on the same track but at their own best speeds; and all concentrate their education in a relatively few areas that encompass the most significant of man's knowledge. It is a competitive system, authoritarian if you like in about the same degree as those of Jefferson and Nock, and built on strong assumptions about the importance of priorities in education and on a highly optimistic assessment of the intellectual possibilities of most men.

Obviously, these four positions, those of Jefferson, Dewey, Nock, and Hutchins do not exhaust the field, but they do represent the fundamental positions with which most others that influence modern education—Maritain, Whitehead or Kilpatrick—have a clear affinity. It is important to remind ourselves that all such views are statements of position, not of fact. They tend to be hortatory, histrionic, and proselytic. Each of them must appeal for support to the collective experience of the race and each is at heart an act of faith not closely related to observable, measurable phenomena. . . .

Let me, then, turn to the question of what rationale seems to me the most valid today for the education of Americans and by extension the education of American teachers. I would not dignify my argument as a "philosophy of education" or even a theory, but I would defend it as a reasonable analysis and a practical program. . . .

It follows, I believe, that man's best hope for his future lies in the maximum cultivation within each person of these uniquely human endowments, for only in this way do we have much chance of narrowing the gap between the real and the ideal. If it is true, as Santayana once suggested, that "perhaps the only true dignity of man is his capacity to despise himself," it is true only because of man's peculiar capacity to see how far short he still falls of his possibilities, how wide the gulf still is between his achievements and his potential, between what is and what might be. The job of education, I believe, is to bridge this gulf.[19]

If Rickover, Bestor, and Koerner may be noted as the best propagandists, then James B. Conant may be considered the most effective agent in securing public and professional acceptance of the essentialist views. Conant's background as an educator and public figure lent stature and dignity to his part of the movement; his thoroughness and obvious devotion to the preservation of the American public, state-controlled, junior and senior high schools were convincing; it appeared that many of his ideas for improvement would be put into practice.[20]

The positions of Mortimer Adler, Ulich, and of idealism generally, will be discussed in a later section, as will that of Paul Goodman, whose *Compulsory Mis-Education* aroused quite a furor in the middle sixties.

EDUCATIONAL ATTITUDES OF THE ESSENTIALISTS

Aims

The essentialists, like the realists of the seventeenth century, have as their ultimate aim "to fit the man to perform justly, skillfully, and magnanimously all the offices, both private and public, of peace and war." In fact, there are those who designate this movement the new realism, setting up as the purpose of education "the adjustment of the pupil to the actual demands of a real external world." For example, Frederick S. Breed states:

> The demands of "environment," of "life," or "society," of "school" and "curriculum" . . . are easily seen to represent in essence the independent objects postulated by the realist, the scientist, and the common man. . . . They are taken deeply to heart if one starts with realistic premises. The source of compulsion and requirement in education . . . is found ultimately to originate in the independent reals with which personality must deal and to which it must make the most endurable or

[19] "Theory and Experience in the Education of Teachers," in American Association of Colleges for Teacher Education, *Strength Through Reappraisal, Sixteenth Yearbook, 1963 Annual Meeting* (Washington, D.C.: American Association of Colleges for Teacher Education, 1964), pp. 15–16.
[20] Of Conant's many works, *The American High School Today* was perhaps the most influential.

satisfactory adjustment. From such a point of view the problem of education, as of life, becomes that of establishing for the individual the most effectual relationships with an environing world, . . .[21]

Bagley, the prophet of this new realism, stated its fundamental admonition thus:

> Should not our public schools prepare boys and girls for adult responsibility through systematic training in such subjects as reading, writing, arithmetic, history, and English, requiring mastery of such subjects and, when necessary, stressing discipline and obedience?[22]

The essentialists do not believe that the essential skills, knowledge, and attitudes needed by the individual in making his adjustment to the realities of life will be gained incidentally. The essentialist insists that adult direction of the immature is necessary and inherent in human nature; that it is the real meaning of the child's long period of dependence on adult care and support; that this plastic period of dependency furnishes opportunities for inducting the young into the heritage of culture. The indispensable cultural objectives of humanity, commonly referred to as essentials, are goals that must be achieved, sometimes incidentally, but more often by direct instruction. The essentialist insists that teachers must be responsible for systematic programs of studies and systematically planned activities in order that the recognized essentials be acquired.

Most essentialists agree that informal learning can share in the attainment of such objectives, but believe that this should always be supplementary and secondary. Most of these essentials are more exacting; they generally require more effort and attention than is provided in the project or activity curriculum. Judd advocated "wise guidance of immature minds" as the aim of education, and raised the question, "Why should we deny children the right and even the duty to adopt the orderly mental arrangements that the race has given to the experiences of life?"

The essentialists, as realists, are concerned with the building of "competencies" in the individual, competencies of mind and body and spirit to meet all the needs, even the emergencies, of life. With the outbreak of hostilities in Europe, and especially after the United States entry into the war in 1941, the emphasis upon a more competent people became pronounced in our country. The Educational Policies Commission declared:

> American education faces a momentous decision . . . it can, if it will, come to grips with the needs of the hour, and direct its vast resources to the task of increasing the civic understanding, the loyalties and the intellectual competence of millions of citizens, with speed and efficiency matched to the exigencies of the time. . . . The home defense which the

---

[21] *Education and the New Realism* (New York: Crowell-Collier and Macmillan, Inc., 1939), pp. 123–124.

[22] See his *A Century of the Universal School* (New York: Crowell-Collier and Macmillan, Inc., 1937), pp. 73–77.

American people must now organize, requires a strategy which is more subtle than the blunt appeal to armed might. It requires, to be sure, close attention to direct military preparedness, as such. It requires also the training of every worker to the highest possible level of effectiveness, and the useful employment of every worker in tasks of importance. It requires confidence in the sincerity and reliability of one's fellow citizens and comradeship in the common search for solutions to the nation's problems. It requires, above all, that common understanding of aims and procedures which leads to united and effective action. Of such elements is the defense of our democracy to be built. In the building of it the schools of America are ready and determined to play their part.[23]

Thus the philosophy of essentialism had its aims greatly reinforced by a realistic recognition of the needs of a people faced with world conflict. The school, as well as the nation as a whole, set up as its goal the preservation of democracy and directed its whole attention toward developing the skills, knowledge, and attitudes essential to this tremendous task, a necessity which was to continue during the decades of the cold war.

At about the same time New York State completed a comprehensive study of education known as the Regents' Inquiry, directed by an agency of the state education department. The results were included in a twelve-volume report and suggested a greater need for guidance, adequate background in reading, oral and written expression, and arithmetic, as well as some preparation for after-high-school cultural and vocational adjustment.[24] Since the various reports appeared at approximately the beginning of World War II it is probable that their influence was somewhat curtailed.

The perennialist views education as a recurring process based on eternal truths, and as such his essentials include the traditional materials of the curriculum. He believes that the literature and the art, the social life and political life, of the peoples of the past will throw much light upon our problems of the present. Robert M. Hutchins, formerly President of the University of Chicago, believes that the study of the great classics serve this purpose. In our zeal for the more immediate essentials of education, we must not neglect these broader and more general needs of our students.

Roman Catholic and other parochial educationalists adhere firmly to perennialism, but utilize religious philosophy and subject matter in their teaching. Their view that the truth is the same yesterday, today, and tomorrow and that its verities have been revealed through the sacred presence makes them intolerant of naturalist, pragmatic, and social education. Catholic thought especially opposes the teaching of history on economic or strictly political grounds, citing the "need to associate the Divine

---

[23] *Education and the Defense of American Democracy* (Washington, D.C.: National Education Association, 1940), pp. 21, 23.

[24] See Francis T. Spaulding, *High School and Life: Report of the Regents' Inquiry* (New York: McGraw-Hill, Inc., 1940).

Tradition with the legitimate heritage of human values and human culture
. . . saving the world from the demolition of Voltaire and Marx."[25] It considers entrepreneurial theories of history debased and stresses the superiority
of moral judgment over economic judgment; it presents history as "philosophy teaching by examples."

Types

Basically, the essentialists were concerned with a revival of efforts
in the direction of teaching the fundamental tools of learning as the most
indispensable type of education. Since investigations had suggested that
many high school and college students were woefully weak in such fundamental skills as reading, spelling, penmanship, and arithmetic, schools were
urged to make them their dominant concern. With the development of the
emergency, this type of training continued to be emphasized as of primary
importance in the defense of democracy, but other kinds of education were
also recognized as essential for this purpose.

In response to many requests from teachers and administrators
regarding the types of education to be stressed during the emergency, the
United States Office of Education in July, 1941, issued a bulletin in its
series on education and national defense under the title, *What the Schools
Can Do.* Action along six fronts was recommended to schools planning
to adapt their programs to the needs of the time: (1) health and physical
education; (2) education for citizenship; (3) education in community,
national, and international relationships; (4) education in the conservation
of national resources; (5) education for work; and (6) education for
personal adjustment.

Physical health has long been recognized as an essential type of education, although it is only in recent decades that the schools have assumed
much responsibility for its development. The early Greeks, Locke in the
seventeenth century, and Spencer in the nineteenth made sound physical
health one of the basic essentials of their educational programs. War always
highlights the need for marked attention to the health, physical well-being,
and mental hygiene of children and of youth. War-minded nations never
neglect this type of education. Health and physical fitness is an absolute
essential for military service both at the front abroad and behind the lines
at home. The physical examinations of 1939 selectees revealed the deplor-
able prevalence of physical defects in our American youth that was discovered in World War I, and aroused schools to the necessity for increased
attention to this type of education. Health, however, is always an essential
for human happiness and efficiency, and must continue as a definite part
of the educational program.

In the summer of 1940, the federal government made appropriations

---

[25] See Christopher Dawson, *The Historic Reality of Christian Culture, A Way to
the Renewal of Human Life* (New York: Harper & Row, Publishers, Inc., 1960, pp.
62, 107–108.

for a summer training program in schools and colleges for workers essential to defense industries. Late in the fall of the same year additional appropriations were made for the training in vocational schools, rural schools, high schools, colleges, and universities of both youths and adults for defense production. Established vocational and trade schools made their facilities available for defense classes, and many new schools were established by the federal agencies. Most of these schools operated on a twenty-four-hour, six-days-a-week basis. Instructors were usually selected on the basis of their practical experience in the trades, and adult trainees were recruited from unemployed men registered with government employment services and from WPA employees. The Civilian Pilot Training Program contributed much to the training of the military flying forces. During the cold war the programs of the Peace Corps and VISTA have been educational to teacher and student.

One of the most essential types of education for war and peace is civic education. It has been a chief concern of educational leaders to promote such understanding, not because other types of education are not vital and important, but because civic enlightenment and citizenship training are even more important in times of domestic unrest than in actual war, when society is by necessity much more regimented. For in the absence of a strong unifying force such as civic education can provide, we would be very likely to lose hard-gained freedom and slip into a regimentation that is as totalitarian as the present menaces to democracy. Citizenship education for all levels of people is just as essential for the preservation of democracy as the industrial and military training of workers and soldiers is for the immobilization of its enemies. Thus, civic education is the first bulwark of internal defense.

From the beginning of the essentialist acceleration—about 1940—realists have insisted upon the provision of craft experiences for most American youth as an essential part of the school's business. Vocational education, especially in the mechanical arts, is being recognized as a requisite to national well-being and security. To supplement or complement the work of the conventional American high school, the Job Corps program, for training or retraining in vocational efficiencies was put into operation in the sixties.

But it is easily possible to overlook the fact that cultural types of education are also essential. The schools must always seek to raise the educational level of the people by providing training to both youth and adults in music, the fine arts, literature, architecture, and home decoration. Cultural education and education in the humanities are doubly essential in times of stress and strain. It is essential that we then impart something of the vital experiences of the human race so that our people may be better able to solve their common problems. The study of history, for example, "may so accumulate years to us as though we had lived from the beginning of time."

Content

Essentialists emphasize the need for a curriculum that transmits significant race experiences, and they believe that this racial experience should be presented to the pupils largely through organized subject-matter courses. They favor the use of individual personal experiences merely as a means toward the end of interpreting this organized racial experience. While it is not their purpose to go back to the formalism and verbalism of an earlier day, they do believe that subject matter can be logically organized and still be presented psychologically, and that there is a definite place in education for exact and exacting studies. They are particularly concerned with the fundamentals of education, the skills and knowledge without which a person cannot be either individually or socially efficient.

Yet there is great variation about what these essentials are among the educators we have considered traditionalist, as opposed to progressive, or left. Hutchins and Adler would seek the essentials for living in the great books. Morrison developed a curriculum, broad and extensive, based upon what he considered the essentials for common living. Parochialists base their content on the eternal verities. The moderates, led by Judd and Bagley, take a realistic view. Bagley says:

> There can be little question as to the essentials. It is no accident that the arts of recordings, computing, and measuring have been among the first concerns of organized education. Every civilized society has been founded upon these arts, and when they have been lost, civilization has invariably collapsed. Nor is it accidental that a knowledge of the world that lies beyond one's immediate experience has been among the recognized essentials of universal education, and that at least a speaking acquaintance with man's past and especially with the story of one's country was early provided for in the program of the universal school. Investigation, invention, and creative art have added to our heritage. Health instruction is a basic phase of the work of the lower schools. The elements of natural science have their place. Neither the fine arts nor the industrial arts should be neglected.[26]

Thus reading, writing, arithmetic, grammar, history, geography, hygiene, elementary science, drawing, language, art, manual training, domestic arts—all the traditional subjects of the elementary school—are given a new justification and a new emphasis as basic essentials in the training of children.

In a democracy everyone should be able to read and write, yet a shocking amount of illiteracy has existed in our country. The revelation of the facts of the selective service examinations in two world wars has awakened us again to the importance of this problem in relation to national defense. In one state 35,000 young men had to sign their registration cards

---

[26] Bagley, p. 202.

for selective service with a mark; in some areas nearly half of the blacks and a quarter of the whites were excluded from the armed services on account of illiteracy. Those too illiterate for military service are undoubtedly also too illiterate for successful civilian life. It would be well to have a new emphasis on the necessity of teaching every child at least to read and write. This is the minimum essential of education.

The essentialists first turned their attention to the elementary school curriculum, and it was much later that the high school and college curriculum was influenced by the Jeffersonian point of view. In the final report of a six-year investigation by the American Youth Commission, under the title *Youth and the Future*,[27] the commission reaffirmed its recommendations for curriculum revision presented in a preliminary announcement, originally issued as *What the High Schools Ought to Teach*. Emphasis was given to the importance of continued instruction in reading as a much neglected element in the high school curriculum. Special emphasis was given to actual experience as a phase of general education second in importance to none. Instruction in the social studies and instruction to prepare young people to meet major personal problems were also stressed as essential elements in a reorganized curriculum.

Science and technology advanced rapidly during the pressure of war and cold war. The first atom bomb appeared in 1945 in the closing days of the conflict with Japan. A little later the hydrogen (fusion) bomb was developed. The use of the jet engine in military and civilian planes caught on rapidly. There was a veritable communications revolution. The first artificial satellite (the Russian Sputnik) went into orbit in 1957. Automation brought vast changes in factory organization and personnel needs. Engineering of all kinds made great strides. The development of rockets and missiles went on apace. Chemistry flourished as never before, while plastics and other synthetic products monopolized fields previously held by metals and natural and plant resources. It was inevitable that the schools would be expected to keep pace with such progress. In 1958 on the heels of the Sputnik shock, Congress passed the National Defense Education Act, designed to aid instruction in science and mathematics.

A new look at the role of science in the curriculum, now partially based on the necessities of the space age, was demanded by Bestor, Woodring, and Conant. Science courses had become essential to the preservation of the nation as well as necessities by which intelligent citizens might be prepared for an understanding of the present together with an anticipation of the future. While it was not expected that every student could profit from rigorous scientific study, levels were established and gradations within them made the basis for suitable offerings. Nor should every student continue further work in science after the basic and explora-

---

[27] (American Council on Education, 1942).

tory courses. By the same token, the able must be encouraged to reach their maximum development both for the sake of insuring their highest potential as well as adding to the brainpower reserve of the nation. In general, the public, science-conscious as never before, agreed.

Woodring called for a whole new organization of the American school system, placing the accent on a rigid course of study and thorough work. Several groupings should be made, he said, allowing the able to pursue uninterruptedly a rigorous study of algebra and geometry, for example, so that they would have a proper preparation for college entrance and professions requiring this knowledge. Woodring believed that if honor rolls are retained in high school their basis should rest on proficiency in conventional high school courses, including science, mathematics, and language rather than on the softer courses frequently utilized to secure higher grade-point averages.[28]

Conant's prescription for the high school curriculum, while allowing course space for the less able and medium-ability student, likewise suggested rigorous programs for the scholastically able. He proposed three levels of instruction indicating that aptitude may place a particular student in the highest section in one subject and lower positions in the others. The highest type course, he advised, moreover, should be thorough. He would require prerequisites for admission to these higher classes. All students would take science, and the course appropriate for them would be determined by their aptitude and previous record. Two types of chemistry and two of physics should be offered for students of different abilities. Conant prescribed foreign languages for the able and insisted that not less than four years in one language should be the standard.[29]

Hutchins has always favored the approach through the classics and, as such may be classed with the perennialist wing of the traditionalists. While concerned, at least in his tenure at Chicago, with college and university education primarily, his conclusions on general education betray his allegiance to the classical on lower levels as well. In *The Higher Learning in America* (quite appropriate for the sixties although originally published in October, 1936), Hutchins maintained that a general education must be given to all young Americans until about their twentieth year. One problem is how to handle the "handminded and functionally illiterate" in such a program; another is the adaptation of "the intellectual virtues," for it is there that men become citizens and that the specialists can, Hutchins hopes, meet on common grounds.[30] His premise that education should draw out the elements of common human nature is reciprocated in his axiom that these elements are the same at any place or in any time;

---

[28] Woodring, *A Fourth of a Nation*, pp. 149–150.

[29] Conant, pp. 49–50, 69–73.

[30] Robert M. Hutchins, *The Higher Learning in America* (New Haven, Conn.: Yale University Press, 1936), pp. 61–85.

hence the same education should obtain everywhere just as the same truth is everywhere present. Truth and knowledge are reciprocals. Obviously, Hutchins favors the Seven Liberal Arts and their classic repositories for such a general education.

Roman Catholic thought considers Christopher Dawson's (1908–) philosophy of history an authentic treatment of the facts of anthropology, history, and education; Dawson maintains that "great religions are the foundation on which great civilizations rest." Catholic educational content includes the history of the church and its saints as well as the general content of an essentialist curriculum.

Ulich speaks of the "consciousness of the transcendent," by which he invokes the universal and the eternal; he calls for persistence and the "Seeing of Relationships," although it may indeed be that few adults as well as adolescents can qualify here.[31] Yet Ulich's contention that secondary schools should so organize instruction need not be entirely lost. The direction can be set even if the goal remains far over the horizon.

The emergency gave reinforcement to all the areas in the curriculum which, as we have shown, have always been utilized by the nationalists. The teaching of history, and civics particularly, is again being emphasized as essential to national welfare. The social studies are essential in such times, but in ways not ordinarily recognized. They meet many sorts of needs, immediate and remote. Some of these needs are obvious; others are more obscure. The latter, involving the larger aspects of national and international life, the rise and growth of nations, the causes of war and the bases of peace, are the more profoundly significant. On the adequacy with which these subjects meet all these needs depend not only military victory, but permanent peace. Trained leaders, thoroughly educated in the culture of the Western world, possessed of the sharp tools of an educated mind, aware of the complexities of the world order, and inspired by the nobler possibilities open to man are urgently needed. The social studies are essential.

Intercultural education has replaced the Americanization movement of World War I. By furthering understanding of the contributions of many diverse people to the culture of America, intercultural education in the school curriculum attempts to advance national unity and morale, to unite the various races and nationalities who have come from the four corners of the earth into a united nation. An expert study in intercultural education[32] deals with what should be done and what is being done in the schools in

---

[31] Robert Ulich, *Crisis and Hope in American Education* (Boston: The Beacon Press, 1951), pp. 94–100.

[32] *Americans All. Studies in Intercultural Education.* Yearbook sponsored by Department of Supervisors and Directors of Instruction, National Council of Teachers of English, and Society for Curriculum Study (Washington, D.C.: National Education Association, 1942). See also, John A. Rademaker, *These Are Americans* (Palo Alto, Calif.: Pacific Books, 1951).

building concepts of racial democracy, conserving cultural resources of various culture groups, rediscovering folkways of various peoples, and giving cultural emphases in foreign language classes. Committees on intercultural understandings are being organized in many states.

In war and in crisis there is a tendency for high schools and colleges to mobilize their efforts toward the special uses their curricula may have for military and defense values. History and geography departments, English and speech departments, biology, chemistry, physics, and science in general, the commercial and industrial departments, mathematics, and physical education all select and teach the items and materials that have immediate preparedness values. While from the nationalistic standpoint this is commendable, there is a grave possibility that the larger implications of education may be brushed aside or sidetracked by such an approach. Thus, in the zeal to provide for defense or to compete in the cold war, it is probable that, through the inclusion of new, specific, and *ad hoc* items, other more permanent essentials of the curriculum will be neglected. Indeed, aggravated by the continuing war in Vietnam, grave controversy over such offerings as the preparation courses in Reserve Officers' Training Corps, certain science courses, and research allegedly geared to aiding and abetting the "military-industrial complex" flared in colleges and universities in the late sixties.

For example, there is a special danger in connection with the industrial arts curriculum. Vocational instructors in the past have tried to give their students basic training in the general skills of a trade, and a broad acquaintance with various phases of work in an industry, so that the worker could more readily adapt himself to a new task when necessity demanded. But in defense-training classes speed is essential. No attempt can be made to give broad training; the trainee is merely given the skills necessary for him to work on a specific job such as milling-machine operator, lathe operator, drill press operator, punch press operator, shaper, grinder, arc welder, wing assembler, cable splicer, fabric applier, and so on. This is true whether the job is in the area of precision instrument making, tool making, aircraft, missile, or boat construction, tank building, or any of the other many fields involved in war production. In such a program of highly specialized training for all-out production, some means must be devised for preserving the broader vocational training of the earlier industrial schools.

Totalitarian nations prepare their youth for war by means of a curriculum that develops blind devotion to their leaders, passionate feelings of patriotism for their countries, and a fervent belief that they are fighting a holy crusade. There are some who insist that the same kind of education is essential to a democracy fighting a cold war. But such a recommendation is clearly based on a misconception of the true nature of democracy.

If education is worth anything, it can accomplish more by developing a genuine loyalty based on rational understanding and calm reasoning. Although national unity is sorely needed, it can be created only through a willingness to serve and sacrifice with a supreme confidence in a durable peace, by teaching the truth rather than by the dissemination of propaganda, and by intelligently and directly attacking our problems.

Another essential is the need to discover the road to a united world, a world of free nations each maintaining a government of its own choice, based on its own culture. Only when nations voluntarily cooperate on a planetary basis will the common good of all, based on peace and justice, be assured. It is the duty of the school to provide a careful study and to foster an understanding of all peoples.[33]

A recent study of student attitudes toward their curriculum indicates the American educational program has failed in some of its responsibilities. This recent poll, conducted by Louis Harris and Associates on the problems of the American high school, student dissent, tensions brought about by overcrowding, and teacher complaints about fiscal policies, indicates changes in thinking about the conventional school subject matter. The following table, based on interviews with 2500 students in 100 schools in representative cities, rural areas, suburbs, and small towns, suggests the necessity for a reevaluation of priorities in the curriculum:

What Students Think of Their Courses[34]

	Most Useful	Least Useful	Most Difficult	Most Important
English Grammar and Composition	33%	14%	21%	52%
Mathematics	28	17	35	30
Science	20	16	22	13
Business and Secretarial	18	5	6	9
History (inc. Black)	15	18	12	12
Current Affairs	9	7	4	7
Foreign Languages	8	13	13	5
Literature	*	2	1	2
Geography	*	2	1	*
Family Planning	*	*	*	1

* Less than one half of 1%.

---

[33] Ulich, as mentioned earlier, is a strong advocate of international education. See his *History of Educational Thought*, pp. 349–350E, and his *Education of Nations*.

[34] Louis Harris, "What People Think about Their High Schools." From the Harris Poll, as published in LIFE Magazine, May 16, 1969.

Agencies

An education in the essentials, particularly those needed for the preservation of democracy and national welfare, cannot confine itself to children and youth in formally organized schools. It must reach the significant body of adults who actually determine public policy and practice. The Educational Policies Commission in its bulletin, *A War Policy for American Schools,* emphasized the fact that foreign and domestic policies are debated and major decisions of public policy made by adults and not by children. Unwise judgments on the part of adult voters will adversely affect the role that America plays in this postwar period. Adult education has become, therefore, a central rather than a marginal responsibility.

There are many agencies for the education of adults. The broadcasting companies have cooperated with educational leaders in providing various types of educational programs for adults as well as for children in the schools. Public evening schools, established in the nineteenth century, are developing more and more into agencies for adult education. The most promising agency for the education of adults is the forum, or discussion group.

Opportunities must be provided also for various forms of cultural, technical, and individual training for men and women who were denied these opportunities in youth. We need to realize the neglected truth that education is a continuous process, and provide extended educational opportunities to all adults. Schools and school libraries must serve as community centers to which adults may turn as places for discussion, information, and other aids to help them intelligently decide on the issues of the hour. Books must be prepared that are not only informative and useful, but easy to comprehend. The Readability Laboratory of the American Association of Adult Education devoted much effort to this problem and issued an experimental series of eleven volumes, called *The People's Library.* Lyman Bryson (1888–1959), its director, and one of the outstanding leaders in the field of adult education, said:

> Since we live in a self-governing nation, in which public institutions must be adapted to the needs and desires of the public, it is important to note here that the public itself undergoes modification. . . . Adult education becomes a more serious problem when there are more people, proportionately, of adult age.[35]

Another development in adult education, somewhat different from that fostered by Bryson, but in harmony with its idea, is the great books study groups. Operating in many sections of the country, meeting in public libraries, churches, or homes, under the leadership of intelligent men and women, either professional or lay, these assemblies read and discuss the

---

[35] *Adult Education* (New York: American Book Company, 1936), p. 8.

masterpieces of literature, past and present. Generally founding their study on the great Greek classics, they move through Rome and the Middle Ages to the Renaissance and Reformation and so on to the contemporary scene. Such a search for the meaning of life is essentially perennialist, and the vogue for this study must indeed gladden the heart of Hutchins and his colleagues in neoscholasticism. (Although the method is Jacksonian, its purpose is Jeffersonian.)

Throughout the preliminaries to war, the Office of Education was an active agency in stimulating the schools to give serious attention to the essential educational needs of the emergency. Early in 1941 an Information Exchange on Education and National Defense was organized as a "defense education clearing house for the federal government." Schools, colleges, and communities throughout the nation dispatched to the exchange publications and reports on defense education activities and services. Organized by educational subjects and school levels, this material was gathered into loan packets which constantly circulated around the country.

The Office of Education was active also in helping to mobilize the educational forces of the nation into a cooperative defense and war effort. On December 23, 1941, all educational institutions and organizations of the country were united in the Wartime Commission to take up the consideration of such important questions as (1) hastening graduation of students by lengthening school weeks and school terms, shortening vacations, and modifying curricular content; (2) utilizing colleges and universities for training various types of military personnel; (3) removing educational handicaps for men rejected in the draft; (4) establishing nursery schools for children of mothers employed in war industries; (5) improving the health and physical vigor of all the people; (6) planning for postwar educational readjustments.

The National Education Association continued its efficient educational leadership by promoting the essential educational needs of the crisis. As noted earlier, its legislative assembly established the Commission on the Defense of Democracy through Education, made up of representatives from the various states, to aid in developing statewide programs of education for democracy and to counteract forces inimical to such programs. In cooperation with the American Council of Education, the NEA organized the National Committee of Education and Defense in which the efforts of sixty or more national educational organizations and agencies were coordinated in the task of adapting education to the essential needs of the war without sacrificing long-term educational objectives.

In January, 1942, this National Committee on Education, sponsored the National Conference of College and University Presidents to deal with the problems of higher education in wartime. At this conference the institutions of higher education offered their "united power for decisive military victory, and for the ultimate and even more difficult task of establishing a just and lasting peace." Such a widespread cooperation of all the educational agencies of the nation in a common cause was something never before accomplished.

During the Great Depression the federal government became increasingly concerned with education, particularly along vocational lines, and set up many agencies to aid in the training of youth. The war accelerated this concern and participation. The National Committee on Education and Defense recommended that no agency be developed through federal funds that paralleled or duplicated existing educational facilities, but that existing agencies be adjusted, expanded, and utilized to meet the needs of the times. This cautious attitude has, of course, been fostered by the long history of decentralization in American education and, possibly, by the strict separation of church and state demanded by the federal Constitution.

As we have stated in earlier chapters, no agency in education is more important than the teacher. Yet, aggravated by the war and the consequent demand in defense industries, the inflationary period which followed World War II placed the teaching profession in a new situation. Personnel were scarce rather than abundant and, while salary rises stabilized the condition temporarily, the problem of securing good, well-qualified teachers soon plagued many boards of education.

The difficulty was compounded by the immense enrollments rising from the higher birthrate of the forties. The first pinch, of course, was felt in the elementary schools, but after a few years, secondary education was also hard hit. The shortage was most acute in rural and village schools and in certain areas such as science, mathematics, home economics, industrial education, and business practice. It was expected that state departments of education would be called upon to "let down the bars" and issue temporary or substandard certificates; and this happened in numerous cases.

Organization

The urgencies of war and cold war enhanced rather than diminished institutionalism in education. There is more of a tendency than ever before to organize all educational endeavors within the framework of a closely knit public school system. The economic depression, followed by the heavy taxation imposed by the demands of war and the resulting inflation have made the position of independent private schools and colleges rather precarious. Both the American Youth Commission and the Educational Policies Commission suggested the need for a unified public policy that will bring together all the educational functioning of nation, state, and local community into one powerful organization of effort.

Certain reorganizations that were proposed earlier have been stimulated by the saturation of the existing conventional agencies. One of the most frequently discussed proposals is the extension of the public school through the fourteenth grade for all. For years the junior college duplicated the work of the first two years of the traditional liberal arts college. A usual justification was the fact that it was making part of a liberal college education available to high school graduates in their home communities, making it unnecessary for them to leave their own locality. Now the junior college is becoming an institution for "terminal" education, providing essential training for such occupations as secretarial work, retail selling, and other types of technical and clerical pursuits and college training as well. Many public junior colleges and technical schools are being incorporated into the school system of the local school districts. It is urged that all students with the requisite abilities should not only be required to attend throughout the fourteen grades but should be enabled to do so by means of such forms of school aid, including part-time work-education programs, as may be necessary. The recent provision of scholarships, from public and private sources, is a step in this direction.

Most of the national defense program was organized around the existing public school program of vocational education. The entire program of defense training in no way supplanted or conflicted with the regular occupational training conducted in the public schools and subsidized by the federal government through funds made available by the Smith-Hughes and George-Dean acts. As in World War I, the nation's schools were given primary responsibility in training workers for defense employment. The public vocational schools provided preemployment training in the occupations designated by the War Production Board as essential to national defense. In addition to such preemployment training, public schools provided upgrading courses for employed workers which made possible their promotion to jobs requiring higher skills.

The colleges reorganized their programs to meet the needs of the return to world conflict. Most of these rearranged their year's work on a three-semester plan so that students might, by enrolling in this accelerated program, complete the regular college course in less than the usual four years, soon enough for many to get their degrees before they reached the minimum draft age of twenty. Some colleges admitted students before they finished high school. Professional schools shortened their programs, and many admitted students before they received their bachelors' degrees. Spring vacations were eliminated and Christmas holidays shortened in this attempt to streamline college education.

Although there was some apprehension that acceleration might lower the standards of higher education generally, this appears not to have happened. However, as a matter of precaution, the executive committee of the North Central Association of Colleges and Secondary Schools issued a statement to members of the association concerning the "attitude of the association toward special adjustments within schools and colleges to meet emergency conditions." Emphasizing that it expected all schools and colleges to devote their energies and resources to the service of the nation, it also dwelt on the necessity for adhering to certain fundamentals in the acceleration of programs: (1) every effort was to be made to insure that there was no loss in the quality of work; and (2) there was to be no dilution; that which was regularly required was to be thoroughly completed. A further condition mandated that all reorganization and readjustment to meet the war emergency must adhere to basic educational principles, which hold true whether a nation is at war or peace.

That the foregoing has more than historic interest was soon shown. Although the prescriptions noted were conceived for the benefit of institutions operating under the rigors of war and defense conditions, peace brought no relief but a serious aggravation of the problem. First, the so-called GI Bill offered college education to thousands who had been unable to attend because of the interruption due to the war and to others who, except for the terms of this most remarkable instrument, could never have financed the operation. As a result the colleges and universities virtually burst at the seams. Secondly, the baby boom mentioned earlier brought the promise of an increased enrollment within a few years. It was predicted that college attendance, based on the enrollment of the early forties, would quadruple by 1970.

Thus the problems of college organization, difficult in wartime, had become even more potentially worrisome in peacetime. Already the University of Chicago had adopted an interesting reform. Under President Robert M. Hutchins the university had decided to award the bachelor's degree at the end of the sophomore year not merely as an emergency measure but because Hutchins believed that the baccalaureate should mark the completion of general education. Hutchins held that it was foolish for a scholarly student to remain in college for four years to secure a degree that might as well be conferred a year or two earlier. This was consonant with his famous Chicago Plan, in which a student could secure his degree when he demonstrated that he had satisfied the requirements, regardless of the elapsed time.

Regardless of the merits or demerits of Hutchins' program, upon his retirement from the university Chicago reverted to the familiar four-year plan for the first degree. Nevertheless, many agree with Hutchins that too much of the student's time is wasted in college and that students, by eliminating certain overlapping, could begin their specialized preparation for the professions at least two years earlier, as has always been the custom in European universities.

Increased enrollment and inadequate facilities must force some decision in these matters of college and university education. And it is easily seen that the conflict between popular Jacksonianism and the more rigorous

Jeffersonianism which has reached even the teachers college is not confined to secondary school curriculum.[36]

Nevertheless, complaint about educational philosophy is a chronic thing and not confined to the present generation. A point which many critics fail to grasp is that the real wonder may be that the American schools, especially the high schools, are as good as they are. A quick summary of the new climate in the secondary school, through its population change, will suffice to demonstrate this.

By 1870 there were scarcely 70,000 students in the American public high school although it was already in its fiftieth year; in 1900 the number had reached 700,000; by the fifties the pupil population had zoomed to 7,000,000. Coupled with this prodigious growth in numbers was the problem of staff, housing, and administration, to say nothing of the evolution of curriculum and academic standards.

In an unprecedented decision, which reversed its stand in Plessy *v.* Ferguson (1896) for "separate but equal" facilities, the United States Supreme Court, on May 17, 1954, declared segregation in the nation's schools unconstitutional and illegal.[37] The court then ordered the removal of every such restriction with "all deliberate speed," this decree to be implemented by the regional federal courts. But for a decade after 1954, desegregation moved slowly, not only in the South but in the northern cities as well, where special problems occurred in middle-class areas. In 1964, however, the Civil Rights Act, banning federal aid to segregated schools, was passed; through this legislation Congress hoped to speed the process of desegregation. Other devices for securing integration were pairing, shuffling of school district boundaries, and bussing of students from one predominant color area to another in an attempt to achieve "racial balance."

Recent figures offered by the Department of Health, Education and Welfare indicate that while in the first ten years after the decision only 1 percent of the country's public schools attained integration, between 1964 and 1969 at least 20.3 percent qualified. Together with these reductions in segregation, blacks (and other minority groups) have also achieved new rights in many other fields of activity. Such improved relationships include parity in public accommodations, transportation, housing, voting, and job placement. But a dilemma still exists in the migration from the cities of nonblacks or nonminority members to the suburbs; this movement has created even larger pockets of unmixed groups and has

---

[36] Karl W. Meyer in "The Passing of the Teachers College," *School and Society*, vol. 87, no. 2160 (October 24, 1959), pp. 416–417, concludes that "the transition of the normal schools into comprehensive institutions is not without its dangers and problems."

[37] Brown *v.* Board of Education of Topeka, Kansas, 347 U.S. 483 (1954).

unsettled tax valuations as well. And, from time to time, protest is heard from black or other minority groups who demand local school control, with courses and teachers especially suited to their racial, or "national," differences. Such concessions would, in the minds of the conservative majority, vitiate the democratic gains of recent years.

Following the enactment of the Elementary and Secondary Education Act in 1965, a number of Regional Educational Laboratories were set up in various parts of the country (Title IV) "designed to make the results of innovation and experimentation in education readily available to the schools."[38] Titles I, II, III, and V provided funds to assist State Departments and individual school districts in planning and implementing better teaching practices.

Early in 1969 the Department of Health, Education and Welfare announced that it had a plan to smooth school desegregation through the cooperation of the Justice Department and the Attorney General's office with the federal courts in desegregation. The Justice Department will file suits against districts which have, in circumvention of the aim of the Civil Rights Act, accepted the loss of federal funds as the price for local segregation. It remains to be seen how much the new approach will affect school authority and organization.

Yet regardless of controversy over organization or philosophy, the American people are proud of their public school system. Single track or not (reference here is made to the existence of a number of private, academy-type schools in the East, South, and Far West and to the fact that virtually each high school beyond hamlet-size offers a variety of curricula, four courses being a frequent organization, with usually one leading to college preparation), Europe did not err when educational statesmen saw something more than quantity and chance in the American fetish of universal education.

Professor Kenneth Richmond, University of Glasgow, finds a uniqueness here that is unparalleled. He concludes a worthwhile study with the following happy phrases: "The Jacksonian lion and the Jeffersonian lamb will lie down together and although their natures are opposed, agree, for strange as it seems, the two are of one flesh."[39]

Methods

Present-day differences between the methodology of the essentialists and that of the progressives are mainly those of degree, neither group giving exclusive emphasis to one extreme or another. The essentialists

---

[38] *Purpose and Potentials, 1968 Report to Members* (Portland, Ore.: Northwest Regional Laboratory, 1968), p. 3.

[39] W. Kenneth Richmond, *Education in the U.S.A., A Comparative Study* (New York: Philosophical Library, Inc., 1956), p. 223.

emphasize habituation more than experience, guidance more than incidentalism, discipline more than freedom, effort more than interest, and self-examination more than expression. They believe also that the realities of environment place distinct limitations on individual freedom and individual interest.

The environment demands from the pupil the performance of certain acts and the inhibition of others. The price of genuine freedom from want, fear, superstition, and error is the surrender by the learner of a certain amount of his liberty, especially the freedom to learn what he pleases and when he pleases. The systematic mastery of the culture that has been acquired by mankind through its long struggle from primitive barbarism is the best source of real freedom. The knowledges and skills, the customs and manners, the attitudes and appreciations, built up through centuries of civilization, are our most precious heritage and the best aids in meeting the emergencies now confronting humanity. The essentialists believe it unwise to waste time in building generalizations by the slower method of induction when the general laws and principles discovered and formulated by generations of thinkers can be acquired by the properly guided pupil in a few hours or days, then used deductively in the solution of immediate and pressing problems.

The essentialists, therefore, first believe that there is a distinct place in our schools for the teaching of inhibitions, the forming of habits, and the development of skills. They agree, to this extent, with William James, who many years ago in his classic chapter on habit, said, "The great thing, then, in all education is to make . . . automatic, as early as possible, as many useful actions as we can." There are certain essential reactions that the realities of life demand of all of us, the essentialists assert, and certain other reactions that our place in life requires from us individually; there is no good reason why these should not be made automatic and habitual to lessen the toll on our time and energy. And, they claim, the daily routine tasks of our lives should be made as effortless as possible, and the repeated acts of our occupations should become skills, habits raised to a high level of accuracy and speed. The most effective methods of forming habits and developing skills are of great concern to the essentialists, and drill is finding a place in our classrooms again.

In the second place, since the essentialists emphasize the necessity of teaching pupils how to think systematically and effectively, we are witnessing a return to the "reasoning lesson." Judd said, "What children need, if they are to get in a short time what the race has evolved in a long time, is guidance in systematic thinking." We cannot do effective thinking by looking at the world en masse, or by acquiring knowledge piecemeal in encyclopedic fashion. We must make use of the methods of systematic analysis and systematic synthesis, the essentialists urge, to separate the essential elements of knowledge from the worthless chaff, and to organize these essentials into meaningful wholes, with close attention to the interrelationship of each of these entities. In teaching the pupil to think we must so guide his learning so that he will come into mental possession of the important elements of truth, the most reliable knowledge available; be able to use this knowledge in the solution of the real problems that confront mankind; and get enough practice in the actual techniques of thinking to learn to escape the pitfalls and errors of faulty reasoning. The pupil must be disciplined in the acquisition and use of "coherent compilations of related content," but the teacher must not make the mistake of insisting that the completed organization of knowledge by the mature scholar be the first material to confront the child, they assert.

Horne, one of the leading exponents of the idealist wing of essentialism, complained that the progressives failed to appreciate the real significance of intelligence by limiting "the formation and free play of both intellectual and ethical ideas. [Dewey's] naturalistic view of intelligence is both inadequate in itself and insufficient as a basis of school procedure. It is inadequate in itself because the course of nature is not its own object; yet it is the object of intelligence."[40] Essentialists strongly advocate subject matter and experiences calculated to both challenge and develop the student's mental capacity and ethical realizations.

Essentialists accept the guidance function as a responsibility of the teacher. Yet often, possibly, they misunderstand the true meaning of guidance and think it means telling the pupil what he must do. Guidance is helping pupils to make their own choices and decisions. Obviously, the prime characteristic of democracy is freedom of thought and action on the part of all. Freedom of choice and freedom of action are the fundamental requisites for the democratic way of life, but they alone do not make a *good* democracy. A people could be free to be depraved, free to be diseased, free to be dishonest, free to exploit; freedom can easily become a state of anarchy. If a democracy is to be efficient and worthy, freedom must be intelligent and socially minded. Intelligence and good will must be concomitants of freedom. A true democracy, then, rests upon these relevant conditions: (1) freedom of choice in thought and action, (2) intelligence of choice in thought and action, (3) socialization of choice in thought and action. Freedom must operate within the laws of intelligence and social welfare if democracy is to succeed and function beneficially for all. The teacher must guide the pupils so that they will come to make not only free choices but intelligent and socially desirable choices. By helping the pupils seek out all the relevant truth about themselves and the alternatives from which choices are to be made, teachers will guide them toward choices that have all three characteristics. This sort of guidance is essential if

---

[40] Herman Harrell Horne, *The Democratic Philosophy of Education* (New York: Crowell-Collier and Macmillan, Inc., 1932), p. 532.

democracy is to be preserved. Nor should it be forgotten that the ultimate goal is self-guidance. The good counselor is one who soon makes himself dispensable.

Essentialism, like progressivism, recognizes that interest is a strong motivating force in learning. Learning, however, that is not immediately interesting and appealing to the child should not be entirely eliminated from education. More valuable and more permanent interests may grow out of efforts that are at first disagreeable and monotonous. Very often the pupil will develop a deep and abiding interest in something that did not attract nor hold his attention at first. It is the duty of the teacher to help the pupil grow into these higher interests rather than limit all school activities to those ephemeral things that appeal only to natural and childish interests.

An important new teaching tool and method, educational television, capitalizes on pupil interest and can be adapted to curriculum needs without interfering with the standard curriculum. Although in the past several approaches to "classrooms of the air" have been utilized including selected radio stations, broadcasting from airplanes, and special programs via regular networks, it now appears that National Educational Television, with congressional appropriations, will eventually overshadow these. Viewing can be handled in two manners: (1) fitting the broadcast into the conventional program or (2) rebroadcasting, using kinescopes or various types of electronic tape, which may not be available to all schools. But the use of programs directly is not too difficult, and these programs have the virtue of being available to the nonschool public, especially preschoolers, dropouts, and the general adult population. There now are approximately 200 noncommercial stations and the number is growing. Recent sample programs include fare assisting children from "disadvantaged" homes in learning the alphabet, numbers, and vocabulary. Other levels include a "magazine of the air" and a "drama hour."

When the essentialists urge that we bring discipline back into our schools, they are often misunderstood. They do not mean obedience to a tyrannical authority. They feel that the basis of all true authority lies in the realities of life. All the desires, projects, and proposals of men are subject to the veto of reality. Therefore, they feel, we must teach our children to face realities, to discipline themselves to the actualities of the worlds of nature and of men. We must teach them to relinquish sentimental and romantic dreaming. True wisdom comes when we bring ourselves in harmony with the realistic laws of physical and human nature. Self-discipline is the goal, but imposed discipline is essential for a while. "The truth will make us free," they maintain, but in the immature years of childhood and youth we need competent, sympathetic, and firm teachers to help us see the truth and adjust ourselves to inexorable facts. This is discipline as the essentialists understand it.

EXISTENTIALISM

Another similar approach to discipline is found in the thought of the existentialists, a "newer" educational philosophy. Based on the work of Kierkegaard, Marcel, Sartre, Heidegger, Buber, Camus, and Tillich (among others), existentialism is concerned with man's apprehension of his own life role, with experiences that define or comment on self. Man's future may be gloomy or glorious, but—say existentialists—since he is terribly alone, he must choose. Existentialist method arises in providing experience and realization geared to individual necessity. Some existentialists study the past as revealed in history and literature to gain guidelines for now; for others, only the present is significant, and even it is marked by exercises in futility and "no exit" signs. Although by its very tenets existentialism appears to be antithetical to organizational symmetry, it is concerned with man as man, with man as nothing, with man and God, man as individual, with death and love. It has little to say about *this* morality, *this* political system, or *that* educational rubric; and existentialists consider themselves as sharing an authentic educational light.

Many existentialists would agree with essentialists that the most important goal of the schools is to teach people to live together in peace. If we learn to be friendly, neighborly, and brotherly in the small-group relationships of the school and the home, then shall we not be more inclined to be friendly, neighborly, and brotherly in our large-group relationships of community, state, and nation, and eventually in our relationships with other nations? Experiences in cooperative living must begin on a relatively small scale at home and in school. Family quarrels, neighborhood jealousies, class struggles, racial animosities, and sectional rivalries are the things that destroy the spirit of the good neighbor and make easier the development of the envies, jealousies, and hatreds that breed wars. Peaceful relations on a small scale may help to bring about peaceful relations on a large scale. If every teacher in every schoolroom in the world could somehow teach his pupils the gospel of brotherly love, then perhaps the day would come when the whole world would remain at peace.

In an address formally opening the golden anniversary White House Conference on Youth and Children, former President Eisenhower declared that the faith of the American people in peace with justice is an absolute. "So," he continued, "among the things we teach to the young are such truths as the transcendent value of the individual and the dignity of all people, the futility and stupidity of war, its destructiveness of life and its degradation of human values."[41] The advocacy of this principle is not the

---

[41] Associated Press release, College Park, Maryland, March 27, 1960.

monopoly of the existentialist; it is the property of all democratic societies and the goal of all true education.

In the past decades the civilized world has been staggered by two terrible blows. A world depression followed by a world at war has left its mark upon education. Along with many other cherished aspects of our civilization, education has been endangered by the ill winds of adversity and the ravage of hot and cold war. But those in charge of education have not surrendered to a defeatist philosophy. They realize the importance of education in such emergencies and insist that the task of education is greater because of the great crisis through which the world is passing.

The schools of each nation must develop in its people an understanding of and empathy with the people of other nations. Most wars are the result of mutual misunderstanding and mistrust, which the study of other languages may help to eliminate. How much of our friendship and support of Great Britain is due to our common language? When one understands the speech of another country and reads its literature, a firmer basis is laid for understanding and rapport. The study of the vital interests and cultural forces of foreign nations in our schools should serve as an effective means for diminishing the danger to international peace. If we place before our students the materials pertaining to a foreign land—ethical, esthetic, historical, economic, political, and cultural materials compiled by scholars and authors representative of that nation—we are building a common bond of understanding and fellow feeling which may help preserve peace between our nation and theirs.

Schools and colleges must make clear that permanent peace depends upon equality of opportunity and freedom of action in all world relationships. Threats to that freedom precipitated the last war and have forced nations into the present cold war. This deadly circle must be broken, and we must learn how to break it. Scientific discovery, the triumphs of surgery (the first successful heart transplant was made in 1968), rapidity of communication and transportation, the conquest of the atmosphere (the first moon walk occurred in 1969), the general increase of knowledge increasing the complexity of human wants have all made world cooperation essential if civilization, as we understand it, is to continue. Perhaps the United Nations and its cultural agencies may prove to be the answer. Perhaps Hutchins' Center for the Study of Democratic Institutions at Santa Barbara, California or similar endeavors may provide solutions. But, whatever the medium, the effort must be made.

The existential movement, through another use of the raw material, offers another alternative. Existentialism being free, yet involved; seeking truth, yet accepting nothing secondhand, and above all *caring*, has the facility for offering and even forcing choices. Some argue that the programs of the Peace Corps and VISTA, mentioned in the preceding chapter, offer many choices. But how difficult is it to make a new curriculum? To recapture appropriate methods? To attract teachers? Is it hopeless to talk of peace and social justice, or shall we say that through existentialism the next advance in education will be made, and cite William Ernest Henley's *Invictus*?

> I am the master of my fate,
> I am the captain of my soul.

New York's commissioner of cultural affairs, a sage observer viewing the threat both to human existence and to interpersonal relationships, has stated what may well be the supreme goal for modern education:

> In projecting the idea of brotherhood, we might each paraphrase a great American poet, and say to ourselves: Each man's folly diminishes me. Since man's worst folly is his inhumanity to his fellow man, we cannot, in our own interest, ignore our responsibility to our fellow man. Brotherhood is not the noble prerogative of a select, dedicated few; it should be the prevailing signpost of every waking hour of the daily life of each person who breathes the air of God's world.[42]

REFERENCES

Adler, Mortimer J., and Milton Mayer, *The Revolution in Education*. Chicago: University of Chicago Press, 1958.

Bayles, Ernest E., *Democratic Educational Theory*. New York: Harper & Row, Publishers, 1960.

———, and Bruce L. Hood, *Growth of American Educational Thought and Practice*. New York: Harper & Row, Publishers, 1966.

Bestor, Arthur, *The Restoration of Learning*. New York: Alfred A. Knopf, 1955.

Boyd, William, *The History of Western Education,* 8th ed. Rev. by Edmund J. King. New York: Barnes & Noble, Inc., 1966. Pp. 412–450.

Brameld, Theodore, *Ends and Means in Education: A Midcentury Appraisal*. New York: Harper & Row, Publishers, 1950.

———, *Patterns of Educational Philosophy*. New York: Harcourt, Brace & World, Inc., 1950. Pp. 265–288, 351–386.

Breed, Frederick S., *Education and the New Realism*. New York: Crowell-Collier and Macmillian, Inc., 1939.

Brubacher, John S., *A History of the Problems of Education,* 2d ed. New York: McGraw-Hill, Inc., 1966.

Broudy, Harry S., *Building a Philosophy of Education*. Englewood Cliffs, N.J.: Prentice-Hall, Inc., 1954. Pp. 3–26.

Butts, R. Freeman, and Lawrence A. Cremin, *A History of Education*

---

[42] Dore Schary, *The Stereotype* (Medford, Mass.: The Tufts Civic Education Center, Tufts University, 1960).

in American Culture. New York: Holt, Rinehart and Winston, Inc., 1953. Pp. 515–562.

Conant, James B., *The American High School Today.* New York: McGraw-Hill, Inc., 1959.

———, *Education and Liberty.* Cambridge, Mass.: Harvard University Press, 1953.

———, *Slums and Suburbs.* New York: McGraw-Hill, Inc., 1961.

Crosser, Paul K., *The Nihilism of John Dewey.* New York: Philosophical Library, Inc., 1955.

Demiashkevich, Michael. *An Introduction to the Philosophy of Education.* New York: American Book Company, 1935. Pp. 381–440.

Edwards, Newton, and Herman G. Richey, *The School in the American Social Order,* 2d ed. Boston: Houghton Mifflin Company, 1963. Pp. 483–650.

General Education in a Free Society. Cambridge, Mass.: Harvard University Press, 1945.

Gross, Richard E. (Ed.), *Heritage of American Education.* Boston: Allyn and Bacon, Inc., 1962. Pp. 423–526.

Horne, Herman Harrell, *The Democratic Philosophy of Education.* New York: Crowell-Collier and Macmillan, Inc., 1932.

Hutchins, Robert M., *The Higher Learning in America.* New Haven, Conn.: Yale University Press, 1936.

Koerner, James D., *The Miseducation of American Teachers.* Boston: Houghton Mifflin Company, 1963.

Maritain, Jacques, *Education at the Crossroads.* New Haven, Conn.: Yale University Press, 1943.

Mason, Robert E., *Educational Ideals in American Society.* Boston: Allyn and Bacon, Inc., 1960. Pp. 41–51.

Mayer, Frederick, *Philosophy of Education for Our Time.* New York: The Odyssey Press, Inc., 1958.

Meyer, Adolphe E., *An Educational History of the American People,* 2d ed. New York: McGraw-Hill, Inc., 1967.

Mulhern, James, *A History of Education,* 2d ed. New York: The Ronald Press Company, 1959. Pp. 668–721.

Nakosteen, Mehdi, *The History and Philosophy of Education.* New York: The Ronald Press Company, 1965.

Park, Joseph (Ed.), *Selected Readings in the Philosophy of Education.* New York: Crowell-Collier and Macmillan, Inc., 1962.

Potter, Robert E., *The Stream of American Education.* New York: American Book Company, 1967. Pp. 472–503.

Pounds, Ralph L., *The Development of Education in Western Culture.* New York: Appleton-Century-Crofts, 1968.

Power, Edward J., *Main Currents in the History of Education.* New York: McGraw-Hill, Inc., 1962. Pp. 450–493.

Redden, John D., and Francis A. Ryan, *A Catholic Philosophy of Education.* Milwaukee: The Bruce Publishing Company, 1942.

Richman, W. Kenneth, *Education in the U.S.A.* New York: Philosophical Library, Inc., 1956.

Riesman, David, Nathan Glazer, and Reuel Denney, *The Lonely Crowd.* New Haven, Conn.: Yale University Press, 1950.

Schleffler, Israel (Ed.), *Philosophy and Education.* Boston: Allyn and Bacon, Inc., 1958. Pp. 263–271.

Ulich, Robert, *Crisis and Hope in American Education.* Boston: The Beacon Press, 1951.

———, *History of Educational Thought.* New York: American Book Company, 1950. Pp. 292–314, 345–350.

——— (Ed.), *Three Thousand Years of Educational Wisdom,* 2d ed., enl. Cambridge: Mass.: Harvard University Press, 1954. Pp. 577–614.

Weber, Christian O., *Basic Philosophies of Education.* New York: Holt, Rinehart and Winston, Inc., 1960. Pp. 35–87, 91–156, 159–236.

Whitehead, Alfred North, *The Aims of Education and Other Essays.* New York: Crowell-Collier and Macmillan, Inc., 1929.

Wingo, G. Max, *The Philosophy of American Education.* Boston: D. C. Heath and Company, 1965.

Woodring, Paul, *A Fourth of a Nation.* New York: McGraw-Hill, Inc., 1957.

SELECTED PAPERBACKS

Alexander, William M., and others, *The Emergent Middle School,* 2d ed., enl. New York: Holt, Rinehart and Winston, Inc., 1969.

Beck, Robert Holmes, *A Social History of Education.* Englewood Cliffs, N.J.: Prentice-Hall, Inc., 1965.

Beggs, David W. III, and S. Kern Alexander, *Integration and Education.* Skokie, Ill.: Rand McNally & Company, 1969.

Bruner, Jerome, *Toward a Theory of Education.* New York: W. W. Norton & Company, Inc., 1966.

Conant, James B., *The American High School Today.* New York: New American Library of World Literature, Inc., 1964.

———, *Slums and Suburbs.* New York: McGraw-Hill, Inc., 1961.

Cornuelle, Richard C., *Reclaiming the American Dream.* New York: Random House, Inc., 1968.

Curti, Merle, *Social Ideas of American Educators,* rev. ed. Totowa, N.J.: Littlefield, Adams and Company, 1959.

Davenport, Russell W., and Editors of *Fortune, U.S.A., The Permanent Revolution.* Englewood Cliffs, N.J.: Prentice-Hall Inc., 1951.

Goldston, Robert, *The Negro Revolution.* New York: New American Library of World Literature, Inc., 1968.

Johnson, Robert H., and John J. Hunt, *Prescription for Team Teaching.* Minneapolis: Burgess Publishing Co., 1968.

Keniston, Kenneth, *The Uncommitted, Alienated Youth in American Society.* New York: Harcourt, Brace & World, Inc., 1965.

Mayer, Frederick, *Foundations of Education.* Columbus, Ohio: Charles E. Merrill Books, Inc., 1963.

Nordstrom, Carl, and others, *Society's Children: A Study of Ressentiment in the Secondary School.* New York: Random House, Inc., 1967.

O'Hara, William T. (Ed.), *John F. Kennedy on Education.* New York: Bureau of Publications, Teachers College, Columbia University, 1966.

O'Neill, William, *Readin, Ritin, and Rafferty! A Study of Educational Fundamentalism.* Berkeley, Calif.: The Glendessary Press, 1969. Pp. 3–137.

Rafferty, Max, *What They Are Doing to Your Children.* New York: New American Library of World Literature, Inc., 1963.

Riesman, David, *Constraint and Variety in American Education.* Lincoln, Neb.: University of Nebraska Press, 1965.

Rippa, S. Alexander, *Education in a Free Society.* New York: David McKay Company, Inc., 1967. Pp. 283–341.

Rudolph, Frederick, *The American College and University.* New York: Random House, Inc., 1965. Pp. 440–482.

Schwartz, Lita Linzer, *American Education, A Problem-Centered Approach.* Boston: Holbrook Press, Inc., 1969.

Stoff, Shelden, and Herbert Schwartzberg, *The Human Encounter, Readings in Education.* New York: Harper & Row, Publishers, Inc., 1969.

Stone, James C., and F. W. Schneider, *Commitment to Learning,* 2 vols. New York: Thomas Y. Crowell Company, 1965.

Tascher, Harold and Associates, *The Quest for Social Intelligence.* Missoula, Mont.: Community Relations Services, 1967.

Trubowitz, Sidney, *A Handbook for Teaching in the Ghetto School.* Chicago: Quadrangle Books, 1968.

Ulich, Robert, *Education in Western Culture.* New York: Harcourt, Brace & World, Inc., 1965.

Whitehead, Alfred North, *The Aims of Education.* New York: New American Library of World Literature, Inc., 1949.

Wiener, Norbert, *The Human Use of Human Beings, Cybernetics and Society,* 2d ed., rev. New York: Doubleday & Company, Inc., 1954. Pp. 41–42, 132–134.

Wingenbach, Charles E., *Guide to the Peace Corps, Who, How, Where.* New York: McGraw-Hill, Inc., 1965.

CHAPTER **21**

Contemporary
Ideologies
and Education

*National rivalries, or antipathies, would be completely out of place here.
The true greatness of a people does not consist in borrowing nothing
from others, but in borrowing from all what is good and in perfecting
whatever is appropriate.*[1]

CHANGING POLITICAL SCENES

Any real assessment of the results and significance of World War II,
like its predecessor in 1914–1918, can be made only in terms that are
basically nonmilitary. In such an analysis three foci immediately suggest
themselves: (1) a multitude of new and resurgent nationalisms; (2) a new
and extraordinary type of satellitism;[2] and (3) powerful new or rejuvenated recourses to education.

Since it is not our purpose to deal with political processes except as
they *effect* educational philosophy and since the developments in nationalism and satellitism oriented both to the Soviet Union and the United States
are well known, we shall consider directly only the renewed responses to
education having their wellsprings in the changed circumstances so apparent, after 1945, in the world.[3]

The post–1944 period presents changed ideologies in educational
philosophy and practice. Although these changes were supranational, our
coverage of this period being of necessity limited, we shall attempt to survey

---

[1] Victor Cousin, *Public Education in Prussia* (London, 1834).
[2] See J. A. Lukacs, "The American Imperial Disease," *The American Scholar*, vol.
28, no. 2 (Spring, 1959), pp. 141–150.
[3] For a balanced picture of the results of World War II and the ensuing cold war,
see Louis J. Halle, *The Cold War as History* (New York: Harper & Row, Publishers,
1967), pp. 30–88.

only the newer relationships in Britain, France, West Germany, the Soviet Union, Czechoslovakia, mainland China, and, coincidentally, the United States. (This is not to say that dynamic developments are not occurring in Africa,[4] the Near East, Latin America, and Japan.) These countries provide a typical representation of the West, the Free World, and an equal representation of the Marxist camp. It will not be possible to develop the entire history of these educational settings, or even to trace their continuity with earlier events.

THE UNITED STATES AND ITS SINGLE LADDER

About and immediately following 1944, the American school system was increasingly scrutinized by the newer nations of the world as well as by the other great powers, together with certain of those countries in the process of transition from former greatness to a less demanding status in world polity.

Possibly because of American success, militarily and industrially, in winning the war, and doubtless because of the contemporary period of American hegemony, beginning sometime after the conclusion of World War I and becoming evident in 1945, the structure and what was taken to be the American educational philosophy gained a respectful attention almost everywhere.

Indeed, what has come to be called the single ladder, or one-track system, in the United States began to evoke at least rudimentary adherence in many European countries and here and there throughout the world. To illustrate: the French *école unique*, the German *Einheitsschule*, the Italian *scuola unica*, and one of the underlying purposes in British reform under the Education Act of 1944, led patently in this direction.

That the United States had in practice qualified its single ladder somewhat was either not known or was blithely disregarded in the haste to show a democratic orientation. This last was in keeping with the new tide that had begun to run strongly during the closing years of the conflict and especially after VE and VJ days. Such an outlook had sprung from popular desires in the new nationalisms and grass-roots movements which had come to the surface during the war's dark hours; it was a response to the demands of a popular front.

---

[4] For these important developments, see David G. Scanlon, *Traditions of African Education* (New York: Bureau of Publications, Teachers College, Columbia University, 1964), for an excellent background of the colonial education position, enlivened by an interesting section devoted to the indigenous Poro. And for a contemporary view, see Basil Davidson, *Africa, History of a Continent* (New York: Crowell-Collier and Macmillan, Inc., 1966); Chancellor Williams, *The Rebirth of African Civilization* (Washington, D.C.: Public Affairs Press, 1961); or Henri Labouret, *Africa Before the White Man* (New York: Walker and Company, 1962).

It was reasoned (perhaps rightly) that America's victory in the war was to a large degree a result of her system of universal education. Moreover, the protestations of the Atlantic Charter and the well-publicized principles of the lately born United Nations served to implement these desires and demands throughout the Western and the Eastern worlds, as well as a rising Africa.

In addition to notions concerning the one-track system, American progressivism, too, had come in for scrutiny and some imitation. This had already been true for a time in the Soviet Union, with a great admiration for John Dewey; now French and Italian cabinets felt disposed to pay lip service to the single track and to concede that new methods and purposes were proper responses to the demands for broadening the base of popular education.[5] That these methods were usually conditioned by some pragmatic philosophy which lent itself to mass education was understood. That many Americans and American schools were becoming more highly traditional and essentialist in outlook was, if apprehended at all, glossed over.

Among the patterns expressing the organization as well as the method was that of the British "modern" school, increasingly the core of a "comprehensive" school.[6] The modern school is the new (1944) popular secondary school, which with the grammar and technical schools offers an alternate education for adolescents. Yet not even in the United States (although the British organization did greatly resemble the progressive American junior high school) was the program lowered to such a level, for, in scholastic terms, it could hardly be called a school, so diluted was the content and so nondirective the methodology.

EDUCATIONAL PHILOSOPHY AND METHOD

In the United States the forces at work in education have frequently been identified as Jeffersonian (the more, traditional, idealistic and academic tendency) and Jacksonian (the pragmatic, vocational, and popular). That pragmatic methods apply in the Jacksonian phase is a natural conclusion; they have to. Nor did the so-called classically oriented school eschew progressivism completely. The pragmatic method was often grafted onto a fairly rigid association of subject matter. Yet circumstances varied, and

---

[5] See Arthur H. Moehlman and Joseph S. Roucek, *Comparative Education* (New York: Holt, Rinehart and Winston, Inc., 1952), pp. 9ff., for a good review of the historical circumstances.

[6] See Robin Pedley, *The Comprehensive School* (Baltimore: Penguin Books, Inc., 1963), pp. 14, 106ff. Pedley lists some 250 schools in England, Wales, and the Isle of Man, which had become "broadly comprehensive in character" as of his book's publication.

the Jeffersonians who utilized progressive methods hardly termed them as such. Yet despite their dedication to a firm idea, the Jeffersonians too perhaps failed to reach their students as thoroughly as they hoped and planned. A new critic, Paul Goodman, wrote of "compulsory mis-education" and called American education largely nonfunctional.[7] And a perceptive sociologist, Edgar Z. Friedenberg, warned that "for all our concern, the hypocrisy and callousness of the marketplace or the political arena have saturated the schools."[8]

But to understand the development of American educational ideology, one has to consider the United States' history and philosophy throughout its unique development, from its beginnings in the seventeenth century, the states' constitutional independence in education; and nineteenth-century rugged individualism. For education was shaped by all these developments; indeed, contemporary American historians are inclined to place education toward the rear as a catalyst determinative of the American way.[9]

Thus, many Europeans may not have fathomed the many and various conditions under which American education had undertaken progressivism. Indeed, the term itself must have caused much confusion. For progressivism in the schools was but part of that great social and intellectual uplift in American life and culture known historically as the Progressive movement. Its roots led to a quest for redress from the slums that had accompanied the rise of the city, the sweatshops of labor, the political rings and bosses, the crushing obligations of farmers to mortgage holders, and even the sterility of the public school of the late 1800s, with its lockstep (or as some preferred, goosestep) and the remoteness of the celebrated American high school, which emphasized almost solely the propaedeutic through a curriculum only a step removed from the class-conscious traditional Latin grammar School (which still flourished under private auspices in some of the older areas of the United States).[10]

To the foregoing must be added the reorganization of American secondary education with junior and senior divisions, the 6–3–3 plan; and

---

[7] See his *Growing Up Absurd* (New York: Alfred A. Knopf, 1960), and *Compulsory Mis-education and The Community of Scholars* (New York: Random House, Inc., 1964).

[8] *Coming of Age in America, Growth and Acquiescence* (New York: Random House, Inc., 1967), pp. 6–7; see his *The Vanishing Adolescent* (Boston: The Beacon Press, 1959).

[9] For example, see Bernard Bailyn, *Education in the Forming of American Society* (Chapel Hill, N.C.: University of North Carolina Press, 1960); Daniel Boorstein, *The Americans, The Colonial Experience* (New York: Random House, Inc., 1958); and Rush Welter, *Popular Education and Democratic Thought in America* (New York: Columbia University Press, 1962).

[10] The classic presentation of the rise of progressivism is that of Lawrence A. Cremin, *The Transformation of the School* (New York: Alfred A. Knopf, 1961). Although the multiform historical factors are presented beautifully by Cremin, some question has been raised as to his finality in terms of philosophical origins and linkages of his subject.

the advent of the public junior college, grades thirteen and fourteen.[11] When these are viewed in relationship to the American Dream, as conceptualized by the historian James Truslow Adams, it appears immediately that with industrialization, urbanization, America's new role in world affairs, and the spectacular rise in population through both immigration and natural causes the American people could hardly fail to be powerfully affected by the currents of change which they saw all about them. That similar developments in education should accrue is a foregone conclusion.

Quite probably what Europe saw so vividly was only the most evident phase of American nationalism and pragmatism. It squared, however, with the myth of the American Dream and with the glamor of popular single-track Jacksonianism in education. Method, too, except in the citadels of New England privatism, where the model in old England of the high British public school discouraged innovation, veered almost 180 degrees until if what Europe saw in American schools of the pre-Potsdam decades was progressivism, then Europe saw not too incorrectly.[12]

Yet, in Europe, academic thought (like that of the Ivy League university in the United States generally) has traditionally considered the art (or science) of education as a technical occupation, having little claim to recognition by the prestigious classical secondary school and humanistic university. The most honored educational theory in Western Europe can be described, in simple terms, as philosophical idealism. Concerned largely with abstract ideas, it is generally intolerant of the scientific method in education and of the findings in educational sociology and social psychology. Educational experimentation and the utilization of practical problems are rare and usually nonexistent. That any modification, particularly of the type suggested earlier, should be permitted to enter such a system of thought represents a veritable revolution in educational theory.

Speaking of the roots of European educational thought, Martin Levit establishes this philosophical base even more definitively:

> In the main [educational theorists] reach back into, and stay within, the philosophical categories derived chiefly from ancient Greece, the Christian tradition, the rationalism of the Enlightenment, and the idealism

[11] See Edmund A. Ford, "Organizational Pattern of the Nation's Public Secondary Schools." *School Life*, vol. 42, no. 9 (May, 1960), pp. 10–12. Ford reports that as of 1959 82 percent of the total secondary school population was attending a "reorganized school." Specifically, 32 percent were in 6–6 organizations; 25 percent in a separate junior high plan; 15 percent in a 6–3–3 organization; and 10 percent in a 6–2–4 reorganization.

[12] As mentioned in Chapter 18, Wilford M. Aikin, *The Story of the Eight-Year Study* (New York: Harper & Row, Publishers, 1942), recapitulates the experiment whereby progressive experience in secondary education was made more popular and thus brought to the attention of the American public. That this picture is presented as a glowing one should not be unexpected. However, following World War II, some of the bloom was extracted from this flower as certain more critical analyses of the results of the study were given wide publicity by the essentialists.

of Hegel and Kant. [Moreover, in areas in which theory leads to sharing certain developments with the existentialists] many theorists seem to be defending the ultimate efficacy of the human will against the influence of external conditions.[13]

EDUCATION IN FRANCE

France found many reasons for not entering wholeheartedly into the reform contemplated under the Langevin-Wallon recommendation of 1947, attempting, insofar as practicable, a one-track system of public education. As a close observer of the French educational scene has commented:

> Judged by modern standards in more experimental countries like the United States and Britain, the system in France is excessively formal and bookish. It bears little relation to the everyday life of the average French community, and even after reform still takes fatally small account of France's urgent need for greater industrialization and modern workaday "know-how."[14]

As is well known, the French system is highly centralized; it is secular and compulsory between the ages of six and, as of 1967, sixteen;[15] it is uniform throughout France, although pupils may attend either a public or a private (tuition) school. Under the 1947 legislation three levels (*degrés*) were conceived: elementary, secondary, and higher. The state maintains a monopoly on approved examinations, which are centrally supervised in a system terribly efficient, with a failure rate frequently as high as 50 percent. Even in Roman Catholic schools, operated under strict supervision, the same examinations are administered from Paris.

King reports:

> The French people are fully conscious of their problems. They try to make the school less formal. [Even] new methods are officially encouraged and demonstrated by the Ministry of National Education. "Pilot classes" are to be found in all regional centers, and "experimental *lycées*" are maintained at six points.[16]

(It will be remembered that the *classes nouvelles* were to be a special feature of the new legislation in 1947.) Such experimentation in a country with as national a system as France's is unusual, to say the least.

---

[13] "Educational Theory in the U.S.S.R. and West Europe," *School and Society*, vol. 87, no. 2145 (January 17, 1959), p. 23. See also Robert Ulich, *Philosophy of Education* (New York: American Book Company, 1961), especially ch. 9, "The Liberal Arts versus Scientific and Practical Education," pp. 176–187.

[14] Edmund J. King, *Other Schools and Ours* (New York: Holt, Rinehart and Winston, Inc., 1963), p. 45.

[15] See William T. Fraser, "Reform in France," *Comparative Education Review*, vol. xl, no. 3 (October, 1967), pp. 300–310, for a thorough evaluation of recent French educational developments.

[16] King, p. 66.

There are, of course, the usual difficulties with the public. The religious faction calls any education except the classical, "godless"; the prosperous call practical education "communistic"; the term *democrat* too is susceptible of different meanings; for one group it means "removing barriers to the successful career of the talented pupil," to others, it appears to mean general education, thus allowing "a much larger proportion of each age-group in the nation" to receive at least a background "before being dispersed into separate channels," as Fraser observes.[17]

French examinations, especially the *baccalauréate* (*bachot*, for short) are severely thorough. However, since 1947 children have been increasingly selected or rejected at the age of eleven on their teacher's recommendation; only those whose status is unclear are now required to take the written examination. (The *bachot* itself, under de Gaulle, was shorn of its oral section.) The reform of January 6, 1959 attempted to relieve the compartmentalization by providing similar syllabi for comparable levels and by permitting the freer movement of teachers from one institution to another, an unusual concession for France.[18]

It has been alleged in defense of the French system, that, regardless of the fact that a small percentage of children are admitted to secondary education, "a surprisingly large number without this would outplay the average American collegian in nimbleness of wits." French educators, it has been said, "for all their insistence on knowledge, are not primarily interested in factual learning; they insist that 'the intellectual faculties shall be developed' and that children's minds shall be 'trained, enriched, and broadened.' "[19] Thus, it appears that, the future of progressivism as well as the implementation (in spirit, no less) of the Wallon reform still is dependent upon the European, and basically French, concepts of philosophical idealism.

Nevertheless, education in France is scarcely fossilized. The most astonishing development, in the light of past French educational history, is that a hard look is being taken at the *baccalauréate*. That this *bête noir* of generation after generation of French secondary school students could be modified is almost as fantastic as Jules Verne's *Autour de la Lune* must have appeared in 1865. Resistant to acute change, though, is the pedagogy of the Gallic secondary school "professor," with its memorization, note taking, analysis, and verbalism, to say nothing of the long hours of homework that *lycée* pupils have traditionally endured. That examina-

---

[17] Fraser, p. 300.

[18] See *The French System of Education* (New York: French Cultural Services, issued periodically).

[19] King, p. 35. See also Theodore L. Reller, "Success and Failure of the Reforms of French Secondary Education," *Educational Administration and Supervision*, vol. 42 (October 1956), pp. 329–342.

tions and the amount of study per week are being reconsidered, as well as a number of innovations in articulation, suggest progress.

Lest it be thought, however, that a loosening of standards is being contemplated, one should be reminded of an old French proverb, The more it changes, the more it remains the same; for, in France, such reforms are always achieved within the existing academic framework!

EDUCATION IN ENGLAND AND WALES

As noted earlier, the British Educational Act of 1944,[20] in addition to attempting to provide a one-track board school (public) to countervail the venerable public school influence, set up alternate routes for its secondary school program. The break comes at age eleven when the British student (or his parents) must make a significant decision which probably will affect the remainder of his life.

Bereday comments as follows on the inequity within the present British system:

> Such proposals as there were for one-stream secondary education which preceded the framing of the 1944 Education Act in England were defeated by the enactment of the tripartite division of secondary schools into grammar, technical, and modern. . . . The inequities and stress inherent in assigning children only eleven years old to definite school careers irked the opponents of the system.[21]

Among these opponents must be classed the British Labour Party, whose advocacy of the comprehensive school (a British version of the American multicurricular high school), generally speaking, served to postpone its early acceptance. With the return of Labour to power a little progress in modifying the traditional has been made,[22] but Labour's majority has been slim and frequently in danger of evaporation. And as Peterson observes, "In England, as perhaps in most countries, the gap between educational reform in theory and in the practical possibilities of change is largely determined by financial and political considerations."[23]

The problem of selection for the swank secondary school has been a particularly difficult one and the methods used have aroused much opposition to the tripartite system, at least from those on the lower socioeconomic

---

[20] *Education in Great Britain* (New York: British Information Services, issued periodically).

[21] G. Z. F. Bereday, "Equal Opportunity," *Journal of Education* (London), vol. 90, no. 8 (April 1959), p. 375.

[22] But see Pedley, pp. 39, 43–44, and A. D. C. Peterson, "Educational Reform in England and Wales, 1955–1966," *Comparative Education Review*, vol. xi, no. 3 (October 1967), pp. 288–299.

[23] Peterson, p. 289.

levels. Although election differs in communities, a usual basis for selection has been an IQ test plus papers on arithmetic and English composition. "The IQ cutting point for grammar schools varies from district to district but seldom falls below 110 and is usually between 114–120," according to one writer.[24]

As alleged by Allison Davis and others in the United States,[25] the relationships between socioeconomic status and success in securing a higher IQ evaluation have not been overlooked by British writers. Himmelweit and Whitfield, for instance, suggest that at least twenty points in a standardized IQ instrument depend on upper-class status.[26]

An idea of the dilemma faced by the average British parents when their offspring reaches the age of decision is reported in his inimitable fashion by Richmond:

> It is to be imagined that Mr. and Mrs. A. (of Muddlewick, Lancs.) are going to have much difficulty in deciding whether their son shall go to the Muddlewick Alderman Smith modern high school or, given half a chance, to Eton College. At one (the old senior school writ large) he would in all probability get on very well, but he would leave it—how shall we say?—without social allure. At the other he might be like a dog without a tail, but wouldn't he be "made" for life? and Eton would give him that indefinable quality which Muddlewick held in admiration and awe—poise.
>
> [But] to be perfectly honest, what they would *really like* best of all (either things being equal) would be for him [to go] to Muddlewick Queen Elizabeth Grammar School: it was nice to know French and Chemistry and things . . . and the blazers were so smart. Possibly Dad had a sneaking idea that his son would be better off at technical school. If so, he either repressed it or thought better to keep it to himself knowing Mrs. A.; anyway the lad hadn't shown any noticeable inclination for that sort of thing . . . though he *did* like his Meccano.[27]

Another problem faced by British education under the 1944 act is that of the public schools themselves. Under the heading "Old Bow Tie" Boris Ford, editor of a leading British education journal, offers some tidbits concerning public school status:

---

[24] Joel B. Montague, Jr., "Some Problems of Selection for Secondary Schools in England—Implications for the United States," *Journal of Educational Sociology*, vol. 32, no. 8 (April 1959), p. 375.

[25] See Allison Davis, *Social-class Influences upon Learning* (Cambridge, Mass.: Harvard University Press, 1948). Also Kenneth Wells, Allison Davis, Robert J. Havighurst, and others, *Intelligence and Cultural Differences* (Chicago: University of Chicago Press, 1951).

[26] H. T. Himmelweit and J. Whitfield, "Mean Intelligence Test Scores of a Random Sample of Occupations," *British Industrial Medicine*, vol. 1 (1947), as quoted in Montague, p. 376.

[27] W. Kenneth Richmond, *Education in England* (Harmondsworth, Middlesex, England: Penguin Books, 1945), p. 160.

The Bow group proposals to "save the public schools" by converting up to half their intake into wards of the Chancellor of the Exchequer have not met with an enthusiastic reception in the Press. This may surprise Sir Robin Williams, author of *Whose Public Schools,* for he writes with an unquestioning conviction of the value of even a minor public school education. . . . The main basis of Sir Robin's argument is that hoary old chestnut still offered without self-consciousness, "character-building. . . ." It would be very difficult to establish that, if the public school does anything for a boy which the [state] grammar school cannot, it is the kind of thing the taxpayer should provide.

In his peroration Sir Robin concludes, bluntly enough, that "to have a son in a Public School is a recognized symbol of success." Obviously, this summation is of a piece with the observation that the "Battle of Waterloo was won on the playing fields of Eton," and has become slightly threadbare to the British man in the street, his attachment to the grammar school notwithstanding.[28]

Bereday pointedly comments:

While England and certainly France revels in the high intellectual training of its elite, its common man is being out-educated not only by the American but also by the German and Russian counterpart. The concentration on education of the most neglected seems to do more for the overall dynamics of a country than the concentration on the most highly endowed in the hope [shades of John Locke!] that they will lift the rest by their genius.[29]

As indicated above, public interest has been focused on the possibilities of the comprehensive school for England and Wales, when and as it can be achieved. As Labour returned to power October 15, 1964, there was the strong possibility that the comprehensive plan would be given a trial. Should Labour act, three of the present difficulties may become more susceptible of solution: (1) the insurance of equality of opportunity, (2) reduction of social disparities, and (3) provision for alternate patterns of school achievement. Bereday thought that "the lessons of the American high school confirm the proposition that mixing children of different social classes can lead to a greater feeling of Equality."[30] Although this has not always occurred in practice in American schools (and recent years have

---

[28] (editorial), *Journal of Education* (London), vol. 90 (February, 1958), p. 41. See also Joel B. Montague, Jr. "The Eleven-Plus Battle in Education in England," *The Clearing House,* vol. 32, no. 5 (January, 1958), pp. 259–262, and "Are Eton and Rugby Doomed by Socialism?" *The Clearing House,* vol. 32, no. 6 (February, 1958), pp. 333–335.

[29] Bereday, p. 47; for a more optimistic picture of Britain's progress in democratization see Richard E. Gross (Ed.), *British Secondary Education* (New York: Oxford University Press, 1965), especially "Schools for the Masses," pp. 45–120, and "Schools for Tomorrow for All," pp. 371–466.

[30] Bereday, p. 47.

been among the most difficult), Bereday has wisely noted the potential. But back in England the current need for austerity has doubtless taken its toll on Labour's plans for school revision. Skeptics point out that Harold Wilson, the Prime Minister, is himself a grammar school product[31] and that education is a live issue in British national politics.

Nor is it clear that there is complete commitment to social equality in England at this time. Richmond argues that "the fact that the comprehensive school is the center of such a bitter controversy in England provides the clearest indication that a fluid society is by no means acceptable by every one in this country as a desirable ideal."[32]

Early in 1969 Sir Ronald Gould, General Secretary of the National Union of Teachers, in comparing the British Newsom Report with the American Conant Report, described the aim of the former as:

> . . . that approximately half of Britain's school children should be trained and entertained. The emphasis is not on finding new educational methods to communicate mathematics, English, a foreign language, mechanics and general science, but rather on providing vocational training, most of which will become obsolete, and social adjustment, which, though valuable, is hardly the answer to all of life's problems. . . . For the young man and the young woman of the future, who are not going to enter higher education, intellectual development in the basic subjects of the technological society is imperative.[33]

Having accented the comprehensive school question in Britain, we may now ask if the success or failure of the modern school is an issue. Generally speaking, it appears that the modern school problem in England is not dissimilar to that confronting the large city multilateral or vocational high school in the United States. The American problems have been aired in films, novels, magazines, and newspapers for some time. Compare an English modern school teacher's dilemma with that depicted in *Blackboard Jungle, Rebel Without a Cause, High School,* or *Up the Down Staircase,* popular books made into films dealing with adolescent delinquency connected with American schools.

Ruth, British, age fifteen, a modern school student, was prevailed upon to express her attitude toward her wishing-to-remain-anonymous mentor. Ruth wrote:

There was an old Hag
Who took from her Bag
All the Books of the Old Hag

<hr>

[31] Associated Press release, Blackpool, England, August 15, 1968: as of this date "organized Labour told Prime Minister Harold Wilson's government to ease its austerity squeeze."

[32] Richmond, p. 144.

[33] "Education and Change," The Grady Gammage Memorial Lecture, Arizona State University, February 11, 1969.

And then
She made us wear out our fountain pens.
She was a BITCH
Who looked like a WITCH
Who also had a big SNITCH. . . .
She would cackle at us
And make a fuss
And her face was like the
Back of a bus.
And when she had a broom-stick
She looked like the NICK.[34]

It is reported that the therapeutic effect of this versification resulted in a feeling of *rapprochement* between pupil and magister.

Of course, it is easy to dismiss the problems of dealing with those of substandard mentality or even of a differing socioeconomic level as being merely issues of valuation. However, as the recent American experience shows, until these frequently antagonistic strata meet, there is little possibility of education, although there may be a certain amount of schooling. Sir Ronald Gould points up this educational ill as follows:

> At the present time . . . only eight per cent of Britain's young people go on to higher education, compared with approximately 40 per cent in the U.S.A.; 75 per cent of Britain's children have left school by the age of 16, whereas in the U.S.A. only 30 per cent leave between 16 and 18 years of age.
>
> In Britain, in the not-too-distant future, and taking little time about it, we shall attempt what you [the U.S.A.] have done in three or four decades. We shall have to accept the consequences of a striking sentence in the Crowther Report: "What is extracted from the pool of ability depends much less on the pool than the effectiveness of the pump." . . . Ways must be found of educating the majority of children up to 18 years of age, to be followed by 35 to 45 per cent going on to some form of higher education. Anything less could well mean a large permanent pool of unemployment measured in millions.[35]

By American experience, change in England and Wales appears to be slow. However, from the British standpoint and considering the longer history of British institutions, transformation, regardless of political and financial inertia, has occurred perhaps too rapidly. As Peterson says:

> Indeed the pace of change is presenting the individual teacher with such a multitude of new challenges that there is a danger that the pace will become too intense. . . . Many are beginning to call for some kind

---

[34] "Portrait of a Secondary Modern School in England," *Journal of Education* (London), vol. 90 (March 1958), pp. 87–89.
[35] "Education and Change," pp. 10–11.

of a moratorium on reform. This pressure is the more intense because the extremely decentralized system of authority . . . puts an unusual burden of responsibility on the individual teacher.[36]

EDUCATIONAL REFORM IN THE SOVIET UNION

An attempt to reduce the prestige problem by upholding several equally recognizable standards, rather than holding to a strictly unitary approach, is offered by the Soviet Union.[37] According to Bereday, in contrast to the situation in France and England, "The Soviet school system has significantly revalued the traditional conception of prestige between liberal arts men and 'engineers.' Even more telling is the superior social position of Stakhanovites in comparison with the lower white-collar workers."[38]

Indeed, a pertinent report from the Soviet Union indicates an even more drastic foreshortening of the gap between mental and manual labor. Soviet comment on the so-called Khrushchev reform which introduced a practical work program into each phase of Russian education, not only serves to justify this departure but reveals a great deal of Marxist strategy as well:

> This is a time of tremendous Soviet progress. The country's economy driving full speed ahead, science and culture are experiencing an unprecedented growth, the working people's living standards are rising steadily. In every field of economic and cultural development the Soviet people—truly masters of life and makers of history—have won outstanding victories they are justly proud of, which are bringing joy and hope to the hearts of millions of friends of peace and socialism and fear and despair to enemies of the working class. . . .
>
> V. I. Lenin taught that the training and education of the young generation, the preparation of highly qualified cadres for all branches of the national economy, science and culture, must always be a matter of central concern for the Communist Party and the Soviet State. . . .
>
> Speaking at the 13th Congress of the Young Communist League, N. S. Khrushchev said, in this connection: "Every boy and girl should know that while studying at school, they must prepare themselves for working, for the creation of values useful to people, to society. For each one of them, regardless of the position of his or her parents, there should be only one road—to study, then having learned, to work."[39]

[36] Peterson, p. 299.

[37] See G. Z. F. Bereday, William W. Brickman, and Gerald Read (Eds.), *The Changing Soviet School* (Boston: Houghton Mifflin Company, 1960), pp. 186–270.

[38] Bereday, p. 47.

[39] "On Strengthening the Bonds of the School with Life, and the Further Development of the Public Education System in the Country. Theses of the Central Committee of the Communist Party in the Soviet Union and Council of Ministers

In this connection—and stripping the report of its overt propaganda —it will be recalled that, a few years ago, a group of leading Soviet medical authorities published a long letter in the *Literaturnaya Gazeta* charging Soviet educational authorities with "endangering the health of school children" by overloading them with lessons and homework. "Chronic over-exhaustion, frequent headaches, weakened memory and vision, proneness to infectious diseases with various complications, result in a general weakening of the child's organism." They complained of the "unbelievable over-burdening" of school children. Children of eleven to thirteen were averaging, including homework, from eight to ten hours a day; and students of fourteen to seventeen, from ten to twelve hours.[40]

Since in the Soviet Union nothing is presumed to happen by chance, this move may be suggested as the preliminary to a reduction in the academic part of the Soviet public school program, which was made in September, 1956. That the present move, undoubtedly to counteract the tendency which was developing in Soviet secondary education (compare with the British problem) of placing prestige on academic attainment in the upper classical and scientific schools, is a way to retreat gracefully from an untenable program is sure. That it was impossible for all to succeed in them and that the prestige factor was seen as inconsistent with Soviet ideology make logical explanations for the proletarian twist.

To return to the polytechnical program:

> Public education must be reorganized along lines that will allow the secondary and higher schools to play a more active role in all of the creative activity of the Soviet people. . . . One of the major defects in the old society was the gulf between physical and mental labor. . . . Marxist teaching has dispelled the bourgeois myth of the inevitable and eternal existence of a grey mass of people, on the one side, whose destiny is submission and grinding physical toil, and on the other, a handful supposedly called by nature herself to do the thinking and ruling, to develop science and literature and the arts. . . .
>
> The idea of uniting instruction with productive labor has long attracted progressive thinkers. Such Utopian Socialists as Campanella, Fourier, and Owen, and the great Russian revolutionary democrat, Chernyshevsky, already in this day, picturing the society of the future, spoke of the close bond of instruction with physical labor under socialism.
>
> The 20th Congress of the CPSU pointed out, as a serious shortcoming in our schools, the fact that instruction is, in a certain measure, divorced from life, and that graduates are ill-prepared for practical activity.

of the U.S.S.R.," *Soviet Education* (an English translation of the monthly *Sovetskaya Pedagogica,* Journal of the Russian Academy of Pedagogical Science, published by the International Arts and Sciences Press, Inc., White Plains, N.Y.), vol. 1 (February, 1959), pp. 3–5. See also George S. Counts, *Khrushchev and the Central Committee Speak on Education* (Pittsburgh: University of Pittsburgh Press, 1959).

[40] As quoted in Robert J. Havighurst, "Is Russia Really Out-Producing Us in Scientists?," *School and Society,* vol. 86 (April 26, 1958), p. 190.

In order to strengthen the bond of the schools with life, it is not only necessary to introduce new subjects into the school curriculum . . . but also to involve them systematically in work at enterprises, collective and state farms, experimental school plots, and school workshops. The curriculum for secondary schools should be revised in the direction of a greater specialization in production so that young people who complete the ten-year (complete secondary school) have a good general education opening the way to higher education, and at the same time, prepared for practical activity, since the greater part of the graduates will at once start work in the various branches of the national economy.[41]

Two stages in providing the program were envisioned. First, a compulsory eight-year school (to replace the seven-year school) from which "the youth as a whole must become involved in socially useful work at enterprises, or collective farms, etc." The second plateau involved continuation schools, secondary general educational labor polytechnical schools, and technical schools with the complete secondary education program. Beginning in the 1959–1960 school year there were to be boarding schools and specialized secondary education programs.[42]

The philosophy of this move was fairly well revealed in the concluding statement of the directive adopted November 12, 1958:

In mastering these qualities, the study of the social sciences plays an important role. A knowledge of the fundamentals of Marxism-Leninism is essential for specialists in all fields. . . . Our youth must be trained in a spirit of implacability towards bourgeois ideology and any manifestation of revisionism.[43]

Such a monolithic attack on the problem which badgers England, Germany, and even the United States confirmed the view of George S. Counts, an American interpreter of the Russian educational world for many years:

Teacher and education as such, moreover, are essentially technicians who translate into practice the general and specific directives formulated by the party leadership. [And] the goals of Soviet education are to be found in the Bolshevik conception of history, the nature of the social structure, the controlling purposes of the party, the cultural heritage from Old Russia, and the shifting tides of change among the nations.[44]

Indeed the polytechnical turn and its ideological counterpart might well be a plagiarization of Lenin's words:

In the field of people's education the Communist Party sets itself the aim of concluding the task begun by the October Revolution of 1917

---

[41] "On Strengthening the Bonds," p. 5.
[42] "On Strengthening the Bonds," pp. 6–7.
[43] "On Strengthening the Bonds," p. 14.
[44] *The Challenge of Soviet Education.* (New York: McGraw-Hill, Inc., 1957), pp. 32, 50–51.

of converting the school from a weapon for the class domination of the Bourgeoisie into a weapon for the destruction of this domination, as well as for the complete destruction of the division of society into classes. The school must become a weapon of the dictatorship of the proletariat.[45]

One would be exceedingly naive to expect each of the phrases quoted above to be taken literally, as meaning that the class system has been annihilated in the Soviet Union. We must note that the problem in the Soviet Union and its satellites has been to devise a working arrangement between Communist ideology and the needs of the Soviet Union. "It seems evident that a growing number of Soviet intellectuals recognize the mythological function of certain elements of the official ideology," surmises Levit in a pregnant paper on Soviet educational theory, and he continues:

> At the same time, the influence of the Marxist-Leninist legacy is strong; it colors even the objection of dissenters. Nevertheless, a reciprocity of influence is discernible between it and other forces—historical Russian traditions, four decades of an embracive Soviet enculturation process, international problems, the development of a giant industrial power, and an increasingly complex social class structure.[46]

Moreover, a higher birthrate than the United States before Pearl Harbor, together with a school system geared to produce a surplus of academically trained young people, which the facilities of the state were unable to assimilate, led to a minor youth crisis. More students were being graduated from the still largely propaedeutic complete secondary school than could be enrolled in higher educational agencies. There was the strange danger of producing an adolescent intelligentsia, whose uncontrolled activities might prove embarrassing to a managed society. The paramount need was that of developing a larger, occupationally skilled, and more variegated middle class. This was the prime reason for the Soviet shift to polytechnicalization, not student eyestrain!

For a long time Soviet schools have been organized on a 4–3–3 basis: elementary school, incomplete secondary, and complete secondary. The Khrushchev reform provided for an eleven-year program, with eight years basic for all and the upper three years available (although actually only the sons and daughters of the managerial class had much chance of receiving them). So the end-product of this famous, but misleading, piece of legislation was really a reduction in education, as it applied to the common student, although a spate of propaganda was issued to herald it as a great new advance in public education.

At any rate, the "reform" lasted for only six years; for, in 1964 a return was made to the ten-year plan, without the removal of the by-then-

---

[45] Counts, p. 47.
[46] Levit, p. 22.

established eight-year pattern for the common group.[47] To the West, this move should have appeared symbolic; to the Russians, perhaps not so, for they have always insisted that their ten-year school accomplished much more than the typical American twelve-year program.

WEST GERMANY'S "EINHEITSSCHULE"

A paradox is offered by the educational arrangements in today's West Germany. In Communist East Germany the organization of the schools on an 8–4 basis gives the appearance of a single track; in West Germany the system is more traditional, although it varies, of course, in the several *Länder* (states), which as members of the federal republic have autonomy (as theoretically do the states in the United States) in arranging their local schools' program, curriculum, articulation and standards. However, an organization of ministers of education (*Ständige Konferenz der Kultus Minister*) from the various *Länder* meets periodically in the interest of achieving as much national unanimity as appears desirable.

While progressive school reform had marked the inauguration of the Weimar Republic in 1919, the older forces of German authoritarianism— the upper social classes, the Junkers, and the military bodies—had, by the 1930s and the advent of Adolf Hitler, restored much of the former practice, that is, a two-track system. Although under Hitler's National Socialism recession from the intellectualism of pre–World War I became a cardinal principle in training an ideologically correct population, regimentation in terms of "scientific" theory (biology and racial hygiene) and through the creation of paramilitary organizations for both boys and girls merely changed the emphasis and authority of educational practice, not its rigors.

Nevertheless, the *Einheitsschule*, or common-track school idea, which had flowered during republican days was not dead. Following the defeat and surrender of the Third Reich, the Allied educational missions in each of the Western zones, British, American, and French, advocated a pattern designed to encourage the development of more equal educational opportunities. (In the Eastern zone the Marxists copied their own Russian prototypes.)

That a single track was not accomplished immediately in the Federal Republic (formed when the three Allied forces relinquished control of their respective areas) need not be taken as a sign of failure. The autonomy of each of the *Länder* plus the still-strong class tradition provided a situation completely dissimilar from that east of the Elbe where class lines as well as provincial boundaries were erased by Marxist fiat under the cloak of "democracy," as a basic strategy in the creation of a Communist state, the German Democratic Republic!

---

[47] See Elizabeth Moos, "Changes in Soviet Schools in 1964," *Comparative Education Review*, vol. 7, no. 2 (December 1964), pp. 264–268.

In East Germany educational preference is ostensibly nonexistent, but the children of workers and former peasants, party members in good standing, and well-recommended elements of certain Marxist youth groups, notably the Organization Ernst Thaelmann, have priority in securing the opportunity for the university or for an education higher than the basic eight or ten years.[48] The former University of Berlin, in Communist territory, has become Marxist and been renamed Humboldt University.

In West Berlin a new institution, the Free University, was established in 1948 for higher and professional education. Developments in the German Federal Republic suggest that modification is in the wind and that the old solidly elite system has lost some ground to the common-track concept. Several *Länder* now possess the equivalent of the 8–4 system; and legislation establishing a *Rahmenplan* (skeleton, or master, plan) has been passed.

Briefly, states adopting the new design now offer a four-year *Grundschule* for all students, to be followed by the two-year *Förderstufe*, a type of middle school. Then a division would occur, with 50 percent of the students sent to the *Hauptschule*, 25 percent to the *Realschule*, and 20 percent to the *Gymnasium*. The remaining 5 percent would already have been siphoned into a nine-year academic program for the gifted.[49]

Volkhochschulen (peoples' evening schools) and *Berufsschulen* (continuation schools) are provided for those taking the modern (*Hauptschule*) route. Of course the *Abitur* is retained for "leaving" the secondary school and for admission to the university. It would hardly be possible for graduates of the evening or continuation schools to enter the university, although there will be some transfers from the *Realschule* to the preparatory *Gymnasium*.

To recapitulate, the attempt is being made to create a unified system, with a *zweite weg* (second path) for non-*Gymnasium* graduates. The *Förderstufe* extends common schooling for six years; like the American junior high school or middle school it pays particular attention to the student with a poor background, allowing him when possible to advance. And there is provided the *Realschule* which holds the possibility for advanced training beyond the common school, but does not lead to the university. Although hardly as free as Americans like to think that their systems are, West German education offers a refreshing contrast to the regimentation of East German education.

---

[48] For a discussion of some external activities in East German education see Kenneth V. Lottich, "Extracurricular Indoctrination in East Germany," *Comparative Education Review*, vol. 6, no. 3 (February 1963), pp. 209–211, and Joseph S. Roucek and Kenneth V. Lottich, *Behind the Iron Curtain, Education and Nationalism* (Caldwell, Idaho: Caxton Printers, Ltd., 1964), "East Germany," pp. 145–166.

[49] For the schools of West Germany see Ursula Kirkpatrick, "The Rahmen Plan for West German School Reform," *Comparative Education Review*, vol. 4, no. 1 (June 1960); see also Theodore Huebener, *The Schools of West Germany* (New York: New York University Press, 1962).

"REFORM" IN CZECHOSLOVAKIA

The dilemma of mass overeducation in a planned society (as reported in the section on the Soviet schools) has also occurred in the Soviet satellites; and, since their educational policies have been largely controlled by Moscow, developments within the Iron Curtain countries, of which Czechoslovakia offers a disturbing example, serve to indicate the completeness with which the polytechnicalization move was formulated. The sudden and shattering invasion of Czechoslovakia by Soviet and Warsaw Pact (the Communist equivalent of NATO) troops on August 21, 1968, should convince all doubting Thomases that the ideology of the Soviet Union is not to be taken lightly by her unfortunate satrapies.

The Czechoslovak polytechnicalization statement, based on the Khrushchev reform plan, began with the usual Marxist polemic:

> All affairs of public education and the system of the Czechoslovak Republic have undergone profound changes during the years the democratic regime has existed. From a school of the bourgeosie, based on social and property inequality, from a servile weapon of the ruling clique of exploiter-capitalist, the Czech schools have been transformed into a really public school which educates conscious builders of socialism.[50]

Then the "extenuating circumstances" leading to the change were recounted:

> Although certain reforms were established in Czechoslovakia on the basis of "The Law of the Unified School" by the National Assembly in May, 1948, and the April, 1953, Act reducing the term of compulsory instruction from nine to eight years and the term of instruction in the complete secondary school from thirteen to eleven years, some dissatisfaction with the program still existed. Among the chief reasons appended for change were (1) overloading and extended homework; (2) failure of the school to enroll sufficient numbers of children from the worker and peasant background; and (3) the adolescent was found, at age 14, in many cases incapable of correctly choosing a future vocation (in this the school could not help him since almost no kind of work in vocational guidance was conducted).[51]

Considering the situation in the Soviet Union, this is a familiar refrain. Then the Kasvin-Shibanov report began to detail the expedient chosen:

> [Thus] the Central Committee of the Communist Party of Czechoslovakia at the 11th Congress proposed a series of measures which will

---

[50] G. A. Kasvin and A. A. Shibanov, "The Reform of the Schools in the Czechoslovak Republic," *Soviet Education*, vol. i, no. 4 (February 1959), pp. 64–70. By permission of International Arts and Sciences Press, Inc., White Plains, N.Y., publishers of *Soviet Education*.

[51] Kasvin and Shibanov, p. 66.

contribute to the further development of public education in the country and to the regulation of the school system with the object of bringing it closer to the needs of socialist construction. . . . In his speech to the Congress, Comrade A[nton] Novotny said, "The chief task of our school must become the training of thoroughly developed people, who possess the basic facts of knowledge in the field of science and technology and at the same time are trained for skilled physical labor and conscious participation in the construction of communist society. To create such a truly socialist school means, by all possible methods to join teaching in school increasingly more tightly with the productive labor of pupils so that they acquire not only working habits, but in the senior classes of the secondary schools, also gain a basic skill in the field of some kind of working occupation."[52]

Czech differences with the Russians will be reported later, but for reasons of clarity, and because of its ideological significance, tables interpretative of this polytechnicalization move (taken from the Kasvin-Shibanov statement) are appended.

The system of training pupils for labor contains three grades, or levels, as follows:

Table I: The First Level, "Lessons in Handiwork" (Classes I-V)

Kinds of Work	Number of Lessons by Years of Study					
	I	II	III	IV	V-1	V-2
Work with small objects used, for example, in teaching safety, to clean up the workplace, etc.	6	0	0	0	0	0
Work with paper and cardboard	10	10	10	10	0	10
Work with plastics and clay	6	6	4	4	0	4
Work with fabrics	0	6	12	12	0	12
Work with wood and metal (soft tin, wire, etc.)	0	0	6	6	26	6
Work in nature corner and on garden plot	7	7	18	18	24	18
Socially useful labor	4	4	10	10	10	10
Excursions connected with handiwork lessons	0	0	6	6	6	6
Total	33x	33x	66	66	66	66

x lessons per week, all others 2 lessons per week

The following table represents a combination of two indexes, the agricultural and the industrial. Where paired figures are shown, the first

---

[52] P. 67. See also E. P. Gusarov, "Labor as a Factor in the Pupil's Upbringing," *Soviet Education*, vol. i, no. 5 (March 1959), pp. 29–32, which contains anecdotes relating to the worth of student labor activity and anthropometrical studies.

refers to the emphasis given in agricultural regions, the second in industrial areas; otherwise the program is similar. The labor lessons are included in a study plan called "bases of production."

Table II: The Second Level, "Bases of Production"
(Classes VI-IX)

Sections of "Bases of Production"	Number of Hours by Years of Instruction, by Semesters							
	VI		VII		VIII		IX	
Bases of technology, ind.	11	0/0	0/0	0/8	0/15	15/15	23	23
Work in craftshops, ind.	29	0/0	0/0	0/30	0/26	33/26	33	33
Socially useful labor, ind.	4	0/0	0/0	0/6	0/4	10/4	3	3
Talks, industrial emphasis	2	0/0	0/0	0/2	0/2	4/2	2	2
Trips, industrial	4	0/0	0/0	0/3	0/3	4/3	5	5
Bases of technology, ag.	0	7/7	7/7	7/0	15/0	0/0	0	0
Work in craftshops, ag.	0	30/30	25/25	25/0	33/8	0/8	0	0
Socially useful labor, ag.	0	6/5	10/10	10/0	10/5	0/5	17	16
Talks, agricultural	0	2/3	3/4	3/0	2/1	0/1	0	0
Trips, agricultural	0	4/4	5/4	4/0	6/2	0/2	0	0
Totals	50	49/49	50/50	49/49	66/66	66/66	83	82

It will be noted that two basic plans have been set up for use (1) in predominantly agricultural regions, or (2) in industrial areas, although every student is given some contact with each at some time during his study in years VI–IX. Likewise the yearly totals progress from 99 hours per year of instruction in class VI to a total of 165 hours in class IX.

In the third grade, Classes X to XII, the general polytechnical education is combined with production training in specialties of a wide range. Training in cities is in the bases of machine building, the leading branches of heavy industry, textile production, and the construction industry. In the agricultural areas, the program is indicated in the tables below:

Table III: The Third Level, "General Polytechnical"
(Classes X-XII) Cities

Component Parts of Production Training	Number of Hours per Week by Years of Study			
	X	XI	XII	Yearly total
Technology	2	2	3	222
Mechanical engineering	2	2	0	132
Production practice and productive labor	6	7	9	700

Table IV: The Third Level, "General Polytechnical"
(Classes X-XII) Rural

Component Parts of Production Training	By Years X	By Years XI	By Semesters XII		Yearly Total
Crop raising	2	1	1 or 2	0	132
Livestock raising	2	1	2 or 1	0	132
Mechanical engineering	0	2	0	3	156
Production practice and labor	6	7	9	9	700

So may the Soviet-inspired polytechnical program (which serves as a complement to the lightened academic phase), in the ancient land of John Amos Comenius, be outlined. Broad in educational outlook though the grand old Moravian was, it is doubtful that he could have approved such a curriculum, disagreeing, if for no other reason, with its materialistic base. Nevertheless, in deference to their greatest educational prophet—indeed, possibly the world's greatest—the Czechoslovakian Academy of Science published, in the tercentenary of his epochal work, a photolithic edition of the Amsterdam imprint.[53] The Introduction (given in the national language, Latin, Russian, English, French, German, and Spanish) reads as follows:

> After three centuries in Komesky's [Comenius'] native country, there arise the conditions that will make possible the realization of even his most daring plans. The socialist society realizes the unified school system from the primary up to the highest school standard, as Komesky has proposed it; in the socialist society all children are given a general education without any discrimination of sex, social origin, and property as it was Komesky's idea.[54]

Other tributes to Comenius follow along with a schedule for republishing his basic pedagogical works.

In the 1961 edition of this book we stated that "only time can reveal whether the Marxist myth is adequate or satisfactory for the stabilizing of the new [educational] system"; recent events in East Europe indicate that it was not. The fall of Comrade Novotny marked the beginning of a resurgence of Czech nationalism. Left to themselves, the Czechs undoubtedly would have devised an educational system of their own choice, for Czechoslovakia has a long and impressive history in medieval and modern Europe;

[53] Joannes Amos Comenius, *Opera Didactica Omnia* (*Editio anni 1657 lucis ope expressa*), 3 vols. (Prague: Academia Scientiarum Bohemoslovenica, MCMLVII). See William W. Brickman, "Three Centuries of Comenius' Contributions to Education," *School and Society*, vol. 86 (April 26, 1958), pp. 193–194, for other publications under Czech auspices of Comenius' great contributions to the science of education.

[54] In the West perhaps the most significant recognition of Comenius' tercentenary was the publication of *Selections, John Amos Comenius*, introd. by Jean Piaget (Paris: UNESCO, 1957).

the ruthless removal of the post-Novotny liberal government, however, will delay whatever changes the Czechs and Slovaks might have made.

THE CHINESE PEOPLE'S REPUBLIC

Turning now to mainland China for another example of the Marxist ideology in education, we find the vocational motif again strongly in front. Until the past few years it was theoretically possible for private schools to exist if they accepted state control and inspection and if their curricula were sanctioned by the state authorities, but the recent upheavals in Red China cast doubt that anything except the official schooling will now be accepted. In mainland China, as in every other Communist country, the monopoly of education is a party prerogative.

According to Lauwerys, three Chinese ministries are concerned with education: (1) the Ministry of Culture, which supervises museums, broadcasting, the theatre, and so on; (2) the Ministry of Higher Education, which is in charge of all technical institutions, research institutes, universities, and colleges; and (3) the Ministry of Education, which controls all elementary and middle schools, all teacher training, all general education provided in part-time schools, and, in addition, operates special schools for handicapped children. At the date of Lauwerys' report there were 62 of these with 65,000 pupils and 960 teachers. The Ministry of Education is in charge also of the rapidly expanding systems, for infants, of nursery schools and kindergartens.[55]

The architect of Chinese education and its Marxist orientation has been, of course, Mao Tse-tung, to whom has been attributed all progress in the Chinese state. Each Chinese student, as well as the leaders and the common people, are expected to commit to memory and practice Mao's aphorisms. His red-backed book is sold even on university campuses within the United States and presumably throughout the world. Mao's section dealing with schooling is significantly headed, "XVI, Education and the Training of Troops," and begins:

> Our educational policy must enable everyone who receives an education to develop morally, intellectually, and physically, and become a worker with both socialist consciousness and culture.
>
> [He goes on to state that] a school of a hundred people certainly cannot be run well if it does not have a leading group of several people, or a dozen or more, which is formed in accordance with the actual circumstances (and not thrown together artificially) and is composed of the most active, upright and alert of the teachers, the other staff and the students.[56]

---

[55] J. A. Lauwerys, *The Journal of Education* (London), vol. 90, no. 1064 (March 1958), pp. 97–98; see also *Soviet Education* (White Plains, N.Y.), vol. i, no. 4 (February 1959), pp. 57–64.

[56] *Quotations from Chairman Mao Tse-tung* (Peking: The Foreign Language Press, 1966), pp. 165–167.

Dr. Theodore H. E. Chen, Director of the Soviet-Asian Studies Center, University of Southern California, states Mao's second observation less ambiguously:

> The Communist way of life is the collective way. One of the chief tasks of moral education is to train children in collective living. Here, again, the Young Pioneers (an organization equivalent to Boy Scouts in the West) are supposed to set the pace. The collective way is fostered by having children study, labor, and play in groups. The class is organized as a collective unit with the teacher at the head, and with Pioneers and party representatives guiding the activities.[57]

(The activities of the Red Guards, a higher age-level organization than the Pioneers, which recently got out of hand in mainland China are well known.)[58]

Red China's highly organized education program was in keeping with her Great Leap Forward, in which the Marxist leadership hoped through persistent individual, local and national effort, and a crash program on her farms and in her factories to overtake the Western democracies. Millions of Chinese of both sexes were taken from their homes, organized into battalions of farm workers, housed in barracks, and separated from their children, who were placed in the hands of the state. The expansion of manufacturing in villages, towns, cities, and other heavy industry centers, was fostered, too, with special emphasis on the creation of metals. But it proved extremely difficult to control the quality of the output and to keep enthusiasm at fever-pitch. Generally, the home industry or village forge movement has been considered a failure. Ominous indeed, however, was Sinic progress in nuclear bomb and rocket development, an achievement disturbing to the Soviet Union as well as to the West.

Vocational middle schools have been placed in the larger centers of population, where there are also polytechnical, normal, premedical, and trade schools. Without repeating the details of a program developed in Czechoslovakia and in the Soviet Union, the mainland Chinese are constructing an ideology which, no doubt, will result in widening the practical approach to education. This, for ideological reasons, including a rift between Peking and Moscow, is favored, although the traditional Chinese parent has always esteemed the classic culture springing from China's ancient Chou and T'ang and the works of her great philosophers. As Lauwerys delicately states, "A difficult point of policy, at present unsolved, is whether it would be wise at the moment, to encourage the increase in the number of the "general schools" or to concentrate resources upon the vocational school. Public opinion among parents favors the former. Economics needs the latter."[59]

---

[57] "Education in Mainland China," pp. 549–596, in Roucek and Lottich.

[58] But see Hans Granqvist, *The Red Guard—A Report on Mao's Revolution* (New York: Frederick A. Praeger, Inc., 1967).

[59] Lauwerys, p. 98.

More blunt, but with the same intention, are the remarks of Lin Ting-yi in "Education Must be Linked to Productive Work," "The majority of bourgeois educational specialists consider that only book knowledge is knowledge . . . that practical experience is not knowledge. . . . Theirs is a blind alley!"[60]

Dr. Oskar Anweiler of Hamburg sees an apparently unanticipated problem in the shift to "polytechnic emphasis" in the schools, from primary through university, in the Communist-oriented bloc—the Soviet Union, mainland China, and the Peoples' Democracies of East Central Europe, Bulgaria, Czechoslovakia, East Germany, Hungary, and Romania (but with the exception of Poland). In addition to certain objections raised by factory managers bent on efficiency and the necessary provision of school buildings with special space for workshops and technical equipment to say nothing of the retraining required to produce adequate school staffs, Anweiler maintains that:

> Here the aim is to preserve the scientific structure of the various disciplines, whilst at the same time paying special attention to their practical applications . . . the children's age, their attitude to work and their participation in "workers' collectives" also present various problems with respect to the methods of teaching and giving work experience.
>
> Seen as a whole, the main educational problem consists in the conflict between, on the one hand, the forms of life and teaching suited to children and young people and, on the other, the early adaptation to and preparation for the adult working world which it is sought to achieve.[61]

Western-trained (Cambridge) T. C. Cheng, more than a decade ago, evaluated the half-work, half-study plan in Communist China with a note of warning to the West, a warning that has been shown through China's recent political activities in eastern and southeastern Asia to be not unrealistic:

> It would be folly to ignore the basic challenge posed by the Peiping [Peking] regime in terms of its aims, industrialization, military prowess, and educational achievement. In spite of the fact that the so-called Communist institutions of higher education are little more than vocational schools, and Communist schools hardly compare with the schools of the Free World as regards their academic standards, they already claimed that in 1958 that 93.9 per cent of all school-age children on the mainland was enrolled in primary schools, and that illiteracy was to be wiped out. . . . [Yet] it remains to be seen whether or not the institutions and ideology of Communist China may eventually succeed in blending the unlettered laborers with the intellectual elite in the years to come.[62]

---

[60] Source noted under footnote 50, *Soviet Education*, p. 58.

[61] Oskar Anweiler, "School Reform Problems in Eastern Europe," *International Review of Education*, vol. vi, no. 1 (1960), pp. 34–35.

[62] "Half-Work and Half-Study in Communist China," *History of Education Journal*, vol. ix, no. 4 (Summer 1958), pp. 88–92.

Cheng's words intimated the rise of a new world military power and an internal revolution of stupendous proportions. The advent of Sinic nuclear capability does little to deemphasize this promise or threat.

POSTSCRIPT

Educational ideologies in seven countries have been examined, admittedly in kaleidoscopic fashion. Comparisons and contrasts are easily suggested, four of these countries being among the leading "democracies" of the West, the remaining trio representing various shades of the Marxist-oriented ideology.

Speaking in philosophical terms, these ideologies vary from the idealism tinged with rationalism of the Western European setting through the idealism and pragmatism of North American education to the frankly dialectical materialism of the Communist group. Yet there is also a peculiar inverted idealism in the Marxist camp and there are strong pragmatic leanings in Britain and elsewhere in western Europe. In the United States, the Progressive Education Association has withered, but the John Dewey Society remains; and in western Europe the New Education Fellowship is not dead. Both France and Germany are engaged in some experimentation, and in America the essentialists have absorbed much of the pragmatic methodology of the progressives. In each half of the West existentialism is gaining ground.

Throwing the bit into the teeth of the experimentalists, who hold that the school's task is primarily social (and paraphrasing Van Cleve Morris[63]), existentialists maintain that "the work of the school is only incidentally social; its primary task is individual." Can current ideology support this viewpoint? Can existential teachers be supplied?

But now to assess other new directions in education which are more visible now than at any time since the close of World War II. Can everyone really be educated? Has the population explosion opened Pandora's box? What new frontiers can replenish a diminishing food supply? Do new developments in popular education represent progress? Will youth movements in high school and college create havoc or initiate a novel cooperative growth toward a more realistic curriculum? Is existentialism valid? What have the rising nationalisms of Asia and Africa to offer the long-favored humanistic curriculum derived from ancient Greek and Latin sources? And is nationalism in the captive East European countries dead or merely dormant? Is Communism as the new world force to destroy the world's democratic achievements, or is it to be liquidated by the very currents it has contrived

---

[63] *Philosophy and the American School* (Boston: Houghton Mifflin Company, 1961), pp. 383–401; see also Maxine Greene, *Existential Encounters for Teachers* (New York: Random House, Inc., 1967).

to liberate? Perhaps such germane questions are too difficult to answer without further experience with the new ideologies in education.

There is change if not progress and this appears to be a healthy sign; the people themselves (although this is only a relative phenomenon) are now making their wishes known in education and sometimes in politics. *Education* as an abstract term is being redefined; and although free, mandatory, universal education has not been attained in much of the world, levels of literacy, under the twin spurs of nationalism and independence, are rising rapidly.[64]

Yet danger is not dead. The ugliness of war has burst forth again, and especially in the United States relations among the races, and indeed the haves and the have-nots, have cast a pall over our vaunted American democracy. No longer can we honestly sing:

> Thine alabaster cities gleam,
> Undimmed by human tears.

In 1965 American soldiers were ordered into combat in Vietnam, after a long period of advising and otherwise assisting a weak but (according to American ideals) democratic government representing only half of a torn and shattered remnant of European colonialism. Once again, as in Korea, Communists are the opponents.

Three prominent Americans have been felled by assassins' bullets: President John Fitzgerald Kennedy, the Reverend Dr. Martin Luther King, Jr., and the martyred President's brother, Robert Francis Kennedy. In one year (1968) student riots erupted in Berkeley, Orangeburg, South Carolina, and at Columbia University, and this was but a prelude to 1969.

Between 1966 and 1968 disturbances occurred in Los Angeles, Detroit, Cleveland, and other prestigious cities in the United States; the city of Washington, the nation's capital, was not spared the fire and smoke from burning and looted stores and homes that, in 1968, must have resembled the furious attack by the British in 1812. In this same year the Poverty March was made on the federal city. And in many other large municipalities teacher strikes began, while billions were being spent in an attempt to end segregation.

Beginning in 1958, the year after Sputnik, the American Congress, hopefully to stem criticism of a lack of science preparedness, has enacted law after law distributing largess and augmenting federal control, for example, the Higher Education Facilities Act, the Libraries Services Act,

---

[64] Robert E. Belding in a small volume, *Students Speak Around the World* (Iowa City, Iowa: Department of Publications, State University of Iowa, 1960), highlights this inclination. Speaking of Britain (pp. 15–25), France (pp. 26–33), and the Soviet Union (pp. 54–63), together with Latin America, Scandinavia, West Germany, and Japan, Belding points up the newer tendencies through illustrations of influences which presently are providing nonclass education to a greater degree than ever before. Moreover, the influence of the student mind is providing a significant new force.

the Vocational and Technical Education Act, the Economic Opportunity Act, and a host of others, including the Elementary and Secondary Education Act of 1965, "An Act to Strengthen and Improve Educational Quality and Educational Opportunities in the Nation's Elementary and Secondary Schools," or so the title ran. A certain sector's resentment of federal "intervention" was to be anticipated, for reasons we have given already.

Summing up, several tendencies may easily be observed: (1) the new demands for literacy, from either nationalistic or monolithic motives; (2) the deaccentuation of class bias in the provision for a greater range of educational opportunities at all levels; (3) the broader base assumed by education in the Soviet orbit through the utilization of work experience plans; (4) a noticeable willingness to educational experimentation, especially by the Western European democracies; (5) the strengthening, particularly in the United States, of educational philosophy and method leading to a synthesis of many of the better features of essentialism and progressivism; (6) the increasingly dominant role being played by high school and college students and youth organizations throughout much of the world; and (7) fresh urges to education, both scientific and academic, springing in large part from the grassroots of societies and from the natural dignity of the newly created independent nations on the older continents, where anticolonial movements (while not without a certain peril) offer great promise.

The joy of brotherhood has, of course, not been won and the millennium appears farther and farther away, but the educational picture is surely brighter than say, in 1939, when it seemed that an overthrow of world civilization, with a return to primordial tribalism, was imminent. (Today there is, however, the threat, political and ethical, offered by world Communism, or by its opposite number, republican regimentation offered as a "defense" against it).

The new world literacy movement and a surer awareness of totalitarian tactics let us hope that the wave of the future will not flow from utopian illusions, but from democratic realities founded on the long history of all races' struggle for individual freedom and a higher existence than that of an anthill society. It is education's role to assure this reality.

REFERENCES

Adler, Mortimer J., and Milton Mayer, *The Revolution in Education.* Chicago: University of Chicago Press, 1958.

Bailyn, Bernard, *Education in the Forming of American Society.* Chapel Hill, N.C.: University of North Carolina Press, 1960.

Bestor, Arthur, *The Restoration of Learning.* New York: Alfred A. Knopf, 1955.

Boyd, William, *The History of Western Education,* 8th ed. Rev. by Edmund J. King. New York: Barnes & Noble, Inc., 1966. Pp. 451–475.

Conant, James B., *The Education of American Teachers*. New York: McGraw-Hill, Inc., 1963.

——, *Shaping Educational Policy*. New York: McGraw-Hill, Inc., 1964.

Counts, George S., *The Challenge of Soviet Education*. New York: McGraw-Hill, Inc., 1957.

——, *Khrushchev and the Central Committee Speak on Education*. Pittsburgh, Pa.: University of Pittsburgh Press, 1959.

Cramer, John Francis, and George Stephenson Browne, *Contemporary Education*, 2d ed. New York: Harcourt, Brace & World, Inc., 1965.

Cremin, Lawrence A., *The Transformation of the School*. New York: Alfred A. Knopf, 1961.

Davidson, Basil, *The History of a Continent*. New York: Crowell-Collier and Macmillan, Inc., 1966.

Davis, Allison, *Social-Class Influences upon Learning*. Cambridge, Mass.: Harvard University Press, 1948. The Inglis Lecture, 1948.

Edwards, Newton, and Herman Richey, *The School in the American Social Order*. Boston: Houghton Mifflin Company, 1963. Pp. 651–672.

General Education in a Free Society. Cambridge, Mass.: Harvard University Press, 1945.

Granqvist, Hans, *The Red Guard—A Report on Mao's Revolution*. New York: Frederick A. Praeger, Inc., 1967.

Huebner, Theodore, *The Schools of West Germany*. New York: New York University Press, 1962.

Kandel, I. L., *The New Era in Education, A Comparative Study*. Boston: Houghton Mifflin Company, 1955.

King, Edmund J., *Other Schools and Ours*. New York: Holt, Rinehart and Winston, Inc., 1963.

Labouret, Henri, *Africa before the White Man*. New York: Walker and Company, 1962.

Mao Tse-tung, *Quotations from Chairman Mao Tse-tung*. Peking: The Foreign Language Press, 1966. Pp. 165–167.

Meyer, Adolphe E., *The Development of Education in the Twentieth Century*. Englewood Cliffs, N.J.: Prentice-Hall, Inc., 1949.

Moehlman, Arthur H., and Joseph S. Roucek, *Comparative Education*. New York: Holt, Rinehart and Winston, Inc., 1952.

Morris, Van Cleve, *Philosophy and the American School*. Boston: Houghton Mifflin Company, 1961.

Myers, Edward D., *Education in the Perspective of History*. New York: Harper & Row, Publishers, 1960.

Potter, Robert E., *The Stream of American Education*. New York: American Book Company, 1967.

Pounds, Ralph L., *The Development of Education in Western Culture*. New York: Appleton-Century-Crofts, 1968.

Richmond, W. Kenneth, *Education in the U.S.A.* New York: Philosophical Library, Inc., 1956.

Riesman, David, Nathan Glazer, and Reuel Denney, *The Lonely Crowd*. New Haven, Conn.: Yale University Press, 1950.

Truscott, Bruce, *Red Brick University,* London: Faber & Faber, Ltd., 1943.

Ulich, Robert, *Education and the Idea of Mankind.* New York: Harcourt, Brace & World, Inc., 1964.

———, *Fundamentals of Democratic Education.* New York: American Book Company, 1940.

———, *History of Educational Thought.* New York: American Book Company, 1950. Pp. 350A–E.

———, *Philosophy of Education.* New York: American Book Company, 1961. Pp. 176–187.

Williams, Chancellor, *The Rebirth of African Civilization.* Washington, D.C.: Public Affairs Press, 1961.

Yesipov, B. P., and N. K. Goncharov, *I Want To Be Like Stalin.* Trans. by George S. Counts and Nucia P. Lodge. New York: The John Day Company, Inc., 1947.

SELECTED PAPERBACKS

Adams, Don, and Raymond Bjork, *Education in Developing Areas.* New York: David McKay Company, Inc., 1969.

Belding, Robert E., *European Classrooms: Schools of Four Nations.* Iowa City, Iowa: Sernoll, Inc., 1966.

———, *Students Speak around the World, A Book of Contemporary Cases.* Iowa City, Iowa: Department of Publications, State University of Iowa, 1960.

Bereday, George Z. F., William W. Brickman, and Gerald Read (Eds.), *The Changing Soviet School.* Boston: Houghton Mifflin Company, 1960.

Beveridge, Sir William, *Social Insurance and Allied Services.* American ed. New York: Crowell-Collier and Macmillan, Inc., 1942.

Bruner, Jerome, *Toward a Theory of Instruction.* New York: W. W. Norton & Company, Inc., 1968.

Burke, John G. (Ed.), *The New Technology and Human Values.* Belmont, Calif.: Wadsworth Publishing Company, Inc., 1966.

Butler, J. Donald, *Idealism in Education.* New York: Harper & Row, Publishers, 1966.

Clark, Burton R., *Educating the Expert Society.* San Francisco: Chandler Publishing Company, 1962.

Cohen, Morris Raphael, *American Thought, A Critical Sketch.* New York: Crowell-Collier and Macmillan, Inc., Collier Books, 1962.

Conant, James B., *The American High School Today.* New York: New American Library of World Literature, Inc., 1964.

———, *Slums and Suburbs.* New York: McGraw-Hill, Inc., 1961.

Coombs, Philip H., *The World Educational Crisis.* New York: Oxford University Press, 1968.

Drake, William Earle, *Intellectual Foundations of Modern Education.* Columbus, Ohio: Charles E. Merrill Books, Inc., 1967.

Education in Britain. New York: British Information Services, issued periodically.

Frankel, Charles, *Education and the Barricades*. New York: W. W. Norton & Company, Inc., 1968.

Fraser, W. R., *Residential Education*. New York: Pergamon Press, Inc., 1968.

The French System of Education. New York: French Cultural Services, issued periodically.

Friedenberg, Edgar Z., *Coming of Age in America, Growth and Acquiescence*. New York: Random House, Inc., 1967.

———, *The Vanishing Adolescent*. New York: Dell Publishing Co., Inc., 1962.

Galbraith, John Kenneth, *The Liberal Hour*. New York: New American Library of World Literature, Inc., 1964.

Goldston, Robert, *The Soviets, Fifty Years from Chaos to World Power*. New York: Bantam Books, Inc., 1967.

Goodman, Paul, *Compulsory Mis-Education and The Community of Scholars*. New York: Random House, Inc., 1964.

———, *Growing Up Absurd, Problems of Youth in the Organized System*. New York: Random House, Inc., 1960.

Gordon, Margaret S., *Poverty in America*. San Francisco: Chandler Publishing Company, 1965.

Goslin, David A., *The School in Contemporary Society*. Glenview, Ill.: Scott, Foresman and Company, 1965.

Greene, Marjorie, *Introduction to Existentialism*. Chicago: The University of Chicago Press, 1959.

———, *The Public School and the Private Vision, A Search for America in Education and Literature*. New York: Random House, Inc., 1965.

Gross, Richard E. (Ed.), *British Secondary Education*. New York: Oxford University Press, 1965.

Hanson, John W., and Cole S. Brembeck (Eds.), *Education and the Development of Nations*. New York: Holt, Rinehart and Winston, Inc., 1966.

Harrington, Michael, *The Other America*. Baltimore: Penguin Books, Inc., 1963.

Hoffer, Eric, *The Ordeal of Change*. New York: Harper & Row, Publishers, 1964.

Hofstadter, Richard, *The Progressive Movement, 1900–1915*. Englewood Cliffs, N.J.: Prentice-Hall, Inc., 1963.

Hollingsworth, August B., *Elmtown's Youth*. New York: John Wiley & Sons, Inc., 1961.

Hu, Chang-tu, *Chinese Education under Communism*. New York: Bureau of Publications, Teachers College, Columbia University, 1962.

Kazamias, Andreas M., and Erwin H. Epstein (Eds.), *Schools in Transition*. Boston: Allyn and Bacon, Inc., 1968.

Kneller, George F., *Existentialism and Education*. New York: John Wiley & Sons, Inc., 1964.

Lee, Dorothy, *Freedom and Culture*. Englewood Cliffs, N.J.: Prentice-Hall, Inc., 1959.

McLuhan, Marshall, *The Gutenberg Galaxy*. Toronto: University of Toronto Press, 1965.

Morris, Van Cleve, *Existentialism in Education*. New York: Harper & Row, Publishers, 1966.

Pedley, Robin, *The Comprehensive School*. Baltimore: Penguin Books, Inc., 1963.

Perkinson, Henry J., *The Imperfect Panacea*. New York: Random House, Inc., 1968.

Richmond, W. Kenneth, *Education in England*. Baltimore: Penguin Books, Inc., 1945.

Rippa, S. Alexander, *Education in a Free Society*. New York: David McKay Company, Inc., 1967.

Roucek, Joseph S., and Kenneth V. Lottich, *Behind the Iron Curtain, Education and Nationalism*. Caldwell, Idaho: Caxton Printers, Ltd., 1964, 1969.

Scanlon, David G., *Traditions of African Education*. New York: Teachers College Press, Columbia University, 1964.

Shermis, S. Samuel, *Philosophic Foundations of Education*. New York: American Book Company, 1967.

Starr, Roger, *Urban Choices: The City and its Critics*. Baltimore: Penguin Books, Inc., 1967.

Stone, James C., and R. Ross Hempstead, *California Education Today*. New York: Thomas Y. Crowell Company, 1968.

Tyack, David B. (Ed.), *Turning Points in American Educational History*. Waltham, Mass.: Blaisdell Publishing Company, 1967.

Ulich, Robert, *Education in Western Culture*. New York: Harcourt, Brace & World, Inc., 1965.

White, Theodore H., *China, The Roots of Madness*. New York: Bantam Books, Inc., 1969.

Wisniewski, Richard, *New Teachers in Urban Schools: An Inside View*. New York: Random House, Inc., 1968.

Index

Monastic education *(cont.)*
 and chastity, 162
 content, 164
 curriculum, 164
 dialectic, 164
 and discipline, 162, 166
 geometry, 164–165
 industrial skills, 163
 literary training, 164
 manual training, 164
 and meditation, 163
 methods, 165
 and mortification, 162
 music, 164–165
 and obedience, 162
 organization, 165
 and poverty, 162
 rhetoric, 164
 types, 163
Monasticism, 160, 162
Mongolians, 19
Monologue on the Method in Which One May Account for His Faith, 167
Monotheism, 67
Monroe, Paul, 223, 229
Montagu, F. Ashley, 25
Montaigne, Michel de, 264–267, 290
Montesquieu, Charles de, 295
Montessori, Maria, 368, 385, 391, 392
Moral censor *(sophronist),* 99
Moral training, 75, 215, 218, 270, 306
Moral virtues: rationalistic education, 295, 296
More, Thomas, 229, 257
Morocco, 196
Morrill Act, 344, 415
Morris, Van Cleve, 559
Morrison, Henry C., 502, 504, 512
Mort, Paul R., 418
Moscati, Sabatino, 77
Moses, 68, 71
Motivating force in learning, 528
Motwani, Kewal, 38
Mulcaster, Richard, 268, 271, 277
Muller, Max, 36
Murray, Lindley, 336
Music, beginnings of, 11
Music school (didascaleum), 99
Muslims, 67
Mussolini, Benito, 347–348
Mysticism, 163

Namlulu, 32
Napier, 268
Napoleon, 324–325, 340, 342
National Association of Directors of Educational Research, 401
National Commission for the Defense of Democracy through Education, 453
National Commission on Vocational Education, 438
National Committee of Education and Defense, 519–520
National Congress of Parents and Teachers, 443
National Defense Education Act, 513

National democratic tradition, 448
National Education Association, 348, 401, 449, 519
National Educational Television, 527
National Factory School Association, 442
National Herbartian Society, 364
National Safety Council, 438
National Society for the Study of Education, 364, 389
National Society of College Teachers of Education, 483
National Society of Sciences and Arts (France), 339
National welfare, 518
National Youth Administration, 443, 482
Nationalism, 318–354
 American, 326–332
 French, 322–323
 Prussian, 323–326
Nationalistic education
 adult training, 336
 agencies, 339
 aims, 332
 content, 335
 curriculum, 336–338
 ideals, 337
 methods, 352–354
 organization, 346–352
 patriotic instruction, 336–339
 physical, 334
 types, 333
Natural History (Pliny), 127
Naturalism, 301–315
Naturalistic education
 agencies, 309
 agriculture, 308
 aims, 303–305
 carpentry, 308
 content, 307–309
 curriculum, 307–308
 discipline, 313
 family, 310
 individuality, 305
 methods, 312–315
 moral training, 307
 organization, 311
 physical training, 306
 types, 305–307
"Naturalistic progressivism," 461–490
Natural sciences, 335
Nature, Rousseau, and, 301–302
 study, 410
Nazareth, 138, 139
Nazi system, 467
Neef, Joseph, 362
Neill, A. S., 491
Neo-Platonism, 148
Nestorian Christians, 191
Nestorius, 191
Neuhof, 361
Nevada Act, 337
New Atlantis, The, 268, 269
New Education Fellowship, 434, 559
New essentialism, 466, 468
New Harmony, Indiana, 362
New Héloise, The, 302